MAMMALS

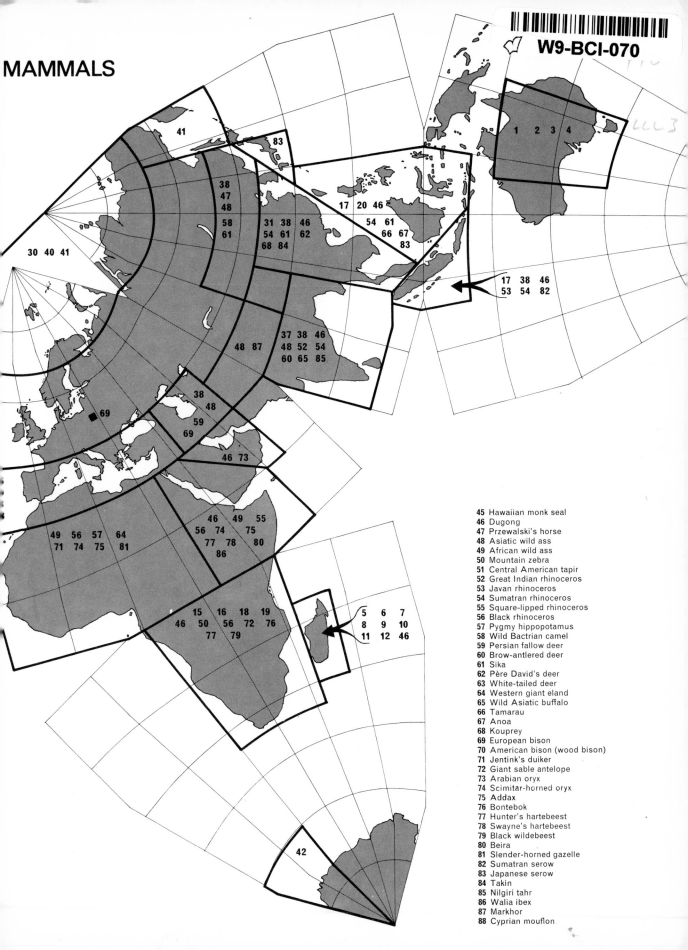

45 Hawaiian monk seal
46 Dugong
47 Przewalski's horse
48 Asiatic wild ass
49 African wild ass
50 Mountain zebra
51 Central American tapir
52 Great Indian rhinoceros
53 Javan rhinoceros
54 Sumatran rhinoceros
55 Square-lipped rhinoceros
56 Black rhinoceros
57 Pygmy hippopotamus
58 Wild Bactrian camel
59 Persian fallow deer
60 Brow-antlered deer
61 Sika
62 Père David's deer
63 White-tailed deer
64 Western giant eland
65 Wild Asiatic buffalo
66 Tamarau
67 Anoa
68 Kouprey
69 European bison
70 American bison (wood bison)
71 Jentink's duiker
72 Giant sable antelope
73 Arabian oryx
74 Scimitar-horned oryx
75 Addax
76 Bontebok
77 Hunter's hartebeest
78 Swayne's hartebeest
79 Black wildebeest
80 Beira
81 Slender-horned gazelle
82 Sumatran serow
83 Japanese serow
84 Takin
85 Nilgiri tahr
86 Walia ibex
87 Markhor
88 Cyprian mouflon

Wildlife in Danger

by

James Fisher, Noel Simon, Jack Vincent

and members and correspondents of the
Survival Service Commission of the International Union for
Conservation of Nature and Natural Resources

Foreword by

Harold J. Coolidge

and

Peter Scott

Preface by

Joseph Wood Krutch

A Studio Book
THE VIKING PRESS
New York

Published in 1969 by The Viking Press, Inc.
625 Madison Avenue, New York, N.Y. 10022

Library of Congress catalog card number: 69-12903

This book was designed and produced in Great Britain by
George Rainbird Ltd., Marble Arch House, 44 Edgware Road, London W2

Printed and bound in Great Britain by
Jarrold and Sons Ltd., Norwich

CONTENTS

ILLUSTRATIONS

Note: Adjacent subjects are not always shown on the same scale.

Colour Plates

Drawings in Black and White

PREFACE

Never in the history of the world has there been so much concern over man's violation of the natural environment and the disappearance of what was once an abundant wildlife. This is an encouraging fact, but it carries a discouraging implication. We are more concerned today than ever before because never before have the destructive processes operated at such a rapidly accelerating rate. Despite new legislation and the establishment of new parks and wilderness areas, the tide is still running against everything except the growth of the human population, and the consequent elimination of everything which is not man-made and man-dominated. Even Africa, which seemed not long ago a great reservoir of the wild and the beautiful, is now threatened by its own "developing nations" despite international concern and the establishment of protected areas.

Pessimists sometimes insist that if the population explosion continues there will be no room for anything except human beings and then, presently, no room even for them. Mankind, as Harrison Brown pointed out, "is behaving as if it were engaged in a contest to test nature's willingness to support humanity, and would, if it had its way, not rest content until the earth is covered completely to a considerable depth with a writhing mass of human beings, much as a dead cow is covered with a pulsating mass of maggots."

If this prospect were absolutely inevitable, then conservation would be no more than a rearguard, or delaying, action. But if it is just possible that the human race will discover in time how to avoid both mass destruction on the one hand and mass starvation or mass suffocation on the other, then it is surely worthwhile to preserve as much as we can of all the beauties, animate and inanimate, of our earth. Destroyed buildings can be rebuilt; destroyed works of art may possibly be replaced by new creations; but every animal and every flower which becomes extinct is lost forever in the most absolute of all deaths.

If the concern which many feel is to be effective, the public at large must know what is happening and must feel very strongly that it ought not to happen. Considerable knowledge is already available, and there are today far more books than ever before extolling the beauties of nature and lamenting their violation. But there is not, to the best of my knowledge, any other book quite like the present one. It is a complete reference library in itself, presenting the facts with encyclopedic thoroughness.

In our own country the destruction of the natural environment and its population has reached a state somewhere between that of Europe on the one hand and Africa on the other. In Africa man is just beginning to threaten the existence of its wildlife, including what Thoreau calls the nobler animals. England and the European continent have been so impoverished by deliberate destruction and, more importantly, by the simple pre-empting of available space, that naturalists can hope for no more than the preservation of a pitiful remnant. We in America, on the other hand, have just recently reached the point where saving rather than clearing the forests typifies what ought to be our ambition, although many continue to talk as though we were still pioneers in an empty land and to boast of inexhaustible resources when, in fact, resources as indispensable as space, pure air, and pure water are approaching exhaustion.

Neither laws aiming at some sort of conservation nor others intended to encourage killing are new. In 1630 the Massachusetts Bay Colony provided a penny bounty for each wolf killed, which was no doubt justified at a time when men had only a precarious foothold on the continent they were presently to conquer all too thoroughly. But we are only now beginning to get rid of the senseless poisoning of coyotes by the government and the bounty-payments on pumas in some of the Western states. Sixty years after the first payment of a bounty on wolves came the first measure directed at conservation, when Massachusetts established a closed season for deer and followed it in 1710 by a law prohibiting the use of camouflaged canoes, or boats equipped with sails in the pursuit of waterfowl. Both were admirable measures, and have been followed by many others. But it is usually a case of too little and too late. Hunters continue to press for the right to use high-powered rifles equipped with telescopic lenses for the slaughter of the nearly extinct mountain sheep in the fastnesses to which it has retreated. In Baja California, Mexico, where most game laws are either nonexistent or unenforced, they have all but exterminated this once plentiful animal.

Who cares? Many do, but not everyone does. It is said that when Audubon sought a subscription to *The Birds of America* from a wealthy citizen he was answered by the declaration "I would not pay that much for all the live birds in the United States, much less for pictures of them." Indeed, it is not uncommon to observe a sort of backlash provoked by increased public concern with conservation. Human needs, it is said, come first, though the question "What needs of what people?" is less often asked. The whole assumption that some contact with the natural world is conducive to physical and emotional health is often rejected. Once proposals to conserve were met with nothing worse than indifference. Now they are sometimes met with rationalized arguments ranging from simple enthusiasm for superhighways to the theory that the aim of civilization is not the preservation of the natural but its ultimate elimination – including the destruction of everything which does not serve the primary needs of an exploding population. As a dean at Massachusetts Institute of Technology recently put it, "in hedonic potential, megalopolis is no more and no less a natural environment for man than Athens or a peasant village."

Today most people would be inclined to reply to his defense of megalopolis by citing recent experimental evidence which seems to demonstrate that crowding not only reduces "hedonic potential" but also produces many disorders unknown where adequate elbow-room is available. Others (and I would include myself among them) are inclined to insist that there is such a thing as human nature and that it needs contact with the natural world of which it is a part. Perhaps the late William Morton Wheeler, an impeccable technical scientist, put the whole thing most succinctly when he wrote about our fellow creatures: "That, apart from the members of our own species, they are our only companions in an infinite and unsympathetic waste of electrons, planets, nebulae and stars, is a perennial joy and consolation."

JOSEPH WOOD KRUTCH

FOREWORD

This book contains information as objective as a global consensus of biological expertise can make it. It is an illustrated collection of facts about some of the more important living things whose survival on our planet is patently in danger.

Its message is of bad tidings: of disaster. Here and there it also carries a message of hope. It is written neither in optimism nor in pessimism, but simply objectively, as part of the duty to focus world attention on wildlife in crisis that the International Union for Conservation of Nature and Natural Resources has charged itself with. To analyse, inform, and prescribe is the I.U.C.N.'s assignment. It has many friends who have helped it with the first two tasks. The third needs money and power; and one of the purposes of this book is to help to raise its money, and increase its power – to turn more of its intelligence files into action files, to spread the conservation message from the committed to the uncommitted. We believe that this may prove to be one of the most important documents that we have so far placed before the general public, and those who form and lead world opinion and are responsible for action.

The I.U.C.N. is a relatively young organization, and it has had a somewhat complicated evolution. In 1934, on private initiative, the O.I.P.N. (l'Office International pour la Protection de la Nature) was founded in Brussels. After an international conference at Fontainebleau sponsored by UNESCO and the Government of France, this evolved into the I.U.P.N. – the International Union for the Protection of Nature. By 1956 its widening circle of supporting naturalists, ecologists, and conservationists felt that its role and new dynamism called for another change of name: and since then its designation has been the International Union for Conservation of Nature and Natural Resources.

The main purpose of the I.U.C.N. is to perpetuate wild nature and natural resources all over the world. It is dedicated to promoting or supporting any action that may ensure this perpetuation. Its devotion to nature is twofold: to its intrinsic cultural and scientific values; and to its values to long-term human welfare, economic and social. Its chief concern is with man's modification of the natural environment through the rapid spread of urban and industrial development and the excessive exploitation of the earth's natural resources, upon which rest the very foundations of man's survival.

It has evolved into an independent international organization whose membership comprises states (irrespective of their political and social systems), government departments, private societies and institutions, and international organizations. It is not a United Nations organization; but it enjoys the support of U.N. agencies such as the Food and Agriculture Organization (F.A.O.), the Educational, Scientific, and Cultural Organization (UNESCO), the Economic and Social Council (ECOSOC), and that of the Council of Europe and other inter-governmental bodies. With all of these it has full consultative status. It also has a special relationship with the International Council for Bird Preservation (I.C.B.P.), an organization of some seniority and experience, first conceived in 1902 and formally founded in 1922, and with the World Wildlife Fund, founded in 1961.

The I.U.C.N. works through six Commissions: Ecology, Education, Landscape Planning, Legislation, National Parks, and Survival Service. This book has been written by the Survival Service Commission (formed in 1949, and now with over fifty members from over twenty countries), whose responsibility is to collect data on, and to maintain lists of, all wild animals and plants that may be in danger of extinction, and to initiate action to prevent it. Since July 1966 the official version of this list – the Red Data Book – has been published in a new, loose-leaf, lithographed form by the I.U.C.N. from its head-quarters in Morges, Switzerland, and a periodic issue is made of new sheets (as the status of organisms changes), which brings the subscribers' information regularly up to date. This present book is an extended, selected, and specially illustrated version of the Red Data Book (which of course continues to expand and maintain its revision service), compiled from the Red Data Book itself, and other sources, by three of the workers most deeply involved.

Jack Vincent, who till recently was responsible for the bird sheets in the Red Data Book, has written the accounts of about half the birds in the present volume. Formerly Director of the National Parks of Natal, South Africa, he represents the International Council for Bird Preservation. Until he returned to conservation service in Natal in the second half of 1967, Col. Vincent was the Secretary of the Survival Service Commission.

Noel Simon, responsible for the mammal (and various other) sheets in the Red Data Book, has written the accounts of the mammals in the present volume. He is responsible for the organization and administration of the I.U.C.N.'s Operations Intelligence Centre. He was founder and first Chairman of the East African Wild Life Society, and Deputy Director of the Kenya National Parks.

James Fisher, at present Deputy Chairman of the Countryside Commission of the United Kingdom, is a zoologist by training and an ornithologist by vocation. He is a Survival Service commissioner and a council member of the Fauna Preservation Society, a British-based international conservation organization of long standing that works in full and whole-hearted cooperation with the I.U.C.N. (The Chairman of the S.S.C. is also Chairman of the F.P.S., and Mr and Mrs R. S. R. Fitter, also Survival Service commis-sioners, are respectively secretary to the F.P.S. and editor of its journal *Oryx*.) Mr Fisher has written the accounts of the rest of the birds, and also the reptiles, in this book.

The S.S.C. gratefully acknowledges the special articles that have been contributed to this volume by Dr Coleman J. Goin (amphibians), Dr Robert Rush Miller and Dr Ethelwynn Trewavas (fishes), and Dr F. Nigel Hepper (plants). It is grateful also for the generous support given to the Red Data Book by the New York Zoological Society and by the World Wildlife Fund.

Harold J. Coolidge, B.S. SC.D.(Hon.)
President of the International Union for Conservation of Nature and Natural Resources

Peter Scott, C.B.E., D.S.C., M.A., LL.D.
Chairman of the Survival Service Commission of the I.U.C.N.

INTRODUCTION

The Red Data Book of the Survival Service Commission of the International Union for Conservation of Nature and Natural Resources was published in a new, lithographed form in July 1966, and is the guiding intelligence document for workers all over the world in forming their policies for the conservation, and indeed preservation, of endangered species of animals and plants. As it is in loose-leaf form, the batches of new leaves are sent to its subscribers as the status of living things changes (which it does often with alarming rapidity).

The "Red", of course, is for Danger. The S.S.C. has another list, which could be called Black for Death, or rather extinction; organisms extinct since 1600 (or believed to be so) are recorded periodically in the *I.U.C.N. Bulletin*.

The year 1600 might be thought an arbitrary date; but it has been chosen for a good reason. The S.S.C., not surprisingly, has more precise information about the higher vertebrates – the birds and mammals – than about any other organisms. Virtually all the mammals and birds known to have become extinct since 1600 are identified by adequate descriptions or portraits, nearly all of them by skins, and a considerable number also by subfossil bones; all but two that we can critically admit have acceptable Linnean or scientific names.[1] The two will doubtless soon be formally named. The year 1600 is the year after which zoologists know at least the colours (more than less) of the extinct birds and mammals. Of course zoologists know of very many animals extinct in historical times, though before 1600: but only in a few exceptional cases, based on very rare early documentary evidence, do they know the colours of these; and only very exceptionally do they possess their skins, or parts of them. So 1600 is accepted by the S.S.C. as the reckoning date for modern extinction. It is a practical date that happens to coincide with the approximate beginning of the civilized epoch's own special attack on wild nature.

To summarize the erosion of the variety of wild life, whose study and cure is the particular duty of the S.S.C., a simple statement can be made.

In 1600 there were approximately 4,226 living species of mammals. Since then thirty-six (or 0·85 per cent) have doubtless become extinct; and at least 120 of them (or 2·84 per cent) are presently in some (or great) danger of extinction.

In 1600 there were approximately 8,684 living species of birds. Since then ninety-four (or 1·09 per cent) have doubtless become extinct; and at least 187 of them (or 2·16 per cent) are presently, or have very lately been, in danger of extinction. Of the single order Passeriformes (the "higher" singing birds), which with about 5,153 species in 1600 represented nearly three-fifths of the living birds, twenty-eight (0·54 per cent) are now extinct and at least seventy (1·36 per cent) presently in danger; of the rest, about 3,531 species in 1600, sixty-six (1·87 per cent) are now extinct and at least 117 (3·32 per cent) in danger.

To sum up: a hundredth of our higher animals have become extinct since 1600 and nearly a fortieth are now in danger. These figures apply to full species: geographical races – or subspecies –

[1] The expression "Linnean name" is used in celebration of the founder of scientific naming, Linnaeus of Sweden, and in preference to the usual expression "Latin name", not as an exercise in pedantry, but because nearly as many Linnean names are derived from the Greek as from the Latin.

of our higher animals have had a similar fate. Among the mammals whose species survive, at least sixty-four races have become extinct since 1600, and at least 223 races are still surviving but are included in the Red Data Book. Among the birds, 164 races have become extinct and at least 287 are presently endangered.

As will emerge, this is a state of affairs that is quite without parallel in the former span of man's life with nature, that is to say, in his less civilized history before 1600. What has happened to the mammals and birds since 1600?

It is not easy to measure, despite the fact that the files of the Survival Service Commission are much deeper and more complete for the mammals and birds than for any other animals or any plants. What we have tried to do is the following.

Every entry in the Red Data Book mentions the causes of the rarity (or extinction) of an animal as completely as the available information warrants. Not all the evidence is of the same value. Some of it is very deep. Some of it is slender. If some of it is obviously guesswork, we have ignored it. But most of our researches and investigations have given us at least leads and pointers, to the extent that in all cases we have been able to identify one or more of five main factors. These are:

Natural causes. Extinction is a biological reality: it is part of the process of evolution. The study of fossils tells us that before man came on the scene the mean life of a bird species was rather over 2,000,000 years, of a mammal species not much over 600,000. No species has yet "lived" more than a few million years before evolving into one or more others, or "dying" without issue. In any period, including the present, there are doomed species: naturally doomed species, bound to disappear through over-specialization, an incapacity to adapt themselves to climatic change or the competition of others, or occasionally some natural cataclysm of earthquake, eruption, flood, or the like.

Hunting. Pressure on species is exerted by the human hunter for food, clothing, sport, or scientific, quasi-scientific, or status-symbol collection, or as a means of "disease", "pest", or "vermin" control; or pressure as a consequence (usually not intended) of the control of other pests, particularly by poisons.

Introduced predators. These exist most commonly in areas colonized since 1600, where mammal predators particularly have been introduced (as in the West Indies, Australia, and New Zealand) to "keep down" the explosive populations of other introduced animals (for instance, rats and rabbits) and have readily turned their predatory attention to the native fauna.

Other introduced animals. Among these are species that have become supplanting competitors in the native habitats of the indigenous animals, or even crude habitat-destroyers (goats in Galápagos), or animals that have brought into the habitats diseases against which the native forms have had little or no resistance (for example, in the Hawaiian archipelago and New Zealand).

Habitat disturbance and destruction. These involve the modification, degradation, and sometimes total destruction of habitat, usually by humans, and most particularly through the felling of forests and the drainage of swamps, for timber, farming space, reservoirs, buildings, airfields, and many other purposes, even sometimes including recreation.

To arrive at some assessment of the relative importance of these main factors, we have awarded eight marks to each species on our list, and shared them in a proportion between the five factors based on our common-sense judgement of the evidence available. This has been a somewhat arbitrary process in cases where the evidence is slender; but we could not think of a better. Expressed as percentages of the total marks that fell to each factor, the results are as in the table opposite.

From this it appears that only about a quarter of the species of birds and mammals that have become extinct since 1600 may have died out naturally: humans, directly or indirectly, may be

	BIRDS			MAMMALS
	Non-passerine (large)	Passerine (small)	Total	
Cause of extinction	per cent	per cent	per cent	per cent
Natural	26	20	24	25
Human				
hunting	54 ⎫	13 ⎫	42 ⎫	33 ⎫
introduced predators	13 ⎬ 74	21 ⎬ 80	15 ⎬ 76	17 ⎬ 67
other introductions	– ⎪	14 ⎪	4 ⎪	6 ⎪
habitat disruption	7 ⎭	32 ⎭	15 ⎭	19 ⎭
	100	100	100	100
Cause of present rarity				
Natural	31	32	32	14
Human				
hunting	32 ⎫	10 ⎫	24 ⎫	43 ⎫
introduced predators	9 ⎬ 69	15 ⎬ 68	11 ⎬ 68	8 ⎬ 86
other introductions	2 ⎪	5 ⎪	3 ⎪	6 ⎪
habitat disruption	26 ⎭	38 ⎭	30 ⎭	29 ⎭
	100	100	100	100

responsible for the extermination of the rest. Also, about four-sixths of the birds and five-sixths of the mammals presently known to be in danger of extinction may have come to their present state because of man's activities. Most, but by no means all, of these live or lived on islands, whose faunas (and floras) are far more vulnerable than those of continents to the influence of civilized man.

In 1965 fossil bones were found in Hungary belonging to our (probably) ancestral species, *Homo erectus,* in a deposit that was laid down in a shortish period of relaxation of the second principal advance (the Mindelian advance) of the European ice systems in the Pleistocene Ice Age. Radio-active and astronomical datings agree that this man lived about 470,000 years ago – nearly twice as long ago as the oldest known *Homo sapiens*, the famous Swanscombe fossil from Kent. The Pleisto-cene period is now generally agreed to have started well over 1,000,000 years ago, and has been characterized by a global climate far more fluctuating than at any time in the previous 10,000,000 years (or so) of Pliocene times. In the northern part of the Northern Hemisphere and in the southern part of the Southern Hemisphere the Pleistocene brought in a series of ice advances and retreats – in the north a succession of four major and up to a dozen minor ice advances, with warmer or even sometimes quite hottish periods in between. Some of these ice advances covered very large areas indeed of the northern continents.

There is no evidence, in fact, that we are "out" of the Ice Ages yet: many geologists think that we are living at present in no more than an "interglacial" period that started about 10,000 years ago and may continue for no more than another 10,000 or so before the ice returns.

Despite the climate's alternation of hot and cold in the Pleistocene, unlike any that had previously occurred (as the rock records show) for millions of years, the mammals and birds adapted them-selves well to it – better than the flowering plants. After a beginning when a number of specialized Pliocene species and groups fell out, the Pleistocene fauna settled down to evolve in its own way, producing all manner of new genera and species, including some specialist forms and even giant species, and one highly successful species whose very success depended on its non-specialist adaptability – man: whose immediate ancestors are now believed beyond any reasonable doubt to have evolved in Africa in the period between the end of the Pliocene about 3,000,000 years ago and the onset of Pleistocene glaciations in the north, with parallel dry and wet periods in Africa, about 1,000,000 years ago.

The stabilized Pleistocene faunas of all the continents are – or were – dominated by highly adapted big land animals, with which big predators and scavengers were associated. Huge elephants and rhinoceroses even became successfully adapted to life in the tundra where the undersoil was permanently frozen.

South America had its huge ground-sloths and glyptodons (super-armadillos); North America its super-elephants, super-bison, super-camels, and super-lions; even Europe its share of elephants and hippos and giant bison. All continents had arrays of giant birds: North America had the vast teratorns – the biggest birds of prey known to science; Europe had its Maltese super-vulture (last heard of at Monte Carlo 100,000 years ago or so) and a super-swan so big that it must have been flightless. Only Africa today – and perhaps for special and complicated reasons – still has a characteristic Pleistocene fauna; and that is now mainly in the national parks and game reserves: big elephants, rhinos, giraffes, vultures, and storks, and a galaxy of magnificent antelopes. The isolated lands had their Pleistocene heyday, too – Australia with giant marsupials; New Zealand with its moa fauna, the tallest (up to 12-foot) birds known; Madagascar with its elephant-bird (the biggest, half a ton) and super-lemur fauna. Even the isolated little Mauritius, Réunion, and Rodriguez islands in the Indian Ocean had their own flourish through (and after) the Pleistocene with their dodos and other curious flightless birds.

By general agreement among geologists and paleontologists (and largely to make definitions and meanings clear), the Pleistocene is considered to have ended "officially" a little over 10,000 years ago. The period we live in is called the Holocene – even if the ice may soon come back (using "soon" in the geological sense), and we may be still in the Pleistocene, in terms of irregular climate-changes. In terms of faunas, the Pleistocene really ended in Europe, perhaps also in most of Asia, more or less at the beginning of the official Upper Pleistocene over 100,000 years ago; in North America about 8,000 years ago; in the West Indies and Central and South America rather later than that; in Australia at the most twenty, but probably only a few, thousand years ago; in New Zealand after A.D. 950. The main reason why the Pleistocene fauna, as characterized by its more exaggerated and highly adapted (and therefore vulnerable) elements, collapsed in these different places at different times seems to be a simple one: the coming of man the hunter, Stone Age man – in the case of the Indian Ocean islands, civilized man.

Now, the Pleistocene fauna has not yet departed from Africa, or rather from the continent south of the Sahara that is the home of the present Ethiopian fauna (this fauna extended sometimes to France up to Miocene times, perhaps 20,000,000 years ago). Yet it was in Africa that man evolved in the Pleistocene period, from higher apes. Is there a paradox here? Probably not. As man evolved, the Pleistocene fauna of Africa evolved with him, and developed defence adaptations as he rather quickly became the most intelligent and skilful hunting animal the world has ever known. Very probably Stone Age man destroyed some large African species; but he did not destroy the Pleistocene fauna. It was when man became an armed invader of new faunal areas that their faunas, without such adaptations, became decimated (in some cases literally so, or more than so).

Sapient man of our own kind was, as we have seen, in Europe about 250,000 years ago. The heavy Pleistocene elements disappeared as his skills improved; the forest elephant and hippopotamus and perhaps the giant vulture about 100,000 years ago; the forest rhino not long afterwards. The bird fauna was already a modern one: of the Pleistocene types, only the French sarus crane and the cave chough lasted until the late Pleistocene times of the sophisticated Magdalenian cave men. The giant deer lasted beyond the official end of the Pleistocene up to the Iron Age. The other last big animals (apart from bison and aurochs) retreated to Siberia, where the last mammoths and woolly rhinos, tundra-adapted, probably survived until the last glaciation, when a warm spell made it too boggy for them to range in the summer.

The impact of man upon the animals of America was much more sudden and sweeping.

The great Rancho la Brea fauna fossilized in the asphalt tarpits of Los Angeles is the most complete and the best worked out array of its kind in the world. As we now know from carbon dating, it survived, at least in part, well beyond the official end of the Upper Pleistocene 10,000 years ago. It is now certain that the earliest Amerindians reached North America at least 15,000 and possibly (or even probably) over 30,000 years ago – that is to say, in the Upper Pleistocene – and rather quickly penetrated to what is now the western United States.

Early man in North America encountered a Pleistocene fauna. From the evidence of the Rancho la Brea tarpits, his bones and atlatl darts are associated there with the fossils of early prehistoric or Holocene age.

Now, of fifty-four different species of mammals in the la Brea tarpits of Upper Pleistocene to prehistoric date (at the broadest from a little over 18,000 to a little less than 4,500 years ago), twenty-four, or nearly half, are now extinct; and of 113 fully identified birds twenty-two, or nearly a fifth, are extinct.

Gone now, amongst others, are the huge dire wolf; the short-faced coyote; the vast short-faced bear; the big sabre-toothed cat, *Smilodon*; the giant lion (or jaguar), *Panthera atrox* (the present lion in linear measurements plus a quarter); the super-camel or super-llama, *Camelops*, 7 feet at the withers; the American mastodon (6 feet 3 inches); the imperial (10 feet 8½ inches) and Columbian mammoths; and the greater (huge), middle, and lesser la Brea ground-sloths. Gone these are indeed; but it seems certain that they did not go until after the coming of man.

Gone too are Rancho la Brea's peculiarly Pleistocene birds, many of them also giants. Nearly all the great latest-Pleistocene birds of North America that we know of are represented in the Rancho la Brea fauna, including all the remarkable extinct birds of prey of that time. From the regions in which their fossils have been found, we can be sure that at least a dozen of them survived to early human times. The asphalt stork was evidently the New World representative of our Old World white and black storks, and stood, on slender limbs, about 4 feet 6 inches high. The extinct la Brea turkey, or ground-fowl, was a robust bird not unlike the surviving ocellated turkey of Mexico that, from the abundance of its bones, must have been the commonest game bird of what is now the Los Angeles district in la Brean times.

Of the great Rancho la Brea raptors, the largest was Merriam's teratorn, which had a 12-foot wingspread and an estimated weight of 50 pounds, and which was doubtless a scavenger on the corpses of the giant mammals. *Teratornis merriami* may have persisted until the tarpit faunas of about 4,500 years ago. Its congener (member of the same genus), the incredible teratorn, *T. incredibilis*, which, with a wingspan of 16 to 17 feet, was the largest soaring bird of prey yet known to have lived, survived not quite so long – in Nevada, until the Upper Pleistocene.

Most important of all among six other birds of prey of Rancho la Brea, for the simple reason that it is (just) with us, and a Red Data Book bird of the Survival Service Commission, was *Gymnogyps*. Males of the California condor (and there are about twenty of them left alive) run to a wingspread of 9 feet 7 inches and a weight of 23 pounds. The California condor, *Gymnogyps californianus*, and what is probably its rather bigger direct ancestor, *G. amplus* (the transition from one species to the other, if separate species they really were, seems to have taken place around the official end of the Pleistocene 10,000 years ago), in Pleistocene years ranged west of the Rocky

Mountains from the border of Washington and British Columbia in the north to that of California and Mexico's Lower California in the south; also in a great strip across the southern states from New Mexico through Texas to Florida. By the time the modern Americans had opened up the West, it had retreated west of North America's great Rocky Mountain spine. To cut a story short, it was confined to a few counties of California with a population of about sixty in 1947; by 1963 was nesting and roosting in but two California counties; and between these two main years of survey (on behalf of the National Audubon Society) had been reduced to a world population of only about forty-two (see p. 198).

To bring the story of the California condor up to modern times has been a digression. Only in the last forty years has the Upper Pleistocene presence of man in America been confirmed, and only lately have archaeologists and paleontologists begun to collate his hearths and flints and other remains with the last of the North American mastodons and mammoths, big tortoises and birds. With the success and spread of carbon dating, the collapse of the North American Pleistocene super-fauna has been narrowed down to a period of between 11,000 and 8,000 years ago; which makes it very sudden. Only a few of the big extinct mammals and birds held on longer. The period of "Pleistocene over-kill", now recognized as a phenomenon that has occurred at one time or another all over man's realm, which means all over the world, was short in North America, and marches with the development of the sophisticated flints of the Clovis and Folsom cultures, tools quite effective enough to kill and butcher an elephant.

New Zealand's higher vertebrate fauna has naturally consisted almost entirely of birds, which had a remarkable adaptive radiation into mammal niches, the great order of the moas taking the place of big grazers. When the first humans – Polynesians – discovered the main islands and the offlying Chatham Islands in about A.D. 950, they were confronted with an array of classic Pleistocene quality, an indigenous bird fauna that can be guessed, from the evidence of the fossil and living examples, to have been over 150 species. Before Captain Cook's time, the Polynesians had killed off at least twenty species of moas, and shortly after the European discovery the last one was killed, on South Island, in the late eighteenth century. The Polynesians and the Europeans (who helped a little towards the end) killed off about a third of the birds of the islands. The fact that the present nesting fauna of the islands is up to about 147 is the consequence of thirty-five successful introductions of non-native birds by the Europeans, and eight known natural colonizations in European times. At least forty-three New Zealand species have been globally lost since the Polynesians arrived, nine of them since 1600. Both families of the moas have been totally exterminated, and with them two flightless geese, a great swan, a great eagle, flightless rails, interesting passerines like the extraordinary huia (this, early in the present century). At least a dozen surviving New Zealand birds are in the Survival Service Commission's Red Data Book. A few, like the famous flightless rail, *Notornis*, the takahé (p. 231), seem to be holding their own under close protection. The very status of others (that is, whether surviving or extinct), like the piopio, or New Zealand thrush (p. 301), and the New Zealand laughing owl (p. 261), is still mysterious. New Zealand is blessed with energetic and skilful ornithologists; but it is a rugged country to work over, and the competition of the introduced exotics may be an important cause of the rarity and "pocket isolation" of the ancient indigenous song-birds at least.

In Hawaii, a still further isolated archipelago, even more exotics have been introduced than in New Zealand. Here the old fauna does not seem to have been destroyed by the first Polynesian colonists, who probably arrived there before they discovered New Zealand. But the Westerners who arrived since Captain Cook have brought about the extermination of fourteen species, and have brought perhaps as many more to Red Data Book status. Destruction of habitat has been as powerful as the introduction of disease and competitors. The status of many species now hangs in the balance, despite the efforts of the excellent farming and conservation authorities, and the watchful Hawaiian Audubon Society. There is a triumph here to report, though. The native Hawaiian goose, or néné (p. 189), with the help of a remarkable programme of captive culture in England at the Wildfowl Trust's Slimbridge and in Hawaii at Pohakuloa, and with the successful release of nearly 200 birds into the wild population, has been restored in numbers from its all-time lowest around fifty just over a decade ago to ten times that. The population of the Hawaiian duck (p. 192) is turning the corner, too; and the Laysan teal (p. 195) is now flourishing both on its isolated home at the western end of the long Hawaiian chain, and in captivity.

Stone Age man, then, has been a fauna-exterminator. If we narrow the period of Pleistocene over-kill in North America to 3,000 years, we can find with some reasons that in or around that time about fifty mammals and forty birds may have been extinguished at most: that is to say, not more than three every century on average. Between the Polynesian colonization of New Zealand in about A.D. 950 and Cook's first voyage there in 1769, about thirty-six species of birds (there were no land mammals save rodents and bats) were extinguished – not more than one every twenty years on average. Since 1769 seven more have gone, or about one every twenty-seven years on average. The world is not comparable with a part of itself; but it seems quite clear that on islands and in other specially vulnerable areas, where most of the modern extinctions have taken place and most of the Red Data Book animals are presently found, modern man has contrived to arrange an extinction rate even higher than that attained by an Old Stone Age community that discovered a fauna hitherto unknown to man. Of the ninety-four birds believed extinct since 1600, only the following became extinct that lived on continents: in Asia the pink-headed duck (1944), the Himalayan mountain quail (1868), Jerdon's courser (1900), and the forest spotted owlet (c. 1872); in North America the Labrador duck (1875), Cooper's sandpiper (1833), the passenger pigeon (1914), the Carolina parakeet (1914), and Townsend's bunting (1833). All the others have become extinct on islands large and small, particularly in New Zealand, Hawaii, and others of the South Seas, the Mascarene Islands of the Indian Ocean, and the West Indies. In the West Indies, from fossil and other evidence, we can calculate that the average expectation of total "geological" life of the larger bird species was about 180,000 years, before any humans arrived (much smaller than on the North American continent at the same time, owing to the specially fast natural evolution rate on islands). It was brought down to about 30,000 years by the aboriginal colonists in about 5,000 years of prehistoric times. It was brought down to a bare 12,000 years or so since 1600, after the establishment of the more sophisticated and civilized Western colonists. The pre-man bird species of Mauritius and Rodriguez in the Indian Ocean seem to have had a mean geological life-span of only about 6,000 years, from the fossils and their likely dating; these islands had no Stone Age phase, and their Western discoverers quickly brought the span, after 1600, down to about 1,000 years.

We have already seen that the suppression of fauna by man has been, and is, attained in several ways, and that hunting and habitat destruction are by far the most important and powerful. Hunting is our own society's almost ineradicable link with Old Stone Age times.

Hunting was the living of our species for 250,000 years or more, in which the Old Stone Age peoples learnt its art and tradition by trial and error. Masters of tools and fire, and, doubtless early on, of speech and pictorial art, the men of the Old Stone Age became food-gatherers, and skilful hunters of all things of the land and shallow waters, from shellfish to honey, from tubers to fruit, from sparrows to ostriches, from rodents to at least eight kinds of elephants and mastodons, rhinos, tapirs, bison, wild cattle, and huge deer. Hyena, wolf, cave lion, sabre-tooth, cave bear were their rivals at the top, and they learnt to master them, usurp their homes, share space and prey with them, and dominate the hunting-grounds. At some time in their evolution, many Stone Age groups encountered the effects of their own Pleistocene over-kill and developed lore of totem, taboo, and self-denying ordinance, cropping and rationing rules. Inventions, often quite independent, carried them over thresholds of hunting power: bolas, hand-dart, spear-thrower, bow-and-arrow, throwing-stick, boomerang, blowpipe, stalking-horse, deadfall, trap, snare, net, decoy; and the domestication of the faithful dog and horse.

With the invention of methods of polishing and grinding stone to make tools for cutting tree and earth, our neolithic ancestors found it possible to settle, to let the nomadic rhythms of a purely hunting life cease or run down, to carve farms from the forests, plant seed, and become pastoralists. But even with metal, first copper and bronze and later hard iron, they never stopped hunting. Hunting became then a facet of their lives, not the main thing in their lives. Its rules and arts became more complex, and its practice began to have a class structure. In the Dark Ages of the early sophistication of iron, a trend began – to organize hunting as a noble pursuit: parks in the Dark Ages became conservation areas under rules in essence no different from (though cruder than) those that exist in modern African game reserves, or syndicate areas in Britain's pheasant woodlands, or in the hills and fields of Pennsylvania at the opening of the deer season, or the wetlands of Russia when duck-hunting begins. High hunting art, the more interesting because of its relative, and perhaps unconsciously fostered, inefficiency, reached its climax with the invention of falconry, probably in several countries quite independently; in the English Bronze Age; at about the same time, or a little earlier, in China (c. 2000 B.C.); and with a wonderful flourishment in Dark Age Persia and Arabia and Europe.

The painters of magical animals of the chase at Lascaux in France have left us what is doubtless the earliest surviving work of art, including a picture of a rhinoceros that can represent (unless the artist took remarkable liberties) none other than Merck's forest rhinoceros, a very close relation of the Sumatran rhinoceros (p. 114), which is not known from any fossil deposits younger than about 30,000 years! The Persian kings of old enclosed little wildernesses of hunting land and called them paradises, and the Norman kings of England did the same and called them parks and chases. The Zulu King Dingaan, himself no mean hunter of elephants and trader in ivory, established a protected game park years before the present game-park system was developed in Africa, north of the Umfolozi River, where today the square-lipped rhinoceros (p. 117) still has a headquarters. The Vikings of a thousand years ago or more established a sea-bird hunting culture in St Kilda and other parts of the Hebrides, and in Faeroe and Iceland, which still thrives in much of its old range (still shared by as many – or more – sea-birds), with very strict rules about the cropping season and the size of the "take". The northern world in America and Eurasia is networked with a complex array of public licence systems, and conservation areas both public and private, designed to foster hunting and at the same time the populations of the hunted; and the enlightened emergent nations are learning and copying and adapting the rules and experience with gratifying speed, especially in Africa.

The statements in the previous paragraph may appear to be somewhat disconnected. They have been so arranged deliberately, to show a common thread that runs through the history of hunting, woven from the facts that hunting has its atmosphere as well as its achievement, and that, even when it no longer supplies the main tribal or national protein, it continues to have, or indeed further refines, its complicated rules. It is when the rules are unknown, or lost and forgotten, or (as has happened lately) ruthlessly ignored, that a situation of over-kill develops.

We have seen that Stone Age people all over the globe attained the power to over-kill and extinguish at varying times in the Pleistocene and prehistoric epochs; and our ancestors learnt wisdom from the warning. This wisdom appears to have been widely forgotten again in our later years of post-Renaissance exploration, and particularly since the Industrial Revolution, and the rapid refinement of guns and other hunting tools, in the early nineteenth century. The over-killing of the whales cleared huntable whale populations out of the Northern Hemisphere before that century had finished, and promises (p. 61) to do the same for the Southern Hemisphere before the end of the present century. The modern over-kills are "investment over-kills", with expensive tools and loaned capital behind them. Such investments of money and skill run contrary to the public good and even to the interest of the investments (without mentioning the future of the animal species concerned) unless they can be planned and controlled. In our late historical times such conservation forces as have been available have resembled a weak, unarmed police force in a town where looting is going on. In the past the looters have often looted until there was nothing left worth looting – witness the whale trade, the seal trade, the sea-otter trade, and some fisheries. The bird-plumage trade has been mostly stopped, before any species became badly endangered by it, but was stopped only just in time. Serious over-hunting persists in many parts of Africa and some of Asia and the Americas – not all of it for protein, some in the name of sport: though, in most of the northern world and much of Australasia, the conservation leaders are perhaps more likely than not to be also experienced hunting sportsmen. Many people, especially those brought up in industrial towns, cannot understand that the roles of hunter and conservationist can be compatible, far less that they have proved compatible in some countries for ages, and long before Renaissance thought. Many people still find it hard to understand that the ultimate protection of nature, and all its ecological systems, and all its endangered forms of life, demands a plan, in which the core is a management of the wilderness, and an enlightened exploitation of its wild resources based on scientific research and measurement.

The latest phase of over-hunting is not quite describable as over-kill, since its products are wanted alive. Private aviculture all over the civilized world has multiplied in the last three decades by geometrical progression. There were about 526 zoos in the world in 1965, the number having doubled since 1946! This fantastic increase is largely due to the escalation of roadside menageries, many of which may never attain the standards and rules of the mainstream zoos, whose relation with the Survival Service Commission is excellent. The wholesale trade in zoo animals, involving illegalities and smuggling on its seamy side, is now turning over millions of pounds annually; and it concerns conservationists and opponents of cruelty to animals very deeply indeed.

Perhaps in the long run the over-kill of the over-capture (for it amounts to over-kill) will be controlled and prevented. That is what the I.U.C.N. is for. But the main battle is now, beyond any doubt, in the ecological field of habitat maintenance. It can of course be truly said that ever since New Stone Age times man has altered his environment deeply, with his power to cut down forests and drain wetlands. When the first men shortly reach the moon, they will probably be able to see the forest slashes of the last century with the naked eye, so accelerated have been the environmental changes of the Industrial Age. Already habitat destruction has contributed a significant share of the extinctions and endangerments of species since 1600. In the future, unless controlled, it may contribute an even greater share. In some tropical forest areas, of which the Philippines and Colombia are examples, lumbering has almost run wild: few scientists have been available to monitor and measure its effects, but insofar as they can be measured they are deplorable.

This book has been compiled from I.U.C.N. files as dispassionately as its compilers could find possible. Confronted with a list of species on the verge of extinction, and the high likelihood that three-quarters of them have become so because of man (and thus avoidably), a certain amount of rage might seem justified. Rage, however, does not cure. We hope that we can arouse righteous indignation with the accounts in this book, which are as true as we, and our many helpful naturalist friends and correspondents, have been able to make them. By the very act of buying it, our readers are supporting the cause of international conservation. We hope that our readers will be able to do more: join their local and national nature conservation societies, if they have not done so already; support their national sections of the International World Wildlife Fund; and help the I.U.C.N. and its Survival Service Commission, beyond the stage where its members and staff have to count the stamps, think twice before telephoning, and hitch-hike to conferences and field programmes. We need more time and power and money to learn, teach, persuade, and dissuade.

J. F.

MAMMALS

Order MARSUPIALIA
Family Dasyuridae: dasyures, etc.

THYLACINE or
TASMANIAN "WOLF"
Thylacinus cynocephalus

Largest of the living carnivorous marsupials, the thylacine shows with remarkable clearness how groups of animals can evolve in parallel. Creatures widely separated across the world may, when similar in habits, grow to resemble each other in appearance to an astonishing degree, if only superficially, even though they have evolved from entirely distinct stocks and under different conditions.

The discovery of the fossil remains of *Prothylacinus,* an animal almost identical with the living thylacine, in Miocene beds near Santa Cruz, is of particular interest in this connection, since it lends support to the theory that the thylacine reached Tasmania in warmer times by way of an antarctic continent linked with South America and Australia. On the Australian mainland no evidence of the animal has been found farther north than Victoria.

The Linnean name of the thylacine means "pouched dog with wolf head": a very apt description of the animal. Its general build is extraordinarily wolf-like, most so in its relatively large, squarish head. Its jaws are remarkable for their very wide gape, opening almost to its ears. Its teeth are similar to those of the dog family: and, like the African wild dog, the thylacine possesses no hallux or "great toe". Its tail is carried rigidly and cannot be wagged, and is also hairless and laterally compressed. At one time, not long after its discovery, the suggestion was made that the thylacine might be of an aquatic disposition. The pouch, a crescent-shaped flap of skin enclosing four mammae, opens aft, and the young are accommodated upside down; but, beyond the fact that three or four are normally carried in a female's pouch, little information is available on the animal's reproductive biology.

Until the 1930s, various zoos in Australia, Europe, and the United States exhibited thylacines. When caught young, the animals adapted themselves well to captivity. They have lived in menageries up to nine years, but have never bred; the Hobart Zoo (now defunct) had several in captivity about 1930, but used them for exchange and made no attempt at breeding.

The animal is about 1 foot $6\frac{1}{2}$ inches at the shoulders and has approximately seventeen transverse chocolate-coloured bands on its back, principally on the hind quarters. These stripes were the reason why the thylacine was dubbed "tiger" or "zebra wolf" by the early colonists. This zebra pattern is unusual among mammals. One of the few other animals to share it is the banded duiker (or zebra antelope), in West Africa; another is the numbat (p. 22).

The thylacine is almost entirely nocturnal, spending the greater part of the day in its lair and emerging at dusk to hunt. Its natural food includes wallabies and smaller marsupials as well as birds and small reptiles. When in pursuit of its prey it runs in a somewhat dog-like manner, but not as fast as a dog. It is said to follow its prey by scent at a steady trot, giving a final burst of speed when the quarry shows signs of exhaustion. Early reports said that, when really hard pressed, the thylacine would sometimes bound along on its hind legs much like a kangaroo.

The extinction of the thylacine on the Australian mainland probably came about through the agency of the dingo introduced by early aboriginal colonists. This feral domestic dog is a more successful animal with which it could not compete. The thylacine was still plentiful in Tasmania, however, no more than a century ago. As settlement increased, it acquired a taste for mutton and inevitably came into conflict with stockowners, because of damage it did to their flocks. This resulted in a relentless campaign to exterminate the carnivore. It was killed at every opportunity and by any means, and was usually so damaged in the process that very few skins and little skeletal material have been preserved for scientific purposes. One man claimed to have killed twenty-four in a single day. Poisoning was tried, but was found useless because thylacines never returned to the same carcass. They were pursued with hounds (although old males generally proved more than a match for several), and were easily snared in traps baited with kangaroo meat.

Between 1888 and 1909 the animal was subject to a Government bounty of £1 for each adult and 10s. for each sub-adult. During this period, and up to 1914, 2,268 thylacines are known to have been killed, but the actual number may well have been much greater.

At the same time the natural habitat was being "tamed" by farming activities, a factor that undoubtedly assisted the decline. A sudden rapid drop in numbers around 1910 is widely believed to have been accelerated by disease.

The westerly advance of settlement, extending from the central part of Tasmania, had the effect of driving the thylacine into the wild rough country in the western part of the state, where it now survives as a tiny remnant in comparison with the numbers that existed in the latter part of the last century. This region is mountainous, covered in parts with almost impenetrable bush, and intersected by numerous steep valleys and rocky gorges. It is a remote area, much of which is inaccessible and therefore free from molestation by trappers and casual shooters. The distribution of the thylacine within this region is presumably dependent on the occurrence of suitable prey species.

Here the thylacine has taken its last stand. Its numbers have declined so drastically that doubts have frequently been expressed whether it survives at all. During a series of investigations undertaken by the Tasmanian authorities shortly before the Second World War, evidence in the form of tracks indicated the existence of at least

half a dozen pairs, and the field studies covered only a portion of the area thought to be inhabited by thylacines. During the last twenty-five years individual animals have seldom been seen; but rare sightings do sometimes occur. There is good evidence that thylacines killed a few sheep in the Derwent Valley near Hobart in 1957. A young male was accidentally killed at Sandy Cape on the Tasmanian west coast in 1961. An animal (possibly a female with pups) used an old boiler as a lair at Mawbanna in the northwest in 1966. The animal is now known to exist in the Cradle Mountain National Park, and other sightings have been made in widely scattered localities, including the Cardigan River, the far north-west coast, and the Tooms Lake region.

The thylacine is now fully protected by law. There are heavy penalties for killing it in any circumstances. The responsible authorities are very conscious of the need to do everything possible to safeguard this interesting marsupial, and the Animals and Birds Protection Board, Hobart, has long been pressing for the establishment of a thylacine sanctuary in the large area lying to the east of Macquarie Harbour. Early in 1966 approval was given to the proclamation of a game reserve of 1,600,000 acres, known as the South-West District, extending from Low Rocky Cape to Sprent, to Kallista, and thence to South-West Cape. Cats, dogs, and guns are now prohibited in the region. The new reserve embraces a large part of the area in which the animal is believed to have survived in the greatest numbers, and where it is least subject to interference. The proclamation of the South-West District is a significant development in retaining a large area of habitat, not only for the thylacine but also for other indigenous fauna, including the rare Tasmanian race of the ground parrot, *Pezoporus wallicus leachi*.

RUSTY NUMBAT

Myrmecobius fasciatus rufus

One of the two races that constitute the numbat species (which is the sole representative of its genus), the "typical" one – *M. f. fasciatus*, the western numbat – occurs in south-western

Australia and is in no immediate danger. But the subspecies *M. f. rufus* is extremely rare.

Usually known as the eastern banded anteater, or rusty numbat, it is a small marsupial, slightly larger than a rat and weighing a little over 1 pound, its head and body combined being about 9½ inches long and the tail a further 7 inches. It is the most brilliantly coloured and patterned of all the marsupials, the general shade of its upper parts being a uniform rich russet, sparsely pencilled with pure white. Its under parts are a tawny ochre, never white as in the typical race. Across its back and rump are six or seven prominent transverse bars, either white or cream-coloured, on a rich brown background. A dark cheek-stripe passes through its eye, and above the eye is a whitish stripe. The outer surfaces of its ears are covered with bright reddish hairs from base to tip. Its tail is clad in long, rather bristly hairs that, when erected, give it a very bushy appearance. Normally the tail is carried horizontally with the tip inclining slightly upwards, but occasionally it is flicked into a vertical position, when its hairs may be fluffed out. The numbat's muzzle tapers sharply; its mouth is small, with a long, thin tongue that can be extended several inches. Its lower jaw has six molars on either side, bringing the total number of teeth up to fifty or fifty-two, more than are found in any other land mammal.

At one time the rusty numbat ranged from western New South Wales, where it lived at the junction of the Murray and Darling rivers, through South Australia as far south as Adelaide, into the eastern part of inland Western Australia. The animal is almost certainly extinct in New South Wales. It probably still survives in limited parts of South Australia and the adjoining part of Western Australia; but this is not certain. The last specimen known to have been collected was taken in 1950 in the Warburton Ranges, Western Australia, close to the meeting-point of South Australia, Western Australia, and the Northern Territory.

Various authors have suggested reasons for the decline of the rusty numbat, including bush fires, land clearance, and such introduced predators as (for example) the domestic dog and cat, and in particular the fox. Very little is in fact known about the animal. The following general observations are based on Calaby's work on the typical race, but they may well be equally applicable to *M. f. rufus*. In a paper published in 1960, Calaby states his belief that the part played by predators in the numbat's decline has been much exaggerated. With convincing logic, he points to the fact that foxes and feral cats are abundant in all areas where the typical race is still reasonably common. Moreover, the fox does most of its hunting at night, when the numbat is secure in its hollow-log shelter.

If fires occurred, they would undoubtedly eliminate the numbat from the burnt area, but bush fires are now so rare in the region favoured by the numbat that for all practical purposes they can be discounted. The normal forestry system of controlled burning appears to have little significant effect on the animal, since such slow burns mainly consume grass, fallen branches, leaves, and other woodland litter and do no harm to trees or sound hollow logs. This belief is supported by observations of numbats foraging in areas that are still smouldering.

The numbat's diet consists almost exclusively of termites. Having located them by scent, the numbat squats on its hind feet and digs rapidly into the subsoil with both paws, constantly stopping to lick up the exposed insects with rapid movements of its long, cylindrical tongue. The animal seldom remains in one place for long, and, even when termites are plentiful, it may abandon a favourable site, move to another spot, and begin digging again. Ants are also consumed, but this is probably accidental: the exposed termites attract the ants, which rush in to seize and carry them off and are then lapped up along with the termites.

Calaby also draws attention to other interesting features of the association between numbats and termites. Not only do termites constitute the numbat's most important source of food; they also consume the heart-wood of the eucalypts, thus providing the hollow-log shelters – essential for its mode of life – from which the numbat seldom ventures far. If disturbed, it will immediately run to a log shelter, and when chased from one it will make for another. Only with extreme difficulty can it be dragged from its log shelter. It will resist strenuously, sinking its claws into the wood and pressing its body against the roof of the cavity.

As a rule, the numbat is a solitary animal, except in spring, when young are present. It is out and about during the day, and much of its time is then occupied in searching for food, with movements that are normally jerky and suggestive of a squirrel. When the weather is not too hot it enjoys basking in the sun, either on the ground or on a log, where it lies on its "stomach" with limbs and tail stretched out. It is a docile animal and, when captured, never attempts to bite or scratch, contenting itself with voicing its protest by a series of rapidly repeated hissing noises or by low throaty growls.

Although a marsupial, the female numbat has no pouch; the young are firmly affixed to the teats, which, as with all marsupials, swell in their mouths. They also grasp the mother's hair with their paws. Females of the typical race normally have a litter of four; the young are born from January to April or May, and are carried or nursed by the mother through the Australian winter. By late August and September they become detached from the teats, and are put into a nest either in a hollow log or in a hole in the ground. By October at least some of the young are already foraging on their own.

Besides being protected by law, the entire known range of the rusty numbat is confined to the Woomera Rocket Range and certain aboriginal reserves. Entry into these areas is very strictly controlled either for security reasons or by the Aboriginal Welfare Departments. Little more, apparently, can or need be done at present to protect this subspecies. It is, moreover, encouraging to have Calaby's opinion that "there is a growing public sentimental attachment to this bright and active little creature which could assure its future in much the same way as public interest has helped the recovery of the koala in eastern Australia".

Family Phalangeridae: possums, etc.

LEADBEATER'S POSSUM
Gymnobelideus leadbeateri

One of the most interesting zoological events in recent years was the rediscovery in 1961 of Leadbeater's possum, a marsupial that for some years had been regarded as extinct.

In many respects *G. leadbeateri* bears a striking superficial resemblance to the sugar glider, *Petaurus breviceps,* but lacks the gliding membrane. It is a much more agile animal than the larger possums, and differs from them by having a tail that is compressed at the sides and narrow at the root but broadens to become bushy at the tip. The under surface of its tail has a distinct middle groove composed of shorter hairs; the tail is not especially prehensile, but it helps the animal's balance when climbing or leaping.

This possum's fingers and toes are spatulate at the tips, with claws short and strong, though the inner toe of each hind foot is clawless. The claws are less well developed than the sugar glider's, but the foot pads enable the animal to climb the trunks of large trees and thin branches with equal ease.

Males and females are similar in size, with a head and body of about 7 inches and a tail as long again; the fur is short, fine, and dense but not so silky as that of the sugar glider. The colour of the upper parts varies from grey to brownish-grey, and the fur of the under parts has a light grey base with dull creamy-yellow tips.

The animal's ears are sparsely covered with brown fur on the outer surface, but are hairless within. A dark stripe, which may vary considerably in width but is normally widest at the centre of its back, extends from rump to crown. There are also two black stripes on either side of its face, one from the upper part of the ear to the eye and the other from the lower part of the ear along the angle of the jaw.

Leadbeater's possum was described in 1867 by Sir Frederick McCoy, at that time Director of the National Museum of Victoria. The two original specimens were obtained in the Bass River valley in South Gippsland, Victoria.

Two further mounted specimens, one obtained in 1900 and the other in 1910, were at first assigned to this area, but later the 1910 specimen was shown to have come from the Koo-wee-rup Swamp (which has since been drained), 30 miles north of the Bass River.

In 1931 a further specimen was discovered among a collection of sugar glider skins. After an intense search, during which everyone within an area of 2,000 square miles was visited in an attempt to locate the donor, so that the place where the specimen was collected could be identified, proof was finally obtained that it came from Sunnyside, Mount Wills, at an altitude of 4,000 feet.

The search for further specimens continued for many years in eastern Victoria, but no more were found, and the species was assumed to be extinct. In April 1961, during a mammal survey in the Cumberland Valley, approximately 50 miles north-east of Melbourne, Mr H. E. Wilkinson, of the National Museum of Victoria, saw what he thought might be a Leadbeater's possum. A later search proved his assumption to be correct, and four specimens were afterwards obtained nearby at Tommy's Bend.

Leadbeater's possum *Cécile Curtis* 1966

Since then single specimens have been sighted elsewhere, one in July 1962 in a stand of shining gums, *Eucalyptus nitens,* at an altitude of 3,000 feet on the slopes of Ben Cairn, and the other in October 1962 among "mountain ash", *Eucalyptus regnans,* north-east of Healesville near the Black's Spur Road. On the 11th March 1963 a dead female was found at Warburton, Victoria, and when Mr Wilkinson visited the district a few days later he sighted a living specimen at Cement Creek, about 5 miles north of Warburton.

The present known population therefore consists of a small colony in the Tommy's Bend area occupying a range of roughly 100 square miles, plus individual sightings in four other areas. These sightings extended the range slightly, although it is necessary to bear in mind that distribution is unlikely to be continuous. The gradually increasing number of sight records may be attributed to the spread of the species from the areas that escaped destruction in the devastating bush fires that swept the Tommy's Bend area in 1939. The species may possibly still survive in the Mount Wills area, a region that contains much suitable habitat, although an earlier search found no evidence of its existence there.

No nest of *G. leadbeateri* has yet been discovered, and little information exists about the animal's social habits and behaviour. Most members of this family use hollow trees for nesting; Leadbeater's possum is assumed to be no exception and, like the sugar glider, may indulge in communal nesting. Little is known about its breeding biology beyond the fact that the gestation period is thought to be approximately two to three weeks; the animal has four mammae, and one specimen was found to be carrying a pair of pouch-young, which is believed to be the normal number.

The areas in which this possum has recently been sighted are all of dense eucalypt forest. The Tommy's Bend area, in the central highlands of Victoria, for example, consists of regenerating "mountain ash", the majority of trees now being 40 to 60 feet high and growing vigorously, interspersed with the skeletons of much larger fire-killed trees, some more than 150 feet in height. At a lower level, below the open canopy of eucalypts, is a dense layer of smaller trees and shrubs. This appears to be the type of habitat favoured by Leadbeater's possum, although, to judge from the few observations that have been made, it seems to have a preference for young saplings and wattles, among which, in its search for insects, it can utilize its nimbleness to full advantage.

The "mountain ash" habitually sheds long strips of bark, which tend to lodge and accumulate in the branches and become attractive to the insects that are believed to form the possum's diet. In the specimens so far examined, no evidence of vegetable matter has yet been found.

The possum is also thought to follow the example of the sugar glider in extracting and eating the larvae of beetles that infest young wattle trees. Captive specimens have rejected most fruits, seeds, blossoms, leaves, and raw meat, all of which have been readily accepted by captive sugar gliders. To start with, the possums also refused mealworms, but these later became an important constituent of the diet.

The nocturnal and arboreal habits of Leadbeater's possum suggest that it is subject to predation by owls and certain carnivorous marsupials. This assumption is supported by the evidence of Mr N. Wakefield, who in 1960 investigated deposits of owl pellets in certain caves in eastern Victoria. Among the older deposits comprising remains of several thousand small mammals were at least fifty specimens of Leadbeater's possum. But the more recent material contained only one, a fair indication that the animal was once rather more abundant.

Other nearby bone deposits, which are believed to have been laid down by the eastern native cat, *Dasyurus quoll*, contained remains of *Gymnobelideus*, and, although the eastern native cat is now extremely rare in Victoria, it may have preyed on the possum; so may other carnivores, including the feral cat, which is not uncommon in the bush. Another potential predator is the common goanna, *Varanus varius*, a large monitor lizard that is an active climber known to prey on many kinds of birds and mammals.

There is, however, no evidence to support the suggestion that normal predation by carnivores had any significant effect on the species or was a factor in its decline. Until the contrary is proved,

it would also be unwise to assume that the surviving possum population is subject to predation by any of these animals, especially as so many more readily available alternative prey species exist throughout both its present and former range.

Leadbeater's possum was already rare at the time of its discovery in 1867, only thirty-three years after settlement had started in Victoria. It seems likely that at one time the species ranged more widely in the state, and extended northwards along the Dividing Range at least into New South Wales, but, by the time settlement began, it had been reduced to a series of small pockets wholly isolated from one another. The assumption is, therefore, that *Gymnobelideus* is a relict species, which over a considerable period has gradually moved closer to the point of extinction as a result of natural factors not yet fully understood.

Possibly the decline began as long ago as the Pliocene and Pleistocene periods, when changes in climate and vegetation caused substantial ecological upheavals. One of them came about when the Tertiary forests of conifers and beeches were replaced by eucalypts and acacia: this change must surely have had a significant effect on the evolution and dispersal of the more successful volant marsupials, with which *Gymnobelideus* had to compete.

So far as can be discovered, the only other phalangerine likely to be in competition with Leadbeater's possum is the sugar glider, a thriving marsupial whose range overlaps and extends well beyond that of the possum. Not only does the sugar glider require a less specialized diet, but it is more aggressive by temperament, as well as having the advantage of a gliding membrane that enables it both to escape more readily from predators and to make use of its environment very much more efficiently. Such slender evidence as exists, therefore, leads to the belief that, in the struggle for the ecological niche that both species seem to occupy, the sugar glider has been the more successful animal both physically and psychologically. Only in the densest areas of forest, where the gliding membrane gives no advantage, has the possum managed to hold its own.

The species is fully protected in the State of

Victoria. Moreover, the exact locations both of the known colony and of the other areas in which sightings have been made are being withheld from the public as a precaution against undue disturbance.

The future of the colony at Tommy's Bend is dependent on the preservation of the habitat. Part of the area is designated permanent state forest, and part has virtually been made inviolate through its reservation as a water catchment zone. There is therefore every reason to believe that the habitat can be kept undisturbed.

SCALY-TAILED POSSUM

Wyulda squamicaudata

Known colloquially as the scaly-tailed possum, this rare and little-known phalanger has a general colour of pale grey, the black tips to the longer hairs giving it a darker and rather mottled appearance. A dark stripe runs from shoulders to rump. Its fine, dense fur is short and soft, its head short and wide; its claws are short and not markedly curved. The most remarkable feature of the animal is its tail, which is unlike that of any other phalangerid, being covered with thick non-overlapping scales, evidently used to assist climbing. One that was shot continued to hang by the tail even when dead.

This species is known only from the Kimberley Division of Western Australia, the two furthest localities being some 300 miles apart.

The type, a female from Violet Valley Station, was described by W. B. Alexander as recently as 1919. This animal died in captivity in the South Perth Zoological Gardens. The second specimen, a male, was collected at Kunmunya Mission and described by H. H. Finlayson in 1942. A further female and pouch young were collected at Wotjulum Mission in 1954 and recorded and described by J. H. Calaby in 1957. In spite of at least two diligent searches, each of several weeks' duration, accompanied by the inducement of substantial rewards offered to the aborigines for specimens, no more were seen for over a decade. Then, at the end of 1965 and early in 1966, Mr W. H. Butler collected several specimens at Kalumburu Mission, close to the most northerly boundary of Western Australia. This discovery represented a considerable northerly extension of range.

Butler described *Wyulda* as not uncommon in the neighbourhood of the mission, in areas of sandstone cliffs containing thick vines, trees, and shrubs. The younger aborigines had never previously seen the animal, but an old witch doctor appeared to be familiar with it. He informed Butler that numbers apparently fluctuate to a large degree: normally it is very rare, but at times it becomes relatively abundant. He said that the animal's principal food is the fruit of a kind of sandalwood that grows among the rocks; but it also eats leaves and insects.

Similarly, at Wotjulum only the older aborigines had previously seen the animal. They call it *illungalya*, and say that it spends the day deep in cavities in the rocks and emerges only at night to feed on the bloodwood (*Eucalyptus*) trees, crossing from one tree to another without ever coming down to the ground. It always returns to its rock home well before dawn. Nothing further is known of this species.

Order PRIMATES
Family Lemuridae: typical Malagasy lemurs

BROAD-NOSED GENTLE LEMUR

Hapalemur simus

This animal is sometimes known as the "reed lemur", which is more descriptive of its mode of life than the more generally accepted name, "broad-nosed gentle lemur".

Of the two species that together constitute the genus, the reed lemur differs from the grey gentle lemur, *H. griseus*, by being larger, and by having a distinctive brownish-yellow rump patch. Its fur is soft and moderately long, and the general colour of its upper parts is dark ruddy-grey tinged with a faint reddish wash. This effect appears because each individual black hair has a grey base and a reddish band near its tip. The sides of the animal's limbs, and the lower part of its belly, as well as most of its tail, have varying shades of dirty grey. Its chin, throat, and chest are off-white or yellowish. Its tail is longer than its head and body combined. Its muzzle is short but broad, its ears small, round, and hairy, its feet and hands short but wide, with prominent pads situated beneath toes and finger-tips. Its skull and teeth have several unusual characters. Except for the molars, all the teeth are equipped with serrated edges specially adapted for cutting fibrous vegetation.

The female possesses two pairs of mammae, one on its abdomen and the other in front of its shoulder. Nothing appears to be known of the breeding biology of this rare animal.

Reed lemurs normally live alone or in small family groups. They are nocturnal, sleeping during the day – head between thighs and tail arched over back – and becoming active after dark. Their call is said to resemble the quacking of a duck.

This lemur is confined exclusively to reed beds along the shore and in the shallower waters of Lake Alaotra, in Madagascar. As the lake was formerly very much larger, the animal once presumably enjoyed a far wider distribution than it does today. For a good many years the lake's surface area has been, and it still is, steadily growing less.

The animal appears to be specially adapted to a humid existence. Its life is spent over or close to water, a fact that gives it effective protection. Nevertheless, this specialization also has the disadvantage of making it practically incapable of adapting itself to any major modification of its environment.

Its diet consists almost exclusively of fibrous material – reeds in the main, especially *Phragmites communis*, known by the vernacular name *bararata*. The bases of the stems are gnawed through, the outer covering is stripped off, and the pith eaten. Its cheek teeth are used for biting, while its sharp lower incisors (which lean sideways) work as scrapers. It seems probable that insects are also included in its diet.

Some reports say that the local people catch these lemurs by firing the reed beds; others, that they are sometimes caught by merely shaking the reeds until the animals drop off.

This species is docile in captivity, and is said to make a charming pet. But none have been captured for a long time. Indeed, many years passed without a sight of any specimens, and fears were expressed that the species might already be extinct. Lately, however, some have been seen by M. Therezien of the Malagasy Fisheries Department. A further indication of its rarity is that it is one of only two species of Madagascar lemurs that the leading authority on this group of animals, Dr J.-J. Petter, has never seen alive.

So little is known of this very rare little animal that a thorough ecological study of it should surely be undertaken before the opportunity is lost for ever. Such a study would furnish precise recommendations for the establishment of a sanctuary to protect the animal, without which it can hardly be expected to survive very much longer.

MONGOOSE LEMUR

Lemur mongoz

This rare animal exists in two races, each with a relict distribution.

The typical race, *Lemur mongoz mongoz*, is found in two localities in the north-west of Madagascar; it also occurs on Mohéli and Anjouan in the Comoro Islands, but not on Mayotte (where a race of *Lemur fulvus*, the brown lemur, is the only lemur to be found).

The typical mongoose lemur has two distinct forms whose inheritance appears to be sex-linked, the females being white-cheeked and the males red-cheeked. This applies to specimens from the Comoros but apparently not to those from the mainland of Madagascar. Otherwise there are no noticeable external differences between the insular and mainland specimens.

Of its genus, the typical mongoose lemur is the least in size, being smaller than a small cat. The male has a white muzzle, blackish rings around its eyes, red cheeks, and a grizzled grey-black forehead. The top of its head, the back of its neck, and part of its back are dark grey, as distinct from the brownish-grey that covers the rest of its upper parts and the sides of its limbs. Its under parts are tawny, with a greyish band across the chest. Its hands and feet are pale, sometimes almost white. The general colouration of the female is similar to the male's, except that its cheeks are pure white, and its under parts and the inner sides of its limbs white. Across its forehead is a black bar. The animal is completely arboreal and diurnal, and is found in troops of never more than three or four. It is very active, running energetically (always with its tail held erect), and leaping vigorously, landing on all fours with a characteristic grunt.

This lemur has been maintained very successfully in captivity, and is said to make a gentle and affectionate pet, although it may be hostile towards strangers. There are records of successful reproduction in captivity, but breeding occurs less readily than with *L. macaco*, the black lemur.

The mongoose lemur has always been regarded as uncommon, and in the past collectors invariably had difficulty in securing specimens. In recent years its habitat has been much reduced, and the typical race is now very rare.

It exists in both the Plateau de l'Ankarafantsika and the Tsingy de Namoroka reserves. The former reserve in particular, extending to 165,000 acres, is of the greatest scientific interest. If this species is to be permitted to survive, the Service des Eaux et Fôrets must be given the necessary powers for the firm administration and protection of this important reserve.

The crowned mongoose lemur, *Lemur mongoz coronatus*, is larger than the typical race of mongoose lemur. Like the smaller animal, it occurs in two sex-linked colour phases, the males being red-cheeked and the females white-cheeked. The males differ from those of the typical race, however, in having a black patch on the crowns of their heads; the females have no crown patch. The tail of the female *coronatus* is reddish, not near-black as in *mongoz*.

At one time, and until quite recently, this lemur occupied a large region in the dry savannah country of northern Madagascar, extending from the Bay of Bombétoka on the west coast, and from the Bay of Antongil on the east, northwards as far as the Montagne d'Ambre, where it was found up to an altitude of about 2,650 feet,

but not in the humid forests of the summit. Until the Second World War this lemur was relatively common, but since then severe destruction of the habitat has reduced the range to a relatively small area near the Montagne d'Ambre, and the animal is now considered rare.

The Parc National de la Montagne d'Ambre embraces part of the range of the crowned lemur, and the establishment of this national park is a notable step in the animal's long-term protection, always supposing that the integrity of the park can be assured.

FAT-TAILED LEMUR

Cheirogaleus medius

The genus *Cheirogaleus* consists of three species. *C. trichotis*, the hairy-eared dwarf lemur, for ninety years after its discovery was known only from the single type specimen in London described by Günther in 1875, and two skins in poor condition in Paris. Until very recently the species was thought to be extinct; but early in 1966 Dr Petter's assistant, M. André Peyrieras, rediscovered the animal on the east coast near Mananara. *C. major*, the greater dwarf lemur, is still abundant. The fat-tailed lemur, *C. medius*, consists of two races, *C. m. medius* and *C. m. samati* – both of which, like the hairy-eared dwarf lemur, are candidates for the Red Data Book.

The fat-tailed lemur is about the size of a large rat, the head and body of the typical race being about 9 inches long and the tail 8 inches; *C. m. samati* is slightly smaller. The prominent eyes, which are made to appear even larger and more conspicuous by the dark rings that surround them, are set in a broad, rather cat-like face whose muzzle is extremely broad in relation to its length and has a distinctive facial streak. The fur varies in colour from grey to rusty brown on the upper parts, while the under parts are whitish. The most distinctive external feature is the white half-collar on the side of the neck.

An interesting feature, from which the common name of the species is derived, is the tail, which at certain times of the year becomes laden with fat, and thus helps survival through the dry season when food is scarce.

The species is entirely nocturnal, and is said to spend the day sleeping in hollow trees in nests made from twigs and leaves. Its movements through the trees on all fours are much more like those of a squirrel than of a typical lemur; when eating, it sits up and grasps the food in its fore paws. Its diet is thought to consist of leaves and fruit and probably insects.

There is considerable uncertainty about the former range of this species, though it has been known from Fort Dauphin in the south-east and the Tsiribihina River in the west; but it is now believed to occur in only two widely separated localities, one near the Betsiboka River in north-western Madagascar and the other in the south-west, near the Mangoky River. As suitable habitat exists between these two regions, however, the range may in fact be more extensive. The only reserves in which the fat-tailed lemur has been lately reported are the 165,000-acre Plateau de l'Ankarafantsika Reserve and the 300,000-acre Montagne d'Ambre National Park.

The species is reputed to tame easily and to submit readily to confinement, but it has never been known to reproduce in captivity. In 1966 three pairs were in captivity at Brunoy and a female at Tananarive.

FORK-MARKED MOUSE LEMUR

Phaner furcifer

This species (the only member of its genus) is distinguished from other dwarf lemurs by the dark stripe running along the greater part of its spine and sub-dividing on the crown of its head – one branch joins up with each of the dark rings encircling its eyes. From this highly characteristic pattern the popular name of the animal is derived.

The general colour of the animal's thick body fur is brownish-grey or reddish-grey, with yellowish-white under parts. Its bushy tail, longer than its body, is also much darker than the body and is tipped with either black or white.

The animal is entirely arboreal and nocturnal, sleeping by day in a hollow tree, frequently sharing it with bees; a popular belief is that this habit was developed to deprive the hives of honey. It is an extremely agile animal, indulging in spectacular leaps and having a piercing cry that is said to resemble a guinea-fowl's.

The distribution of this mouse lemur does not appear to be well known. It is reliably reported from only three widely separated localities, in the north-west of Madagascar near Ampasindava, in the more humid parts of the Montagne d'Ambre and in the south-west near Tulear. It is possible, however, that the range may be more extensive, since there is suitable habitat between these two regions.

The species was considered abundant until the 1930s, since when it has certainly declined along with the forest, but there is not at present enough information to enable a reliable assessment of its current status to be made. In view of this uncertainty, a thorough ecological survey of the species and its environment would be invaluable.

Family Indriidae: indris and sifakas

WESTERN WOOLLY AVAHI
Avahi laniger occidentalis

The genus *Avahi* consists of a single species, the woolly avahi, subdivided into an eastern and a western subspecies. The eastern or typical one, *A. l. laniger*, is still relatively abundant and is not, therefore, a candidate for the Red Data Book. The western race, *A. l. occidentalis*, may be less immediately endangered than any of the other western sifakas, but, like all the west-coast prosimians, it is threatened by the destruction of its forest habitat through uncontrolled clearing and burning. The inhabitants also snare these animals for food, but this factor would be of minor significance if only the habitat were secure.

Unlike the other Indriids, *Avahi* is nocturnal, and much more arboreal than they are; it is seldom seen on the ground. It goes through the

Verreaux's sifaka, typical race *Maurice Wilson* 1965

trees by leaping from one vertical stem to another. C. S. Webb reported that, if pursued, an avahi will cling motionless to the trunk of a tree in an attempt to avoid detection. If that ruse fails, it bounds away, leaping from trunk to trunk in much the same manner as a tree kangaroo. In contrast with the diurnal species, which are gregarious, *Avahi* occurs only singly or in pairs. The animal spends the daytime sleeping in dense undergrowth or, more usually, either in the fork of a tree or clinging to a vertical stem. Its diet is believed to be exclusively vegetarian, consisting of leaves, buds, and bark.

The western woolly avahi is a small animal, its head and body being about 1 foot 6 inches long and its tail slightly longer than its body. It has thick, soft, woolly fur, which on the upper parts is normally greyish-brown, with a yellowish-brown tinge; there is however a degree of variation, some individuals being much more reddish. Its eyes are large, but its ears small and almost hidden in its fur. Its face is whitish and covered with short hair. Its hands and feet are yellowish-brown, its forearms and under parts creamy white, and its tail reddish-brown.

The western subspecies is restricted to coastal forests in the north-western part of Madagascar, from Ampasindava Bay in the north to Bombétoka in the south. The inland limits of the range do not appear to have been well defined. This race occurs in both the Plateau de l'Ankarafantsika and the Tsingy de Namoroka reserves.

The four members of the Indriid family do not like confinement even in their native climate; they become apathetic and listless and rarely survive long. Few have ever reached Europe alive, and there are no records of breeding in captivity, although births have occurred among wild caught specimens freshly arrived at the Tananarive Zoo.

VERREAUX'S SIFAKA
Propithecus verreauxi

The genus *Propithecus*, with its two species, is (or was) widely distributed in Madagascar. The type species, the diademed sifaka, *P. diadema*, which occurs in suitable forest and scrub along almost the entire length of eastern Madagascar, is not yet a candidate for the Red Data Book, but *P. verreauxi* on the west coast has been less fortunate: all five races that together constitute Verreaux's species have suffered serious diminution during the past thirty to fifty years, and are now regarded as endangered.

The species as a whole differs from *P. diadema* by being smaller and having a relatively larger tail, and by the greater density of its rather long silky fur. Otherwise it does not markedly differ either in appearance or in skeletal characters from the other Indriids.

These sifakas are probably the most conspicuous animals living in the western coastal forests, where they are met with in troops of six or eight. The colour of their fur varies according to race, but the general body colour is of varying shades of near-white, with darker colours on the limbs and on top of the head, the sole exception being *P. v. deckenii,* which is nearly all white. In all races the face (which is hairless), the ears, the palms of the hands, and the soles of the feet are invariably black. The naked black face is encircled with a fringe of long white hair, which almost hides the small ears, and there is a transverse black streak on the crown of the head. The legs are about a third as long again as the arms. The foot is a good deal larger than the hand, as well as being narrow and elongated. The great toe is almost as large as the rest of the foot, and provides the animal with a powerful grasping instrument. The hand is longer and narrower than in the Lemuridae, and the fingers are all equipped with pointed nails.

Verreaux's sifakas are arboreal animals, performing without apparent effort spectacular leaps of 30 feet or more from tree to tree. Extending on either side of their bodies, stretched between the front and rear limbs, is a narrow vestigial gliding membrane that assists the animal in making such immense leaps. Although essentially arboreal, these sifakas are sometimes seen on the ground, where they move on their two feet in rather an ungainly manner by means of a series of short hops, balancing themselves by holding their hands above their heads or in front of the body in much the same manner as a gibbon.

They are diurnal, but are not normally active during the heat of the day, when they prefer to rest in a secluded part of the forest. At this time they like to squat with tail curled up between their hind limbs, hands resting on knees or held away from the body, apparently to make the most of the sun. When asleep they sit erect with their heads resting on their chests and covered by their arms, their tails either hanging straight down or curled up between their legs.

Their diet is strictly vegetarian and consists mainly of leaves, bark, flowers, and very occasionally fruit. They seldom use their hands when picking up food, preferring to stoop and seize it by mouth.

Little is known of their breeding biology beyond the fact that a single young is born after a gestation period of approximately five months. The new-born young clings to its mother's ventral fur, but when older it shifts position to her back.

These lemurs are of gentle disposition, seldom biting or fighting except during the period of rut, when there is a tendency for the males to fight among themselves. They are relatively silent members of a noisy family, but when frightened or angry are said to make a sound that resembles the clucking of a hen. They also utter a sharp bark.

Like other members of the family, this species appears unable to tolerate captivity, and until a few years ago there appears to have been only a single record to show that any representative had been exhibited abroad – a specimen of *P. v. coquereli* at the Berlin Zoological Gardens in 1912. More recently, a pair has been successfully maintained at New Haven, Connecticut. The scarcity of records may be due to the difficulty of providing the animal with the specialized diet, notably the foliage of indigenous trees, that is essential for its survival both during the long journey to its destination and after its arrival at a zoo. Even in its native country, only a very few specimens have successfully adapted themselves to confinement. Osman Hill gives particulars of one that lived for more than six years at the Tananarive Zoo, and recently a specimen of the typical race at the same zoo has reproduced with success, while on three occasions, in 1954, 1955, and 1956, the Tananarive Zoo managed to breed a hybrid by crossing a male *P. v. coronatus* with a female *P. v. deckenii*. It seems that plenty of space and a degree of liberty are essential for the animal's well-being.

The five races may be described as follows:

Verreaux's (typical) race, *Propithecus v. verreauxi*

The typical race exists in parts of the south and south-west of Madagascar, extending from the neighbourhood of Fort Dauphin in the east to St Augustin's Bay in the west. The limits of its original range are uncertain, but are known to have included a large part of the south-western coastal region, although it is not known how far inland they extended.

A young specimen of this race is entirely white as a rule, except for a dark brown patch on the crown of its head and a ruddy tinge on its belly. Of the adults, the limbs and under parts are white; but the white is usually tinged with yellow, and is therefore less pure than that of van der Decken's or Coquerel's races, while the back is washed with very light grey. The black or dark brown crown patch is separated from the black face by a white band across the forehead.

PLATE 1 (*a*) Rusty numbat; (*b*) Scaly-tailed possum; (*c*) Thylacine *Barry Driscoll* 1966

(a)

(b)

(c)

(a)

(b)

(c)

(d)

On some individuals there is a greyish patch in the middle of their backs.

At one time tribal taboos protected the animal from slaughter, but in recent years these have been disregarded. Hunting is, therefore, a relatively new and still only a contributory factor in the decline of this sifaka, the principal cause being the widespread and uncontrolled destruction of the original forest by clearing and burning.

This race exists in two reserves, the Tsingy de Bemaraha and Lac Tsimanampetsotsa, and possibly also in the Massif d'Andohahela Reserve.

Coquerel's race, *P. v. coquereli*

An unusually distinctive race, this one has back, head, and hind limbs of almost pure white, while much of the thighs and of the trunk at the front is maroon. The maroon patch on its arms is fringed with long white hairs. Its face, ears, palms, and the soles of its feet are black, but down the centre of its nose runs a patch of short white hairs.

The race exists in the north-west of Madagascar round the Bay of Mahajamba. Formerly its range was more extensive, but much of the suitable habitat has been destroyed, and survival now depends to a very great extent on the security afforded by the Ankarafantsika Reserve (165,000 acres), the only reserve in which the race is known to be. Unfortunately, the protection given by this reserve is inadequate, and, unless it can be strengthened, the future of this interesting sifaka must remain uncertain.

Van der Decken's race, *P. v. deckeni*

This race is virtually an albinistic phase of the species, the fur being entirely white, although the albinism does not extend to the naked parts of the animal's face, ears, palms and foot soles, all of which are black. The white is tinged with yellow or, occasionally, ash-grey on its neck and the front parts of its limbs. Its chest is reddish; its tail is white except for a tawny base. On some individuals the grey marking is limited to a spot on the back of the neck; in others it appears as a collar.

P. v. deckeni lives on the extensive plains between the Manambolo and Mahavavy rivers; it has also been recorded from Betsina, to the south of Lake Kinkony, but within this relatively large area reliable sightings have been made in only two localities in recent years.

Like so many of the prosimians inhabiting the western part of Madagascar, this race has been seriously reduced by uncontrolled destruction of habitat. It is protected in the Tsingy de Namoroka Reserve (14,200 acres), but nowhere else.

Crowned race, *P. v. coronatus*

This sifaka differs from all other races of *P. verreauxi* by having a broader muzzle and wider nostrils. The patch of short white hairs on the nose is, however, the same. Surrounding its face is a fringe of black or dark brown hair, extending from its forehead down past either side of its ears, meeting at its throat, and broken only by a small patch of white on its ears. The upper parts of its body are of a rather dirty white; its arms and legs and the base of its tail are of the same general colour but are tinged with rust. The rest of its tail is pure white; so are its hands and feet. Its throat, chest, and abdomen are a rich mahogany, the colour being deepest on its chest.

Within this general colour scheme is a wide range of individual variation. Some specimens have reddish upper parts and a very dark brown chest; the abdomen and parts of the limbs are bright red. According to Osman Hill, these more brightly coloured members of the race are found in the southern part of the range, near the Manerinerina Forest.

Half a century ago this sifaka was reported as common, but since then its range and numbers have been greatly reduced, and it is now confined to an area west of the Mahavavy River. It is protected in the Tsingy de Namoroka Reserve.

Forsyth Major's race, *P. v. majori*

This partly melanistic subspecies is the most localized and the most gravely endangered of all the races of *Propithecus verreauxi*. However,

---

PLATE 2 (*a*) Broad-nosed gentle lemur; (*b*) Mongoose lemur, typical race; (*c*) Fork-marked mouse lemur; (*d*) Western woolly avahi *Barry Driscoll* 1966 despite its extreme localization, it occurs in the same forest as the typical race, which is much more widely distributed. If full geographical overlap is discovered, it may prove to be either a melanistic phase of *P. v. verreauxi* or a full species.

The face, snout, and ears of this race (if it is a race) are hairless and black, the face being encircled by a wide band of long white hairs, interspersed with a few dark hairs, which meet at the throat. The crown of the head and the back of the neck are black. Much of the back is dark brown; the upper parts are otherwise white, though the large white patch on the shoulders is flecked with brown hairs. The limbs are white, but with large areas of chocolate colour; the tail is white; the throat, chest, and abdomen are dark brown.

This sifaka now occurs only in the Sakaraha Forest, in the south-west of Madagascar. The survival of the race is therefore entirely dependent upon the degree of protection given to the Sakaraha Forest, an area of considerable botanical and zoological significance. Petter believes that it would be an excellent area for studying the extreme diversity of forms that can exist in a relatively small region. This might lead to a better understanding of the problems presented by the distribution of fauna over Madagascar as a whole.

INDRIS
Indri indri

Largest of the living lemuroids, the indris is about 3 feet high when standing erect. Its head is relatively small, appearing strangely disproportionate to its body, and its tail differs from that of other members of the family by being little more than a stump. Its muzzle is bare and rather shortened, giving the animal a somewhat monkey-like appearance in contrast with the almost fox-like look of some of the Lemuridae. All four lateral toes are joined by webs, which cause them to work as a single unit, in opposition to the first toe, allowing its foot an effective grasp.

The colour and pattern of the indris's fur are highly variable; and to a lesser extent certain dental, cranial, and other characters may also vary. These differences are apparently individual, and seem unrelated to the district from which the animal comes or to ecological factors.

Indrises are arboreal and diurnal, sometimes living singly or in pairs, but more usually in troops of three to five. They are rather localized, usually occupying the larger branches of trees, through which they move by leaping from one vertical stem or branch to another. Sometimes they squat on horizontal branches, but their characteristic position at rest is clinging to vertical boughs, rather than to the horizontal ones favoured by most arboreal animals.

These shy creatures are more often heard than seen: their voice is remarkably loud, and they have been described as the noisiest of the lemurs, if not of all the Malagasy animals. Osman Hill states that many early writers refer to the vernacular name *amboanala*, meaning "dog of the forest", an allusion to its remarkably dog-like howls. Other authors have recorded that at a distance the wailing is strangely human and has a ventriloquial effect, so that one can hardly judge where or from how far off it comes. An alternative explanation is, of course, that a troop will frequently call when moving at speed through the trees. The call can be heard at almost any time of the day, and sometimes at night, but it is particularly frequent in mid-morning. It is usually given in company for several minutes at a time, and then, after a pause, repeated.

Indris *Maurice Wilson* 1965

Sonnerat discovered the indris at the same time as the aye-aye and the avahi. He named the animal *indri*, assuming it to be the vernacular name, whereas the word was in fact an exclamation meaning "There it is".

Early writers were impressed by the refusal of the inhabitants to do anything that might harm an indris. Several tribes regarded the animal as sacred, and many myths and legends are associated with it. These tribes were said to believe that if a man rashly aimed his spear at an indris, the animal would retaliate by catching the spear in flight and, with unfailing accuracy, hurl it back at the sender. Some of the tribal beliefs were recorded by Sonnerat and other early writers, but they have been denied by more recent ones. This does not imply that Sonnerat was inaccurate, but merely that, through increasing sophistication, the Malagasy people now treat these matters less seriously than did their forebears. Generally speaking, they no longer regard the animal as sacred. This is confirmed by Rand, who recorded in 1935 that some tribes had no compunction in killing and eating the animal; others, though they would not eat the flesh, were content to help in locating specimens for collectors to shoot.

Sonnerat also stated that the natives caught young indrises and schooled them like hounds for hunting, while Pollen said that they were trained for catching birds; but others have refuted these stories.

Normally the predominant colour of the indris's dense silky fur is black; but this is subject to considerable individual variation, ranging from all black to nearly pure white, with every intermediate shade between. Most indrises have a parti-coloured black, grey, and white coat, but on some specimens the white is limited to a small patch over each eyebrow, or on the ankles or heels; others are almost totally albinistic. Parts that as a rule are entirely black include the crown of the head, the ears, shoulders, back, and arms as well as the hands and feet. On the rump there is usually a large triangular white patch, framed in black. Sometimes this hind patch is washed with orange or red. The under parts are usually grey, except on the abdomen, which has a slightly brown tinge. The forearms are sometimes inclined to be reddish.

The throat is grey-white, and the chest a darker shade of grey. It was this wide variation in colour that caused Gray in 1872 to adopt the now discarded name of *I. variegatus*.

The indris lives in the forests of eastern Madagascar, in the volcanic mountains situated between the Bay of Antongil in the north and the Masora River in the south, which is approximately halfway along the east coast. Its diet is strictly vegetarian, and it is reputed to eat fruit, nuts, leaves, buds, and flowers.

As already mentioned, the indrises prefer the more vertical branches of trees, clinging to them in an erect posture, and leaping from one branch to another, grasping with their powerful hind feet. When climbing they employ a somewhat slow, hand-over-hand motion, and when descending come down tail first in a very ungainly manner. At rest, they may sprawl on a branch with their limbs hanging over the side, although more commonly they rest clinging to an upright branch.

The animal is not exclusively arboreal, however, and is often seen on the ground, where it walks upright or moves with a series of short hops or leaps, its hands extended in front of the body. Like other members of the family, it enjoys basking in the sun with arms held clear of the body to allow the under parts maximum exposure, a practice that has resulted in the legend that the animal worships the sun.

The indris does not thrive in captivity even in its native country. Very few have ever reached Europe or America alive, and, of those few, all have proved difficult to rear, and none have reproduced. No precise explanation has been found for this apparent inability to tolerate captivity, but the cause may well be partly physical and partly mental. The delicately adjusted digestive system is probably unable to adapt itself to changed conditions; in captivity indrises very soon become listless, apparently losing the will to live.

Until recently the indris was reported to be relatively abundant in much of its range, but the widespread destruction of original forest has made the species decline sharply. In this respect the indris holds a similar position to that of most other prosimians of Madagascar, but it is more vulnerable because of its extremely local distribution, which could bring about its early disappearance.

The decline has been especially severe in the central part of the animal's range. Here the habitat consists of a great many small forested hills and ridges: until recently a separate troop of indris occupied practically every ridge, but uncontrolled burning and extensive deforestation have deprived the ridges of suitable cover.

The species exists in two *réserves naturelles intégrales*, the Massif de Betampona (4,000 acres) and the Fôret de Masoala (52,000 acres), as well as near the Perinet forestry station. Unfortunately, administration of the reserves is not effective enough to ensure adequate protection.

These reserves were selected and the boundaries drawn up by competent botanists, and they conform to the criteria laid down by the 1933 London Convention; but no zoologist appears to have been consulted at the planning stage. In fact, no systematic inventory of the fauna of Madagascar has ever been made – an omission that requires early rectification. Moreover, certain boundaries now require to be adjusted as a result of nearby "development".

Most of the Malagasy reserves resemble small oases standing out in contrast to the denuded zones surrounding them. Such areas can hardly survive in isolation. Moreover, having destroyed so much of the original forest and vegetation, the local people are turning covetous eyes upon the few intact areas that remain.

Infringements of the boundaries of the reserves have become increasingly flagrant during recent years, to say nothing of pressure from officially sponsored proposals for the use of other natural resources within the reserves. One can under-

stand the farmers' wish to intrude upon the forests, because freshly burnt forest land gives (for a few years) an unusually high yield with minimum effort, whether the crop be cereals or fresh green pasture for the growing herds of scrub cattle.

The intensity of habitat destruction is hard to describe. In much of Madagascar the destruction is almost total, to the ruin of the country and the loss of an irreplaceable natural and scientific treasure.

Moreover, many politicians do not comprehend either the importance of the reserves or the real values at stake; and, being intent upon immediate economic results, they often attempt to gain votes by saying that previous undertakings are "outmoded" or "no longer in tune with proper development of the country".

The Service des Eaux et Fôrets, a forceful and efficient organization with responsibility for administering the reserves, thus finds its authority undermined, and all the time has greater difficulty in obtaining the support it requires for the fulfilment of its responsibilities. It is therefore being compelled to defend its position against both the farmers and the politicians, and finds itself in an increasingly isolated state.

Never was there a better example of the truism "Take care of the habitat, and the animals will look after themselves". All too few of those in authority as yet appear to understand the importance of the original flora and its associated fauna, either to Madagascar or to the world at large. A carefully devised and directed publicity campaign is needed to improve the general outlook. Meanwhile the Government should, as a matter of great urgency, do everything possible to protect existing reserves.

Family Daubentoniidae: aye-aye

AYE-AYE
Daubentonia madagascariensis

Probably the most remarkable, and certainly the rarest and most gravely endangered of all the mammals in the I.U.C.N.'s Red Data Book, is the aye-aye. *Daubentonia madagascariensis* is the

sole surviving representative not merely of a genus but of a family, and it is doubtful whether more than about fifty individuals remain in the wild state.

The only other known member of this family is a fossil form (probably from the Holocene deposits of the post-Pleistocene period of the last 10,000 years), similar in general appearance but substantially larger, whose remains have been discovered in the south-west of Madagascar. This species, *Daubentonia robusta*, is believed to have still existed at the same time as man, and it was probably exterminated by human agency. Osman Hill quotes a report that the skin of a very large aye-aye, which may have been one of the last survivors of this species, was seen by a French government official in the hands of an inhabitant of the Soalala district about 1930.

Aye-aye *Peter Scott* 1967

Anything less like the traditional concept of a primate would be hard to imagine; and it is not difficult to see why Gmelin, who first described the animal in 1788, eight years after its discovery by Sonnerat, believed it to be related to the squirrels and therefore classified it among the Rodentia. For many years there was a conflict of opinions about its classification, and almost a century passed before Owen, in 1860, finally established it as an aberrant type of lemur and set up a new family to accommodate it.

The aye-aye is descended from the same stock as the Indriidae, and it retains various features associated with the primitive ancestral primates. It is a squirrel-like animal, the size of a large cat, covered with coarse, straight hair, black or dark brown, with a long bushy tail, but differing from any rodent by having hands and feet essentially of primate pattern, with an opposable great toe, although the thumb is not truly opposable. All its digits have claw-like nails, with the exception of the first toe, which has a flat nail.

Characteristics of particular interest include its curved, rodent-like incisors, which are very large in relation to its skull and are separated from its cheek teeth by a wide gap. A further dental peculiarity is that its canine teeth are absent in the permanent dentition, though present in the first set, being shed as a result of continuous growth of the permanent incisors.

There are many other interesting skeletal and anatomical features, including the aye-aye's skull, which is rather like that of the squirrel but possesses structural affinities with the primates'. Its brain, which is relatively large but of very primitive structure, also contains features indicating a link between the primates and other mammals.

Perhaps the most striking features of the aye-aye are its highly specialized hands, notably their third "finger", which is extraordinarily long and thin. This finger and the rodent-like incisors are adaptations for an insectivorous diet, consisting mainly of wood-boring insects and their larvae. Sonnerat and others have reported that the aye-aye's highly developed sense of smell and hearing enable it to detect larvae embedded in the timber. The animal then taps the wood with the tip of its long middle finger in much the same way as a woodpecker taps with its bill, using its gnawing-adapted incisors to break open the wood and its middle finger to extract the larvae. Its diet is apparently supplemented by birds' eggs and vegetable matter. The aye-aye is said to consume the pith of bamboo by gnawing the shoots, as well as sugar cane and fruit of various kinds, whose pulp is scooped out with its middle finger. This all-purpose tool is also employed to comb its fur, to scratch, and generally for cleaning. While grooming itself the animal sometimes hangs suspended by its hind feet in a manner reminiscent of a loris. When drinking, the aye-aye inserts its middle finger into the liquid and draws it rapidly sideways through its mouth.

The aye-aye's eyes are large and well developed, as befits an essentially nocturnal creature. The animal lives either singly or in pairs in dense forests or bamboo thickets, sleeping during the day with its fore limbs covering its head, and its tail wrapped round its body. It emerges at dusk, when it becomes quite active, leaping from branch to branch in typical lemur fashion. It is normally silent, but occasionally utters a cry that Lamberton, in 1911, likened to the noise made when two pieces of metal are rubbed together. Sonnerat adopted the Malagasy name *aye-aye*, which was reputed to be the native rendering of the sound associated with this strange nocturnal note.

Hardly anything is known of *Daubentonia*'s breeding biology, although it is believed to give birth to a single young. The female is known to construct a spherical nest, some 2 feet in diameter, in the fork of a tree, consisting of rolled-up leaves and lined with twigs and dry leaves, and with a single opening at the side.

Many prosimians seem unable to adapt themselves to changed conditions, but the aye-aye appears to survive well in captivity. Specimens have lived at the Jardin des Plantes in Paris for up to eight years, in the London Zoo for nineteen, and in the Amsterdam Zoo for twenty-three. However, the species has never been known to breed in captivity.

The distribution of the aye-aye is limited to the north-eastern coastal forests of Madagascar between Antalaha (north of Maroantsetra) and Mananjary. At one time the animal must have ranged much more widely: it is believed to have existed until less than a century ago in most of the eastern part of the country. Sonnerat obtained his original specimens from the north-west coast, where an isolated population appears to have survived between Ambilobe and Analalava, but there have been no records from this area since 1932. In 1967, however, Petter visited the Ampasindava Peninsula (an area in which the aye-aye was not previously known to occur), where he obtained evidence that the species survives, although precariously.

Osman Hill records that the aye-aye has long been regarded with superstitious dread by the Malagasy people, some of whom believed it to be an ancestral reincarnation. If unintentionally trapped, the animal was therefore always freed. But today, when so many traditional beliefs appear to have been abandoned, some local people are provedly killing aye-ayes in the belief that they are harbingers of death; and others will do everything possible to drive them away from the coconut plantations because of the damage they are said to cause.

Madagascar possesses a very diversified fauna and flora, which has long been isolated from the mainland of Africa, and is therefore unique and of inestimable scientific value. The Madagascan prosimians form one of the most interesting groups of animals anywhere in the world, and their loss would be a zoological catastrophe. Their survival is already in the balance, however, and none is closer to extinction than the aye-aye.

Since the end of the Second World War, much of the original forest on the island has been replaced by plantations of exotic trees, or eradicated by uncontrolled felling and burning to open up new areas for cultivation or to accommodate the ever-increasing herds of domestic cattle. Much of the wild fauna is protected by law, but no amount of legal protection can compensate for loss of habitat, especially that of so highly specialized an animal as the aye-aye. The coastal forest has now almost entirely disappeared, and, although two national parks, twelve *réserves naturelles intégrales*, and twenty-five forest reserves (these last are being commercially exploited) have been established in Madagascar, the aye-aye is not represented in any of them. Even the existing reserves are vulnerable to the specious argument put forward by vested interests that the country's economic development is incompatible with the "protection of butterflies".

The fauna of Madagascar cannot hope to survive without its flora. Destruction of the habitat is therefore the essential reason for the disappearance of the aye-aye. Almost all the fauna of Madagascar is endangered to a greater or a lesser degree, but the first to disappear will inevitably be the highly localized and specialized birds and lemurs.

Part of the Ambato Malamo Forest, in Tamatave Province, extending to 346 acres, was proposed as a reserve following the 1956–7 Jean-Jacques Petter Mission, which had noted the existence of aye-ayes in the area. Unfortunately, the authorities later decided to construct a road through the forest, and the aye-ayes quickly vanished.

In a final attempt to safeguard the species, the I.U.C.N.'s Survival Service Commission supported a proposal made by Dr Petter that the small island of Nossi Mangabé, off the northeast coast of Madagascar in the Bay of Antongil, should be set aside as a *réserve intégrale*, and this has now been done. The island is regarded by the Malagasy people as sacred, and the flora, which resembles that of "mainland" Madagascar, is untouched. By 1967 André Peyrieras had captured four males and five females on the mainland and released them on the island. This appeared to be the only hope of preventing the early extinction of the aye-aye; and the state of the released animals, which have settled well in the forest, was studied by the 1967 I.U.C.N. Mission, which recommended an immediate investigation of the zoologically unexplored forest on the western side of the Masoala Peninsula, to see whether the species occurs there. If it does, the Malagasy Government will be asked to declare the area another reserve.

The only aye-ayes in captivity in 1967 were a young pair in the care of André Peyrieras in Madagascar.

Family Cebidae: New World monkeys

WOOLLY SPIDER MONKEY
Brachyteles arachnoides

The genus *Brachyteles* consists of this single species, which is the rarest and one of the least known of all the New World primates.

As its common name implies, the animal's fur is woolly and its limbs are long and slender. Its tail, longer than its body, is naked near the tip and prehensile. Its thumb is either vestigial or entirely lacking. The predominant colour of most individuals is yellowish-grey or ash-brown; but some specimens are mainly reddish. The animal's head is usually either dark brown washed with yellow, or grey tinged with brown. The crown of its head is sometimes chestnut, and the back of its neck and forehead reddish-orange. Its hairless face is often bright red, particularly at times of anger or excitement. Possibly the variation in colour is sex-linked; but it may be merely individual or due to geographical location.

The woolly spider monkey is found in a very restricted area in south-eastern Brazil, extending from the southern part of the state of Bahia to São Paulo and inland as far as Minas Gerais. Within this region the animal is confined to coastal mountains and the Tupi Forest. In former times the range was more extensive, but reduction of the forested habitat for agricultural purposes and for human occupation has reduced the population to a precariously low level, and the animal is now believed to be on the verge of extinction.

Hardly anything has been recorded about the behaviour, biology, and requirements of this primate except that it is arboreal and diurnal. Its diet is believed to consist largely of fruit.

There is an urgent need for a study to be made by a competent ecologist while the possibility still exists, with the object of assessing the status of the animal and its environment and of making firm proposals for the protective measures that could ensure its survival.

There are very few records to show that the woolly spider monkey has been maintained successfully in confinement, and it has never been known to breed in captivity. The Leipzig Zoo had a specimen in the 1930s, and the first to reach the United States was an immature female, which was kept at the Bronx Zoo for just over a year in 1959–60. At first apparently thriving, the animal could not be kept in good health, and it finally wasted away and died through the effects of internal parasites.

GOELDI'S TAMARIN
Callimico goeldii

This genus of New World primates is represented by a single species, which is of unique interest as a link between the two existing families of Ceboids, the Cebidae and the Callithricidae. It is usually placed in a special subfamily of its own, the Callimiconinae. The structure of its foot, face, and claw-like nails resembles that of marmosets; but its teeth and skull are similar to those of the Cebid monkeys.

The adult male has soft, silky fur, almost wholly coal-black, but occasionally tinged with dark brown, particularly on its hind quarters. Some specimens may have irregularly distributed pale spots and patches on head, back, and other parts of the body.

Perhaps the most distinctive external characteristic of Goeldi's monkey is the coif of erect hair that envelops the crown of its head. It has also a mane-like growth of long hair covering neck and shoulders like a cape; elongated rump hairs extend like a skirt over the root of its tail.

This species was described in 1904: but, during the sixty years since it was first made known to science, hardly anything appears to have been learnt about its biology, habits, and ecological requirements in the wild state. Even the animal's present range has not yet been adequately defined. The few available specimens came from the head-waters of the Amazon in northern Bolivia, eastern Peru, and western Brazil (Acre Territory, Rio Xapury), where the species is said to exist in troops of up to twenty or thirty. Its intelligence, and the speed at which it is capable of moving through the trees, make its capture difficult.

Unfortunately, however, there has in the last few years been a rising demand for this lively little primate by the pet trade; as a result, strenuous and successful efforts have apparently been made to overcome the difficulties involved in its capture. This demand is having a very harmful effect, particularly as the mortality rate among newly exported specimens is high.

It therefore seems essential for the governments of the three countries concerned to limit or prohibit, by joint or coordinated legislation, the export of Goeldi's tamarin. At the same time, an ecological study by one or more competent field workers should be undertaken without further delay, to assess the current status of the animal and to make recommendations concerning the measures needed to give it adequate protection.

Until 1954 the only specimens kept in confinement were one at the London Zoo (in 1915) and another at the Goeldi Museum at Para, Brazil. Between that year and 1963, the Bronx Zoo obtained six specimens, one of which, a male received in September 1959, lived until March 1964, a little over four and a half years. The Cologne Zoo had its first, a female, in 1961, and has since kept a male for five and a half years. Of twelve imported into Germany, seven survived in 1966. Dr L. Rane of Miami University has the distinction of being the first person to have succeeded in breeding this animal in captivity; so far about a dozen have been captive-bred, all in private establishments save one in the San Diego Zoo.

Family Cercopithecidae: Old World monkeys

TANA RIVER MANGABEY
Cercocebus galeritus galeritus

Cercocebus, the genus of the mangabeys, was revised in 1928 by the systematist Schwarz, who recognized four species (widely distributed from the west to east coasts of equatorial Africa) and divided them into a total of ten races. No race of the grey-cheeked, black, or sooty mangabey seems to be in any (present) danger; but the Tana River race of the agile mangabey qualifies without doubt for inclusion in the Red Data Book.

Peters, who originally described this form in 1879, stated that the upper parts of its body are covered with long, soft hair, grey at the roots and mainly grey-green and brown, almost black, at the tips; the effect of this is to give the fur a crimped appearance. The sides of its head, and its under parts, are inclined to be yellowish, the inner side of its limbs being yellowish-grey. The hair of its tail has yellowish rings and becomes lighter towards the tips. On top of its head is a flat coif of longer hair, which forms a distinctive fringe on its forehead. This mangabey's long tail, which is normally carried high over the back, is not fully prehensile but is sometimes seen to be curled round a branch to maintain the animal's balance.

Very little has ever been recorded about the Tana River mangabey since Peters first obtained his solitary specimen close to the confluence of the Osi and Tana rivers, and only a few people have ever seen a living specimen. The 1963

Los Angeles County Museum zoological expedition kept a careful look-out when they studied the Tana River, but saw none; and the Kenya Game Department warden in the area has tried to obtain specimens for two years without success.

The writers have been able to trace only one person, Reggie Destro, a professional hunter, who has seen these mangabeys in recent years – a troop of eight, on only one occasion, in June 1961. Destro believes that the mangabey exists in a very limited part of the lower Tana, on the south bank at about the point where the Tiva River joins the Tana. He considers that it probably does not extend upstream beyond Mnazini. Neither he nor anyone else knows whether the animal also lives on the north bank of the Tana.

Peters records that the mangabey was frequently seen in troops of four to six and that the Wapokomo tribesmen were well acquainted with the animal, which they named *garau* in imitation of its high-pitched screech. It is clearly dependent on the gallery forests, which until recently stretched in a narrow unbroken belt along either bank of the lower Tana – two strips of lush green forest, varying in width but seldom more than a few hundred yards wide, and contrasting with the semi-desert country that stretches away from the river far to north and south.

Unfortunately, however, the fertile soil of the forest floor has long been coveted by local tribesmen. Until recently they were prevented from intruding; but during the last five years or so they have attacked the forest with axe and fire until, for many miles along both banks, a few charred stumps amidst the cultivated *shambas* are the only remaining evidence of the forest's former existence.

This cultivation has compelled the mangabeys, along with much other fauna, to abandon the neighbourhood of the river, retreating into flood-water channels in an inaccessible piece of country about 4 miles away. Its inaccessibility has saved it from cultivation, but, like all the lower Tana region, it is an area in which a great deal of game-trapping takes place. Fortunately mangabeys are not deliberately caught or killed, except occasionally in the name of crop-

protection, but the status of this race is nevertheless so precarious that even accidental trapping could have serious consequences for the surviving remnant.

The animal is fully protected by the Kenya Game Department, and no capture permits are issued in any circumstances, but the law does not make any provisions for preventing slaughter by the local tribesmen or, most important of all, for protecting the limited habitat from further human encroachment. Unless such protection is given, the Tana River mangabey cannot long survive.

TANA RIVER RED COLOBUS
Colobus badius rufomitratus

The magnificent leaf monkeys of the genus *Colobus*, the colobus monkeys or guerezas, are peculiarly African animals much persecuted for their fur, which is of considerable commercial value; and the status of all three species is being carefully watched by the Survival Service Commission. Here we single out the form most in danger, one of the fifteen or so races of the red colobus, *C. badius*: the Tana River subspecies, *C. badius rufomitratus*.

The widespread destruction of the gallery forest on the lower Tana River seems to have had nearly as disastrous an effect on the red colobus of this zone as it has had on the mangabey reported upon above.

The red colobus has a slender body, a long tail, and a vestigial thumb. The hair of its head inclines to the rear, except on its forehead (where the hair is vertical) and in a vertical "comb" between the ears. Its shoulder hairs are a little longer than those on its back. The last third of its tail is a dark olive-brown; so is most of its body fur, except for the chest and stomach, which are greyish-yellow, and the front of its neck, the inner sides of its legs, and the under surfaces of its forearms, all of which are greyish. The top of its head is rust-coloured, apart from its eyebrows and "comb", which are a brown that approaches black.

At the time of writing, the red colobus is perhaps in a less precarious position than the mangabey and is locally not uncommon. But its numbers are very limited, and the 1963 Los Angeles County Museum zoological expedition saw only about twenty or thirty specimens at a spot approximately 40 miles downstream from Bura on the western bank of the Tana.

The genus *Colobus* is regarded as the most arboreal of all the groups of African monkeys; its members rarely descend to the ground: the Tana River race thus depends for survival wholly on the strip of riverine forest in which it lives.

The red colobus is fully protected by the laws of Kenya, but this alone is not adequate to ensure the animal's survival. Nothing less than the rigorous protection of gallery forest along the lower Tana River can ensure the survival of the two special monkeys, as well as of many other interesting fauna and flora, some of which are found nowhere else.

Family Pongidae: apes

ORANG UTAN
Pongo pygmaeus

The orang utan is the only representative of the great apes now living outside central Africa. It is a large animal with remarkably human facial characteristics, the adult male being a little more than 4 feet tall, with long, shaggy russet-brown hair. Its arms are extremely long, reaching almost to its ankles when it stands erect. Every night, the animal constructs a "nest" or platform of branches in the fork of a tree, and there it sleeps.

Fossil and archaeological evidence indicates that at one time this primate had a much wider distribution. Remains have been discovered in such far-apart places on the Asian mainland as the Siwalik Hills of India and the provinces of Kwangsi, Kwangtung, and Yunnan in China; and among the great islands fossil bones have been found in parts of Borneo and Sumatra beyond the present range, as well as in Java and Celebes. Teeth, all probably of fossil origin, have been sold in apothecaries' shops in Shanghai, Peking, Hong Kong, and Manila in the Philippines.

Today the orang utan is found only in parts of Sumatra and Borneo. It prefers the lowlands below 2,000 to 2,500 feet, but may range up to 4,500 feet. Until the Second World War, it was estimated to occur in about 50 per cent of the primary forests of Atjeh, the state in the north-western quarter of the island of Sumatra, but since the war its range has been substantially reduced, and it is now restricted to the Löser Reserve (about 1,090,000 acres) and one or two smaller forested regions.

The largest surviving population occurs in Sabah, extending over the border into adjacent Kalimantan (Indonesian Borneo), where orangs are found in limited numbers in the north-east and west; they also occur in Sarawak, but have been exterminated in neighbouring Brunei.

No population estimates exist from before 1959, but it is known that numbers have declined drastically during the last century and particularly since the Second World War. The best available estimate indicates that the total population is now not more than 5,000 and is continuing to decline. Of these, there are estimated to be about 2,000 in Sabah. Kalimantan and Sumatra each have approximately 1,000 and Sarawak about 700.

There are several reasons for the decline; these are applicable in greater or lesser degree to all the territories in which orangs exist.

For its survival the orang is dependent on a certain type of primary or old secondary forest, and it is doubtful whether it will ever adapt itself to any other type of habitat; but in recent years much of the suitable indigenous lowland forest has been used for commercial timber production. As a result, the orangs have been either destroyed or driven from their natural habitat and forced into regions, such as mountainous areas, that do not contain the rather specialized food (notably the fruit of the durian) on which they feed, or that are unsuitable for other reasons.

Widespread destruction of the habitat is probably the principal cause of decline; but an equally serious factor is the large illicit trade in young animals, which are smuggled into Singapore, Bangkok, and other eastern ports and towns where they find a ready market. The high price paid for captive orangs is an irresistible temptation to smugglers to break the law.

Under favourable conditions, there seems to be no great difficulty in capturing orangs. Their movements are normally rather ponderous, and this fact puts them at a disadvantage on the ground. Occasionally an immature animal may be isolated from its mother and captured, but the method most commonly employed involves shooting the mother; after that the young is easily taken. Shooting is a simple matter, as orangs normally show little fear of human beings and, animated by curiosity, do not flee when approached. In these circumstances a small-calibre rifle or shotgun is perfectly adequate, since it can be fired from close range. Larger animals may be driven into a suitable tree. The surrounding trees are felled and the creatures are left isolated, often for many days, until forced to the ground by hunger and thirst; they are then so weak that their capture is easy. Sometimes the tree is felled and the animals are caught as they crash to the ground. Sometimes the orangs are smoked out of cover.

Young orangs are delicate and especially prone to human infections. Many of those that have been caught are kept under primitive and unhygienic conditions; they are compelled to exist on an unnatural diet and die from malnutrition or disease. It has been estimated that only one in three survives the rigours of captivity.

Even in an undisturbed natural state the reproductive rate of the orang is slow. Mature females produce a single infant about every fourth year, but, because the infant mortality rate is about 40 per cent, the actual lifetime reproductive potential may be as low as two or three young per female.

Though the orang is a "protected" animal throughout the greater part of its range, generally speaking such protection is merely nominal. In Sumatra, for example, a relatively new factor in the situation is the presence of Indonesian soldiers who are reported to hunt orangs with rifles, and even with automatic weapons, for the high prices offered by smugglers.

The combination of deliberate slaughter and reduction of the habitat, both for logging and to provide areas of cultivation for the ever-expanding human population, is splitting the survivors into small, often isolated, groups. The more fragmented these groups, the more vulnerable they become in the struggle for survival.

Most of the orangs in Sarawak and Sabah occur in "forest reserves", a term implying that the areas are protected. Unfortunately, the implication is misleading. These forest reserves are essentially areas that the Government has set aside for timber extraction, the work being undertaken by licensed contractors, with the Government deriving a return from royalties. Conservation of wildlife takes second place.

Because the orang depends on primary forest, the survival of the animal must surely require the creation of at least one large national park, or similar reserve, designed especially for the long-term protection of the species in Sarawak and Sabah, besides the one that already exists in Sumatra.

This fact was recognized by Sarawak's Maias Protection Commission as long ago as 1959, and has since been stressed by several ecologists and naturalists, yet nothing has been done to carry out their advice.

The killing and capture of the orang for any purpose must be effectively prevented. Smuggling of young orangs will continue only as long as a market for them exists; and there is an urgent need to remove the legal loopholes that still leave smugglers free to carry on this traffic.

Until recently many of these smuggled orangs found their way through unscrupulous middlemen and dealers into the world's zoos. In an attempt to control this illegal trade, the International Union of Directors of Zoological Gardens agreed to introduce stringent regulations prohibiting the purchase of orangs through illicit channels, but unfortunately many zoo managers remain outside this body. Several of the institutions in the United States that use orangs for medical research have agreed to establish their own captive breeding stock of orangs and other primates, thus reducing to the minimum the need for captured wild animals.

All these measures are constructive and will undoubtedly help to arrest the decline, but the urgent need is to allocate certain areas for the protection of the orang within the preferred natural range of the species, even though these areas may be desirable for commercial or agricultural purposes. This immediately sets the problem of choosing between the requirements of wildlife conservation and those of economic development. The ultimate solution lies squarely in the hands of the Governments of Indonesia, Sarawak, and Sabah. Unless they are prepared to set aside forest sanctuaries – adequate in extent and efficiently protected – to ensure the perpetuation of the species, it will be only a matter of time before Asia's sole great ape ceases to exist, except perhaps in captivity.

In the post-war period the orang breeding record in zoos has improved. The first orang to be born and bred entirely in captivity arrived in the (West) Berlin Zoo on the 12th January 1928. In the same year births also occurred in the Nuremberg and Philadelphia Zoos. By now at least two dozen zoos have reared orangs. Berlin has a particularly good record; so has Phila-delphia, where the famous Guarina, now at least thirty-six years old, gave birth to her ninth baby in 1955. In the summer of 1964 at least 278 orangs were known to be in captivity in at least ninety-six zoos; only thirty-seven of the animals were captive-bred in a rather small minority of those zoos. Besides these, many were captive in research laboratories. A careful estimate of the total captive stock in November 1964 arrived at a figure of just over 500, or perhaps one-tenth of the world population. In 1967 the first baby orang was born in the wild (in Bako National Park, Sarawak) to a female released from captivity; the father was completely wild.

T. H. Harrisson is chairman of a special orang utan committee of the Survival Service Com-mission.

PYGMY CHIMPANZEE
Pan paniscus

Considerable divergence of opinion exists among zoologists about the classification of this species. At one extreme, some believe it to be simply a well-differentiated race of the chimpanzee, *Pan troglodytes*; others think that it differs enough to justify its being placed in a separate genus.

Pygmy chimpanzee *Maurice Wilson* 1965

There are certainly several important anatomi-cal differences. *Pan paniscus* is less than half the size of any race of *P. troglodytes*; its body, relatively more slender, is reminiscent of a tailless spider monkey. Its hair, though fine, is rather long and dense, and is glossy black all over except for a small white rump patch. Its head is small and its face long and narrow, its ears small and partly hidden in fur, and the hair of its head has no division. Moreover, the second and third toes of the pygmy chimpanzee are partly joined together.

It also differs greatly in temperament. *P. troglodytes* has an uncertain temper and is given to uncontrollable fits of rage. *P. paniscus*, on the other hand, is extraordinarily placid and seldom attempts to bite unless seriously provoked. Its call is said to be quieter and less shrill than that of its larger relative.

The existence of a chimpanzee to the south of the Congo River had been suspected for some years. The British Museum had a specimen in 1895, and one that probably was of this species was exhibited for a short while in 1923 at New York's Bronx Zoo, but it was not until 1929 that the animal was actually described. Vernon Reynolds has lately shown that the original specimen described by Tulp, upon which Lin-naeus's *Simia satyrus* of 1758 (a name now suppressed) had been based, was doubtless a pygmy chimpanzee; it was said to have come from the coast of Angola, but this is doubtful.

The pygmy chimpanzee is apparently restric-ted to a relatively small area of humid rain forest on the south bank of the Congo River. The southern limit of the range appears to be the Kasai and Sunkuru rivers, where the animal becomes less plentiful as the rain forest gradually gives way to increasingly large stretches of savannah country.

Hardly anything appears to be known about this primate in the wild state. As far as can be ascertained, the local tribesmen have not yet made any serious attempt to molest the animal except on occasions when induced to do so by European collectors. The greatest potential threat to the species lies in destruction of the high forest that constitutes the animal's native environment, and without which it cannot survive.

There are about twenty specimens now in various of the world's zoos, where they make gentle and affectionate pets. The Frankfurt Zoo achieved the distinction of successfully breeding the animal for the first time in captivity on the 22nd January 1962 and again on the 22nd December 1963.

MOUNTAIN GORILLA
Gorilla gorilla beringei

For more than 100 years after its first scientific description, from West Africa in 1847, the gorilla remained something of an enigma. The remoteness of the dense forests inhabited by the animal – and its massive size and strength, which gave it a reputation for ferocity now known to be unwarranted – discouraged more than brief and superficial observations.

In 1959–60, however, all this changed. For twenty months George Schaller and his wife lived among mountain gorillas mainly in the Virunga Volcanoes. His first-hand observations resulted in what is surely the most thorough study of a wild primate ever made. His published monograph on the animal is a model of its kind; as a result, the gorilla has changed from being one of the least known to one of the best-documented primates. Nearly all the following notes are extracted, quite unashamedly, from Schaller's classic work *Mountain Gorilla* (1963).

The full species occurs in the dense equatorial forests of western and west-central Africa. It has been subdivided into two widely separated races,

the lowland gorilla, *G. g. gorilla*, which is restricted to the Congo River basin, and the mountain gorilla, *G. g. beringei*, which is found in the mountainous regions in the eastern Congo extending very slightly into south-western Uganda and western Rwanda. The status of the lowland race is being carefully watched, and it is not at present endangered: but the mountain gorilla is.

During his remarkable walk from the Cape to Cairo in 1898, Ewart Grogan came across the skeleton of a gigantic ape, bigger than any he had ever seen, in the neighbourhood of the Virunga Volcanoes. This appears to have been the first record of the mountain gorilla, and, if Grogan had thought of sending the skeleton to England, he would undoubtedly have been credited with the animal's discovery. However, four more years were to pass before the subspecies was first made known to science from a specimen collected by Captain Oscar von Beringe on Mount Sabinio in October 1902.

Gorillas are the largest and by far the most powerful of all the living primates. Together with their relatives, the chimpanzee and the pygmy chimpanzee of Africa and the orang utan of eastern Asia, they are known collectively as

Mountain gorilla *Barry Driscoll* 1967

the great apes. It is a sobering thought that three of the world's four great apes have the doubtful distinction of a place in the Survival Service Commission's Red Data Book.

An adult male mountain gorilla may weigh 300 to 400 pounds or more (a few have reached what were probably abnormally high weights in captivity) and stand 5 feet 6 inches tall when fully erect, with an arm-spread greatly exceeding its height; females are much smaller, weighing 150 to 250 pounds. Their bodies are thickset, their arms very powerful but their legs relatively weak. Their heads are massive and have a prominent crest, with a low forehead and heavy ridges over the eyes. Their eyes and ears are small, their nostrils large. Their hands are very large, with thumbs larger than fingers. Their hair is brownish-black to blue-black, males over the age of about ten years being distinguished by a prominent silvery-grey saddle. Individuals vary greatly in appearance.

The mountain gorilla differs from its lowland relative by having a somewhat narrower head with a prominent fleshy callosity on its crest, arms somewhat shorter, legs longer and fur denser. Gorillas often stand erect; but prolonged movement on two feet is rare, and the normal walking position is on all fours with the knuckles on the ground.

Although their large canine teeth might give a contrary impression, gorillas have a diet believed to be wholly vegetarian. Captive gorillas eat meat, but there is no evidence that they do so in the wild. They consume the juicy stems of wild celery, bamboo shoots, the fronds of tree-ferns, the bark of certain shrubs, leaves, berries, wild fruits, and a variety of other herbage. Occasionally they raid standing crops in native *shambas*. At no time did Schaller see them drink, and they probably obtain their liquid requirements from heavy morning dew and succulent vegetation.

They are able to climb trees but, being primarily terrestrial animals, spend most of the time on the ground, where their preferred food is more abundant.

Rough platforms are built for sleeping at night or for rest during the day, either in a tree or on the ground. Adult males usually prefer the ground. A gorilla rarely takes more than a few minutes to make a nest, either standing or sitting in a central position, and pulling in the surrounding vegetation, which it tucks under and around itself. According to locality and circumstances, the nests are made in a crude and casual way or may be much more elaborately built, but they are not normally occupied more than once.

The mountain gorilla lives in groups of any number between two and thirty (according to the area) but probably averaging between six and seventeen. Factors determining the size of each group are little understood, but may be dependent to some extent on the availability and type of forage. Each group is dominated by a silver-backed male.

The mountain gorilla inhabits a region shaped like an inverted triangle, and extending about 300 miles south from the equator and about 220 miles from east to west at its widest point. The southern limit of the range is near Fizi, where the forest gives way to savannah and cultivation. The total range covers roughly 35,000 square miles; but within this region the area actually used by gorillas is much less since most groups are concentrated in sixty or so isolated areas varying in size from a few to 200 square miles and separated by anything up to 30 or more miles. Some groups undoubtedly come into contact with each other, but many live in isolation. The area actually occupied by gorillas is less than a quarter of the total range, or roughly 8,000 square miles, although stragglers, usually lone males but occasionally small groups, may sometimes wander into the large areas of forest surrounding the resident populations.

Within this range, the density of the gorilla populations varies from roughly three animals per square mile in the Virunga Volcanoes, where there are about 400 or 500 in all, to about one and a half per square mile in the Kayonza Forest, and one or perhaps a fraction of one per square mile in the Utu region. The entire population has been estimated at between 5,000 and 15,000 animals.

The mountain gorilla is found in three types of environment: lowland rain forest below 5,000 feet, mountain rain forest from 5,000 to 11,500 feet, and bamboo forest from 8,000 to 10,000 feet. An estimated three-quarters of the population inhabits lowland rain forest west of the Rift Valley; and most of the remainder lives in the mountain forests of the Rift escarpment. The bamboo zone is relatively unimportant to the subspecies, as it contains little suitable dry season forage and is in any event of limited distribution. The most favoured habitat consists of secondary forest; and the rotational felling of primary forest, and its subsequent regeneration, under the slash-and-burn system of shifting agriculture used in the past by primitive agriculturalists, undoubtedly created conditions favourable to the ape.

Females are believed not to reach sexual maturity until the age of six or seven, and males at about nine or ten years, when the hair of the black-backed males starts changing to silver, a process that may take at least two or three years to complete. The gestation period of four captive specimens varies from 251 to 289 days. There is no evidence of a breeding season, but mature females normally produce a single young every three and a half to four and a half years, unless the young dies in infancy, in which event the interval is reduced. Mortality is high and probably between 40 and 50 per cent of the progeny die during the infant and juvenile periods.

The young remains with its mother for about three years, during which time she does not again conceive. On the assumption that a mature female reproduces about once every fourth year, her lifetime reproductive expectancy is probably about four or five young, assuming none dies in infancy.

Losses through predation by leopards or other carnivores are believed to be insignificant. By far the most important predator is man. Notwithstanding nominal legal protection, some tribesmen continue to hunt the gorilla, mainly for food, and notably in the Utu and Mount Tshiaberimu regions, by a variety of methods including nets, snares, and pitfalls. Schaller quotes a 1928 missionary report that tribesmen had killed and eaten eleven gorillas in a single day. He also mentions a mine official who admitted shooting nine for sport, and cites an instance of the shooting of females by collectors to obtain the young, including an occasion about 1948 when sixty were killed near Angumu to acquire eleven infants, only one of which eventually survived.

Gorillas are subject to a wide variety of diseases and other ailments: virus diseases, bacterial infections, and various internal parasites may be responsible for the majority of gorilla deaths.

The numbers slaughtered every year for food are believed to be substantial, but do not so far appear to have had any serious effect on the total population. Losses from this cause can be sustained just as long as killing rates do not rise much above their present level through the acquisition by the killers of more sophisticated weapons. A more immediate threat to the animal occurs in areas such as the Virunga Volcanoes, the Kayonza Forest, and the Mount Tshiaberimu region, which are gradually being taken over by agriculturalists and pastoralists.

The latest threat to the gorilla, as well as to many other species of primates, is the increasing demands of medical research and the pharmaceutical industry.

Because only relatively small differences separate the mountain and lowland races, it is believed that their divergence must have been fairly recent. The distribution of the species was once probably continuous throughout the rain forest north of the Congo River; today a gap of about 650 miles separates the two races, but it does not result from any limitations of suitable habitat. Indeed, rain forest stretches unbroken throughout the region.

The dispersal of gorilla populations is restricted by the extent of humid forest that readily provides their favoured forage, such as vines and succulent herbs: they avoid grasslands and large areas of open woodlands. Moreover, although gorillas use fallen trees for crossing streams and small rivers, they are apparently unable to swim and seem to avoid even quite shallow streams. Deep, swift rivers, such as those of the Congo and Ubangi-Uele systems, would have formed impassable barriers.

With these limiting factors in mind, Schaller speculates that at one time the gorilla inhabited country to the north of the Uele River, and penetrated into its present habitat by way of the headwaters of that river. Although the region north of the Uele River is not now suitable for gorillas, there is evidence that during the late Pleistocene the rain forest extended farther to the north than it does today, thereby linking East and West Africa by way of the northern edge of the Congo Basin. This hypothesis is supported by evidence that several species of East African montane forest birds are not even differentiated by subspecies from their counterparts on Mount Cameroon in West Africa. Furthermore, Lake Chad during the late Pleistocene was almost five times the size of the present Lake Victoria, which means that it must then have received twenty times more water than it does today. The resulting precipitation would have permitted the occurrence of suitable humid forest vegetation north of the Uele River.

Later a dry climatic period caused the forest to regress, leaving the two populations isolated from each other by the 650-mile gap. Additional evidence in support of the theory that the gorilla spread from north to south in the relatively recent past arises from the fact that colonization is more extensive in the northern than in the southern part of the range.

The colonization of the Virunga Volcanoes and the Kayonza Forest presumably occurred by way of forest bridges across the grasslands, which were afterwards severed by agriculture and burning, so that the populations became isolated. Failure to colonize the Ruwenzori Range, which contains much suitable habitat, is probably because the Semliki River formed an insurmountable barrier to penetration.

Schaller's work has shown conclusively that the mountain gorilla is not at present on the verge of extinction, as was thought when it was placed among the Class A mammals by the International London Convention of 1933. His study has revealed that both the range and the population are larger than previously supposed. The total area occupied by the subspecies is nevertheless small, and without doubt the animal is extremely vulnerable to direct destruction as well as to reduction or alteration of habitat. In some parts of the range, this form of indirect destruction constitutes a more serious and immediate threat than in others, particularly in areas such as the Virunga Volcanoes, where there is a dense and expanding human population that requires grazing for the constantly increasing herds of scrub cattle.

A notable step towards the protection of the

mountain gorilla was the establishment in 1925, and the subsequent enlargement in 1929, of the Albert National Park, which was designed primarily for the long-term protection of the gorillas inhabiting the six dormant cones that constitute the Virunga Volcanoes. The park authorities have had a constant struggle to prevent violation of the park's boundaries, and in 1958 they were compelled to relinquish 47,500 acres of forest land. Wherever agriculturalists have been admitted, the forests have disappeared within a few years. In spite of the difficulties that have beset them in recent years, the Congo National Park authorities deserve the highest commendation for their vigilance in safeguarding the park in the face of almost insuperable difficulties.

On the Uganda side of the Virunga Volcanoes, the northern slopes of Mounts Muhavura, Gahinga, and Sabinio were declared a gorilla sanctuary in 1930; but in 1950 the reserve was reduced from over 8,000 to less than 6,000 acres. The part cut out contained the most suitable gorilla habitat, much of which is now under cultivation, and the area is therefore subject to heavy disturbance.

The Kayonza Forest, otherwise known as the Impenetrable Forest, was declared a forest reserve in 1932 and became a wildlife sanctuary of nearly 74,000 acres in 1961. Selective use of the forest, mainly by a limited number of licensed pitsawyers, has been permitted since 1940, but it apparently causes little more than temporary disturbance in the areas actually being worked, and it may indeed benefit the gorillas by providing additional forage in the regenerating areas. Gorillas are seldom molested in the reserve, although occasionally a few may be unintentionally killed in traps set for wild pigs, and their status in the Kayonza Forest appears at present to be satisfactory.

The Mount Tshiaberimu massif is included within the boundaries of the Albert National Park, but is hemmed in by cultivation on three sides. Beyond the boundaries of the park the forest is being rapidly replaced by permanent agriculture. Furthermore, tribesmen in this

PLATE 3 Orang utan *Barry Driscoll* 1966

Common Rorqual

Sibbald's Rorqual or Blue Whale. BO

region slaughter the gorilla for food. Failure to introduce and enforce more effective protection of the forests must sooner or later lead to the elimination of the ape from this region.

The situation is much more satisfactory in the extensive montane forests of the Rift and the huge areas of lowland forests lying to the west of Lake Tanganyika. Except around the towns, of which there are few, the human population is thin; and shifting cultivation will probably continue as in the past, a method of agriculture that in fact benefits the gorilla. True, African tribesmen undertake communal attacks on gorillas, and many of the animals are slaughtered, but the rate of kill is limited by the weapons and techniques employed, and the gorilla population should be capable of withstanding those losses so long as modern firearms are not made available.

Schaller concludes that it is essential for the mountain gorilla to remain on the list of fully protected animals, which would involve doing everything possible, such as banning modern firearms, to prevent large-scale killing orgies by local tribesmen. A strict limit should be introduced, and enforced, on the numbers collected for zoos, museums, medical institutions, and so forth; and the technique of killing the female to obtain the young should be outlawed.

Strong measures should also be taken to prevent intrusion by agriculturalists and pastoralists into the existing gorilla sanctuaries, which should be extended to embrace more of the animals' natural range, notably in those areas where permanent agriculture is feasible. At the same time consideration should be given to the establishment of spacious reserves in the great, and at present almost uninhabited, areas of lowland rain forest while the opportunity still exists – as a precaution against the day when the expanding human population changes over from the present pattern of shifting cultivation to a more stable system of husbandry.

In mid-1965 thirteen gorillas of the mountain race were in captivity in six zoos. A number of further specimens have been subsequently acquired. The lowland race, of which nearly 200 are captive in zoos alone, had successfully bred in them ten times by early 1967, the first at Columbus, Ohio, in 1956, the last (the only twins) at Frankfurt. Adult pairs of mountain gorillas have lately been kept in captivity, and one pair bred at Antwerp in 1968. Other captive adult pairs are now reaching breeding age, and there is no reason why they should not breed as well. At least two babies have been born to females already pregnant when brought captive to Congo holding camps.

Order LAGOMORPHA
Family Leporidae: rabbits and hares

RYUKYU RABBIT
Pentalagus furnessi

The genus *Pentalagus* consists of this solitary species, which exists exclusively on two small islands, Amami Oshima and Toku-no-Oshima, south of the island of Kyushu, which is itself in the southern part of Japan.

The animal is covered with thick, woolly fur, dark brown above, reddish-brown on its flanks, and somewhat lighter underneath. It has a tail

of little more than $\frac{1}{2}$ inch, ears that are proportionately smaller than those of the common rabbit, and curved claws that are unusually long and heavy. Hardly anything appears to have been recorded about its breeding biology, but the females are said to bear only a single young.

Until 1921 the rabbit was very much hunted, partly for food and partly because of its reputed medicinal properties. The demand was so heavy that the animal diminished drastically in numbers. In 1921 the rabbit was officially designated a special natural monument, thus being given complete protection against shooting and capture. Unfortunately there were other hazards, which the law could not so readily

PLATE 4 (*a*) Fin whale; (*b*) Blue whale *Archibald Thorburn* 1920 control. Among them was the increase of stray dogs, resulting in a further serious setback to the rabbit population. Deforestation was also permitted. The animal has therefore been deprived of large areas of suitable habitat.

These hazards appear to have been especially severe on Toku-no-Oshima, where the animal is now almost extinct. On Amami Oshima it has a rather more favourable position, and in certain parts is thought to be holding its own. No accurate census of the population is possible, but numbers have been assessed at between 500 and 900 all told.

Ryukyu rabbit *Barry Driscoll* 1966

Although several attempts have been made to breed the animal in captivity outside the islands, none so far have succeeded. Apparently the only practical method of safeguarding the species for posterity would be a twofold programme – the establishment of reserves embracing sectors of the forested habitat, and an officially sponsored campaign for the eradication of stray dogs from both islands.

A further suggestion that might usefully form part of any programme for the rescue of the species might be the setting up in suitable parts of the islands of large dog-proof enclosures, where at least a sample of the limited habitat could be protected from disturbance and maintained in a suitable state.

VOLCANO RABBIT
Romerolagus diazi

This genus consists of a single, and probably relict, species that is markedly different from most other members of the family, but has been described as bearing a striking superficial resemblance to the northern pika or cony of the genus *Ochotona*. Not only are they both tailless, with short ears, but both have the habit of living under rock piles and both possess high-pitched, penetrating voices that they use frequently: no other members of the family Leporidae, besides *Romerolagus*, are normally vocal.

The volcano rabbit is covered with fur, which is a uniform dark brown on its back and dark brownish-grey beneath. Its legs and feet are short, its ears small and rounded, and its tail so rudimentary that it is invisible.

The *teporingo*, to use one of its colloquial names, exists only on the middle slopes of Popocatépetl and Ixtacihuatl and some of the nearby ridges on the southern side of the Valley of México, where it is further restricted to elevations between 9,000 and 10,500 feet. Within this narrow zone its preferred environment consists of open pine forests under which is a dense ground cover of coarse *zacaton* grasses. Only among the mingled pine and *zacaton* on the edge of this one valley does the volcano rabbit exist. It thus has the most restricted range of any mammal in Mexico.

It lives in burrows either beneath the ground or in rock talus, and makes its way through the tall, coarse tussocks of grass by a series of well-maintained paths. Little is known of the animal's food habits, but it probably consumes the aromatic mint, *Cunila tritifolium*, which grows in this region. Sometimes the rabbits smell strongly of the plant.

During fine weather the animal spends much of its time above ground; usually it rests during the heat of the day and becomes active in the evening and early morning. When disturbed or alarmed, it will utter its sharp cry and dash to take refuge in a nearby burrow.

The underground burrow normally has several openings for escape; in the breeding season, it contains a nest, lined with a combination of pine needles and the animal's own fur. Breeding takes place from March to early July. Litters vary between one and four young; three is the usual number.

Nominally the species has complete protection, but this has not prevented it from becoming very scarce in recent years. The reason is partly because of increasing encroachment on the habitat for agricultural purposes, which involves burning the vegetation, and partly because of casual hunting by people from Mexico City. Apparently nobody is interested in killing the animal for food, perhaps because its diet of strong mint imparts an unpleasant flavour to the meat; but sportsmen occupied in hunting game birds regard the rabbit as useful for target practice or as dog meat.

Considering its rarity and limited range, and the lack of effective protection, the volcano rabbit is unlikely to survive for many more years unless the Government of Mexico takes protective measures.

Order RODENTIA
Family Sciuridae: squirrels, etc.

KAIBAB SQUIRREL
Sciurus kaibabensis

The Kaibab squirrel, so much admired by visitors to the North Rim of the Grand Canyon National Park in northern Arizona, is either a race of, or a full species descended from, the tassel-eared squirrel, *S. aberti*, of the South Rim and neighbouring parts of this state of great deserts and forests. The tassel-eared form, with its dark tail, has been isolated from the northern form by the mile-deep Grand Canyon itself, perhaps for the 1,000,000 years or more that this great rift, now well over 200 miles long, has been eroded deeply enough by the Colorado River to be impassable to squirrels. But whether the Kaibab squirrel rates the rank of a full species or not, it is now very different in appearance from its cousin 10 miles away across the world's greatest river-rift.

Sciurus, the genus of the tree squirrels, embraces at least thirty-seven species, which are widely distributed throughout the world from the tropics to the temperate regions.

The Kaibab squirrel is of about the same size as the well-known grey squirrel, or a little longer. Its back is a dark grizzled grey, with a tinge of reddish-brown from rump to shoulders. It has black under parts. Its ears have prominent black tufts; its large, bushy tail (unlike that of its relative across the Canyon) is white, with an indistinct greyish stripe running along the centre of its upper side.

It is found only on the Kaibab Plateau, on the northern side of the Grand Canyon, in an area of about 30 by 70 miles, wholly within the national park or in part of the Kaibab National Forest of Arizona, among yellow pines and Gambel oaks. In this sanctuary the animal has been legally protected for many years.

The squirrel feeds almost exclusively on the cambium layer of the yellow pine, and its existence may be intimately linked with this tree. The suggestion has been made that the policy of fire prevention on the Kaibab Plateau during many years has been so effective that the stands of this tree have deteriorated – an interesting example of how over-protection may have unexpected results. Other contributory causes of decline include disease and a surprisingly high number of casualties inflicted by road traffic through the area.

For reasons that are not fully understood, the squirrel population appears to fluctuate from year to year. According to Dr Joseph G. Hall, who for five years has been making a special

Kaibab squirrel *Barry Driscoll 1966*

study of the animal, the population reached its peak about thirty years ago but is now lower than it has been for half a century. The Arizona Game and Fish Commission, however, believes that the present population, estimated at about 1,000, is the optimum number for the limited habitat and that the species is not endangered. Further studies will undoubtedly be needed to assess the relative merits of these divergent opinions.

DELMARVA PENINSULA FOX SQUIRREL
Sciurus niger cinereus

The familiar fox squirrel of the eastern United States, so common in many areas, has at least one of its ten races at present in danger of extinction – the Delmarva Peninsula form, *S. n. cinereus.*

This race is rather larger than the typical race of the grey squirrel, with which it shares its range. Its upper parts are a light grizzled grey, its under parts and feet white. Its tail has a prominent black stripe on the outer edges. A melanistic form also exists.

At one time this subspecies was widespread over the Eastern Shore counties of Maryland, as well as parts of Delaware and south-eastern Pennsylvania, but its range has now declined to only six of the Eastern Shore counties. The northern part of the range includes several small insular populations, including one on Eastern Neck Island, which is roughly 2 by 3 miles and is situated south-east of Baltimore across Chesapeake Bay. Some 10 or 12 miles further south another colony lives on Wye Island in Queen Anne's county, where it is restricted to a strip of loblolly pine, *Pinus taeda*, covering no more than 75 acres.

In addition to these isolated populations, the squirrel is found in parts of Talbot and Dorchester counties in a strip that probably does not exceed 50 to 75 by 25 miles.

The island populations are unlikely to amount to more than a few hundred specimens, and the total population therefore may not be more than a few thousand.

The decline of the squirrel, and much of Maryland's other native fauna, has come about through the steady elimination, reduction, or spoliation of habitat. Felling the trees – particularly during the last century, when much of the heavy timber was cut out – and, more recently, road-building and other forms of construction have all contributed to this process.

As the distribution of the species appears to be closely associated with mature stands of loblolly, its survival in the long run largely depends on protecting areas of suitable forest. The establishment of the Blackwater National Wildlife Refuge and the Pocomoke State Forest is a notable advance towards this goal. The United States Fish and Wildlife Service is trying to acquire Eastern Neck Island as a waterfowl refuge. If this attempt proves successful, the island will have proper woodland management, to the great benefit of the squirrel.

UTAH PRAIRIE DOG
Cynomys parvidens

The prairie dog genus, *Cynomys*, was once widely distributed and abundant on the short-grass plains of North America. The opening of the great plains for settlement brought these prolific rodents into immediate conflict with cattlemen, who regarded the enormous colonies of prairie dogs as competitors for the available grazing. As a result the animals were heavily persecuted, and many hundreds of thousands destroyed by strychnine and other means.

Like so many commonly accepted names for wild animals, "dog" in this case is quite wrong; it probably arose from the creature's characteristic bark. *Cynomys* is not related to any dog, but is a type of ground-squirrel adapted for burrowing.

The Utah prairie dog is a rather large, plump rodent with a flattened head, covered in uniformly brown coarse fur. It has a short white tail and short legs.

In a year it normally produces a single litter, consisting of four to six young, after a gestation period of about twenty-eight to thirty-two days. The young are weaned after about six or seven weeks; they reach full growth at fifteen months and become sexually mature at about three years.

The prairie dog has achieved an impressive level of social organization and lives in "towns", which extend over a wide area and often consist of several thousand individuals controlled by a hierarchy of dominant males. Each burrow extends almost vertically for several yards underground, with smaller passages leading off to each side; in these a nest of grass is built. Earth from the excavation is piled up around the entrance, often to a height of 2 feet and as much as 4 feet in diameter, forming a mound that prevents surface water from flooding the burrows. The prairie dog spends a great deal of time and energy in maintaining this crater-shaped mound, and can often be seen near the entrance squatting on its haunches in an upright position, alert for any sign of danger.

Unlike most other species of prairie dog, *C. parvidens* has never been particularly widespread or abundant, and, as far as is known, it has always been restricted to Utah. During the last thirty years it has greatly declined. A survey undertaken in 1962 showed that it now exists in only five counties of south central Utah, whereas in 1935–6 it was known to have existed in nine counties.

It is the least common and most restricted of all the prairie dogs, although it is also regarded as the one least subject to interference. Nevertheless the population continues to decline. This may be through the outbreak of sylvatic plague that recently affected the species, although the extent of the mortality does not appear to have been recorded.

Today the largest concentration is on Packer Mountain, where an estimated 1,500 prairie dogs occupy an area of about $15\frac{1}{2}$ square miles. The total population is not known, but 2,775 animals were counted in nine "towns".

The United States Fish and Wildlife Service has issued instructions to all personnel engaged in control measures to avoid disturbing the species, and there seems little further protective action that can be taken at present.

Family Cricetidae: New World mice, hamsters, lemmings, voles, gerbils, etc.

BLOCK ISLAND MEADOW VOLE
Microtus pennsylvanicus provectus

The genus *Microtus* includes more than forty species and many more subspecies widely distributed over the greater part of North America, northern Europe, and northern Asia. Of these species the widespread meadow vole of North America is typical, with twenty-three currently accepted races. Among these, one island race, *M. p. provectus*, is in the Red Data Book.

Microtus pennsylvanicus provectus is possibly a relict form that once inhabited the mainland coast, and it differs very little from the common meadow vole of the mainland. Whatever its past history may have been, it is now restricted to Block Island, some 8 miles long and 2 to 5 miles wide, situated off the north-eastern tip of Long Island.

Meadow voles are extraordinarily prolific. A female is capable of breeding when only twenty-five days old and may produce up to thirteen litters a year, each consisting of four to eight young, after a gestation period of three weeks. The birth of a litter is followed immediately by a fresh mating; the young are weaned at about ten to fifteen days old. A single female can probably produce 100 young in a year.

It may seem strange that an animal that reproduces itself on this scale should be regarded as in any way endangered. The explanation is that the construction of roads and buildings, and the cultivation of large parts of Block Island, have altered the very restricted habitat and made it less suitable for the meadow vole. It is also probable that, with the protective grass removed, storms and hurricanes have increased the degradation of the habitat. Certainly great ecological change has taken place on the island since Bangs, who described this race in 1908, first collected specimens there.

The status of this insular race is not easy to

assess, particularly as all members of the genus, even under satisfactory conditions, seem subject to violent fluctuations in their numbers. But the animal is thought to have recently declined, and it may be endangered. The only practical method of helping its recovery would be to ensure the continuation of suitable perennial grasses. If that were done, the Block Island meadow vole would be well able to look after itself, for the species is capable of withstanding a degree of cold and privation that would kill most other small rodents.

BEACH MEADOW VOLE

Microtus breweri

This is another insular meadow vole, closely related to *Microtus pennsylvanicus* but with fur that is longer, coarser, and paler; it differs also in certain less obvious ways. It may be, indeed, a very well-marked race of *M. pennsylvanicus*, which has no other representative on its island. The beach meadow vole is a further example of a relict form that inhabited a sandy plain, which no longer exists, but at one time extended along the coast of North America from New Jersey to Newfoundland.

M. breweri lives only on Muskegat Island, off the extreme western end of Nantucket and some 30 miles south of Cape Cod. Muskegat is separated from Nantucket by a strip of very shallow water, 6 miles wide and broken about midway by Tuckernuck Island, and on the south side is cut off from the sea by long narrow beaches. These beaches constantly change their shape and position through the tidal forces that sweep over them; but, however much they may fluctuate, the three islands remain permanently isolated from each other.

Perhaps no other small mammal lives under such harsh conditions. During the greater part of the year the only protection against the force of the weather is the scant grass, fortified by pieces of driftwood that may be swept on to the beaches. The sand, moreover, is so coarse and loose that the mouse cannot make more than the most primitive and inadequate burrow, except for a short period during the winter when the surface of the ground is frozen. The beach mouse has been compelled to modify its habits accordingly.

Like the mainland meadow vole, the Muskegat form undergoes violent fluctuations of number. In 1869, for example, the population was extremely abundant, but in 1890–1 there was virtually no sign of any. By 1892 the situation had apparently returned to normal, and reports were made of a "thriving colony"; by the following year the situation had once again been reversed, and the colony had apparently vanished. There was a fairly high population in 1965.

The history of the beach meadow vole indicates that these cycles are a normal part of the animal's existence, and do not in themselves constitute a threat to the species. In attempting to assess the status of this vole, it is necessary, however, to take other factors into consideration. The increase in building and the rise in the number of feral cats threaten the meadow vole. An even more serious potential danger arises from natural causes. During the past quarter of a century hurricanes and storms are thought to have become more intense: erosion on the island has increased, and it could conceivably sweep away the small world of the beach meadow vole.

Muskegat Island has been declared a refuge for nesting terns, and this measure will naturally also benefit the mouse; but, in the interest of both tern and mouse, steps must be taken to eliminate the feral cats.

Family Capromyidae: hutias and coypu

CUVIER'S HUTIA
Plagiodontia aedium

DOMINICAN HUTIA
Plagiodontia hylaeum

The curious genus *Plagiodontia*, the hutias or zagoutis, consists of four species, two of which (*P. ipnaeum* and *P. spelaeum*) are extinct and known only from prehistoric skeletal remains. The two living species, *P. aedium* and *P. hylaeum*, are in the Dominican Republic and Haiti. So far as is known, Cuvier's hutia lives in the western and southern parts of the island of Hispaniola and the Dominican hutia in the north-east. The genus is unknown on the mainland or in any other part of the Antilles.

Cuvier's hutia is about 1 foot long. Its naked tail is almost half as long again, with small, non-overlapping scales; its fur is dense and, on the upper parts, consists of fine silky hairs, grey with tawny tips and intermixed with longer black hairs. Its under parts are paler, its "whiskers" long, and its hands and feet all equipped with claws, the one on the thumb being short and blunt. *P. hylaeum* differs from *P. aedium* by having a larger body and a shorter tail; its feet are narrower, its claws sharper and longer, the scales on its tail and feet smaller. In general its fur is darker, the under parts being almost the same colour as the upper parts, and not pale as in *P. aedium*.

P. aedium was originally described by the famous French naturalist, Frédéric Cuvier, in 1836, from a single specimen obtained by Alexander Ricord from Hispaniola ten years earlier. For more than a century no further specimens were collected, and the animal was assumed to be extinct. Then, in 1947, the scientific world was surprised to learn that a second specimen had been discovered in a remote part of the island, where native hunters stated that it was still relatively abundant.

In 1923, Dr W. L. Abbott obtained ten adults (including three females) and three immature specimens at a place not far from Samaná Bay in the Dominican Republic. At first they were assumed to be identical with Cuvier's hutia, but later they were recognized as a distinct species, which was described by Miller in 1927. Ten years afterwards two further specimens were obtained for the Museum of Comparative Zoology and apparently the species still exists in the same general area, near Samaná Bay in the north-eastern part of the Dominican Republic.

The decline of both species is probably due to three principal factors. Because of the hutias' vegetarian diet, their flesh was regarded as very good to eat, with the result that they were so heavily hunted by the local people that even in Cuvier's day they had already become very scarce. It is significant that, of the two extinct species of hutia, one is known only from fragmentary cave material, and the other from abundant kitchen midden deposits. This suggests that early man may have persecuted them with such enthusiasm that they were virtually hunted out of existence. At the same time the expanding human population made inroads upon the original forests, thus decreasing the habitat available to the hutias. The third factor that may have tipped the scales against the hutias was the introduction of the Burmese mongoose into the island. Although they can climb to some extent, hutias are almost entirely terrestrial in habit, a fact that renders them particularly vulnerable to the mongoose, as well as to dogs.

Dominican hutia *Barry Driscoll* 1966

Hardly anything appears to have been recorded about the habits of the two surviving species, although they are believed to be nocturnal, hiding during the day, possibly in hollow trees. They probably eat fruit, roots, and other vegetable matter. The hutias' reproductive rate is thought to be very low, with the females bearing only a single young.

Order CETACEA

WHALES AND WHALING[1]

In recent years there has been increasing awareness of the need for wildlife and wild places. Man's preoccupation with problems of his own survival may have made him slightly more sympathetic toward the other animals with which he shares this planet. There is also perhaps a dawning realization that, while it is permissible to use the income derived from some of the things of beauty, interest, and value that are part of man's natural heritage, the capital must be handed down intact to future generations. Indicative of man's growing concern over the prodigal squandering of nature are a mirror and accompanying sign set up at the Bronx Zoo; the sign states, simply but emphatically, "You are looking at the most dangerous animal in the world. It alone of all the animals that ever lived can exterminate (and *has*) entire species . . ."

The oceans of Antarctica sustain the largest animal the world has ever known (considerably larger than the most massive of the dinosaurs that dominated the Mesozoic era); it is also one that has earned a high place on the list of mammals in the service of man. An adult blue whale, up to 98 feet long and weighing perhaps as much as 160 tons,[2] dwarfs any other animal in the whole of creation; even its new-born young are larger than a full-grown elephant and are reputed to consume more than $\frac{1}{2}$ ton of milk a day. But it may not be long before the blue whale joins the dinosaurs in the museum of oblivion. The demise of the dinosaurs remains veiled in mystery and surmise, but there is no need to speculate on the reasons for the disappearance of the blue whale; the rapaciousness of man is wholly responsible. Seas and oceans comprise 70 per cent of the earth's surface, and one would have thought this ample habitat allowed more than enough space for the whale's survival, but pursuit of the whale has been so persistent that nowhere on the face of the sea or in its uttermost depths, however remote or vast or forbidding, is there any longer a true sanctuary beyond the reach of man's ruthless exploitation.

Written records of whaling in Europe extend as far back as the ninth century, and small whales have been hunted certainly since Neolithic and probably since Mesolithic times. In medieval times the Basques hunted the Atlantic right whale from the shores of the Bay of Biscay, and later constructed sea-going vessels that enabled them to extend their activities out into the Atlantic, eventually reaching as far as Iceland and the New World.

By the end of the seventeenth century, stocks of the Atlantic right whale had been so depleted (it is no longer found on the Biscay coast) that attention was transferred to the Greenland or Arctic right whale. The northern whale fishery was a flourishing industry for almost three centuries, but by 1913 it was finished, and the Arctic right whale, once so common around Spitsbergen and Jan Mayen Island, is now seldom seen. The final redoubt of the bowhead, as this whale is called in North America, was the Sea of Okhotsk and the area to the north of the Bering Strait.

The history of the North Pacific fishery differs only in that the end came much more swiftly. American whalers entered the area in the early 1840s, and they pursued their quarry with such determination that by 1908 the fishery was finished. The Pacific right whale, the counterpart of the Atlantic species, was practically fished to extinction south of the Aleutians by the same time, though some continued to be taken for about three more decades. The right whales survive, but they are now extremely scarce.

The sperm whale industry, based on New England, was for all practical purposes an American monopoly; it flourished from the end of the eighteenth to the middle of the nineteenth century. The industry reached its peak in 1846 with several hundred vessels in operation. The discovery of petroleum some thirteen years later was one of the factors that caused the sperm whale industry to begin its gradual decline until

[1] Adapted, with permission, from *Science*, Vol. 149, No. 3687, 27 August 1965.

[2] *Brachiosaurus*, a giant even among dinosaurs, weighed only an estimated 50 tons.

it expired in 1925. During the past two years it has revived, especially in the Southern Hemisphere.

The wide-ranging activities of the sperm whalers led almost incidentally to the near-elimination of two further species. The southern right whale (once abundant off the coasts of South Africa and elsewhere, but now seldom encountered) was taken in great numbers, and

is particularly valuable commercially, as it yields about 140 barrels of oil, or twice the yield of the fin whale.

Before 1904 whaling was almost entirely restricted to the Northern Hemisphere, and the Southern Hemisphere whale populations on the Antarctic feeding-grounds were free from human exploitation. Improved ocean-going catchers, and the growing scarcity of whales in northern

Sperm whale *Archibald Thorburn* 1920

by 1900 it had almost gone. The Pacific grey whale – which, during the course of its migration, was hunted in the breeding lagoons along the coast of California – was also practically exterminated. Following its recent total protection, however, it has increased satisfactorily, and the population is now estimated to exceed 8,000. This species once had an Atlantic population that may have been racially distinct; the last known example was apparently "fished" off New England in the early eighteenth century.

During the heyday of the old-time whaling industry, only the smaller whales, which could be pursued in open boats, were hunted. The speed and size of the large rorquals (the blue, fin, and humpback whales) rendered them safe, but in 1865 their natural immunity was lost through the invention of the harpoon gun and the development of the steam-powered catcher[1] as a vehicle for the new weapon. These inventions gave fresh impetus to a flagging industry, but, at the same time, they sealed the fate of the great rorquals, notably the blue whale, which

waters, encouraged the industry to break new ground, and in 1904 the first ship began whaling from South Georgia in the South Atlantic. The start of deep-sea whaling in the Antarctic was followed by the development of new and increasingly efficient techniques. The factory ship, with a slipway built into the stern, up which whales could be winched for flensing on deck, greatly extended the radius of operations. After that, expeditions could operate freely throughout the oceans of Antarctica, wherever whales were to be found, the covey of catchers in combination with the factory ship making virtually a miniature task force, the whale oil being transferred in bulk to attendant tankers for transportation to the home base.

Postwar refinements include the use of helicopters for spotting whales, sonar devices developed from wartime designs, more efficient harpoons (both explosive and electric-powered),

[1] A modern whaling fleet consists of a factory ship, working in conjunction with a varying number of powered vessels known as catchers, each of which mounts a harpoon gun and is designed for the pursuit and slaughter of whales.

and the modern factory ship, which processes the carcass of a fin whale in half an hour (disposing of a blue whale takes a little longer). Every part of the animal is utilized; the products from the various species include edible oil, sperm oil (which is not edible but has many industrial uses), frozen meat for human and animal consumption, meat meal, bone meal, vitamin-rich liver oil, spermaceti, ambergris, and pharmaceuticals such as hormone extracts.

At first Antarctic whaling was unrestricted, and catches were immense. By the 1930s it was apparent that certain species, especially the blue and the humpback whales, were being over-exploited, and that some form of restriction was necessary if the Antarctic whaling industry was not to go the way of the northern fisheries. Shortly before the Second World War the British, German, and Norwegian governments agreed to the placing of certain limitations on Antarctic whaling, and in 1946 the International Whaling Convention was signed, and the International Whaling Commission was established.

The Commission is empowered to regulate the whale catch, and thus to ensure the effective conservation of the world's whale stocks. To this end, it has introduced regulations specifying the species that may and those that may not be caught, the length of the hunting season (this varies for different species), the areas in which fleets may operate, measures for protecting nursing females and their young, and the size below which mature whales are protected.

Moreover, the Commission sets a limit on the total number of whales that may be taken in any season.[1] The basis on which the annual permissible total is calculated is the "blue whale unit formula": one blue whale unit (1 b.w.u.) = one blue, or two fin, or two and a half humpback, or six sei whales. Up to 1953 this total was fixed at 16,000 b.w.u., but reductions have had to be made in subsequent years, and the limit for the 1963–4 season was 10,000 b.w.u.

Because of the apparent deterioration in the whaling situation, the International Whaling Commission decided in 1960 to appoint a special group to undertake a study "on the condition of the Antarctic whale stocks, on the level of sustainable yield that can be supported by these stocks and on any conservation measures that would increase this sustainable yield".

Following a comprehensive survey, this "Committee of Three Scientists"[2] issued a strongly worded report based on accumulated scientific evidence, and made a number of far-reaching proposals designed to alleviate the critical situation that had by then developed. The report confirmed the "drastic need for action" and left no doubt that "the stocks have been over-exploited and a programme of conservation should be initiated if the industry is to be maintained on a continuing basis".

The study indicated that the blue and the humpback whales "are in serious danger of extermination unless adequate protective measures are taken immediately. Fin whale stocks have been seriously depleted and are far below the levels of maximum sustainable yield". The Committee therefore recommended, among other proposals, that there should be a complete cessation in the catching of blue whales "for a considerable number of years", that the humpback should be fully protected throughout the Southern Hemisphere, and that "the quota of fin whale catches be reduced to 7,000 or less" to allow stocks to recover.

The Committee concluded that the "absolute upper estimate of 1953/54 stock is about 14 to 15 thousand blue whales, and a likely value is about 10 thousand or less", and that the 1961–2 population (apart from pygmy blue whales) was between 930 and 2,790. "By 1963 the stock will be reduced below even the present level, probably to between 650 and 1,950 whales – which is a level at which there must be a distinct risk of complete extinction . . ." In fact it is now probable (1967) that the world stock of the blue whale is no more than 600.

In setting up the Committee of Three Scientists, the International Whaling Commission had made a commitment to bring its regulations into line with the scientific evidence by July 1964. It was therefore confidently expected that the meeting of the International Whaling Commission, held at Sandefjord, Norway, in June

[1] Whaling is permitted for only a limited period each year; the season starts late in one year and finishes early in the next.

[2] The Committee has more recently been expanded to a Committee of Four.

1964, would unhesitatingly accept the scientific advice of a committee that the Commission had itself appointed, and would thus resolve the critical situation that had arisen. Unfortunately these hopes were not fully realized, and the commitment was not honoured.

The Sandefjord meeting agreed that the blue whale and the humpback should be fully protected throughout the Antarctic, but in September 1964 Japan exercised her right to lodge an objection within ninety days, and this decision was therefore smothered almost at birth. It is true that protection is to continue in the North Atlantic (although not in the North Pacific) for a further five-year period,[1] but it is an ironic circumstance that this belated and inadequate protection has been accorded only when both species have been so drastically reduced in numbers that, for all practical purposes, they are already regarded commercially as extinct. Blue and humpback whales are no longer of any commercial importance because both have been exploited to the brink of extermination, and the whaling industry can therefore now afford to tolerate their protection.

D. B. Finn of Canada, who, until early in 1964, was head of the United Nations Food and Agriculture Organization's Fisheries Division, states: "[The blue whale] has all but vanished from the seas because the nations that hunted it were unable to agree on a common and enlightened conservation policy for the world's whale resources. It used to be said that no one owned the oceans beyond the territorial waters. In law this was called *res nullius*. The blue whale was a victim of *res nullius*. The whales were there, nobody owned them, and everyone was free to hunt. True a treaty was drawn up among whaling nations, but it was a bad one for the simple reason that it did not work. In the future, if the sea's natural resources are to be intelligently protected, the *res nullius* concept must be replaced by that of *res communis* – that the oceans belong to all rather than to none".

With the example of the blue whale before it, the industry might surely have recognized the need to prevent a similar catastrophe befalling any other species. One would have thought it very much in the industry's own interests to ensure the continued existence of the fin whale,

which has become the most important commercial species and furnishes the bulk of the Antarctic whale catch. Further depletion of this species would undoubtedly result in the disruption of most of the whaling industry. Therefore the requirements of the industry would presumably best be served by the introduction of a policy designed to conserve the species on a basis of sustained yield.

Although the permissible quota for the 1963–4 season, as set by the Commission, was reduced from the 1962–3 quota by one-third, from 15,000 to 10,000 b.w.u., the actual catch amounted to only 8,413 b.w.u. The three scientific advisers had estimated that to fill the reduced quota would require a kill of 16,000 fin whales together with the anticipated catch of other species, but had concluded that the existing fleets, however hard they tried, would be unable to take more than 14,000 fin whales, a prediction that was borne out when just under 14,000 were taken during the season. The significance of this figure is at once apparent when it is related to previous seasonal catches. Of the 27,176 rorquals taken during the 1955–6 season, 25,289 were fin whales. By 1962–3 the figure had dropped to 18,668. This decline occurred despite a steady seasonal increase both in the number of catchers and in the efficiency and hunting capacity of the whaling fleets.

The decline of the fin whale in recent years is shown by the following statistics for estimated average population size, published by the International Whaling Commission:

1955–6	110,000	1960–1	59,700
1956–7	101,700	1961–2	45,300
1957–8	89,000	1962–3	40,000
1958–9	88,600	1963–4	32,400
1959–60	65,700		

In the light of this situation the Commission's scientific advisers agreed that the 1964–5 season's catch should be limited to 4,000 b.w.u., this figure being progressed to 3,000 b.w.u. in 1965–6 and 2,000 b.w.u. in the 1966–7 season; the figure of 2,000 b.w.u. would have permitted the recovery of the whale stocks to begin, and would

[1] Protection in the North Atlantic was introduced by the International Whaling Commission in 1960 for an initial period of five years. The Sandefjord meeting agreed that this protection should be extended for a further five-year period, starting in 1965.

therefore have been acceptable as a kind of conservation measure. This proposal did not secure the three-fourths majority necessary for its acceptance. The four[1] countries that engage in pelagic whaling in the Antarctic later reached agreement outside the Commission to limit the 1964–5 season's catch to 8,000 b.w.u., which was double the quota accepted by the scientists; a further serious reduction of fin whale stocks therefore became inevitable.

Actual catches for the 1964–5 season fell short of the unofficial target by almost 1,000 b.w.u., substantiating the scientific advisers' prediction not only that whale stocks were so low that a quota at that level "could not be considered either as a restraint or as a conservation measure in any sense", but also that the available whaling fleets could not secure such a catch, even on a short-term basis.

Seven thousand fin whales were taken, the total stock of this species being thereby reduced to an estimated 34,000 or 35,000, which is about one-third of the number estimated to have existed less than ten years ago.

The statistics also show that the whalers concentrated much more effort on catching the sei whale than they had done in any previous season. This shift can be attributed in part to the scarcity of other species, but it is also accounted for by the increasing value of whale meat, meat extract, and other products. The catch of sei whales was four times that of the preceding year, 20,000 being taken from an estimated total population of 55,000.

No species of whale can long withstand this rate of exploitation, and it is clear that, unless a realistic catch limit is introduced and unfailingly enforced, the sei could within a few years be reduced to the same precarious status as the blue whale.

Stringent reduction of the Antarctic whale catch during the next few years would allow stocks to recover and thereby pave the way for a progressive expansion of the industry. At the Sandefjord meeting the proposal for such a reduction was supported by all but four of the fourteen participating countries (the four were Japan, the U.S.S.R., the Netherlands, and Norway), but, since the Commission has no legal powers of enforcement, the minority view

prevailed. A situation had in fact arisen in which nine commissioners, backed by their own governments, failed to obtain the agreement of the Antarctic whaling countries to reduce the quota of catches in accordance with scientific advice and in accordance with the industry's own long-term interests.

The governments whose representatives at Sandefjord voted to give effect to the scientists' recommendations regarded the failure to take effective action as a threat to other international agreements for the conservation and rational use of marine fisheries' resources. These governments indicated that continuing failure to reach agreement through the Commission might compel them to seek a solution through the United Nations, where many more countries not at present engaged in whaling would make evident their opposition to the destruction of a valuable food resource through unrestricted predation by a few.

Mounting dissatisfaction over the failure of the Sandefjord meeting led to the calling of the first Special Meeting ever to be convened by the International Whaling Commission; this was held in London from the 3rd to the 6th May 1965. Its purpose was to reach agreement on an overall maximum quota for the Antarctic pelagic-whaling fleets for the 1965–6 season.

Scientific evidence was presented to show that only if the total catch for 1965–6 were held to less than 2,500 b.w.u. (made up of not more than 4,000 fin and 3,000 sei whales) could it be ensured that stocks of fin and sei would not be further depleted. The basis for discussion was a report by a group of scientists, and submitted by the Food and Agriculture Organization, of analyses of data supplied especially by the Bureau of International Whaling Statistics, the Commission having made no arrangements for appraisal of the recent scientific data. This report, together with the F.A.O.'s consistent refusal to be associated with a policy that could ultimately lead to the destruction of the whale resources, were factors of the greatest importance to the meeting.

[1] At the time of the Sandefjord meeting there were four pelagic-whaling countries, but since then the Netherlands has sold her one remaining fleet to Japan. Thus there are now only three such countries – Japan, the U.S.S.R., and Norway.

There was unanimity among the countries represented at the meeting as to the desirability of reducing catches to within the sustainable yield, and of ultimately reducing them still further, so that whale stocks could increase to the point where maximum sustainable yields could be obtained.

Four separate proposals, submitted respectively by the representatives of the U.S.S.R., Norway, Japan, and the U.S.A., were examined by a special committee whose essential purpose was to obtain the agreement of the three pelagic-whaling countries to any one of the proposals, and preferably to the one giving the highest degree of protection to the whales.

This committee failed to reach agreement, in spite of a last-minute attempt by the U.S.S.R. and the U.S.A., who put forward what were virtually identical amendments proposing the adoption of a quota of 4,000 b.w.u. for the 1965–6 season.

The amendments contained the proviso that each member of the Commission should bind himself to recommend to his own government that it should agree to further reductions in the 1966–7 and 1967–8 quotas – reductions designed to ensure that the 1967–8 quota would be lower than the sustainable yield of both fin and sei stocks at that time.

The Japanese finally offered to accept the proposal of the U.S.S.R. and the U.S.A., provided that the 1965–6 quota was raised to 4,500 b.w.u. The Canadian representative and others attempted to have the clause concerning further reduction in quotas defined more precisely and made more binding, but their efforts were unavailing. The Japanese amendment was put to the vote and carried.

The official press release issued by the International Whaling Commission after the meeting states that "there is thus for the first time a plan for the effective conservation of whales in the Antarctic", but this optimistic assertion appears to be premature, since the agreement is open to the following objections:

1. The 1965–6 quota of 4,500 b.w.u. is almost twice as high as the 2,500 b.w.u. that the scientific advisers regard as the maximum for the 1965–6 season if stocks of fin and sei are not to be still further depleted.[1]

2. The wording of the statement on the reduction of quotas for the two subsequent seasons to within the sustainable yield of existing stocks is very imprecise, and the Japanese delegate was notably evasive in giving his interpretation of it.

3. The intention, implicit in the agreement, is that the reduction should be to the level that would permit basic whale stocks to increase, but this essential requirement is not clearly stated.

4. The quota applies only to pelagic whaling and takes no account of the catch from shore stations. The 500 b.w.u. taken from South Georgia, for example, during the 1964–5 season is a significant amount in relation to the overall pelagic catch.

5. The quota continues to be expressed in blue whale units, a procedure that gives inadequate control over the killing of individual species. Thus, in theory, the entire quota could be taken in either fin or sei, with disastrous results to either of those species.

Therefore, although it is true that the agreement recognizes the need to conserve whale stocks in the Antarctic, this need is unlikely to be met unless further measures are adopted, along the following lines:

1. The proposal to reduce the catch to the level of sustainable yield by 1967–8 should be unequivocally stated as part of a firm policy directive by the Commission; indeed, the quota for that season should be set sufficiently *below* the sustainable yield to allow some significant increase of whale stocks to begin.

2. The system of basing quotas on the blue-whale-unit formula should be abandoned, and quotas for each species should be laid down.

3. Quotas should cover both shore-station and pelagic catches.

4. Both the blue whale and the pygmy blue whale should be specifically accorded absolute protection throughout their entire range. (At the Sandefjord meeting the Commission

---

[1] Just who was right can be gauged from the news that the whalers were able to catch only 4,091 b.w.u. in the 1965–6 season. Most of these were represented by 17,583 sei whales, whose Antarctic stocks were once again reduced by more than a third. The catch of the large fin whales fell from 7,308 to 2,318. In the 1966–7 season 3,511 b.w.u. were taken, represented by four blue, 2,893 fin, and 12,368 sei whales. The 1967 Commission meeting decided to extend the ban on killing blue whales and humpbacks to all oceans, and to reduce the b.w.u. quota from 3,500 in 1966–7 to 3,200 in 1967–8. Though no blue whales are involved, the equivalent of 3,200 "b.w.u." is still too high.

recommended the complete prohibition of the capture of blue whales in the Antarctic, but the pelagic-whaling countries subsequently objected to this decision, so it is now null and void.)

5. Urgent steps should be taken to prevent the whaling fleets that cannot, because of reduced quotas, be employed in the Antarctic from destroying stocks elsewhere, as in the North Pacific.

6. The International Observer Scheme,[1] on which the Commission has already agreed in principle, should be put into practice without further delay.

Unless there is firm agreement along these lines, the prospect will continue to be as disturbing to conservationists as it must presumably be to some sections of the whaling industry. As S. J. Holt of the F.A.O., one of the three scientific advisers, has observed, "cut-throat competition, eventual extermination of species and the death of the Antarctic whaling industry could result unless last-ditch agreement is reached in the Antarctic whaling crisis – stocks are now so small that only the most drastic action can save the whaling industry from complete collapse within a very few years, after which it will be generations before the residual stocks recover to a productive level. Some of them may never recover".

Holt has stated that the maximum sustainable yield of Antarctic whales would be slightly more than 1,500,000 tons a year after the stocks had been allowed to build up; this is perhaps two-thirds of the potential world whale catch. At current prices this would be worth some £70,000,000 each year. It seems almost incomprehensible that a sustainable natural resource of this magnitude should be allowed to become virtually extinguished, and a valuable industry halted, because a minority of its members are motivated by what has been aptly termed a "plunder now, pay later" policy.

Rational use of this resource is perfectly legitimate, but exploitation to the point of non-existence is both inexcusable and short-sighted. Quite apart from ethical considerations, total destruction of whale stocks does not make very good economic sense. Yet not only has international agreement so far failed to prevent irresponsible over-exploitation of this valuable and irreplaceable natural resource, but the whaling industry itself has entirely failed to consider the future and to plan long-term operations in the light of the scientific evidence available. Adoption by the Commission of the recommendations of its own scientific advisers would involve no surrender to sentiment, but would provide a plan both for ensuring the continuance of whale stocks and for securing the whaling industry's own means of existence.

The unrestricted slaughter that resulted in the near-extermination of whales in the Northern Hemisphere during the last century could be in part excused on grounds of ignorance. That excuse is no longer valid, yet an identical result is now likely to be achieved quite deliberately – even at the cost of the industry's self-destruction.

The classification of the whales mentioned is:
Physeteridae, sperm whales
  Sperm whale, *Physeter catodon*
Eschrichtidae, grey whales
  Pacific (race of) grey whale, *Eschrichtius gibbosus glaucus*
Balaenopteridae, rorquals
  Sei whale, *Balaenoptera borealis*
  Fin whale, *Balaenoptera physalus*
  Blue whale, typical race, *Balaenoptera musculus musculus*
  Blue whale, pygmy race, *Balaenoptera musculus brevicauda*
  Humpback whale, *Megaptera novaeangliae*
Balaenidae, right whales
  Greenland right whale, *Balaena mysticetus*
  North Atlantic right whale, *Eubalaena glacialis*
  North Pacific right whale, *Eubalaena sieboldi*
  Southern right whale, *Eubalaena australis*

[1] Under the International Observer Scheme, an officially appointed foreign observer would be attached to each whaling fleet to ensure that all ships engaged in whaling conform to the regulations.

Order CARNIVORA
Family Ursidae: bears

MEXICAN GRIZZLY BEAR
Ursus nelsoni[1]

The most powerful, fearless, and majestic of all the native mammals of Mexico is unquestionably *Ursus nelsoni*, the indigenous grizzly bear. Although somewhat smaller than its northern relatives, it is nevertheless a massive animal weighing up to 670 pounds or more and often attaining a length of over 6 feet, although the size of individuals varies considerably. Adults are distinguished by a huge head, small ears, distinctive shoulder hump, and claws that, unlike those of the American bear, *U. americanus*,[2] are only slightly curved. The general colour consists of varying shades of brown.

The Mexican grizzly appears to have preferred the foothills to the higher parts of the mountains, and was usually found in the belt of scrub oak beneath the pine forest, the explanation being that in such forest its favoured food could not be obtained. The bear is omnivorous, eating nuts, acorns, roots, shrubs, and a wide variety of other vegetation, as well as insects, honey, and occasionally small mammals. Its chosen habitat therefore coincided with the zone most favoured by man for his domestic animals, a situation that resulted in conflict, inevitably to the bear's disadvantage.

Little is known of the breeding biology of the Mexican grizzly, but it is thought that breeding age is not reached until the fourth or fifth year and full growth not until the age of eight or ten. Only rarely do litters consist of more than one or two cubs, and mature females do not normally give birth more often than every second or third year. The young develop even more slowly than those of American "black" bears, and remain under maternal care and control for two complete seasons before they are capable of an independent existence. This low reproductive rate explains the inability of the species to withstand excessive exploitation.

The Mexican grizzly remained undescribed until 1914, but had been known more than a century before, when it existed in northern Lower California and parts of New Mexico and Arizona. It is not certain when it was exterminated in Lower California, but no specimen has been recorded there for several decades. In the northern Sierra Madre grizzlies were abundant in 1855 when the international boundary between the United States and Mexico was being marked. The animal was said to be particularly numerous in the San Luis Mountains and at Los Nogales.

Even as recently as 1892, when the second international Boundary Survey was in process, grizzlies were still plentiful in the San Luis Mountains, and Dr E. A. Mearns, who participated in the survey, considered the presence of

[1] No famous animal (or group of animals) has a more confused classification than the great bear of North Africa (where it is now extinct), Europe, northern Asia, North America, and northern Mexico. Its vernacular names are reasonably stable: in the Old World "brown bear", in western Alaska "big brown bear", in the rest of its New World range "grizzly". Through the years, though, at least 108 specimens have been first named as full species and at least fifty-one specimens first named as subspecies – excluding a large number of fossil forms. Few of these are even valid as races among what is now a very broadly scattered world population, with many relict sub-populations, some of which have become extinct in historical times. The European systematic authorities prefer to regard all as forms of one highly variable species, *Ursus arctos*. The American authorities, such as Hall and Kelson in 1959, prefer to leave the question in suspense. Ellerman and Morrison-Scott, in 1951, from a large number of synonyms, accepted only seven races as valid in the whole Old World, and cite *U. a. crowtheri*, the Atlas brown bear, known to have existed in western North Africa, but certainly extinct for over a century, as a doubtful subspecies. On the other hand, Hall and Kelson list as many as eighty-six other forms as peculiar to the Americas, in an alphabetical order (no fewer than seventy-six of them as full species), though they admit that "it seems almost certain that the majority of these are at most subspecifically distinct" and suggest that some names may even apply just to family groups. By European standards of systematics, these names (and a few others that are certainly synonyms of them, being later names for the same form) may probably belong to only about nine valid races. Supposing we accept the American populations as all of one species, we may arrange them under the name *Ursus arctos* if we want a broad classification, or under the first American name for a grizzly bear if we hold them in a separate species. This is *Ursus horribilis* of the naturalist Ord, published in 1815; and there is little doubt that the form named *Ursus nelsoni* by Clinton Hart Merriam in 1914, the Mexican grizzly, is a valid subspecies of it even if Merriam was perhaps unduly concerned with divisions.   J.F.

[2] This native bear of North America and northern Mexico is quite a different species unknown in the Old World. It shares nearly all the present range of the grizzly and occupies eastern North America (including Newfoundland) besides. It has eighteen races, according to Hall and Kelson, one of which, *U. emmonsi*, the glacier bear of Alaska, is of some concern for the Red Data Book. The commonly used vernacular name of the American bear is "black bear", which is almost as confusing as the scientific names of the grizzly, for the American bear has black, brown, and cinnamon colour phases – and these can be found in the same litter.   J.F.

the grizzly and Billy the Kid and his band of desperados the reasons why this wild region should be avoided by law-abiding folk.

At that time grizzlies had already become scarce along the border of Arizona and Sonora. Merriam's type specimen was collected in 1899 by Dr E. W. Nelson (after whom the species is named) in Chihuahua near the Casas Grandes and Colonia Garcia, but the status of the animal in that region does not appear to have been recorded at the time. The last specimens in this area were killed in 1928 and 1932, and, when Starker Leopold went there in 1937, the animal was no longer to be found. He wrote: "Thus in a period of less than half a century the grizzly bear was reduced from abundance to extinction along the United States border and in the northern Sierra Madre".

The Mexican grizzly has now ceased to exist throughout its range except in a small patch of territory about 50 miles north of the city of Chihuahua, in the Cerro Campana and the adjoining Santa Clara and Nido ranges.

Within this small area of rough country no more than twenty to thirty survive; and the number of both grizzly and black bears, which exist together in this region, continues to decline. The few survivors are constantly menaced by uncontrolled hunting. A further source of danger has arisen more recently from the use of sodium fluoroacetate (the poison 1080) in the area. A female and her two cubs have already been found dead of this poison, and there may well have been other casualties.

It is clear that little time remains to prevent the extermination of the Mexican grizzly. It is so nearly extinct that one can say without fear of contradiction that, unless the Mexican Government gives the species total legal protection without delay and ensures enforcement of the law, this magnificent animal will soon be a creature of the past.

A field survey to determine the exact size and distribution of the population would be an essential first step towards effective proposals for the protection of the surviving remnant. These might well include the establishment of a national park in the Sierra del Nido for the sake of the grizzly and of the other interesting fauna still to be found in that area.

POLAR BEAR
Thalarctos maritimus

The male polar bear averages about 900 pounds, although specimens twice as heavy have been recorded. It stands about 5 feet at the shoulders and is 7 to 8 feet or more long; but some individuals are considerably bigger, and there are grounds for regarding it as the largest carnivorous land mammal, the other claimants to this distinction being the Kodiak and other west Alaskan forms of the big brown (or grizzly) bear. The polar bear's fur is uniformly white tinged with yellow; its neck and head are long, its limbs powerful and feet broad, with soles covered in fur.

The polar bear is found in the Arctic, distributed around the Pole. For much of the year it lives in the pack-ice of the Arctic Ocean, well beyond international territorial boundaries. Individuals have been seen as far north as 88° N.; but such reports are exceptional, and only seldom are they made from the zone of permanent polar ice. This is understandable when it is remembered that the animal, which except in the short summer is almost exclusively carnivorous, preys very largely on several species of seal, and therefore favours areas of open water where seals are abundant, but where pack ice is also present to provide both cover and a raft to facilitate hunting. From autumn through winter to early spring seals constitute by far the most important part of the diet; but during the summer break-up of the ice the bears are compelled to leave the ocean and move to the land, where suitable food is very limited. During this lean period they will eat berries, roots, and various types of vegetation, as well as carrion or almost anything else that happens to come their way, including Eskimos' cached meat supplies.

It can therefore be seen that the distribution of the polar bear is also governed by its need for land during part of each year, particularly when seals are scarce and alternative sources of food must be found, as well as during the denning period. These ecological requirements mean

PLATE 5 (*a*) Atlantic right whale; (*b*) Humpback whale
Archibald Thorburn 1920

Pl. 42

that the actual land area used by the bear is a relatively small portion of the vast Arctic regions.

In Canada mating normally occurs in April, and the bear's gestation period averages approximately eight months. It is thought that delayed implantation may occur, and that the development of the foetus does not begin until late September or early October; but this hypothesis has yet to be proved. Denning may start in October, the young being born about early December. Like those of all members of the bear family, the young are extremely small at birth, but they grow rapidly on the rich milk provided by their mothers. The family leaves its den in March or April, and moves towards the sea to begin hunting for seals. The summer is spent as a family group along the shore, the young remaining with their mothers until the beginning of the following spring, when the females again mate.

Young females, which become sexually mature at about three years of age, often give birth to a single cub; but mature females will usually produce twins, sometimes even triplets, and very rarely quadruplets. An adult female does not normally breed more often than every third year, unless she loses her cubs, a fact indicating that the recovery of a depleted population can take some time. Polar bears are much more at home in the sea than on land. They are exceptionally powerful swimmers, having often been observed many miles from the nearest land, and are known to be capable of swimming long distances under water. At sea, cubs will clamber aboard their mother's back to rest.

With the onset of winter, pregnant females move inland to seek out denning sites, usually remaining fairly close to the coast, but sometimes going many miles from the sea. Each female selects a suitable snow-bank and excavates the den in which she will give birth. During the whole of the denning period she subsists entirely on the thick layers of fat that have accumulated in her body during the previous summer.

Soviet investigations have shown that only pregnant females spend the winter in hibernation. Males and dry females occupy temporary snow shelters during snow storms or bad weather, but move on as soon as the storm abates, in constant search for food. However, in the colder parts of the animals' range, such as for example northern Greenland, males may be forced by the extreme cold to hibernate.

It may seem paradoxical that an animal apparently occupying a vast environment in a remote region that is not physically attractive to man should be in any way endangered. At one time there was no such paradox. The decline of the polar bear dates from the seventeenth century, when the opening up of Arctic waters to shipping led to vigorous hunting. During the next two centuries white bears were heavily hunted in Spitsbergen, Novaya Zemlya, islands in the Bering Sea, Baffin Bay, Hudson Bay, and many other places. The decline of the whaling industry in the latter part of the nineteenth century caused the whalers to transfer their attention to sealing, which in turn led to mounting pressure on the polar bear, notably in the Canadian Eastern Arctic, the Greenland Sea, Franz Josef Land, and Spitsbergen. As the fur trade developed, the exploitation of the bear was further stimulated.

Compared with most other parts of the earth, the region favoured by the polar bear is indeed practically uninhabited by humans, except for a few Eskimos and Indians who live scattered throughout the area. Until a few decades ago the indigenous people lived in harmony with their harsh environment, and their predation on the bear and on the other wild animals with which they shared their habitat had no significant effect on any species. In recent years, however, the tendency for the people to turn from the traditional subsistence economy to a more sophisticated mode of life has included new and more efficient methods of killing, although in Canada hunters are still obliged to confine their work to foot and sledge. Furthermore, the Arctic regions have in recent years been increasingly penetrated by geologists, prospectors, and officials.

For countless years the Arctic seas have provided the polar bear with adequate security; but it is practically defenceless against hunting with

PLATE 6 (a) Polar bear; (b) Spanish lynx *Maurice Wilson* 1965 precision weapons from powered boats (which are growing very popular in some parts of the animal's range) or from aircraft. Hunting from aircraft has recently become a favourite sport in Alaska, where polar bears are fairly common on the ice that lies north of Bering Straits, although they do not den or forage on the Alaskan mainland. This form of hunting has now been banned over the mainland and territorial waters; but there is at present nothing to prevent the technique from being employed in international waters beyond the three-mile limit. That is not to condemn polar-bear hunting, which could make a valuable contribution to the economy of a remote and unproductive region, but to emphasize the need for very careful regulation of hunting based on reliable biological data.

Dr S. M. Uspensky, the Russian authority on the species, believes that in recent decades the range of the polar bear has been gradually reduced, as a result of the onset of milder climatic conditions in the Arctic. Water temperatures have risen around the limits of the Arctic, causing the bears to move to the northern extreme of the region frequented by their principal prey species, *Phoca hispida*, the ringed seal. A contributory factor has been the increase in the numbers of humans and domestic livestock in the Arctic in recent years, which has resulted in a higher incidence of disease, notably from the *Trichinella* parasite, which has inevitably affected the bear.

The largest and most flourishing white bear population is found in the Canadian Arctic, where 6,000 or 7,000 are estimated to exist – possibly more than half the world's total. The east coast and, more particularly, the heavily fiorded north-eastern coast of Greenland are very suitable for the animal, mainly because of the abundance of seals there. Since the 1930s, however, there has been a pronounced decline in the bear population in Greenland as a result of excessive hunting, especially along the western and south-eastern coasts.

A similar numerical reduction has occurred during the same period in the Soviet sector of the bear's range, and this has also been attributed to over-hunting: but, for reasons that have already been given, climatic and environmental change, together with disease, are believed to

have been powerful and possibly dominant factors in the decline in this region.

It is therefore heartening to record that, after the resolution of the 1955 I.U.C.N. General Assembly recommending that the Arctic countries should take measures to protect the polar bear, the Soviet Parliament adopted a special decree in 1956 that imposed a ban on the shooting of polar bears throughout the Soviet Arctic. At the same time the catching of cubs was prohibited except under special licence. As a result of these protective measures, the bear population in the Soviet Union has remained stable since 1960, and may have increased slightly.

A further constructive measure taken by the Russian authorities has been the establishment in 1960 of a reserve on Wrangel Island, one of the most important denning grounds in the Soviet Union. Other good denning areas in the U.S.S.R. include Franz Josef Land, Novaya Zemlya, Severnaya Zemlya, and the New Siberian Islands. Dr Uspensky estimates that about 10 per cent of the pregnant females occurring in the Soviet Arctic use Wrangel Island for denning, a fact that underlines the importance of the reserve to the polar bear. Dr Uspensky is currently engaged in a study of denning ecology in the reserve.

In the Norwegian Arctic, the polar bear is protected on King Karl's Land and in nearby waters, and there are certain restrictions on the capture of cubs. Apart from that, polar bears may be hunted in any part of the country throughout the year, the sole limitation being a bag limit of one bear for each foreign sportsman.

On the north-east coast of Greenland, hunting is prohibited between the 1st June and the 31st October, although there appears to be no restriction on the number taken by residents. As in other parts of the Arctic, changing climatic conditions have altered pack-ice conditions around Greenland, which has greatly influenced the distribution and status of the polar bear.

Protective measures taken by the Canadian Government include the prohibition of bear-hunting for sport in Manitoba, Ontario, Quebec, and the Northwest Territories. The only people permitted to hunt the animal in Canada are Eskimos, Indians, and the very few holders of general hunting licences, who are believed to have taken about 600 bears annually in the 'sixties, though more in 1965–6. In 1961 the Canadian Wildlife Service started a five-year study of the polar bear, reviewing the effectiveness of present protective legislation, and attempting to acquire and collate data that would fill some of the wide gaps in our knowledge of the animal.

Among other things, it is hoped that the study may lead to the development of an effective method of marking polar bears. If an internationally coordinated marking programme could be introduced, there should in time be a better appreciation of the extent to which the management of the polar bear is an international problem. Until such basic information is forthcoming, it is impossible to learn enough about numbers and movements to start really sound management programmes.

Because so much of the life-cycle of the polar bear takes place in the Arctic no-man's-land beyond territorial boundaries, it is clear that international cooperation and agreement are extremely important to guard against the possible extinction of the species.

A notable initial step in this direction was the First International Conference on Polar Bears, held at the University of Alaska, Fairbanks, in September 1965. The conference invited the I.U.C.N. to accept responsibility for collating scientific data in polar bear research for dissemination among the conservation zoologists of the nations directly concerned. Since accepting this commitment, the I.U.C.N. has maintained regular communication with the governments of the five Arctic countries – the U.S.S.R., the U.S.A., Canada, Norway, and Denmark – that together encompass the full range of the species.

The development of a pan-Arctic management plan for the species was obviously of first importance. There was agreement on the desirability of this objective – but understandable reluctance on the part of the governments to enter into any commitment until the answers to various critical scientific questions had been obtained.

The general consensus of opinion was that progressive improvement in the global status and management of the polar bear depended on starting and developing a carefully considered and well-coordinated circumpolar research programme, designed to obtain the fundamental data on which an internationally acceptable management programme could be based.

Until lately, each of the five nations concerned had been conducting its own independent research with little understanding of the requirements of the others or knowledge of what they were doing. It was to achieve more effective and continuing collaboration that the I.U.C.N. invited leading polar bear specialists to participate in a working meeting at its headquarters in January 1968.

The meeting was a valuable and highly successful experiment in international cooperation. There was a wide exchange of scientific data, and agreement was reached on a coordinated research plan. The happy outcome was the formation of a permanent international committee of scientists engaged in polar bear research. This "polar bear group" will function under the auspices of the I.U.C.N.: Dr S. M. Uspensky of the Soviet Union was unanimously elected first Chairman.

This working meeting was important not only in advancing the scientific study of the polar bear, but also in establishing a mechanism for improving scientific study and cooperation internationally. This could have obvious value both in connection with broader questions bearing on the Arctic fauna and environment as a whole, and with ecological situations elsewhere in the world that can be satisfactorily resolved only at the international level.

Family Procyonidae: raccoons and pandas

GIANT PANDA
Ailuropoda melanoleuca

The giant panda was first brought to the attention of the Western world by the noted French naturalist Père David during the second of his three expeditions to China in 1869. Hunters in his employ spent several weeks acquiring two female specimens, one adult and one immature, from which he wrote the original description of the animal.

The first specimen to be shot by a white man was collected by Theodore and Kermit Roosevelt in 1929. Subsequently this specimen, together with a second skin purchased from the local people, was used for the Chicago Natural History Museum's well-known habitat group. The publicity resulting from this fine exhibit started a spate of expeditions in search of the animal, which was further made popular in 1936 when the Chicago Zoological Park obtained the first living specimen ever to be seen outside China, a young male that was named Su-lin. This inspired expeditions to collect living specimens for other zoos.

Superficially the giant panda appears to resemble the bears, and at first it was assigned to the bear family (Ursidae). Anatomically, however, it is more closely related to the raccoons, kinkajous, and their allies, which together form the family Procyonidae. It is a somewhat aberrant member of the family and the only living representative of its genus.

Adults may reach a length of 6 feet excluding the stump of a tail, and weigh more than 300 pounds. The thick, woolly coat is white, the legs, ears, and eye-patches are black, and a black band reaches from the forelegs across the shoulders. Its head is massive, the skull deep and equipped with large ridges, to which are attached the masticatory muscles that complement the powerful teeth required to chew the tough, fibrous material constituting the animal's main diet. Each forepaw has the unusual feature of a small pad, presumably to assist in grasping bamboo. Under the tail are large scent glands, which, it has been conjectured, may be used during the breeding season to enable these normally solitary animals to detect one another in the forest and dense bamboo thickets.

The giant panda spends most of the day feeding on the ground; but local hunters assert that it is capable of climbing trees and does climb them when pursued by the dogs that as a rule are employed locally for hunting. It is thought to use caves and hollow trees for shelter, particularly during the winter, when heavy falls of snow occur in its region, but it does not hibernate like the bears, although it may possibly do so for short periods during exceptionally cold weather.

The range of the giant panda is restricted to the bamboo forests in an isolated mountainous region of western Szechwan in western China, at an altitude ranging from about 5,000 to 10,000 feet. At the higher altitudes, roughly above the 10,000 feet contour, the bamboo gives way to rhododendron, into which the panda probably does not wander. Other rare mammals sharing the same habitat include the golden monkey, *Rhinopithecus roxellanae*, and the takin, *Budorcas taxicolor tibetana*.

With the exception of the specimen obtained by the Roosevelt brothers, which was taken at Yehli on the slopes of the Ta-liang Mountains, all specimens have come from the Chuing-lai Mountains. This gives the animal a very restricted habitat – little more than 175 miles from north to south. Sowerby (1932), however, believed that there was indisputable evidence from native hunters of the animal's existence in south-western Shensi, as far south as the little known mountainous region on the Yunnan border.

A recent unconfirmed report provisionally extends the range a further 300 miles to the north on to the open steppe of the Plateau of Tibet near the upper source of the Yangtze River. Hung-shou Pen, who recorded the sighting in 1943, speculates that the existence of a specimen in the plateau country may indicate an annual summer migration on to the plateau, with a reverse movement during the winter back to the less harsh conditions in the mountains.

The fossil record shows that the animal

Giant panda *Peter Scott* 1967

since his original field notes on the species were published in 1871, extraordinarily little has been added to his observations.

The actual status of the animal is not accurately known, and any attempt at a census would be extremely difficult owing to the nature of the environment. The region in which the giant panda is known to exist is so restricted, however, that it is reasonable to assume that the population is small. It is unquestionably rare: but, at the same time, it would be misleading to assume that it has declined in recent years. There is no evidence to support such a conclusion. The skin is of no commercial value; and there is no reason to suppose that the giant panda has been severely hunted. Moreover, it appears to be without natural enemies, with the possible exception of the leopard and the red wolf. The only occasion on which the species is known to have suffered a setback was in the 1930s, when the sudden demand for zoo and museum specimens made local hunters believe there was a demand for skins, as a result of which some were slaughtered; in other circumstances they would not have been molested.

The giant panda is now strictly protected, and, although no special reserve has been established, the Chinese are justifiably proud of the species. There is therefore every reason to feel optimistic about the animal's future.

Until very recently no giant panda had ever been born in captivity; but in September 1963 the Peking Zoo succeeded in breeding it for the first time. Since then the same zoo has repeated its outstanding achievement, and more recently the Shanghai Zoo has also successfully bred the animal.

There are now more than twenty specimens in captivity, the great majority being in China.

existed over a far wider region within relatively recent geological times. Pleistocene remains have been found in the northern Shan State in Burma, over 500 miles south-west of the limits of the present known range. Pliocene material has also been unearthed on the Yangtze in eastern Szechwan, some 250 miles to the east.

Hardly anything is known about the breeding biology of the giant panda in the wild state, but captive specimens have revealed that the gestation period is approximately 148 days; it is thought that only a single young is born, possibly not more often than every alternate year. It says much for Père David's competence and ability that, during the intervening period

---

Family Mustelidae: weasels, badgers, skunks, otters, etc.

BLACK-FOOTED FERRET
Mustela nigripes

The black-footed ferret could be described as probably the rarest mammal native to the United States. It also has the distinction of being

the sole North American representative of the Old World group of black-bellied weasels.

Adult males are about 1 foot 8 inches long, with a relatively short tail of about 5 inches. This ferret's fur is a pale yellowish-buff; its face, throat, and belly are almost white. Across its eyes is a black mask, and its legs and feet and the tip of its tail are either black or blackish-brown. During the winter its fur is only a little paler than in summer.

The species was once distributed across the North American prairies to the east of the Rocky Mountains, extending from northern Montana and Alberta in the north to central New Mexico. The range still embraces much the same area as formerly, except that the animal almost certainly no longer exists in Texas, Kansas, and Oklahoma, and that in the rest of its range it has ceased to exist in all but a few localities.

The range was in fact almost identical with that of the prairie dogs (*Cynomys*); and it is believed that the welfare and indeed the very existence of the ferret may be intimately connected with these rodents. In the Arkansas valley it was in fact known as the "prairie dog ferret". Not only is the ferret thought to depend on the burrows of prairie dogs for shelter, but it preys very largely on these hosts. The probability is that it also feeds on other small animals; but there is little evidence to substantiate this belief, although Cahalane records one seen carrying a thirteen-lined ground squirrel (*Spermophilus tridecemlineatus*).

Very little appears to be known about the black-footed ferret; and the reasons for its rarity are imperfectly understood. Recent attempts to study the animal for a better understanding of its habits and requirements have been frustrated by the difficulty of locating specimens.

The original description was based on a single damaged skin, and nearly a quarter of a century passed before any further report was received. It seems that the animal was already scarce at the time the West was first being opened up for settlement.

When Walt Disney made the well-known film *Vanishing Prairie*, three specimens of unknown sex were trapped in central South Dakota and starred in the film. Later these animals were released in Wind Cave National Park, and, although they are assumed to be still there, none have since been seen. An attempt by the American Museum of Natural History in 1961 to study the ferret in the park had to be abandoned, as none could be found.

The elimination of the vast herds of bison and

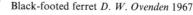

Black-footed ferret *D. W. Ovenden* 1967

other species of large native mammals from the Great Plains during the latter half of the last century resulted at first in an increase of the prairie dog population through the removal of competition for grazing. The rodents were not permitted to enjoy this advantage for long, however; and, as more of the West was won, the settlers looked with increasing disfavour on the prairie dogs, which they regarded with some justification as being in strong competition with their cattle for the grazing.

During the last sixty years or more a vigorous poisoning campaign has been undertaken in an attempt to exterminate the prairie dogs. Various types of poison were used, ranging from strychnine in the early days of the campaign to the much more sophisticated sodium fluoroacetate (1080) after the Second World War. The campaign was successful in achieving its purpose, but one of the side-effects seems to have been that, along with its host species, the black-footed ferret was reduced. The destruction of the original grasslands and the ploughing in of burrows may have been another factor in this reduction.

In 1952 the American Committee for International Wildlife Protection began a survey of the status of the ferret, with the object of ascertaining the facts and deciding what action could best be taken to improve the situation. Allowing for possible duplication of sightings, the survey revealed between fifty and seventy reported from forty-two localities during the period 1946–53, principally in South Dakota,

Montana, Nebraska, and Colorado. Approximately one-third of the animals seen were specimens that had been trapped, shot, or killed by road traffic.

Since 1955 there have been more than fifty-five sightings, six of them road kills. During this period ferrets have been reported from fifteen counties in South Dakota and one county in North Dakota.

In 1954 the United States Fish and Wildlife Service entered into an agreement with the National Park Service by which all black-footed ferrets that could be live-trapped in areas scheduled for rodent-control operations should be released into sanctuaries, such as Wind Cave National Park in South Dakota or Theodore Roosevelt National Memorial Park in western North Dakota, where prairie dog colonies could be permitted to exist undisturbed. At the same time employees of the Fish and Wildlife Service have been instructed to do everything possible to discourage the destruction of the ferret, and to maintain records of any sightings that they may make. It is important that secrecy should be maintained over sightings to avoid the possibility of molestation or disturbance by the public.

GIANT OTTER
Pteronura brasiliensis

The *lobo de rio*, to use its vernacular name, is the largest of the world's otters, averaging between 5 and 6 feet from nose to tip of tail, though specimens of over 7 feet have been recorded. It is placed in a genus of its own, though superficially it looks very like a larger version of the common otter (*Lutra*), except that most specimens have a relatively more extensive cream-coloured chest-patch and the under side of its flattened tail has a shallow "keel" on either side. The fur on its back is a rich chocolate colour, fading to a lighter tone on the under surface. Its head is flat and wide, and its small rounded ears are placed far back. Its feet are well webbed and set on short, stout legs, which are used with great effect in the water, but are almost useless on land, when the animal tends to haul itself along on its belly in much the same ungainly manner as a seal.

The giant otter is found in slow-running streams and rivers in South America, from Venezuela in the north through Brazil to Paraguay, Uruguay, and north-eastern Argentina, and extending along the Peruvian Amazon.

With its wide distribution, covering the greater part of South America, the animal might be expected to be fairly well known. But very little has been recorded of it. No doubt the lack of data is at least partly due to the difficulty of observing the animal, in spite of the fact that it is active by day and normally exists in small groups. At the first sign of danger it submerges rapidly and disappears from sight, although it is less shy in undisturbed areas.

The giant otter's food consists principally of fish, which it usually eats on land. Molluscs and crustaceans are also eaten; and it is said that birds, eggs, and small mammals are included in the diet on occasion.

Hardly anything is known of the animal's breeding habits in the wild state. However, it is believed to be monogamous, with a litter of one to three (normally two) young, which are born, after a gestation period of approximately three months, in dens made in the banks of rivers. It is not known whether breeding takes place more than once in the year.

The status of the giant otter is hard to determine, owing to the lack of sufficiently precise information. In some parts of its huge range the animal is said to be relatively abundant; but such localities are few, and in the greater part of its habitat the animal is believed to be scarce and continuing to decline. In Venezuela, for example, the species is not in imminent danger of extinction, although undoubtedly much decreased in rivers, such as the Apure, that are easily accessible to hunters. Along the Peruvian Amazon, on the other hand, it is questionable whether more than a small number still survives.

The decline has been caused by heavy persecution of the animal for its fine pelt; each one is valued at about U.S. $1,700. An indication of the extent and value of the trade can be gained from the statistics of *lobo de rio* skins exported abroad (mainly to the United States) from Iquitos, in Peru, alone. In the late 1940s the mean was 1,400 (maximum 2,170, 1946); in the 1950s, 1,338 (maximum 2,169, 1955); in the

1960s, a reduced 526 (maximum 1,002, 1960), hinting at a fall in yield due to over-cropping; the crop in 1966 (210) was the lowest on record. Lately the mean export value of Peruvian skins has been about U.S. $36 each. Pelts originating in Venezuela are usually marketed in Colombia, where a better price is obtained.

Apart from the need for measures to be taken to protect the giant otter in the wild, there is a further clear need, in the interests of the survival of the species, for the governments of the countries directly concerned to control the trade in otter pelts; but this could only be effective if all of them cooperated.

SOUTHERN SEA OTTER
Enhydra lutris nereis

The sea otter, the most highly specialized of the whole otter subfamily, has a special genus to itself. Formerly the species occupied a wide coastal sweep of the Pacific Ocean extending from the Kurile Islands, along the coast of the Kamchatka Peninsula, across to the west coast of North America by way of the Commander and Aleutian islands, thence southwards to the coast of Lower California. Within this considerable area the southern race, *E. l. nereis*, at one time occupied the region extending along the Pacific Coast from Washington State to central Lower California. Though hunting once reduced the other, northern, race severely, it has now recovered under protection, and it is the southern form that is in the Red Data Book.

Superficially the northern and southern races are identical, the distinction of subspecies being based entirely upon minor cranial differences. The sea otter weighs up to about 80 pounds and, including its tail, is about 4 feet long. Its fur is glossy and thick, the under-fur being especially dense, and varies in colour from black to dark brown sprinkled with white-tipped hairs, its head, throat, and chest being creamy white. Its ears are practically invisible in the fur. Its forefeet are relatively small, but its hind feet long, broad, webbed, and flipper-like. It is the only carnivore equipped with four incisors in the lower jaw; it also possesses unique cheek-teeth, its molars being specially adapted for crushing the shells of clams, crabs, sea-urchins, mussels, abalones (ormers), and other shellfish that form its diet.

The southern sea otter has rarely been observed more than a mile from shore, preferring shallow waters off a rocky coast. Most of its time is spent in the water; it seldom goes ashore, and then never ventures more than a few yards from the sea.

Individual sea otters remain in one locality, seldom moving far from their favoured beds of kelp, where they spend their time swimming, or floating on their backs. It is in this position that they usually feed, smashing shellfish against stones on their chests – they are among the few animals to make regular and deliberate use of a tool.

The mother also adopts the same position when nursing her young: she swims on her back with the young resting on her chest cradled in her arms. There is no particular breeding season, and the single young (twins are rare) is born at sea on the kelp beds after a gestation period of about eight to nine months. Probably the normal time between births is two years; so the reproductive rate is slow. The pup as a rule is highly developed at birth; its eyes are open, its fur and milk teeth fully formed; and it can swim.

Southern sea otter *D. W. Ovenden* 1967

During the nineteenth century the sea otter existed along the coast of California in great numbers; but the animal was exploited for its valuable fur with such ruthlessness that it was rapidly brought to the point of extinction. By the beginning of the present century it was so rare that pelts were regarded as the most valuable of all furs, fetching as much as U.S. $1,000 each. By 1876 the southern race had been exterminated off the Washington and Oregon coasts, and the last specimen in California was reputedly killed in 1911 south of Fort Ord.

In 1910 the United States Government introduced a law prohibiting its capture within American waters, and simultaneously entered into negotiations with other interested governments for parallel protection elsewhere.

For more than a quarter of a century the southern sea otter was thought to be extinct. Then, in 1938, it was rediscovered off Bixby Creek on the Monterey coast of California. Since then it has gradually increased in numbers, and has extended its range southward to Point Conception and possibly as far as the Channel Islands. There has, however, been only slight expansion northwards. Today the animal can regularly be seen in Carmel Bay and off parts of the coast of the Monterey Peninsula.

Strict enforcement of protective measures by the United States authorities has been responsible for retrieving the southern sea otter from the brink of extinction, and the population is now estimated at about 850 to 900.

Unfortunately there is little prospect of re-establishing the animal in the part of its former range that extends northwards along the Pacific coast of the United States and Canada, unless oil pollution can be greatly reduced or, better, totally eliminated. Unlike most other marine mammals, sea otters do not have a deposit of fat under the skin to protect them against cold: they are wholly dependent on air entrapped in their fur. If the fur becomes polluted by oil, it quickly loses its insulating properties, and the animal may die from cold and exposure.

Family Felidae: cats

SPANISH LYNX
Felis lynx pardina[1]

The study of fossils and animal history tells us that the handsome lynx was distributed in latest Pleistocene (or Ice Age) times all over the forests of the northern world, from Britain and Ireland in the west of Europe to Newfoundland in eastern North America. It was contemporary with New Stone Age man in Britain and Ireland. Its relict type distribution has become accentuated in later historical times, particularly in Europe, where it is now very rare indeed except in some parts of Scandinavia and northern Russia.

The Spanish race of lynx, *F. l. pardina*, at one time ranged over the greater part of the Iberian Peninsula possibly as far north as the Pyrenees. A few may still exist in three parts of the Pyrenees – Gave d'Aspe, Massif de Néouvielle, and the Capcir. There is some doubt, however, whether the Pyrenean population belongs to the Spanish or to the typical race, the European lynx, *F. l. lynx*, which may possibly still survive in the Massif Central of France, but is otherwise found now no nearer than Scandinavia, Poland, and Czechoslovakia.

Widespread deforestation resulted in the elimination of much of the animal's habitat,

added to which it was, like so many of the larger European carnivores, relentlessly persecuted for the damage it inflicted on domestic livestock. The Spanish lynx has now been exterminated in most of its range except certain controlled hunting areas, known as "cotos", in the delta of the Guadalquivir in southern Spain. The total population is unknown, but may possibly amount to several hundred, including an estimated 150 to 200 in the Coto Doñana, which is believed to hold the largest remaining population.

This region is one of only two major areas of unspoiled wetland and wilderness remaining in western Europe, and thus has a significance out of all proportion to its size and extending far

[1] The systematics of this hunting cat's races (of which there are or were at least eight) have clearly not been fully worked out, especially as regards the (apparently) nameless population that still inhabits parts of Greece and perhaps also still neighbouring parts of the Balkans. This population, another in the Transylvanian Alps and Carpathian Mountains of Romania and Russia, the extinct population of Italy and Sicily, the Sardinian race, *Felis lynx sardiniae* (which is almost certainly also extinct), and the Spanish lynx, *F. l. pardina*, are regarded by some authorities as a species separate from the rest, the pardel or pardine lynx, in build more rangy, in coat almost uniformly spotted, with lozenge-shaped dark brown flecks, and with a more rounded black tail-end than the northern forms, whose rounder spots (on adults) are clearly evident upon their legs alone. It is possible that in the western Carpathians the northern and pardine groups may coexist; if so, the pardine lynx should be regarded as a full species, *Felis pardina*. Fossil evidence supports this.

The Spanish population, *Felis lynx pardina*, would carry the name *Felis pardina pardina* if the species status of the pardine lynx be admitted.   J.F.

beyond the borders of Spain. It is therefore heartening to be able to record that in June 1965 approximately half the Coto Doñana (16,000 out of a total of 32,000 acres) was declared a nature reserve. The title deeds were formally handed over to the Spanish Government by representatives of the World Wildlife Fund, which had accepted the challenging task of raising part of the large sum of money required to secure the area, the rest being contributed by the Consejo Superior de Investigaciones Científicas.

It is hoped to purchase about 7,500 acres of the Marismas de Hinojos, adjoining the Coto Doñana to the south-east, to forestall the possibility of development and drainage and link up with a further area of reserve, due to be taken over by the Spanish Government, so as to form a single unit.

The acquisition of these as areas of nature reserve is a notable advance in the preservation of the Spanish lynx. The animal is still included on the list of verminous animals, for which there is no closed season and which could be killed at sight, but this will no longer be applicable within the new reserve.

The problem of devising a wildlife management plan for the reserve has still to be faced, and not the least of the difficulties confronting any attempt to include provision in such a plan for the Spanish lynx is the lack of reliable information on its biology, habits, and requirements. Dr José Valverde, the Director of the Coto Doñana Reserve, proposes to remedy this deficiency by undertaking an ecological study of the animal.

FLORIDA COUGAR
Felis concolor coryi

Variously known as cougar, panther, puma, or mountain lion, the species *Felis concolor* is widely distributed over northern, central, and southern America.

The Florida race, *Felis concolor coryi*, which formerly existed from the lower Mississippi River valley (in Louisiana and Arkansas) eastwards to southern South Carolina and the Florida peninsula, differs from the eastern puma by being smaller and more brightly coloured and by having smaller feet. It is a large, unspotted cat, up to 7 feet long, and pale brown with dull whitish under parts.

All fifteen (or so) races of the cougar have diminished greatly during the last seventy-five years, but none has declined more drastically than *coryi*, one of two races currently listed in

Florida cougars, *D. W. Ovenden* 1966

the Survival Service Commission's Red Data Book. In the latter part of the nineteenth century the animal was still fairly abundant in those parts of its range that had not then been taken over for settlement. The expansion of settlement inevitably brought the cougar into increasing conflict with man, and from the beginning of the century the decline accelerated rapidly.

Unfortunately for the "tiger", as *F. c. coryi* was locally known in parts of Florida, it could not resist the temptation to make an easy living from the settlers' domestic animals, and in those parts of the country where horses were plentiful the carnivore developed a particular taste for colt flesh. Indeed, one of the races whose range includes Wyoming, Colorado, and parts of Utah has been named *F. c. hippolestes*, "horse-killer". Stock losses caused the wrath of the stockmen to be vented on the entire species: the animal was outlawed and was slaughtered at every opportunity and by any means. In Florida hunting was usually undertaken with dogs. When flushed, the cougar generally runs only a short distance and then takes refuge in a tree. The pack keeps the animal at bay, allowing the hunters to shoot what is literally a sitting target.

Ruthless pursuit of the slaughter policy, coupled with a general decline in the deer population, which constitutes the panther's principal food, quickly achieved its purpose, and within a relatively few years the cougar had been exterminated everywhere east of the Mississippi River except for a remnant that held out in what is now the Everglades National Park. In this wild region, parts of which are very difficult of access, the subspecies has taken its final stand.

At one time the Florida cougar was thought to be extinct, but the firm protection accorded by the national park authorities has enabled it to increase gradually, and, although the size of the population is not known with certainty, numbers have been estimated at about 100. Recent sightings have indicated that the animal may now be slowly spreading into parts of the park where it has not been known for many years, such as the neighbourhood of Bear Lake and the Ten-Mile Corner area. This improved situation is believed to be partly due to the increase in the deer population since the Everglades acquired the status of a national park.

The eastern cougar, *F. c. couguar*, also deserves a mention. Formerly ranging from the eastern United States in the deep south to provincial Canada west to the edge of the Plains and Alberta, this race has been extinct in the United States since the end of the last century. It was almost eliminated in Canada as well, but, although still rare, it is now believed to be gradually increasing its range. This improvement is due to pulpwood operations that incidentally create range conditions ideal for grouse and deer and therefore beneficial to the cougar.

ASIATIC LION
Panthera leo persica

In size and general appearance there is little to choose between the lions of Asia and Africa.[1] The Asiatic lion is said to have a scantier mane than the African, as well as a thicker coat, a longer tail tassel, a more pronounced belly fringe, and a more prominent tuft of hair on its elbows. However, some workers do not think that these characteristics warrant full systematic differentiation between the two, particularly as there is wide individual variation among African lions in general colouration, length of mane, and

---

[1] Fossil evidence shows us that the lion enjoyed a vast distribution in Pleistocene or Ice Age times, extending west into England and Wales, east through Holland, France, Germany, Switzerland, Austria, Czechoslovakia, and Russia into at least the western parts of Siberia, south through virtually the whole of Africa, and south-east to Asia Minor, Arabia, and the Indian sub-continent as far as Ceylon. Its Palearctic, or European-Siberian, population of the fossil deposits has been named *Panthera leo spelaea*, the cave lion: it is known in Britain from early Pleistocene times, of 500,000 years ago or more, from the Cromer Forest Bed of Norfolk, and persisted in Wales, and in England as far north as Yorkshire, until about 50,000 years ago (perhaps less) during the rise of native Old Stone Age hunters. In south Germany there were still lions in the time of the Magdalenian Stone Age culture of about 30,000 years ago. Lions, which some believe to have been of the cave race (though there are no contemporary bones to prove it) were still in Greece in 480 B.C., when they attacked Xerxes' baggage train during his march through Macedonia. By the time of Aristotle, who wrote his *History of Animals* about 150 years later, the lion was already rare in southern Europe. In the last decades of the first century A.D., Dio Chrysostom, the Greek sophist, wrote that lions were extinct in Europe: "There are no longer any more; but formerly they dwelt in the district of Macedonia and in other places".

If we exclude the cave lion, and the lion of classical European times (whatever race it was), we find a typical relict distribution for the great cat in historical times (except in parts of Africa), with eleven races, of which two, the typical race, *P. l. leo*, or Barbary lion of Africa north of the Sahara, and the Cape lion, *P. l. melanochaitus*, of southernmost Africa, have become extinct in the present century, and a third, the Asiatic lion, *P. l. persica*, is in grave danger of extinction and is the main subject of this essay.   J.F.

all the other alleged points of difference between the two races. Only if additional Asiatic specimens can justifiably be collected, for comparison with the large quantity of African material that already exists in museum collections, will a final classification be possible. Even if the Asiatic lion is only of a borderline race by modern systematic standards, its population is nevertheless quite discrete, and the problems of its survival seem to be of as much concern to all as if it was a full species.

The gradual expansion of Arabian and Asian human population inevitably brought the lion into conflict with man's interests, principally through predation on domestic livestock, but also, though to a much lesser degree, as a potential threat to human life. This process occurred throughout the whole area occupied by the carnivore; and pressure on it was intensified as the efficiency of weapons improved.

Until relatively recent times the lion was distributed widely throughout much of Asia Minor, Arabia, Persia, and India. In Israel, where it was common in Biblical times, it was exterminated in the thirteenth century, when the last specimen was hunted at Lejun, near Megiddo. In some of the more remote parts of Arabia outside the desert areas, however, it survived into the present century.

In the early part of the nineteenth century lions were still fairly plentiful in many parts of Iraq, but by the beginning of the present century they had been exterminated throughout most of the region. The last two specimens to be taken alive in that country were captured on the Khabur River in Upper Iraq and were seen shortly before 1914 in the possession of the Turkish Governor of Mosul. Even as recently as 1866 the animal was not considered rare in the vegetation along the Turkish sector of the upper Euphrates, but after the First World War it had ceased to exist along the Tigris and Euphrates.

Between the two world wars it was assumed that the lion was extinct everywhere in Persia. It is true that from time to time reports of its existence continued to be received from tribesmen. These statements were regarded as of doubtful validity, however, mainly because the vernacular word *nim'r*, or some variation of it, is used indiscriminately to refer to lion, tiger, leopard, cheetah, and various other members of the cat family.

However, in 1941 R. N. Champion-Jones saw a lion on the banks of the Kharki River in wild and mountainous country about 40 miles north of Dizful, in south-western Persia. A further report was received from the same area (possibly of the same animal) in the following year.

This region and the nearby Bakhtiar Mountains are ideal lion country, being extremely wild and sparsely populated, and very difficult of access. Since reports of the killing of cattle by lions still persist it has for some years appeared very probable that the carnivore still survives in this little-known part of the country.

In Pakistan, where it was once common along the Indus and all its tributaries, the lion is now believed to be extinct. The last recorded specimen was killed in 1842. There does not appear to be any firm evidence of its having ever existed in Afghanistan within later historical times, although occasional unconfirmed reports from there mention it in the recent past.

The range in India included parts of the Punjab, Bengal, Baroda, and the Kathiawar Peninsula. The last specimen surviving in the Indian subcontinent outside Kathiawar was killed in 1884, since when the species has been restricted to the neighbourhood of the Gir Forest, in the south-western part of the Kathiawar Peninsula. Here a small remnant – possibly no more than 100 – was protected by the Nawab of Junagardh, in whose state the greater part of the Gir Forest is situated. In 1900 the lion was officially declared a protected animal, with the Nawab still retaining the right to allow important guests to shoot a limited number of specimens each year.

This protection permitted the lion to increase. A census undertaken in 1936 revealed a population of 289 lions; numbers remained more or less constant for some years, and they were probably close to the maximum the area can accommodate. The estimate for 1968 was about 162. A lion's breeding potential is high, and the total would undoubtedly increase if it were not that numbers are killed each year, mainly by poisoning.

The Gir Forest covers an area of approximately 309,000 acres, having shrunk from over

768,000 acres in the 1880s, and it is the only large forested area remaining in the seasonally arid thorn-scrub desert country that constitutes the greater part of the Kathiawar Peninsula.

About half the area consists of open teak forest, from which the commercially valuable timber has long been extracted, leaving only the secondary growth and scrub timber, most of which has been spoiled by indiscriminate hacking of branches and browsing by domestic animals.

The rest of the area surrounding the stands of teak consists of thorn scrub, and ranges from dense acacia thickets to practically bare earth, interspersed with patches of cultivation. The only real source of cover during the dry season, for wildlife inhabiting the area, is the narrow evergreen strip of vegetation along the banks of the rivers and streams that rise in the area.

During the wet season when the lower-lying parts of the forest tend to be temporarily inundated, many of the great cats move out of the forest, no doubt following the herds of domestic animals that are moved to the flush of new grass beyond the forest boundaries. At this season lions are frequently reported several miles away from their usual haunts.

There is little competition for water, which is apparently readily available throughout the greater part of the year, but there may well be competition for seclusion. The shortage of suitable cover during the critical dry season is very probably a limiting factor for the lions, and Talbot suggests that manipulation of natural cover in the forest might be a possible means of managing the lion population.

The fundamental problem affecting the Gir Forest and all the wild fauna it contains is the large increase in the human population and their livestock that has taken place during the past century. More than 7,000 human inhabitants and approximately 57,000 domestic animals make use of the forest. Most of the livestock consists of water buffalo; each consumes double the quantity of fodder needed by a zebu cow. The rest is made up of cattle, together with work oxen and a few herds of camels and goats.

The number of domestic animals in the reserve is at least double the optimum. This situation has naturally resulted in extreme over-grazing, which has led to the elimination of undergrowth and seedling trees, so that there is no possibility of natural regeneration. Those parts of the forest that have died or been cut out are invaded by thorn scrub; eventually overgrazing eliminates even that, all vegetation gives up the unequal struggle, and the land reverts to desert. The spread of the nearby Gir Thar Desert, which is calculated to be advancing at the rate of $\frac{1}{2}$ mile a year, cannot be attributed to climatic change or any other "act of God", but simply to continuing degradation of the land through gross over-stocking.

All types of wildlife inhabiting the region are naturally affected by this abuse of the land. Over-grazing deprives wildlife of food and cover, particularly during the critical dry season, and concentrations of domestic animals inevitably breed internal parasites and spread disease.

The situation has resulted in the elimination or heavy reduction of several species of wild ungulates that constitute the lion's normal prey. As a result, the lions have little alternative but to resort to taking domestic animals; and it is said that they kill between ten and twenty a day, mainly water buffalo. The owners of the herds do not slaughter any of their own stock, and they apparently seem content to accept these losses as part of the price they must pay for the privilege of grazing the government-owned forest land. Certainly the lions are performing a useful function in helping in a small way to reduce excessive numbers of domestic livestock, but one could scarcely expect the herders to share this point of view. Talbot concludes that, even if numbers of human beings and domestic animals do not rise above their present level, land degradation will continue unabated and the Gir Forest will be unable to survive much longer than another twenty years.

Enough has been said to show that the future of the lion in India is intimately linked with the Gir Forest, and that the outlook for the forest does not give much cause for optimism. Over-stocking is the basic cause of the problem; and the answer lies in a drastic reduction of the numbers of domestic animals inhabiting the area, not merely for the sake of the wild fauna, but also in the long-term interests of the people themselves – for of what use will the forest be to them when the desert takes over? In July 1966 the surviving 500 square miles of the forest were set aside as the Gir Wild Life Sanctuary, with a superintendent in charge.

The difficulties of making an effective management programme in Gir are formidable. The problem is partly religious, because the Hindu religion forbids the slaughter of bovines, thereby making it almost impossible to arrange a system of culling. Moreover, the herds of domestic animals represent wealth, as well as providing milk and draft animals: the herd owners are therefore unlikely to agree to any voluntary reduction. Politics also plays a part, since grazing control and land use are local political issues.

Another possibility involves the capture of surplus Gir lions and their reintroduction into other sanctuaries. A useful start has already been made in this direction with the translocation of three lions into Chandraprabha Sanctuary in Uttar Pradesh in 1957. This nucleus has since increased very satisfactorily.

An ecological study of the Gir Forest is desirable, and a recommendation that one should be undertaken was approved by both the I.U.C.N. and the Indian Board for Wild Life in 1956. Such a study is now being carried out, in the course of three years, by two Ph.D. students, P. Joslin and K. Hodd, under scholarships from the Royal Society and a grant from the World Wildlife Fund.

TIGER

Panthera tigris

In historical times the tiger's range,[1] like that of the lion, has become steadily reduced, and of the seven currently accepted races all but one, the Bengal tiger, are in the Survival Service Commission's Red Data Book. For the sake of completeness, all are discussed here.

Chinese tiger, *P. t. amoyensis*

This race has a wide distribution in China ranging from about the 38th to the 40th parallel southwards throughout the greater part of eastern, central, and southern China, and extending along the larger river valleys to the moun-

tainous regions in the western part of the country. Tigers are known by tradition and from classical Chinese literature to have existed in the past as far west as Szechwan and Kansu, but no recent records appear to have been made in this area, and the boundary between the Chinese and Bengal races has never been satisfactorily determined, although the latter has recently been reported in the extreme south of Yunnan.

Tiger bones are greatly prized by the Chinese as a medicine that, in powder form, is reputed to give vigour, strength, and courage.

The tiger is now extremely scarce in China, and, although the Chinese have done much to protect many of the rare species in their country, the tiger has been excepted because it lives in relatively populous regions and is considered a menace to human life.

Bengal tiger, *P. t. tigris*

The nominate race has up to now been the only one of the seven races of tiger to avoid inclusion in the Red Data Book. Recent information, however, indicates that its status is deteriorating, so that its name too will before long have to be added.

Sumatran tiger, *P. t. sumatrae*

Until the Second World War, the Sumatran tiger was not regarded as endangered, even though it was known to have declined during the previous few decades. After that the animal's numbers are believed to have been seriously reduced by hunting and trapping. Although hardly any precise information appears to be available on its current status, the tiger is said to exist chiefly in the northern parts of Sumatra as well as in the mountainous regions of the south-west.

It is smaller than the Bengal race, and a live adult male specimen stood only 2 feet 5 inches at the shoulder. It is also more fully striped, the white being less conspicuous than in the typical race.

---

[1] The tiger may have originated in highland Asia, for a fossil skull of late Pliocene age from Szechwan in China has been referred to the present species. Despite rumours of bones from the Sudan in Africa (which may have been confused with those of the lion), no wild tiger has ever been found outside Asia. In the Pleistocene (Ice Age) past, like the lion, the other of our greatest living cats, the tiger came to enjoy a wide distribution, extending to Japan, as fossil evidence shows. But by historical times it was already split into separate populations.   J.F.

Caspian tiger, *P. t. virgata*

A medium-sized or rather small dark-coloured tiger, the Caspian race ranged until relatively recently over an extensive region, stretching from Transcaucasia and northern Iran to northern Afghanistan, thence to the Aral Sea and Lake Balkhash in Kazakhstan. At one time it was distributed even more widely, reaching as far north as the Irtish basin and the Altai. Material collected (probably near Bagrash Kul) in Chinese Turkestan may also belong to this race.

Tigers are now very rare in Turkmenia. The latest authentic report comes from the Talysh Mountains, in Lenkoran District, not far from the shores of the Caspian Sea, in extreme south-eastern Azerbaidzhan, close to the Iranian border, where tigers were sighted at the end of 1964. Another was caught in January 1954 in Gozli-dere Canyon in the western portion of Kopet Dagh in the Karakal District of Ashkabad Region, the mountain range on the Soviet–Iranian border in southern Turkmenia. There are spasmodic post-war reports of tigers in the Amu Dar'ya basin, where the last specimen was captured in 1947, although others were rumoured to exist there until 1951. Since then nothing has been heard of the animal in this region despite the year-round presence of a great many muskrat hunters, who would certainly have reported the presence of any large carnivore. The widespread propagation of the muskrat and its intensive use have, of course, greatly modified the prevailing natural conditions in the Amu Dar'ya delta, and have reduced the tiger's chances of survival.

Along the Syr Dar'ya the last tiger was killed in 1933, although others were occasionally reported until 1948. On the Ili River, which flows into the southern part of Lake Balkhash, the last one was killed in 1935, but they were still seen there until 1948. From the River Vakhsh, in Tadjikistan, the most recent report was received in 1953. However, almost without exception, these reports refer to tigers that have crossed into the U.S.S.R. either from Iran or from Afghanistan, and apparently there is no longer a resident population of Caspian tigers anywhere in the Soviet sector of the animal's range.

About fifteen or twenty tigers are thought to exist in Iran along the Caspian littoral – in the vicinity of Mazanderan, Gilan, and Gorgan, but not in the western portions of this region. Others exist in northern Afghanistan, but the animal's distribution in that country is not known, beyond the fact that it is probably restricted to the northern part; no numerical estimate has ever been made there. Some authors consider that Afghanistan harbours the largest surviving population of the Caspian race. This belief may be correct, but there is no firm evidence to support it.

The decline of the tiger in Turkmenia was brought about partly by excessive hunting, and partly as a result of clearing the dense *tugai* vegetation when the country was given over to extensive cotton growing. In Kazakhstan the tiger inhabited dense reed thickets in the river valleys. The burning of these thickets was an important factor in driving the animal from the region.

It is not entirely clear why the tiger has declined in northern Iran. The skins are highly prized, and hunting, both legal and illegal, has helped to reduce the population, but irrational destruction of the magnificent original Caspian forest, together with a decline in the tiger's prey species (the wild boar excepted) have probably been the principal causes of decline. In recent years an important contributory factor is believed to have arisen from the control of the centuries-old incidence of malaria along the Caspian coast. This has led to a more healthy and active human population, so that the number of hunters has increased and pressure on the few surviving tigers, as well as on their principal prey species, has also sharply increased.

The killing of tigers is now strictly prohibited in the U.S.S.R., and if specimens were to become established in one or more of the Soviet reserves the future of the race would be less bleak. Unfortunately, the tiger's wandering propensities render this difficult.

The tiger is also nominally protected in Iran, but law enforcement is not always effective, and there is little doubt that illegal hunting continues. It is hoped that the establishment of the well-protected 260,000-acre wildlife sanctuary about 60 miles east of Gumbat-i-Kabus, in north-eastern Iran, will help the animal, but it is not known how many tigers inhabit the reserve.

Siberian or Amur tiger, *P. t. altaica*

Largest of all tigers, the nomadic long-haired Siberian tiger can be over 13 feet long and weigh up to nearly 600 pounds. Formerly its northern population ranged rather widely in Siberia from Lake Baikal north to the upper reaches of the Lena River and through Transbaikalia to the valleys of the Amur and Ussuri river systems; whence south through eastern Mongolia, Chihli, and Manchuria to Korea and the Hwang-ho. It is now stable, probably, in no more than one mountain system in Korea, the remotest parts of Manchuria, and some protected areas of the far eastern U.S.S.R. In Russia its present headquarters is in the river systems of the Sikhote Alin Mountains east of the Ussuri River, particularly the reed thickets of the rivers Iman, Bikin, Bira, and Anyur, where the large Sudzukhe (250,000 acres) and Sikhote Alin (320,000 acres) reserves have been established and may be further extended. The Russian population (over 100) is protected by law; each year a few young are captured under controlled conditions for zoos (which have quite often bred this race); and measures have been taken to foster wild boar populations to divert the animals from stock-predation. Nevertheless a decline has been marked since 1962, and in the winter of 1964 only two sets of pug marks of wandering tigers were found in the larger reserve.

The Chinese-Korean population is reduced in Korea to the highlands of Mount Baekdu and neighbouring Machonryung and Rangrim ranges only, where there are believed to be between forty and fifty individuals. No tiger has been captured in South Korea since 1900. In Manchuria a population, believed to be of the same approximate size, survives only in the Changpai Mountains and the Lesser Hsingan Mountains in the provinces of Kirin and Heilungkiang, where up to ten a year were taken for zoos in the early 1960s. Much hunting for the pharmaceutical trade may be a primary cause of the decrease of this population, which is now protected in Korea.

Javan tiger, *P. t. sondaica*

Numerous a century ago, this race may now survive in only five places, including the Udjong Kulon Reserve (where the last population

estimated was nine) and the Betiri Reserve in South Djember, East Java (five). Though shooting permits have been required in Java since 1940, uncontrolled hunting has brought this tiger and the Javan rhinoceros to the most parlous state of all the great mammals of Indonesia. This race has been bred in zoos.

Bali tiger, *P. t. balica*

Some authorities have suggested that the tiger was originally introduced to Bali from Java by human agency. Whether this was so or not, the Bali tiger has racial characteristics that distinguish it fully from the present Javan population. Formerly fairly common in the western half of the island, the tigers of Bali are now exceptionally rare if not extinct. The results of any recent first-hand observation are not available; but reports hint that there may still be a few in the two national parks in the extreme western part of the island. In this area, parks notwithstanding, hunters from Java still pursue them.

BARBARY LEOPARD
Panthera pardus panthera

Panthera pardus panthera is a large leopard, variable in both pattern and colour, and not differing to any great extent from neighbouring races.[1] Its range includes Morocco, Algeria, and Tunisia, and within this region it was at one time relatively abundant. Twenty years ago, for example, it was found in the Rif and in the Upper Atlas in the hinterland of Marrakech, but no longer exists there. Today it can be found in Morocco only in the Central Atlas and in montane forests in the Oulmès region.

[1] In Pleistocene times the leopard, *Panthera pardus*, the greatest climbing cat of the Old World, seems to have occupied much the same vast area as the lion and tiger combined; it is found as a fossil in Europe west to England. Since the Ice Ages it has become restricted to Africa, the Caucasus, Arabia, the Asian mainland, Ceylon, Sumatra, and Java. Its populations, some of which have become more isolated and reduced in historical times, have been grouped in about thirty living races. Of these the Barbary leopard is indeed a relict form, separated, as it now is, by hundreds of miles from any other; and it well merits an entry in the Red Data Book.   J.F.

PLATE 7 (*a*) Asiatic lion; (*b*) Chinese tiger *Barry Driscoll* 1966

(a)

(b)

There is little reliable information on its current distribution in Algeria, and the only place in that country where its survival is confirmed appears to be the Akfadou National Park: even there it is diminishing in numbers.

Its existence in Tunisia is uncertain, but there is a reasonable prospect that it still survives in the forests between Bizerta and Tabarka, as well as in the almost impenetrable thickets of the mountains at Tamerza, even though no confirmation of this assumption could be obtained by questioning the local people.

Numbers are difficult to assess, but it is considered unlikely that more than 100 are still living in the forests of Morocco: there must be even fewer in the remainder of the animal's range.

The reasons for the decline of the Barbary leopard are to a greater or lesser extent applicable also to the reduction of the species in most other parts of Africa. The widespread elimination of the carnivore's natural prey species, usually as a direct or indirect result of human activity, has left the leopard little alternative but to prey on the increasing herds of domestic livestock that have largely replaced the native ungulates formerly existing throughout the region. Herdsmen and shepherds avenge themselves for stock losses by waging ceaseless war on the leopard.

Losses from this cause would probably not in themselves prove disastrous if that were all the leopard had to contend with, but during the recent past a more impelling factor has come to dominate the situation. Leopard skin is regarded not only as a sportsman's trophy *par excellence*, but since the Second World War the value of pelts has increased so much that illegal hunting has become an irresistible temptation to people whose income does not usually exceed a few pounds a year. But it should not be imagined that illegal hunting is the monopoly of the poor and needy. On the contrary, the damage is often caused by those in high places who appear able either to disregard or to circumvent the law that, in theory, accords the leopard total protection.

Barbary leopard *Barry Driscoll* 1967

One can therefore hardly avoid concluding that, under present conditions, it is only a matter of time before the Barbary leopard becomes extinct, and that only a revolution in local attitudes towards wildlife resources could perhaps still prevent the situation at the eleventh hour.

Order PINNIPEDIA
Family Odobenidae: walrus

ATLANTIC WALRUS
Odobenus rosmarus rosmarus

The family Odobenidae consists of a single living genus and species, subdivided into an Atlantic and a Pacific race. The two forms differ only

slightly. The Pacific race, *O. r. divergens*, though carefully watched, is not now in the Red Data Book; but *O. r. rosmarus*, the Atlantic walrus, is.

The walrus is a large animal, the males being 10 to 12 feet long (even larger individuals have been recorded) and weighing up to 3,000 pounds. The cows are smaller, but even they may weigh a ton.

The walrus's brownish-grey hide is heavily wrinkled and almost devoid of hairs. Its skin is

PLATE 8 (*a*) Przewalski's horse; (*b*) Persian wild ass
Maurice Wilson 1965

very thick; under it is a layer of blubber several inches deep. Two conspicuous facial features are its prominent, bristly moustache and its tusks, up to 2 feet long, which are thought to be used for prizing molluscs from the sea-bed. These tusks also help the animal to lever itself on to the ice, and serve for defence. The walrus's cheek teeth are specially adapted for crushing molluscs, although there is no evidence that crushed shells are swallowed, and the suggestion has been made that shellfish may be sucked from their shells.

The walrus's fore flippers are about a quarter the length of its body, each having five digits and a roughened, warty under surface that assists traction over ice. Its eyes are small and pig-like, and it has no external tail. The animal is capable of making a trumpeting sound rather like that of an elephant.

Walruses normally live in mixed herds of 100 or more, and are found on islands, rocky shores, coastal waters, and ice-floes. In Hudson Bay births are believed to occur on the pack-ice from April to June. Normally a single calf is born each alternate year after a gestation period of about ten to eleven months. The young are nursed for a long period, possibly as much as two years, before they are able to obtain their own food.

The distribution of the walrus is governed by the extent of sea-ice and the availability of the molluscs that form its principal diet. It occurs in the Kara Sea, Novaya Zemlya, Franz Josef Land, Barents Sea, the Greenland Sea north of Scoresby Sound, Baffin Bay, Ellesmere Island, Foxe Basin, Hudson Strait, and Hudson Bay (as far south as the Belcher Islands). According to Ognev, the dividing line between the Atlantic and Pacific races runs north from the Lena River Delta through the Nordenskiöld Sea.

Walruses also inhabit the Laptev Sea, and are apparently resident there throughout the winter. Chapsky (1936) has conjectured that the Laptev herd, which is small and has never been large enough to exploit, may be of a race intermediate between the Atlantic and the Pacific forms.

At one time the range of the Atlantic walrus was much more extensive, reaching along the entire Labrador coast as far south as Massachusetts; its most southerly breeding outpost was once Sable Island off Nova Scotia. The animal was also once common around islands off the north of Finland, but by the early part of the seventeenth century had been exterminated on that coast as well as on Bear Island. Although abundant around Spitsbergen, Franz Josef Land, and Novaya Zemlya, it has rarely been recorded from Iceland. There is, however, an early record from the English Channel, and a few wanderers have reached Shetland in the present century.

Commercial exploitation for hides, tusks, and oil began in the sixteenth and early seventeenth centuries and resulted in extermination of the

Atlantic walruses *D. W. Ovenden* 1967

walrus on some coasts. More recently, the introduction of modern firearms and power-boats has led to an increased rate of kill by Eskimos. A further factor has been the increase in the number of Eskimo-owned dogs (each of which requires considerable quantities of winter meat) as a result of the change from a hunting to a fur-trapping economy.

The walrus plays an extremely important role in the Eskimo economy, and almost every part of the animal is used, for food, shelter, or other purposes. In addition to hunting, Eskimos also catch walruses on baited lines. Inefficient and wasteful methods of hunting have endangered the existence of the walrus in some localities.

By an act of 1931, the taking of walrus in the Canadian Arctic was restricted to Eskimos and certain white residents, and the export of unworked ivory and skins was prohibited. In 1949 the act was amended by the introduction of more explicit regulations designed to prevent excessive exploitation. The purpose appears to have been accomplished in most areas—although poor hunting techniques in some may have tended to offset the advantages achieved elsewhere. The species is protected under Norwegian and Dutch law; in the U.S.S.R. the killing of walruses, except by the Eskimo and Chukchi people, has been prohibited since 1956.

There is no doubt that, until the introduction of the protective legislation mentioned in the previous paragraph, the walrus was over-exploited. The present situation is hard to determine, but Loughrey, who has made a valuable study of the position in the Canadian sector of the animal's range, believes that three discrete populations may exist between north-western Greenland and southern Hudson Bay, one of which appears to be over-used and the other two more or less stable. The average annual kill in the eastern Arctic-Atlantic is estimated at about 2,666, of which 90 per cent are taken by Eskimos. The annual increment has been estimated at 12 to 20 per cent, which suggests that a minimum population of 23,000 is required to sustain the present rate of kill. The herds in the Barents, Kara, and White seas, which at one time were large, are now reported to have been reduced almost to the point of extinction, and the total population of the race, estimated in 1966 as about 25,000, cannot withstand the present rate of cropping.

More precise information is needed on distribution, potential rate of increase, population movements, and range-carrying capacity, as a basis for planning the management of this economically important species.

Family Phocidae: seals

RIBBON SEAL
Histriophoca fasciata

The single species of seal in the genus *Histriophoca*[1] gets its name from the prominent yellowish bands that stand out distinctly from the rest of its chocolate-coloured body. The bands are much fainter on females and young, which also differ by being of a paler colour. The only other banded pinniped is the harp seal, *Phoca groenlandica*, which is doubtless the ribbon seal's closest living relative, and Atlantic counterpart.

Ribbon seal *D. W. Ovenden* 1966

The ribbon seal has a wide distribution extending in Asia from Hokkaido, Sakhalin, the Sea of Okhotsk, and the Kurile Islands northwards to the Bering and Chukchi Seas as well as to the eastern part of the East Siberian Sea. In North America the animal is found from Point Barrow south to Bristol Bay. Occasional specimens have been recorded as far as the tip of the Alaska peninsula and the Pribilof Islands.

Nowhere within this large region is the ribbon seal abundant. The total population has been variously estimated at from 5,000 to 20,000, the largest numbers being on the southern edge of the pack-ice during winter and spring. It has been conjectured that during summer and autumn the animal may be pelagic – operating far out to sea – in the Okhotsk and Bering seas, but this is not known with certainty.

As far as is known, the ribbon seal has always been scarce within historic times, long before the white man first appeared on the scene. Its skins have a low market value, and the animal is therefore not hunted in North America except by Eskimos. The largest numbers are taken in the Sea of Okhotsk and off Hokkaido, where Japanese sealers use them for oil, meat, and leather.

No protective measures have been taken in North America. There is in fact a state bounty of U.S. $3 per animal offered in Alaska for this and all other species of phocid seals. The bounty was introduced primarily as a means of controlling the ringed or harbour seal, *Phoca vitulina*, which was held responsible for preying on salmon and for damaging salmon fishermen's

[1] By several authorities this is regarded as a subgenus of the widespread northern genus *Phoca*.

nets. More recently the bounty has been extended to include all species of "hair seals" in both coastal and inland waters of the state. In practice the bounty has very little effect on the ribbon seal, because the animal is usually hunted only by Eskimos, who in any event will continue to catch all they can.

Little is known of the breeding habits of the species. Like the Ross seal, it is of solitary habit and does not gather in concentrations at breeding time. The gestation period is thought to be about nine months, and mature females probably do not breed more often than in every alternate year, the young being born on the ice during March and April.

ROSS SEAL
Ommatophoca rossi

The Ross seal is generally regarded as one of the rarest of the pinnipeds; it is certainly one of the least known. Until 1898 the species had been known only from two specimens presented to the British Museum by Sir John Ross after his return from his 1839–43 expedition to Antarctica. In 1898 two more were obtained, and there were nine further records between 1903 and 1907. Despite the increasing number of expeditions to the antarctic regions, the total number of recorded specimens until 1945 was believed to be fewer than fifty. The animal is still little known, but is now believed to be somewhat less rare than was previously supposed: the population has been calculated at between 20,000 and 50,000, including 10,000 in British Antarctica.

The Ross seal is the smallest Antarctic seal, adult specimens rarely being more than about 6 feet 6 inches to 8 feet long and weighing perhaps 300 to 475 pounds. Its coarse fur is greenish-yellow on the upper surface, with yellowish stripes set at an oblique angle on the sides; its under parts are paler. Its eyes are extremely prominent; at one time the animal was known as the "big-eyed seal".

The Ross seal is the only seal that is confined wholly to Antarctic seas, where it is extremely local in distribution. It feeds along the edge of the pack-ice and is believed not to winter under the ice.

Most of the records consist of solitary individuals. Immature specimens were collected in the South Orkneys in 1903; but breeding concentrations have never been seen. The suggestion has been made that the species may not follow the normal pinniped practice of gathering in rookeries during the breeding season, and that births may take place on the pack-ice. By remaining in the pack-ice the animal obtains additional security: it is said that its great agility in the water renders it safe from attacks by the killer whale.

Ross seal *D. W. Ovenden* 1966

The Antarctic Treaty, which came into force in 1961, and the measures that were subsequently agreed to in 1964 for conserving the Antarctic fauna and flora – an exceptionally important landmark in conservation history, since this was the first occasion when agreement on this subject had been reached at the international level – have given the Ross seal as much safety as human ingenuity can assure. It is possible, however, that the animal is a waning species that is gradually disappearing from evolutionary causes or other unexplained reasons.

MEDITERRANEAN MONK SEAL
Monachus monachus

The genus *Monachus* consists of three species, all of which are confined to subtropical waters in the Northern Hemisphere, but are widely separated from each other, one in the Mediterranean region, one in the Caribbean, and one in the Hawaiian Islands in the Pacific. With the exception of the California sea lion of the genus *Zalophus*, the monk seals are the only pinnipeds existing in subtropical regions. All three living species are included in the Red Data Book.

An adult male Mediterranean monk seal may be 8 to 9 feet long, with upper parts ranging in colour from brownish-grey to greyish-yellow, and with contrasting white or yellowish-white under parts. Its fur often has a white ventral patch, which is entirely absent on the other two species. Its fore flippers have well-developed claws, but those on the hind flippers are small.

The distribution of the species centres on the Mediterranean, but extends eastwards to include all the shores of the Black Sea, and westwards to Madeira and the Canary Islands as well as the north-west coast of Africa southwards as far as Cape Blanc. Nowhere within this range is the monk seal common, and it is mostly found in a series of about twenty to thirty very small colonies. Only two big colonies are known to exist. Some interchange of individuals may take place between the different colonies, but this is not certain.

The monk seal was once numerous and well-distributed along the entire Mediterranean coast, as well as on many of the offshore islands in that region, and along the Atlantic seaboard. It was found in the Danube delta, and was abundant along the Black Sea coast, notably on the southern and south-western coasts of the Crimea, where the last survivors were exterminated shortly after the Second World War.

The largest existing colony, consisting of up to 200 seals, is in Rio de Oro, occupying two caves on the western side of Cape Blanc at a place called Las Cuevecillas. Individuals are reported to have been seen moving along the coast of Rio de Oro, and it is assumed that they originated from this colony. Recent aerial observations confirm that the Las Cuevecillas colony is the only one along the coast of Rio de Oro. There the animals are now protected, as a result of which they have become comparatively tame. Numbers remain more or less constant; this suggests that the natural increase is probably being slaughtered elsewhere, possibly in the Banc d'Arguive in Mauritania, where in former times the monk seal was commercially exploited, and where a recent record states that a solitary immature specimen was seen on a beach.

Between 1940 and 1957 many observations and records were obtained of the other important colony, which breeds in caves near Villa Sanjurjo,

in the Bay of Alhucemas, Morocco. Dr José A. Valverde believes that this colony is of unusual importance, since it may have acted as the reservoir for replenishing stocks of monk seals in several parts of the western Mediterranean in recent years. A constructive measure for the protection of the monk seal would be to give these caves proper protection with the status of a nature reserve. The species may also still exist on the Chafarinas Islands, where several specimens were killed between 1945 and 1950. In 1961 a live specimen was obtained from nearby Beni Enzar and sent to the Casablanca Zoo.

Algeria formerly had a resident monk seal population, but there does not appear to have been any record of the species in that country since 1943.

In Spain the species was once dispersed along the coast between the Gulf of Alicante and Almeria and around the Balearic Islands, but has been exterminated. There appears to have been only a single record from one of the southern islands in 1957 and another in 1960 from near Tuent, on the north coast of Majorca.

Other smaller colonies may survive in the Desertas Islands (south-east of Madeira), islands off the coasts of Tuscany and Sardinia, and the tiny island of Galata off Tunisia. Monk seals no longer occur on the south coast of France, where they were once common, but each year they have bred and attempted to rear their young in a cave near Calvi, in Corsica: these efforts have usually been frustrated by the local people, who seem determined to kill them.

At one time the monk seal was common around many parts of the Adriatic coast, but the animal has now almost entirely vanished from this sheltered and busy sea. Solitary individuals are occasionally seen on the islands off the Dalmatian coast, and there is a small colony in the Illyrian Islands.

A small but static population exists along various parts of the coast of Greece. The seal may also be dispersed through the Ionian Islands and the Cyclades.

Two small colonies can still be found in Bulgaria, one at Cape Caliakra and the other at Cape Maslenos.

Colonies also exist along the Black Sea coast of Turkey, as well as in the Bosporus and the

Sea of Marmara. On the Mediterranean coast of Turkey specimens have been recorded from the Dalaman estuary and the Bay of Iskenderun, and lately Israeli naturalists have found a number of colonies in sea caves along Turkey's south coast which they urge should be declared nature reserves.

Seven or eight small colonies survive along the coast of Cyprus, where young are occasionally seen. Numbers have apparently much declined, but, as far as can be ascertained, this decrease has not been caused by direct human interference so much as by the increasing scarcity of fish in Cyprus waters.

In the winter of 1958–9 a male monk seal was killed near Beirut, Lebanon, but no more recent information is available from this part of the Mediterranean coast.

A specimen was seen on the coast of Israel near Dor in 1958, and another the following year near Rosh-Hanikrah.

In the early part of the nineteenth century the species was abundant along the coast between Alexandria and Benghazi, but since then has been almost exterminated. The last authentic report was one seen off El Arish about 1940; but it is possible that individual specimens may from time to time still come ashore on some of the remoter parts of the Egyptian and Libyan coasts.

The slow reproductive rate of the monk seal does nothing to assist the rehabilitation of the species. Mature females do not breed more often than in alternate years. Their single pup is normally born on land during September or October after an eleven-month gestation. The young is nursed for six or seven weeks, and is believed to remain with its mother for about three years; it does not reach breeding age until about four years.

Nearly all the currently existing monk seal colonies appear now to have adapted themselves to living in caves, often with submarine entrances: in the past they commonly inhabited open beaches. The only logical explanation is that the seals have been obliged to adopt this practice to avoid man, who has reduced the population to a low level by constant persecution, either for skins, oil, and meat or because of (reputed) damage to fisheries. A modern factor contributing to the decline is believed to be disturbance in and around the last remaining colonies by skin-diving enthusiasts.

The entire monk seal population is now estimated at no more than 500 individuals. Unless firm measures are taken to halt the decline, the species can scarcely be expected to survive many more decades.

The Mediterranean monk seal is legally protected in France, Italy, Yugoslavia, Greece, Bulgaria, and Spanish Sahara, but the law is extremely difficult to enforce, and there is no doubt that illegal slaughter occurs whenever opportunities arise.

The establishment of reserves or sanctuaries is clearly essential for safeguarding the remnant. The two largest colonies, one at Las Cuevecillas in Rio de Oro and the other at Villa Sanjurjo in Morocco, are in particular need of such protection.

CARIBBEAN MONK SEAL
Monachus tropicalis

This species is very like its near relative the Mediterranean monk seal, its general colour being brown with a tinge of grey, which is caused by the light shade of the extreme tip of each hair. Its sides are paler, gradually lightening to yellowish-white on the under surface.

The West Indian seal, as it is often called, was once distributed around the shores and among the islands of the Caribbean and the Gulf of Mexico, extending from approximately the latitudes of Texas in the north to Honduras in the south. The numerous places around the Caribbean bearing the names Lobos Keys, Seal Keys, or other variants, attest the former occurrence of the seal; and it was once abundant in the coastal waters of the Bahamas.

During his second voyage in 1494, Columbus found seals on the islet of Alta Vela off the south coast of Hispaniola, eight of which were killed by his crew for food. The Caribbean monk seal was in fact the first New World animal to be recorded. Paradoxically, no specimen ever reached a museum until the middle of the last century, by which time it was already rare!

No less an authority on the Caribbean region than Dampier, the famous buccaneer, states that in the late seventeenth century the seal gave rise to a profitable oil industry; and there is evidence that in the early part of the eighteenth century as many as 100 were sometimes taken in a single night, their oil being much in demand for lamps. Like Steller's sea cow, the Caribbean monk seal assisted its own demise by being too well-disposed towards man. As its movements were so slow, and it was devoid of fear and mistrust, a man could walk up to any animal and slaughter it with little difficulty. The West Indian seal was quickly reduced.

The last known concentration of the species occurred on the Triangle Keys, a series of small, low-lying, sandy islets off the west coast of Yucatan. In 1911 a party of fishermen practically exterminated the 200 seals remaining there; a few may have escaped.

Nearer our own times the animal was for some years thought to be extinct. Hope had almost been abandoned when, in 1949, two specimens were seen in Jamaican waters, where it was recorded again in 1952. Since then the captains of several shrimp and turtle boats have reported seeing occasional specimens, and have expressed the belief that the seal undertakes a seasonal migration between remote cays off British Honduras and the Caribbean coast of Mexico.

Whether or not this conjecture proves accurate, the surviving population must be very small. To avoid any possibility of premature exploitation, and to allow opportunity for numbers to build up, there seems to be a very real need for the Bahaman Government to introduce regulations protecting any seals that may have survived in and around the Bahamas. At the same time the Mexican Government should introduce and enforce total protection of the animal on islands off the coast of Yucatan.

HAWAIIAN MONK SEAL
Monachus schauinslandi

The isolation from each other of the three living species of monk seal has caused much speculation. One theory is that the Hawaiian species originated in the Caribbean region during the Tertiary epoch, when there was a direct sea link with the Pacific. Towards the end of the Tertiary, the land bridge between North and South America was re-established, leaving *M. tropicalis* in the Caribbean and isolating *M. schauinslandi* in the Pacific.

The Hawaiian monk seal does not differ greatly in appearance from the Caribbean species, although there are a number of differences in its skull that distinguish it from its Mediterranean relative. Further study may possibly show that *M. schauinslandi* should be treated as only a subspecies of *M. tropicalis*. The three species of monk seal are the only warm-water representatives of a family most of whose members occur in cold seas.

Hawaiian monk seal *D. W. Ovenden* 1966

M. schauinslandi is a moderately large seal, the males averaging about 7 feet in length and weighing about 375 pounds; females are larger and heavier, averaging about 450 pounds but weighing much more (550 to 600 pounds) when pregnant. Adult females have two functional pairs of mammae, which are extruded only when they are actually nursing. With one other exception, all species of earless seals have only a single pair.

Unlike most mammals, which moult individual hairs, the monk seal sheds its entire coat in large patches in a somewhat reptilian manner, after the breeding season. The elephant seal is the only other mammal known to moult in this way.

The Hawaiian monk seal is restricted to the waters of the Leeward Islands, the chain stretching 1,200 miles to the north-west of the main Hawaiian group. The entire population breeds on five atolls in the western half of the Leeward chain; on Kure Atoll, Midway Atoll, Pearl and Hermes Reef, Lisianski Island and Laysan Island, as well as on one atoll, French Frigate Shoals, in the eastern sector. The last named is a crescent-shaped atoll comprising a dozen small islets surrounded by the only extensive area of shallow water in the eastern part of the chain. Occasional stragglers are seen among the main Hawaiian Islands, including Kauai, Lehua, Oahu, and Hawaii, as well as at Maro Reef and Nihoa in the Leeward chain.

The preferred habitat of the Hawaiian monk seal consists of near-tropical coral atolls. The more important of its requirements include shallow water over coral reef or sandy bottoms where it can feed; low-lying, preferably sandy, sloping beaches on which it can haul out; and, for pupping purposes, secluded beaches or sand-spits above the high-tide level, sloping gently into very shallow water and protected from heavy waves. While on the beaches the seals sometimes root and roll to form shallow depressions, in which they lie, presumably for coolness and for some protection against flies.

During many thousands of years the monk seals survived undisturbed in their remote habitat at the western end of the Leeward chain. Early man did not intrude into the region, so the seals were left in peace; but the tranquillity of generations was forcefully interrupted in the early part of the eighteenth century, when the sealers discovered their retreat and exploited the population with such ruthlessness that within half a century it had practically ceased to exist.

The monk seals are remarkably tame and placid, possibly because there are no natural land predators in their realm (although sharks probably inflict casualties); and this characteristic lack of fear undoubtedly contributed to their decline. The seals barely escaped extermination before the scientific world had become aware of their existence. It happened that Dr Schauinsland visited Laysan Island in 1896, where he was given the skull of a seal, one of only seven that were killed on the island during the subsequent fifteen years. Nine years later Matschie recognized that the skull represented a hitherto undescribed species.

Favourable climatic conditions permit this seal's breeding season to be much more prolonged than that of the seals of northern waters: it extends from late December to early July, the majority of births occurring from the middle of March to late May. At this time the females do not object to each others' presence on the beaches – but they take strong exception to interference by any other seals, notably amorous males, that may attempt to join them.

When she first comes ashore to give birth, the female as a rule is enormously fat. At birth her pup weighs less than 40 pounds and is covered in velvety jet-black hair, which, at about the eighteenth day, starts to shed. White is the normal birth colour of most cold-water seals: it is thought that the black serves to protect this warm-water animal from the strong tropical glare. Within about a month the black birth coat is replaced by one more nearly resembling that of the adults, silvery-grey above lightening to white on the under parts. From the age of four days the pup starts to swim, at first for short periods in shallow waters but soon becoming more adept.

Dale W. Rice, who has made a valuable field study of the monk seal, records that with frequent nursing the pup puts on weight at an almost unbelievably rapid rate. At birth it is a gaunt creature weighing under 40 pounds; within about fifteen days its weight has doubled; by the twenty-sixth day it has tripled; and by the thirty-fifth day it has quadrupled to more than 140 pounds – by which time the animal is so fat that it can scarcely move. By this time also, the mother, who in constant attendance on the cub has had neither time nor opportunity to feed, has become a mere shadow of her former self, as the frequent nursing has exhausted all the natural reserves accumulated during the months before giving birth. Finally, after about thirty-five days, the mother can no longer stand the strain of fasting, and she suddenly deserts her offspring while it lies sprawled asleep on its back satiated with food.

At this point the pup, which until then has enjoyed an entirely carefree existence, is suddenly thrown on its own resources, a situation for which it is ill-prepared. The accumulated fat helps to see it through the difficult and critical period of learning to catch its own food. As its weight steadily falls, it is gradually forced to fend for itself. Those young which do not start this period with enough store of blubber are unlikely to survive their apprenticeship. Rice suggests that "the physiological strain of rearing a pup probably prevents females from becoming pregnant again until they have regained their store of blubber during at least one entire year of uninterrupted feeding".

In 1951 the total Hawaiian monk seal population was estimated at fewer than 500. By the summer of 1958 the figure had increased to an estimated 1,350, and, although no subsequent full census has been conducted, today's population is believed to be about 1,500. The net rate of increase has been estimated at about 12 per cent per annum, and is apparently being well maintained. The limiting factor to the expansion of the population will probably be imposed by the relatively small area of suitable habitat that exists in the Leeward Islands.

The animal has been legally protected against capture and molestation since 1909, and, with the sole exception of Midway, all the islands used by the monk seal are now included in the Hawaiian Islands National Wildlife Refuge (formerly the Leeward Islands Bird Reservation), which is administered by the United States Fish and Wildlife Service. Entry is prohibited except under permit from the Federal Government. Nevertheless, the recovery of the species from near-extinction may be attributable more to the isolation of the breeding-grounds, and the fall in demand for seal oil (the need has been reduced by petroleum products), than to any threat of punishment under the law. Its further survival depends on whether the breeding-grounds stay free from disturbance by man.

The large seal populations at Pearl and Hermes Reef, Laysan Island, and Lisianski Island, all of which are uninhabited by man, are thriving. These three atolls are not patrolled, but prominent warning notices are displayed at all their potential landing-places. Unauthorized landings are in fact unlikely owing to the remoteness of the atolls and the dangerous surrounding reefs.

French Frigate Shoals and Kure Atoll are occupied by United States Coast Guard units, the personnel being briefed on the protected status of all wildlife within the refuge. Despite the presence of the coastguard station on French Frigate Shoals, there are numerous remote islets offering secluded hauling-grounds, and the seal population therefore has abundant space for expansion. At Kure Atoll, however, the situation is much less satisfactory, as the coastguard station and airstrip are on Green Island, the only area above the spring tides and therefore the only suitable pupping area.

There is abundant evidence to show that the monk seal population cannot thrive in the presence of permanent human intrusion. On Midway, for example, where the main island, Sand Island, is now the site of a naval station, the seal has undergone a severe decline since 1957 to the point almost of extinction. It now occurs in very small numbers only on isolated sand-spits that are seldom visited by military personnel.

Because of possible human interference, direct or indirect, it would greatly benefit the species if entry to parts of certain beaches on both Midway and Kure could be prohibited during the breeding season between the 1st March and the 15th June each year to prevent curiosity-seekers from harassing the animals to the point where they may prematurely desert their pups. Since the seals tend to concentrate on a few favourite parts of the beaches, the prohibited sectors could be small.

So far eight animals have been kept captive in Honolulu and San Diego; none survived more than three years.

Order SIRENIA
Family Dugongidae: dugong

DUGONG
Dugong dugon

The genus *Dugong* consists of a single species, which inhabits coastal marine waters in tropical regions extending from Madagascar northwards along the east coast of Africa from Delagoa Bay, Mozambique, to the Red Sea, thence eastwards to the coasts of Malabar, India, Ceylon, the Andaman Island, and the Mergui Archipelago, the Ryukyu Islands, Formosa, Malaysian waters, the Philippine Islands, the Palau Islands, New Guinea, the Solomon Islands, New Caledonia, and northern Australia. These sirenians are never far from the coast, and have seldom been reported from river mouths or other freshwater localities.

Dugongs attain a length of up to 10 feet, and adult males may weight up to 375 pounds or more; the females are smaller. Their general colouration is variable, but is usually brownish or bluish-grey, their under surfaces being lighter. Their tails consist of two lateral flukes separated by a central notch and pointed at the tips. Their eyes are small and their ear orifices almost invisible. Two of the upper incisor teeth of the male are enlarged to form constantly growing tushes.

their melodious voices. For, although the calf is said to bleat like a lamb, the adult dugong is mute: the only noise it can utter is a singularly unmelodious snort caused by the inhalation or exhalation of air through its nostrils.

Dugongs usually live in pairs or in small family groups, but larger herds have sometimes been reported. In July 1893, for example, a herd in Moreton Bay, near Brisbane, which must have consisted of many hundred individuals, was reported to have extended over an area 3 miles long and 300 yards wide.

They are dull-witted and slow-moving animals that browse largely on marine vegetation grow-

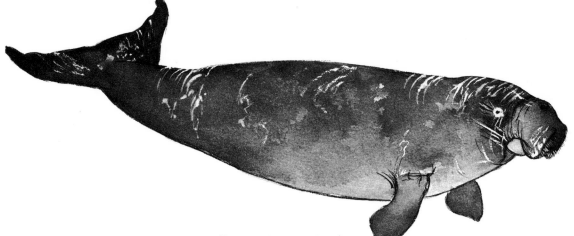

Dugong *Maurice Wilson* 1965

Very little has been reported about the breeding biology of this remarkable animal. The fact that young have been seen at different times of the year suggests that there is probably no definite breeding season. The gestation period is thought to be about eleven months. Only a single young is born, which is suckled from a pair of mammae; and the fact that the mother is obliged to surface at irregular intervals to breathe may have given rise to the fanciful stories told by early mariners of mermaids who nursed their progeny in a remarkably human manner.

The mind rebels at the suggestion that the sirens of mythology may have been dugongs, and at the thought that Odysseus made his crew bind him to the mast for such unprepossessing creatures; credulity is strained beyond the limit at the further thought that the Greek hero's ears were stopped with wax to avoid enticement by

ing in shallow water, although it is possible that other foods are also eaten. Its somewhat prehensile upper lip, coupled with the stiff hairs and bristles surrounding its muzzle, assist the animal in feeding. Troughton quotes Solomon Islanders' reports that dugongs root in the sand for shellfish, in the manner of a pig, the females using their leathery snouts and the males their tushes.

The confinement of the animal to a narrow strip of shallow water immediately adjacent to the shore line, its low reproductive rate, and its total lack of any means of defence (except for an acute sense of hearing) have rendered it extremely vulnerable, particularly to modern methods of slaughter. Its highly palatable flesh is said to resemble a cross between pork and beef; so the animal has been remorselessly hunted wherever it exists.

Another valuable product is the oil, which is

rendered down from its blubber, an adult female in good condition yielding between 5 and 6 gallons. The oil has been popular for a variety of ailments, including lung complaints, and, although there is no evidence that it is superior to many other animal oils, Troughton states that it is still held in high repute by some coastal aborigines and by the Torres Strait islanders.

In Madagascar the upper incisors of dugongs are ground into powder and used as an antidote against contaminated food; other parts are employed to cure headaches or as a laxative. Red Sea fishermen are said to prize the teeth highly.

In Ceylon dugong flesh is in much demand among certain castes, as it is credited with being an effective aphrodisiac. The seventeenth-century Chinese apparently used certain "stones", probably the tympanic bones, found in the head of the dugong, which, according to Allen, were reputed to have the "property of clearing the kidneys of every kind of sand and gravel and of removing obstructions from the lower parts afflicted by them". In the waters around the Ryukyu Islands and Amami-Oshima, the dugong was once subjected to an annual hunt undertaken by feudal lords for tribute.

In Australia it has been hunted not only for meat. Its hide was used to make excellent leather or was processed into glue; its bones had the reputation of making the highest-quality charcoal, used in sugar-refining, and its tushes were turned into knife-handles.

At one time the dugong was relatively abundant along the coast and among the off-shore islands of Madagascar, but nowadays it seldom appears in the markets.

At the northern extremity of its African range, the animal was also apparently plentiful a century ago in many parts of the Red Sea. In 1932, however, Flower reported that it was by then rare on the Egyptian Red Sea coast and seldom appeared further north than 25° N. At that time it was said to be captured more frequently south-east of Assab than elsewhere in the Red Sea. It is now uncommon throughout the region, as well as along the Somali coast. Further south along the coast of Kenya it still occurs in reasonably satisfactory numbers (especially round Lamu and Patta Island), fifty-two being seen together on one recent occasion.

East of Aden there are only cursory records of it. Thesiger (1949) states that the "sea-cow" is common in the straits of Al Bazam, on the Trucial Oman coast, where it is known as *bagar al bahr*. "The Arabs catch them in nets and there is a big demand for their meat and for their hides which are used to make sandals."

Further east it exists sparingly on the Malabar coast of India. It is more numerous on certain parts of the coast of Ceylon, although much reduced compared with sixty or seventy years ago. Specimens are frequently netted among coral reefs, and at one time live dugong were sent by train to the Colombo fish-markets. That barbaric practice is now reported to have ceased.

Further east still the dugong exists, but is rare, in the Straits of Malacca, along the coasts of Thailand, Sumatra, and Borneo to the Philippines. Distribution then follows the Japanese current, extending northwards to Formosa and the Ryukyu Islands, where the animal has been reduced almost to the point of extinction. There are no records from the coast of China, and, according to Sowerby, there is no evidence in Chinese literature of its having existed there.

The Indonesians slaughter dugong at sight along the south and south-east coasts of Borneo; and none of these animals have been reported along the west coast in recent years. Small numbers still appear in the north-east, and, in spite of being legally protected in Sabah, one was offered for sale in Sandakan market as recently as April 1965. The problem, of course, is to prove that the animal was deliberately killed, as new and more efficient types of fishing-nets catch much that previously escaped without difficulty.

In Australian waters the dugong exists from Broome in Western Australia around the northern coast, and down the east coast inside the Great Barrier Reef as far south as Moreton Bay. Remains from aboriginal middens have yielded evidence of its former existence as far south as the north coast of New South Wales. On the west coast it was known to have occurred at least as far south as Shark Bay.

From Troughton's description, the aboriginal method of hunting dugong is strangely reminiscent of the one employed in parts of Africa for hunting hippos. A barbed dart, to which a length of rope is attached, is fitted into a socket at the end of a heavy spear. The hunters station themselves either on rafts or platforms above the grazing-grounds, or drift gently along in their canoes looking for the tell-tale signs of grass floating on the surface that betray the animal's presence. As it rises to breathe, the hunter strikes, aiming at the tail to entangle it in the line. The stricken animal rushes away, towing the canoe in its wake, until eventually it weakens enough to enable further spear thrusts to be made.

The early settlers in Australia were partial to dugong meat, but their attempts to hunt on a commercial scale appear to have been short-lived and were abandoned – possibly because the numerical decline in any locality was so rapid that hunting could not long be sustained on a scale that was economically sound.

The dugong is protected by law in many parts of its range, including East Africa, Mozambique, New Caledonia, and elsewhere; but control of offshore fishing is seldom feasible, and the law is therefore extremely difficult to enforce. An illustration of the problem is afforded by the 371 specimens known to have been taken off Ceylon during the two years from July 1957 to June 1959.

In spite of these difficulties, more vigorous attempts need to be made to protect the animal. Appropriate penalties should be imposed for selling or possessing dugong meat. Sanctuaries should be established in certain selected parts of the animals' range. Along the Great Barrier Reef, for example, the presence of dugongs undoubtedly enhances the amenities of this superlative natural region, which is a strong contender for the title of the world's most interesting and important marine wonderland.

Measures should also be taken to educate public opinion to a greater appreciation of this inoffensive and useful animal. Such an approach might be particularly successful in a country like Ceylon, where there is much strong religious opposition to the taking of life. Insofar as anyone in Ceylon has considered the matter the dugong is regarded as a fish; but by trying to explain that it is a mammal and, moreover, is harmless to man and does not prey on fish, Buddhists might be prepared to use their influence to reduce the present rate of slaughter.

The precise status of the dugong is extremely difficult to assess, but it is believed to have declined throughout the greater part of its range, and probably few now remain in the Red Sea and around the coasts of Ceylon and Malaysia. The largest and most stable population is in Australian waters, notably along the coast of Queensland, and on the southern coasts of New Guinea. This is confirmed by a five-month survey undertaken in 1965 by Dr G. C. L. Bertram and his wife, who consider that on some parts of the north-east coast of Australia the animal may have recovered from the over-exploitation of the nineteenth and early twentieth centuries.

In Australian waters, hunting is now restricted to aborigines, many of whom are in process of changing over to a money economy, which sophistication may have the advantage of decreasing the pressure on the dugongs. On the other hand, there are probably some areas where increase in the aboriginal population has resulted in a rising rate of kill.

There is a need for the recent investigation by the Bertrams to be followed by the collection and collation of additional data, not only from Australian waters, but also from as many other parts of the range as possible, to enable a world-wide assessment of status and trends of the various dugong populations to be made, as a first step towards lifting the veil of ignorance that has surrounded the animal for so long.

The acquisition of these basic data appears to be a necessary first step towards carrying out a plan for conservation of the species as an important source of meat production.

The dugong is an animal occupying an ecological niche that is unusual for several reasons. Most important is the fact that it is equipped to convert types of aquatic vegetation into high-quality protein, without in any way being in competition with any of man's domesticated animals. Regrettably, its potentialities do not yet appear to have been generally appreciated by those in authority.

Order PERISSODACTYLA
Family Equidae: horses, asses, and zebras

PRZEWALSKI'S HORSE
Equus przewalskii

Equus przewalskii is the sole surviving species of wild horse. It is the size of a pony (13 to 14 hands), stockily built, with a heavy head and long tail; and it is distinguished from all other horses by its stiff, erect mane (about 6 to 8 inches long) and absence of forelock. The colour of its summer coat is a light yellow, becoming almost white on its under parts; its muzzle is white; a well-marked dark vertebral stripe extends the full length of its back; and it has an inconspicuous shoulder stripe. In winter its coat changes to yellowish-brown and becomes more shaggy. The lower parts of its limbs have black markings, usually with distinct bars up to its knees. Its voice is shrill.

Statements on the former range of the animal vary considerably and are often contradictory; but it appears most likely that the principal area occupied in its heyday extended from the Altai Mountains, in extreme western Mongolia, across the border into Dzungaria, the northern part of Sinkiang.

The decline of the wild horse dates from the acquisition of modern firearms by Chinese and Mongolian hunters, coupled with the spread of man and his domestic animals into previously unoccupied areas, thus competing with it for grazing and, particularly, for the limited water. At the same time there is a strong probability that the basic stock has been gradually diluted with an admixture of domesticated Mongol ponies. There are a good many records of mating between domestic mares and wild stallions. Numerous authors have commented on the variations in colour of the wild horse in different regions, and according to Carruthers (1913) there were "immense droves of horses running half wild all over the prairies" in southern Dzungaria. It is not even possible to know with certainty that the type specimen was of true pure-bred wild stock.

Today the species survives in only one area, the Takhin Shar-nuru massif in south-western Mongolia, close to the frontier with China. Its range extends about 190 to 220 miles from north to south and 60 to 90 miles from east to west. The region is of mountainous, semi-desert country; and the animal is known to move seasonally into the Gobi Desert as well as over the border into China in search of suitable pasturage.

There is considerable difference of opinion on the current status of the species in the wild. Not least of the difficulties found when attempting to assess the situation is the ease with which the Przewalski horse can be mistaken for the kulan, or Mongolian wild ass, which inhabits the same general region. Both species are so shy and alert that it is extremely difficult to get even moderately close to them; and even the most experienced observer can make a mistake in identification after a distant view. Further difficulty arises from the fact that some of the wild horses inhabiting this inhospitable and little-known region are in all probability feral.

The U.S.S.R. Academy of Sciences lists four sightings made during the last twenty-five years. Between 1942 and 1945 several specimens were captured in the northern branches of Batjak-Bogdo and Takhin Shar-nuru (the only survivor of this group is a mare now living at Askaniya Nova in the Ukraine); in 1947 a Soviet botanist, A. A. Yunatov, saw a herd of six or seven at the bottom of Takhin Shar-nuru; between 1949 and 1952 what was probably the same herd was sighted in the same place. In August 1955 the expedition sent by the University of Ulan Bator discovered evidence of wild horses on the summit of Takhin Shar-nuru, as well as a solitary individual that looked like a wild horse but behaved more like a domestic animal.

It appears, however, that there have also been recent sightings by Mongolian hunters. In 1965 Ivor Montagu wrote: "Between 1958 and 1963 they have several times seen what they distinguish as 3–4 separate herds, not more than 7–8 to a herd, usually in autumn and led by a stallion. The leader drives younger and weaker stallions from the herd, which explains why solitary stallions are seen more often. These have been encountered on the western slopes of the massif, particularly near Khorin-us ('sheep-water'), a desert oasis, where rushes and various grassy desert shrubs are abundant". This report indicates that at best the animal must be very rare. More recently there has been an increasing volume of evidence that the pure-bred animal still exists in the wild state. Dr Dashdorj of the University of Ulan Bator, an authority on the subject, is of the firm opinion that at least some of the 1966–7 sighting reports are acceptable, and that a small herd of pure-bred *E. przewalskii* has managed to survive in the Gobi-Altai region.

The most recent threat to the survival of the species arose from the bitter weather experienced during the winter of 1963–4. Losses among Mongolian domestic livestock were heavy, and both the wild horse and the wild ass are known to be susceptible to severe winter conditions.

The best hope for the future of the species lies in the fact that (although it is gravely reduced in numbers) its last stronghold is a harsh region that shows no early prospect of being used by man. According to Montagu, the improved methods of livestock husbandry recently adopted by the nomadic pastoralists have had the effect of halting their expansion into the habitat occupied by the wild horse. He states that the region is "never visited by nomad herdsmen on the Mongolian side of the frontier, and almost certainly not visited by them on the Chinese side either".

The species is now under strict protection in the wild state, with severe penalties imposed for any breach of the law. A further important development has been the maintenance by the Prague Zoo of the *International Studbook of the Przewalski Horse* (an annual publication that registers all specimens living in captivity), kept by Dr J. Volf.

The number of *E. przewalskii* in captivity has increased satisfactorily from thirty-six in 1956 to 153 in 1968, 39 per cent of which are from the Prague stud. The probability is that captive specimens are more abundant than wild stocks; and at a later stage it is hoped that the Soviet authorities will agree to the establishment of a special reserve into which a breeding nucleus of captive-born specimens can be released. Prof. A. G. Bannikov of the U.S.S.R. is chairman of the Survival Service Commission's special wild-horse committee.

ASIATIC WILD ASS
Equus hemionus

Of the five accepted races of the native wild ass of Asia, all are endangered to the extent that they have full entries in the Red Data Book, and one is almost certainly already extinct.

There are minor differences between the races, but all have certain characteristics in common, including a sandy-coloured coat (the shade varies with the race), lightening to white on the belly, with a dark spinal stripe; and all have large ears (but smaller than those of the African species), an erect mane, and a tufted, black-tipped tail. The races differ in size, the kulan (the "typical" race *E. h. hemionus*) standing about 4 feet 3 inches at the shoulder.

The Syrian wild ass, *E. h. hemippus*, formerly ranged (if some confusion in the records allows a general statement) rather widely over Syria, Palestine, Arabia, and Iraq. Its last stronghold was around the greater Syrian desert, and its last refuge the Jabal Sinjar north of the Euphrates, where none has been seen since 1927. Rumours of the continued survival of an ass of this race in South Arabia and Oman probably refer to domestic animals that have gone wild.

The kiang of Tibet, *Equus hemionus kiang*, whose range extends, or formerly extended, as far north as the Koko Nor in Tsinghai, and south to Ladakh, Nepal, and Sikkim appears, according to Chinese sources, to be rare but in no immediate danger. Its fully Indian counterpart, the Indian wild ass, *E. h. khur*, formerly ranged widely in dry north-west India and West Pakistan, but is now reduced to under 1,000 individuals, mostly in the Little Rann of Kutch, a few in southern Sind. The status of this race is of concern: but the two that follow are in a positively parlous state.

Persian wild ass, *Equus hemionus onager*
The Persian wild ass, or onager, is somewhat smaller and more slenderly built than the other

Asiatic wild asses. It has a narrow backbone stripe continuing to the tip of its tail, lined on both sides with a pale border. Its lighter body markings are not so well defined as those on *E. h. hemionus* and *E. h. kiang*. The onager differs from all other races in that its body colouring continues on to its legs, only the inner sides of which are whitish. There are small but well-defined hoof stripes.

It was once distributed right across the southern part of Russia, and may possibly have existed in the Danube Valley before historical times. However, the boundaries between the old range of the onager and the neighbouring extinct subspecies, *E. h. hemippus*, have never been satisfactorily determined.

By 1919 the range of the animals of this race in the U.S.S.R. had been reduced to two isolated zones – the eastern part of Turkmenia, where they were found in Badkhyz and at the base of Kopet Dag, and in Kazakhstan around the shores of lakes Balkhash and Zaysan and in the Bet-Pat-Dala Desert.

By the end of the 1930s the range had been still further reduced by the elimination of the Kazakhstan population, the last reported sighting being in 1935–6. Bannikov records that severe winters with snow more than 15 inches deep and an ice-crust may have a serious effect on the kulan (as both this and the Mongolian race are called in Russia). The decline of the animal in Kazakhstan has been attributed to the severe winters of 1879–80 and 1891–2; and in 1934 there were heavy losses in Turkmenia from the same cause – as there have also sometimes been in the population of *E. h. hemionus*.

The onager now exists in the U.S.S.R. only in the Badkhyz Reserve of 290 square miles, which was established in 1941 specifically for its protection, and contained then about 300 individuals. For several years, however, it was impossible to accord the animals adequate protection, and numbers declined, reaching their lowest point in 1952–3, when fewer than 150 remained. A fortuitous immigration from across the nearby border with Afghanistan caused a rise in the population to 200 by 1955. Since then there has been a steady increase, and, from 1959 onwards, numbers have been stabilized at about 700, under most stringent protection.

In 1953 a stallion and seven mares were transferred from Badkhyz to the island of Barsa Kel'mes, a game reserve in the Aral Sea. The solitary stallion unfortunately proved impotent, and not until 1955 could arrangements be made to send a replacement to the island. Births occurred two years later, and between 1957 and 1963 (when there were thirty-eight births and five deaths) the annual increase fluctuated between 15 and 44 per cent of the population, an average of 28 per cent.

As one of its common names implies, the Persian wild ass also occurs in Iran. Here, too, both range and numbers have been much reduced. Until the latter part of the last century, the onager appears to have been widely distributed and was locally abundant in much of the north-eastern part of the country, notably around the fringes of the Great Salt Desert; but it did not exist in the south, west, or north-west or in the Caspian region. It is still found also in the salt steppe to the east of Gum, as well as east and south of Meshed, towards Isfahan. Herds have been noted by pilots flying over the area south of Meshed.

Moreover, although the onager once existed in the north-western part of Afghanistan, recent information indicates that it is now extinct in that sector of its range.

For many centuries it was the practice to capture onager foals alive. They fetched a substantial price, as they were much in demand for stud purposes; their progeny, used for riding, were far superior to the lowly domestic ass employed as a beast of burden. The onager has also long been heavily hunted for its flesh and hide; its chase was a sport of the Persian nobility, its meat being considered a great delicacy. Other parts of the animal were used for a variety of medicinal purposes.

The onager's speed and powers of endurance were reputedly such that it could not be taken in the open by a single horseman. It was therefore ridden down by relays of horsemen assisted by hounds. In the dry season, when water holes were scarce, hunters also waited in hiding until the onager had drunk its fill, when it could the more readily be overtaken. With the coming of modern firearms these techniques became superfluous; and the recent practice of shooting from cars has been largely responsible for the accelerated decline.

The present status of the animal in Iran is somewhat obscure. A 1959 report assessed the population at between 400 and 1,000. More recent estimates suggest that the figure may now be substantially less, but accurate evidence is lacking. True, the animal is legally protected; but the exhibition of warning notices at the police stations does not apparently deter the police themselves and others in positions of influence from disregarding the law, for the meat is greatly esteemed.

Mongolian wild ass, *Equus hemionus hemionus*

The Mongolian wild ass, or kulan, was once widely distributed from the upper reaches of the Amur River through parts of Mongolia, Siberia, Manchuria, and Chinese Turkestan as far north as 50° N., to European Russia, at least as far west as the Odessa region.

During the last 2,000 years its range has steadily diminished, until today the animal exists only in the southern and south-western parts of the Mongolian People's Republic, extending over the frontier into China.

Before the Second World War, the kulan was considered abundant and in need of no protection, but since then the situation has deteriorated; and the Chinese now regard it as rarer than its cousin the kiang. No accurate census has been made, and estimates of population size and range vary considerably. In 1965 Ivor Montagu stated that numbers in Mongolia "cannot be less than several thousand", in spite of substantial losses caused by the severe winter of 1948.

The kulan is almost as fast as a racehorse and has wonderful stamina. A foal is fleet of foot almost from the day of its birth, an attribute that enables it to outrun its principal canine predator, the wolf. Bannikov records that adults can attain a speed of 37 to 44 miles an hour, and maintain it for 6 miles. A speed of 25 to 30 miles an hour can be kept up indefinitely. A herd is, moreover, extremely alert and in open country cannot be closely approached.

For these reasons the kulan was seldom caught by man, except in cunningly prepared ambushes, until the introduction of firearms. From that point, numbers declined rapidly as both hide and flesh were highly prized. In 1929 Lattimore described the meat as "something like beef but a sublime beef. It is very dry, with a coarse grain and a strange aromatic sweetness. Chinese and Mongols put it above any other game, and it undoubtedly ranks with the noblest venison."

During the rutting season the stallions gambol about the herd, neighing, sometimes rolling on their backs on the ground. The young males are not tolerated close to the herd; they are driven away and compelled to watch the antics of their elders from a respectful distance. At this time vicious fighting takes place between stallions, who finish the season virtually covered with scars. The steppe is dotted with stallions roaming about in search of mares or of herds led by young males; and the males may be seen standing for long periods on hillocks or prominent hill features as they scan the countryside for possible rivals.

According to Bannikov, the distribution of the kulan is governed primarily by the availability of water. In winter, when there is snow or surface water, and in spring, when lush green grass is plentiful, it is not dependent on permanent water and can therefore roam over a wide region. During the dry season, however, watering places assume a special significance. This wild ass can probably survive for two or three days without drinking, but no longer. Regular watering is therefore essential to its existence. During the summer the herds will normally station themselves within a radius of 6 to 9 miles from a source of water and, if undisturbed, will remain nearby for a long period. But, even when they suffer severely from thirst, wild asses will shun any place inhabited by man. The steady increase of human activity in the kulan's range, with mounting numbers of cattle and other domestic livestock, has reduced the numbers of open watering places available to it. This is the main reason why it has left areas where it once flourished.

The kulan is now strictly protected both in China and in Mongolia; but perhaps the greatest hope for its survival lies in the extreme remoteness and inaccessibility of the country that forms its final redoubt, and is not yet coveted by man.

AFRICAN WILD ASS
Equus asinus

As Linnaeus first gave the name *Equus asinus* in 1758 to the domestic donkey of the "near east", the "typical" name is not used for any of the wild races of the African wild ass – which is the donkey's ancestor. Authorities differ as to the number of wild races that should be recognized, some holding to as many as five. Here three are accepted, of which one, *E. a. atlanticus*, the Algerian wild ass, which formerly ranged over Algeria and the adjacent part of the Atlas, has been extinct for many years (probably in a wild state since Roman times of A.D. 300!), though (like the other races) it certainly contributed to domestic stock. The two others are both in the Red Data Book; and the most useful vernacular names for them are geographical – the Nubian and Somali wild asses. Both are somewhat larger than the Asiatic species; and their bray is entirely different, being similar to that of the donkey.

Nubian wild ass, *Equus asinus africanus*

The Nubian wild ass is readily distinguishable from its Somali relative by having a short stripe across its withers, at right angles to the narrow dorsal stripe, and by the absence of dark crescent-shaped bands on its legs. It has, however, a dark patch on each side of the front fetlocks. The animal stands about 3 feet 9 inches to 4 feet at the shoulder, although Sir Samuel Baker gave the height of a male from the Atbara River as 4 feet 7 to 8 inches. Its general colour is a greyish fawn. Baker's description has never been bettered: "Those who have seen donkeys in their civilized state have no conception of the beauty of the wild and original animal. . . . The animal in its native desert is the perfection of activity and courage; there is a high-bred tone in the deportment, a high-actioned step when it trots freely over the rocks and sand, with the speed of a horse when it gallops over the boundless desert. No animal is more difficult of approach; and, although they are frequently captured by the Arabs, those taken are invariably the foals, which are ridden down by the fast dromedaries, while the mothers escape".

Until relatively recently the Nubian wild ass was distributed over Nubia and the eastern Sudan from the Nile to the Red Sea, extending as far south as the Atbara River. It is interesting to note that on the island of Socotra, off the extreme north-east coast of Somalia, are herds of either wild or feral asses that are said to be similar to the Nubian race but somewhat smaller. They are reputed to be descended from stock originally brought to the island by ancient Egyptian incense-collectors.

For a good many years there has been considerable difference of opinion about the existence of true wild asses in the Sahara. Selous, Lavauden, and others consider that they could not be found west of the Nile. Other authors cite the populations of wild asses in the Hoggar massif in southern Algeria, for example, or those in the hills north of Tibesti-Ennedi in Tchad, where there are known to be several hundred. The consensus of opinion is that the various populations that now survive west of the Nile are almost certainly feral, being descended from domestic animals that have for generations run wild.

The doubt remains, however, and the question may never be satisfactorily resolved. The most recent report to come to the attention of the I.U.C.N. concerns the existence of a small herd in the salt marshes of Giarabub, to the north of the northern edge of the Great Libyan Sand Sea. They are well known to the local people as *himar wahash* (wild or, more accurately, ferocious ass). They appear to be secure, since the local people do not molest them, and when approached they gallop into the *shott* (salt-marsh), where it is almost impossible to follow owing to the treacherous nature of the surface.

Brocklehurst, writing of the Sudan in 1931, stated that the animal "had been strictly protected for a number of years, and although by no means common there is not, at present, any danger of their being exterminated".

Powell-Cotton secured two specimens in 1934 in the area south of Tokar, not far from the Eritrean border, and was informed that the animal was more numerous on the Eritrean side.

In 1954 Mackenzie described the species as "very rare". Since then the total absence of reliable sight records has led to the assumption that the pure-bred wild animal may by now be extinct and that all surviving stocks are feral.

The principal reason for decline appears to have been, in T. R. H. Owen's words, "less persecution than a gradual deterioration and extinction of the true stock through inter-breeding with tame donkeys . . ."

Somali wild ass, *Equus asinus somalicus*

The Somali race is said to be more powerful than the Nubian, standing about 4 feet 3 inches at the shoulder. Its general colour is a sandy fawn, but, according to Pocock, it changes to light grey during the hot season. Its vertebral stripe is not very pronounced, and there is no dark stripe across its withers. The front of its forelegs is distinguished by a series of dark bands up to the level of its body.

The subspecies formerly occupied the coastal plain extending from Massawa in the north to the Webi Shebeli in the south, and extending inland across the plains of the Danakil country to the Awash Valley. Thesiger, who traversed the Danakil country in 1933, found it quite common at that time.

Reports mention the existence of herds in the Bale region of Ethiopia on the upper reaches of the Juba River, but opinions differ on whether these were wild or feral. Other reports extend the range even further. Sir Harry Johnston, for example, writing in 1900, stated that the wild ass was "indigenous to the desert region round the northern shores of Lake Rudolf and possibly also between Lake Rudolf and the Upper Nile". He added: "It has long been domesticated by the negroid inhabitants of the Rudolf countries . . ."

It may have been his report that caused the name of the wild ass to be added, as a pre-cautionary measure, to the Uganda Game Schedule in 1906 (the province had not at that time been transferred to Kenya). Other authors, however, consider it extremely unlikely that true wild asses ever existed in the neighbourhood of Lake Rudolf, and believe the most likely explanation to be that Johnston's animals were of feral breed, such as the handsome asses of the Turkana tribe, which Teleki and von Höhnel first recorded during their epic journey of discovery to Lakes Rudolf and Stefanie in 1888. The ass had long been domesticated in that

region, and the stock gradually spread through neighbouring tribes in the Rift Valley at least as far south as Masailand. In those parts of Ethiopia and Somalia where wild herds existed, the quality of the domesticated stock was maintained through the practice of tethering mares at some distance from human habitation, so that they should be served by wild stallions.

An indication of the speed and extent of the decline can be gained from Swayne's 1905 estimate that, in the maritime hills in the eastern part of the Somaliland Protectorate alone, there were approximately 10,000 wild asses. The size of today's population is not known with certainty, but is believed not to exceed a few hundred.

Somali wild ass *Barry Driscoll* 1967

Major I. R. Grimwood, formerly Chief Game Warden, Kenya, and a member of the I.U.C.N.'s Survival Service Commission, who recently investigated the status of the wild ass in Ethiopia, considers the population in the Sardo area to be the last major group remaining in that country: he estimates numbers at about 200, with a possible maximum of 300 to 350. There are no reliable figures for any of the other herds, but it is thought unlikely that they total more than a few hundred at most. Various small groups are known to survive in a few isolated parts of the animal's range. It is possible, of course, that unknown herds still persist, and one uncon-firmed statement quoted by Grimwood men-tions the existence of wild asses "in large numbers" at a place called Buri, south of Massawa, as well as at several other spots along the coast of Eritrea.

Hardly any reliable information is available from Somalia, but it is said that the animal still exists in small numbers in the Wadi Nogal. The region is practically uninhabited, and the herd is therefore thought to be reasonably secure.

Most of the range of the wild ass is in country occupied by Muslim pastoralists. This has led to the widely held supposition that the animal enjoys a degree of protection because religious beliefs inhibit the eating of ass-flesh. This may be true as far as it goes, but it is not the full story. There is irrefutable evidence that the Somalis, to give but one example, hunt wild asses for the fat, which they regard highly as a medicine against tuberculosis.

The most serious current threat to the wild ass, in a region where the annual rainfall averages 4 inches or less, arises from competition with domestic livestock for the very limited available grazing; in places this competition is severe.

If the wild ass is to survive, it is therefore important to establish national parks, game reserves, or equivalent sanctuaries in areas where the animal is known to exist, and from which humans and domestic livestock must be rigidly excluded. Before that can be done, however, additional surveys will certainly be needed to ascertain the status of the animal throughout its range in Ethiopia, Somalia, and French Somaliland, so that the most suitable areas can be selected.

MOUNTAIN ZEBRA
Equus zebra

This species comprises two races, the Cape mountain zebra, *E. zebra zebra*, and Hartmann's mountain zebra, *E. zebra hartmannae*, both of which are in the I.U.C.N.'s Red Data Book. The former was the first of the zebras known to Europeans, and is the smallest of them all, being approximately 4 feet high at the shoulders. It is more donkey-like in general appearance than the common zebra, *E. burchelli*, and differs from all other members of the family by having a

definite dewlap on the throat. Its stripes are narrow and set close together, except on its rump, where they broaden out. The arrangement of its stripes is also distinguished from that on other zebras by the gridiron pattern on top of its rump set at right angles to its backbone.

According to Blaine, Hartmann's mountain zebra is a much larger animal than the Cape race, "approximating to a Grévy Zebra in size", and Shortridge agreed that it is "certainly the largest of the South African zebras". A further difference is that the stripes of Hartmann's race are more widely spaced, so that the black no longer predominates, thus giving the impression that it is lighter-coloured than the Cape race.

Since its discovery, the "typical" Cape race has always been restricted to the mountain ranges of Cape Province, South Africa, and particularly the mountains in the south-western and western sectors of the province.

Cape mountain zebra *Peter Scott* 1967

It has never been numerous, and it was accorded special protection by Jan van Riebeeck as early as 1656, more than a century before it was first scientifically described and named by Linnaeus in 1758. When the British took over the Cape in 1806, the hunting laws were generally relaxed, with the result that many zebras were wantonly destroyed.

More recently, closer human settlement and increased development caused a gradual reduction of the race's range, and it was forced into less suitable areas. At the same time there was competition from domestic animals, notably merino sheep, for the limited grazing available. As the numbers of the Cape zebra declined, inbreeding may possibly have weakened the stock.

By 1937 the population was down to a total of about forty-seven individuals. In that year the Mountain Zebra National Park was established and stocked with six animals, only one of which was a mare. By 1950 only two stallions remained, and both had to be destroyed. A few weeks later a fresh start was made with the introduction of eleven more animals (five stallions and six mares) presented by Messrs H. K. and J. K. Lombard, one of several herds that had been maintained on private property.

In 1964 the size of the park was almost trebled by the acquisition of a further 12,700 acres, comprising some of the most suitable mountain zebra habitat available – and the "Doornhoek" herd purchased from Mr C. Michau and his brother, which amounted to thirty animals. More recently the Government has undertaken to introduce fresh stock from the small numbers of animals still remaining outside the park, to prevent excessive inbreeding.

As a result of these efforts, the number of animals in the Mountain Zebra National Park in September 1965 had increased to fifty-eight, comprising twenty-five stallions and thirty-three mares. Another seventeen animals existed elsewhere in South Africa, including several farms in the Outiniqua Mountains, bringing the total to seventy-five.

The Cape mountain zebra came perilously close to extinction. But the constructive measures taken by the authorities in recent years have improved its status to such an extent that, within the national park, conditions for survival are now more favourable than they have been for a long time.

Hartmann's mountain zebra, on the other hand, although much more numerous, appears to be moving in the opposite direction.

This race exists in South-West Africa and was formerly distributed along the chain of arid mountains on the western edge of the Namib

Desert. The animal ranged down to the coast, where Blaine recorded having seen its spoor on the wet seashore at low tide. According to Shortridge in 1934, it was never found far from these mountains: nowhere did it occur more than 100 miles inland; and it was most commonly encountered within 50 miles of the coast. The range extended from the Orange River in the south across the Cunene River in the north into south-western Angola at least as far as Elephant Bay, 100 miles to the north of Mossamedes. Present distribution is similar, with more than 80 per cent of the population north of 24° S.

Until a few years ago, the subspecies was considered abundant and certainly not in any way endangered. As recently as 1958, for example, Bigalke stated that "within its restricted range, Hartmann's mountain zebra is numerous". A series of population counts undertaken during the last few years has revealed a substantial reduction of the whole population, to about 7,000 in 1967. The decline is at least partly attributable to the increasing erection of "game-proof" veterinary fences, some of which stretch for many miles and effectively restrict normal seasonal movements, sometimes cutting off the herds from access to the limited sources of water.

This situation has arisen despite the fact that Hartmann's race is classified as "protected game" under the Game Ordinance, which means that it may not be hunted except on a special licence, granted by the Administration only when crops or grazing are endangered. The necessity for this proviso can be understood from Bigalke's statement that "when the rains have been favourable it ranges deep into the desert and may sometimes cause severe damage on nearby farms".

It seems clear that special protective measures will have to be introduced as a matter of some urgency if Hartmann's mountain zebra is not to follow the same course as the Cape race.

In 1966 seventy-eight animals of this race were in zoos, at least forty-seven of them females, and thirty-two zoo-bred.

Family Tapiridae: tapirs

CENTRAL AMERICAN TAPIR
Tapirus bairdi

The tapir family is represented by a single living genus comprising four species, three of which exist in parts of South and Central America, and one, *T. indicus*, in South-East Asia. This is a typically relict distribution, and fossils show that substantial parts of the tropics between the Americas and South-East Asia were inhabited by (now extinct) forms of tapir until the Pleistocene Ice Ages.

The Central American, or Baird's, tapir is a stoutly built animal about the size of a donkey, with short legs and standing about 3 feet 6 inches at the shoulder. Its tail is very stubby, and its snout elongated to form a short trunk. Like other members of its genus, it has four toes on its fore feet and only three on its hind feet. Its general colour is dusky brown; the species is distinguished from the others by the white on parts of its face, throat, and chest, by its white-tipped ears and white lips, and by the absence of a mane (which is replaced by bristles) on the nape of its neck.

Tapirs are the only living native American representatives of the order Perissodactyla, and Baird's tapir is the least known of all the tapirs. It occurs in suitable parts of Central America as far north as Veracruz in Mexico, as well as in Ecuador and Colombia on the western side of the Andes. Its habitat comprises damp tropical forests ranging from marshy lowland to montane forest up to a high altitude. Hershkovitz records "well-worn tapir trails at 3,350 meters altitude near the very summit [of Volcán de Chirigui in Panama]".

The combination of water and undisturbed rain forest is essential to this tapir's existence; it is an exclusively herbivorous animal that spends much time in water or mud wallows. It is a strong swimmer and, when alarmed, often takes refuge in water, sometimes swimming submerged for long distances.

Tapirs are shy and cannot tolerate disturbance by man or his domestic animals. In recent years much of the original forest, both highland and lowland, in which this animal lived has been taken over for settlement. Reduction of the forest has been accompanied by more rigorous

Central American tapirs, adult and young *Cécile Curtis* 1966

persecution by man, and the animal has there-fore been eliminated from much of its former range. That this is not an entirely new factor is shown by Starker Leopold, who states that the Central American tapir had already disappeared from Yucatan by the time of the Spanish conquest, "presumably as a result of Mayan settlement and clearing of the forest". The same author asserts that "there remains no secure and assured population anywhere" in south-eastern Mexico.

Because of the inability of the species to adapt itself to the changed conditions resulting from settlement and transformation of the environment, only a few have survived in some of the more remote areas. The only hope for its continued existence appears to lie in the estab-lishment of well-protected national parks or similar sanctuaries to embrace some of the few areas of virgin forest that, almost miraculously, still exist.

Starker Leopold, writing of Mexico in 1959, states: "One such area that might well be designated as a permanent rain forest reserve for tapirs and other elements of the wet tropical fauna and flora is the north-eastern slope of Volcán San Martín in the Tuxtla Range of southern Veracruz. There may still be other suitable sites in southern Campeche, Quintana Roo, or Chiapas. The creation of one or more rain forest preserves and the extension of effective legal protection to tapirs everywhere in southern Mexico are steps that should be taken quickly to save this unique member of the Mexican fauna from ultimate extinction".

Leopold's proposal is applicable with almost equal urgency to the other countries in which the species still precariously exists.

Family Rhinocerotidae: rhinoceroses

GREAT INDIAN RHINOCEROS
Rhinoceros unicornis

The genus *Rhinoceros* (the one-horned rhino-ceroses) is represented by several species in the fossils of the Pleistocene Ice Ages, when it appears to have ranged through Eurasia from Europe to Taiwan and Japan, and through the Asian mainland to Sumatra, Java, and Ceylon. It is now represented by only two relict living species, the great Indian rhinoceros, *R. unicornis*, and the Javan rhinoceros, *R. sondaicus*. The former is the largest of the three living species of Asiatic rhinoceroses, and more heavily built than the Javan one-horned species, attaining a height of over 6 feet at the shoulder and a length of more than 14 feet. A fully grown specimen may weigh over 2 tons.

The most striking feature of the great Indian rhinoceros is its thick hide, which has several loose folds, notably on its neck, behind its fore-quarters, and in front of its hindquarters, giving the impression that the animal is encased in armour-plate. This illusion is heightened by the convex tubercles, looking almost like rivets, with which the sides and upper parts of its legs are studded, and by the almost total absence of hair on its skin, except for a bristly fringe around its ears and the tip of its tail. Its head is large, its eyes small, and, like that of the black rhino-ceros of Africa, its upper lip is prehensile. Its lower jaw contains a pair of sharp incisors that have developed into tushes, which are used with considerable effect on the rare occasions when the animal attacks.

The animal's massive bulk and somewhat intimidating appearance are deceptive, since it is normally shy and inoffensive and seldom acts aggressively unless wounded or with young.

The great Indian rhinoceros is an animal of territorial habits (although to what extent has yet to be determined), and is never far from water, in which it bathes daily, or mud, in which it wallows. Its food consists mainly of grasses, shoots, and reeds. Normally it feeds in the early morning and evening; for the remainder of the day it rests or wallows, especially during the hot weather – a practice that may alleviate the persistent attacks by hordes of insects in the swamps.

A single young is born after a gestation period of 474 to 486 days (Dr Ernst Lang). On the assumption that she suckles her calf for at least six to ten months, an adult female will not normally breed more often than every third year. If, as has also been suggested, the calf is suckled for two years, births may possibly occur only once in four years.

During the Middle Ages, the Indian rhinoceros was distributed over much of the northern part of India and Nepal, extending from Peshawar and Kashmir in the west, along the Himalayan foothills as far as the frontier with Burma. The southern limit of its former range is uncertain, but, because the animal is so closely associated with water, it may not have existed beyond the plain of the Ganges river system. Earlier reports of its existence in South-East Asia are questionable, and may refer to one of the other two species of Asiatic rhinos. On the evidence available, it seems unlikely that *R. unicornis* ever extended eastwards more than a short distance beyond the borders of Assam and Bengal.

Increasing pressure on the land by the human population, and the consequent drastic alteration of its natural habitat, have driven the Indian rhinoceros from most of the region in which it formerly lived. The fertile lowlands were first taken over by agriculture. The rhinos retreated to the hills, but, as these in turn came gradually under cultivation, the animals were eventually eliminated everywhere except only in the most remote or inaccessible parts of their range. In more recent years, increased hunting has accelerated the decline of the tiny remnant of a species already greatly reduced in numbers through loss of habitat.

An indication of the relative abundance of the animal less than a century ago can be gained from the fact that, as recently as 1876, the Government of Bengal was offering a bounty of Rs.20 to anyone who shot a rhinoceros, on the ground of damage to standing crops. In the fields of the Terai, the Nepalese used to build raised platforms of bamboo on which, as harvesting time approached, people would beat gongs and ring bells to frighten the rhinos away.

By about 1910 numbers had been so reduced that the hunting of rhinos in Bengal and Assam had to be prohibited; and a series of sanctuaries was proclaimed in the upper Brahmaputra valley and Bengal for the purpose of protecting the species and parts of its natural habitat. But the creation of sanctuaries was not in itself enough protection against well-organized gangs of poachers; and on more than one occasion the Assam Rifles had to be called in to help in restoring order.

There has long been a considerable demand for rhino horn in India, but, following the near-extermination of the Javan rhino in South-East Asia (which had previously met much of the demand from China), the market value of horn multiplied (*see also* p. 115). A lucrative trade developed, and poaching became widespread.

The Indian rhinoceros is now confined to eight reserves in India and Nepal. Occasional reports of individuals in other areas nearly always refer to stragglers wandering beyond the boundaries of sanctuaries. Small, isolated populations may still exist, however – for example, in the Tirup Frontier Tract in Assam, where unverified reports mention the presence of a small group.

The total number in 1966 was estimated at about 740, of which 575 were in India and the rest in Nepal. By far the largest and most important stock in India existed in the Kaziranga Sanctuary (166 square miles) in Assam, where the numbers were estimated at about 400. A major shortcoming of the reserve is that domestic animals are permitted to graze within its boundaries. In theory stock is allowed to use only a very small part of the sanctuary, about 3 miles long and 1 mile deep; but in practice supervision is negligible, and little attempt is made to keep the regulations. A considerable threat to the rhino and other wild animal species has therefore developed through competition for the limited available fodder; and there is a possibility that disease may spread. It seems essential that measures should be taken to exclude all domestic animals from Kaziranga, so that it could become a sanctuary in fact and not only in name. Poaching is also strong in Kaziranga: no fewer than thirteen rhinos were killed in 1966.

The largest stock of Indian rhinos in Nepal in 1966 consisted of 165, which inhabited the Chitawan Rhinoceros Sanctuary, in the Rapti valley. It is hoped that this sanctuary will shortly be given national park status. Since Chitawan has an exceptionally important bearing on the future of the species, and because the recent history of the area is such an outstanding example of effective practical conservation, its story needs telling.

Until the downfall of the Rana Prime Ministers in 1952, the Rapti River valley was a wild and sparsely populated region used by the powerful Rana family as a hunting-ground. It was here that lavishly organized tiger hunts were staged in honour of visiting royalty. In addition to many other species of wild animals, 800 Indian rhinos were estimated to inhabit the western end of the valley.

Following 1952, large numbers of land-hungry hill people took advantage of the period of political instability to move into the valley. At the same time the Government sponsored a scheme designed to eradicate malaria from the valley and encourage the large-scale settlement, in the open grasslands, of many thousand immigrants from the hills.

Within a few years the new settlers began to encroach upon the forests; as a consequence, the rhinos were driven from their principal habitat into the swamps south of the Rapti River and on to islands in the Narayani River.

In 1958 the I.U.C.N. received a report that, during the previous year, a gang of Indian poachers had been operating in the Rapti valley and were believed to have killed a very large number of rhinos. The I.U.C.N.'s Survival Service Commission thereupon arranged for one of its members, E. P. Gee, to visit Nepal, investigate the situation, and make proposals for proper protection of the species.

Gee visited the valley early in 1959, and estimated that the population had been reduced to about 300. By 1961 the number had declined still further to approximately 165. The results of Gee's investigation, and his subsequent recommendations for improving the situation, were incorporated into his *Report on a Survey of the Rhinoceros Area of Nepal, March and April 1959*, which was prepared for and adopted by the Survival Service Commission.

In 1963, as a result of strong representations made to the Government of Nepal by the Forest Department, a committee of inquiry was appointed to investigate the chaotic situation that had by then developed in the Rapti valley. The inquiry was followed by the appointment of a Land Settlement Commission, with responsibility for determining which settlement was legal and which illegal, and with full powers to remove illegal squatters and resettle them elsewhere.

By the time the Land Settlement Commission had completed its work in 1965, some 22,000 people had been removed from the forest areas, including 4,000 from the rhinoceros sanctuary itself, some of them on the personal instructions of King Mahendra. The whole of the rhinoceros sanctuary and the proposed national park is therefore now clear of settlement; as a result, poaching has been brought under firm control, and the outlook for the rhinoceros has immeasurably improved. If poaching can be kept down, there is every reason to think that the rhinoceros population will prosper.

It is difficult to exaggerate the significance of this almost unprecedented action for the survival of the Indian rhinoceros. By its timely and forthright intervention, the Government of Nepal has set a splendid example to other countries of what can be done with drive and determination to safeguard an endangered species.

JAVAN RHINOCEROS
Rhinoceros sondaicus

The Javan rhinoceros is similar in appearance to the Great Indian rhinoceros, except that it is rather smaller, its shoulder height being on average about 6 inches less. There are, however, some obvious differences. Both sexes of the Indian rhino are equipped with horns, whereas the female Javan rhino has none or at most only a very small one. It is in fact the only one of the five species of rhino in which the females are almost always hornless. Moreover, the male's horn is normally less than half the length of its Indian relative's. The skin folds also differ, the Javan rhinoceros having an additional fold in front of the shoulder, while the skin structure lacks the "rivets" of the Indian rhino, being marked overall with a pattern of scale-like disks.

Javan rhinoceros *Cécile Curtis* 1966

The tail stands out more prominently from the hindquarters through lack of a deep fold across the rump.

In Pleistocene (Ice Age) times, as fossils show, the Javan rhinoceros extended as far west as East Punjab, and a form of it lived in Ceylon. Little more than a century ago it was still found throughout most of South-East Asia, from the Sikkim Terai and Brahmaputra River valley in Assam and Bengal eastwards to the southern border of China, and possibly extending over the border into Yunnan and Kwangsi, notably along the Mekong and Song Koi rivers. Until as recently as the First World War, the species was said to be abundant along the greater part of the Mekong valley, and was hunted in the marshy plains not far from Saigon.

There is considerable uncertainty, however, about the identity of the rhinos formerly existing in parts of South-East Asia, through the failure of early reports to differentiate clearly enough between the three Asiatic species.

The Javan rhinoceros also formerly existed over the greater part of the islands of Java and Sumatra. In Sumatra the last specimen in South Palembang was said to have been shot in 1928, but a few lingered on in other parts of the island until the Second World War, since when there has been no evidence of the animal's continued existence.

During the last 100 years the human population of Java has increased more than tenfold, with the result that agricultural expansion has deprived the rhino of much of its natural habitat, forcing it to retreat into more inaccessible areas, where the remnant has been persistently hunted for its horn.

The horns were valuable enough to form part of the annual tribute sent by the King of Luang-Prabang to the Emperor of China and the Emperor of Annam; and a rhino horn was frequently included in the dowry of the royal princesses of Luang-Prabang.

The horn trade (*see also* p. 115) has been responsible for the virtual annihilation of the Javan rhinoceros throughout its range, with the exception of the Udjong Kulon Reserve in extreme western Java. It is possible that a few specimens may still exist in the Tenasserim area on the south-western borders of Thailand, where it is known to have once been especially abundant, and where local tribesmen claim still to hunt the species.

Until there is definite evidence to the contrary, though, Udjong Kulon must be regarded as the last remaining stronghold of the Javan rhinoceros, and thus the reserve can justifiably claim to be one of the most important in the world. It is also of considerable botanical interest, as it is the only area of the lowland forest indigenous to Java that remains. It extends over approximately 117 square miles, and in January 1967 contained, as estimated by Dr J. Verschuren, a population of not more than forty rhinos.

A disturbing feature of the present situation in Udjong Kulon is the apparent lack of an adequate number of young rhinos. Lee Talbot, during his 1955 field mission on behalf of the I.U.C.N., suggested that the population had reached such a low level (about forty) that adequate reproduction might no longer occur. During the subsequent ten years only six calves were reported, and approximately twice as many animals died or were killed. Such a low replacement rate is not enough to replenish losses. The fact that no sightings of young have been recorded may, of course, be partly due to the retiring habits of the species. In dense forest it is extremely difficult to see them.

Even in ideal circumstances, the reproductive rate of the Javan rhino is low. Its gestation period is about seventeen months; and, since the single calf is suckled for as long as two years, mature females probably do not breed more often than every fourth or fifth year.

The Netherlands Indies Government set aside the Udjong Kulon Peninsula as a nature monument in 1921, essentially for the protection of the Javan rhinoceros, the Javan tiger, and the banteng, all three of which appeared to be endangered.

Some ten years later the status of the area was changed to that of a game reserve. All human habitation has been excluded, and even the headquarters of the reserve are situated on an island off the peninsula's north-western coast.

Apparently the rhinos are found mainly on the low-lying central plateau and in the southern sector of the reserve, but, since they wander for considerable distances, they probably use other areas, at least to some extent.

Talbot records observations indicating that the favourite food of the Javan rhino appears to be the very peculiar "tepus" plant, *Amomum coccineum*, one of the ginger family, resembling the cardamom, which throws up 18-foot broad-leaved spikes, but carries its red flowers at or even below ground-level. The animals also eat young bamboo leaves and fruits of various kinds. Sometimes they push over trees up to 6 inches in diameter to get at the foliage and possibly the fruit. Talbot also states that the director of the reserve "reported seeing the rhinos knee deep in the sea and he believed they ate the intertidal Rhizophora".

Udjong Kulon Reserve has the further distinction of harbouring the world's rarest predator, the Javan tiger, of which fewer than a dozen are believed to exist. Talbot states that, shortly after the Second World War, a gang of poachers entered the reserve with the intention of slaughtering the rhinos for their horns. One of the poachers was killed by a tiger, and, as the local villagers refused to cooperate in taking action against the carnivores, because of the belief that tigers harbour the souls of their departed ancestors, the poachers decided to leave.

Although it is possible that a tiger could kill a very young rhino calf, losses from this cause are no longer very probable. There is such an abundance of alternative prey species, and so few remaining tigers, that a tiger can have little need to risk an attack by such a formidable opponent as a cow rhino defending its calf.

Various proposals have been made for ensuring the survival of the Javan rhino. In considering the merits and demerits of the various schemes, it becomes clear that all hope for the future of the species hinges on the Udjong Kulon Reserve.

The Government of Indonesia – and in particular the Forest Service, which is responsible for administration of the peninsula – deserves high praise for having maintained the reserve in the face of almost insuperable difficulties since the Second World War. So long as this protection continues, there is cause for optimism. To strengthen the hand of the Indonesian authorities, however, it is essential to learn more about the animal and its ecological requirements. With the aid of the Fauna Preservation Society and the World Wildlife Fund, the I.U.C.N.'s Survival Service Commission, in cooperation with the Indonesian Forest Service, has started a series of ecological studies designed to provide the scientific data for planning the effective management of the rhinoceros and its habitat.

Pending the outcome of ecological investigations, every possible step should be taken to protect the reserve and, in particular, to prevent intrusion by poachers, whether civilian or military. Only the most stringent protection can save the species from becoming extinct.

SUMATRAN RHINOCEROS
Didermocerus sumatrensis

The Sumatran rhinoceros[1] is the smallest of the world's living rhinos. Adult specimens are seldom more than 4 feet 6 inches high at the shoulder; they are 8 to 9 feet long, and weigh 1 ton. This rhino is readily distinguishable from the other Asiatic species not only by its smaller size but also by its two horns. Its front horn is the larger, being generally about 15 to 20 inches long on adult males, while its hind horn is much

[1] The genus *Didermocerus* (some authorities prefer the name *Dicerorhinus*), was represented in (and before) the Pleistocene Ice Ages very widely, and by a succession of species that penetrated, when the climate was suitable, as far west as Europe (including the British Isles); they were observed by Stone Age Europeans, painted on the walls of Lascaux's famous cave (whose rhino is certainly not the plains and tundra woolly rhino), and hunted by some of them. Indeed, these two-horned hairy forest rhinoceroses ranged over wooded Eurasia (including Asia Minor) to north-eastern China and Yakutia in Siberia, and their fossils have also been found in Africa north of the Sahara. The sole living survivor is indeed but a relict of a successful Pleistocene genus.   J.F.

smaller – usually little more than a large boss protruding only a few inches. On some specimens it is so small that it appears to be missing, which may account for earlier reports of one-horned specimens. Both sexes carry horns, but those on the female are about one-third the size of the male's.

A further difference is that the Sumatran rhino's skin folds are rather less conspicuous than those of the other two Asiatic species; and the skin itself is relatively thin and smooth. Immature animals have a covering of hair, which appears to vary in density according to geographical locality, but which seems to diminish as the animals mature.

Two subspecies are usually recognized, the "typical" race, *D. s. sumatrensis*, being restricted to Sumatra and Borneo, and the race *D. s. lasiotis* (usually known as either the Chittagong or hairy-eared) living on the mainland. The latter is reputed to be somewhat larger than the island race, and to have paler and somewhat longer hair, a shorter and more fully tufted tail, and a more strongly developed fringe on the edges of its ears.

The habits of the Sumatran rhino are apparently similar to those of the Javan species. Both favour forested hill country, often at a considerable height, and both live within reach of water so that they can bathe and wallow. Lydekker quotes a report that "in the Mergui Archipelago a rhinoceros, which may have been this species, is stated to have been seen swimming from island to island . . ." Talbot confirms that they are strong swimmers, and refers to a 1954 report by U Tun Yin of a rhino seen swimming off the coast of Burma "near High Island which is a good twenty miles from the mainland although there are islands in sight all round".

At one time the Sumatran rhino was distributed over a wide region, extending from parts of East Pakistan and Assam, throughout Burma, much of Thailand, Cambodia, Laos and Vietnam, Malaya, Sumatra, and Borneo. In the two big islands its fossil remains have been found in prehistoric human sites far from its present limited haunts.

Like the other two Asiatic species, *D. sumatrensis* has been hunted almost to extinction throughout its range because of the widespread belief in the value of its horn, and almost every other part of it, as an aphrodisiac. The principal market is China, where there is evidence of a substantial trade in horn going back many hundreds of years. The price is said to have reached its peak shortly before the Second World War, when horn was nearly worth its weight in gold. In Thailand at that time there was even a special customs duty levied on it.

It seems impossible to shake the belief of the Chinese that rhino horn is one of the most powerful aphrodisiacs: they will pay almost any price to obtain it. Every part of all three Asiatic species is used by Chinese pharmacists, including horns, hide, meat, various organs, blood, bones, and even urine.

Although the Sumatran rhino lived in inaccessible regions remote from human habitation, the price offered proved an irresistible incentive and it was hunted ruthlessly wherever it existed. The Dayaks of Borneo, for example, made a very good business of hunting it for sale to the Chinese. The nomadic Punans of Central Borneo were reputed to have developed the method of silently following the animal, if necessary for weeks, until they found an opportunity of using their blowpipes and poisoned darts.

In Sumatra the Battas were said to creep up close to the rhinoceros and hamstring it with a sharp knife. Other hunting tools included deadfalls made from weighted spears suspended over rhino paths, or well-camouflaged pitfalls dug in the ground along their trails.

As the human population increased and spread, the rhino's habitat diminished correspondingly, and pressure on the remaining population thus multiplied. During the last 100 years this multiplication has even further accelerated, the fate of the species being finally sealed in most areas by the introduction of more sophisticated weapons.

Small and isolated populations of Sumatran rhinos still exist in a few widely separated localities in Burma, Thailand, Malaya, Sumatra, and Sabah. Others may possibly have survived in the Lushai Hills and the Tirup Frontier Tract in India, and in the Chittagong Hills of East Pakistan, as well as in parts of Cambodia, Laos, Vietnam, and Kalimantan.

The total world population is estimated at between 100 and 170, and is distributed as follows: Thailand (on the Tenasserim border) six; Cambodia possibly ten; Borneo perhaps ten to thirty; Burma twenty to thirty; Malaya possibly thirty; Sumatra possibly sixty.

As recently as the 1920s the species was abundant in the Mekong valley, and at an earlier period it was widely distributed throughout Cambodia, Laos, and Vietnam. It has now almost entirely disappeared from that large region.

Only two of the existing reserves in Burma are thought to have resident rhinos. More sanctuaries are therefore needed to cover the range of the largest possible number of the surviving stock. Unless such sanctuaries are made and actively protected, it will be only a matter of time, and not a very long time, before the last specimen is exterminated.

In Malaya the pace of rural development, which has notably accelerated during the last five or six years, has caused large areas of wild country to be put under cultivation. Pressure on the few surviving rhinos is therefore constantly mounting. Only ten are definitely known to exist in the entire country, but a recent report suggests that there may be about thirty. They are scattered throughout the country, and consist mainly of solitary specimens or pairs. The maximum number in any one group is estimated at four, a situation suggesting that the few survivors are now so widely separated, and are subject to such disturbance, that breeding may possibly be inhibited, though David L. Strickland found evidence in 1966 that viable groups may survive in the Sungei Dusun Game Reserve and possibly in the Bintang Hijau Forest Reserve in northern Perak.

The most recent report from Sumatra estimates the total rhino population at sixty animals. Some of them live in the Löser Reserve of 1,090,000 acres in northern Sumatra; others are known to be in the wild and little known South Sumatran Nature Reserve. But the largest number is said to be in the low-lying swampy regions of Riau.

Less than a century ago, the Sumatran rhino was widespread in Borneo and in some localities was regarded as common, but the decline came rapidly. According to Tom Harrisson, it is doubtful whether more than thirty individuals have survived in the whole of Borneo, and the animal has definitely ceased to exist in Sarawak. The only bright spot in an otherwise depressing picture is the recent report indicating the presence of a few specimens on Mount Kinabalu, an area that has recently been proclaimed a national park.

The species is legally protected over the greater part of its range, but the law is extremely difficult to enforce. In Burma, for example, there is a strange legal anomaly: although the animal is "fully protected" by law, the sale of rhino blood and other parts is perfectly legitimate. Moreover, several cases are known in which senior (Burmese) officials have been officially authorized to kill rhinos "for medicinal purposes".

Law-enforcement is essential if the species is to survive; but in several countries the law needs revision to plug the loopholes that prevent it from being fully effective.

At the same time there is a pressing need to reinforce the protection of the few reserves in which the species is known to exist, and to create new reserves wherever significant numbers of the animals are reported. But much additional survey-work is needed to ascertain precisely where these groups of survivors are, and to fix suitable boundaries for areas designed to protect them. This will not be easy, because the species is a wanderer; and reserves will have to be of a substantial size.

It is, of course, possible that the wandering habit may be to some extent a direct result of human disturbance, and that, if undisturbed, the animals might conceivably settle down in quite a restricted area. Not the least effect of the rising price in rhino products is that it is now very difficult for an investigator to obtain any information concerning the whereabouts of any surviving animals, because anyone with such knowledge would almost certainly want to keep it to himself and turn it to his own advantage.

Any attempt, therefore, to draw up a plan for the conservation of the Sumatran rhino is frustrated at every turn by the fact that so very little is known about the habits and requirements of the species. This is illustrated by the ignorance surrounding the animal's breeding biology. Thus a female Sumatran rhino captured near Chittagong in 1868 was eventually purchased by the Zoological Society of London and reached England in 1872. While in the docks the animal gave birth, and, according to Lydekker's account, "from facts that came to his knowledge, the late Mr A. D. Bartlett was led to conclude that the period of gestation in the species was only a little over seven months". This statement is still quoted in recent publications, but is obviously inaccurate in view of the known gestation periods of the other two Asiatic species, which are almost three times as long.

In terms of practical conservation, the overriding fact that emerges from any discussion of the status of the three species of Asiatic rhinos is that Indonesia has the largest surviving stocks of two of them, *D. sumatrensis* in Sumatra and *R. sondaicus* in Java. The survival of these species is therefore primarily in the hands of the Government of Indonesia, a privilege and a responsibility that, if accepted and acted upon with vigour, would ensure Indonesia a leading place among the countries that have risen to the challenge of conserving the world's rarest species.

The sole animal presently in captivity, a female, has been in the Copenhagen Zoo for some years.

SQUARE-LIPPED *or* WHITE RHINOCEROS
Ceratotherium simum

The genus *Ceratotherium* consists of a single species, with two living subspecies. It is the largest living land mammal after the elephant, an adult male standing 6 feet 6 inches at the shoulder and weighing 3 tons or more. Notable features are a massive head, a prominent shoulder hump, the twin horns, and a characteristic broad muzzle from which both the animal's common names are derived: the most convincing explanation of "white" rhinoceros is that it is a corruption of the Dutch *wijd*, meaning "wide". This rhino's front horn sometimes reaches a great length; the record is $62\frac{1}{4}$ inches for the southern race, $47\frac{1}{4}$ inches for the northern.

The square-lipped rhinoceros is essentially an animal of perennial grasslands, and at one time it occupied an extensive range in Africa south of the Sahara wherever suitable savannah country could be found. Indeed, in Pleistocene times, as fossils tell us, it ranged to Morocco and Algeria, north of the present Sahara. The living races are now restricted to two regions separated from each other by more than 2,000 miles.

Until the latter part of the nineteenth century the northern race, *C. s. cottoni*, was widely distributed from the west bank of the Nile in the Sudan to Lake Tchad, roughly between 9° N. and 13° N. Since the beginning of the century, however, both range and numbers have drastically declined.

Today, the northern race exists in the southwestern Sudan west of the White Nile, in parts of the West Nile Province of Uganda along the western bank of the Albert Nile, and in the Garamba National Park in the extreme northeast of the Congo.

A few square-lips also cling precariously to existence in the Ndende and Birao areas of northern Ubangui in the Central African Republic. For more than fifty years no reliable information on the survival of the animal in that country could be obtained, and the species was assumed to have been exterminated there. In 1965, however, the I.U.C.N. received information that three individuals had been sighted, and that there might be up to a maximum of ten in the area. Earlier reports of extermination may, of course, have been correct, and the present animals may possibly be recent immigrants from the Sudan.

Until a few years ago, the most stable population was found in the Garamba National Park, where a census undertaken in 1960 showed a total of about 700 rhinos; by 1963 the figure had increased to perhaps 1,000. A little poaching by raiders from across the Sudanese border was kept firmly under control by the park's wardens and rangers. In 1963, however, the situation deteriorated abruptly when rebel forces crossed the border from bases in the Sudan, virtually occupying the entire national park and a large adjacent region. The rebel soldiery, who were armed with the most modern weapons, indulged in a great slaughter, as a result of which it has been estimated that at least 900 rhinos were killed. It is thought unlikely that more than 100 survived the massacre – and this may be an over-optimistic estimate.

The situation in the Sudan is obscure. No wildlife survey has been undertaken in either the Bahr-el-Ghazal or Equatoria, the two provinces in parts of which square-lipped rhinos exist. Thus there are no reliable population figures, and estimates vary from a few hundred to 2,000. It is known that the subspecies was strongly protected until at least 1963, as a result of the rigorous measures taken by the Sudan Government against poachers; and it is possible that the southern Sudan harbours the largest numbers of square-lipped rhinos in the world, though no up-to-date information is available.

In Uganda there has been a very severe decline in numbers since the Second World War. Despite the efforts of the Game Department, poaching has for some years been rife in the strip of land (about 70 miles long and 20 to 30 miles wide) in which the animals existed; and numbers decreased from about 350 in 1955 to fewer than eighty in 1962. Because the situation was clearly hopeless, measures have been taken to capture some of the survivors on the West Nile and move them into the Murchison Falls National Park. Since 1961, a small breeding nucleus has been successfully introduced into the park, and it appears to be prospering. In view of the gradual development of the West Nile District, which includes proposals for the construction of new roads and a railway as well as increased settlement throughout the area, the survival of the species in Uganda appears to be wholly dependent upon this newly established group and any other specimens that can be added to it.

Enough has been said to show that the status of the northern race is unsatisfactory, and that a drastic decline has taken place throughout its entire range. The record during the last few decades, and particularly during the last five years, suggests that in prevailing circumstances the only practical means of safeguarding such a vulnerable animal lies in strongly administered national parks where it can be adequately protected.

This view is supported by the recent history of the species in South Africa. In historical times the square-lipped rhino was widely distributed in the southern third of Africa as far south as the Orange River.

Before the coming of the Europeans it was extraordinarily abundant, and, being almost without natural enemies, it had (according to that great hunter, Selous) "increased almost to the limit of its food supply. Within fifty years, however, of the time when Cornwallis Harris had met with the white rhinoceros in almost incredible numbers . . . thousands upon thousands of these huge creatures were killed by white hunters, and natives armed with the white man's weapons, and the species had become practically extinct".

In spite of its huge size, the square-lipped rhinoceros, unless provoked, is normally an inoffensive animal that is ridiculously easy to approach and to kill. Not only were its horns in considerable demand, but its flesh was much esteemed: Selous declared the meat to be "superior to that of any other game animal in South Africa". In addition, its hide was valuable for making whips, which were widely used in those days, when ox waggons were the usual means of transport.

Selous recorded an instance of one trader who supplied firearms to more than 400 natives to hunt rhinos on his behalf. He also stated that the animal was still abundant in 1872 in what is now Rhodesia; but, from about 1880 onwards, it steadily declined. Fifteen years later almost every square-lipped rhino between Salisbury and the Zambezi had been killed.

Farther south the story was the same. By 1880 the animal had vanished from the northern Cape Province, South-West Africa, and Botswana; by 1896 it had been exterminated in Transvaal; and by the end of the century had ceased to exist in Mozambique.

The position today is that the southern race, *C. s. simum*, has been wiped out everywhere except for a small pocket in the south-eastern extremity of the range in Zululand comprising the Umfolozi and Hluhluwe game reserves and the land immediately adjacent. Stringent controls introduced by the Natal Parks, Fish and Game Preservation Board have given full protection to the animal, and each year for more than thirty years the population has steadily increased. As a result of sound conservation measures, the southern race, once on the brink of extinction, has been restored to abundance, and its name has therefore been taken out of the Red Data Book. The very success of the Board's measures has in fact created a situation where sheer pressure of numbers has become almost embarrassing.

The Board's predicament is better appreciated when it is realized that, properly protected, the rate of reproduction of this rhino can be surprisingly rapid: the net annual increment in Natal is at least 12½ per cent and is thought to be increasing. Breeding may begin at the relatively early age of four or five years; and a single calf (there are occasional records of twins) is born after a gestation period of about eighteen months. The calf is able to accompany its mother within twenty-four hours of birth, and is suckled for about a year. Adult females may often be accompanied by two (and sometimes three) calves at different stages of development, ranging from new-born through half-grown to almost mature.

In August 1965 there were 606 square-lipped rhinos in Umfolozi, a figure that is well beyond the area's optimum carrying capacity, a further seventy-five at Hluhluwe, and about 130 in neighbouring parts of Zululand. To help the survival of the southern race, it will be necessary to reduce the population and so preserve the strictly limited habitat.

No fewer than 330 have been already introduced into other national parks in South Africa, Rhodesia, and even as far afield as Kenya, and a further 63 have been sold to zoos. The park authorities are offering specimens to interested conservation organizations. There are limits, however, to the numbers that can be disposed of in this way, mainly on account of the high costs arising from the time and effort involved in the capture and translocation of these bulky animals. Each year the total population increases by about eighty, and at this rate the market is quickly saturated.

The recovery of the southern race is an outstanding recent example of what practical conservation can achieve. As long as the habitat can be properly protected against the effects of overstocking, the future of the southern subspecies seems assured.

BLACK RHINOCEROS
Diceros bicornis

The genus here consists of a single living species; but some authors also include its closest living relative, the white or square-lipped rhinoceros, in *Diceros*. The "black" rhino is smaller than the "white", standing about 4 feet 9 inches to 5 feet 6 at the shoulder and weighing about 1½ to 1¾ tons. The muzzles of the two species are markedly different in that the black rhino's upper lip is pointed and its tip prehensile, thus stressing the fact that it is essentially a browser whereas its relative is a grazer. The black rhino's "hooked" lip is used for stripping leaves and twigs from the bushes and shrubs on which it feeds. Both sexes have a pair of horns, the front one being the longer, averaging about 20 inches although the record is 53½. Individuals with more than two horns have occasionally been recorded. The species is normally associated with arid thorn-scrub country, but in Kenya it can also be found in the high forests of Mount Kenya and the Aberdare Range, sometimes existing at an altitude of more than 10,000 feet above sea-level.

Black rhinoceros *Peter Scott* 1967

The black rhino appears to have no particular breeding season; and a single young is born after a gestation period of about twelve to eighteen months. The calf stays with its mother for as long as two years, often remaining with her after the birth of the subsequent calf. Sexual maturity is reached at about five years of age. Under normal conditions the net annual population increase has been estimated at about 5 to 8 per cent – considerably less than that of the square-lipped species.

The black rhino also differs substantially from its relative in temperament. Its reputation for being thoroughly bad-tempered has probably been exaggerated, but without question it is unsociably disposed and can be aggressive. Its truculence may be partly due to its poor eyesight, although it is keen of scent and hearing. When disturbed, it may undertake a blustering charge towards the source of the disturbance. It may equally well dash off at a tangent. In spite of its huge bulk, it is surprisingly agile and can "turn on a sixpence" as impressively as any polo pony.

The black rhino's poor eyesight is to some extent compensated by its association with tick birds. This association is mutually advantageous, the birds feeding on the parasites of their host, who is warned by their alarm notes of any potentially hostile intruders.

The black rhino is generally found alone or in pairs, and usually in a definite locality, which the male will defend vigorously against rivals. On occasion this apparently territorial be-haviour can react to the animal's disadvantage, as, for example, during the 1960–1 drought, when 282 rhinos were known to have died of malnutrition in Kenya's Tsavo National Park. Almost all the casualties occurred along the Athi and Tsavo rivers. The rhinos could have saved themselves had they moved only a few miles over the Yatta plateau to the Tiva River, where browse was relatively abundant, but they preferred to remain in their own territories to the bitter end. By the time the rains came, approximately half the total number estimated to be living in the area had died.

The species was first encountered by Euro-peans in 1653 near Cape Town. At the time of its discovery, it was widely distributed in Africa from Cape Province and south-western Angola to eastern Africa, including Somalia, south-western Ethiopia, and the southern Sudan. From there the range extended westward along a relatively narrow strip between the southern edge of the Sahara Desert and the northern limits of the dense rain forests of the Congo and Nigeria, as far as Lake Tchad and Cameroon. Within this huge region there were, of course, areas where rhinos were absent, as, for example, along the coasts of Kenya and Tanzania and between the Chobe and the Zambezi rivers.

The greatest retraction of range has taken place south of the Limpopo, where the species now exists only in Zululand, and south of the Cunene, where it is now found in small numbers only in the northern part of South-West Africa.

Elsewhere the black rhino has been reduced to a remnant, except in a few national parks and other sanctuaries where special measures have been taken to protect it. Hobley, writing in 1936, estimated that during the previous twenty years the rhino population had declined to about 20 per cent of its former numbers. Since then, of course, the rate of decline has not lessened, and in most parts of Africa it has accelerated – a trend that continues with scarcely a check.

Africans do not attribute any magical or superhuman qualities to rhino products. The Masai greatly prize a *rungu*, or knobkerrie, carved from the horn, although nowadays examples are seldom seen; and the Somalis value the hide for making the small circular shields in which they take such pride. According to Swayne, rhinos were killed in the western part of Somalia especially for their hide, "which cuts up into seven good shields, leaving besides some strips for making whips". Some tribes will eat rhino flesh; but most Africans regard rhinos from an entirely mercenary standpoint, knowing that they can obtain a good price (although but a fraction of the true value) from the un-scrupulous Asian traders and middlemen who control the smuggling rings.

A survey undertaken by the I.U.C.N.'s Survival Service Commission in 1960 indicated that the total black rhino population was between 11,000 and 13,500. By far the largest surviving numbers (about half the total) are in Tanzania and Kenya. These figures show that the black rhino is the least rare of all the five living species. But it has been eliminated at an alarming rate,

PLATE 9 (*a*) Great Indian rhinoceros *C. F. Tunnicliffe, Brooke Bond* 1963; (*b*) Sumatran rhinoceros *Peter Scott, Brooke Bond* 1964; (*c*) Southern square-lipped rhinoceros *Peter Scott, Brooke Bond* 1964

(a)

(b)

(c)

The alphabetical references (b) and (c) should be transposed.

and the decline shows little sign of slowing down. Hobley mentions "one area in Kenya of about 1,600 square miles which twenty years ago contained several thousand rhino; today [1936] they have entirely disappeared from that region. European licensees may have killed a few hundred, the remainder have been poached. This rate of slaughter is widespread and not confined to one region".

A rather more recent example occurred shortly after the Second World War, when the Kenya Game Department commissioned J. A. Hunter to exterminate rhinos in the Makueni District so as to open an area of 50,000 acres for a Kamba agricultural settlement scheme. His final tally was 1,088 rhinos killed.

The Makueni rhinos were destroyed in order to make way for a settlement scheme on marginal land that was incapable of supporting more than the crudest form of subsistence agriculture. Between 1946 and 1959, a total of £307,535 was spent on bush clearance and the installation of water supplies, and a further £15,377 in the form of loans and grants. This heavy expenditure did not prevent the scheme from becoming a failure through lack of co-operation from the Wakamba settlers. Thus the destruction of the Makueni rhinos – animals ideally adapted to the prevailing harsh environment that made the region unsuitable for conventional forms of agriculture – does not appear to have served any constructive purpose.

In many other parts of Africa similar situations have arisen, although on a smaller scale. The presence of rhinos was incompatible with settlement: in many places they were systematically exterminated. The animals' huge bulk, stupidity, and blundering tendencies make them an easy prey to modern firearms. The species is legally protected throughout the greater part of its range; but legal protection alone is not enough to counter the dual threat to its existence: loss of suitable habitat as development proceeds, and illegal hunting for its horn.

The best hope for the future of the species appears to lie in the national parks and equivalent reserves where adequate protection can be given. Efforts should be made to transfer animals from those areas where they conflict with development, or where they cannot be adequately protected, into suitable sanctuaries. During the last few years there have been some notable advances in the types of drugs and the techniques used for the immobilization of wild animals. The importance of these developments to the future of the black rhino and several other endangered species can scarcely be overstated: they have opened up entirely new fields of practicality. Ten years ago the only means of dealing with an "unwanted" rhino was to kill it; today it can be immobilized with drugs and transported to a sanctuary with relatively little difficulty.

Several countries have already used the drug and translocation method to introduce or re-introduce rhinos. The Kenya Game Department, for example, has for several years used a special "capture team" for the purpose, while Tanzania has succeeded in introducing more than twenty rhinos on to the island of Rubondo in Lake Victoria, transported there on rafts after being captured on the mainland in areas where they were in conflict with human interests.

Farther south, the National Parks Board of South Africa is considering the reintroduction of black rhinos into the Kruger National Park as soon as the programme for restocking the park with square-lipped rhinos has been completed.

PLATE 10 Wild Bactrian camels *D. W. Ovenden* 1966

Order Artiodactyla
Family Hippopotamidae: hippopotamuses

PYGMY HIPPOPOTAMUS
Choeropsis liberiensis

At a casual glance the pygmy hippopotamus might be mistaken for a juvenile common hippopotamus, but it differs so substantially from *Hippopotamus amphibius* not only in size but in many other characteristics, that it has been placed in a separate genus of its own. Adults stand about 2 feet 6 inches at the shoulder, are about 6 feet long, and weigh from 390 to 500 pounds or more. Its skull is proportionately smaller than that of the common hippo, and carries only a single pair of lower incisor teeth, whereas that of its larger relative has two pairs. Its canine teeth, on the other hand, have developed into prominent tushes. Its colour has been described as "shining greyish blue-black".

Deposits reveal that the animal's forebears were widely distributed during the Pleistocene; but its modern distribution is confined to a relatively small part of West Africa from the extreme south-east of Guinea to the Ivory Coast (where it is reputed to be most abundant), including parts of Liberia and Sierra Leone. It is also reported to exist in part of the Rivers Province of Nigeria.

Within this range the pygmy hippo inhabits dense, low-lying swamp forests, and marshy regions. It is nocturnal, spending the day lying up in riverine thickets. Although it swims well, it is much less aquatically inclined than its larger relative. When alarmed, the common hippo's inclination is always to head for the nearest river; the pygmy hippo, on the other hand, makes for the forest.

The common hippo forms herds, sometimes very large, but the pygmy is of a solitary disposition, usually being found alone or in pairs. Some reports state that it is more placid than the big species; but such statements do not come from those who have handled it in zoos.

The animal is believed to be territorial in habit and to adopt a more or less standardized ranging routine, using the same paths at the same time each day. But very little is known of its habits or ecology, and study of it is made difficult by the nature of the habitat. It is reputed to be everywhere thinly distributed; although its trails – which in places resemble tunnels through the dense undergrowth – are very obvious, it is possible for a naturalist to spend a long time in its country without seeing one. Despite these difficulties, it is vital that an ecological survey should be attempted: without a reasonably accurate estimate of the animal's current status, no precise prescription of the measures likely to safeguard it can be arrived at. That such action is needed is abundantly evident.

Information on human predation of the pygmy hippo is conflicting. Some reports state that the local tribesmen make no special effort to kill it: Büttikofer, on the other hand, spoke of the natives' "relish for the flesh which tastes like that of wild pig", from which one must conclude that at least in parts of its range it is probably deliberately hunted.

This suggestion appears to be supported by the fact that in 1887 Büttikofer collected the animal on the banks of the Du Queah River in Liberia, whereas in 1930 Strong stated that "these animals are rapidly disappearing and we were unable to find one in Liberia". Blancou, writing in 1960 of other parts of the range, says that "in spite of total protection it is nevertheless diminishing alarmingly".

The first record of a living specimen outside Africa seems to be one at the Dublin Zoo, where

Pygmy hippopotamus *D. W. Ovenden* 1966

it was recorded by Sclater (1873), but it did not survive for long. Almost forty years passed before Europe saw another.

In 1912, following a two years' field trip, Schomburgk delivered five specimens to Karl Hagenbeck, the well-known animal-dealer on whose behalf he was acting. Three of them (two males and a female) were sold to the New York Zoological Park, where one of them lived for thirty-eight and another for thirty-nine years.

Since then the species has become well established in captivity, where it appears to thrive. The Basle Zoo has been outstandingly successful in breeding the animal and has already raised more than thirty. In mid-1965 there were eighty-five animals in thirty-three zoos – thirty-eight of them zoo-bred. Its continued existence is therefore doubtless ensured by what has become an important zoo bank (of which a stud book is being planned) – but the need still remains for a field investigation into the status of the species, which can be used as a basis for recommendations leading to the protection of the animal in its natural habitat.

Family Camelidae: camels

WILD BACTRIAN CAMEL
Camelus bactrianus ferus

The genus *Camelus* has two living species, the one-humped *C. dromedarius*, which probably originated in Arabia but which now exists only in domesticated form, and *C. bactrianus*, the two-humped camel from Mongolia and Chinese Turkestan. It has been found generally convenient to regard the "typical" domesticated form, widely used as a beast of burden, as racially distinct from the surviving wild stock, described by the great Russian naturalist Przewalski in 1883 as *Camelus bactrianus ferus*.

The validity of *C. b. ferus* has sometimes been called into question on the grounds that its wild population may have become mixed with domesticated stock run wild; but the weight of evidence that has now accumulated appears to support the contention that it is a true wild stock, carrying no genes from domestic stock.

Compared with the domestic form, the wild camel is more slenderly proportioned and less hairy, with shorter snout and ears, smaller humps and feet; it is less heavily built. Individuals vary in colour, ranging from dark brown to lightish grey.

The wild camel is well able to endure the extreme temperatures of the harsh environment it lives in. During the great heat of the summer, herds climb into the mountainous regions to an altitude of 11,000 feet or more; in winter they return to the desert. They can drink the brackish water of the Mongolian steppe that is un-palatable to most animals.

Until the 1920s *C. b. ferus* could still be found throughout the greater part of the Gobi. Numbers then dwindled; and for some years after the Second World War the subspecies was believed to be extinct. This fear has recently been proved unfounded. It is now known that the herds are split into two main groups – one in the south-western part of Mongolia, and the other in north-western China between lakes Lob Nor and Bagrach Kol. The Chinese sector of the range is close to the Silk Road and covers about 12,000 square miles.

No recent information is available about the status of the animal in China, except that it is believed to be extremely rare. In Mongolian Gobi it is apparently stable, and the principal population has been assessed at about 400 to 500 animals. Other less numerous groups exist, but their total has not been accurately estimated.

The wild Bactrian camel declined partly as a result of heavy persecution by hunters – its meat, which in the autumn is very fat, was used for food and its skins for clothing – and partly through competition for the scarce water and grazing with increasing herds of domestic animals. As far back as 1879 Przewalski wrote: "Twenty years ago, wild camels were numerous near Lake Lob, where the village of Chargalik now stands, and farther to the east along the foot of the Altyn-tagh, as well as in the range itself. Our guide, a hunter of Chargalik, told us that it was not unusual in those days, to see some dozens, or even a hundred of these animals together. He himself had killed upwards of a hundred of them in the course of his life (and he was an old man), with a flint and steel musket. With an increase of population at Chargalik, the hunters of Lob Nor became more numerous, and camels scarcer. Now, the wild camel only frequents the neighbourhood of Lob Nor, and even here in small numbers. Years pass without so much as one being seen; in more favourable seasons again the native hunters kill their five and six during the summer and autumn . . ." Dementiev suggests that in recent times the wide dispersal of fragmented herds has probably contributed to the decline.

The Mongols also used to catch young wild camels to train as riding animals. In the 1880s Younghusband was told that they could travel 200 miles a day for a week; but such claims should be treated with caution, as owners no doubt exaggerated the prowess of their beasts. There is general agreement that the wild camel could never be broken to carry a load.

The wild Bactrian camel is now fully protected both in Mongolia and in China. Hunting of the animal is forbidden, and heavy penalties are imposed for any infringement of the law.

As far as can be ascertained, the only specimens in captivity are one in Peking Zoo (mid-1965), the survivor of a pair of young captured in Chinese Inner Mongolia in 1959, and a small semi-domesticated herd that is maintained in the province of Gobi-Altai in the Mongolian People's Republic – where there is also a herd of hybrids between wild and domesticated camels. There appears to be no record that *C. b. ferus* has ever bred in captivity.

Family Cervidae: deer

PERSIAN FALLOW DEER
Dama mesopotamica

The genus *Dama* embraces two living species, one the subject of this article and the other the European fallow deer, *D. dama*, which is native to the Mediterranean region but has been widely introduced into many countries in Europe and elsewhere.

The Persian species is a good deal larger than the common fallow deer, and much more brightly coloured. Like its relative, it is spotted on the neck and upper parts of its body; but the white spots along each side of its dark dorsal stripe blend into one another to form an unbroken line. The antlers of the two species also differ: those of *D. dama* are flattened at the tips, whereas those of *D. mesopotamica* are not – indeed, they represent a type unique among the Cervidae.

During the Pleistocene the Persian species was widely distributed over parts of the Middle East and north-eastern Africa. It was well known in biblical times. In an interesting paper published in 1965, Charles A. Read has drawn attention to bas-reliefs near Kermanshah in west-central Iran of hunting scenes during the Sassanian Dynasty (A.D. 226–641), one of them depicting fallow deer hunted in an arena by a royal personage. After that, the animal seems to have faded from sight until its rediscovery by Sir Victor Brooke, who first named it scientifically in 1875.

Within about fifty years of its rediscovery, the species was generally regarded as extinct. "Last specimens" were reported to have been shot in northern Iraq in 1917 and in Luristan (Iran) in 1906.

In 1955 Dr Lee M. Talbot, then the I.U.C.N.'s Staff Ecologist engaged in a field mission in the region on behalf of the I.U.C.N.'s Survival Service Commission, obtained information that small numbers of *D. mesopotamica* could still be found in the dense riverine vegetation along the banks of the Dez and Karkeh rivers in Khuzestan, south-western Iran.

Talbot passed this information to Werner Trense, who in the next year visited the region and was able to confirm the accuracy of the report. In 1957 Dr Georg von Opel arranged for Trense to return to the area. One of the results of his expedition was the capture of an immature stag; the following year a doe was added, both being taken to Kronberg in Germany, where Dr von Opel proposed to establish a herd. The first birth occurred in 1960, but unfortunately the stag died in the same year, and it was not possible at that time to obtain a replacement.

The species is now known to survive in only two small areas (each about 2,500 acres) of riverine thicket along the Dez and Karkeh rivers. Because of the nature of the habitat, numbers are difficult to assess, but in 1966 the total population was thought to be no more than thirty to forty individuals. Almost all of them are believed to be along the Dez River, the group along the Karkeh River having been reduced to an estimated three individuals.

Talbot also said there was a possibility that fallow deer might still survive in one place in Iraq, close to the Persian border between Maidan and Halabja, the area being malarial and therefore avoided by man. In 1959, however, Hatt concluded that, if the species still managed to exist in Iraq, it must be exceptionally rare.

The Persian fallow deer was long ago hunted to the point of extinction throughout almost its entire range; and the few animals clinging to existence in Khuzestan owe their survival to the nature of the riverine vegetation, which in places over a stretch of about twenty miles is almost impenetrable.

Although man cannot himself penetrate the thickets, the deer's ultimate refuge has during the last few years been increasingly assailed by domestic livestock, notably the ubiquitous goat, but including cattle, camels, and water buffalo. The marginal cover has also been reduced by the villagers who cut the wood for fuel.

Suitable agricultural land is scarce, and, as the area occupied by the fallow deer is potentially valuable for agriculture, pressure from the rising human population inevitably means conversion of the habitat to man's use. According to Reed, Khuzestan is "destined to be the granary of Iran again as it was in the time of Darius".

For this reason, the only way of ensuring the survival of the species lies in capturing as many specimens as possible and translocating them to areas where adequate measures can be taken to protect them.

The Game Council of Iran is very conscious of the need for effective action, while opportunity still exists, and it has already begun the establishment of a breeding nucleus. Several animals have been captured and placed in the 50-acre Dasht-e-Naz Reserve, situated on the south-eastern shore of the Caspian, about 16 miles north of Sari, the capital of Mazanderan.

The Game Council plans to allow stocks to breed in the Dasht-e-Naz Reserve, and hopes, after a few years, to introduce breeding groups into other protected areas, spreading the species as widely as possible to minimize the risk of losses through disease or other factors.

As an additional form of insurance against the future, the Survival Service Commission would also like to see other breeding herds established in Europe and elsewhere. Dr von Opel made good the loss of his stag by one acquired in 1965, and in 1968 the Kronberg herd consisted of three males and four females.

The concern of the Game Council of Iran is very laudable, and it is to be hoped that the Council's earnest attempts to rescue from oblivion a species that is unique to the country, and one of the noblest members of the deer family, will meet with success.

BROW-ANTLERED DEER
Cervus eldi

This South-East Asian deer has three races, of which the Burmese, *C. e. thamin*, is not at present in danger of extinction. But the other two races have sheets in the Red Data Book.

The Thailand race, *C. e. siamensis*, formerly abundant in the plains and forests from southern Thailand and Cambodia through Laos and Vietnam to Hainan, is now reduced and split into relict populations in all areas, excepting parts of Cambodia.

The typical race, *C. e. eldi*, the Manipur brow-antlered deer, is now so rare that it gives the greatest concern to the Survival Service Commission.

C. e. eldi stands about 4 feet at the shoulder and weighs up to 250 pounds. In winter coat stags are of a uniform dark brown, whitish below, changing in summer to chestnut with pale brown under parts. Hinds remain a paler reddish-fawn throughout the year; young fawns are spotted with white. The hooves of the Manipur race are adapted to the special conditions of its habitat and are unlike those of the other two subspecies. The pasterns are horny and greatly elongated to help the animal in moving over the dense mass of vegetation, known in the vernacular as *phumdi*, that carpets the surface of their last refuge, the Logtak Lake.

Phumdi can be described as a floating mat, varying in thickness from a few inches to several feet, and comprising a base of dead or decaying organic matter on which grow reeds, grasses, and other vegetation. It is comparable to the *schwingmoor* of Europe. The deer, when crossing the *phumdi*, has been described as appearing to proceed "on its hind legs, the body being held almost vertical".

The Logtak Lake is situated in Manipur State, India, and the deer exists only in the southwestern part of it. It is the largest lake in the area. Nearby are many smaller lakes, or *jheels*, which are almost or completely dry at certain times of the year. During the rainy season, much of the surrounding valley is flooded to a depth of a few inches, at which time rice is extensively cultivated.

Heavy rain takes time to seep through the *phumdi*, and the weight of water causes it to sink deeper into the lake. At that time the deer leaves the lake for drier areas, and is then believed to wander considerable distances. As the inundated vegetation dries out, it gradually rises higher in the water; and the deer returns to it. This seasonal movement creates difficult problems in protecting the animal from human and canine predators. The Bombay Natural History Society reported during the 1930s, for example, that "in time of high flood the animals are driven out of their haunts to isolated places of high ground and slaughtered regardless of sex or age".

At one time the subspecies (locally known as the *sangai*) may have occupied a more extensive range, possibly into the nearby foothills, before agricultural development and human pressure on the land compelled the population to withdraw to the lake, almost the only part of the original range that was not taken over for human use. The present habitat may therefore not be of the animal's own choosing; but this is only conjecture. What is certain is that the

animal has substantially declined since 1842, when Eld reported having "frequently seen herds of two or three hundred" after the annual grass-burning. Although no accurate census is possible in such difficult terrain, E. P. Gee estimates the present-day population at about 100.

Until 1891 the subspecies was strictly protected by royal edict – the penalty for killing being amputation of a hand; but, when the British assumed responsibility for the country's administration, the local people lost no time in taking advantage of the relaxation of this traditional practice, and many deer were surrounded and speared by groups of men mounted on buffalo.

The recent diminution of the surviving stock derives from the unsettled conditions during and immediately after the Second World War. The decline was sufficiently drastic to compel the Manipur Forest Department to conclude in 1951 that the deer had become extinct. This conclusion later proved premature: in 1952–3 strenuous efforts by a few interested local naturalists confirmed the fact that small numbers still existed.

In October 1953 the Logtak Lake was officially designated a sanctuary by the Government of Manipur. Less than a year later, however, the lake, excepting the southern part in which the deer lived, was opened to shooting. This left an area of approximately 13,000 acres known as the Keibul Lamjao Sanctuary. The surface area was afterwards further reduced to 7,000 acres.

The deer has been legally protected since 1934; but its survival has been due less to legislation than to the impenetrable nature of its habitat and – most important of all – to the fact that most of the villagers in the region are vegetarian Manipuris who do not hunt or kill the deer.[1] This does not detract from the praise due to the Government of Manipur for the constructive measures it has taken to safeguard the animal in the face of considerable difficulties.

Not the least of the problems relating to protection of the deer lies in the presence of

---

[1] Not far from the sanctuary, however, are four Muslim villages whose inhabitants would have no such compunction.

villages along the sanctuary's southern and western boundaries. The villagers own large herds of cattle and water buffalo. Although cattle are unable to enter the *phumdi*, the buffalo regularly graze about 1,600 acres of the sanctuary. Rice is grown on a substantial scale; and land along the western boundary – as well as a 60-acre strip thrusting into the centre of the sanctuary – has been cultivated. Moreover, an estimated 1,000 dug-outs are engaged in fishing throughout the entire sanctuary area, penetrating the *phumdi* along narrow tracks where the vegetation is thin or absent.

There is therefore an unquestionable need to strengthen the protective measures already taken. Gee, in his valuable report to the I.U.C.N. in 1961 on the status of the Manipur brow-antlered deer, recommends among other measures the prohibition of rice cultivation within the sanctuary; the prohibition or severe restriction of grazing by domestic buffaloes; control of fishing and reed-cutting inside the boundaries; the appointment of adequate permanent staff; and an ecological study of the subspecies and its unusual habitat.

SIKA
Cervus nippon

The sika was once widely distributed through Japan and Formosa, as well as on the Asiatic mainland from the southern part of the Ussuri district of Eastern Siberia through Manchuria and parts of eastern China as far as northern Kwangtung.

There is some difference of opinion over classification, but the consensus of opinion of most modern authorities recognizes seven subspecies, which vary considerably in size and general appearance. All are to a greater or lesser extent spotted with white when in summer coat; and all possess a distinct throat and neck mane during the winter, together with a conspicuous erectile rump patch edged with black. All are forest dwellers in the wild state, but in captivity they readily adapt to open grasslands.

Stock of several races of this fine deer has been introduced in various parts of the world, where the animals have become feral – for instance, in the British Isles. Five of the seven races are now regarded as in danger of extinction in their native lands: the only races that are not (yet) held to be so are the "typical" race, *C. n. nippon*, of the Japanese archipelago, and the Manchurian race, *C. n. hortulorum*, of Russian Ussuriland, Manchuria, far-eastern China, and Korea. Each of the Red Data Book races can be treated separately, as follows:

Formosan sika, *Cervus nippon taiouanus*

The Formosan sika has been described as the most handsome of all the deer family. It is smaller than the northern mainland races, standing about 2 feet 11 inches at the shoulder, but larger than the Japanese race. Its background colour in summer coat is light chestnut, with prominent white spots, a deep chestnut tinge on the hinder part of the neck, and a strongly marked dorsal stripe. In winter its coat is thicker and darker and its spots less noticeable. The record size of antler is $19\frac{3}{4}$ inches.

According to Sowerby, the Formosan sika formerly lived in the high central mountains of Taiwan, parts of which were covered in perennial snow, where it seems at one time to have been quite common.

The decline has come about very rapidly. Under the Japanese occupation, the sika was stringently protected; but, within a few years of the end of the war, it had been hunted with such persistence that it had been killed out in the greater part of its range. At the same time the forested habitat – indispensable to its survival in the wild state – was ruthlessly destroyed. It seems that the animal does not have even nominal protection.

Philip Wayre, whose excellent *Advisory Report on the Wildlife of Taiwan* (1968) contains the most up-to-date information on this subspecies, provides evidence that it must now be close to extinction in the wild state. However, it still occurs in small numbers in the central mountains of the Taitung region. The continued existence of a relict wild population is confirmed by recently caught specimens in the Taipei Zoological Gardens and by others in Taitung, several of which were maimed through being trapped by aborigines in the mountains. Occasional specimens also pass through the hands

Formosan sika and Ryukyu sika *D. W. Ovenden* 1966

of animal traders in Taitung, who purchase live animals from the aborigines for sale to restaurants.

In addition to the fifty or so sika at the Taipei Zoo, a herd of about 100 to 200 is maintained on Lu-tao (Green Island) about 18 miles east of Taitung. They are farmed for venison, not for the antlers, which, according to Wayre, are of small value compared with those of the sambar (Swinhoe's deer) *Cervus unicolor swinhoei.*

A few captive herds (over 300 animals) have been established in other countries; at Woburn and Whipsnade in England, for example. It is to these that one must look for the continued survival of the subspecies. There is nonetheless a pressing need, even at this late hour, for the Government of Taiwan to make a serious attempt to remedy its own previous neglect by establishing reserves to protect not only sika, but also various other representatives of the insular fauna, much of it unique and almost all of it gravely reduced, even to the point of extinction.

North China sika, *Cervus nippon mandarinus*

The white spots on the summer coat of this race are individually larger but less numerous than those of the Manchurian sika, *C. n. hortulorum,* and are retained throughout the year. Further distinctions in comparison with *hortulorum* are that its antlers are more wide-spreading, its general colour paler, and its belly not white but of the same colour as its flanks.

In the distant past this deer was probably widely distributed in the north-eastern part of China. Sowerby, writing in 1937, stated that at that time the only place in which wild living specimens still existed was in the Tung Ling area or Imperial Hunting Grounds, in Jehol (now known as Chengteh). It was also kept in captivity on deer farms in the same area.

Until the overthrow of the Manchu dynasty in 1911–12, the deer had been strictly protected; but Manchu soldiers encamped in the Imperial Hunting Grounds slaughtered many of the animals, and in later years no attempt appears to have been made to protect the remnants of the Imperial herds.

The position today is obscure. Some reports state that the subspecies is now extinct in the wild state, and such tenuous evidence as exists tends to support this belief. It is possible that small numbers may still survive on a few deer farms in Shansi Province; but no particulars are available.

South China sika, *Cervus nippon kopschi*

The south China race of sika is a small animal, only a little bigger than the Japanese race, and standing about 2 feet 10 inches at the shoulder. Its upper parts are mottled brown, with a dark vertebral stripe extending the full length of its back from head to tail and bordered on each side by a series of indistinct white spots. Its belly and the inner sides of its limbs are of varying shades of white.

This subspecies once existed over a large part of the lower Yangtze valley, extending southward into Chekiang and Kiangsi provinces, thence into northern Kwangtung and possibly even further south. In the 1880s and early 1890s it was still to be found in fair numbers in some localities. In 1915 Wallace wrote: "They inhabit rough, stony bush-clad hills about 4,000 feet high, and always keep in the densest cover"; but a quarter of a century later Allen stated that, although they normally frequent heavily forested country, they may descend in summer into open valleys with patches of thick cover.

Sowerby wrote in 1937 that by that time the race was almost extinct, but was to be found in a small area in the mountains of southern Anhui and the adjacent parts of north-western Chekiang and south-eastern Kiangsi.

Before the Second World War the animal was accorded no protection of any kind, and Sowerby recorded that it was "hunted mercilessly by local hunters", as a result of which "their extermination in the near future [was] certain".

The sika was the most heavily hunted animal in China, with the possible exception of the musk deer. All deer were, of course, ruthlessly persecuted by the Chinese; but the sika was at a particular disadvantage in that its antlers when in velvet were reputed to make one of the most potent aphrodisiacs known. In 1929 a pair of south China sika's antlers would fetch between £40 and £70. Glover wrote, in 1955: "The persistent hunting that results from such prices might do little harm if it were only done by stalking stags with a rifle, but the Chinaman makes free use of set-guns, snares and pitfalls also. The destruction of the deer themselves goes hand in hand with the destruction of their habitat; and the methods of slaughter used spare neither hind nor calf".

Hardly any information is available on the current status of the south China sika. Many authors have expressed the belief that *C. n. kopschi* is extinct in the wild state, but a recent report states, without giving details, that a few still exist in the Yangtze valley. It is now said to be rigidly protected by the Chinese authorities.

Shansi sika, *Cervus nippon grassianus*

This is one of the four larger races of Chinese sika deer, standing 3 feet 6 inches at the shoulder, the weight of an adult male being about 220 pounds. It is readily distinguishable because the spots, so distinctive a feature of the other races, are almost invisible on it both in summer and in winter. The general colour of its body is dark greyish-brown, becoming a rich brown on its back and the lower parts of its legs. Below the heel of its outer hind leg is a patch of long white hair edged with black.

According to Sowerby, the subspecies was at one time distributed "throughout the whole of the mountainous area of West Shansi, as well as in the mountains that extend in a north and south line between Shansi and Chihli".

The final stronghold of the race is (or was) in the highest parts of the montane forests of western Shansi, where Sowerby states that the last specimen known to have been shot was killed in 1920 by a Chinese hunter-guide.

The antlers of this sika were said to be in their prime in August and September, during which months the animal was most diligently hunted. The antlers were cut off, the velvet removed, and the horn dried and shredded before being boiled in soup and consumed.

Ceaseless and entirely uncontrolled hunting has coincided with widespread degradation of the once magnificent forests that were the sika's natural habitat, and without which the animal cannot survive in the wild state.

The current status of the Shansi sika is not known with certainty. It was practically extinct even in Sowerby's day. Indeed, it would be almost miraculous if any free-living specimens have survived the intervening thirty years. A recent report states that some of the leading Chinese zoos exhibit the animal: but no details are available.

Ryukyu sika, *Cervus nippon keramae*

This subspecies bears a close resemblance to the "typical" race that inhabits Japan. It was first described by Kuroda in 1924, and is distinguishable from *C. n. nippon* by the small size of its body and skull, as well as by its antlers, which are smaller and have more warty appendages.

The animal was, in fact, introduced into the Ryukyu Islands from Japan many years ago: the date of introduction is not known, but there is a record of deer in the islands in 1757. Its long isolation has resulted in the development of an insular form with distinctive characteristics.

The sika exists on three small islands in the Ryukyu group: Yakabi-Shima, Kuba-Shima, and Keruma-Shima.

The number of deer on Yakabi and Keruma in 1955 was approximately 160. Since then there has been a steady decline and the population is now down to about thirty.

The islands are very small (Yakabi, for example, is only $\frac{1}{2}$ square mile), and their forage is of a poor quality, possibly through the presence of goats, much of it being *Miscanthus sinensis*. There is also a shortage of water on the islands at certain times. There have, moreover, been various casualties. Some deer have fallen into a disused copper-ore separator tank that was built before the Second World War. Others have fallen from the steep cliffs (over 700 feet high) during the frequent sparring that takes place in the rutting season.

In January 1955 the Ryukyu sika was officially designated a natural monument, thereby acquiring full legal protection. Other measures that have been taken to safeguard the race include the demolition of the disused copper-mine constructions and the building of an artificial catchment for the provision of water. Plans have also been made to improve the grazing on Yakabi-Shima by the introduction of leguminous plants and the elimination of all goats from the island.

PÈRE DAVID'S DEER
Elaphurus davidianus

The history of Père David's deer provides an outstanding example of the role of captive herds in safeguarding a rare animal. The sole living representative of its genus, this species was destroyed in its country of origin, and would have become extinct everywhere but for the existence of a few specimens in European zoos. The initiative of one man was instrumental in bringing the few animals together to form a small breeding nucleus, which virtually ensured the survival of the genus.

The general colour of Père David's deer is tawny red tending to grey, its lower limbs being paler and under parts whitish. Its muzzle and a patch surrounding each eye are white. Its tail is tufted and longer than that of any other deer, reaching to its hocks. Its hooves are unusually broad. Its antlers also differ from those of any other member of the family in that their hind prongs are forked. A further unique feature is that two sets of antlers are sometimes grown in the same year, the second pair being smaller than the first. Young are marked with very prominent white spots.

The animal has never been domesticated, but, paradoxically, neither has it ever been known to science as a truly wild animal.

Within historical times the species was abundant and widely distributed across the great alluvial plain of north-eastern China, from a point north-east of Peking southwards as far as Hangchow and east to Lo-yang in Honan Province.

Père David's deer ceased to exist in the wild state at the time of the Shang dynasty (1766–1122 B.C.), when the Chihli Plains, in the swamps of which it lived, were brought under cultivation. For almost 3,000 years the animal survived in parks. At the time of its scientific discovery the only surviving herd was contained within the Non Hai-tzu (or Southern Lake) – the Imperial Hunting Park south of Peking.

Père David's deer *D. W. Ovenden* 1966

The species was made known to science by the eminent French missionary and naturalist, Abbé Armand David, after whom it was named, when in 1865 he succeeded in looking over the wall of the strongly guarded park, entry to which was strictly forbidden to Europeans.

In the following year Père David contrived to obtain two skins, which were sent to Paris, where they were described by Milne-Edwards. Later, several live specimens were shipped to Europe and their progeny distributed among a number of zoological gardens.

In 1894 the flood waters of the Hun Ho River breached the brick wall, 45 miles in circumference, which surrounded the Imperial Hunting Park; and the deer escaped into the surrounding countryside, where they were killed and eaten by the famine-stricken peasants.

The few animals to survive this disaster were destroyed in 1900 during the Boxer Rebellion, when the international troops stationed in the park shot the remaining deer and sold the meat to the Chinese. Only a handful of specimens survived the Rebellion, and these were taken to Peking. By 1911 only two remained alive in China; ten years later both were dead.

Meanwhile, as a result of events in China, the Duke of Bedford decided to establish a herd at Woburn by bringing together all available specimens from the various European zoos. Between 1900 and 1901 he acquired a total of sixteen animals. The Woburn herd increased satisfactorily and by 1922 totalled sixty-four.

After the Second World War, numbers had risen to the extent that surplus animals from Woburn were made available for the establishment of herds in several countries; and by 1963 the total exceeded 400. By 1964 the wheel had turned full circle, when the London Zoo sent four specimens back to China, where they were installed in the Peking Zoo, half a century after the species had been exterminated in that country.

An annual register of the world population, compiled by E. H. Tong, the Director of Whipsnade Zoological Park, is published in the *International Zoo Year Book*.

WHITE-TAILED DEER
Odocoileus virginianus

The principal game deer of the northern Americas has a vast distribution over the temperate and tropical woodlands of North and Central America from Canada to Panama, except the south-western United States. Thirty races are currently recognized, of which two are in some danger of extinction.

The Columbia River race – the westernmost subspecies, *O. v. leucurus* – was formerly widespread from the west of Washington State through western Oregon from lower Puget Sound to Roseburg in Douglas County. It is now reduced to a small but viable population of 300–500 (late 1964) in the southern part of its original range.

On the other side of the United States, however, the "Florida Key deer" gives rise to greater concern. *O. v. clavium* is the smallest of the eastern races of the white-tailed deer, paler than the mainland form, with small teeth and very small antlers. It is short-coated throughout the year.

The subspecies has never been known to exist outside the confines of the chain of keys, or small islands, that extends south-west from the southern tip of the Florida peninsula. It lived on most of them, readily swimming from one island to another. In recent years it has been eliminated from several of the keys on which it formerly existed and, according to the last report, is confined to an area from Little Pine Key to Cudjoe Key.

The decline resulted from a combination of factors, beginning with human occupation of the islands, and gradually becoming more adverse as the limited habitat was modified through development by man.

For many years the Key deer was heavily hunted by all means and with no rules. Packs of dogs and hunting by night with spotlights were two of the methods employed. According to Glover M. Allen, parties of hunters came from as far away as Cuba. Hurricanes and fires – particularly fires – also had disastrous effects and played a part in the animal's decline. By 1949 the total population had been reduced to about thirty individuals.

The deer now has full legal protection,

and the keys are regularly patrolled by wardens; as a result of this, hunting has been brought under firm control and the population has built up to some 300, with a ratio of about one male to three females.

In 1953 the Key Deer National Wildlife Refuge was established for the more effective protection of the subspecies. The refuge extends to 6,745 acres and includes the greater part of the animal's habitat. Of this total, 834 acres are federally owned; the Government holds the remainder on lease.

Currently the two most serious factors affecting the deer are loss of suitable habitat and the casualties caused by motor vehicles on the road that runs the full length of the keys.

At present the most urgent need is for the federal authorities to acquire legal title to other more important parts of the habitat not yet under their control before the opportunity is lost for ever.

Family Bovidae: antelopes, cattle, goats, and sheep

WESTERN GIANT ELAND
Taurotragus derbianus derbianus

The genus *Taurotragus* has two living species, the common eland, *T. oryx*, which is widely distributed in eastern, central, and southern Africa, and the giant (or Lord Derby's) eland, which exists locally from the south-western Sudan to Senegal, and is the largest living antelope.

The giant eland is, in fact, only a little larger than its common relative, except for its horns, which are much more massive, the record being $47\frac{5}{8}$ inches. The species as a whole is rather uncommon throughout its range, but only the western subspecies (the typical *T. d. derbianus*) is at present listed in the Red Data Book. The western giant eland is distinguished from the other three subspecies (of Cameroun, Congo, and Sudan) by being of a more ruddy colour, with fourteen or fifteen white vertical stripes on its sides.

Before the Second World War the western giant eland was found in the Ivory Coast; but it

has since been extinguished in that country. It now exists in very small numbers in three isolated areas – the Niokolo-Koba National Park in Senegal, the Haut-Bafing region, and Bakoy on the borders of Mali, Senegal, and Guinea. In 1937 numbers in the Gambia alone were estimated at about 1,000. Today the total

Western giant eland *Cécile Curtis* 1966

population is no more than a few dozen individuals.

For many years the animal has been nominally protected by local game regulations; but little attempt appears to have been made to enforce the law. It yields a large amount of high-quality meat; and its hide makes excellent leather. As a consequence many have lately been killed by hunting tribesmen, who have no compunction about the means they employ and do not hesitate to hunt at night. It also seems probable that rinderpest has caused substantial losses: it is known that the genus is particularly vulnerable to this disease.

Since rinderpest was first introduced into Africa at the end of the last century, various epidemics have swept the continent and have substantially reduced eland populations. This was particularly true in the earlier years of the present century.

Recently, however, the elands, and several other susceptible indigenous mammals, have benefited from the work of various territorial veterinary services in immunizing cattle against rinderpest, as a result of which these devastating scourges have been successfully checked. This is true particularly of the Central African Republic and Cameroun, where the species is in a stronger position than it has been for more than half a century. Unfortunately the same cannot be said of much of West Africa – where the value of preventive treatment does not appear to have been appreciated in time to help the western race.

The subspecies is now so gravely reduced in numbers, and the protection accorded the few survivors is so ineffectual, that the western giant eland is unlikely to survive for many more years unless immediate measures are taken by the governments concerned to safeguard the few that remain.

WILD ASIATIC BUFFALO
Bubalus bubalis

The "Indian buffalo" exists as a domesticated animal in many countries in southern Asia and elsewhere, where it is widely employed in the service of man. In the wild state, however, it is now very uncommon.

Wild Asiatic buffalo *Peter Scott* 1967

It once occupied the greater part of the Brahmaputra and Ganges plains from eastern Assam to Uttar Pradesh, extending through the eastern part of the Central Province and the eastern coastal plain from Bengal southwards slightly beyond the Godavari River.

Even as recently as the end of the last century, the wild buffalo was still plentiful in some areas: in 1892 Kinloch described it as "extremely abundant" in Assam. Since then the animal has been eliminated from the greater part of its former range, and it now exists in only three regions – the Brahmaputra valley in Assam; the lower reaches of the Godavari River at the confluence of the borders of the states of Orissa, Madhya Pradesh, and Andhra Pradesh; and the Saptkosi River in Nepal, close to the border with India.

Reports of wild individuals from other areas (such as, for example, Ceylon) should be disregarded, since they invariably refer to feral animals. Some authors have maintained that "wild" buffalo occur in Borneo, but the consensus of recent opinion is that all "wild" buffaloes in Borneo are descended from imported domestic stock.

The wild buffalo is very different from its less powerful domesticated relative. It is a massively built animal, standing almost 6 feet at the shoulder with huge, black, backward-sweeping horns which have been recorded up to 78 inches, and are longer than those of any other living member of the family Bovidae.

It is a powerful beast, with an aggressiveness that makes it a dangerous adversary. There are a good many records of tigers that have been killed by wild buffalo, often by the action of the herd, which, it is said, does not hesitate to attack in combination.

Like its domesticated relative, the wild buffalo enjoys wallowing in mud, often wholly immersing its body and leaving only its head exposed. The coating of mud affords protection against the hordes of biting insects that ceaselessly pester it.

The wild buffalo's favoured habitat consists of extensive grass plains plentifully supplied with water, and its decline was brought about by the fact that these conditions are also the most attractive for human occupation. As cultivation spread, the habitat available to the buffalo became smaller. The introduction of firearms meant that many of the animals were killed in the name of crop-protection; and their hide, horns, and meat were (and are) much in demand. Moreover, the practice of allowing domestic cattle to graze in areas occupied by wild buffalo resulted in heavy losses from rinderpest, a disease to which the buffalo is particularly susceptible.

In 1966 the total population was estimated to be a little under 2,000. Almost all of them (about 1,425) occurred in Assam, with approximately 700 in the Kaziranga Sanctuary, 400 in the Manas Sanctuary, 100 in the Pabha Sanctuary, 50 at Laokhowa, 75 at Sankos-Manas, and 100 at East Lakhimpur. In peninsular India the herds along the Godavari River totalled 400 to 500; Nepal had about 100 individuals on the Kosi River.

The wild buffalo has been fully protected by law for many years, and its survival has been much assisted by the creation of the Kaziranga, Manas, and Pabha sanctuaries. The most recent development in its protection has been the decision by the Government of Nepal to establish the Kosi River Sanctuary, in the eastern part of the country, principally for the benefit of the species. The Government of India is now considering new recommendations for the ecological study and conservation of the Godavari population, including the formation and extension of reserves.

TAMARAU
Anoa mindorensis

The tamarau is a dwarf buffalo native to the island of Mindoro. It is the largest animal endemic to the Philippines, and is not known to have existed anywhere except this one island within historical times. Its name has been spelt in a variety of ways, including *tamaraw*, *tamarou*, and *timaraw*; but none of these names would be intelligible to the local hill people, who know it as *anuang*.

The tamarau bears a superficial resemblance to its relative the anoa, which exists in the Celebes. It stands about 3 feet 3 inches at the shoulder, bulls being stockily built and thick-necked. Its horns are short and stout, roughly triangular at the base and directed backwards and slightly upwards, the tips somewhat incurved. Its general colour is greyish-black, occasionally tending to dark brown. A bull photographed by Talbot displays a prominent white chevron on the throat.

Less than a century ago the species was distributed throughout Mindoro (about 4,000 square miles), including the lowlands, particularly in the neighbourhood of swamps, marshes, and rivers. Its range is now much reduced and extends along the central ridge from the neighbourhood of Mount Calavite in the north through the forests of the Baco Range in the south as far as Mount Iglit. Within this area the animal is only thinly distributed, and most of the suitable habitat that remains is now widely fragmented, and is being steadily whittled away by various forms of agricultural and commercial activity.

Before the Second World War the species was not endangered. Since then, however, large quantities of modern firearms have come into general circulation, and little attempt appears to have been made to enforce the hunting regulations. According to Talbot, who in 1964, on behalf of the I.U.C.N., investigated various conservation problems in the country, "the Philippines probably has one of the highest percentages of actively armed, non-military citizenry of any country in the world. It also has a numerous well-armed military and a variety of law enforcement groups, and considerable numbers of U.S. military personnel stationed in the country. In addition to firearms, dogs and traps of all kinds are very widely used in hunting. Most present 'big game hunting' is done at night with spotlights."

Tamarau *D. W. Ovenden* 1966

These circumstances have, moreover, coincided with a marked increase in the human population. Man is gradually extending into regions previously uninhabited, and is using them for agricultural and pastoral purposes or for exploitation of the original forest.

In 1920 an area of about 100,000 acres on Mount Calavite was set aside as a preserve for the protection of the tamarau. It seems, however, that this reserve was little more than a paper exercise, and its effectiveness can be gauged from a statement by Manuel in 1957 that, "obviously due to accessibility to centers of civilization, there are more tamaraws killed in Mount Calavite and in Mount Iglit than in other ranges combined. Mount Calavite preserve can be reached within 10 hours from Manila by automobile, motor boat and a short hike . . . people prominent in their respective communities and who can afford expensive hunting parties organize these parties to hunt the tamaraw for its meat, its hide, its horns, or just for fun".

In 1961 a preserve, known as the Mount Iglit Game Refuge, was established in the southeastern part of the island. Nominally the refuge extends to more than 19,000 acres, but it has apparently never been surveyed, and there is difficulty in locating the boundaries on the ground.

The refuge is situated in rugged country

rising to about 3,000 feet, and was at one time covered with forest, almost all of which has disappeared. Only small clumps of trees now remain on the exposed highlands, which are used for cattle ranging. Absence of tree cover is attributable to the ranchers' practice of regularly burning the vegetation early in the dry season, and to the *kaingin* system of shifting agriculture (burning and clearing the forest to provide new areas of cultivation, which are abandoned after a few years) practised in Occidental Mindoro for generations. The cover now consists mainly of coarse grasses, some species of which form dense stands taller than a man. On the steep slopes at a lower level is a belt of forest scarred by fire and interspersed with patches of cultivation. Below this again is grassland and open woodland used for ranging and rough cultivation.

The centre of the refuge is occupied by the Korienoff Ranch, which was granted a grazing permit shortly before the reserve was created. Access to the ranch by foot is difficult, but ranchers and their friends overcome this problem by flying in to the private airstrip.

In the early days of the ranch, tamarau could be seen grazing openly during the day and were relatively placid; but, after a few years of constant harrying, the animals have been obliged to adapt themselves to changed circumstances by becoming nocturnal in habit. They have also acquired a reputation for aggressiveness, no doubt with good cause, for many have been wounded by the assortment of weapons that have been used against them.

Talbot suggests that the tamarau's favoured environment probably comprises the forest fringe, which provides a combination of open grasslands for grazing, thick cover for refuge, and water close at hand. For this reason commercial exploitation of the environment, including selective felling (which improves the cover through encouraging increased secondary growth), and even limited burning, would not adversely affect the habitat, and might actually improve it, were it not for the side-effects, such as increased hunting pressure, that inevitably accompany environmental changes of this kind. The effect of hunting is best summarized in Talbot's own words: "Hunting is clearly the major limiting factor. Cattlemen on all the ranches from which we were able to obtain information shoot tamarau for food whenever they have the opportunity. Ranch owners and their friends fly in from Manila or other cities for sport hunts. When fires are lit during the dry season it is reported that any animal that is seen fleeing from the fire is shot. Everyone in this area is armed. Outside of the ubiquitous sidearms, there is an amazing variety of sporting, defence, and ex-military weapons, ranging from fine sporting rifles and ·22 caliber target rifles to full automatic military carbines and Thompson sub-machine guns. With the armory available, precision shooting is apparently not necessary. We spoke to one cattleman who told us of the last tamarau he had helped kill with a group of cattlemen armed with a variety of weapons, mostly automatic. The animal had been shot 167 times".

Primitive hill people, such as the Mangyans in eastern Mindoro and the Batangans in the Mount Iglit region, have for generations hunted the tamarau whenever opportunity occurred. The spears, traps, and other simple methods used by them for the purpose have not, however, contributed to the decline. Several early reports declare, on the contrary, that the aboriginal inhabitants of Mindoro seldom attempted to hunt the tamarau as they were much too afraid of it. The Mangyans' fear of the tamarau is said to be such that in no circumstances will they approach a supposedly dead tamarau unless someone else first does so.

The tamarau has excellent sight and hearing, and the reputation of being swift and utterly fearless. If wounded, it is said to attack on sight, "coming on with the speed and recklessness of a rhinoceros". It has also been said to be impossible to tame, and so fierce that a young calf captured and put to a tame buffalo would promptly attack its foster mother.

In theory the tamarau is legally protected, but in practice there appears to be no case on record in which the law has ever been invoked. In any event, there is a legal loophole that permits the animal to be killed in defence of life or property.

Whitehead, writing in 1898, stated that the tamarau was "not uncommon in the huge forests that nearly cover the entire island of Mindoro". His statement is confirmed by several other authors writing at that time, but since the beginning of this century the situation has greatly deteriorated. By 1957 Manuel estimated the number of tamarau in Occidental Mindoro at approximately 244 in nineteen herds, and the total population is now believed to be fewer than one hundred. The accelerated rate of decline clearly indicates that, if the species is to survive, firm action will have to be taken at once. This must include the strengthening of existing legislative protection and the simultaneous establishment of reserves that are sanctuaries in fact and not merely in name.

The Parks and Wildlife Office has so few staff at its disposal that it cannot, as it stands, contribute effectively enough to the protection of the animal. It is impossible for the Department to fulfil its function without additional staff, a point made clear by the fact that a single warden is responsible for the whole of Mindoro, his principal charge being the Naujan Lake National Park. Up to the time of Talbot's going there, only a single visit to the Mount Iglit Refuge had ever been made by a representative of the Parks and Wildlife Office.

A further necessity is a field study to locate the surviving specimens, to determine what proposals should be made for their proper protection, and to acquire further knowledge of their habits and ecological requirements. This information would form the basis for a sound management plan, and for the establishment of a proper system of reserves. These would of course need to have their boundaries clearly marked on the ground, and would require adequate personnel to man them.

Talbot suggests that because the key to the survival or extinction of the tamarau rests largely in the hands of the ranchers and cattlemen, their cooperation should be sought in establishing a series of effective sanctuary areas within suitable parts of their own estates.

It is to be hoped that the Government of the Philippines will enhance national prestige by acting decisively to safeguard the tamarau. In both scientific and practical terms the species is

PLATE 11 (a) Persian fallow deer; (b) Brow-antlered deer, Thailand race *Maurice Wilson* 1965

a potentially valuable animal, of unusual interest to the world at large. Unique to the Philippines, the tamarau would make an appropriate national emblem in which the Filipinos could take pride. Its liking for untamed country, and its determination and courage whatever the odds, symbolize much that is admirable in the national character and history.

ANOA
Anoa depressicornis

This species has three races, all of which are restricted to the Celebes, and all of which are included in the Red Data Book. These tropical bovids are unknown on the Asiatic mainland, and there is no evidence that they ever existed anywhere except Celebes.

The anoa is the smallest of the wild cattle, the lowland anoa, *A. d. depressicornis*, standing about 3 feet 2½ inches at the shoulder; the mountain anoa, *A. d. fergusoni*, 2 feet 6 inches; and Quarles's anoa, *A. d. quarlesi*, 2 foot 1 inch. All three races are sturdily built, with heavy bodies, thick necks, and short legs. The colour of adults ranges from dark brown to black, males being darker than females, with small white patches, which vary with the individual. Many mature specimens are almost hairless: calves are of a lighter colour, and their coat is woolly. The horns have a triangular base (except those of *quarlesi*, which are conical), and are lightly ringed and almost straight, reaching a length of up to 15 inches. Anoa hide is exceptionally thick.

Some authors consider the race *A. d. quarlesi* to be of questionable validity, and synonymous with *A. d. fergusoni*. There is no doubt that much confusion has arisen over the arrangement of this species, and it may be that differences between these two races are not enough to warrant subspecific distinction. This question may never be satisfactorily resolved, as there is unfortunately not enough material in collections to enable any adequate comparative study to be

undertaken, and the prospect of obtaining fresh specimens in the field appears to be remote and receding.

Until the end of the nineteenth century, the lowland anoa was widely distributed throughout northern Celebes. Heller, writing in 1892, stated that increasing human population and spread of cultivation were compelling the animal to abandon the coastal regions, where it was once common, and to retreat into the more remote mountainous interior. Even as recently as 1937, however, it was still reasonably abundant in parts of its range, notably Gorontalo in northern Celebes.

Before the Second World War, the species was protected by the game regulations; and the Dutch administrators had established a series of nature reserves for its benefit. Moreover, the anoa was seldom hunted by the local people, as (like its relative the tamarau) it had a reputation for ferocity. Tribesmen, armed only with primitive weapons, were understandably reluctant to risk provoking it.

Quarles' anoa, known as *tokata* by the Toradja people, is reputed to be much less vicious than the typical race – a belief that appears to be confirmed by the fact that they hunt it with dogs and spears, a technique that would be dangerous to attempt with the lowland race.

Since the Second World War, the faunal situation in Celebes has radically altered. The introduction of modern firearms has enabled the people to overcome their earlier reluctance to hunt the animal; the game regulations are no longer enforced; and the nature reserves, once so assiduously maintained, are no longer effective and appear to have been abandoned. The most serious slaughter of anoas, and of much other local fauna besides, has been caused by bands of military personnel, apparently subject to little control, and without overmuch to occupy themselves, armed with modern automatic weapons and apparently unlimited supplies of ammunition. The killing has been immense.

Possibly because of its shyness, the anoa has been little studied. Hardly anything is known of its habits and requirements in the wild state, and its population status is not known with certainty. From the tenuous evidence that is

PLATE 12 (*a*) Giant sable antelope; (*b*) Arabian oryx; (*c*) European bison *Peter Scott, Brooke Bond* 1964

Anoa *D. W. Ovenden* 1966

available, however, it appears that all three races have been greatly reduced and are close to the point of extinction. Anoa meat is extremely palatable, and for that reason the animal is hunted by the local people at every opportunity. It is also taken for its hide. According to Harper, the Koela people "use the hide, tanned while with the tail still on, as a dancing dress".

Although both the mountain anoa of central and south-eastern Celebes and Quarles' anoa of south-western Celebes have much more restricted ranges than the lowland form, it is possible that they may be in a slightly better position. This apparent paradox arises from the greater degree of security these two races gain in the densely forested mountainous parts of the country. The lowland race is now believed to have been exterminated almost everywhere except in the swampy forests of northern Celebes.

The fate of the anoa rests very largely in the hands of the Indonesian military authorities. Unless they can be persuaded to impose some degree of control in the matter of hunting, whether for sport or meat, and have the means to make it effective, there is no doubt whatever that, with many other interesting and valuable species of the native fauna, the anoa will be obliterated within a short time – if indeed it has not already gone.

KOUPREY
Bos sauveli

The kouprey is the most recently discovered of the true wild cattle, having been known to science only since shortly before the Second World War.

Several authors have suggested that the animal may be a hybrid arising from a cross between the banteng and possibly the gaur. Others (Tate, for example) consider that, although in some respects the kouprey may be intermediate between the gaur and the banteng, it is not a hybrid. The suggestion has also been made that the kouprey may be one of the ancestors of the humped zebu cattle of India.

It is a primitive type of wild bovid, whose bulls stand more than 6 feet at the shoulder and whose cows are rather smaller. Its general colour is blackish-brown, its under parts being lighter. The lower parts of its legs are white, with black hoofs and with a dark stripe on the front of each foreleg. Its forehead, a patch on either side of its muzzle, and a patch surrounding each eye are chestnut. It has a prominent dewlap. Characteristic of the species (and a feature in which it differs from all the other wild cattle of Asia) is the shape of its horns, which, next to those of the buffaloes, are the largest and have the widest spread of any living wild cattle. They are lyre-shaped in the cow, but curve inwards in the bull. The horns of adult bulls sometimes become conspicuously frayed at their tips, leaving the last few inches of inner horn polished and exposed.

The kouprey exists in two localities of northern Cambodia 156 miles apart and separated by the Mekong River. On the right bank the range covers about 4,600 square miles, and on the left bank an area about half that size. The animal also occurs in eastern Cambodia and western Vietnam.

Sauvel estimated the 1938 population at about 800; and two years later Coolidge considered the figure had increased to about 1,000. By 1964, however, the number had declined to about 350, and since then has been reduced to about 200.

The decline has been primarily due to uncontrolled hunting by military personnel, who over a period of several years during the war in Indo-China occupied the region and to a large extent lived off the land.

A contributory factor is believed to have been the kouprey's low reproductive rate, possibly arising from lack of calcium and phosphorus in the area in which it lives.

The species is legally protected. Of the wild-life sanctuaries recently established by the Government of Cambodia, one, the Koulen Prom Tep Refuge, extending to 3,700,000 acres, has been specifically designed for its protection.

EUROPEAN BISON
Bison bonasus

Two living species comprise the genus: *Bison bison*, the American bison, which until relatively recently existed throughout much of North America; and *B. bonasus*, the European bison, or wisent, which was once widely distributed in Europe. The latter is divided into two subspecies: the Lithuanian (or lowland) bison, *Bison bonasus bonasus*; and the Caucasian (or mountain) bison, *Bison bonasus caucasius*.

The wisent stands higher at the shoulder than the American bison, and has longer legs, and a longer and less barrel-like body. Its head is smaller and is carried higher. Its hindquarters are more powerfully built and well proportioned. Its mane is thinner, but the fur on its hind-quarters heavier. The wisent has poor eyesight, but is keen of scent, and is a wilder and more wary animal than its American relative. It was much more difficult to hunt and was said to be almost unapproachable. The American bison's heavy forequarters and weak hind legs placed it at a disadvantage when chased uphill; but the wisent's build meant that it could give an equally good performance on either steep or level ground.

The European bison is essentially a woodland animal and a browser,[1] the American species being primarily an animal of the open prairies and a grazer. This fact caused the American bison to undertake lengthy seasonal migrations in search of grazing, whereas the European species was relatively static. The depletion and, eventually, the almost total eradication of the indigenous forests of Europe was therefore the principal reason for the latter's decline. Hunting was a contributory factor, but of less significance than destruction of the forested habitat.

The original range of the species was known to have included western and southern Europe as far east as the Caucasus, and northward as far as the Lena River in Siberia. By the beginning of the twentieth century, the only surviving wild herd of the typical race was in the Bialowieza Forest in Poland, on the border with the U.S.S.R., where since 1803 a herd was main-tained for the personal use of the Russian Imperial family. The animals were carefully protected, although a few were shot by privileged visiting sportsmen and a small number was presented to zoological gardens.

In 1914 there were 737 animals in the Bialo-wieza herd; but not a single one survived the First World War. The only survivors were about forty-five specimens of Bialowieza origin, which some years before had been distributed among various of the zoological gardens of Europe, and the herd in the Pszczyna Forest[2] (Pless) on the Duke of Hochberg's estate in south-western Upper Silesia. This reserve was established as a breeding centre in 1865 with a bull and three cows from Bialowieza presented by Tsar Alexander II. By 1921 the Pszczyna herd numbered more than seventy: but only three animals, a cow and two bulls, survived the political upheavals in Upper Silesia in that year.

These three, together with two cows purchased from Sweden and another bull from Germany, were sent in 1929 to Poland, where they were kept under semi-captive conditions in a special fenced enclosure of 507 acres in part of the Bialowieza Forest, of which 74 acres were cleared and sown to pasture grasses. They formed the basis of the various herds that have since been re-established in that country.

In 1923 a proposal by the Polish zoologist Jan Sztolcman led to the founding of the Inter-national Society for the Protection of the European Bison. The Society, with headquarters in Frankfurt, made a significant contribution to the rehabilitation of the species. Among other matters, it was responsible for compiling a stud book – the result of devoted work by Dr Erna Mohr, Jan Zabinski, and others – containing particulars of all living pure-bred specimens of

[1] The Bialowieza bison cause surprisingly little damage to the forest, less than is caused by small game. The bark of the common sallow, poplar, and European aspen is eaten, as well as the bark of broad-leaved trees such as lime, maple, and ash (although birch bark is scarcely touched). Young spruce and pine shoots are occasionally browsed, but acorns are the preferred food: during the season when the oaks shed their fruit the bison subsist exclusively on acorns.

[2] Incorporated into Poland in 1923.

B. bonasus. The first *Pedigree Book of the European Bison* published in 1930 contained data on forty animals. New editions of the stud book have subsequently appeared at irregular intervals.

By 1939 there were thirty animals in Poland and thirty-five in Germany, as well as a few others elsewhere in Europe. In spite of heavy losses, the Second World War was not as disastrous for the bison-breeding centres as the First World War, and forty-six animals were recorded as surviving in Poland in 1946. At that time no more than a dozen remained in Germany, in the Springe Reserve and at the Hellabrunn Zoo, Munich.

After the Second World War, Poland took the lead in the bison-breeding programme. In 1949 Zabinski stated that the basic material then available at the three Polish breeding centres comprised nine pure-bred cows of the typical race at Pszczyna; three pure-bred cows at Bialowieza, together with a further three having a small admixture of Caucasian genes; and four cows at Niepolomice all containing Caucasian genes.

Zabinski adds that the Polish Ministry of Forestry proposed to place the hybrids "in a separate reservation and to interbreed them in order to maintain a possible accumulation of genes of the extinct race . . . It is difficult to foresee whether it would be possible to reconstitute the Caucasian bison from this material, as Bashkirov in the U.S.S.R. is planning to do. All the animals in question have a very low percentage of Caucasian blood, representing the fifth or sixth generation in relation to their only Caucasian ancestor, the bull Kaukasus . . ."

More recently the number of breeding centres in Poland has increased to five: Bialowieza, Pszczyna, Niepolomice, Smardzewice, and Borki.

In 1956, measures were taken to release some wisent into the Bialowieza Forest. The experiment involved liberating animals that for several decades had been living in semi-captivity, and giving them the opportunity to adapt themselves to a wholly wild existence.

Not enough time has passed to enable firm conclusions to be drawn; but initial results are encouraging. The free-ranging herd is in excellent condition (better than that of the semi-captive herd), and calves born in the wild state have developed admirably.

By the end of 1962 the free-living herd numbered fifty-seven, of which thirty-four had been born since the release. The Polish authorities estimate that 2,500 acres of forest will support two bison without damage to the habitat. Bialowieza is therefore capable of carrying up to approximately 100 to 115 individuals.

The rehabilitation of the species calls for reintroductions on a larger scale. There are now enough specimens to achieve this desirable aim, but the difficulty is that no suitable locality extensive enough for the purpose exists except in the Soviet Union. In the meantime, the Polish authorities are anxious to distribute the bison widely over the globe as an insurance against the possibility of catastrophic losses from disease or other causes.

The original range of the Caucasian race, *B. b. caucasius*, is not well known, partly because of confusion with the auroch, *Bos primigenius*, and partly because it was not scientifically described until 1906, when it was already restricted to the Caucasus region. At that time the range embraced an area of about 1,280,000 acres on the northern side of the Caucasus around the headwaters of the Bielaja and Malaja Laba rivers, both of which flow into the Kuban. At the end of the last century Prince Demidoff saw tracks in the snow at an altitude of 8,000 feet and heard reports of the animal's existence on the southern slopes of the Caucasus, from which he concluded that the wisent crossed over the main range.

This region remained outside proper administrative control until after the 1860s, when a system of protection was instituted that caused considerable resentment among the local Tcherkess people.[1] Even the Grand Duke in whom the local sporting rights were vested was not permitted to kill a wisent without the Tsar's express authority, and in no circumstances were more than three kills allowed in any season.

Under these conditions the wisent flourished; but, when the gamekeepers were swept away by

[1] In 1915, Van der Byl wrote: "Much ill-feeling has been created by making the natives vacate their grazing grounds, to which they have considered themselves entitled from time immemorial".

the Revolution, the local herdsmen appear to have had ample opportunity to give vent to their pent-up feelings of resentment. Many bison were killed during hostilities in 1920, and by 1921 not more than about fifty survived. Fortunatov was of the opinion that by 1923 only about fifteen to twenty remained alive. In 1924 the Soviet Government accorded the species protection and established the Kuban (Caucasus) Wisent Reserve (700,000 acres), embracing the known range of the animal. Unfortunately, little was done to implement the decree; and three years later, when a team went to investigate the area, they could find no living specimens – but they did find enough evidence to indicate that deaths during the previous two to three years were not attributable to natural causes. It is generally believed that the last free-living wisent in the Caucasus was destroyed about 1925.

The only surviving representative of the sub-species at that time was a bull presented as a yearling by the Tsar in 1908 to Karl Hagenbeck, the Hamburg animal-dealer. This bull, named Kaukasus, sired a number of calves, but all were out of cows of the typical race originating from Bialowieza. He died on the 26th February 1925.

The recent history of the wisent in the Soviet Union is also of particular interest: only a single pure-bred European bison survived the Second World War in the U.S.S.R. Between 1946 and 1951 seventeen pure-bred specimens were obtained from Poland, and a comprehensive programme for the rehabilitation of the species was drawn up by Dr Zablocki, which included the establishment of special stud farms.

By January 1966, the number of pure-bred bison in the Soviet Union had reached 250, of which sixty-nine were in the Bialowieza Forest, adjoining the Polish reserve of the same name, and 181 had been introduced into the Caucasus. This comprises more than a third of the total world population.

In addition to the pure-bred herd mentioned above, there is a further herd in the Caucasus National Park; it contains a small admixture of American bison genes.[1] This herd numbers 500 specimens and occupies a range of 75,000 acres, which is extended each year by approximately another 4,000 acres.

The aim of the Soviet authorities is not only to increase numbers, but also to re-establish the species under free-living conditions. More than a hundred wild-bred bison already exist in Central Russia.

In summary, the present position is that the Caucasian race, *B. b. caucasius*, is extinct, and pure-bred stock of the typical race, *B. b. bonasus*, survives in modest but increasing numbers.

In addition there is a substantially larger number of European bison that contain genes of both races, and some with a small admixture of American bison genes.

Dr Erna Mohr of Hamburg, Germany, estimated the world population of the species on the 1st January 1967 as 860.

WOOD BISON
Bison bison athabascae

The wood bison is one of the two surviving races of the American bison, *B. bison*. It is distinguished from the typical race of the plains by being rather larger and darker, with a denser and more silky coat, and longer and more slender horns and horn cores. It is regarded as being rather more closely allied to the European bison, *B. bonasus*, than is the plains bison, *B. b. bison*.

In the early part of the nineteenth century the wood or northern subspecies ranged through central Saskatchewan and Alberta, extending from the North Saskatchewan River northward to Lac la Martre and the Horn Mountains in the Northwest Territories, and westward to the eastern slopes of the Rocky Mountains following the line of the Rockies as far south as Colorado.

At one time the species occupied the greater part of central North America east of the Rocky

---

[1] American bison genes appear to have been introduced in a misguided attempt to improve the European stock. Zabinski records that in the 1920s there was thought to be a "decrease of vitality . . . and an almost unanimous expression of opinion even among responsible specialists . . . that the European bison was a degenerating species . . ." Mohr (1949) quotes a report to the effect that in 1928 at Saupark, Springe, American bison cows were put to a European bison bull. Of the resulting calves, all the males were slaughtered and the females retained for the eventual mating with a bull of the European species. Under this system, the characteristics of the American bison were believed to have been eliminated by the third generation. This programme of cross-breeding ceased at Springe in 1934.

Mountains in numbers estimated to have totalled 60,000,000 animals. Within a relatively few years the huge herds had been wantonly destroyed, and by 1889 only a few hundred specimens remained.

The extinction of the southern herds of plains bison was followed by heavy exploitation of the northern herds, and by 1875 bison had almost ceased to exist south of the Peace River. By 1891 the northern race had been reduced to about 300 animals in a remote area of wild country situated to the south of Great Slave Lake and west of the Slave River.

Wood bison *Cécile Curtis* 1966

In 1893 it was estimated that 500 northern bison survived in what later became Wood Buffalo Park, and in that year the subspecies was accorded protection by the Federal Government, although no rangers were appointed until 1911. By 1922 the population was estimated to have reached about 1,500 to 2,000, and in December of that year the Canadian Government established Wood Buffalo Park, which embraced the full known range of the subspecies. The park now covers 11,000,000 acres, and in 1961 contained about 10,300 animals, the largest population of bison existing anywhere in the world.

Between 1925 and 1928, 6,673 plains bison (*B. b. bison*) were moved by train and barge from the Wainwright Buffalo Park in Alberta, where the restricted range had become overcrowded, and released into Wood Buffalo Park. Inevitably the two subspecies interbred freely, and it was assumed that the northern form had disappeared as a distinct race.

In 1957, however, during an aerial reconnaissance of the area, Novakovski discovered a segregated group of bison in the extreme northwestern part of the park, 75 miles from the nearest hybrid herds and isolated by almost impassable country. Subsequent field studies showed that these were pure-bred bison numbering about 200 and occupying a restricted range on the upper Nyarling River.

Since its rediscovery, the subspecies has undergone a numerical decline and, in 1965, Novakovski estimated that fewer than 100 animals remained in the fully wild state in the Nyarling River area. The population in Wood Buffalo Park has been limited to a great extent by disease. When the plains bison were introduced into the park in the 1920s they brought tuberculosis with them. In 1962 Fuller concluded that tuberculosis was the highest single cause of mortality, causing annual losses of from 4 to 6 per cent of the population.

Since 1962 a control programme has been in operation in the park. Annual round-ups have been held and large numbers of bison tested for tuberculosis. Reactors are slaughtered, and in this way it is hoped that the disease can be kept under control. Contagious abortion has also been diagnosed in the park; but calves now receive routine injections against it.

More recently an outbreak of anthrax close to the park boundary resulted in the death of over 500 bison. In spite of the stringent control measures taken to prevent this highly infectious disease from spreading, infected bison were found within the park in the summer of 1964.

To preserve the wood bison, and because of the threat from tuberculosis, Bang's disease, and anthrax, the authorities decided to adopt a policy of decentralization. An independent breeding herd was therefore established west of Great Slave Lake and north of the Mackenzie River with the translocation of eighteen bison to Fort Providence in the summer of 1963. By 1965 this herd had increased to twenty-four.

A second independent herd has been established at Elk Island Park in central Alberta. Forty-three bison were captured in February 1965 and held for a year in quarantine before being moved into this park.

The wood bison narrowly escaped extinction

at the hands of man, only to come under an equally serious threat from disease. In recent years, protection has progressed to carefully planned management, as a result of which there is every reason to hope that the subspecies may now be secure.

JENTINK'S DUIKER
Cephalophus jentinki

A prominent whitish collar around the fore-quarters of Jentink's duiker separates its grizzled grey body from its almost jet-black head. The animal is very similar in size and general conformation to the yellow-backed duiker.

Very little is known about this rare duiker. It was discovered by F. X. Stampfli in an area close to the coast of Liberia, east of Monrovia, and named for his collector F. A. Jentink. Three specimens, all females, were collected in the triangle formed by the Junk, Du Queah, and Farmington rivers, the first in 1884 and the others in 1887. Johann Büttikofer sighted a fourth specimen in the forest near Fali, north-west of Monrovia, but failed to collect it. The type specimen was described by Oldfield Thomas in 1892 and is now in the British Museum. The other two are in the Leyden Museum. For more than half a century these were the only known specimens, and no male, either living or dead, has ever been seen. It was not until 1948 that P. L. Dekeyser and A. Villiers collected the skull of an adult male in the Dyiglo region.

The meagre information on this species led to the assumption that it was confined to the small region where it was originally discovered. This is close to the large Harbel Firestone Plantation, where it is certain that the animal no longer exists. Only recently has information come to light suggesting that the range may be much greater than previously supposed. Dekeyser and Villiers have recorded specimens from a good deal further east, one in the Klosoké region (about 5°20′ N., 8°0′ W.) and another, already mentioned, from Dyiglo (about 5°45′ N., 8°0′ W.). Moreover, they no longer consider it to be an exclusively Liberian species. Tribesmen from the Man region (Ivory Coast) know this duiker under the name of *nienagbé*, a word very close to the one used by the people of Klosoké, who call it *nyagbé*. However, H.-J. Kuhn states that this name is used indiscriminately for both Jentink's and the yellow-backed duiker.

Jentink's duiker may possibly be part of a residual population based on the Cavally River. This observation appears to be supported by M. J. Coe, who in 1964, during the course of his work on the Liberian side of Mount Nimba, was informed by Mano hunters that they knew the animal well and could describe it. Although Coe himself saw no positive evidence of its existence, he was assured that it still appears in the neighbourhood of Putu and on the other side of the Nimba Range in the Ivory Coast.

This duiker may possibly exist also in Sierra Leone. In 1933 A. H. W. Haywood recorded that "according to Captain Stanley it is quite common there"; but this information has not been confirmed from any other source. If it does in fact exist in Sierra Leone, it is most likely to be found in the Gola Forest in the eastern part of the country.

The 1933 London Convention listed Jentink's duiker as an endangered species, but it has not been accorded special protective measures in Liberia or elsewhere. Its status certainly needs special investigation.

GIANT SABLE ANTELOPE
Hippotragus niger variani

The sable antelope has four races, the greatest of which, the giant sable antelope, is of particular interest to the I.U.C.N. There is only a slight difference in shoulder height between the giant sable antelope, *H. n. variani,* and the other and more common races, but the former is readily distinguished by the majestic sweep of its huge scimitar-shaped horns (the record length is $64\frac{7}{8}$ inches), which are among the finest hunting trophies possible to obtain.

Mature giant sable bulls are jet black, with contrasting white under parts and facial markings, and prominent black manes. Females are of a much lighter colour, with smaller, less curved horns. Immature males are similar in colour to the females, but can be readily identified by their black faces.

The subspecies is isolated from the others; and there are no records of its former existence outside that part of central Angola situated between the Cuanza and Luando rivers.

It was the last of the large African mammals to be discovered, the type specimen being obtained in 1913 by H. F. Varian, then Chief Engineer on the Benguela Railway, and described by Oldfield Thomas three years later.

The animal is now restricted to the southern part of the Luando Reserve in the Malange District of Angola, bounded by the Luando, Cuanza, Dunda, and Luasso rivers. It also exists in the Cangandala region, roughly 25 to 30 miles north of the confluence of the Luando and Cuanza rivers. In this last area there are thought to be about 100 to 120 animals; and the total population is estimated at between 500 and 700.

The present restricted range suggests that the giant sable antelope may never have been particularly abundant. No early population estimates are available for comparison with present day numbers; but uncontrolled hunting appears to have been a major factor in its decline. During the 1870s, for example, numbers of Boer immigrants living in the interior of Angola used to raid the area in which the giant sable lived. Varian records one such raid that occurred in 1912, and "heads up to 61 inches were the result". A further raid was planned for the following year, but Varian prevailed upon the governor of the district to close the area to shooting.

The species has been legally protected from about 1926, since when it might be killed only on special licence, very few of which are granted. This restriction was unfortunately inadequate, since it imposed no embargo on the sale of trophies. In practice, therefore, it was effective only against foreign sportsmen. Local residents promptly made a lucrative business of shooting the bulls for their horns and the cows for their meat and hides. Several authors record that traders offered them as many heads as they cared to buy, and P. N. Gray stated in 1933 that he "heard several Portuguese brag of killing ten sable in a month. At that rate, this magnificent animal will soon be extinct."

African hunters also took advantage of the situation, and in 1932 Varian wrote: "The greatest number and the largest heads have been accounted for by the pit traps of the local natives. One of the largest heads recorded was traded for something less than a shilling from the natives".

The Government of Angola, alarmed at the decline, introduced more stringent protective measures, with severe penalties for infringement of the law – and, later, established the Luando and Cangandala reserves, which together embrace the entire known range of the species. In recent years the species has moved from the northern part of the Luando Reserve and concentrated in the southern sector, much of which is still little known. The reasons for this situation are not clear, but it is thought likely that they are not entirely related to any human activity.

The Institute of Scientific Research of Angola in Luando, in collaboration with the Overseas Research Board in Lisbon, recently began a comprehensive ecological survey of the Luanda Reserve and the giant sable antelope. It was hoped that the study would reveal why the animal evacuated the northern part of the reserve, and would thus show whether it would be feasible to attempt reintroductions. Another purpose of the study was to try to define the full extent of the antelope's range, which has never been accurately determined, with the object of undertaking any adjustments to the boundaries of the reserve that might prove necessary.

Unfortunately this study was discontinued not long after it had begun, and, as far as can be ascertained, proposals for its completion have made no headway. It is to be hoped that the authorities will agree to continue this important investigation. It is hard to see how sound recommendations for the effective protection and management of the giant sable antelope can be made, in the absence of basic data, which can be obtained only by a thorough ecological study.

ARABIAN ORYX
Oryx leucoryx

The Arabian oryx is the smallest (3 feet 4 inches or less at the shoulder) and the rarest of the three species of oryx that together comprise the living members of the genus. Its colour is almost pure white, with dark chocolate markings on its legs, all of which are darker in front than behind and have white pasterns. There is a slight but distinct shoulder hump. Its tail is white, with a prominent black tuft, and there are black markings on its face. In some specimens there is a faint flank stripe. Its hooves are broader and rounder than those of any other oryx species. Its horns are almost straight, diverging gradually from the base with a slight backward curve, and up to 29 inches in length.

The preferred habitat of this oryx is the *jol* (a gravel plain, interspersed with sand and stones, that occurs around the fringes of the sand desert), where the vegetation on which it feeds is more abundant; but it may move into the desert proper either when disturbed, or, in the event of rain, to take advantage of a sudden flush of herbage. In summer, however, the heat in the sands is too great even for the oryx, although it is capable of going for long periods without drinking. Oryx cover considerable distances in search of grazing; Stewart records one animal – tracked by the 1962 expedition and apparently unaware that it was being followed – that moved 58 miles in under 18 hours, mostly at a walk. During the day, hooves and horns will sometimes be used to scrape out a shallow depression under a bush or on the side of a dune to seek shade and possibly a degree of concealment. Even from close range the animal blends well with its surroundings and its horns can surprisingly easily be mistaken for desert vegetation.

The species was at one time distributed over most of the Arabian peninsula, wherever suitable habitat could be found, at least as far east as Mesopotamia, and westward to the Sinai Peninsula. The northern limits of the range have never been satisfactorily determined, but the animal is known to have existed as far north as the Syrian desert, and was hunted and kept captive by the ancient Egyptians.

By the end of the last century, the oryx survived in only two parts of the peninsula. The northern population occupied the region known as the Great Nafud, and the southern the Rub'al Khali. Stragglers were occasionally reported from other areas. In Jordan, for example, small numbers existed until about 1930.

The Great Nafud population had died out by the early 1950s, when the southern population had also drastically declined. The position today is that the few survivors are confined to a small part of Oman, in a quadrilateral about 250 miles long and 100 miles deep. There are occasional reports of individual oryx or very small groups outside this section, notably in the Duru and Wahiba country to the east of the great sand area; and it seems possible that altogether a few hundred specimens may still survive.

The decline of the Arabian oryx began with the introduction of modern firearms, and accelerated rapidly following the coming of the motor vehicle. Until then, the traditional method of hunting involved tracking the oryx on foot or by camel, a laborious and time-consuming procedure that could be used only in the cool season, and might last up to a fortnight (the maximum time a camel could go without water), and resulted in the bagging of relatively few animals each year.

Almost every part of the animal is used. Its flesh is greatly esteemed and fetches a high price not only as a delicacy but because it is reputed to impart strength, courage, and endurance; its hide makes valuable leather; its fat is applied for a variety of disorders, a mixture of fat and blood being regarded as a cure for snake-bite. According to Thomas in 1932, the Bedouin consume the gastric juices with evident relish, and give the solid stomach-contents to their camels.

The decline of the Arabian oryx can be attributed to the invention of the internal combustion engine. From oil was derived the new-found wealth that served to open up the peninsula for development; and oil not only financed but also provided the mode of propulsion for the vehicles used in hunting the animal. Stewart summarized the position when he wrote in 1963: "Oil companies, soldiers, and local citizens have all joined in the slaughter. In the last two years there have been two raids within the Eastern Aden Protectorate by Arabs from Qatar, on the Persian Gulf; in well-equipped vehicles and with water and petrol bowsers they have come in the winter months (December–January) prepared to follow oryxes both within the sands and on the *jol* for weeks at a time. Forty-eight animals were killed on one such occasion and thirteen on another. Since animal tracks remain obvious for months on the ground throughout most of its habitat the oryx has little chance of escaping such persistent hunting from motor vehicles."

In 1962 Grimwood wrote: "The Arabian oryx is, by its vigilance and ability to travel great distances, more than a match for the Beduin hunting on foot or camel back. . . . But the oryx is helpless against motorized hunting parties, for on the *jol* ninety-nine per cent of the country carries a good spoor and ninety-five per cent of it can be traversed by car. It is therefore simply a matter of following up an animal till it is sighted – spooring at speeds of twenty miles per hour being possible – and then running it to a standstill."

The continued existence of oryx in Muscat and Oman is attributed to the Sultan's personal interest in the species and his decrees protecting them. Even in a country where such protective measures are exceptionally difficult to enforce, the local Bedouin observe the Sultan's instructions. Unfortunately, the principal cause of decline elsewhere has been not so much the activities of local Bedouin hunters as the highly organized and well-equipped motorized hunting parties originating from other territories farther north.

Motorized hunting is sometimes conducted in the grand manner. An indication of the scale of operations was given in 1960 by Talbot, who stated that a hunt of average size employed forty to sixty vehicles, but that other hunts might use as many as 300, some of which would be hunting cars and the remainder support-vehicles carrying the expedition's supplies and servants. "The hunting cars fan out into a sort of skirmish line, driving down and shooting virtually everything that moves. Repeating shotguns are used more than rifles, and often the animals are run until they drop from exhaustion and their throats are cut by servants. St John Philby told me of riding with the late King Saud when the King personally shot over one hundred gazelles in a day. Between January and April 1955, in a royal goodwill tour around northern Saudi Arabia the retinue numbered four hundred and eighty two cars at one point. Hunting was a part of this excursion and this vast army of vehicles spread out, crossing the desert, and shooting every-

thing. As a result of the incredible blood lust of the past twenty years, virtually all of the abundant wildlife of Arabia has been extirpated from areas accessible to automobiles. In the last eight years the Arabs have been also using airplanes for hunting. It is hard to see how any animal can survive this attack. The Arabian ostrich has been exterminated, the bustards greatly diminished, three species of gazelle (once present in vast herds) reduced to the danger point, the cheetah almost exterminated and the oryx reduced to one or two hundred individuals."

In recent years, oil company prospectors and their escorting soldiers – who, according to Talbot are Arabs "over whom by government decree the companies have little control" – have gradually but persistently expanded their operations into remote areas which hitherto were a secure refuge for the oryx.

The publication in 1960 of Talbot's *A Look at Threatened Species* did much to focus attention on the plight of the Arabian oryx. His assessment of the situation led him to conclude that "the only way to assure survival of this interesting species is to transfer some specimens to a safer habitat . . . This should be done as soon as possible, to be assured of finding enough animals".

His recommendation was acted upon by the I.U.C.N.'s Survival Service Commission, as a result of which it was decided that, in conjunction with the Fauna Preservation Society, an operation should be mounted in the Eastern Aden Protectorate to capture enough oryx to form the nucleus of a captive breeding herd, as an insurance against the extermination of the species in the wild. In May 1962 the team participating in "Operation Oryx" under the leadership of Major I. R. Grimwood, Chief Game Warden, Kenya, succeeded in capturing three oryx (two males and one female) as well as obtaining much fresh information on the animal's distribution, biology, and habits. The expedition also had the effect of stimulating interest in the species; as a result of this, sighting reports and other data began coming in from the eastern part of the range, thus enabling a much more comprehensive assessment of the animal's status to be made than had hitherto been possible. Valuable information was received from officers of the foreign and consular services of both Britain and the United States, as well as the Sultan of Muscat and Oman's Armed Forces, the Trucial Oman Scouts, the Hadhrami Bedouin Legion, the Desert Locust Survey, the Shell Company of Qatar, the Arabian American Oil Company, and a good many private individuals.

After a period in holding-pens at Isiolo in northern Kenya under strict veterinary supervision, the three wild-caught specimens were transferred to the Phoenix Maytag Zoo, Arizona, where they were soon joined by additional specimens generously donated by Sheikh Jabir Abdullah al Sabah of Kuwait and King Saud of Saudi Arabia, and another given by the London Zoo, to form a viable breeding herd. A second well-managed breeding herd also exists at Riyadh in Saudi Arabia and a third at Slamy in Qatar. In October 1966, the Phoenix Zoo herd consisted of eleven males and five females, the Riyadh herd of eight, and the Slamy herd of nine males and six females. Some of the females are of course pregnant, and breeding has occurred readily and normally.

In summary, therefore, the position is that a wild population, possibly to be numbered in the low hundreds, still survives in one relatively undisturbed part of Oman where it is protected by the Sultan. It is difficult, however, to see how such protection can be permanently effective over an extensive enough region in face of the natural inclinations of the local people. This is based on the traditional nomad attitude, which involves killing while the chance exists and allowing the future to look after itself – knowing that, if the opportunity is permitted to pass, somebody else will certainly take advantage of it. Even if this difficulty could be resolved, the greater problem remains of preventing border violations by highly mobile raiding parties who owe no allegiance to the local ruler, and who strike without warning and are gone before any counter-action can be taken.

Three small captive herds have been established as a precaution against the possible extinction of wild stocks. They comprise a nucleus that may in future be used for the reintroduction of oryx into parts of the original range, once national parks or other sanctuaries have been established for the effective protec-

tion of the highly interesting fauna of the Arabian peninsula.

SCIMITAR-HORNED ORYX
Oryx tao

The scimitar-horned oryx is rather similar in size and build to the beisa oryx, *O. gazella*, of East and South Africa, an adult male being about 4 feet at the shoulder and weighing about 450 pounds; but, instead of being almost straight, its horns, as its name implies, curve backwards. Its general colour is much paler than that of the beisa, being white with a faint tinge of chestnut on face, neck, flanks, and upper limbs.

The species was once well distributed around the fringes of the deserts of northern Africa from Senegal in the west to the Nile in the east, with a pocket in the Sudan isolated east of the Nile. Although, unlike the addax, it normally avoids true desert country, the scimitar-horned oryx is adapted to existence under conditions that would be intolerable to most other mammals.

Less than a century ago, the species was abundant in the south of Morocco and parts of Algeria and Tunisia, but it has since been extinguished in those countries. It had gone from Egypt by about 1850. It is now close to extinction in Rio de Oro.

In short, the animal has been killed off in most of the northern part of its range. But it still exists in relative abundance in the southern sector, occupying a narrow strip extending along the southern edge of the Sahara, from Mauritania to the Red Sea.

The most important remaining concentrations live in the northern part of Tchad and in the Ténéré region of Niger, to the east of the Aïr Mountains. The total population may be more than 10,000 of which an estimated 4,000 are in Tchad.

Gillet, who has made a valuable study of the species, believes that in Tchad there may be two distinct populations that do not intermix. Animals of the northern group (called *Haouach korollo*), are distinguishable by their smaller size, stockier build, and paler colour. Moreover, this population remains all the year round in the neighbourhood of the Haouach, Emera, and

Sofora wadis. The southern population (*Haouach abruck*), on the other hand, undertakes a seasonal southerly migration; it is more slenderly built, with darker markings, and is regarded as less robust than the northern.

The days of the large herds, often of more than 1,000 animals, have now passed. Perhaps one of the last Europeans to witness such a large assemblage was the hunter-guide who, as recorded by Gillet, on the 20th January 1959, counted 800 oryx in a herd in the neighbourhood of the Wadi Emera. Throughout much of its range, the decline is attributable to degradation of the specialized habitat of the species by encroachment of the desert, almost always as a consequence of overstocking by domestic animals. At the same time, mounting pressure has been exerted by uncontrolled hunting.

Scimitar-horned oryx *D. W. Ovenden* 1966

This oryx is hunted by the local tribesmen wherever it occurs. Perhaps the leading hunters are the Haddad, a tribe inhabiting northern Tchad, whose entire life and culture depend exclusively on the oryx. The Haddad have perfected a hunting technique that involves mounted men driving the animals into nets manufactured from oryx leg tendons. The animal's reaction when netted is to fight with its horns, the only result of which is for it to become more enmeshed. Its meat, considered superior to that of any other wild animal, is said to be comparable with top-quality beef and is eaten either raw or cooked. The Haddad have organized a widespread trade in sun-dried meat, either in the form of biltong or ground into meal. Oryx hide, particularly that of the neck, makes high quality leather, for which there is much demand, as it is durable and able to withstand rough treatment. The Haddad are beyond the reach of the law, and cause immense destruction to the oryx. In 1964 Gillet stated: "If a herd falls into their hands everything is slaughtered, including females and young".

Other nomadic tribes have evolved a system by which horsemen ride down an animal to the point of exhaustion. The oryx invariably runs up-wind, occasionally pausing to look back at its pursuer. After 6 to 9 miles it can go no further. The horseman dismounts and, holding his reins in one hand, hurls his spear, which is attached to his wrist by a cord. The oryx flees again, but,

exhausted and wounded, soon gives up and stands resignedly to await the finishing blow. It has no chance of escape. A camel that has been following up the tracks soon arrives on the scene to carry the oryx away. Gillet records that the horses are esteemed for the number of oryx they have ridden down in this way.

Certain Sudanese nomads use a similar technique, but are mounted on camels and helped by packs of dogs. Their activities have resulted in the near-extinction of the species in that country.

During recent years an additional cause of slaughter has arisen from the presence of oil surveyors and motorized troops, many of whom have no compunction about shooting from a vehicle and sometimes use automatic weapons.

The animal is constantly losing ground. It is obvious that, if uncontrolled slaughter continues on the present scale, the species will not survive. This would be particularly serious for tribes such as the Haddad, whose very existence is so intimately bound up with the oryx that they need to be saved from the inevitable results of their own folly and shortsightedness.

There is a pressing need for the establishment of a national park in the Oum Chalouba region of northern Tchad, adequately staffed to enforce protection, and embracing a large enough section of the animal's natural range to cover its wandering propensities. An authority is also needed that could have exclusive and absolute control over hunting throughout the whole of northern Tchad. Such an organization would need to control an area of perhaps 144,000 square miles, with resources proportionate to the task of instituting an effective system of management of this important and irreplaceable animal.

ADDAX
Addax nasomaculatus

Addax *D. W. Ovenden* 1966

The genus *Addax* comprises a single species that, with no exaggeration, can be regarded as unique. It has become adapted to existence under some of the most forbidding environmental conditions anywhere in the world. It is a true creature of the desert, deriving moisture only from the plants on which it feeds, in circumstances under which no other mammal, not even the scimitar-horned oryx, could survive.

The addax is a sandy-coloured animal with white under parts, standing about 3 feet 6 inches at its shoulder, with a conspicuous tuft of chestnut-coloured hair on its forehead. The colour of its coat varies seasonally, being darker in winter. Its hooves are short and broad, to assist it in crossing sand.

The original range of the addax extended throughout the greater part of the Sahara, from the Rio de Oro (possibly Senegambia) and Algeria eastward to the Nile, with a very small population isolated in the Sudan east of the Nile.

The addax has been extinct in Egypt since about 1900. It has also been exterminated in Tunisia, southern Algeria, and Rio de Oro. Recent reports of sightings in this last country appear to refer to occasional strays. In Tripolitania, its extinction was accelerated by Italian military patrols who perniciously machine-gunned the herds. The animal is now very scarce in the Sudan.

The last refuge of the addax in the western Sahara is the vast sand region, incorrectly named "El Djouf" on the maps, situated between the Mauritanian Adrar, the Tagant, the Dahr Tichit-Walata, the Azaonad, and the Hank. This area extends to about 193,000 square miles and is waterless and uninhabited. Monod states that, when in this area a few years ago, he had to travel about 560 miles between two wells. Addax are still abundant in the region, but are hunted by three groups of nomadic tribesmen.

In 1931 Brocklehurst described the method of hunting used by the Arabs in Darfur in the western Sudan. "Carrying enough water for six or seven days, a small party of these Arabs mounted on camels and accompanied by their dogs push into the desert until they strike the fresh spoor or actually sight a herd of Addax . . . and by following the undulations of the ground, the party is able to get within a few hundred yards of their quarry without being observed. The Addax being short-legged and heavy, is incapable of any great speed, and the cows and calves are soon brought to bay, and even some of the old bulls are run down and speared."

These primitive techniques have given way to modern firearms, and slaughter is therefore on the increase. Moreover, this hitherto impenetrable region has in recent years been opened to motorized transport and entered by military personnel and oil prospectors.

Not a single game reserve exists in the whole of the huge expanse of territory in which the animal can be found. Monod does well to draw attention to the fact that "Mauritania and Mali have the privilege of possessing on their common border the last remaining large addax habitat refuge in Africa. These two countries therefore have a very particular responsibility to the world for effectively safeguarding the species". There is certainly a need to establish a national park in the Oum Chalouba region of northern Tchad that, if extensive enough, would serve to protect both the addax and the scimitar-horned oryx.

The ecological niche occupied by the addax enables it to claim an unusual distinction: neither directly nor indirectly can it come into competition with man or his domestic livestock. It is thus clear that, if intelligently managed, the addax could become a valuable, indeed an irreplaceable, animal in the service of man – and particularly in the service of those nomadic tribes whose culture and ultimate existence are so closely interlinked with the only mammals capable, as it were, of converting the desert into protein.

BONTEBOK
Damaliscus dorcas dorcas

The bontebok has often been mistaken for its near relative the blesbok, to which it bears a close resemblance – a fact that has given rise to much confusion, particularly in the early literature. Indeed, the two animals are now regarded as belonging to the same species and the blesbok, *D. d. phillipsi*, though extinct in the wild, has such a large population on South African farms that it does not rate a sheet in the Red Data Book. Both animals stand about 3 feet 4 or 6 inches at the shoulder. The general colour of the bontebok is a rich dark brown, with flanks, upper limbs, and the sides of its head a glossy plum colour, the blesbok being a somewhat redder brown, lacking any purple gloss, and with other less conspicuous differences. The bontebok's limbs are white below the knee except for a brown stripe on the front of its forelegs. Some individuals also have a brown patch on the front part of their hind legs immediately above their hooves. The front of the bontebok's face is white. It has a much more prominent pure white rump patch than the pale rump patch of the blesbok. Its horns incline towards the lyre shape and are up to about 16 inches long.

When the first Europeans arrived at the Cape in the latter part of the seventeenth century, the bontebok was restricted to a narrow strip of land in the south-western part of the Cape Province between Swellendam and Caledon, sandwiched between the mountain ranges in the north and the coastal belt in the south. But within this area the animal was from all accounts abundant.

The region was soon absorbed by settlement. With its very restricted range, the animal was particularly vulnerable to hunting, and before long had been severely reduced in numbers. Unrestricted hunting and pressure on the land forced the survivors into the sour lands of the coastal belt, where the poor grazing, deficiency of trace elements, and heavy parasitic infestations formed a combination of circumstances under which it was impossible for them to thrive.

The bontebok would almost certainly have been extinguished along with the quagga but for the initiative of a few local landowners, notably Mr Van der Byl, who in 1864 succeeded in driving a herd of about 300 bontebok into a large enclosure on his land. Mr Van der Byl's example was followed by one of his neighbours, Dr Albertyn, and later by other interested landowners. But, in spite of stringent legal protection, numbers continued to decline, and in 1931, in an attempt to meet the situation, the authorities established the National Bontebok Park (1,784 acres), situated about 16 miles from Bredasdorp: this was specifically for the protection of the subspecies, and had then a stock of twenty-two animals.

At one time the policy of the National Parks Board was to encourage interested farmers to establish small herds on their land, and to help with the provision of stock for that purpose. This system did not work out as had been hoped. Small herds on adjacent farms attempted to link up with each other, and many were killed or injured on the fences in the process. Moreover, there was a tendency for the males in these small enclosed groups to kill not only each other, but also calves. This policy had therefore to be abandoned.

In the National Bontebok Park all went well for the first few years: by the end of 1953 numbers had increased to about 120. Unfortunately the park was not well sited. During the winter much of it was inundated. Parasitic infestations spread in the land. By the end of 1960 the position had deteriorated so seriously that it was decided to transfer the animals to a new park at Swellendam. Another herd was established on the Provincial Wildlife Farm de Hoop. Both these reserves are more favourably situated. There are also other herds, on private land in the Swellendam and Bredasdorp districts; and a large one in the Albany district. As a result of these measures, the future of the subspecies now appears to be secure.

HUNTER'S HARTEBEEST
Damaliscus hunteri

Hunter's hartebeest is perhaps best described as having the general appearance of a small kongoni (Coke's hartebeest) but the lyre-shaped horns of an impala. Its skin has the texture of a topi, but the colour of a kongoni. Stretching from eye to eye is a conspicuous white chevron, and it has prominent glands beneath its orbits. It is interesting to speculate how such a distinctive member of the genus evolved in such isolation from its nearest known relatives.

The species is confined to a narrow strip of semi-desert thorn-scrub country in the Garissa District of Kenya, extending from the north bank of the Tana River behind the coastal rain forest into the south-western part of the Somali Republic, where it appears to exist as far as the Juba River.

The bulk of the population is believed to inhabit the Kenya sector of the range, a major dry-season concentration area being in the neighbourhood of the Tana River.

As far as can be judged, the total population probably does not exceed about 1,500, of which an estimated maximum of about 200 live in Somalia. Although no reliable early population estimates exist, the suggestion has been made that numbers may now be as high as ever before, largely through the efficient protection that has long been accorded the species by the Kenya Game Department.

The remoteness, and inaccessibility of the habitat, coupled with the fact that the Somali tribesmen do not molest the species, are the main reasons why it has survived so satisfactorily to the present day.

Why, then, does it figure in the Red Data Book? The explanation is that in November 1962 an announcement was made to the effect that the United Nations Special Fund had agreed to finance a survey of the lower Tana River basin with the object of selecting a large area of land suitable for concentrated development under irrigation. The area to be surveyed, on the left bank of the river, coincided very closely with the range of *D. hunteri*; and the proposal failed to include any provision for studying or taking into consideration the likely effects of the scheme on Hunter's antelope or other native fauna. The purpose of the project being the settlement of 75,000 African families, it seemed unlikely that Hunter's antelope would survive, since the natural range is so small that any substantial change in land use within the area could lead to its extermination.

More recently, the Government of Kenya is reported to have agreed to modify the original proposal by limiting the scheme to the south bank of the Tana River. The habitat of *D. hunteri* will therefore no longer be directly affected. In view of this satisfactory development, the species has been given a green sheet in the Red Data Book, thereby indicating that it is no longer directly endangered.

Indirectly, however, the threat has not been entirely removed. If the irrigation project goes through, the presence of many settlers adjacent to the animal's habitat, even though separated by the Tana River, will inevitably lead to poaching. In such circumstances, the only practicable solution appears to lie in the establishment of a national park or equivalent reserve to embrace as much as possible of the natural range of the species on the north bank of the Tana.

In the Somali Republic, much of the animal's range has been incorporated in the trans-Juba Reserve. Only a single specimen is permitted annually to holders of A type licences; and it is said that the species is seldom hunted by local tribesmen, because its hide is practically worthless.

In October 1963, in an operation conducted jointly by the Game Department and the National Parks of Kenya, a herd of thirty specimens was captured on the Walu Plains on the north bank of the Tana River and transferred to the Tsavo National Park (East). It was hoped in this way to establish a breeding herd within the park such as might secure the survival of the species if the carrying out of the irrigation project placed its existence in jeopardy.

The original plan envisaged holding the animals in pens at Bura for several weeks until they had settled down, before transporting them by lorry to the Tsavo Park. Although the captured animals quickly became tame and fed readily, they did not thrive in the pens. Several died for no obvious reason: and post-mortem examinations failed to reveal the cause. Some months later it was found that the deaths were attributable to muscular dystrophy, a deficiency disease well known in domestic livestock but not previously known in wild animals.

The first of the hartebeest to be moved by air and by road failed to survive the journey, and the situation became so serious that there appeared to be no alternative but to abandon the operation. At this point, the arrival in Mombasa of the British aircraft-carrier H.M.S. *Ark Royal* solved the problem. Her captain at once generously offered to allow the carrier's helicopters to be used for the operation. This permitted the animals to be loaded into the helicopters at the point of capture and flown straight to the Tsavo Park, where they arrived in perfect condition within about $2\frac{1}{2}$ hours of being caught.

More would have been transported in the few days before the onset of the rains, but the breakdown of the capture vehicles, caused by the rough conditions under which they were working, brought the operation to an end.

After a short period in holding pens, the hartebeest were released near Voi as the rains broke. They dispersed into the park and for almost two years all attempts to locate them again failed. It was assumed that the translocation had been unsuccessful, and that the animals had either died or moved out of the park.

On the 10th April 1966, however, when all hope had been abandoned, a small herd consisting of seven animals was spotted about 8 miles from Aruba. Four of them were juveniles that must have been born in the park. Another was seen near Maunga. There is therefore the strong possibility that others may also have survived, and that "Operation Antelope" may after all prove to have been successful.

SWAYNE'S HARTEBEEST
Alcelaphus buselaphus swaynei

The common African hartebeest has fifteen races, of which the bubal hartebeest, *A. b. buselaphus*, of North Africa, and the red hartebeest, *A. b. caama*, of the Cape are extinct, and Swayne's hartebeest, *A. b. swaynei*, is in danger of extinction. Swayne's is one of the smallest of the hartebeests next to the extinct bubal hartebeest. It is a close relative of the tora hartebeest, *A. b. tora*, from which it is distinguished by a darker body colour, which is a deep reddish-brown. Its face and the upper part of its body have dark markings. Adult specimens have a somewhat silvery appearance, as their hairs are tipped with white. Specimens from eastern Somalia are said to differ from those of Ethiopia by having an almost purplish tinge, with less prominent facial markings. According to Swayne, horns vary greatly in shape and size.

In 1891–2 Brigadier-General E. J. E. Swayne, who discovered the animal, was the first European to visit the area, well south of the Golis Range of Somaliland and about 120 miles from the coast, inhabited by the hartebeest. In this region was a series of open grass-covered plains, about 4,000 to 6,000 feet above sea-level, occasionally intersected by broken ground covered with thorn scrub, some of which extended for 30 or 40 miles.

His brother, H. G. C. Swayne, described these plains as "covered with hartebeests, there being perhaps a dozen herds in sight at one time, each containing three or four hundred of these antelopes. . . . The largest herd I have seen must have contained a thousand individuals, packed closely together, and looking like a regiment of cavalry, the whole plain being dotted with single bulls".

Within a few years of this discovery, the "immense herds" in the Haud and Ogo that Swayne observed had dwindled to such an extent that by November 1905 he estimated that only about 880 remained. He described the

PLATE 13 (*a*) Bontebok; (*b*) Hunter's hartebeest; (*c*) Black wildebeest *Barry Driscoll* 1966

(a)

(b)

(c)

(a)

(b)

(c)

Swayne's hartebeest *Barry Driscoll* 1967

subspecies at that time as "very greatly diminished and in danger of extinction".

The reason for this drastic decline was the series of rinderpest epidemics that swept Africa during the last decade of the nineteenth century. Swayne stated that the 1897 outbreak caused very heavy losses among the hartebeest in the western part of Somaliland. The magnitude of the disaster is perhaps best shown by his cryptic comment that the Somalis "went out daily on foot and with their hands pulled down the sick animals in order to get the hides".

The rinderpest caused a calamitous setback to the fauna of Somalia from which it was never able to recover, for it was followed by a series of military campaigns about the beginning of the century, notably against the Mad Mullah, during which time much of the interior of the country was beyond effective administrative control.

Apart from the activities of the Mullah and his numerous followers, the military forces were habitually permitted to kill as much game as they wished without restriction. Arms flowed into the Horn of Africa and, to add to the general confusion, the Ethiopians took advantage of the unsettled conditions to send paid Midgan hunters into the country. They performed their

PLATE 14 (*a*) Slender-horned gazelle, typical race; (*b*) Sumatran serow; (*c*) Walia ibex *Barry Driscoll* 1966

task so conscientiously that within a relatively short time they had succeeded in almost destroying the remnants of the hartebeest and oryx herds.

The position today is that *A. b. swaynei* no longer exists in the Somali Republic; but about 200 individuals survive in Ethiopia, where J. Blower recorded a herd on the Alledeghi Plains in 1966, and small groups have been seen near lakes Zwai, Awaya, and Chamo. The Ethiopian Government has taken the precaution of placing the subspecies on the List of Protected Animals; but, at the time of writing, there is no means of enforcing protection.

BLACK WILDEBEEST
or WHITE-TAILED GNU
Connochaetes gnou

The genus *Connochaetes* has two living species: *C. taurinus*, the common blue wildebeest, which is widely distributed in eastern, central, and southern Africa; and *C. gnou*, the black wildebeest, also often called the white-tailed gnu.

The black wildebeest had a relatively smaller distribution than the blue, being restricted to an area extending from the Karoo (central Cape Province) to the high veld country of the Orange Free State and southern Transvaal up to the Vaal River. Selous recorded the species in southern Bechuanaland in 1872 and again in 1880. Within this range it was once abundant, an indication of numbers being gained from Bryden, who wrote in 1899: "If it had not been for a devastating disease known as the 'brand-sickte', or burning sickness, which periodically thinned the herds of these and other game their numbers would have been far too many even for that vast country to have supported . . ."

The general colour of the black wildebeest is dark brown or charcoal, with a black face; its mane consists of stiff hairs, parti-coloured black and dirty white. A beard extends from its lower jaw to its lower chest; and its whitish horse-like tail extends almost to the ground. Males stand about 3 feet 10 inches at the shoulder and weigh about 360 pounds; females are a good deal smaller.

From the earliest days of the Cape Colony,

the Boers regarded the white-tailed gnu and the quagga as a convenient source of food for their African labourers, and skins were used for a variety of purposes including, among other items, *riems* for work oxen, harness, ropes, and even sacks for storing grain.

For more than a century the black wildebeest was subjected to constant unregulated persecution, culminating in the 1870s with the activities of hide-hunters, who slaughtered immense numbers solely for the paltry value of the skins, which were shipped in quantity to Europe. Selous doubted whether a single specimen remained alive anywhere in the Transvaal by the end of 1885. He estimated that the species would almost certainly have been wiped out had it not been for the initiative of Messrs Du Plessis and Terblanc, two Boers living in the Orange Free State, who succeeded in protecting a herd of about 300 animals on each of their farms.

Until 1936 the only specimens surviving were all on private land. Mainly as a result of repeated representations by the Wild Life Protection Society of South Africa to the Provincial Administration of the Orange Free State, five cows were released into the Somerville Game Reserve in October of that year. The following year a bull was introduced, and in April 1939 a further bull and six cows. From this nucleus, numbers in the reserve had risen to fifty-two by 1945. When the Somerville Game Reserve was abolished, the herd was transferred to the Willem Pretorius Game Reserve in the Orange Free State, and by 1966 it had increased to 370.

The position today is that several herds have been established in game reserves and on private land. In addition to the Willem Pretorius Reserve, the most important herds are those in the Mountain Zebra National Park, the S. A. Lombard Nature Reserve, and Natal's two mountain reserves – Giants Castle and Royal National Park.

The species is now well protected, and numbers are increasing satisfactorily. This is best illustrated by comparing the total population of 1,048 in 1947 with the 1965 figure of 2,117.

As a result of its recently enhanced status, the black wildebeest has been given a green sheet in the Red Data Book, to indicate that the species is no longer threatened with extinction.

BEIRA
Dorcatragus megalotis

The sole representative of its genus, the beira is a little-known antelope that, when first described, was regarded as a type of klipspringer (*Oreotragus*). It was later recognized as being more closely allied to the dik-diks (*Madoqua*), by the similarity of their foot-glands.

The beira stands about 1 foot 10 inches at the shoulder and weighs about 20 pounds; it is therefore substantially larger than the dik-dik. It is covered with dense, coarse hair, reddish-grey on its upper parts and white below; it has fawn-coloured legs and a yellowish-red head. A distinct dark line runs along each flank. Its ears are exceptionally large in proportion to its head, the inner surface being lined with white hairs. Horns are present only on the male. Its tail is bushy and short; and the under surfaces of its hooves are equipped with gristly pads, which permit the animal to move in a manner strikingly reminiscent of the klipspringer, among the rocky regions it inhabits.

The beira usually lives in pairs or in small parties of from three to seven animals (occasionally more), of which one or two are males. Each group establishes its own territory, usually on a small hill. Its habitat is largely waterless and the beira probably gets its needed water from dew and the vegetation it feeds on.

The beira's protective coloration merges very effectively with the landscape. This antelope is also fast, agile, and wary. Moreover, as a hill species it occupies a habitat that by its very nature is not yet coveted by man. These factors, in combination, suggest that the beira's chances of survival are probably better than those of many species living in the plains of the Horn of Africa.

The same reasons may explain the fragmentary and frequently contradictory information that exists about the animal. Even its distribution is not well known. The general consensus of opinion is that it is restricted to the mountainous regions in the north and north-west of the Somali Republic as far south as the Nogal Valley. It is also said to occur in parts of Ethiopia; but the Ethiopian sector of the range has never been satisfactorily determined.

SLENDER-HORNED GAZELLE
Gazella leptoceros

The species comprises two races, *G. l. leptoceros* and *G. l. marica*, both of which are listed in the Red Data Book, but are here treated together for the sake of convenience.

The rhim, to use the name by which the animal is usually known, is a medium-sized gazelle about 2 feet 4 inches at the shoulder and weighing about 60 pounds. It is readily distinguished from other members of the genus *Gazella* by its very light (almost white) sandy-fawn colour with extremely faint markings, and by its long, thin, almost straight horns. Its tail is darker, with a black tip. Its hooves are long and narrow, and rather splayed to help the animal in moving over sand.

The typical race is widely distributed in a range covering the greater part of the northern half of the Sahara, from Algeria to Egypt and the north-western Sudan and the mountains in the extreme north-west of Tchad. The race *G. l. marica* exists in the Arabian peninsula.

Like the addax, the slender-horned gazelle is a true desert species, occupying sand-dune regions in which few other mammals would survive. In times of unusually severe drought it may leave the dunes in search of food.

Few naturalists have seen this gazelle in the wild state, although at one time it was regarded as the most common of the Saharan mammals. Hartert wrote, in 1913: "Owing to the hilly nature of the dunes and the noiseless walking on the sand, the Reem is easily stalked, and generally killed with shot by the Arabs, who have no idea of sportsmanlike shooting: they often catch the young (with or without the help of dogs), then make it squeak, and kill the mother when coming to the help of her young. In this way, and by patiently waiting for days and nights in ambush, these and other Gazelles are decimated, and they will soon be rare or disappear from all the more or less frequented districts of the northern Sahara."

Whitaker, writing of Tunisia in 1897, said that the Arabs "kill a good many, and every year some 500 to 600 pairs of horns of this species are brought by the caravans coming from the interior to Gabès, where they find a ready sale among the French soldiery".

In the Arabian peninsula the rhim's survival is threatened by motorized hunting parties, whose activities have already been mentioned in the account of the Arabian oryx (p. 148). It is probably less severely menaced, however, than the Arabian gazelle (*G. gazella arabica*), because it favours sandy regions that are impenetrable to motor vehicles, as distinct from the *jol*, or gravel plains, where the going is good.

The remote and inhospitable nature of its environment has so far prevented any detailed study of the species. Knowledge of the animal is therefore very superficial, and its current status is difficult to assess owing to lack of precise details. Information that does exist is enough, however, to indicate that the remorseless persecution to which the rhim has for several decades been exposed has resulted in a substantial decline, although the position may not yet be critical.

Nowhere in its huge natural range is the slender-horned gazelle protected, nor is it represented in a single national park or equivalent reserve. This regrettable fact applies also to several other desert species that have the distinction of being adapted to survival under conditions hostile to most mammalian forms of life. It would be both tragic and short-sighted to permit the extinction of species that possess these unique attributes and that, if properly husbanded, could be of exceptional value in supplying planned protein for man in circumstances under which domestic livestock could not survive.

SUMATRAN SEROW
Capricornis sumatraensis sumatraensis

The serow species is divided into eleven races, which are widely distributed from eastern and southern China through Nepal and Assam to Kashmir, and extend through much of South-East Asia into Sumatra. Only the typical race – that of Sumatra – at present has a sheet in the Red Data Book; but it is possible that others will need to be included as further information on these little-known animals becomes available.

The serow was once distributed throughout the higher parts of Sumatra wherever suitable habitat was to be found. Little recent information is available concerning the animal; but, as far as can be ascertained, it is still to be found in the Tapanuli Mountains, the Padang Highlands, Kerintji, Ranau, and the Lampongs. It spends the day in thick cover or in some sheltered spot, feeding only during the hours of darkness, at which time it may descend to a somewhat lower level. It has the ability to move about on almost perpendicular cliff faces with extraordinary ease and speed.

This shy animal appears unable or unwilling to coexist in areas occupied by man. The continual spread of cultivation has thus caused it to retreat into the more remote and inhospitable parts of the island; and it is now believed to exist in and around the higher reaches of some of the volcanoes along the mountainous western portion of Sumatra.

It has long been nominally protected by law. This, however, does not seem to have deterred the local people from hunting it at every opportunity; its flesh and hide are much in demand, and its horns are used as charms. It is either caught in snares or hunted with the aid of dogs – methods that were so successful in the past that the serow was extinguished throughout all but the most impenetrable parts of its range.

The rugged nature of the terrain in which the Sumatran serow has taken its last stand accords it a degree of protection from man; but persecution is so persistent that the only real hope for the animal's survival lies in the establishment of reserves specially designed for the purpose. Such reserves were in fact created before the Second World War, but since then their existence appears to have been overlooked.

JAPANESE SEROW
Capricornis crispus

The genus comprises two species of goat antelope: the serow and the Japanese serow, *C. crispus*, which is subdivided into two races, one of which (*C. c. crispus*) is restricted to Japan and the other (*C. c. swinhoei*) to Taiwan.

The Japanese serow is smaller than the mainland serow, with woollier and thicker fur and a more bushy tail; but it lacks the heavy mane of the mainland form. Its general colour ranges from grey-black to red-brown, with whitish under parts, and with white markings on its legs, throat, and muzzle. Both sexes carry short curved horns.

At one time the serow existed throughout much of the higher forested regions of the Japanese islands of Honshu, Shikoku, and Kyushu; but it is now restricted to the mountainous areas of Honshu (excluding the Chugoku District) and Kyushu (where only small numbers remain).

The reduction of the original forests, which has taken place on an increasing scale during the last half-century, has greatly reduced the area of habitat available to this woodland animal.

According to Nagamichi Kuroda, serow meat is more tasty than sika venison – and its skins are popular as carpets. For these reasons the animal was heavily hunted. By 1924 only a few remained. In that year the serow was declared a special nature monument – a designation that accords complete protection against hunting and capture. More recently, several reserves have been established specially for the animal's protection. These measures have proved effective and have permitted the population to build up to an estimated 1,500.

The Formosan serow, *C. c. swinhoei*, which is endemic to the island of Taiwan, is now restricted to a few of the more remote and inaccessible parts of its mountains.

The animal normally occupies rugged forest at a high altitude, where it lives either singly or in small groups of up to about half a dozen individuals. It is remarkably sure-footed and, although not fast, is capable of traversing steep and difficult rocky slopes. It rests during the day in cover or beneath the shelter of an overhanging rock, and feeds in the evening and early morning. It is reputed to be capable of defending itself resolutely and vigorously with its horns.

Wayre reports that the serow is frequently seen by forestry workers in the remoter parts of the Ali-shan Mountains in central Taiwan, which in places rise to more than 11,000 feet. Although locally not uncommon, the total population is small and is unlikely to be capable

Japanese serow *D. W. Ovenden* 1966

of withstanding the degree of uncontrolled hunting to which it is currently subjected.

The aborigines – of which there are about a dozen families in the Ali-shan area – capture the goat-antelope by means of large steel traps, usually during the months of September to December, at which time the animal is particularly vulnerable, as it is then compelled to leave the protection of the forest in search of grazing at the lower altitudes.

The aborigines drink the fresh blood before smoking and selling the meat to the Chinese, who have unshakeable faith in the medicinal properties that are believed to be inherent in almost every part of the animal's anatomy, and are the reason why the demand for serow meat is far greater than the supply.

The Taiwan Government has made no attempt to safeguard the serow, or indeed any other native fauna; and there can be no doubt that, unless appropriate protective measures are taken in the near future, it will be only a matter of time before a good many species cease to exist on the island. It is probably already too late to save several of them; but there is still time to ensure the future of the serow, provided that prompt action is taken.

TAKIN
Budorcas taxicolor

The genus comprises a single species, which is subdivided into three races: the Mishmi takin, *B. t. taxicolor*, of Assam and Bhutan; the Szechwan takin, *B. t. tibetana*; and the golden takin, *B. t. bedfordi*. The two last-named sub-species are both included in the Red Data Book.

The takin is a powerfully built animal, having affinities with the serows and the musk ox. Adults stand about 4 feet 2 inches at the shoulder, with short legs, a distinctive bulbous nose, and horns somewhat resembling those of the wildebeest. Their tails are short and hidden beneath long fur.

During the summer season the takin lives in large-sized herds at or above the timber line; but, during the winter, herds break up into smaller groups that move to lower country. The animals are very shy, and generally spend the greater part of the day in cover, emerging into the open in the evening to feed, retiring again in the early hours of the morning. When alarmed, a herd will seek shelter in dense thickets.

The older bulls lead a solitary existence except during the rutting season, which is in July, calves being dropped at the end of March or early in April. Normally a single calf is born; it is capable of keeping up with its mother within three days of birth.

Szechwan takin, *Budorcas taxicolor tibetana*

The Szechwan takin has horns thinner, more arched, and less ridged than those of the typical race. Summer males have golden yellow coats washed with iron grey, and go grey in winter; the females are much greyer than the males.

This race appears to be confined to Szechwan, north to the Kansu border, west to the Omei Shan Mountains, south nearly to the great bend of the Yangtze. Here it was fairly plentiful in the first third of the present century; but the Chinese authorities now regard it as a rare mammal and, disturbed by the hunting pressure (in winter the takins come down to the sheltered valleys from their summer range in rhododendron and dwarf bamboo between 8,000 and 14,000 feet), have, it is reported, protected the race.

Two males were in Peking Zoo in 1965.

Golden takin, *Budorcas taxicolor bedfordi*

The golden takin is readily distinguished from the other races by the striking colour of its shaggy coat, which Lydekker describes as "bright golden buff colour . . . the golden tint being rather darker in the males and creamy in the females".

The subspecies exists only in part of the Tsing Ling Range, called the Tai-pei-san (or Great White Mountain), in southern Shensi, where it lives in isolation. Its food consists of bamboo grass, which is abundant at that altitude.

Its habitat is at an elevation of from 9,000 to 11,000 feet, and consists of precipitous and inaccessible country, which the animal is able to cross with extraordinary agility, and which provides extremely effective natural protection for it.

The golden takin was first described in 1911, since when the rugged nature of its country has effectively discouraged both foreign sportsmen and local hunters from shooting specimens. The animal has, moreover, the unusual distinction of being one of the very few native mammals that the Chinese have not hunted almost out of existence. Sowerby noted, in 1937, that the takin were hunted "only to a limited extent for food, there being nothing about them that is considered of any particular value for medicinal purposes, as is the case with so many other large mammals in China".

Under the new regime, the golden takin has been accorded special protection. No census has ever been taken, but it is thought likely that its total population can be numbered in the low hundreds; and there is every reason to believe that its future is assured.

The only captive golden takins in the world in 1965 were in China. The Peking Zoo possessed a male and two females, and Shanghai Zoo had a solitary male.

NILGIRI TAHR
Hemitragus hylocrius

The genus *Hemitragus* embraces three living species: the Himalayan tahr, *H. jemlahicus*; the Arabian tahr, *H. jayakari*; and the Nilgiri tahr, *H. hylocrius*. The two last both have sheets in the Red Data Book.

The Nilgiri tahr is the largest of the three species, standing more than 3 feet at the shoulder. It is readily distinguished from its Himalayan relative by a shorter, stiffer, and coarser coat. Its

females have a single pair of teats; females of the Himalayan species have two pairs. Its general colour is a dark yellowish-brown, becoming paler on its under parts. Females and juveniles are greyer, old males darker. The most conspicuous feature of old males is a whitish saddle-shaped patch on their backs; they are locally known as "saddle-backs".

The Nilgiri tahr lives in the mountainous regions of southern India at an elevation of 4,000 to 6,000 feet, from the Nilgiri Hills to the Anamallais and southwards along the Western Ghats. Tahr normally occupy forested slopes; but the Nilgiri species is said to prefer the scarps above the limits of the forest. The animals feed in the early morning and evening, lying up in the shade during the heat of the day. Several females at a time maintain vigilant watch, which makes a herd difficult to approach.

This tahr seems to have no definite breeding season. Kids are seen throughout the greater part of the year; but most births occur at the beginning of the hot weather, following a gestation period of about six months. Normally a single kid is born; twins are rare.

The population totals rather more than 800 animals, half of which are in four sanctuaries in the Nilgiris. There may be a few others in areas where no census has been undertaken because of inaccessibility.

Losses occur through natural predation, particularly by leopard and probably by dholes (wild dogs), which hunt in packs. Such losses are made good through natural increase, and could therefore be sustained were it not for excessive shooting, which has taken place in spite of the protection accorded the animal by law, and to which the decline of the tahr is chiefly attributable.

Davidar gave his opinion in 1963: "The herd on the eastern slopes [of the Nilgiris] around Glen Morgan has been wiped out by poachers, thanks to the ban imposed on shooting and the consequent absence of licence holders who provide a check on illegal shooting . . . In the Kundah Hydro-Electric Scheme area roads are being laid in the tahr country and forest wattle plantations are also being pushed through. This seems a crucial stage in the protection of this species . . . I may state that unless the licence holder is allowed to pursue the saddle-backs, most of which are useless for breeding purposes, and thus patrol the area, there is no doubt that tahr will eventually share the fate of the Glen Morgan herd".

In 1965 three males and two females were in captivity in the Trichur Zoo (Kerala), which has reared three kids since 1959; and a female at Trivandrum.

WALIA IBEX
Capra walie

This species is the Ethiopian representative of the ibex, *C. ibex*, of which it is regarded by some as a very well-marked race.

The walia ibex is larger and more powerfully built than the nearest race of ibex, the Nubian ibex, *C. i. nubiana*, which ranges to the neighbouring Sudan. It stands about 3 feet 2 inches at the shoulder, and has much more massive horns than the Nubian ibex – up to 45 inches long. It also has a prominent bony protuberance on its forehead. Its general colour is a deep chestnut, with whitish under parts. Females are paler and a good deal smaller than males.

The species is confined to a narrow belt of precipitous crags and narrow ledges on the almost sheer cliff face, between the 8,000- and 11,000-foot levels, on the north-western escarpment of the Semien Mountains, in the Province of Begemder, Ethiopia, about 60 miles northeast of Gondar. When Maydon and Blaine visited the area in the 1920s, the walia occupied a larger range and was much more abundant than it is today.

Recent visits to the Semien Mountains have been made by Leslie Brown and John Blower. Blower describes them as "one of the largest and certainly the most spectacular mountain massifs in Africa. They consist of a high undulating plateau deeply intersected by a number of rocky valleys, the average altitude of the plateau being 11,000–13,000 feet, but rising to 15,158 feet at its highest point (Ras Dashan). To the north and east the plateau drops away in immense vertical precipices 2,000–5,000 feet in height, which extend in an unbroken wall for some 40 kilometers or more, and are guarded by outlying pinnacles rising like immense Gothic cathedrals from the broken country beneath the cliffs almost to the height of the plateau itself. This indescribably spectacular landscape is generally agreed by those who have seen both to exceed even the Grand Canyon in its breathtaking grandeur and beauty".

Brown describes the scenery as the "most spectacular of its kind that I have seen anywhere, and certainly some of the most astonishing in the world. Maydon found that words failed him, and had to say, like me, that the Semien were like no other mountains to be seen anywhere."

The animal has long been persistently hunted by local tribesmen for the meat, hide, and horns – these last are used for drinking vessels. The hunters' usual technique has been to lie up over a favourite shelter or water-hole and wait for the animal to appear. The rugged nature of the habitat has always made hunting unusually difficult, and has served to protect the ibex in its isolated retreat, a situation that prevailed until the introduction of modern firearms.

According to Brown, local tribesmen maintain that the species underwent a catastrophic decline during the Italian occupation of the country. At that time the Semien Range became a hide-out for guerilla fighters, many of whom spent a long period in the mountains, living to a large extent off the country. After the Second World War the species gained a short respite, when the guerillas emerged from hiding and returned to their former mode of life. But this was not for long: once normal conditions had been re-established, the local people, armed with more efficient weapons than before, began hunting the ibex for food.

Brown explains that "it is convenient to blame the Italians for almost anything bad that has happened in Ethiopia, either directly or indirectly. The facts appear to be that legal protection by the Government means very little, that Walia are hunted indiscriminately by local people, and that the main reason for their survival is that some of them, at least, live in places beyond the wit of man to reach without a great deal of trouble".

In theory the walia is protected by law, but in practice such protection is merely nominal. Brown writes that he was "assured by the

District Governor at Davarik that there were guards charged with the duty of protecting the animals. However, none of these guards contacted us, though we enquired about them." He concludes that "if protective edicts had gone out they had either not reached Geech or were largely ignored, and that the only thing that would cause any local hunter to spare a Walia was difficulty in recovering the body. Our guide appeared to regard as absurd the idea that female Walia with kids should be spared to breed some more. 'Someone else would shoot them before they could breed' was his verdict."

Brown rightly emphasizes that any account of the wildlife of Semien must not fail to take into account the human situation. The number of human beings living in the neighbourhood has increased since the Second World War and threatens serious poaching. The herds of domestic livestock have correspondingly risen, and crops are being grown on an ever-wider scale. Cultivation is frequently begun on steeply sloping land, often to the very foot of the cliffs or on any accessible spurs; and even the most elementary principles of soil conservation are totally ignored. The little soil that exists, together with the natural vegetation that alone keeps it in place, is eroding away. At the higher levels the giant heath, twenty feet high, and other interesting native trees and shrubs are being cut down for fuel, while cattle dung is collected for the same purpose. The thought of planting quick-growing trees for fuel does not seem to have occurred to anyone.

Brown writes: "The extent of cultivation and grazing in the Semien highlands is alarming and it can be said that the cultivators, both at the lower levels and on the plateaux at 10,000 feet and above, are destroying or seriously damaging their own habitat with an energy and industry which would be highly commendable if it were not certain, in due course, to lead to large scale human tragedy. Cultivation extends in many areas to 12,000 feet, and slopes are being cultivated which cannot be cultivated by any method known to man without causing erosion. The mere act of ploughing throws clods and stones downhill. As the soils are often not deep, a situation must inevitably arise in which rock is exposed on the steeper slopes and the large areas now under cultivation will have to be abandoned, except for a few pockets where the soil is deeper or the slope more gentle".

These various hazards represent a serious and continuing threat both to the survival of the walia and the uniquely interesting habitat itself. Brown's recent estimates indicate that the walia populations can be numbered in the low hundreds, in an area of potential grazing of about 1,000 to 1,200 acres. The status of the species will give cause for concern until effective action is taken to protect both animal and habitat.

The solution lies in establishing a national park in the area, a recommendation made by Grimwood and Brown in 1965 in their *Report on the Conservation of Nature and Natural Resources in Ethiopia*. The Government of Ethiopia has approved this proposal in principle, but unfortunately has not yet taken adequate practical steps towards its implementation.

In conclusion, enough has been said in this brief summary to indicate that, although the numbers of the walia ibex have seriously declined compared with those of forty years ago, the residue is adequate to ensure the survival of the species and to allow it gradually to reoccupy its former range, provided adequate protection is given while the opportunity still exists.

MARKHOR
Capra falconeri

The genus *Capra* has six living species, widely distributed from western Europe through the Mediterranean to India, extending north as far as Siberia and south to Ethiopia.

The markhor, *C. falconeri*, is subdivided into six races, which differ mainly in their horns, and inhabit different rugged mountain ranges from extreme eastern Iran along the Afghanistan–Pakistan border, extending into southern Russia and the western Himalayas.

Reliable information on the current status and distribution of the markhor is available only from the Soviet sector of the range. Thus, although *C. f. jerdoni* is at present the sole representative of the species listed in the Red Data Book, further investigations may possibly reveal the need to add others.

The markhor is the largest and most power-fully built of all the wild goats, an adult ram standing up to 3 feet 5 inches at the shoulder. The horns vary from the wide spread and open twist of the Astor race, *C. f. falconeri*, of Kashmir and Baltistan, in which the spiral does not exceed one and a half turns, to the tight cork-screw formation of the Suleiman or straight-horned race, *C. f. jerdoni*, of the Punjab, with a maximum of three full turns. Male horns often reach a length of 60 inches, the record being 63 inches: female horns are much smaller, but of the same general form. The old males are further distinguished by having a heavy beard extending down to the chest. The markhor's summer coat is long and silky and a deep russet-brown, changing to varying shades of grey in the cold season.

In Tadjikistan and Uzbekistan the markhor is never found higher than 8,000 feet. For the greater part of the year the animal frequents open forested regions, preferably where there are also steep rocky scarps or cliff faces, as well as herbaceous clearings where it can feed un-disturbed. In summer it moves higher to the limits of the timber-line, in some places going as high as the alpine meadows, but always keeping below the snow-line. In winter it descends to lower levels.

Markhor usually live in groups of four or five individuals, but form larger herds, up to twenty or thirty, during the winter. Adult rams spend the greater part of the year apart from the females; but during the mating season, which in Tadjikistan is from mid-November to December, they establish small harems, with bitter duelling.

The kids are born at the end of April or early June after a gestation period of five to five and a half months, and are not weaned until the next mating season. Young females usually give birth to a single kid; but adults bear twins.

Cobb has lately stated that the name markhor is derived from the Persian *mar* (snake) and *khor* (eater), and that he considers the name to be apt. Over a century ago Hutton wrote that the Afghans call the animal "snake-eater" because they believe it deliberately seeks out and eats snakes. For that reason they also believe that if a man is bitten by a snake the effects of the poison will be counteracted by eating markhor meat. Moreover, the "bezoar", which is some-times found in the animal's stomach, is believed to have the power of extracting poison from the wound.

Numbers have decreased in recent years throughout the greater part of the range as a result of indiscriminate shooting. The animal lives in remote areas where the law could not be enforced, even if it accorded theoretical protec-tion. The introduction of modern firearms has been largely responsible for the accelerated decline; but an important contributory factor has been competition for the limited grazing from increasing numbers of domestic livestock.

In 1936 Stockley wrote that markhor in the Suleiman Range were "persecuted by all and sundry at all times of the year, while the local inhabitants are well-armed, and the peace which has lately invested that country has only given the tribesmen more leisure to hunt. Small wonder that the markhor have decreased almost to vanishing point and are likely to decrease still further unless measures are adopted for their protection. Such measures are difficult to enforce in country where my last four trips have had to be carried out with an escort of forty rifles, but at least the authorities might make some effort in places immediately under their control, instead

Markhor *Peter Scott* 1967

of encouraging the local soldiery to shoot markhor and corial for meat in lieu of meat rations, using government ammunition to do it."

T. J. Roberts reported that in 1966 the straight-horned markhor survived in only six or seven isolated groups in inaccessible mountain ranges. The largest herd, probably, was in the Toba Kakar on the Baluchi–Afghan border, the most southerly in the Gorshani Hills in the southern Suleiman Range; a few (ten to fifteen) still lived in the Chiltan Reserve, a few probably in the Takhatu Reserve near Bostan, and perhaps no more than twenty in the Kaliphat Range (11,400 feet) nominally also a reserve but heavily poached. Late evidence suggests also that a few may survive in the north in the Takht-i-Suleiman (11,100 feet) on the Baluchi–Waziri border (about 20 square miles) and possibly in the Khanori Hills in Malakand. Formerly the race extended to Mithankot, the neighbourhood of Quetta, and into Afghanistan as far as Kandahar.

The race is severely threatened because protection is largely nominal and enforcement hampered by lack of funds to pay game guards.

The only country in which the markhor receives adequate protection is the U.S.S.R. There the animal had at one time been reduced to a precariously low level, but since 1936 it has been strictly protected, as a result of which its status has considerably improved, and the population is now estimated at about 1,000.

CYPRIAN MOUFLON
Ovis orientalis ophion

The group of sheep known as Asiatic mouflon, red sheep, and urial are all forms of *Ovis orientalis* – one of several wild species that together comprise the genus of the domestic sheep, which is widely distributed, with representatives in both the Old and the New World. The number of species now living is seven, if Dall's sheep, *O. dalli*, of Alaska and the Yukon is regarded as distinct from *O. canadensis*, the bighorn.

The Cyprian mouflon, *O. o. ophion*, is at present the only race of *Ovis orientalis* to warrant a sheet in the Red Data Book.

A mature male mouflon of Cyprus is a strongly built animal standing about 2 feet 2 inches at the shoulder, with heavy sickle-shaped horns of triangular cross-section. Females are hornless. The mouflon's thick winter coat is a dull brown, with a prominent light grey saddle across its withers and a black throat-mane. The lighter summer coat is brown, with light under parts.

The mouflon is the only large wild mammal native to Cyprus. During medieval times it existed throughout much of the island, not only in each of its two prominent mountain ranges, but also in the foothills.

A popular sport at that time was coursing the mouflon with cheetah. It was also hunted with hounds; and Waterer states that, to judge from the "numbers regularly taken in the chase, it is clear that Mouflon must have been very plentiful in nearly all parts of Cyprus".

By the time of the British occupation of Cyprus in 1878, the mouflon had already undergone considerable numerical reduction and was restricted to the southern range of mountains. It was still common in both the Troödos and Paphos forests, however; and, since its meat was extremely palatable and no serious attempt was

Cyprian mouflon *Barry Driscoll* 1967

made to regulate hunting, it was killed without restriction.

During the next half century, the increase in human population and the development of the island inevitably brought new pressures on the mouflon. The construction of summer resorts near Troödos, the establishment of a mining community at Amiandos, and the development of a network of roads to open up previously inaccessible areas (to give but a few examples) coincided with the introduction of modern firearms. These and other factors combined to bring the mouflon close to extinction.

By 1937 the Troödos population had been extinguished and all that remained of the subspecies was a small herd of fifteen animals in the Paphos forest.

At this point the plight of the mouflon was brought to the attention of the Society for the Preservation of the Fauna of the Empire (as it was then called) and other organizations, and a representative of the Society visited the island in 1938 to assess the situation. His report aroused considerable interest in many quarters and led to swift remedial action.

The entire Paphos forest, extending to 148,500 acres, was declared a game reserve in which it would be illegal to carry firearms for any purpose. The law was amended to provide effective legal protection to the mouflon; and forest guards were appointed to patrol the reserve. Perhaps the most important measure involved the exclusion of all goats from the forest. Until then large flocks had resided permanently in the forest, and their herdsmen, all of whom were armed, were primarily responsible for shooting the mouflon. Their expulsion resulted in an immediate improvement in the mouflon's status, and since then, in spite of occasional poaching, the situation has steadily improved.

The Paphos forest is in a mountainous region rising to a maximum height of 4,619 feet, with eleven valleys radiating more or less from the centre of the area. During the summer, mouflon occupy the higher sectors of the range, moving down to the valleys during the winter. For the greater part of the time they remain within the forest, but on rare occasions emerge and cause damage to orchards and vineyards.

Much of the Paphos forest consists of the evergreen dwarf oak *Quercus alnifolia*, which is unknown outside Cyprus. The reserve also contains the only surviving stands of the magnificent cedar *Cedrus brevifolia*, another tree that is unique to the island. It is therefore of very great botanical and scenic, as well as faunal, interest.

Not the least important result of the protective measures has been the improvement of the forested habitat through the expulsion of domestic livestock. The forest has thickened up, and the fire hazard has been substantially lessened. Waterer, describing the situation in 1949, considered that "conditions for Mouflon life in the Paphos Forest are now more favourable than they have been at any time during the past hundred years. In such circumstances it should now only remain to enforce strict protection and Mouflon should be able to breed up to any required strength over a period of years".

These hopes, unfortunately, have not been wholly realized. The struggle for independence from 1955–8, and the subsequent unsettled conditions, resulted in a further period of uncontrolled slaughter. Once again the mouflon population was severely reduced.

No accurate assessment of the population has been made in recent years, but it is believed to total between 100 and 200 animals.

Perhaps the best hope for the mouflon lies in the fact that the declared policy of the Department of Forests involves the management of the forest estate in a way that will ensure the effective conservation of the island's native flora and fauna. Forestry management has reached a remarkably high standard in Cyprus, and the Department is fully aware of its special responsibility to protect the mouflon, even though circumstances during the recent past may not always have permitted the carrying out of this obligation to the extent that the Department itself would have wished.

BIRDS

Order PODICIPITIFORMES
Family Podicipitidae: grebes

GIANT PIED-BILLED GREBE
Podilymbus gigas

In the south-west highlands of Guatemala, at a height of about 5,100 feet, lies the big lake of Atitlan, an irregular oval with a shoreline of about 155 miles. Here in 1862 was collected a grebe that, though peculiar, was not recognized as anything special until 1929, when Ludlow Griscom visited Atitlan and realized that it was of an undescribed form.

Griscom gave the Atitlan grebe the name *Podilymbus gigas*, finding that it was a giant form of the common pied-billed grebe of the Americas, widespread on both continents. Later the systematist Wilhelm Meise called it a race of the pied-billed grebe, and K. E. L. Simmons a "semispecies" of it. But it seems to be a good, full species, nearly twice the size of its common pied-billed cousin (and presumed ancestor); high up in the Guatemalan mountains, it replaces the common species. Its wings are so small and weak that it can fly scarcely, if at all; and its colour is darker, and its beak-mark darker – in fact, altogether black.

All expeditions since Griscom's confirm that the giant pied-billed grebe is entirely confined to Lake Atitlan. Griscom, who toured most of the lake in 1929 with his companion Crosby, estimated a population of about 100 pairs; so did Alexander Wetmore, who visited Atitlan in 1936.

Though Atitlan is rather isolated, there are at least five Indian villages around its shores, with inhabitants who hunt the grebes; and visiting shotguns invade the area periodically from the lowlands. Despite the Guatemalan Government's declaration of the lake as a waterfowl refuge in 1959, hunting still continues. However, a wardening system is being planned; and when

Mrs A. La B. Bowes and her husband, C. V. Bowes Jr, visited the lake in 1960 to photograph the grebes and make a census of their population, they found, after covering a substantial stretch of the shoreline, that the numbers were probably of the same order as those estimated by Griscom and Wetmore. Later (in 1963) they returned for further study, photography, and sound-recording; and a census in December 1964 suggested no more than 100 birds surviving. In November 1966 only eighty-six birds could be found.

Besides hunting, a new danger confronts the giant pied-billed grebes. In 1957 Atitlan was stocked with two non-native fishes, the small- and large-mouth bass. The Boweses believe that these fish are "serious predators on the downy chicks, and compete directly with juveniles and adults for food". Future conservation depends certainly on the strengthening of a warden system begun in 1965, and of law-enforcement (a decree protecting the reed beds from cutting has been lately passed), and would be helped by the presence of a biologist resident at least in the breeding season.

Giant pied-billed grebe *Albert E. Gilbert* 1966

Order PROCELLARIIFORMES
Family Diomedeidae: albatrosses

SHORT-TAILED ALBATROSS
Diomedea albatrus

The great albatrosses, so the fossils tell us, go back in geological time over 50,000,000 years – if a breastbone found in an Eocene deposit in Nigeria belonged to this most highly adapted of the soaring sea-bird families, as most paleontologists think it did. *Gigantornis*, if it was an albatross, must, as far as we know, have been the biggest that ever existed – with a wingspread probably of nearly 20 feet; the great wandering albatross, the biggest of the dozen living species of today, has a maximum wingspread of about 11 feet 6 inches.

Doubtless the albatrosses, as a family, originated in the stormy southern oceans. Most of the species live now in the southern hemisphere. None nests any longer in the North Atlantic Ocean, though over 500,000 years ago the now extinct English albatross lived in East Anglia, and bones quite a few million years earlier found in Florida may have belonged to the same species. But outpost-albatrosses still survive in the North Pacific – the waved albatross of the equatorial Galápagos Islands, the black-footed and Laysan albatrosses of the islands farther north, and the short-tailed (or Steller's) albatross of the Pacific north-west, the most northerly member of its family.

All four of the northern Pacific albatrosses are carefully watched by the I.U.C.N., for their nesting status is vulnerable. But the short-tailed species – when adult, a white-bodied, dark-winged bird with a wingspread of 7 feet – is in real danger, and now has only a relict distribution and a tiny population.

From fossil evidence, we know that in the late times of the Pleistocene Ice Ages the short-tailed albatross visited California; and in prehistoric times lived – and was caught and eaten by Indians and Eskimos – along the coasts of California, Oregon, and Alaska as far north as St Lawrence Island in the heart of the Bering Sea. Its bones have been found in no fewer than ten Eskimo middens in Alaska, varying in age from

around 500 B.C. to the nineteenth century A.D. But when modern ornithologists discovered it, in the last two centuries, it was probably already on the decline, aided by Asian fowlers and feather-traders. A few specimens were taken off California in the nineteenth and early twentieth centuries. Ornithologists know for certain of only eight nesting-places that were occupied in this period, and three more that may have been – all of them on little islands in the old Japanese empire on the western side of the North Pacific. Near Formosa the albatross probably bred on small islets in the Pescadores to its west; on Kita Daito Jima (into the present century) and probably Okino Daito Jima, to its east; and possibly on an islet to its north. It also nested on Chia-u-su, or Kobisho (last known egg 1930), in the Ryukyu Islands' Senkaku Archipelago. Further east into the main Pacific it may formerly have nested on Iwo Shima in the Kazan Retto (Volcano Islands); and it certainly did, until hunted out, on about four of the Bonin Islands – probably Muko-shima and Yome-shima, and certainly Nishi-no-shima (last known egg 1924) and Kita-no-shima (last known 1936, when there were about fifty birds). Now it breeds only in its last stronghold, on Torishima, very nearly the southermost of Japan's "Seven" Isles of Izu, where it has barely survived. So near was it to total extinction that it was recorded as extinct by some of the best Japanese and American scholars of the 1940s.

Torishima's population has been affected periodically through the destruction of nesting-grounds by volcanic eruptions and hurricanes; but until the Japanese rediscovered a surviving Torishima population in the 'fifties, and in 1957 declared the island a special nature reserve, the fowlers and feather-hunters wreaked the major havoc there. It has been estimated that, after the islands were settled in 1887, the fowlers killed over 500,000 short-tailed albatrosses and their young on Torishima in the seventeen seasons of 1887 to 1903. In 1903 an eruption killed all the feather-hunters, but others came, and by 1929 the albatross population was estimated at only

2,000. Persecution continued at least until 1934, though in the previous year Japanese ornithologists had already tried to start a programme of conservation and scientific observation of this island colony, which by then they suspected to be unique in the world. This did not stop a fowlers' slaughter of over 3,000 birds in the 1932–3 season, at the end of which the visible survivors were under 100 birds. After the war the population was believed to have disappeared entirely; but in 1953–4 ten pairs were discovered back on Torishima (sixteen birds by another account). The adventures of the colony in the previous intervening years had been rather obscure. Lava flows are thought to have destroyed the main breeding areas in 1939 and 1941, and apparently no birds were seen on the islands at all in 1946–9.

The short-tailed albatross lays its single egg in October or November; thus its young, after a long incubation and fledging period typical of albatrosses, can fly in June or July after the months of good food supply. In the 1954–5 season, at least sixteen adults had seven eggs or young, but all the young may have died; in the 1957–8 season twenty-eight adults were seen with seven chicks; in 1958–9 over thirty-eight adults with eighteen chicks. But in 1959–60 the chicks hatched were said to have been all eaten by Steller's sea eagles. Regular counts began to be made in the season 1961–2, when twenty-three eggs were laid and nineteen young (by another account eleven) hatched, presumably by at least twenty-three pairs, of which the maximum number seen at one time was thirty-five, and ten young were eventually fledged. In 1963 birds (maximum seen forty-four) hatched eleven young, of which ten were fledged; in 1964 birds (maximum seen forty-four) laid twenty-five eggs, of which eleven were fledged; in 1965 birds (maximum seen fifty-two) hatched twelve young, of which eleven were reared.

In October 1965, however, a volcanic eruption forced the evacuation of the weather station (normally now the only home of humans since the feather-hunters departed, when the sanctuary was declared). Occurring as it did just around the production of the 1965–6 crop, it may once more have endangered a global population of birds. However, in April 1966 Y. Yamashina and H. Elliott McClure flew low searches over Torishima and saw twenty-three birds apparently occupying safe sites on the normal territory.

Old haunts of the short-tailed albatross, like Kita-no-Shima, have been lately visited and found negative. It seems certain that the surviving world population is presently attached only to Torishima.

Without doubt the short-tailed albatross is one of the rarest birds in existence. Fortunately its late period of trial coincided with a time of renaissance in practical nature conservation by the Government of Japan; and, with anxiety mitigated by reasonable confidence in its recovery, the world watches the progress of this remote, vulnerable, and unique island population of beautiful birds.

Family Procellariidae: petrels

DIABLOTIN or
BLACK-CAPPED PETREL
Pterodroma hasitata

This remarkable petrel, known to the early post-Columbian West Indians as the "little devil", or diablotin, was formerly an abundant nester in burrows on the high hills and cliffs of Guadeloupe, of Jamaica, and Hispaniola (Haiti), and of Dominica and Martinique in the Lesser Antilles, where remains have been found at the pre-historic site at Paquemar. A bone, also pre-Columbian, that probably belongs to this species has been found in an ancient kitchen-midden at Magen's Bay on the north coast of St Thomas.

The diablotin was first discovered by J. B. du Tertre in the middle of the seventeenth century on Guadeloupe: he thought it a rare bird of the mountains. (Quite a number of petrels nest on inland and even wooded hills, in burrows.) In 1696 J. B. Labat described a remarkable hunt for diablotins on the Soufrière of Guadeloupe, using eight-foot poles, hooked at the end, in the burrows; six men caught 213 in a morning. Already, Labat commented, the settlers were wiping the birds out. By the nineteenth century it was rare, and most of the surviving burrows on the Soufrière were destroyed by a great earthquake in 1847. But one diablotin was caught by a dog on Guadeloupe "a few years" before 1891.

On Dominica, Labat recorded it in 1696; it was known in 1791, and recorded as "abundant" as late as about 1858. After this it seems to have quickly vanished; between the 1870s and 1961 no fewer than four deliberate searches have been made by ornithologists for it on the Morne Diablotin – its ancient breeding-place in the north of the island – without result, though one individual was found on Dominica in 1932, not in a nesting burrow.

From Martinique we have no recent information at all, though records show that the early French settlers took young there, as on Guadeloupe, and found them a valuable source of food. The last news was that in 1847 an earthquake had destroyed a main breeding-ground and many birds. Likewise, the early settlers on Haiti knew, and made use of, the breeding birds; an individual was recorded on the Haiti mainland in 1928, and another found alive there in 1938 was a young one not long out of the nest.

Until quite recently the only real evidence of the continued existence of the diablotin was from records at sea. Normally confined to the neighbourhood of the Caribbean, the diablotin has wandered (sometimes after hurricanes) at least a dozen times to the seaboard of eastern North America and occasionally some distance inland. The single record for Europe is an old one: a diablotin was caught alive on a heath at Southacre, near Swaffham in Norfolk, in March or April 1850. Ten years ago the number of sight records at sea in the triangle between the West Indies, Bermuda, and the Azores left one of the present writers certain that "the survival of a small breeding population upon some Caribbean hillside is scarcely a matter of doubt". In 1963 D. B. Wingate solved the problem; he discovered a colony of rather unexpected strength, estimated at no fewer than 4,000 breeding in-

dividuals, upon the Morne la Salle in Haiti, just where James Bond, the expert West Indies ornithologist, had long suspected it might survive. This is now the only known nesting-place, though the possibility that inhabited burrows may be found in the Lesser Antilles still seems fair; a great area of scrub-covered mountains still has to be searched on Guadeloupe, Dominica, and Martinique before anybody can be certain that the diablotin is extinct there.

The Jamaican race, or dark-colour phase, named *P. h. caribbaea*, may however be fully extinct. It disappeared entirely from the island "some years before 1891" and has not been seen since except in museums, unless a dark bird seen at sea west of the Bimini group in the Bahamas, around 1930, was of this form. Greenway and other experts link its disappearance (and indeed the reduction of the species generally) in part with the introduction of the Burmese mongoose into Jamaica and the French Antilles shortly after 1872. It is conceivable, though, that it may still survive. In 1965 Dr W. R. P. Bourne, quoting G. S. Ritchie of Jamaica, reported that birds are still said to call at night in the John Crow Mountains in the north-east part of the island.

Like all petrels, the diablotin must lay only one egg a year, and is unlikely to re-nest if egg or young is destroyed. Its future must depend largely upon the introduction and enforcement of protective legislation in Haiti.

CAHOW
Pterodroma cahow

This almost legendary petrel bred on Bermuda in vast numbers until the islands' discovery by man in the sixteenth century. Fossil evidence and the earliest accounts, such as that of Diego Ramirez, a famous Spanish captain, indicate that it nested everywhere, even on the main island. But by the early seventeenth century it was already much reduced in numbers, except on the lesser offshore islets, as a result of the depredations of introduced pigs.

In 1609 the first permanent colony of British settlers became established on Bermuda, and soon afterwards the black rat was accidentally introduced. The explosive increase of rats that resulted caused a famine, and the settlers were forced to turn to the cahow as a source of food. So rapidly and ruthlessly was the last major nesting colony on Cooper's Island exploited that governors of the island were obliged to pass bird-protection orders in 1616 and 1621 to save the species from extinction. The few remaining cahows were soon forgotten, and their earlier abundance was remembered only as history. For nearly three centuries nothing more was heard of the bird, and many in scientific circles presumed it to be extinct. Even its taxonomic status remained obscure until R. W. Shufeldt, writing in 1916, associated the historic cahow with the bones of a *Pterodroma* petrel found in abundance in mid-Pleistocene and sub-recent deposits in Bermuda's limestone caves.

It was then realized that a petrel collected on the Castle Harbour Islands by L. L. Mowbray in 1906, and described as *Æstrelata gularis* by Bradlee in the same year, was in fact a cahow and was accordingly renamed as the type by Nichols and Mowbray in 1916. After that, more specimens appeared, and late nineteenth-century reports of the bird, formerly rejected as cases of confused identity with the still extant Audubon's little shearwater, *P. assimilis lherminieri*, were given more credence. Fishermen of that period were apparently well aware that there were two kinds of nocturnal sea-birds, and the true cahow was known to them as the "Christmas Bird", because it was most active and noisy at night in mid-winter.

On the 8th June 1935 a boy on a bicycle brought a bird to William Beebe in his research laboratory at New Nonsuch, Bermuda, from the lighthouse-keeper at St David's. It was a young bird, probably only a few days out of the burrow, and had died by flying against the light. Beebe sent it to R. C. Murphy, who confirmed that it was the second known specimen of *Pterodroma cahow*. The bones of this bird were, rather luckily, preserved; and they proved to be identical with the subfossil and recent cave-floor material described by Shufeldt. So there was no doubt that *Pterodroma cahow* was the old cahow, and that it survived and bred in 1935.

A third specimen of cahow was killed in June 1941 by striking a telephone wire on St George's, Bermuda, but it was not until March 1945,

during the wartime construction of a giant United States Air Force base in the Castle Harbour, that two military officers and ornithologists, Fred T. Hall and his companion Anton, came across positive evidence of the location of the cahow's last breeding-ground. In addition to recent bones and feather fragments, Hall obtained an almost fresh carcass of an adult that has been washed ashore on Cooper's Island.

Inspired by these late records, R. C. Murphy and Louis S. Mowbray (son of the cahow's first rediscoverer) arranged a special search expedition in January and February 1951, to locate the nest sites of any cahows that might still survive, and if possible to help them by protection measures. Murphy's expedition was an outstanding success, and no fewer than seven nests were brought under close observation for the first time. This made possible the launching of a programme of research and protection, which, thanks to the generous financial support of Childs Frick and the New York Zoological Society, has continued ever since.

It was immediately evident, after 1951, that the cahow was rediscovered only just in time to be saved from extinction. Because man and his domestic animals had reduced the species to the most marginal portions of its original breeding habitat, on rocky offshore islets, the birds were unable to find enough soil to dig their own nesting burrows, and consequently had to use natural holes and crevices of cliffs instead. Here more than 60 per cent of the population came into conflict with another cliff-nesting sea-bird, the tropic bird *Phaethon lepturus*, which returns to breed somewhat later in the season just after the helpless cahow chicks have hatched. As a result, nearly all the chicks were being killed, and breeding success was extremely low.

A solution to this problem became the first concern of the conservation programme, and in 1954 one of the first wardens, Richard Thorsell, devised a baffler to prevent tropic birds from entering cahow nest sites. This was simply an artificial entrance-hole of precise dimensions fitted over the front of each nest hole and taking

PLATE 15 (*a*) Abbott's booby; (*b*) New Zealand rough-faced (king) shag; (*c*) Cahow; (*d*) Short-tailed albatrosses, adult (left) and immature *Albert E. Gilbert* 1966

(a)

(b)

(c)

(d)

GILBERT

(a)

(b)

(c)

advantage of the size difference between the two species. The smaller cahow was able to squeeze through while the larger tropic bird was excluded. By using this device on all burrows, in conjunction with other protective measures, mortality of cahow chicks due to tropic birds was gradually reduced to zero by 1961, and the production of young has been doubled.

Since 1958 the cahow conservation programme has been conducted on a full-time basis by David Wingate, a Bermudian naturalist. A concentrated search for additional breeding pairs begun at that time resulted in the discovery of several more nest sites in concealed situations. Some of these were not subject to occupation by tropic birds, and this helped to explain how the cahow had survived. It was not until 1961 that the entire breeding population totalling eighteen pairs was finally located. Since then it has risen by one pair per year to twenty-four pairs in 1966. Productivity on the other hand has shown a slight decline owing to a radical reduction in the percentage breeding success. The table immediately below makes this clear.

Cahow Breeding Statistics 1961–6

from David Wingate

A pair of cahows lays only a single egg in a season.

Date	Maximum potential productivity with protection	Actual productivity (number of young leaving burrows)	Probable productivity without protection	Number of occupied burrows	Per cent of breeding success
1961	11	8	4–5	20	40
1962	8	8	4–5	20	40
1963	9	8	4	22	36·3
1964	8	7	2	22	32
1965	8	8	4	23	34·8
1966	6	6	1	24	25
Total	50	45	20	Rate of increase: 1 per annum	Mean: 34·7

At first, this reduced breeding success was thought to be due to an advancing senility of the older established pairs. This seemed a plausible end-result in a population of long-lived birds that had been unable to replace itself owing to competition with tropic birds. By 1967, however, it became apparent that mortality of chick embryos, either in the egg or at hatching, was becoming the chief cause. Because a parallel phenomenon, with identical symptoms, has recently been reported on a wide scale in hawks and other terrestrial carnivorous birds under circumstances that implicate pesticides, the dead cahow chicks and eggs were subjected to analysis and found to contain an average of 6·44 parts per million D.D.T. residues. In view of the cahow's pelagic way of life, these residues can have been obtained only by concentration through the oceanic food-chain.

It is not yet conclusive that pesticides are the cause of the cahows' declining breeding success, but, should this cause-and-effect relationship be established beyond a doubt, the future of the cahow, and indeed of many other sea-birds, will be in grave jeopardy, dependent on international treaties of pollution-control rather than on local conservation measures.

The plight of the cahow is still critical, but, assuming that its present problems can be overcome, the opportunities for its recovery are excellent. In 1961 the Bermuda Government designated as bird sanctuaries more than 25

PLATE 16 (*a*) Chinese egret, 1966; (*b*) Oriental white stork, 1961; (*c*) Japanese crested ibis, 1961 *Shigekazu Kobayashi* acres of islands, including 15-acre Nonsuch Island, with its deep soil cover suitable for petrel burrows. These islands are now maintained free from all potential predators by the warden and are capable of supporting a population of cahows in the order of 25,000 pairs. Meanwhile, on the smaller soil-less islets to which the cahow is at present restricted, petrel burrows are being constructed artificially in sites where colonization by the cliff-nesting tropic birds is unlikely. In this way it is hoped that the two species can be separated back into their original breeding niches more quickly, thus lessening the need for "bafflers", which require constant checking.

STEJNEGER'S PETREL
Pterodroma longirostris

Petrels wander widely over the oceans and seas, and mostly breed in burrows on remote rugged islets, or even far inland on wooded hills. It is not surprising that their large family is very little known; and even the full identity of the numerous species and races remains still to be worked out, despite years of research by a good number of people on whom this family has cast a spell. Vast areas of the Pacific and Indian Ocean archipelagos, and even some in the Atlantic, must still be deeply investigated before the true pattern of the petrels begins to emerge.

Before writing of Stejneger's petrel, we should say that there are probably about twenty-two certain species in the gadfly genus *Pterodroma*, and there may well be over a couple of dozen. The system of the group will continue to be doubtful until a good deal more exploration, and a certain amount of legitimate collecting, has been done. Is the Réunion petrel, *Pterodroma aterrima*, a race of the great-winged petrel or a true species? All that is known of this bird, for certain, is a group of three specimens taken on the little-known island of Réunion (or Bourbon) in the Indian Ocean before 1890, two of which were young birds doubtless reared on the island; another probably from Mauritius; a further one taken at sea in the Indian Ocean; and a few recent sightings in the northern Indian Ocean. Another gadfly petrel, *P. baraui*, or Barau's

petrel, has just been discovered on Réunion, where it nests; it was described only in 1964. It is very closely related to the diablotin and cahow. Nothing is yet clearly known about the status of either species.

The bird of providence, *P. solandri*, is now probably extinct on Norfolk Island, and may nest only on Lord Howe Island (the other isolate between Australia and New Zealand). Again, little is known of its status.

In 1867 the Italian research ship *Magenta* was working in the Pacific, and its scientists collected a petrel, markedly different from other gadfly petrels, which was named *P. magentae* and is still "based", as a species, upon a unique skin in Turin. Lately, however, Dr Bourne has looked at this specimen and found that its proportions conform with a good sample of subfossil bones from Chatham Island, east of New Zealand. Within the last 100 years a mysterious petrel, the "Chatham taiko", was well known to the Chatham Island colonists. It has long been thought extinct. Is it?

Another *Pterodroma*, not named until 1949, is *P. ultima*, Murphy's petrel. It is now no longer a great mystery, for a breeding colony of some strength has come to light on Oeno, one of the most easterly of the Pacific islands. Another is still mysterious, for Beck's petrel, which may be a race of the larger Tahiti petrel *P. rostrata*, is still based only on two specimens collected north of the Solomons in the 1920s. *Pterodroma (rostrata) becki* could easily breed in burrows on the vegetated higher hills of the Solomons; prolonged nocturnal expeditions by ornithologists could find it – but it might take years! Again, the Fiji petrel, *P. macgillivrayi*, is still known only from a single fledgeling in the British Museum, taken at Ngau 100 years ago. There is plenty of hilly bush in Fiji still to be explored.

Stejneger's or the "Japanese" petrel, *P. longirostris*, was first named in 1893 from one of two specimens taken in Matsu Bay at the north end of Honshu, the main island of Japan. The typical form of this petrel is still known from only ten skins all taken within 600 miles of Japan, the latest in 1929. This does not mean, necessarily, that the petrel breeds in Japan: it might well be a visitor (all the known dates are in August) from miles away in the Pacific, and probably another hemisphere. In 1913 a series of petrels was taken off the Juan Fernandez islands in the South Pacific, and in 1917 their species, later named *P. masafuerae*, was found breeding on Mas Afuera, the westernmost of the two main islands – nearly 500 miles west of Chile. Ornithologists now accept *P. masafuerae* without much doubt as a race of *P. longirostris*; and some who have studied the skins and measurements believe that the Chilean material is so close to the Japanese material that the birds are not racially separable. In the technical words of systematics, there is a case for "sinking" the name *P. longirostris masafuerae* in *P. l. longirostris* as a synonym. The fact that the Japanese specimens and practically all the others taken north of the Equator are in full or considerable condition of moult suggests that they are, indeed, wintering specimens of the Juan Fernandez breeders.

A racial status (that is, a trinomial one) may still, however, be necessary, for in 1932 Dr Falla discovered and shortly afterwards named a very closely related petrel, breeding on the Hen and Chickens Islands, off North Island, New Zealand. In 1940 G. A. Buddle found it breeding on the Poor Knights not far away. As it turns out, the population was, in fact, first discovered on the Chicken Islands – the home of another Red Data Book animal, the tuatara (p. 322), with which it shares burrows – by the pioneer New Zealand naturalist Andreas Reischek in 1880; but Reischek thought it was an example of the closely related Cook's petrel. Nothing is yet known of the ocean range of *P. pycrofti*, which must be known as Pycroft's petrel if it is maintained as a full species. It should probably be regarded as a race of Stejneger's petrel, with whose measurements its own overlap, though not so broadly as those of the Mas Afuera race. It does not seem to be in danger in New Zealand, and indeed was discovered nesting in some numbers on yet another island, Red Mercury, in 1962. But the Mas Afuera population's size is quite unknown. The Chilean island is uninhabited, and is very seldom visited by naturalists.

Dr Falla records that birds of the typical *P. longirostris* race (in which he positively sinks *P. masafuerae*) were washed up, recently dead, on North Island beaches, New Zealand, in the summer of 1961–2. One was found on the shores of Cook Strait in December, and two in the Bay of Plenty in January. In the new *Field Guide to New Zealand Birds*, 1966, he and his colleagues hold Stejneger's petrel as a monotypic species whose only known breeding-place is on Mas Afuera; in 1962 Dr Falla still held Pycroft's petrel as an "anomalous" and separate species, and the *Field Guide* maintains it so.

Order PELECANIFORMES
Family Sulidae: gannets and boobies

ABBOTT'S BOOBY
Sula abbotti

Abbott's booby was first described for science from Assumption Island, on the western side of the Indian Ocean, in 1893, and was shortly afterwards found to be part of the native fauna of Christmas Island, 220 miles off Java in the north-eastern part of that ocean. It has nested nowhere else in the world, as far as anybody knows, and is now extinct on Assumption, a coral island with a rich and heavily used deposit of guano. It seems likely that the guano-workers of the early part of the present century may have driven Abbott's booby away. The birds were certainly breeding in some numbers on bushes in (at 88 feet) the relatively high sand-dune area in the south-east of the island when J. C. F. Fryer was there in 1905, though the experienced ornithologist M. J. Nicoll, who visited the island in the following year, made no mention of it. However, a small population seems to have bred there, perhaps intermittently, until later. Birds were still attempting to nest in 1930, and adults frequented the island for some years after that, though none has been seen there since 1936.

The Christmas Island population occupies a much larger and higher island (about 64 square miles), where it nests inland in the crowns of tall trees some way up the slopes of the central plateau, which is 600 to 1,000 feet high. Here the late Dr Carl Gibson-Hill, ashore on war duty in 1941, estimated a breeding population of about 1,000 to 1,500 birds, which was then doubtless the world (breeding) population of the species.

Both islands have been settled and worked for guano since the late nineteenth century, but the guano trade on Christmas Island, has not affected the Abbott's boobies so terribly as it did on Assumption Island; and the breeding groups on the forested slopes are officially protected by the Australian Government.

Though visitors in 1964 and 1965 could not find more than a few hundred birds, Dr and Mrs J. B. Nelson's thorough exploration in 1967 found not fewer than 2,000 pairs in a scattered distribution nesting on the jungle trees mainly on the central plateau, and in some cases near noisy settlements. As long as the woods remain uncleared, the species could have a future; already some key "tree islands" have been proposed as nature reserves.

Family Phalacrocoracidae: cormorants

NEW ZEALAND ROUGH-FACED (KING) SHAG
Phalacrocorax carunculatus carunculatus

The handsome king shags of the southern and subantarctic waters have a fine representative species in the main New Zealand archipelago, which can be generally gathered under the name *P. carunculatus*, the rough-faced shag. It is difficult to name the populations, for the systematists who like lumping groups together would prefer to fit all the six well-marked races concerned into one species, while others would split the two smaller and more delicately built races of the relatively remote Auckland and Campbell Islands into a separate species, *P. campbelli*. The Auckland Island race is common, and the Campbell Island race less abundant, though there is no present danger to its population.

Similarly, the races of the main group on Bounty Island, on the Chatham Islands, and on Stewart Island and the southern part of South Islands, are in no danger. Only one is in the Red Data Book: the most northerly race, *P. carunculatus carunculatus*, the "New Zealand" race. It is well distinguishable (in the field as well as in museums) from the other South Island race that nests no further north than the Otago Peninsula; the latter is dimorphic, about half its population being of a uniform "bronze oily green", as it was described in the new *Field Guide to New Zealand Birds* by Falla, Sibson, and Turbott.

The "New Zealand" race of the king shag is encompassed, in its breeding range, within a radius of about 30 miles in the Marlborough Sounds, from the White Rocks in the east to the Trios in the west. It nests on White Rocks, Sentinel, Duffers Reef, North Trio, and lately on Stewart Island (not to be confused with the big Stewart Island to the south of South Island). In recent years there has, indeed, been a slight increase in numbers, for, besides the colonization of Stewart Island, the size of the stations on Sentinel Island and the Duffers has built up. But Brian Bell, of New Zealand's Wildlife Branch, who has given this rare race much study, is convinced that the total population does not yet exceed 500 birds. Today the New Zealand king shag is fully protected by law – a fact posted up conspicuously at the breeding colonies; and field officers and local residents collaborate to warden the colonies that now have reserve status.

Persecution by fishermen in the past may be the cause of this fine bird's slender numbers. Only lately have even sophisticated societies like that of New Zealand come to realize that cormorants may eat fish, but have not been proved to compete with fishermen to any significant extent. In the pre-colonial Maori days, of course, cormorants were also fair game, and bones of the rough-faced king shag have been found in two South Island Maori middens. One of them, at Tai Rua in North Otago, was within the Stewart Island race's present range. But the other – though its bones have not shown the race concerned – was at Lake Grassmere in the Marlborough Sounds area. As we have seen elsewhere (p. 16), human predation through both Polynesian and post-Cookian times has disastrously reduced the variety of New Zealand birds. The rough-faced king shag of Marlborough Sounds may have been rescued just in time from a fate no worse and no better than death.

Order CICONIIFORMES
Family Ardeidae: herons

NEW ZEALAND LITTLE BITTERN
Ixobrychus minutus novaezelandiae

The little bittern is a well-distributed and successful bird of the Old World wetlands. The Palearctic race is found all over Europe, in western Siberia, and in north-west India. Ethiopian Africa, and Madagascar, have their own races; so does Australia (perhaps one in the south-west and another in the east).

In 1871 a bird collected in Westland, in New Zealand's South Island, was named *Ardeola novaezelandiae*. It was later recognized as a little bittern, and the name was used racially to cover also the eastern Australian little bitterns (and, by some, all the Australian little bitterns); for, at least when the *Checklist of New Zealand Birds* was published in 1953, opinion was that the Westland bird was one of the first of about twenty South Island records (mostly in the same area) in the nineteenth century, and that all were windblown from Australia. A sight record of one at Meremere in North Island, regarded as unsatisfactory (like the only other North Island record, of 1836), is the sole twentieth-century record on the books.

Yet there may be a little bittern peculiar to New Zealand. Dr Falla and his colleagues have lately re-examined the few New Zealand skins in museums, and have found them so markedly distinct from Australian material as to make it most unlikely that they could have come from that continent. It has, according to Dr Falla (unpublished), plumage features nearer to the strongly patterned least bittern, *I. exilis*, of America than to any of the known races of *I. minutus* or of the Asiatic *I. sinensis*, the Chinese least bittern. These three species are in need of further study in regard to their relationships.

Westland is the least explored area of New Zealand. Could there be a colony of *I. minutus novaezelandiae* nesting in its still extensive swamps? This is a question that the current New Zealand *Field Guide* asks. The Red Data Book holds the bird in the limbo between extinct and endangered until more information comes from new field work.

CHINESE EGRET
Egretta eulophotes

After it was first scientifically named by Swinhoe in 1860, the Chinese egret had little attention from virtually a generation of ornithologists. As Dr H. G. Deignan points out to us, many were misled by the great systematist Bowdler Sharpe, who in one of his rare mistaken moments believed that the species was the same as the common eastern reef heron, *Egretta sacra*.

Certainly, by the time the bird-explorers of China and Korea began to build up a geographical plot of this interesting and beautiful heron, the plume-traders must have already made certain that there was little to plot. Maps of the old breeding range so far published are very tentative, including E. P. Spangenberg's in the second volume (1951) of the standard *Birds of the Soviet Union*. But it does emerge that in the early years of the present century the species had two breeding headquarters, one in Korea and the other in the wetlands of some coastal provinces of China. Here, as Spangenberg and others record, it had already ceased to breed in Fukien at the end of the nineteenth century; but it bred in Kwangtung, Kiangsu, and Shantung. In Korea it bred on the mainland, and possibly also on Tsu-shima and Quelpart islands, and on Yob-do in the northern Yellow Sea.

Some present scholars of Asian ornithology believe that a small colony surviving in Korea may be the last. It seems possible that a breeding population may still also persist in China, whence recent information is scant. The most likely place seems to be Shantung, or Kwangtung, opposite which lies Hong Kong, whence came the suggestion, yet to be confirmed, that some egrets bred there in 1964.

Lately (1967) V. I. Labzyuk and Yu. N. Nazarov have published a note indicating that the Chinese egret may range, if not breed, further north than was thought. In Russian Primor'ye (Amur-Ussuriland), where previously only two records had been made, they found it a regular spring visitor to the south in 1956–7, especially in the Olga Bay area, and also at the mouth of the Shmiltovka River and on Bolshoi Pelis Island in the Rimskii-Korsakov group. Some appeared to be on passage north.

The Chinese egret in its heyday was a summer breeder in the range described above, and a winter visitor to Taiwan (Formosa), the Philippines, and Celebes, from all of which have come rumours of nesting – all improbable except for one case that may have occurred in the last century in the Tamsui area of northern Taiwan. There is a June record of one on Iriomote, the nearest largish island of the Ryukyus. Records from Hainan are probably of passage birds; and in Singapore Island (two September adults and another bird), peninsular Thailand (one, rather doubtful), Sarawak (seven examples), the Maritime Province of Russia (Cape Olympiada, one June adult), and Honshu, Japan (doubtful), the records are almost certainly of vagrants.

With the Chinese egret we may have the last victim of the plume trade, rampant in the early years of the present century and not yet at an end. It is obviously now a very rare bird indeed, and the chances that measures will be taken for its conservation seem at present rather slender.

Family Ciconiidae: storks

KOREAN *or* ORIENTAL WHITE STORK
Ciconia (ciconia) boyciana

The well-loved white stork of Europe, one of the most intensely studied birds in the world, is a migrant that winters in Africa south of the Sahara. Another race, the Central Asian white stork, has a breeding headquarters around Russian and Chinese Turkestan, and some of its stock may winter in north-west India. Still further east, another white stork is the subject of this sad story. Most authorities class the oriental white stork, first named in 1873, as another race of the typical white stork; but Dr Vaurie, whose opinions are to be respected, believes (1965) that, with its larger black (not red) bill, its red (not black) eye-skin, and its larger size, it is worthy of status as a full species. Full species or not, its survival status is the cause of widespread concern.

The oriental stork's nesting-grounds were known to science a little before it was first named as a separate form; for in the 1860s the great Russian naturalist Przewalski found about twenty nests in three places in the basin of Lake Khanka, in the southern part of the U.S.S.R.'s Primorskaya Oblast (in Ussuriland, the most south-easterly corner of Siberia, close to China's Manchurian border). He heard also of nesting storks further north down the Ussuri valley. The River Ussuri flows into the Amur. Much later, in the 1930s, storks were also found nesting in Amurland on the Krasnoi River at Novorusanouka, and in two river valleys (Samarga and Botcha) on the eastern (Pacific) side of the Sikhote Alin range. The northerly birds seem (or seemed) to use Lake Bolen Odzhal in the lower Amur valley as a migration assembly place, and have been seen as far up the Amur as Blagoreshchensk. A bird seen in Yakutia, near where the River Botoma enters the Lena, on the 20th May 1935, was doubtless a stray.

Outside Russia the oriental stork is suspected, though not proved, to have nested in eastern

Manchuria, bred in Korea, at least at Hwanghae Do, until 1936 at the latest, and it certainly breeds in Japan. It used to winter in its summer range, except for the Russian part, and south as far as Fukien in east China, occasionally Formosa, and the southern Ryukyus. Recorded from Sakhalin, it was there probably in passage. Records quoted from Assam, Manipur, south Bengal, and Burma are very doubtful, especially the last, and rejected by the latest authorities on the fauna of India and Burma. Clearly the oriental stork is not in the same league of migrants as its western counterpart – and perhaps this is another reason for considering it different enough to earn the rank of a full species.

In Japan we first learn of the stork as a "common and well-loved bird", as Drs Austin and Kuroda put it, at the time of the Tokugawa shogunate, which began early in the seventeenth century. It continued to be protected for the best part of two centuries, and was fairly common, at least on the main island of Honshu, in the late 1860s and 1870s. But after this it declined fast.

It is not known exactly how widely the oriental white stork nested in Japan in its heyday. The three largest islands (Hokkaido, Honshu, and Shikoku), and Tsushima between Japan and Korea, have been quoted as within the zone of occupation. But by the end of the nineteenth century good records show that it was probably breeding only on one hill, Tsuruyama, in the prefecture of Hyogo in west-central Honshu. For seventy years this place had been a kind of sanctuary; and it is doubtless this that saved the storks, though hunters have continued to disturb the area until quite lately. In 1904 the reserve, or natural monument, was newly dedicated and the administration of its 6 square miles and more was strengthened, though the bird continued to nest only at Tsuruyama. By 1920 it had spread to at least five neighbouring places; by 1931 it was nesting in at least four villages with eleven nests at Tsuruyama. Despite wartime disturbance, about fifty birds had more than six nests in the area in 1944.

Unfortunately, by 1948 the number of storks had apparently fallen to a mere sixteen, and only three nests were found. In 1950 the sole ones known were a pair that had a nest but no eggs, and pairs in two other villages that raised three young. However, in 1957 two new pairs colonized part of Fukui prefecture further east, which was quickly made another special natural monument. The latest news from Hyogo prefecture is of a population of about twenty birds in 1961; in 1963 of sixteen birds with five known nests, with four eggs, from which no fledgelings were reported; in 1964 fourteen birds (two adults had died) laid at least seven eggs but reared no chicks; in 1965 ten birds (four adults had died) laid at least four eggs, which were infertile; in 1966 nine birds (one adult had died) reared no chicks. Two of the birds that died in 1965 contained what was probably more than a lethal dose of mercury, probably taken in loaches from water polluted with chemical pesticides.

In the present century wanderers or passage birds have been recorded elsewhere in Japan, including a stray (May 1923) from Hokkaido and birds in four other prefectures of Honshu and in Shikoku. Apart from the stork's extension into the Fukui prefecture, there is no sign of the spread of breeding populations beyond Hyogo.

The western forms of white stork breed well in captivity; and the oriental race or species thrives in zoos, having been kept with success in Europe in the last century. The Japanese ornithologists have, since 1964, been working on a captive-breeding project, which all hope will provide a cure for the dangerous state of the population, though results so far have been negative through infertility. The species is now doubtless extinct as a breeder in Korea, where only one stray (which was offered, dead, in Seoul market in January 1958) has been recorded in the last thirty years. The Russian breeding area seems, however, to have been a fairly broad one thirty years ago; unfortunately we have not received any later news of it. If a good population survives there and can be encouraged to increase by conservation measures, it may save the species.

Family Plataleidae: ibises and spoonbills

GIANT IBIS
Thaumatibis gigantea

The giant ibis might well be known as the Mekong ibis, for it has never been proved to breed outside the great area of South-East Asia's mainland drained by this river and its tributaries. Only three birds have been recorded, as far as we can find, out of this area; all were collected over fifty years ago, between December and April in peninsular Thailand on the other side of the Gulf of Thailand, and can be presumed to have been vagrants.

Cambodia seems always to have been the heartland of this fine and rare bird, though its range apparently extended into the Mekong valley wetlands of eastern Thailand fifty years ago and into the Saravane district of southern Laos forty years ago. It was doubtless nesting near Phu-Rieng, north of Saigon in South Vietnam, in 1925, though it appears now to have withdrawn from this area, close to the delta country of the mouths of the Mekong – and, indeed, probably from South Vietnam altogether.

Giant ibis *Shigekazu Kobayashi* 1966

O. Milton, who encountered the giant ibis in pairs and small parties on the border between Cambodia and Laos in March 1964, confirms our impression that this shy, wary, and seldom-collected bird has not suffered any recent decline. It seems likely that breeding-grounds are still scattered over a stretch of lowlands from the

Mekong in the Laos border area, up to 200 miles south-west to the north shore of Tonlé Sap, the Great Lake of Cambodia, with what is perhaps the headquarters along the valley of the River Sen for 30 or 40 miles north of Kompong Thom – a region where Dr Jean Delacour found them numerous in 1927–8.

The giant ibis, through its shyness, may be not so rare as has been supposed; but it is far from common, and its world population may be no more than a few hundred. Its wetland habitat is being both reduced and disturbed; it is a bird to be carefully watched and, as opportunity and resources provide, conserved. Since the Pacific Science Congress of 1961, the Government of Cambodia has been internationally urged to give the Mekong ibis complete and effective protection.

JAPANESE CRESTED IBIS
Nipponia nippon

A century ago the lovely Nippon ibis nested over a vast area of the Far East, from Ussuriland in the north (the Primorskaya Oblast of Russia and the neighbouring parts of eastern Manchuria, centred on Lake Khanka) to the Chinese province of Chekiang in the south; and from south Shensi (or possibly even Szechwan) in west China, to parts of Japan 2,000 miles east.

It is now on the verge of extinction. Everywhere its history has been one of decline, accelerated by human persecution and by deforestation of the wooded wetlands. In Ussuriland it was known ninety years ago to the great Russian naturalists Przewalski, Dybowski, and Taczanowski, as a nester on the Ussuri's tributaries Lefu and Muren; and here it seems to have hung on as a breeder in one place at least until 1917, possibly to 1927. No breeding has been proved since then in Russia. In Korea this beautiful bird may have bred; but only very few have been seen there since 1930 – a record in 1950; a dead male offered for sale in a Seoul market in January 1954; a record of ten in flight in North Korea in March 1965, and three seen together at Panmunjom in February 1966, two of which may also have been seen at Chollanamdo a week earlier. In China, where the crested ibis was once widespread and may have nested in as many as nine provinces (it was still a common breeder in Shensi in 1904), the last certain breeding records we know were at Wutu in southern Kiangsu in 1925, and in Shensi to 1958, when the last colony's trees were felled.

In the Tokugawa times of Japan (from 1615 to 1865) the Nippon ibis was, as Drs Austin and Kuroda tell us, probably a not uncommon breeder on the main island of Honshu, and on Kyushu, as well as on the northern island of Hokkaido (at least in the Hakodate area). But few seem to have survived the collapse of animal protection after the Meiji restoration in 1867. A colony apparently held out at the Satuga shrine in Aomori in the north of Honshu until about 1875. After that the bird seems to have been almost totally extirpated on the main islands of Japan, although there is some evidence that a group may have continued to breed on Oki Island until about 1920. By 1925 the Japanese population appeared to be only twenty birds, at Sue on the Noto Peninsula.

Fortunately, in the period between the two world wars, there seems to have been a partial recovery. By 1930 between twenty-five and forty birds appeared to be established in the Ishikawa prefecture of central Honshu's western coast, on the Noto Peninsula (five to ten birds), and on offlying Sado Island (twenty to thirty). But the population has never shown any sign of improving its numbers since; indeed, the late trend has been a slow decline of this tiny group: the Sado population was twenty-seven in 1941, twenty-one in 1952, fourteen in 1953, and twelve in 1954. In 1956 there were five birds on Noto, and two young fledged. In 1957 only twenty-six birds were known in the whole of Japan – eleven on Sado, fourteen (including two chicks, the last reared here) on Noto, and a single bird (found dead) in Fukui prefecture to the south of Ishikawa. In 1958 there were only nine on Sado. The 1960 population appears to have been only twelve (five on Sado, seven on Noto), that in 1961 only ten (six, four), that in 1962 nine (six, three); and the latest censuses the present writers have are of ten (eight, two;

two fledged on Sado) in 1963; twelve (eleven, one; three fledged on Sado) in 1964; eleven (ten, one; two fledged on Sado) 1965; and ten on Sado (where two died and two were fledged) and one on Noto in 1966. There were eight ibises left on Sado in 1967. The population has been threatened by earthquakes, and by a project to fell trees to pay for road improvement, in spite of the fact that the Japanese crested ibis is completely protected by law, and indeed has been a national natural monument since 1934. The Sado breeding forests were bought by the Government in 1962.

The whole future of the species doubtless depends upon the present work of Japanese conservationists, whose efforts are supported, and are watched with sympathy and anxiety.

In the old days the flourishing world population was migratory. Birds were sometimes recorded in Russia in places on both the upper and the lower Amur River some distance north of the wetlands of its Ussuri tributary, which used to be the most northerly breeding place of the species; the last such was seen down-river from Kharbarovsk in August 1949. The ibises ranged south as far as Hainan, Formosa, and the Ryukyus, but have not been seen in any of these wintering places for nearly half a century. Nevertheless a few spring and autumn birds were recorded passing in the Vladivostok area of Russia with modest regularity at least through the 1940s. Although it seemed certain to Dr Spangenberg, in 1951, that the species no longer bred in its old haunts at Lake Khanka or on the River Lefu, it may yet be possible that a colony survives in Ussuriland.

The Nippon ibis was kept in captivity in the heyday of its population, in the London Zoo amongst others. Though we have no evidence that it bred there, the members of the ibis subfamily include many that breed steadily in confinement in well-managed zoos such as those at Basle and San Antonio. If the tiny Japanese population is the sole breeding.nucleus left in the world, it is probably too small to permit a culture-breeding experiment; but a zoo bank would be a sound insurance for the species, if an increase of the wild Japanese stock, or rediscovery of a population in Ussuriland or China, enabled such a bank to be started.

Order ANSERIFORMES
Family Anatidae: wildfowl

TRUMPETER SWAN
Cygnus buccinator

The greatest swan of North America, the proud trumpeter, is a magnificent bird: adult cobs often weigh over 27 pounds. Just as the smaller whistling swan is the counterpart of the Eurasian Bewick's swan, so is the trumpeter the counterpart of the whooper. But, while the two lesser swans are so close that they are now almost universally regarded as races of the same species, the trumpeter has an immensely long windpipe, which bends twice within its specially adapted breastbone, and can rank for this reason alone as a separate species.

The trumpeter is a fairly old bird, in the geological sense, for its fossil bones have been found in the Middle Pleistocene Fossil Lake formation in Oregon, probably deposited about 300,000 years ago. When man first arrived on the American scene some 10,000 years ago, or probably even a little earlier, he seems soon to have learnt to hunt the great trumpeters. At least fourteen Indian and Eskimo sites have disclosed bones of this big swan, in Alaska, Illinois, Iowa, and Ohio: some of these have been dated by radiocarbon and other techniques; the Eskimos of Kodiak Island in Alaska ate trumpeters from about 2,000 years ago until post-Russian times. In Illinois the swan-eating Indians of Snyder ate them at perhaps about the time of Christ, those of Cahokia in the two or three centuries before Columbus; two sites in Ohio are dated as having been occupied by swan-eating cultures as long ago as about 2,500 years.

The heyday of the trumpeter, as a widespread breeding bird on the lakes in the wetlands of the open northern forest zone and other habitats of the forest-prairie margins, lasted until the European hunters became widely distributed and powerful in the nineteenth century. The trumpeter had a wide breeding and wintering range in the early nineteenth century, before the shotgun, the hunter's ever-hungry pot, and the fur companies' feather and swan-skin trade began to tell. This account is based primarily on the fine analysis made by Winston Banko when he was manager of the Red Rock Lakes Refuge in Montana, the greatest trumpeter reserve of all, which to this day usually holds about half the breeding population of all North America outside Alaska. Banko shows that, while the spread of farming into trumpeter wetlands has contributed to its ousting, the main pressures on the species, which reduced its population to a miserable remnant by 1930, were those of hunters, for commerce and more lately for sport. Nevertheless the total protection of the trumpeter at all times and in all places in Canada and the United States came in time; indeed this is a success story, and told here really as an example of what conservation can do, and has done, to save a species. That the trumpeter swan is one of the earlier endangered birds to be saved, is largely due to the fact that it is a famous, popular, and beautiful creature that sportsmen feel bound to respect.

The dark ages of the trumpeter were dark enough. It probably nested for the last time in Missouri in the first decade of the nineteenth century; in Wisconsin and perhaps also British Columbia in the 1840s; in the 1860s it began a decline in the hunter and fur-trader lands of western Alaska, the northern Yukon, Mackenzie, Saskatchewan, and the Hudson's Bay provinces of Manitoba, Ontario, and Quebec that resulted in extinction there by the 'nineties. (Wherever it nested, the population that used to winter on the eastern seaboard of the United States had disappeared by the 1830s, in Audubon's time.) Some time in or before the 1890s the trumpeter also last nested in Indiana and Nebraska; from Iowa it had gone in or shortly after 1883, from Minnesota in about 1885. It held on in North Dakota till 1895, and in the state of Washington until 1918. But by 1932 the population of adults on nesting-grounds in the continental United States (outside Alaska) was no more than an estimated fifty-seven, which reared a dozen cygnets, all of them within the region that covers parts of Montana, Wyoming, and Idaho. They bred in all three states then, and have done ever

Trumpeter swan *John James Audubon* 1838

since; but at that time the majority (twenty-nine adults) were occupying territories in the great Yellowstone National Park, in Wyoming; there were nineteen adults at Red Rock Lakes. Besides these, in 1932 there was a population breeding also in Alberta, in south-eastern Alaska, and possibly also in southern Yukon; but it was doubtless small. It may well have been that fewer than 100 adult trumpeters survived to attempt breeding in 1932 outside Alaska.

Fortunately the main sanctuary of the trumpeter south of Canada was within, or close to, an area already long dedicated to nature by one of the most far-seeing conservation measures the world has known. On the 1st March 1872, President Ulysses S. Grant signed a bill that had been voted in Congress after a formidable and altruistic lobbying campaign, and enacted that "the tract of land in the territories of Montana and Wyoming, lying near the headwaters of the Yellowstone River . . . is hereby reserved and withdrawn from settlement, occupancy or sale under the laws of the United States, and dedicated and set apart as a public park or pleasuring ground for the benefit and enjoyment of the people".

Yellowstone was the world's first National Park, in the modern sense. It was founded as a direct consequence of the campaign by a group of young businessmen and lawyers who were sent to explore the Yellowstone area for commercial exploitation. Round a camp fire in the Yellowstone, on the now annually celebrated evening of the 19th September 1870, these men – all highly educated intellectuals and most of them directly inspired by the New England idealism of Thoreau, Emerson, and Hawthorne – decided that commercial exploitation and private ownership could not be tolerated in the Yellowstone's spacious paradise. We can thank revenue-man Nathaniel Pitt Langford, army surveyor General Henry D. Washburn, his navigator Lieutenant Gustavus C. Doane, Judge Cornelius Hedges, and banker Samuel Hauser for the chain of consequences that pre-adapted the area for its role as a refuge where a swan has been able to raise again its noble head. And here it is appropriate to hand over the account to refuge manager (and swan-master) Winston Banko, from whom we now, with his permission, quote:

"The farsighted Congressional legislation which originally provided for the protection of wildlife in Yellowstone National Park, the Lacey Act of May 7, 1894, furnished essential protection for the ancestors of the few pairs of trumpeter swans which were discovered breeding in this famous Park in the summer of 1919. The early protective wildlife regulations which grew out of this initial National Park legislation were forerunners of continentwide laws which first applied specifically to waterfowl and later to waterfowl refuges. Each link of legislation which protected the trumpeter was forged as part of a greater plan to perpetuate portions of the representative native fauna in their natural environment.

"Unfortunately, the passage of the second Lacey Act in 1900, the Weeks-McLean Law in 1913, and the Migratory Bird Treaty Act in 1918 arrived much too late to prevent the extirpation of the trumpeter over most of its United States breeding range. For two decades after 1900, a number of prominent American scientists interested in the problems of species survival commented on the fate of the trumpeter swan. In 1913 William T. Hornaday reported that in 1907 these swans were regarded as so nearly extinct that a doubting ornithological club of Boston refused to believe on hearsay evidence that the New York Zoological Park contained a pair of the living birds, and a committee was appointed to investigate in person and report. In 1912 Edward Howe Forbush, an eminent ornithologist, lamented: 'The trumpeter has succumbed to incessant persecution in all parts of its range, and its total extinction is now only a matter of years . . . The large size of this bird and its conspicuousness have served, as in the case of the whooping crane, to make it a shining mark, and the trumpetings that were once heard over the breadth of a great continent, as the long converging lines drove on from zone to zone, will soon be heard no more.'

"Passage of the Migratory Bird Treaty Act 6 years later placed a closed season on both species of native swans for the first time when it became effective in 1918. This was the first aid to survival of the few trumpeters which still existed outside Yellowstone Park boundaries and which were to be so important in the eventual restoration of the species.

"In 1929, the Migratory Bird Conservation Act authorizing the acquisition of land for waterfowl refuges was passed by Congress. When supported with funds in 1934, this basic waterfowl legislation was as important in providing for the future increase of the United States trumpeter flock as the Migratory Bird Treaty Act was in protecting the remnant populations.

"Under the Migratory Bird Conservation Act, the Red Rock Lakes Migratory Waterfowl Refuge in southwestern Montana was established by Executive Order in 1935. This area, containing thousands of acres of historic trumpeter swan breeding habitat, was subsequently staffed by the Biological Survey, a predecessor of the United States Fish and Wildlife Service. The 22,682-acre area originally set aside under this Order was enlarged in September of the same year, when about 18,000 additional acres were included in the Refuge in order to complete the breeding-ground acquisition and to bring under management certain warm spring-water areas important to the swans during the winter months. Although several management problems remained, the establishment of this Refuge provided the upward turning point for this species in the United States. While the status of the trumpeters in Yellowstone Park before the establishment of the Refuge was marginal, it was apparently improving slowly. But the existence of this species outside the Park was actually in jeopardy by the early 1930's."

Banko, who served as assistant, and later as manager, of the Red Rock Lakes Refuge from 1948 to 1957, shows that protection in the Montana Refuge, in the neighbouring part of the Yellowstone in Wyoming, and on other waters in these two states and in Idaho, has proved remarkably worth while. A successful breeding population was established in one place (Jackson, by Wyoming's National Elk Refuge) through the translocation of adult swans. The adults on all these breeding-grounds numbered only forty-six when the Montana Refuge was created in 1935. After three years they had doubled (ninety-eight in 1938). After six more years they had doubled again (207 in 1944). After seven more years they had doubled for a third time (417 in 1951). Since 1951 the population has become more or less stabilized, doubtless to the swan-carrying capacity of the land, at an average of 476 adults (a maximum of 560 in 1954) annually producing ninety-four cygnets (a maximum of 118 in 1951).

Translocations of birds to the National Wildlife Refuges of Malheur in Oregon, Ruby Lake in Nevada, and Lacreek in South Dakota have produced breeding stock – after intervals of some years. A small group sent to the Delta Water-fowl Research Station in Manitoba in 1955 first bred in 1959. A limited number of birds trans-located to carefully chosen zoos and waterfowl gardens have also succeeded in breeding. The trumpeter breeds in captivity, but not very easily; the first known record was in the London Zoo in 1870 (four years after translocation): later successes are known from France and Holland. At Slimbridge in England the present trumpeters date back to 1952, when Queen Elizabeth II deposited five birds presented to her by Canada; they first bred successfully in 1964.

In 1963 (before the Alaskan discovery reported later in this paragraph) the world population of the trumpeter swan, adults and cygnets com-bined, was estimated at approximately 1,700. Only at Slimbridge (three) and West Berlin Zoo (two) were any living outside their North American home. About half the believed popu-lation was in the main United States, still chiefly in the great nucleus in Montana, Wyoming, and Idaho, but building up elsewhere. An estimated record crop of 300 cygnets was reared. No fewer than seventy-nine birds were in North American zoos and waterfowl collec-tions. The Alaska and Canada population also certainly improved markedly, though the preci-sion with which it could be measured could not match that in the nuclear area until 1964, when it was finally confirmed that the swans nesting in interior Alaska were not, as had been hitherto believed, whistling swans (*Cygnus columbianus columbianus*), but trumpeters! James G. King and Peter E. K. Shepherd, "by examining swans and their nests and eggs", as the Bird Protection Committee of the American Ornithologists' Union reports, "have identified trumpeters during the breeding season from Fort Yukon to Lake Minchumina, and their breeding range is thought to extend westward at least to the Koyukuk River valley". On the basis of this discovery, Henry A. Hansen's reassessment of swan counts estimated the Alaskan-Canadian trumpeter population in 1961 at about 1,300 birds; so it is likely that the world population is over 2,000; the Bureau of Sport Fisheries and Wildlife estimated 2,200 at the end of 1966.

HAWAIIAN GOOSE *or* NÉNÉ
Branta sandvicensis

One of the present writers, in a recent book,[1] has tried to show how zoos and avicultural collec-tions can contribute, and have contributed, to restoring the fallen fortunes of animals in danger. This essay is based on the section in it devoted to the Hawaiian goose, brought up to date with information from the Wildfowl Trust and other organizations concerned with the néné.

When the Polynesians first came to Hawaii, some time between the fifth and ninth centuries A.D., they seem to have fallen into an easy relationship with its striking and unique native fauna. Although they took many skins of several very pretty birds to weave into the great feather cloaks of their kings, there is no evidence that these colonists ever put a bird in danger of extinction. They led their quiet and uncrowded lives all over the archipelago without upsetting nature very much, so far as we can tell. Indeed, their effect on nature, before the Westerners came, appears to have been quite different from that of their race on the much older, highly specialized, and vulnerable bird fauna of New Zealand (p. 16).

Paul H. Baldwin, a great scholar of Hawaii, believes that among the birds that the Poly-nesians lived happily upon and with were the little Hawaiian geese – birds in the same genus as the brent and barnacle geese, but coloured russet rather than near-black, and with neck feathers arranged in a different pattern from other members of the genus *Branta*. Without doubt the Polynesians hunted the nénés in the craters of Mauna Loa, Mauna Kea, and other volcanoes, where they lived during their flightless state of moult, when they had their goslings. But Baldwin thinks that the Hawaiian geese main-tained a steady population of at least 25,000 until white men came to the islands.

The fauna of the Hawaiian Islands has been peculiarly vulnerable ever since the coming of Western man, and in strictly historical (that is, in Western) times there have been more bird extinctions there than on any other archipelago in the world. It is difficult to say what factors

[1] *Zoos of the World* by James Fisher, London, Aldus, 1967.

have contributed most to this state of affairs; but among them are the extension of agriculture, accompanied by the felling of forests, and the introduction of alien species. Native birds have also suffered from disturbance by pigs, and dogs, that have gone wild, and from hunting (by Westerners, not by Polynesians). Altogether, no fewer than fourteen species of birds have been extinguished; many of those that survive have become so rare as to cause great concern to the Survival Service Commission.

Among those in mortal danger has been the Hawaiian goose. Not much more than a decade ago it was thought by many to be doomed. We have no evidence of any change in the population status of the néné before Captain Cook visited Hawaii in 1770, but we are certain that a slow decline began not long after. By about 1800 this little goose was still living in the lowlands of Hawaii itself and the neighbouring island of Maui, but its numbers were decreasing. Soon after 1850 it became restricted to the wilder parts of high ranges on both islands. By 1900 the néné was rare even in mountainous areas of Hawaii, and on Maui it was probably extinct. In the next few years it would almost certainly have died out had it not been for the work of zoos and some landowners.

Let us see what was happening to the Hawaiian goose in captivity during its century and more of decline in the wild. The first nénés to reach Europe were sent to Lord Derby's great private menagerie at Knowsley Park in Lancashire, England, in 1823. They happily bred in 1824 and in the following years. They had fully entered aviculture. In 1832 Lady Glengall, who had some connections with Hawaii, presented a pair to the London Zoo. One of these became the type of the species; that is to say the species was formally described from it (in 1833) by the Secretary of the Zoological Society of London, Nicholas Aylward Vigors. He called it *Anser sandvicensis*, after Lord Sandwich.

The birds started breeding in the London Zoo in 1834, and the breeding pair continued to rear young for many years. These were distributed among other zoos and private collections all over Europe. If only the European aviculturists had been aware of the rapidly declining state of the néné in the wild, they might have paid more attention than they did to keeping the captive stock breeding. By 1910 there were only a few captive birds left, and they had lost the urge to breed. The stock had not been refreshed from Hawaii for years, and was by then probably senile. One male néné reared in Holland in 1898 was transferred to Jean Delacour's collection at Clères in France. When it died or disappeared during the German invasion of 1940, it was the longest-lived waterfowl ever documented.

The task of saving the néné from the verge of extinction was now taken up in Hawaii itself by Harold C. Shipman, a landowner and aviculturist. In 1918 he started to keep and breed a captive flock of nénés at Keaau, near Hilo. In 1927 the Hawaiian Board of Agriculture and Forestry started a similar venture. During the next thirty years the Shipman farm reared forty-three birds, though some of these disappeared during the tidal wave that struck the island in 1946 and others (more valuably) reverted to the wild. The Board of Agriculture built its own flock up to about forty-two. But for some reason this was broken up in 1935 and distributed to private aviculturists; it virtually disappeared. By 1947 only fifty nénés – wild and captive – were estimated to be left on Hawaii, and none anywhere else in the world.

The Hawaiian Board of Agriculture quickly started a new farm at Pohakuloa, with a couple of pairs of nénés from Shipman, a gander from the Honolulu Zoo, and a wild goose caught in 1949. (There were a very few wild birds still existing then.) In April 1950 John Yealland (now Curator of Birds at the London Zoo, but then Curator to the Wildfowl Trust) flew from Hawaii to Slimbridge in England with two Shipman birds. Early in 1951 both these birds laid eggs! However, a cable and aeroplane brought a gander over from Pohakuloa within a week.

Kamehameha, named after the great Hawaiian king, settled down at once with his geese, Emma and Kaiulani; and nine young were reared from the trio at Slimbridge in the following year. When Kamehameha died in 1963, he was the ancestor of more than 230 birds. At least 170 of Kamehameha's progeny were living in captivity in Europe, a dozen in the continental United States, and fifty had been returned to the wild in Hawaii, where they were used to restock the island of Maui. Meanwhile the breeding stock at Pohakuloa was also building up, and was being used to restock the island of Hawaii. By 1962 the total world population of the Hawaiian goose, captive and free, was estimated at 427. In January 1964 it was about the same; after further translocations there were fewer in Europe but probably more free in Hawaii. By April 1966 there had been yet further translocations from Slimbridge to Maui, and the world population was over 500.

The captive stock in Europe has now been spread over more than a dozen collections, as an insurance against disease or parasites or other hazards of aviculture. This European stock has its headquarters at Slimbridge, the main home of the Wildfowl Trust, with other groups in England at Peakirk (a satellite of the Trust), Leckford and other private collections, London and Whipsnade Zoos, and on the Continent at Antwerp, Basle, West Berlin, Clères, Cologne, Copenhagen, and Rotterdam Zoos.

The world population of nénés – about fifty between 1947 and 1951 – had doubled by 1957, doubled again by 1959 or 1960, and doubled yet again by 1962 or 1963. A doubling every three or four years is progression indeed. The foresight of the Hawaiian farming authority and of Peter Scott, Director of the Wildfowl Trust (and Chairman of the Survival Service Commission), has been rewarded in full measure.

The headquarters free population on the island of Hawaii – a mixture of indigenous and liberated birds – is now well established in its old haunts on the lava flows at between 5,000 and 8,000 feet on the eastern slopes of Mauna Loa, Mauna Kea, and Hualalai; and re-established on Haleakala Mountain on Maui. Official protection (in the sense of a hunting ban) goes back to the first decade of the present century. In 1964 the Fish and Wildlife Service reported that two sanctuaries totalling 18,000 acres had been established for a period of ten years; and large sums of private and government money are now supporting the essential ecological research and reserve management.

It is scarcely necessary to add that the néné is also fully protected by public opinion in the State of Hawaii: it is indeed, now, the official bird of the fiftieth state of the Union.

CRESTED SHELDUCK
Tadorna cristata

The crested shelduck is one of the world's most mysterious birds, and found its way out of the Survival Service Commission's list of extinct species and into the Red Data Book just in time to catch the printing of this volume.

The species was first recognized by Japanese aviculturists, and was figured and described as the "Chosen-Oshi", or Korean mandarin duck in a book published in Japan about 1750, which stated that it was often imported to Japan from Korea between 1716 and 1736. It was described in 1803 in a Japanese nature encyclopaedia. Japanese paintings of around 1700 and of the nineteenth century also figure it; a pair, caught at Furubori, Ipponji, near Kametamura, Hakodate, on Hokkaido in October 1822 was figured from the Shogun's living collection in the following year, and other pairs were drawn from life in about 1850 and 1854. The duck was also figured on old Chinese paintings and tapestries.

Only four specimens exist: the first, a female collected near Vladivostok, in Russia, in April 1877 was never scientifically described, as it was deemed to be a hybrid between a ruddy shelduck, *Tadorna ferruginea*, and a falcated teal, *Anas falcata*. The second, a male, was taken at the mouth of the Kum River near Kunsan, in Korea, in late November or early December 1913 (or 1914). The third, a female taken on the Naktong River near Fusan in Korea on about the 3rd December 1916 was the type of Nagamichi Kuroda's scientific description of 1917.

Crested shelduck *D. M. Henry* 1958

The fourth, a male, was taken at the mouth of the Kun-Kian River not far from Seoul, in Korea, in the summer of 1924. Three taken from a flock of six in north-west Korea in March 1916 were apparently not preserved. Nothing was heard of this bird since then, apart from a possible sight record reported to Yasukichi Kuroda from Chushinhokudo, in Korea, in late March 1943; and the species was lately believed extinct, and was logged in print by James C. Greenway and Jean Delacour as most probably so, and by two of the present authors as certainly so.

It may not be so. On the 16th May 1964 V. I. Labzyuk and Yu. N. Nazarov recorded three crested shelducks in a small flock of harlequin ducks on an isolated skerry in the Rimskii-Korsakov archipelago south-west of Vladivostok. From their account a drake stood out from the harlequins by his colour pattern and large size, easily visible without binoculars. When Labzyuk and Nazarov came to within 25 yards of the skerry the drake flew off with the harlequins and was joined by two ducks, which rose from behind the skerry: the birds flew south-east. Later a pair was seen for a few days on a small lake on Bolshoi Pelis Island in the same archipelago, and the drake was in full breeding plumage on the 10th June.

Subsequently, in a letter to Prof. L. A. Portenko, Labzyuk (known to our Survival Service Commissioner Prof. G. P. Dement'ev as an experienced observer with a knowledge of the literature) confirmed that the drake was "sharply three-coloured", with pinkish bill and legs and a crest on its head. Confirmation of such sight records as these is vitally important, and these details (not published in the observers' paper of the 18th February 1967) seem fully convincing. The records suggest that the breeding-grounds are more likely to be in Russian Ussuriland (south Primor'ye) than in Korea.

HAWAIIAN MALLARD or KOLOA
Anas platyrhynchos wyvilliana

The common mallard, *Anas platyrhynchos*, is more widespread and more fertile than any other kind of duck. But, considering that it occupies virtually the whole of the temperate and sub-arctic world, it has comparatively few valid races. The typical birds of Eurasia and the main North American continent are virtually indistinguishable and are held to be of one race, *A. p. platyrhynchos*. Greenland, Mexico and New Mexico, and Florida have valid races of their own, it is true. Many authorities have classed the Laysan ducks (p. 195) of the Hawaiian archipelago as a race of mallard; but these are certainly more teal-like and are now held to rank as a full species. In the Pacific Marianas a small group of odd ducks, named *Anas oustaleti* in 1894, were thought to be an outlying, isolated race of mallard, but are now regarded as a "swarm" of wild hybrids of the mallard and the grey duck, *A. superciliosa*.

The special indigenous ducks of the main Hawaiian Islands do, however, appear to rank as members still of the full mallard species, though after generations of isolation they have evolved into a smaller and very well-marked race of it, with a dullish male plumage intermediate in pattern between that of a duck and of a drake in eclipse plumage of the typical mallard. Drake koloas have the purplish-blue speculum or wing-mirror shown by the common mallard's drake and duck; duck koloas have a green one.

There is little doubt that in the nineteenth century, when pioneer Hawaiian field men like R. C. L. Perkins knew it well, the koloa inhabited small pools and forest wetlands all over the main islands of the archipelago with the exception of Lanai and Kahoolawe. But in the present century the drainage of wetlands, hunting, and possibly also the pressures of introduced predators had extinguished it in the larger eastern islands of Molokai, Maui, and Hawaii by the 1940s. Now it breeds, and lives as a resident, only in the coastal wetlands and some hill-streams of Niihau, Kauai, and eastern Oahu. It is watched anxiously by the State Game Department of Hawaii, which has now worked out plans for the special study and aided

PLATE 17 (*a*) Nénés, male (right) and female *F. W. Frohawk* 1893; (*b*) Koloas, two males *J. G. Keulemans* 1900; (*c*) Laysan teals, male (right) and female *J. G. Keulemans* 1893

(a)

(b)

(c)

propagation of the species with the backing of the World Wildlife Fund.

In the post-war years the endangered status of the koloas has encouraged exploration to measure the world population; some of it, in the fortunately still wilderness country of inner Kauai, has been difficult even for experienced rangers. It seems that there were about 500 individuals surviving on Kauai and fewer than thirty on Oahu in 1946–7; but in the whole archipelago only about 300 remained in 1950, probably fewer in 1951, and as many as 500 in 1957 and 1960, but perhaps only about 300 in 1961, and possibly only 200 in 1962. However, the state investigators estimated a world population of about 500 again in 1964 (most on Kauai), and, though this included sixty or seventy in zoo and other waterfowl collections, it suggests that the present status of the bird is fairly good (though not good enough), and that it is relatively safer for the time being than many other birds in the Red Data Book. Kauai, the island with the largest undisturbed wilderness, holds the bulk of the present population, though, before its Mana marsh area was drained for sugar-cane farming in 1923, this wetland alone is believed to have supported over 2,000 koloas. On Oahu, the most highly populated island, the birds may have been fewer than thirty – possibly only a dozen – in 1964, and probably confined to the eastern peninsular area around Lanikai and Kailua, where they were modestly surviving twenty years ago, with a headquarters on the offlying, mongoose-free, twin isles of Mokulua.

Aviculture is, quite rightly, part of the present programme of resuscitation of the koloa. Unfortunately the birds have not taken quite so readily to breeding in captivity as the néné and Laysan teal – the other endangered Hawaiian waterfowl. The species probably first bred in captivity in the Honolulu Zoo, in Europe first at Slimbridge in 1951, after a pair had been flown over from Paul Breese at Kapiolani Park, Oahu, in the previous year. In Europe the clutches have usually been only half the apparent wild norm of eight eggs, and the breeding success not

spectacular, despite the special skills with rearing possessed by Slimbridge and Clères (France). Only about four birds survived in Europe in 1964, though at least sixty-three koloas, some breeding quite well, were then in United States zoos, notably a flock of thirty birds at Hawaii's Pohakuloa, of néné fame. As experience grows, and despite the difficulties of fine European aviculturists with the birds, a zoo bank should develop, as a valuable insurance against further diminution of the wild wetland habitat of these unique mallards – a process now resolutely opposed by the Hawaiian Audubon Society.

LAYSAN TEAL
Anas laysanensis

Towards the remote western end of the Hawaiian archipelago, the small island of Laysan has its own species of duck. Lord Rothschild, who first named it in 1892, was probably quite right to hold it a full species. Jean Delacour, in his 1956 volume of the *Waterfowl of the World*, held it to be an "undersized, inbred sub-species" of the mallard. But, although it somewhat resembles the koloa, which doubtless is a mallard, and its ducklings are rather like those of koloa ducklings, Peter Scott and other authorities consider now that this duck could most usefully be spoken of as a teal, and at all events as a full species. It is certainly of teal style, even if, in the process of evolution, it may have shared ancestry more lately with the mallard and koloa group than with the typical teal group of the genus *Anas*.

Like many birds confined to islands, the Laysan teal is tame and disinclined to flight. Its habitat is a rushy, salty lagoon that occupies the heart of an island of 709 acres, less than 2 miles long, and 1 mile wide. Near the lagoon it nests under *Chenopodium* and *Scaerola* bushes, within which it occasionally feeds on insects and round which it hunts moth larvae and crustaceans. Its population, always small, appears to have fluctuated: an early collector, in 1900, found the teal generally in pairs, sometimes in groups of a dozen or more. W. K. Fisher estimated under 100 birds on the island in 1903; later in the same year, after a visit of Japanese feather-hunters, it was down to about twenty-four. In 1909 another

---

PLATE 18 California condor, old male *John James Audubon* 1838

Japanese feather-raiding party seems to have almost exterminated the species – presumably they were unaware of, or more certainly unrestrained by, Theodore Roosevelt's bird reservation order of the same year, which embraced Laysan. When Homer R. Dill and W. K. Bryan, then conservation inspectors, landed in 1911 they could find no more than six ducks. A. M. Bailey could not find more than seven in 1912.

By 1918, however, the population had recovered to an estimated thirty-five. A distinguished United States ornithologist found only twenty birds in 1923 and collected six of them. No further information on numbers seems to be available until 1936, when between nine and eleven were observed, though only in a short stay (there may have been more). In 1950 there were at least twenty-six adults and seven young of the year; and the population of 1951 was counted as thirty-nine. Another visit, in 1955, gave a count of 161, and in 1957 Richard E. Warner, the Laysan teal's thorough historian, and his colleagues found between 400 and 600. The explosive success of the population at this time was confirmed by Warner and Dale Rice in the following year, when they estimated a population of 594 after a very careful series of transects. The fortunes of the Laysan teal had certainly improved. Some authorities link the increase of the 1950s with the recovery of the plant-cover after the earlier disappearance of the population of rabbits. Rabbits were introduced in 1903 by the manager of a guano company. By 1911 they had already made inroads on the vegetation, and by 1923 had virtually destroyed it. Before the rabbits were finally eliminated by United States biologists (last, about 1926), they contributed greatly, by depriving the teal of feeding-ground, to the slowness of the recovery of the duck's population from the Japanese raid.

By 1961, another careful census by Warner and his companions showed that the Laysan population of native teal was close to 688. After that there was a sudden decline, for in 1963 the island population was believed to be down to about 200, not long after a hurricane. Perhaps this was an under-estimate, for the United States Bureau of Sport Fisheries and Wildlife estimated 475 to 500 in 1964. Doubtless the hurricane swept a fairly large part of the population so far to sea that, with their reduced powers of flight, the victims could not get back. It is a paradox that an island population of birds, in an area liable to violent winds, is at an advantage only if it is either of particularly strong fliers, or of almost or entirely flightless birds. The Laysan teal appears to be still in the vulnerable intermediate position.

The disaster of 1963 was just one of the hazards of Pacific life, even if it belies the ocean's name. It came, fortunately, when the population on Laysan was strong enough to stand it, and when, for the first time in history, the insurance of the species had become underwritten elsewhere. In 1957 and 1958 the wild population was believed strong enough to stand a crop of (eight and thirty-six) birds for aviculture; and, as it turns out, the translocation from Laysan to aviculture has proved entirely justified. Live birds were deliberately taken under United States Government licence and placed in enlightened zoos. The pair that reached Slimbridge in England in 1958 produced one offspring in the next year, and Dillon Ripley, President of the International Council for Bird Preservation, also bred the species at Litchfield in the U.S.A. In 1960 the Wildfowl Trust reared three young at Slimbridge, and Laysan teal also successfully bred in three other establishments.

By 1962, when the Wildfowl Trust reared twenty-five young at Slimbridge, there were at least seventy Laysan teal captive in five establishments. In 1963 the Wildfowl Trust reared no fewer than fifty-five young at Slimbridge and Peakirk; and in the spring of 1964 there were 107 birds in ten zoos and about fifty others in other avicultural collections, which means that the hurricane-depleted population of Laysan in that year was backed by a zoo bank that brought the world census to a third as much again.

No further comment seems necessary upon the question whether aviculture has a role to play in the world conservation of vulnerable and endangered species. But, as Richard Warner says: "Our success in preserving the bird under artificial conditions must not be a justification for relaxing vigilance in the protection of the wild population on Laysan Island".

BROWN TEAL *or* PATEKE
Anas aucklandica

The brown teal, a dabbling duck indigenous to New Zealand, was first collected in 1840 on Auckland Island and at about the same time on the main archipelago, and was scientifically named in 1844. It is closely related to the chestnut teal of Australia, *Anas castanea*, though duller in plumage and markedly smaller-winged. Indeed, though flocks will occasionally travel quite swiftly across valleys, the brown teal of the main New Zealand islands is a reluctant flier, and lives a highly resident life. Its vulnerability has no doubt been increased by its reluctance to cross water-partings and recolonize valleys from which it has become extinct.

At some time in the history of the colonization of New Zealand by the species (presumably from Australia) a population seems to have discovered and colonized the Auckland Island archipelago, over 300 miles to the south of South Island, and settled down to evolve into a markedly different race (the "typical" one, *Anas aucklandica aucklandica*), which is generally known as the Auckland Island flightless teal. It is indeed flightless, with short wings, and, since introduced cats went wild on the mainland, has become confined to Adams, Disappointment, Rose, Ocean, Ewing, and Enderby islands, where it still seems to be plentiful, feeding mainly at night on shore and among the coastal kelp. In 1886 a flightless teal was also collected on Campbell Island, about 150 miles further away to the south-east, and, from the rather poor single specimen, named *Anas aucklandica nesiotis*. Flightless teal were not seen on Campbell Island again until 1943, when a coast-watching party was stationed on this normally uninhabited island; and a pair, collected in 1944, showed slight differences from the Auckland Island race. Whether the Campbell Island flightless teal should be classed as a valid race or not (the *Checklist of New Zealand Birds* accepted it as a good race in 1953), it is certainly very rare or perhaps even extinct; indeed, the only subsequent records to guide us are those of Kaj Westerskov, who, ashore on Campbell Island in early 1958, saw only four birds that he was "inclined to think" might be of this form. Dr Alfred M.

Bailey, who led an expedition to the island in 1958, thinks it likely that the few Campbell Island birds recorded are "mere stragglers from the Auckland Islands", though 150 miles seems a long way for a flightless and sedentary bird to swim.

The New Zealand brown teal, *A. a. chlorotis*, as the race of the main New Zealand archipelago is generally called, was certainly widely spread over those islands (North, South, Stewart, and Chatham). It has a normal power of flight, though it may use it (*see* above) reluctantly. Bones dating from the prehistoric period (that is, since the Polynesian colonization of about A.D. 950) have been found on South Island at a human site at Lake Grassmere and in the famous moa deposits of Pyramid Valley.

The brown teal was probably always most abundant on South Island. On Chatham Island it became extinct some time before 1915. It died out early in the twentieth century in the Wellington Province (North Island), where Lake Horowhenna and the lakes near Himatangi in Manawatu County were once strongholds. It was found on Kapiti Island off the west coast in 1873, but later it died out, and in 1907 some of the flightless Auckland Island form were introduced at this sanctuary without success. Some time between 1910 and 1925 it became extinct in Hawke's Bay Province, where it used to be found in the Mahia Peninsula and – perhaps at the last – at Tutira Lake. It is now restricted to the province of Auckland, where it still survives in Northland from Waipu to Kaeo, with populations probably also at Whangarei, Kara, Helena Bay, the Bay of Islands, Kerikeri, and Takou Bay. In 1964–5 it was found in unrecorded haunts on the Coromandel Peninsula and ponds at Auckland. It still breeds in some hundreds on Great Barrier Island. In the rest of Auckland Province it seems to have held on at least until the 1950s, but not later, in the Rotorua district on the mainland and on Mayor Island.

On South Island we know from the prehistoric records that it was once in the fauna of both Marlborough and Canterbury provinces. It was in Canterbury that its nest was found for the first time in 1870. Now it is extinct in these more northerly provinces, and indeed is known only from Southland, where its last

New Zealand brown teals *Peter Scott* 1964

strongholds lie in south-west Fiordland, and in the Stewart Island archipelago, though it may still breed also on Ruapuke Island.

With its retiring habits and nocturnal feeding, the brown teal is not easy to find; but it seems certain that even in the Stewart archipelago, which stoats have not yet reached, the duck is becoming rare. It probably has a surviving population on Big South Cape (or Long) Island, and possibly on the east side of the main island at Half Moon Bay; but at Codfish Island, once a stronghold, and where several birds were seen feeding at night late in 1934, only one was seen in a long exploration in 1948, and none in 1965.

Pending fuller explorations of the Fiordland and Stewart areas, still bushy and difficult to penetrate, an estimate of the world population of the brown teal must be a considerable guess. Peter Scott, in 1957, suggested 1,000 to 1,500 birds, but put the word "perhaps" before this; at that time he believed the teal was probably increasing. This now seems rather unlikely.

New Zealand's protective legislation is now good; the future of the teal must depend surely on improved information and the management of some of its survival areas, especially on North Island. A zoo bank is in present circumstances also a sensible thing to build up. The flightless Auckland Island form was exhibited in the London Zoo in 1895; no examples of it have been in Europe since; a few kept captive in New Zealand years ago did not breed. The first "New Zealand" birds were imported to England in 1934; stock reached the London Zoo, and from there the Wildfowl Trust received a duck at Slimbridge in 1949–50. One of two pairs that came direct to Slimbridge from New Zealand in 1957 reared three ducklings in 1960 – the first ever bred in captivity. Three more were reared in 1961, twenty-two in 1962, ten in 1963, and eight in 1964. This, the only stock now outside New Zealand, may need refreshment; an aviculture experiment in New Zealand itself would no doubt be prudent.

Order FALCONIFORMES
Family Cathartidae: condors and New World vultures

CALIFORNIA CONDOR
Gymnogyps californianus

The California condor is the only great bird of the Rancho la Brea fauna (see p. 15) that survives. Most authorities, as a matter of fact, hold the Pleistocene California condors to be of a different species, *Gymnogyps amplus*, named so by Loye Miller in 1911 on the basis of Upper Pleistocene bones from Samwel Cave in California. *Gymnogyps* bones have now been found in at least twenty-five places in the United States and Mexico, and it is virtually certain that the slightly larger and more robust *G. amplus* is the direct ancestor of the modern *G. californianus*, and that the transition from one species to the other took place around the very end of the Pleistocene, as is borne out by the difficulties paleontologists have had in referring bones of this particular time to one species or the other. Here we will call the two together the California condor, in celebration of the fact that *G. amplus* should probably be rated as a time-race (or paleosubspecies), *G. californianus amplus*.

In the great days of the Pleistocene fauna the shadow of the California condor, with its wing-spread of over 9 feet and weight of up to 23 pounds (doubtless a little larger in the *amplus* period) fell on California, Nevada, Arizona, New Mexico, Florida, Texas, and Nuevo León in north-eastern Mexico, as the bones tell us. If we add the information from bones of the prehistoric period, and from early sightings during the first modern exploration of the West, we can arrive at a heyday range for this condor on the west side of the Rockies from British Columbia south to the northern mountains of Mexico's Lower California, and Arizona, and in a great strip east of North America's mountain spine from New Mexico to north-eastern Mexico, Texas, and Florida. The bones so far discovered in Florida are the earliest at present known, coming from the Reddick beds, which are of the Middle Pleistocene and are around 200,000 years old, and from the Pamlico formation, which is of the early Upper Pleistocene and probably well over 100,000 years old. No later bones from Florida have yet been found. All the prehistoric deposits in which the condor bones have been found seem to have been associated in some way with man; including the Five Mile Rapids Indian midden in Oregon (by carbon-dating, a little under 8,000 years old), tarpits at Rancho la Brea (the youngest, probably about 4,500 years old by carbon-dating), the Gypsum Cave deposits in Nevada (with more sophisticated atlatl darts than those at Rancho la Brea, but quite early prehistoric), and the Indian shell mounds at Emeryville near San Francisco, perhaps 4,000 to 3,000 years old.

The California condor was not recorded by "Western" eyes until the end of the eighteenth century, being first named by Shaw from the coast of California in 1797. Among the earliest pioneers of the West to encounter it were the famous explorers Lewis and Clark on the Columbia River near Sprague in Washington in 1805. It seems certain that when the species was first logged it had already withdrawn as a breeder to states west of the Rockies, for no sightings from the "fossil" areas east of them are on record. During the nineteenth century the range withdrew still farther – from Oregon and Washington probably in the first half, from southern British Columbia perhaps a little later; the last probable sighting in this province of Canada seems to have been at Lulu Island in about 1889. When the century turned, the species was probably breeding only in California, though ranging still to the northern mountains of Lower California, where the last sightings seem to have been of single birds at Encantada

in the Sierra San Pedro Mártir in 1934 and 1935, and to Arizona, where the last sightings appear to have been near Williams in about 1924 and in Yuma County before 1934.

As far as we can establish, no actual nest of the species has ever been formally recorded outside California – and range-records must be taken as giving only an indication of the old breeding range. However, this condor is resident, though with an operational range of up to 150 miles. The presumption that old sight and fossil records are indicators of breeding within such a range is high; though they mean, for instance, that the old southern British Columbia sightings may have been of Washington breeders. By 1943 the breeding range of the species had withdrawn to a relatively small area of south-western California in the southern parts of the Coast Range and the Sierra Nevada, and California's ornithological geographers, the late Joseph Grinnell and Alden Miller, believed that the total number of existing individuals was "in the near neighbourhood of 100". This was, it turns out, already an optimistic figure: between 1939 and 1947 Carl B. Koford made, for the National Audubon Society, a study of the population that was a model in the evaluation of data; it was initiated, and at the end of the survey it was accepted, by Grinnell and Miller. The figure for the population in that period, after the most complex checking and collation of counts from selected stations, was in fact very close to sixty; in 1946–7 it could be broken down into thirty non-nesting adults (in nature both the California and Andean condors nest every other year, so long is the fledging period), ten adults at five nests, and twenty others chiefly immature.

The National Audubon Society formally decided in 1961 to resurvey the condors. Once more the work was under the direction of the late Alden Miller, this time with the rancher-naturalists Ian and Eben McMillan as field men, and with the Koford techniques to elaborate on, and for comparison. The observations they used were spread over the years 1959–64, particularly 1963–4; and their conclusions were that in seventeen years the population had fallen by 30 per cent to an estimated forty-two. In 1963 (after a deep study of the observations) the accepted analysis was twenty non-nesting adults, eight adults at active nests, and fourteen others of which at least ten were immature. The breeding-places in the period were confined to the parts of Santa Barbara and Ventura counties in the Transverse Range that unites the Coast Range and Sierra Nevada, the most active sites being in Ventura County. In October 1966 the California Department of Fish and Game organized another count and identified at least fifty-one living individuals: it is possible that the apparent increase since 1963 may be due (at least partly) to a different system of analysis and (or) more complete coverage in some areas.

Miller and the McMillans published their report in 1965, and they concluded that the greatest losses among condors in recent years have been from illegal shooting. Their records show that, in the period after the Koford survey that ended in 1947, at least nine birds were provedly shot, and that the number we may conclude from circumstantial evidence to have died by shooting, or in some cases by poisoning, was of the order of twenty, which approximately equals the estimated population drop in the period. Judging by the shooting pressures, and the number of hunters (12,000 in August 1964 in the Mount Pinos district of Los Padres National Forest alone), and their behaviour (which can only be felt as lurid by readers of the 1965 report) in the autumn forests and hill-tops of the condor area, the chances that more condors had been shot, beyond the circumstantial evidence, are great – alarmingly great. The Audubon report of 1965 accentuates the inadequate enforcement of the law, the failure to educate hunters, and their "increased

penetration, legally or otherwise, of private and public lands". It adds: "The heavy increase in human population near the range of the condor and the great development of road, trails and other types of accessways have materially contributed to this serious loss from wanton shooting." The staple food of the California condor continues to be dead cattle and sheep, especially cattle; dead deer are also important. "Starvation and limited food supplies are not factors under existing conditions," says the report, and it suggests that the future of North America's greatest bird relic of the Pleistocene depends on improvements in human behaviour, and in the law and its enforcement. In particular it suggests that the great bird should itself be designated a national monument, and that the whole system of hunting and trail access (and low-flying air access) to its heartland refuges should be immediately reorganized. Under California law the killing of a condor, though long illegal, has only recently been made a felony. Moreover, the Topatopa dam project and its construction roads still threaten the main breeding-ground.

The California condor is doubtless doomed unless the great, rich state of California, with its highest of human increase-rates of all the fifty, can adopt the bird as a badge of conscience and its survival as an omen. There is little hope of a zoo bank. Though the Andean condor has bred in several zoos with success, the California condor, as far as we know, has been kept in zoos only in Washington's National Zoological Park, New York's Bronx Zoo, San Diego, and (years ago) London. None bred, though a female at Washington laid several infertile eggs (one a year) half a century ago.

Family Accipitridae: Old World vultures, eagles, and hawks

AFRICAN LAMMERGEYER
Gypaetus barbatus meridionalis

Most authors have considerable difficulty in classifying this magnificent bird. It certainly belongs to the family Accipitridae, which contains all the Old World vultures, hawks, harriers, buzzards, and eagles, but there is no unanimity

about whether or not it is closely related to the vultures. Some writers consider that true vultures form one subfamily and the lammergeyer another, monotypic one (that is, one with only a single representative); but others place this species in the subfamily Accipitrinae between the eagles and buzzards, close to the sea eagles and the palm nut vulture of Africa.

African lammergeyer *Rena M. Fennessy* 1966

The "bearded vulture" really behaves little like any vulture, from which it can be distinguished by its pointed wings (a 9-foot span) and long, wedge-shaped tail. It is a carrion-eater, yet it favours bones: these it will drop from a considerable height on to stones and rocks, before devouring the marrow and bone-fragments. This habit of dropping things has been recorded for hundreds of years, first perhaps by the Roman writer Pliny, who described how the poet Aeschylus was killed by a lammergeyer that dropped a tortoise on his bald head, which it had mistaken for a stone. Disbelief was followed by an admission that bones were in fact dropped, but then the contention was made that the dropping came about accidentally, when the birds were fumbling with the bones in the air. Much more recently, however, there has been adequate evidence to prove that the bones are indeed dropped intentionally.

The lammergeyer inhabits the big mountain ranges of the Palearctic and Ethiopian regions. One race of it, *Gypaetus barbatus aureus*, is very well known, for it had an immense range from Spain through the Alps to the Himalayas, Tibet, and China. The other Palearctic race, *G. b. barbatus*, survives quite well in Africa north of the Sahara. The bird is still numerous and familiar in the Himalayas, but it disappeared from the Alps as a breeding species in the latter half of the nineteenth century. During recent years a few individuals have restarted summering in the Alps, but the subspecies is still comparatively rare west of the Himalayas, though there is a fairly flourishing population in Spain.

It is the African race, *G. b. meridionalis*, that is now considered to be in some danger, where it exists in the mountains of the Yemen, Eritrea, Ethiopia, Kenya, Uganda, Tanzania, Basutoland, and the Republic of South Africa. In these various African localities of rugged mountain grandeur, it is only in the northernmost and southernmost parts of the range that the birds are at all common, and only in Ethiopia that they are locally abundant. In most of the areas they inhabit, lammergeyers are seldom seen or recorded, and they have populations of perhaps a few pairs only. But it is not for this reason alone that we must consider them to be in some danger as a species. The threat to their survival is a new one – the indiscriminate use of poisons.

Quite apart from the misguided endeavours of some people to destroy all large eagles or eagle-like birds, the intensification of farming and the increased production of wool have caused a big spread of jackals, and a great deal of poison is now used to combat their increase. It is also interesting to note that in the Drakensberg Mountains true vultures, which find it difficult if not impossible any longer to obtain dead animals, have taken occasionally to killing domestic beasts. Poison is now used to kill them too, and lammergeyers are prone to take baits put out for both predators.

Many old records accuse lammergeyers of attacking and carrying off quite large animals, in one case even a human baby, but there is no authentic account of such a thing. Indeed, the talons of a lammergeyer are comparatively blunt and not at all suitable for such lethal offences. The species breeds slowly, the female probably taking many years to reach maturity and laying only one egg a season. It is a common duty to ensure that this unique and splendid bird receives everywhere the maximum protection.

Though widely exhibited in zoos, the lammergeyer seems to have bred in captivity only in the

Zoological Gardens at Sofia in Bulgaria, where, in a cage 20 by 23 by 26 feet, a pair reared as many as eleven young between 1916 and 1929.

EVERGLADE (SNAIL) KITE
Rostrhamus sociabilis plumbeus

The giant freshwater snails of the genus *Pomacea* (or *Ampullaria*) provide abundant food in many parts of the subtropical and tropical world, and several groups of birds – openbill storks, limpkins, and various birds of prey – have developed specially adapted beaks to take advantage of this source of protein. In the Americas several kites have beaks of specially fine build, with a curved and very sharp point to the upper mandible that can paralyse the snail prey and prepare it, with the aid of grasping feet, for quick shelling. The most famous of them is *Rostrhamus sociabilis*, the snail kite, which ranges from South America to Florida.

At present four races of this species are recognized. It was first identified and named by the zoologist Vieillot from Corrientes and the Rio de la Plata in Argentina in 1817. The typical form ranges from central Argentina, at the latitude of the mouth of the la Plata River, northwards through more wetlands of South America to eastern Panama. In Central America *R. s. major* is found in the marshes of the tropical lowlands, from Costa Rica through Nicaragua (Lake Nicaragua) and Guatemala (Lake Petén) to Mexico's Gulf and Caribbean states of Quintana Roo, Campeche, and Vera Cruz. The Cuban race, *R. s. levis*, was not long ago locally common in the marshlands of western Cuba, and local and rather rare on the Isle of Pines. More lately it has become scarcer through the draining of marshlands, and its status is of some concern to the Survival Service Commission. But the status of the "Everglade kite", the subject of this essay and the most northerly outpost race, never recorded from any other region than the state of Florida, is really alarming. It seems likely that the world population of *R. s. plumbeus*, first described (and then recognized as of racial status) by Ridgway in 1874, was as few as fifty breeding birds in 1953. A decade later it was a quarter or less of that small number, with

juveniles included perhaps amounting altogether to not more than ten or twelve.

The Everglade (snail) kite seems to have enjoyed a wide distribution in Florida into the present century, but has withdrawn rapidly with the draining of marshlands, particularly the Everglades. Since the early 1950s, indeed, the sole breeding group appears to have been confined to the south-western part of Okeechobee, the biggest lake in North America outside the Great Lakes, where it is protected by law and a wardening network: at least part of the tiny population nests in the Loxahatchee National Wildlife Refuge. Dr William B. Robertson Jr, Park Biologist in the Everglades National Park, reports that the 1961–4 remnant was more or less confined to Loxahatchee and the area west of Fort Lauderdale; in 1963 a wandering immature male appeared at the north edge of Everglades National Park, the first record in that area since 1955. This may have been no sign of recovery; despite good wardening, abnormal nest failure has been recorded as lately as 1963, when two occupied nests at Loxahatchee produced but one fledgeling, and disturbance both by humans and by grackles, which are predators of the contents of nests, has been hard to prevent. In 1964 fifteen birds spent the summer at Loxahatchee Refuge, where at least two young, possibly more, were fledged; although a pair was seen at Okeechobee earlier, it is thought that they may have moved to join those further south. In 1965 only ten birds were counted.

Everglade (snail) kite *Fenwick Lansdowne* 1966

Habitat restoration and maintenance is still the obvious prime necessity for the recovery of this race, particularly in the northern Everglades, where the descent of the water table in the last decade or two has been significant. Fortunately supplies of the main food snail seem to be still fairly widespread over Florida, including the Everglades National Park, whose recolonization from Okeechobee, the source of the Everglade river system, must surely be a prerequisite for the snail kite's survival in the U.S.A.

GALÁPAGOS HAWK
Buteo galapagoensis

The word "hawk" is generally used in the New World for the vernacular name of (amongst others) the broad-winged birds of the genus *Buteo* that English-speaking people of the Old World call buzzards. The Galápagos hawk is typical of the large group of American *Buteos*, and is perhaps closest to Swainson's hawk, *B. swainsoni*, of western North America and to the zone-tailed hawk, *B. albonotatus*, of the southernmost United States and tropical Central America and northern South America. Indeed, it may well share an ancestor with these species more lately than with any other, having a strong resemblance as a juvenile to the zone-tailed species which is found in the nearest part of the mainland – Ecuador, 600 miles away.

The Galápagos hawk was, in fact, described a decade before its more widespread cousin – in 1837 by the English naturalist and painter John Gould, from material collected in the isolated equatorial archipelago by Charles Darwin in 1835. In its heyday – and it was found to be common by all expeditions up to 1924 – it was widespread throughout the whole archipelago, except on the north-westerly small outlying islands of Culpepper and Wenman. However, since the setting up of the Charles Darwin Foundation for the Galápagos Islands in 1959, under the auspices of UNESCO, the I.U.C.N., and the Government of Ecuador, field studies in this unique archipelago have been intensified. Among the many Red Data Book animals in the Galápagos, the native hawk has been the object of particular study by Raymond

Galápagos hawk *Albert E. Gilbert* 1966

Lévêque in 1960–1, A. Brosset in 1962–3, and Dean Amadon in 1964.

It is now clear that the Ecuadorean law of July 1959, totally protecting the Galápagos hawk and other peculiar indigenous vertebrates of the Galápagos, may have come only just in time. In the last four decades, human colonization has been continuing fast, and widespread destruction of the interior vegetation by feral goats has taken place. The Galápagos hawk has been widely shot as an enemy of chicken farmers. By the 1960s it seems to have disappeared from Pinta (which is also called Abingdon and is still uninhabited), the northernmost island of its old range, from Floreana (Charles), and from San Cristobal (Chatham), the substantial easternmost island. On Santa Cruz (Indefatigable) it was dangerously rare by 1961, having been cleared by the colonists from Academy Bay and other inhabited parts about two decades previously, and reduced to a few birds in the interior and on small offlying islands. Its population on Santa Fé (Barrington) and the southernmost island, Española (Hood), is also reduced, though it was still proved to breed on these islands in the 'sixties. On Fernandina (Narborough), Isabela (Albemarle), Marchena (Bindloe), Santiago (James), and the rather small islands of Rábida (Jervis) and Pinzon

(Duncan) it has been met with by all surveyors, and seems to preserve its status best: nevertheless a careful estimate by Brosset indicates that the world population in 1962 was certainly not more than 200 birds.

What little is known of the Galápagos hawk's food indicates that it has a wide range of prey, including the indigenous land and marine iguanas, snakes, birds, centipedes, and carrion. The enforcement of the law, and the persuasion of the chicken-farming colonists to share the islands with these unique buzzards, are main preoccupations of the Darwin Foundation.

HAWAIIAN HAWK
Buteo solitarius

Like the Galápagos hawk, this species of *Buteo*, indigenous to the island of Hawaii (only) in the Hawaiian archipelago, may share a latest ancestor with the zone-tailed hawk of the mainland Americas or one of its close allies. Wherever it came from originally, it seems never to have spread from the largest and most easterly island of the chain to any other; or on Hawaii itself (4,030 square miles) beyond the rather open forest (now much cut up by blocks of farm and grassland) above 2,000 feet.

Within this big range the io – to call it by the onomatopoeic name that the Polynesians gave it from its typically buzzard-like, thin, high-pitched cry – has happily lived a harmless life, its present diet being largely rats and mice, doubtless introduced over 1,000 years ago by the Polynesian colonists, as well as insects and birds. It has been persecuted in the past by sportsmen and farmers, and, though now protected by state law, it doubtless suffers from the reduction of its primary forest habitat. The opinion of naturalists is that the population has undergone a steady reduction, at least in the present century, and may now (from a report of 1965) be fewer than 200 individuals, perhaps even fewer than 100. This small chunky buzzard, with its light and dark colour phases, the only resident hawk of Hawaii, is under careful watch by state and private conservationists. It cannot yet exactly be described as rare, but it could quickly become so if the present favourable temper of public opinion in the state of Hawaii were to change.

MONKEY-EATING EAGLE
Pithecophaga jefferyi

This magnificent bird, of immense size, must now regrettably be numbered among the rarest in the world. Its near-extinction has been notably assisted by man's greed for money; but the monkey-eating eagle has suffered from another and more unusual threat.

There has undoubtedly been – and there still is – a great deal of wasteful and senseless killing of nearly all large birds of prey by ignorant folk who believe that any bird with a hooked beak must be harmful to their interests. More especially, this vast eagle has for long been in demand by animal dealers and zoological gardens. The presence of a bird so spectacular in a zoo really does rattle the turnstiles – and the rarer the spectacle, the quicker the rattle. Happily, today, some of the better zoos decline to deal in such rare eagle species; and there is now a tendency in the Philippines to debar the export of this particular species.

Although this severe drain on the endemic population of *Pithecophaga* has now to some extent dwindled, a special threat to it is that it has become a prestige item among the inhabitants of the Philippines as a mounted specimen. Because of this ridiculous development, there is such demand by taxidermists and others that to shoot or trap the birds has become locally worth while. The resulting pressure is not only dangerous and difficult to control, but is likely to require a long-term educational programme for its elimination.

As though these three direct threats to the existence of the monkey-eating eagle were not enough, there is still a fourth and very grave one. That is the steady destruction of its habitat. This eagle lives largely by snatching tree-top mammals in really primeval forests of big timber. There seems to be a sad lack of control in the Philippine Islands over the farmers and lumbermen who are rapidly cutting down the original evergreen forest for the timber trade, or are clearing new patches for cultivation; and since the Second World War the habitat in which the birds can exist has shockingly decreased.

The relict population of this largest of Philippine eagles may already be doomed. It is confined mainly to Mindañao Island, with a smaller population more recently recorded from Luzon Island, where one bird is known to have been shot in 1963 and another in 1964. In comparatively recent years it lived also on Leyte and Samar: Samar is the type locality, because from it came the specimen originally described by Ogilvie-Grant in 1897. At present the total population of the species is estimated by Prof. D. S. Rabor as being probably fewer than 100 birds. Some effort must be made very quickly, to enforce such laws as do protect these eagles, and to protect the remaining areas of habitat.

The monkey-eating eagle lays only one egg a year, and, like all the larger eagles, does not begin to breed until it is a great deal older than most people realize. This must already greatly

Monkey-eating eagle *Robert Gillmor* 1966

inhibit the recovery of a bird species whose numbers have been allowed to fall to a total of only 100 individuals. If experience with comparable species like the California condor is a guide, this must mean an annual total of active nests that is most unlikely to exceed ten. It needs reiteration that hunting for stuffed trophies is probably the greatest threat to the monkey-eating eagle, particularly as there is some

competition to see who can bag the most outstanding specimen. The present export and hunting regulations in the Philippines are not enough. It is time that a new law should be passed and enforced, to prohibit entirely both sale and possession of live or dead birds without a written permit.

SPANISH IMPERIAL EAGLE
Aquila heliaca adalberti

The handsome imperial eagle is a northern Old World species of some age; fossil material from the Kirov beds of the early Upper Pleistocene (Ice Age) period lie within the present range of the species, which is "western Palearctic". The great bird of prey has a European distribution, with extensions into the western Himalayas and central Siberia, and a foothold in North Africa.

The typical form (which in post-Ice-Age times, probably warmer than now, seems from fossil evidence to have extended as far north as Lake Ladoga) is not in the Red Data Book. But the Spanish imperial eagle, *A. h. adalberti*, as a race, is probably the most endangered European bird listed in it.

In historical times the Spanish race of this eagle seems to have been separated by a large gap from the nearest members of the typical race in the Balkans. It probably extended from the Pyrenees over most of the drier parts of Spain and Portugal, and throughout Morocco and Algeria south at least to the Atlas Mountains. Four decades ago it had disappeared so completely from Portugal that it was known only from a few museum specimens, and the memory of two that had been kept in captivity at Oporto "many years" before that.

During the present century, indeed, a decline – which had doubtless begun earlier – has been so marked that the race was lately estimated by Guy Mountfort to number only about 100 birds in Spain, where it is now confined to the central and southern mountains, and to the Coto Doñana, where about seven nests active yearly doubtless entitle this great international nature reserve to rank as the world breeding headquarters of the form. Robert Etchécopar's recent account states that no nests have been reported from either Morocco or Algeria in the last two decades. The Spanish imperial eagle may, in fact, be extinct in Algeria now.

So far, the only protection this magnificent bird enjoys is in the Coto. As long as Iberian and Moroccan farmers maintain old attitudes to the raptors, the recovery of the Spanish imperial eagle and its range seems in grave doubt. Fortunately the wardening system in the Coto Doñana is improving fast, and the slow rise of stock in this area seems probable. The question is: what will be the fate of these birds' offspring when they prospect outside Spain's only major bird reserve?

The species has very seldom been kept in captivity, and the possibilities of a helpful zoo bank are inconsiderable. So far not much more

than 4 per cent of the big hawk-eagle family (about 270 species strong) have ever bred in aviculture.

Spanish imperial eagle *Rena M. Fennessy* 1966

Family Falconidae: caracaras and falcons

MAURITIUS KESTREL
Falco punctatus

A century ago this little falcon – a well-differentiated species of its own, but doubtless related to the larger African kestrel, *F. rupicoloides*, and the Madagascar kestrel, *F. newtoni* – seems to have been very common on its rather isolated Indian Ocean island. Fifty years ago it was still well distributed. But, when Dr J. C. Greenway published his authoritative work on extinct and vanishing birds in 1958, it was already rare. Dr Greenway believed that persecution by shooters, who had in mind the local name *mangeur de poules*, was largely responsible, together with the agricultural destruction of habitat. Probably the shooting pressure is the most important factor; in 1963 J. Vinson thought so, and he reported a further decline, estimating no more than ten to fifteen birds in the whole island.

It seems clear that, while public opinion is led by an energetic though small group of naturalists on this island of unique and sometimes perilously endangered forms (with one of the worst extinction records in the world), it has a long way to move before we can be sure that even legislation and enforcement can save this bird.

Mauritius kestrel *Rena M. Fennessy* 1966

SEYCHELLES KESTREL
Falco araea

The "katiti", as this little falcon is called by the Seychellois, was once a common bird on many islands of the Seychelles group, and even as recently as 1940 was reported from most of them. During the intervening twenty-five years, however, there has been a catastrophic decline in the population of this unique kestrel, and by 1959 it could not be found by Dr John Hurrell Crook in its former strongholds on Cousin, Cousine, Marianne, or Félicité. The species is now believed to be entirely restricted to the main island of Mahé, where it is considered much rarer than has been commonly supposed. Its numbers may for long have been seriously over-estimated, because the few remaining birds so commonly frequent buildings as to give the impression of belonging to a considerable population in the rest of the island.

That the species (a member of the same group of kestrels as the previous species) is now very rare and seriously decreasing in numbers, is beyond doubt; but it is not easy to be precise about the reasons for its decline. The kestrels feed mainly on lizards, caught in the characteristic way – swooped upon at considerable speed and struck with the talons, after which they are usually taken to a perch to be eaten. There has been no decrease in the lizard population, so lack of food is not a threat to the survival of the kestrels. Nevertheless several reasons for their increasing rarity have been put forward; one is that the birds are remarkably tame, and many have become easy prey for

Seychelles kestrel *P. Oudart* 1846

children with catapults. Another and more important factor has probably been some disturbance by, and fierce competition for suitable nesting and roosting sites from, the introduced and alien barn owl. The barn owls were regrettably introduced into Mahé, it is said by Government authorities and from South Africa, to prey upon an excessive population of introduced rats that were damaging agricultural interests. They have become particularly fierce and – finding difficulty in catching rats – are now said to be doing harm themselves, by preying upon such birds as the attractive little fairy terns.

Order GALLIFORMES
Family Megapodiidae: megapodes

LA PÉROUSE'S MEGAPODE
Megapodius lapérouse

The mainly Australasian game-bird family of the megapodes or mound-builders has penetrated some distance into the Pacific archipelagos, and the two full species treated here have reached isolated island groups, where they now show the typical vulnerability of island specialists.

La Pérouse's megapode was first described from Tinian in the Marianas in 1823; and in 1868 what was then believed to be another species was described from the Palaus. Reduced now to the status of a race, this form, *M. l. senex,* was established as common in the whole Palau group of the West Carolines (to which it is confined) by Otto Finsch in about 1880. Despite a drop in the human population at the end of the Second World War, the general tendency has been one of increase, and the inhabitants, mainly fishermen and copra-farmers, now number well over 7,000, mostly concentrated on Koror. The destruction of the natural habitat, and predation on wild game, have increased.

Ornithological recording is an irregular process on Pacific archipelagos, but it is certain that by the early 1930s the Palau race of La Pérouse's megapode was either very rare or extinct on the largest island, Babelthuap, and on the most densely populated, Koror and its neighbour Arakabesan. At all events, the last birds must have disappeared here between 1932 and 1945. Dr Rollin Baker's survey of four of the more southerly islands in 1945 proved breeding on three of them, but produced a population estimate of under ten on Angaur, five to ten on Ngabad, ten to twenty on Peleliu and neighbouring islets, and twenty to thirty on Garakayo, making forty-five to seventy in all. His expedition was unable to visit other islands from which breeding was still reported in the early 'thirties – Ngesebus and (some distance to the north) Kayangel. Though no further population figures seem to be available, it is likely that the world population of this race is under a hundred.

Considerably farther to the north-east, the Marianas (typical) race, *M. l. lapérouse*, was first named by Gaimard, the naturalist of a famous French exploring expedition, from a Tinian specimen taken in 1820. It is confined to the archipelago, a stretch of volcanic islands extending over 500 miles from Uracas in the north to the largest and most densely populated island of Guam in the south, with a human population of nearly 60,000 in 1950; and once lived on at least nine islands from Asuncion at the north end to Guam. No positive evidence about its status on any of them appears to be available much after 1940, when the race was still breeding on the inhabited islands of Agrihan and Pagan in the north, and recorded as still present on Almagan and uninhabited Asuncion. In the southern islands the megapodes were not found after a wide search in 1945 on four of the five islands the birds had been recorded from;

La Pérouse's megapode, Marianas race *N. W. Cusa* 1966

and they may survive only on Agiguan, which is normally uninhabited but was garrisoned by the Japanese from the American invasion of the Marianas in 1944 until the surrender in 1945. Rollin H. Baker, who with Joe T. Marshall Jr confirmed the extinction of the species on the other southern islands in 1945, was not able to visit Agiguan, but suggested that the Japanese forces "may have used the birds for food and depleted the population seriously".

The Marianas race of megapode survived on Saipan until after about 1930, when specimens were taken. Here the human population was nearly 7,000 in 1953, and practically the whole of the island had been planted with sugar-cane during the Japanese mandate from 1919 to 1945; doubtless the destruction of habitat was the main cause of the final extinction of the bird. On Tinian and Rota, also inhabited though much less densely, the extinction is less easy to explain or date. On heavily populated Guam, where the pristine habitat was earliest destroyed and hunting pressure was doubtless also high, La Pérouse's megapode, from the accounts of the older inhabitants to L. N. Linsley in the middle 1930s, probably disappeared by 1890 at the latest.

It is quite certain that protective measures are needed for La Pérouse's megapode, and a new survey of both populations, particularly that of the Marianas, is badly needed.

PRITCHARD'S MEGAPODE
Megapodius pritchardi

This most easterly of all megapodes has a

curiously isolated distribution, being found on only one volcanic island, Niuafo'ou, which lies off the Tongan group about halfway between Samoa and Fiji. This island rises to 853 feet and is well wooded; and it had a human population of 1,277 (all but fifteen were Tongans) in 1932. *Megapodius pritchardi*, from the slender accounts given since its first description in 1864, appears to have a small population on this rather small island, and to be holding its own. The continual vulcanicity of the island is such that (according to reports) the bird buries its eggs in hot volcanic ashes rather than in the decaying leaf-piles used as incubators by its congeners. There is no evidence that the population has been endangered by the irregular eruptions of 1853 (when there was much loss of human life), 1867, 1886 (when all the villages were destroyed), 1887, 1912 (when one village was destroyed), 1929 (when the same village was destroyed again),

Pritchard's megapode *N. W. Cusa* 1966

and 1935. A survey is needed, even if it may prove that not the megapodes, but the Niuafo'ou Tongans, should be in the Red Data Book.

Family Cracidae: guans, curassows, and chacalacas

HORNED GUAN
Oreophasis derbianus

This beautiful bird was first obtained by the collector J. Quiñones for a dealer who supplied the English aviculturist and amateur zoologist Lord Derby, after whom it was named in 1844 by G. R. Gray. The first specimens came from Volcán de Fuego in Guatemala, where in 1861 the birds were first seen in the field by an ornithologist, the Englishman Osbert Salvin.

Few other scientists have studied the species: altogether only about thirteen trained biologists appear to have encountered this very rare bird in the field, and it has been so far reported or collected (according to the recent analysis of Dr Robert F. Andrle) from only twenty-four localities in the highland forests of south-east Mexico and south-west Guatemala – from the Sierra Madre in easternmost Oaxaca and southern Chiapas, to Guatemala's rugged chain of volcanoes and high ridges east (formerly, if not at present) to Cobán, the Tecpán Ridge, and Volcán de Fuego.

The horned guan appears to be confined to the humid mountain forest, mostly broadleaf evergreen but in places mixed with cypress or pine, from about 6,000 feet (occasionally lower) to nearly 11,000 feet toward the tops of such great wooded mountains as Volcán Tajumulco (13,805 feet) in western Guatemala and Volcán Tacaná (13,335 feet) on the Chiapas border. In many parts of its range this rather tame bird has been reduced in numbers and distribution, by both shooting and forest-slashing. One of the best-known localities, El Triunfo in Chiapas, has lately been occupied by two Mexican families who run livestock in the forest, and, though Dr Andrle, our artist Albert E. Gilbert, and their colleagues found a small guan population surviving in March 1965, they were greatly concerned about the birds' decrease in numbers and the extent of hunting and habitat-disturbance.

In Guatemala the horned guan has apparently not been recorded from Volcán de Fuego and Volcán Santa Maria in the present century or from the Tecpán Ridge since between the two world wars, but this may be due principally to

Horned guan *Albert E. Gilbert* 1966

lack of field work. However, even though there are probably guan populations remaining in these places, volcanism, deforestation, and hunting have evidently caused their decline.

There is recent evidence that populations survive now in Guatemala on Volcanes Tolimán, Atitlán, and San Pedro on the south side of Lake Atitlán, on Volcán Tajumulco, on the Zunil Ridge, and in the Cuchumatanes Mountains some distance further north. In Mexico there are late, but unconfirmed, reports of a surviving relict population on Volcán Tacaná, and post-war certain records from at least three widely separated places in the eastern Sierra Madre de Chiapas, including El Triunfo. In the western Sierra Madre late reports appear to be reliable from near Tonala and near Cintalapa in western Chiapas, and from Mexicans in this range in extreme eastern Oaxaca. Dr Andrle's latest publication, however, accentuates that considerable areas in the Sierra Madre and in the Guatemalan highlands remain both densely forested and ornithologically unexplored, and may be suitable habitat for horned guans that have not yet been discovered. He concludes that in Guatemala "there is an evident need for effective legal protection of the Horned Guan as

well as for the creation of adequately controlled mountain reserves to ensure the perpetuation of the species". Although in Mexico the federal game law now permanently prohibits the hunting of the horned guan, Dr Andrle does not find very hopeful the bird's long-range preservation prospects in Chiapas, and he shows that "the establishment of some extensive tracts of forest habitat as refuges for it and other montane wildlife will be required". Sr Miguel Alvarez del Toro, director of the Museo Zoológico in Tuxtla Gutierrez, Chiapas, and field companion of Andrle on his investigation in 1965, has been trying to establish a nature reserve of this kind around El Triunfo, where the horned guan is still illegally hunted. Success will doubtless involve difficult problems of relocating people, and also of patrol and enforcement. These are problems that all conservationists hope the state of Chiapas will quickly and permanently overcome.

PLATE 19 (*a*) Chinese monals, male and (background) female *J. Wolf and J. G. Keulemans*; (*b*) Western tragopans, male and (background) female *J. Wolf and J. Smit*; (*c*) Blyth's tragopan *J. Wolf and J. G. Keulemans*; (*d*) Sclater's monal *J. Wolf and J. Smit*. All 1872

▲ (a)   (c) ▼   ▲ (b)   (d) ▼

LOPHOPHORUS L'HUYSII

CERIORNIS BLYTHII

Family Tetraonidae: grouse

PRAIRIE CHICKEN
Tympanuchus cupido

The fate of the prairie chicken, one of the noble game birds of North America and perhaps the most famous, is a classic example of the effect of the destruction of habitat on a once widely and densely distributed species.

The Committee on Rare and Endangered Wildlife Species of the United States Bureau of Sport Fisheries and Wildlife is emphatic in assigning the main cause of the prairie chicken's decline to loss of undisturbed prairie grasslands resulting from agriculture. "The tall grass prairies which were the main habitat of this species," they wrote lately, "are exceptionally fertile and tillable and are the most extensively utilized croplands of the Continent."

The U.S.B.S.F.W. is certain that the marginal populations at the edge of the original range "were eliminated early, probably in part by over shooting". Possibly the decline set in during pre-Columbian times; for there are fossil records from Tennessee, and subfossil Indian midden bones known from parts of Ohio, which are outside even the old historical range of the species. As all four races of the prairie chicken have, or have had, a grave survival history, they are here treated individually.

Heath hen, *T. c. cupido*
The "typical" race of the prairie chicken is now extinct. In early Columbian times it ranged certainly over the New England states from Massachusetts southwards, through southern New York, eastern Pennsylvania, New Jersey, eastern Maryland, and Delaware to the Potomac River in north-eastern Virginia. By 1830 it was confined to the Island of Martha's Vineyard off the Massachusetts coast; and here it gradually declined. The last birds were seen here in 1926 or, as some believe, 1932.

PLATE 20 Whooping crane *John James Audubon* 1834

Greater prairie chicken, *T. c. pinnatus*
Formerly widespread over the prairies of southern Canada and the central United States, this race now has a "classic" relict distribution. In Canada there is still an outpost of a few birds in central Alberta. The last wild bird (probably) in Saskatchewan was seen in the southern part of that province by Roger Tory Peterson and one of the present writers (James Fisher) in August 1959. Small populations survive in southern Manitoba and in three areas of southern Ontario, including Manitoulin Island.

In the U.S.A. this grouse has everywhere a relict pattern, though it survives fairly well in parts of the Dakotas, Minnesota, Wisconsin, Michigan, Nebraska, Illinois (perhaps 1,500 birds in small colonies in about twenty-five counties), north-east Colorado, south-east Kansas (over 80,000 killed in 1958, about 4,000 in 1961, and another 4,000 in 1962), Missouri (about 6,000 birds, south of the Missouri River), and Oklahoma. In many of these states large prairie areas have been acquired, or are being negotiated, for conservation management, often linked with programmes of biological survey, for the bird is rapidly being accepted as a national and state problem. Small colonies also hold out in the south-east corner of Wyoming; and in Indiana, where the state population was estimated at only ninety-eight birds in the spring of 1960, still fewer in 1962, and thirty-two in 1966. The bird has lately become extinct in southern Iowa; prairie chickens recorded recently in north-eastern Iowa may only be stragglers. It is probably extinct in Saskatchewan, and certainly so in Ohio, Kentucky, Tennessee, Arkansas, and Texas. No estimate of the full population of this race is available.

Attwater's prairie chicken, *T. c. attwateri*
This race of the most open coastal prairie of the deep south, formerly ranged from south-west Louisiana over the coastal plains of Texas almost to the Mexican border. It was extirpated in Louisiana by 1919. In 1937 a deep investigation by V. W. Lehmann produced a total

Greater prairie chickens, two males (upper and right) and female *John James Audubon* 1834

population estimate of about 8,700; since then the population has been shrinking continuously, and was believed to have been reduced to about 1,300 birds in 1963, fewer than 750 in 1965 (about half in the original prairie in Colorado County), breeding in only four distinct areas in eleven counties.

Lesser prairie chicken, *T. c. pallidicinctus*

By many authorities considered a distinct species, the lesser prairie chicken does not now overlap in range with the neighbouring greater prairie chicken; more significantly, there is no real evidence that it ever has. John W. Aldrich and Allen J. Duvall, Fish and Wildlife Service game-bird experts, hold it firmly in the category of a geographical race. The lesser prairie chicken is still found in all the former states of its old range – (eastern) New Mexico, (south-eastern) Colorado, (south-western) Kansas, (western) Oklahoma, and (panhandle) Texas. F.W.S. estimates of population in its somewhat reduced present range in these states gave about 12,000 in Texas in 1937 and nearly 15,000 in Oklahoma in 1944; an estimate for the full population, including the relict colonies in the three other states (where it is most abundant in New Mexico) was about 30,000 two decades ago. The population fluctuates markedly and seems to have had an all-time low record in the 1930s: that of New Mexico may fluctuate between 10,000 and 50,000 birds. The race continues to decline.

Family Phasianidae: quail, partridges, and pheasants

MASKED BOBWHITE
Colinus virginianus ridgwayi

Perhaps the most popular game bird of the United States, the bobwhite – the best-known member of its New World subfamily, the American quails – has a broad natural distribution from southern Ontario and the eastern and the central United States south to Cuba and through Mexico into western Guatemala. And of twenty-one currently accepted races, some have been successfully introduced west of the

Masked bobwhite *Albert E. Gilbert* 1966

Rockies, and into Hawaii, New Zealand, and the West Indies.

The distribution of the bobwhite species is generally one of a successful bird, well adapted to conquering new lands after human introduction; and indeed the impression from a map is one of withdrawal in recent historical times, doubtless under the pressure of agriculture, only to a certain extent from the margin of the old range. The real exception to this is the decline of the well-marked masked race – the one race isolated from the rest by some distance.

The masked bobwhite, *C. v. ridgwayi*, about the time it was first described in 1885 from near the Arizona border in the state of Sonora, Mexico, seems to have ranged about 50 miles into the central part of southern Arizona and south through most of the desert scrub of Sonora. Some time probably in the first decade of the present century (certainly by 1912) it was extinguished in Arizona; only lately was it seen in Arizona again, as a result of unsuccessful attempts at reintroduction. The most recent of such, begun by the Arizona-Sonora Desert Museum with a captive stock in 1963, is moving from the acclimatization stage, but after some vandalism and winter losses it is yet too early to assess its fortunes. In Sonora it is now extremely rare and localized in the southern part of the state, particularly around Guaymas, at 3,500 to 4,000 feet.

The Arizona experiment has shown that this rare race – fully in the Red Data Book – can breed in aviculture and that the zoo-bank system may be of positive assistance in rehabilitating this fast declining and very interesting race of American quail.

Tribe Phasianini: pheasants

PHEASANTS

Judging by the past (including fossil) and present distribution of the forty-eight living species that constitute this handsome tribe of game birds, the pheasants probably originated, in the course of evolution, on the mainland of South-East Asia, as part of the oriental avifauna (of which no fewer than forty-two species are still members) and spread naturally, at the latest by middle Miocene times (about 15,000,000 years ago or a little more) into the Palearctic fauna of northern Asia, Europe, and Africa; also into the East Indies (the green junglefowl, *Gallus varius*, here east of Lombok into the Australasian fauna). The domestic fowl, *Gallus gallus*, and the common pheasant, *Phasianus colchicus*, now have a somewhat cosmopolitan distribution after human introductions. Apart from these, the only true pheasant native to any other

fauna is the Congo peacock, *Afropavo congensis*. In 1913 the late J. B. Chapin's attention was drawn to a peculiar feather in the hat of a native of the Ituri Forest of the Congo. It had apparently come from some gallinaceous bird larger than a guineafowl. He brought this secondary quill feather home, showed it to many other ornithologists, but could find no bird from which it might have come. In the following year the museum of the Belgian Congo acquired from another Belgian museum some mounted birds that had mostly been collected before 1900. When these skins reached the museum (at Tervueren, Belgium), two of them, which bore a slight resemblance to the peacock and which were already labelled *Pavo cristatus*, were put on top of a cabinet in a room not used by ornithologists. "There they stood in seclusion until early August 1936," writes Chapin. "At that time I happened into the room, noticed the birds, and stood dumbfounded . . . Here at last, I realized, was the bird from which my feather had come." Later Chapin was told by a Belgian friend of a strange bird he had eaten in the Congo forest in 1930: this man drew a sketch of its head which showed that he meant the same bird. It had become clear that in the Congo forest lived a large member of the pheasant family resembling a peacock.

This, the first and only member of the true pheasant tribe known from Africa, Chapin named *Afropavo congensis* in 1936. Since then the Congo peacock has been found to be not uncommon in many parts of the Congo forests, so much so that it is not considered rare enough for the Red Data Book, though careful watch is kept on it. It has been imported into several zoos and aviaries outside Africa, where it has bred since 1960.

The Congo peacock is not (yet) in the Red Data Book; but all races of no fewer than fourteen of the forty-eight living species of pheasants unequivocally are, in the first place doubtless as a consequence of increased human predation in Asia with increasingly efficient weapons, and also – an important factor – the destruction of the primary and secondary forest of vast areas of Asia: all pheasants demand at least forest-edge or scrubland and hedgeland cover for successful life. Indeed, were it not for aviculture's triumphs in the last 100 years, the fate of some species might have by now become hopeless. The zoo bank and aviculture bank of these popular ornamental fowl, now so carefully and intelligently cultured in captivity – in North America, Britain, and France particularly – is likely to become, soon, an investment that may be the main factor in preserving some of these gems of the game-bird world from extinction. As far as the records of aviculture (kept, fortunately, by six generations at least of bird-loving scholars with respectable accuracy) show us, only seven of the pheasant tribe had been known in Western captivity by the end of the eighteenth century, of which six had by then bred in aviculture. A spate of importations brought exactly half the now-known species into captivity, by the 1860s, of which nineteen had by then bred. By the end of the nineteenth century thirty-seven species had been kept

captive, of which thirty-two had bred. When Jean Delacour published his *Pheasants of the World* in 1951, he could report that all but one species (Rothschild's peacock pheasant, *Polyplectron inopinatum*, of the Malay Peninsula mountains) had been kept in captivity, and only seven of the world's forty-eight had not been known to have reared young in aviculture – of which two were bred successfully after his great monograph was published. Apart from Rothschild's peacock pheasant, the only species not yet bred in culture, as far as we know, are four: Salvadori's pheasant, *Lophura inornata*, and Bulwer's pheasant, *L. bulweri*; and two Red Data Book species, Sclater's monal, *Lophophorus sclateri*, and the Chinese monal, *L. lhuysi*. This means that there is a zoo bank, or a potential one, for twelve of the present Red Data Book species and – so well do pheasants respond to skilled modern management in captivity – every prospect that the remaining species may soon successfully rear young and multiply in aviculture; indeed, one of the greatest problems of modern exotic pheasant culture is that of the importation of new stock from the wild for genetic refreshment.

Much of the information about the Red Data Book species treated in their sections below is derived from Dr Delacour and from Philip Wayre, another great aviculturist, of the Ornamental Pheasant Trust, Great Witchingham, in Nofolk, England.

Western tragopan, *Tragopan melanocephalus*

This is one of the rarest pheasants, with a tenuous foothold in the surviving deep pine and dry temperate forests of the south side of the Karakorum and western Himalayas (in the broad sense), from the Duber Valley in Swat, northern Pakistan, through Hazara east of the Indus in western Kashmir, and east to between the Kator and Billing rivers, south-east to the River Bhagirathi in Gathwal. It has been reported from Ladakh. Nothing has been heard of it since 1939, when two live pairs were in captivity in Bombay. Though the species was imported to western aviculture first in 1864, and first successfully bred in captivity in 1894, it disappeared from avicultural collections outside Asia in about 1900.

Blyth's tragopan, *Tragopan blythi*

Two races are recognized of this very rare pheasant. The typical form, *T. b. blythi*, appears formerly to have ranged through Assam south of the Brahmaputra valley in the Petkoi, Naga, and Barail ranges. south to Manipur, the Lushai Hills, and the adjacent Chin Hills of Burma. Wintering down to 5,000 feet, this form normally summers in the moist temperate forest from 6,000 to over 10,000 feet. The range now appears to be reduced to a zone from the Naga Hills to Cachar, the north-west Burma border, and the Chin Hills; and even in the wild Naga Hills it seems now very scarce; Naga trappers operating from Kohima for some months in 1962 obtained only two males.

T. b. molesworthi, the northern race, has been found from south-eastern Tibet through the mountain zone (6,000 to 12,000 feet) of moist, temperate, and coniferous forest across the bend of the Brahmaputra to the Mishmi Hills. Later records seem to be only from Bhutan to the Dafla Hills in northern Assam, some distance west of the Brahmaputra bend; but exploration by ornithologists is infrequent towards the old limits, and a withdrawal of range cannot yet be assumed.

Blyth's tragopan reached   Western aviculture in 1870 and was first successfully bred in 1884, and a breeding stock survived in Europe until the Second World War. After this war it declined, doubtless lacking genetic refreshment, and in mid-1964 only two cocks and a hen were believed to be in captivity outside Asia.

Cabot's tragopan, *Tragopan caboti*

This very rare bird was first described by John Gould in 1857 from a specimen of unknown origin. It was rediscovered by the missionary, explorer, and naturalist Père David in 1873, when he was at Kuatun in north-west Fukien. It seems to be confined to the mountain forests of the Fukien and Kwangtung provinces of south-east China, where it has certainly withdrawn lately with the destruction of forest and increased human persecution. The western avicultural stock was eleven birds (nearly all captive-bred) in the Ornamental Pheasant Trust collection in Norfolk in 1967. The last bird trapped in China, a male, reached Norfolk via Hong Kong in 1965. Fortunately this tragopan does fairly well in expert aviculture, which it reached in 1882 and first successfully bred in during 1884. Philip Wayre has since 1960 been developing a breeding stock in Norfolk earmarked for wild "replanting".

Sclater's monal, *Lophophorus sclateri*

An extremely rare bird, with a montane range from 9,000 feet to the limit of the moist temperate and conifer forests, Sclater's monal has not been seen in the wild since 1938. Its range appears to be, or to have been, in the area where the Brahmaputra and Salween rivers break through the eastern prolongation of the Himalayas, including the south-east corner of Tibet, the northern salients of highland Assam, and Burma and the adjoining mountains of south-western Sikang and north-western Yunnan in China. One bird, the type of the species, came to the London Zoo in 1870, and none seems to have been captive since then.

Chinese monal, *Lophophorus lhuysi*

As rare as Sclater's monal, the Chinese monal seems – as far as records show – to have enjoyed a limited range in highland China, from 10,000 to 16,000 feet in summer, and down to 9,000 feet in winter at the upper limit of coniferous forest, and in summer beyond it into the alpine meadows and scrubland of the mountains of north-east Sikang, north-west Szechwan, Tsinghai south-east of the Koko Nor, and south Kansu. It is perhaps now restricted to Szechwan, after severe hunting.

A single male reached the London Zoo in about 1900, and a male and three females were brought to Europe in the 1930s. The species has never bred in aviculture, and may now be in captivity only in the Peking Zoo.

Imperial pheasant, *Lophura imperialis*

The imperial pheasant was discovered in 1923 by Jean Delacour and Pierre Jabouille when in Annam; they were sent a live pair by two missionaries from the limestone hills of Dong Hoi and northern Quang Tri provinces on the Vietnam-Laos frontier. No later student has extended the range of this – the last of the pheasants to be discovered – any further: it is a limited area on either side of what has been since 1957 the boundary of North and South Vietnam.

Stock from Jean Delacour's original pair (the type and cotype of the species, which first bred at Clères in France in 1925) continues to survive in captivity and is thought to total now about twenty-five birds in the United States and Europe. It has never been genetically refreshed from Vietnam. The wild range of the species, though limited, is rugged, heavily forested, and sparsely populated by humans. Its survival future is impossible to predict until new field exploration follows settled times in Vietnam.

Edwards's pheasant, *Lophura edwardsi*

Edwards's pheasant, discovered by the missionary Père Renauld in interior Quang Tri in 1895, marches in range with, and doubtless shares a rather recent (in the geological sense) common ancestor with, the imperial pheasant. Dr Delacour and others are emphatic, however, that it is a full species and that *L. imperialis* is not a race of it. The crest of the cock imperial pheasant is dark; that of the cock Edwards's pheasant is bright white. There are other important differences in shape and wing-covert pattern; and the imperial pheasant mates when two years old, Edwards's when only one.

Until 1923 Edwards's pheasant was known only from four Renauld skins in the Paris museum; but in 1923–4 Delacour and Jabouille obtained no fewer than twenty-two alive, of which a group transferred to Clères in France in 1924 first bred in 1925 and has provided the principal, if not the only, ancestry of the 200 or more captive in the West at present and still breeding in small numbers – about a quarter of them in public zoological gardens.

Since the Delacour-Jabouille expedition, there has been no evidence that Edwards's pheasant has any other native range than a strip in the rugged limestone hills of what is now northernmost South Vietnam from central and southern Quang Tri to Faifo. The dangers to its wild population are no better known than those to its closely related neighbour, the imperial pheasant; whatever they may prove to be, the introduction of new stock to the present zoo bank would greatly help the conservation of this beautiful pheasant.

Swinhoe's pheasant, *Lophura swinhoei*

When John Gould first described what is certainly the most beautiful of the *Lophura* pheasants (or gallopheasants) in 1862, he named it after Swinhoe, the collector-naturalist and British Consul in what is now called Taiwan. After a whole century, very little is still known about this pheasant's range in the hill forests of Taiwan, except that it may always have been rare, probably never extended into the highest parts of the forests of its large home island, and may lately have been under new pressures of forest-destruction and hunting as the human population of Taiwan has rather rapidly increased. The wild stock, indeed, may now be at a very dangerous level; and some local conservationists are deeply worried about the enforcement of the present hunting laws and believe that the existing captive stock may be greater than the wild population.

Swinhoe's pheasant certainly now has the largest aviculture bank, in Europe and North America, of any endangered pheasant, with an estimated captive population of nearly 600, of which about half are in at least sixty-five public zoos. Most of this stock is descended from a single pair imported to France's Jardin d'Acclimatation in 1866, which first bred in the same year, and whose progeny remained fertile for nearly a century – apparently without any genetic refreshment from Taiwan since the 1880s. Fortunately in 1958 the Ornamental Pheasant Trust received a pair of these birds that had been wild-caught in Taiwan. After this genetic refreshment, no fewer than 120 were bred in Norfolk in the next seven years. In May 1967 Philip Wayre of the Ornamental Pheasant Trust personally liberated six Norfolk-bred pairs in the Experimental Forest of the University of Taipei at Hsitou in Taiwan, and left nine other pairs in the care of Taiwan aviculture to produce further stock for release.

White eared pheasant, *Crossoptilon crossoptilon*

The "white" eared pheasant – not all races of which are white, and which has the shortest eartufts of the "eared" pheasant genus *Crossoptilon* – is found in the high forests up to the snow line in eastern Tibet and the adjoining highland provinces of China. Despite some unconfirmed

Swinhoe's pheasant *Shigekazu Kobayashi* 1966

reports from the Abor and Mishmi hills, it is doubtful whether it has ever been recorded in the northern salient of Assam, that is to say in India.

The whitest race, with (in some cases) only brown flecks on the plumage apart from its iridescent greenish-black tail, is the Tibetan *C. c. drouyni* from south-eastern Tibet and northern and western Sikang. The brown-winged "typical" Szechwan race, *C. c. crossoptilon*, ranges from Szechwan (except its northern part) through eastern and central Sikang to north-western Yunnan. *C. c. lichiangense*, with light grey wings, has been so far collected only on the Lichiang Mountains in the buckle of the upper Yangtze River in north-western Yunnan, at 14,000 feet, and has been sunk by Charles Vaurie in 1965 in the race *C. c. crossoptilon* as not sufficiently separable from it. *C. c. dolani*, or Dolan's eared pheasant, pale grey and not white in its mantle plumage, is a good race so far known only from the region of Yushu in southern Tsinghai. Harman's eared pheasant, *C. c. harmani*, is so blue in its mantle plumage and under parts that it may merit full species status: it is the most westerly geographical representative of the group or species and is confined to the mountains and valley of the eastern stretch of the Brahmaputra, through Tibet and to the south.

So difficult is distributional information to obtain from the "white" eared pheasant's demesne, that it is impossible to say whether its gross range has definitely withdrawn in recent times. Up to the Chinese occupation, the Tibetan races were known to be relatively abundant and were protected on religious grounds. Forest-felling and human persecution have doubtless affected the status of the bird in the last two decades at least; and no individuals of any race seem to have reached Western aviculture between 1937 and 1960. There is reason to believe, therefore, that all populations are now rare, relict, and localized, and that the species as a whole deserves full Red Data Book status. Seventy aviculture individuals of the typical race were introduced from Tatienlu in Szechwan (to the London Zoo) in 1891, but did not breed. However, Leland Smith bred some first in California in 1938 from stock imported in 1936, and F. M. Bailey had some of Harman's race captive at Gantok in Sikkim over fifty years ago, and imported a pair to England in 1937, though apparently they did not breed. At present about thirty individuals, presumably all of the typical race, are believed to survive in aviculture. A female of the typical race reached the Ornamental Pheasant Trust via Hong Kong in 1960; and in 1965 about six pairs were sent from China to some European zoos.

Elliot's pheasant *Shigekazu Kobayashi* 1966

Brown eared pheasant, *Crossoptilon mantchuricum*

This fine bird has a confined and obviously relict distribution in highland China in the upland mountain scrub and zone of birch and stunted conifer, in the mountains of southern Chahar in Inner Mongolia, in northern and western Hopeh, and in north-western and central Shansi. Formerly it also extended into the uplands of Chihli, but has probably been extinct in this province for over three decades. The withdrawal of the species seems to have marched with the vast human assault on the forests of this heartland of China. The species has an uncertain wild status and future. No examples have been secured or recorded by the Peking Museum since 1949.

However, the brown eared pheasant reached Western aviculture as long ago as 1864 (one male and two females) and first bred in captivity in 1866. Although it has had no detectable importations since the latter year, what is virtually a "pure line" of captive breeding birds has survived until the present day, when the avicultural population of Europe and North America appears to be at least 120, of which about eighty are in public zoos.

Elliot's pheasant, *Syrmaticus ellioti*

Like the brown eared pheasant, the lovely Elliot's pheasant has a peculiarly Chinese distribution, much the same as that of Cabot's tragopan, south of the Yangtze in the eastern provinces of Chekiang, Fukien, and (southern) Anhwei, where it is becoming relict under the pressures of mountain forest clearance and doubtless also trapping; trappers who up to 1961 supplied Hong Kong do not do so now, possibly because the population is too low to crop.

The aviculture bank of this prized species is therefore comforting: the bird reached Western collections in 1874, first bred in 1880, and its captive population has been refreshed by wild stock until the last decade. At present this appears to be of not fewer than 350 birds, of which over a third are in public or mainstream zoos, where it fortunately does well.

Hume's bar-tailed pheasant, *Syrmaticus humiae*

This rare pheasant has two races. The "typical" *S. h. humiae* ranges through the steep, moist, temperate forest, from about 4,000 to 10,000 feet, over the mountains on the left bank of the Brahmaputra in Assam, India (the Barail, Patkai, Naga, Lushai, and Manipur hills), possibly extends west to the highlands just over the East Pakistan border, and extends east over some ranges of northern Burma on the right bank of the Irrawaddy, and south through Burma's Chin Hills to Mount Victoria. On the left bank of the Irrawaddy it is replaced by the Burmese race, *S. h. burmanicus*, in the northern highland salient of Burma and in the Shan highlands, whence it ranges beyond the Salween over the Chinese border into south-west Yunnan and some distance into northernmost Thailand. There is no evidence of a recent decline in range, though the population at least in the Naga Hills has been lately reported as low, possibly through hunting and trapping.

Though a few specimens of the Indian race have been kept in culture in Asia since 1888, none seem to have reached Western collections until four pairs came to England in 1962; by mid-1964, much as the result of captive breeding, forty-two birds were in aviculture outside Asia, of which twenty-seven were in public zoos or bird gardens.

Mikado pheasant, *Syrmaticus mikado*

In many ways the handsomest of the five long-tailed *Syrmaticus* pheasants, the mikado pheasant, like Swinhoe's pheasant, is confined to the mountains of Taiwan, where it lives between 6,000 feet and the 10,000-foot tree-line. The first description was based on two tail feathers out of a hunter's head-dress, from Mount Arizan; the mikado pheasant was subsequently found on the Racu-Racu Mountains and other parts of the central ranges.

It is now rare and known to be decreasing; an educated estimate suggests that possibly only a few hundred survive, and that hunting

pressure has caused the decline, despite legal protection.

With the cooperation of the Taiwan authorities, a reserve is now being planned into which captive-bred stock can be released. The species first reached Western aviculture in 1912 and bred in the following year, and reached Japanese aviculture in 1918 and bred in 1922. Since then a trickle of stock, caught wild, has continued to refresh the living collections, and by mid-1964 nearly forty birds were in captivity, thirty of them in public zoos, and about half captive-bred. This aviculture bank seems to be the best insurance for the future of this magnificent bird, though the captive stock in Europe and North America had almost ceased to breed by 1964. However, between 1962 and 1966 the Ornamental Pheasant Trust received four males and three females from Taiwan and in 1966 bred five young. It is hoped eventually to send Norfolk-bred birds back to Taiwan for release.

Palawan peacock pheasant, *Polyplectron emphanum*

Confined to Palawan, the most south-westerly substantial outlying island of the Philippines, this beautiful miniature pheasant (sometimes known as Napoleon's peacock pheasant) was once fairly common in the dense, moist forests of Palawan's lowlands and foothills. It is now restricted in range and, since systematic clearance of the Philippine forests began in earnest after the Second World War, nowhere common.

First imported to North American aviculture in 1929, this pheasant first bred in the following year. Although it is a slow breeder (twin-egg clutch once a year), captive stocks in America and Europe, refreshed from Palawan, have built up gradually, and now total over 100 birds. However, the species does not yet breed easily in captivity, though Dr K. C. Searle had some success in 1966 in the warm climate of Hong Kong. It may require some years of experiment before aviculture can produce a nucleus for "replanting" it in an appropriately protected natural habitat in Palawan, if opinion and law-enforcement in the Philippine archipelago make this practical.

Mikado pheasant *Shigekazu Kobayashi* 1966

Order GRUIFORMES
Family Gruidae: cranes

JAPANESE or MANCHURIAN CRANE
Grus japonensis

The history of the magnificent Japanese crane is rather confused. It has been known to science for nearly a couple of centuries. About 100 years ago its haunts in Russian far-eastern Asia were explored by the naturalists Shrenk, Maak, and Przewalski, who recorded summer migratory birds but found no nests. Indeed, no proof of nesting by this crane on the Asian mainland was recorded by A. M. Sudilovskaya in her account of the species in 1951 in the compendious *Birds of the Soviet Union*. However, it seems certain that the Japanese crane bred in Manchuria in the nineteenth and perhaps twentieth centuries, and still breeds in the valley of the River Amur and along some of its Russian tributaries. G. P. Dement'ev reports that in 1964 the Russian population was 200 to 300 birds, and that thirty to thirty-five breeding pairs were recorded on the south-eastern shores of Lake Khanka. The pattern of the summer distribution (outside Japan) that emerges from the rather slender literature confines the crane to Amur tributaries and their marshy valleys; on the right bank of this great river, to the Khalka River in northern Manchuria on the eastern border of Outer Mongolia, where a passage was observed in September 1928; to the Sungari (and probably also the Nonni) river systems in north and central Manchuria (a special breeding reserve is now said to be established in Heilung-kiang Province); and to the Ussuri systems, including Lake Khanka on the Manchu-Soviet border, down to the confluence of this river with the Amur, down the Amur itself as far as the Gorin River confluence, but not in Mariinsk or at the Amur mouth, and on the Amur's left bank in the valley of the Bureya and perhaps also that of the Zeya.

This continental population in the old days regularly wintered in southern Korea and in Kyushu in Japan, occasionally reached the lowlands of the Yangtze River near its mouth, and straggled exceptionally to Sakhalin and Taiwan. According to Oliver Austin, winterers were still not uncommon in Korea in 1946. They seem to have given up later; Chester M. Fennell, who spent nine watchful years recording birds in Korea, and collecting others' records, from 1953 to 1962, logs none. But one bird was illegally caught in Korea in 1964, at least six in 1965, and a few were recorded in 1966. It is possible that the Manchurian crane may soon be no longer Manchurian, and that it may also be extinct in some of its other old haunts in south-eastern Siberia, apart from Lake Khanka.

Of the six species of cranes known in Japan, *the* crane, as Oliver Austin puts it, is *Grus japonensis*, with its great accompaniment of legend, folk-lore, history, and superstition. In medieval times it certainly bred in the big islands of Hokkaido and Honshu, and perhaps also in Shikoku and Kyushu; and was rigidly protected and conserved by the noble and ruling classes right up to the end of the Tokugawa period in 1867. At the Meiji restoration, its Japanese population rapidly collapsed under hunting pressure, and, despite new game laws in 1892, had probably by then become confined to the one area of inaccessible marshy plain in eastern Hokkaido, where it survives as a resident population – which may now, indeed, be the only breeding stock in the world outside captivity. Only a few individuals appear to migrate, turning up sometimes in winter with other species in the crane sanctuaries (natural monuments since 1921) of Akune and Arasaki in Kagashima at the south end of the most southerly big island of Kyushu.

In eastern Hokkaido the crane's last stronghold is in Kuccharo Marsh near Kushiro (though a few may nest also somewhat further east near Nemuro). Kuccharo Marsh was inaccessible enough in summer – it is a 3,000-acre complex of deep bogs, which freezes, though usually not entirely, in winter – to remain undiscovered as a Japanese crane stronghold until H. Saito found it to be one in 1924, when he estimated the population to be fewer than

Japanese crane *Shigekazu Kobayashi* 1966

twenty birds, with only three of six nests active. On his report, the area was promptly made into Kucharota National Refuge in 1925. By 1934 the resident birds were about thirty, by 1949 thirty-five or thirty-six, by 1952 fifty, in 1953 about forty, in 1959 about 150, in 1960 about 130. In 1962 a detailed census of the December population around Kushiro gave 186, in 1963 147, in 1964 154, and in 1965 (with birds also at Nemuro) 172. The low 1963 population was doubtless the consequence of severe weather. It is gratifying to record this recovery of a population that continues to enjoy full protection (and some cereals provided by public generosity) despite present threats to cultivate the marsh, and could (and indeed soon should) begin to spread again in a Japan that – although now rather short of suitable wetlands – begins to enjoy a climate of conservation opinion once more resembling that of the Tokugawa days, when many noble animals were virtually regarded as sacred. Since 1935 the species has been designated a natural monument by the Japanese Government.

Since the Japanese crane was first successfully bred in captivity in England in 1918, it has done well in aviculture and the basis of a zoo bank already exists. Mainstream zoos have lately reared young in public collections – Japan's own Tama and Ueno zoos at Tokyo in 1960, Whipsnade in 1962, Frankfurt-am-Main in 1963. In early 1966 there were about 134 birds in captivity in zoos alone (about fifty in Korean and thirty-four in Chinese zoos), of which perhaps 40 per cent were captive-bred. About a third of all the Japanese cranes now living may be in captivity.

WHOOPING CRANE
Grus americana

Like the California condor, the stately, lovely whooper, North America's tallest living bird, can be described as a Pleistocene relict. All the evidence gives a picture like that of the California condor: a broad distribution over North America (except eastern Canada and New England) in Pleistocene times; probably a withdrawal in prehistoric times from the western and eastern parts of its Ice Age range; and a nearly disastrous collapse in historic times, particularly in the last 100 years. Six different bones found in the Glens Ferry formation of the Hagerman lake beds in Idaho, which are Upper Pliocene (about 3,500,000 years old by potassium-argon dating) are not distinguishable from modern bones of this species; and bones of this species have been found in the asphalt pits of latest Pleistocene Rancho la Brea in California, far to the west of any historical sighting; and worked whooper bone has been found among the remains of the prehistoric Indians of Kentucky.

The distribution of the whooping crane in the mid-nineteenth century establishes it then as a migrant (mainly) with a population estimated by that deep analyst, the late Robert Porter Allen, as of the order of only 1,300 to 1,400 individuals in 1860–70, breeding from the inaccessible muskegs of Great Slave Lake (and perhaps further north to Simpson and Resolution) in the Mackenzie region of the Canadian Northwest, south through Alberta, Saskatchewan, and Manitoba over the United States border to Illinois, Minnesota, Iowa, probably Nebraska, the Dakotas, and probably Montana; and migrating broadly, but chiefly by the central flyway, to winter mainly on the Gulf Coast and into Mexico as far as Jalisco, Guanajuato, and north Tamaulipas. A rather small non-migratory population also bred in Louisiana and probably also eastern Texas; the Louisiana breeders seem to have continued until 1939 (when indeed they were really rediscovered!), but probably failed in 1940 and have since disappeared; other nests in the present century were recorded with certainty only from Alberta, Saskatchewan, and Manitoba. But no nest of the whooping crane was seen by anyone from after May and June 1922 – when the last examples were recorded near Baliol and at Muddy Lake in western Saskatchewan by the provincial game guardian Neil Gilmour and the game commissioner Fred Bradshaw – until the 16th May 1955, when William A. Fuller and Ray C. Stewart of the Canadian Wildlife Service saw, from a chartered bush plane, a bird sitting on its nest on a swampy island in a small lake in the muskeg of the Sass River country within the vast Wood Buffalo Park, a little-explored area of nearly 11,000,000 acres straddling the Alberta-Mackenzie borders.

The breeding whoopers were on the Mackenzie side; and by a brilliant follow-up programme by land and air – the culmination of nine years of search largely organized and inspired by Robert Porter Allen of the National Audubon Society – it was established that the world population of the whooping crane then had only two main "addresses": in summer the Wood Buffalo muskegs of the Sass, Klewi, and Nyarling rivers south of the Great Slave Lake; and in winter the Aransas National Wildlife Refuge on a peninsula between San Antonio and St Charles bays, near Austell on the south coast of Texas. The families that Allen, Fuller, Roy Stewart, and Robert E. Stewart of the United States Fish and Wildlife Service found in the muskeg after their exhaustive and exhausting search in the summer of 1955 amounted to over half the twenty adults and eight young of the year that appeared around Aransas Refuge on migration that autumn.

Apart from a small captive population, the world population of the whooping crane has now wintered solely on the Aransas Refuge, Matagorda, and other nearby Texan islands for the last quarter of a century; and as far as we know has bred only in Wood Buffalo Park for the last decade at least. The protection of this extreme relict population is thus reasonably well assured at both ends of this migratory line, over 2,300 direct miles apart, which the cranes appear to travel in spring and fall at an average of about 100 miles a day. Wood Buffalo Park is not only a large statutory reserve, but contains one of the largest areas in the world of virtually unexplored muskeg, that peculiarly Canadian complex of slow water and swamp forest possible only for (terrestrial) humans to travel in swiftly during the frozen winter, or to survey on a large scale in summer if they become airborne. Aransas Refuge, on the Blackjack Peninsula, lies mostly in Aransas County, partly in Refugio County, Texas, and was acquired by the United States Fish and Wildlife Service in 1937 as a migratory waterfowl (now national wildlife) refuge, just when it was realized that it had already become the centre of the only regular wintering place of the whoopers in the world, apart from the Louisiana population, which died out after 1940.

Strictly wardened and observed throughout its quarter-century and more as the last winter stronghold of the whoopers, Aransas has a bird log that gives us the fluctuating fortunes of this giant Pleistocene crane with real precision.

Every fall the crane arrival is watched and dated, and the number of (easily detectable) young of the year among the population established. Every spring the number leaving for the muskeg north is likewise measured. Figures are thus available for winter mortality (small), for the combined mortality of adults on spring and fall passage and on the summer grounds, and for the production of young on the summer grounds that survive the first fall passage. Now that the main breeding-ground has been discovered, and the incredibly difficult job of making a census of it is being mastered, passage mortality may soon be also separated from breeding-ground mortality. All this is essential if the future of this very vulnerable bird is to be assured; for the wild population of the whooping crane was only fourteen on Aransas in 1937 and 1938, and the whole population estimated at thirty in 1933, twenty-nine in 1938, thirty-five in 1939, thirty-one in 1940, down to twenty-three in 1941, and twenty-eight in 1942 (from which year virtually all wild birds wintered in the Aransas area). Since then it has climbed unsteadily, and with worrying fluctuations, to a highest of forty-four birds in the spring of 1966. It had climbed to the uncertain thirties in 1943–51, only to fall back to the twenties in 1952–7; it wavered in the thirties again from 1958 to 1963: not until 1964, when the cranes had an excellent year, did the Aransas flock reach over forty. Of the twenty-six adults and seven young that wintered in 1963–4, all but one young, that is, thirty-two birds, went north in the spring of 1964. All thirty-two of them returned that fall, bringing (for the Aransas log) the record number of ten new young with them, and having also produced, in Wood Buffalo Park's Sass marshes, another (injured) young one, which was rescued and flown to the Fish and Wildlife Service Endangered Species Research Station, then in Colorado (but subsequently at Laurel, Maryland), where it recovered except for a still useless wing in summer, 1966. All forty-two birds survived winter, 1964–5 at Aransas and left in spring for the north; in the fall of 1965 thirty-six returned with eight new young, all of which also survived. In 1966–7 thirty-eight adults and five new young survived the winter.

At Aransas, in the thirteen years from 1954 to 1966, the wintering population averaged thirty-four birds, of which an average of five or six of the fall arrivals were young of the year. But in 1954 and again in 1962 the birds returned from the Canadian Northwest with no young at all. The maximum clutch of the whooper is of two eggs in the year, and only seldom is more than one young reared; so the output of eight young in 1955, nine in 1958, seven in 1963, ten in 1964, and eight in 1965 can be regarded as good.

In mid-June 1967 nine nests (with eighteen adults and eight young) were found in Wood Buffalo Park, and six eggs were transported to Patuxent in Maryland for hatching. Four young reared from these eggs are now fully grown, bringing the total young reared in 1967 from Canadian eggs (wild and captive) to thirteen. An additional young bird was produced in this year at the San Antonio Zoo in Texas. At the end of 1967, thirty-nine adults and nine young were on the wintering grounds of Aransas.

The whooping crane, demonstrably one of the rarest birds in the world, is not in a hopeless state. Much of its range is now controlled, and the losses on migration by uncontrolled and ignorant shooting have certainly become small (though not negligible: one bird lost is not negligible) in the last two decades. United States and Canadian public opinion, and the government management based on it, are slowly beginning to give good results. And, besides, there has been a small zoo bank since 1940, when a crippled female, the last of the Louisiana population, was mated to a male crippled by a hunter during migration. After some unsuccessful attempts at breeding, this pair first reared (two) young in the New Orleans Zoo in 1957 and another in 1958. Excluding the old Louisiana female that died in 1965, there were six birds at New Orleans in that year, which with the young bird at Laurel brought the true world population to fifty-one. In 1967 five young had hatched from the eggs at Patuxent and were doing well. Whoopers in captivity in early 1968 numbered four in New Orleans, two in San Antonio, and six at Patuxent. The zoo output should doubtless be improved now that the four captive-bred birds in New Orleans are themselves old enough to breed.

SANDHILL CRANE
Grus canadensis

From fossil records, the sandhill crane of North America may qualify as the oldest living species of bird, for bones in the Upper Snake Creek beds of Sioux County, Nebraska, of Lower Pliocene age (about 9,000,000 years old), have not so far been distinguished from comparable material of the modern species. Like most cranes and other big birds, it seems to have had a Pleistocene heyday, when it was widespread over the continent as breeder and migrant. In prehistoric times it may, from the suggestion of subfossil eggs, have even bred 1,000 years ago as far south as the Vallé de México.

The prehistoric distribution in general, though, from the evidence of at least seventeen midden sites, conveys the impression that pre-Columbian men, as well as climatic change, may have reduced the crane's range somewhat, and the broad pattern of historical records shows what is probably a withdrawal from the Atlantic seaboard, virtually complete by the early nineteenth century days of Wilson and Audubon, and a further withdrawal, generally correlated by the sandhill crane's biographer Lawrence Walkinshaw with the surges of human population over Canada and the United States Middle West and West, which marches inexorably with the last dates of known nesting in various provinces and states: about 1862 (unreliably reported later until a very recent rediscovery, probably a recolonization) in Ontario, 1886 in Arizona, 1890 in Illinois, 1904 in Nebraska, 1905 in Iowa, shortly afterwards in Colorado, 1910 in South Dakota, 1911 in Alabama, 1915–20 in North Dakota, 1919 in Louisiana, 1926 in Ohio, 1929 in Indiana, and 1939 (a semi-captive pair) in Kansas.

The sandhill crane is now classified in five races, though the "typical" or nominate lesser sandhill crane, *G. c. canadensis*, and the other migratory race, the greater sandhill crane, *G. c. tabida*, have a zone of breeding-ground overlap in central Canada, where an intermediate population, whose type came from Fawcett, Alberta, has lately been described by Walkinshaw as *G. c. rowani*. Further south two isolated breeding populations, apparently resident and non-migratory, survive endangered in the southeastern United States and Cuba – the Florida sandhill crane, *G. c. pratensis*, and the Cuban sandhill crane, *G. c. nesiotes*.

Under least pressure, by virtue of its northernmost breeding-grounds from the eastern tip of Siberia across Alaska and the muskegs of the Canadian Northwest, the lesser sandhill crane still has a big population, perhaps 97 per cent of the world population in the 1940s and probably an even higher percentage now. It winters in the southern tier of the United States from California to Texas and south to central Mexico, with its main battalions in west Texas and eastern New Mexico, where nearly 135,000 birds wintered in 1960–1, over 165,000 in 1961–2, 207,000 in 1963–4, 214,000 in 1964–5, 198,000 in 1965–6, 139,000 in 1966–7, and 210,000 in 1967–8, according to the surveys of the U.S. Fish and Wildlife Service.

The greater sandhill cranes tend to be segregated in winter from the more migratory lessers, and to concentrate in winter in restricted areas of California and the Rio Grande valley of New Mexico and neighbouring Mexico, some also wintering in south-eastern Texas and in Florida. The greater sandhill population of the United States was last estimated for the spring of 1944 by Walkinshaw, who found a population on the summering grounds of 1,300 to 1,850 cranes, and believed the Canadian population to be of the same order at that time. (Lately Jim Baillie has rediscovered nesting birds in Ontario between Lake Superior and Hudson's Bay.) It seems very likely that, if the population of *G. c. tabida* was over 3,000 then, it has increased in the last two decades. A late estimate is around or over 6,000; increase has taken place mostly in the west and to some extent in Michigan. In southern Michigan (twenty-seven to thirty-five breeding pairs in 1944, forty-nine in 1952, forty-seven in 1953, forty-three in 1954, forty-four in 1955, forty-eight in 1956, forty-seven in 1957, fifty in 1958), there has been some stability, and there were probably over 100 pairs in the middle 1960s. Up to 6,000 greater sandhills wintered in 1963–4 in the Bosque del Apache National Wildlife Refuge in southern New Mexico, according to Erwin L. Boeker.

Since Walkinshaw's years of survey of *G. c.*

pratensis, the Florida sandhill crane, in 1940–5, this population has remained fairly constant, though it may have decreased in some areas, particularly in Mississippi. Its older historical breeding range may have extended west to Louisiana (extinct after 1919),[1] to the Texas border, and through Mississippi (where a hitherto unsuspected population, which still survives, was first proved to breed in 1938, but probably was an old one), Alabama (extinct after 1911), and southern Georgia to Florida. By Walkinshaw's survey, over fifty birds were on the breeding-grounds of southern Mississippi in April 1940, and in October 1965 Robert Noble counted forty-two there. In 1945 at least 200 were breeding in the great Okeefenokee Swamp, their Georgia headquarters. For the early 'forties Walkinshaw estimated a total population of the race at about 2,650, but noted that in Florida, at least, only about 40 per cent of the population were then breeding.

After two more decades of vast drainage, rationalized agriculture, and human immigration into Florida, the Florida sandhill crane has now come to a low but fairly stable state. Aerial surveys by United States game management agents produced an estimate of a total population of 2,000–3,000 in 1964 – excluding the southern Mississippi group that still existed at a very low level (under fifty). Fortunately the headquarters of the cranes in the Okeefenokee is now part of a federal refuge, and in Florida the breeding-grounds at Loxahatchee are also on a national wildlife refuge. Conservationists are still striving for a sanctuary in the Kissimmee Prairie, where the cranes can now be most easily seen by the public in natural surroundings, threatened though these are by developers.

The status of the Cuban race is poor, but too mysterious at present for us to say how poor. In his survey of 1945 Walkinshaw found only a small remnant of the good population earlier recorded on the Isle of Pines. On the mainland the race was already confined to the central and western parts in the 1940s. In 1951 there may have been some increase on the Isle of Pines, for an estimate of 100 birds was then reported by Walkinshaw. A possible, and lately unexplored, small surviving headquarters may also be on two islands off the Zapata Swamp peninsula. On the

Sandhill crane *John James Audubon* 1835

mainland of Cuba it had almost disappeared. There is evidently little legislation to protect the crane in Cuba, and no precise information about its status there since 1951.

The sandhill crane does fairly well in captivity, and was first successfully bred in England in 1899. In late 1964 there were eight individuals of the Florida race captive in five United States zoos – part of a population of at least forty captive birds of different races, of which several breeding pairs were at the Fish and Wildlife Service Endangered Species Research Centre.

In 1966 this centre was moved from the Monte Vista National Wildlife Refuge in Colorado to Laurel in Maryland, where there were fifty-nine birds in that year, of which

[1] George Lowery, an authority on Louisiana birds, tells the present writer that at Louisiana breeding records are suspect. He is convinced that E. A. McIlhenny obtained his downy young specimen (labelled Louisiana) in Mississippi. However, the habitat in Louisiana is similar to that in Mississippi, and the cranes could have nested there.

forty-six (including five breeding pairs) were greaters, nine lessers, and four of the Florida race.

Crane-hunting is now permitted in Canada, New Mexico, Texas, and (since October 1967)

Colorado. Apart from the danger (at least in Canada) of involving whooping cranes in the bag, the National Audubon Society regards this licence as very poor management in the present state of our knowledge of the species.

Family Rallidae: rails

ZAPATA RAIL
Cyanolimnas cerverai

This curious and isolated member of a family of birds in which special isolates and island forms are peculiarly common, was first described as recently as 1927 from Santo Tomás in the Ciénaga de Zapata (or Zapata Swamp) in western Cuba – so far perhaps the wildest region of lowland Cuba and the only home of one other unique species of bird – the Zapata wren. James Bond, the principal authority on the birds of the West Indies, believes it may be most closely related to the near-black rail, *Rallus nigricans*, of northern and tropical South America, though deserving of the special genus it was put in when first described by Barbour and Peters.

The Zapata rail is, according to Bond in 1950, "known only from that part of the Zapata Swamps directly north of the heavily wooded territory known as Santo Tomás where apparently confined to within a mile of the high ground". This part of the swamp is covered with dense brush of *Myrica* and other scrubby plants and some low trees, and has open stretches of saw-

Zapata rail *Albert E. Gilbert* 1966

grass. Here also breed very few land birds indeed; but among them the peculiarly Zapatan bird *Torreornis i. inexpectata*, a race of the Zapata sparrow. This bird, like the Zapata wren, is confined to a very few square miles of this Cuban wilderness, and is found nowhere else in the world; and both would be in global danger if present proposals to drain the Zapata Swamp were put into effect.

HAWAIIAN GALLINULE *or* HAWAIIAN MOORHEN
Gallinula chloropus sandvicensis

The moorhen, as people in the English-speaking Old World rather oddly call this cosmopolitan water-loving gallinule, has a widespread distribution in tropical and temperate areas of the world, except the deserts and drylands, Australasia, and southern South America. About fifteen races are currently recognized, of which only one, *Gallinula chloropus sandvicensis*, the Hawaiian gallinule (to give it the American vernacular name) is in the Red Data Book. This is one of two highly isolated island forms doubtless originating in the past from stormborne colonists across great sea-gaps: the other is confined to the Palau Islands in the Micronesian West Pacific, has been found on at least four of them, is apparently in no danger of extinction, and is racially not yet fully determined.

George Munro, Hawaii's bird historian, shows that the gallinule of Hawaii was regarded by the first Polynesian colonists as a great benefactor. "Fire was unknown to the people,"

PLATE 21 (*a*) New Zealand shore plovers, adult (left) and immature *J. G. Keulemans* 1873; (*b*) Audouin's gull *Edward Lear* 1837

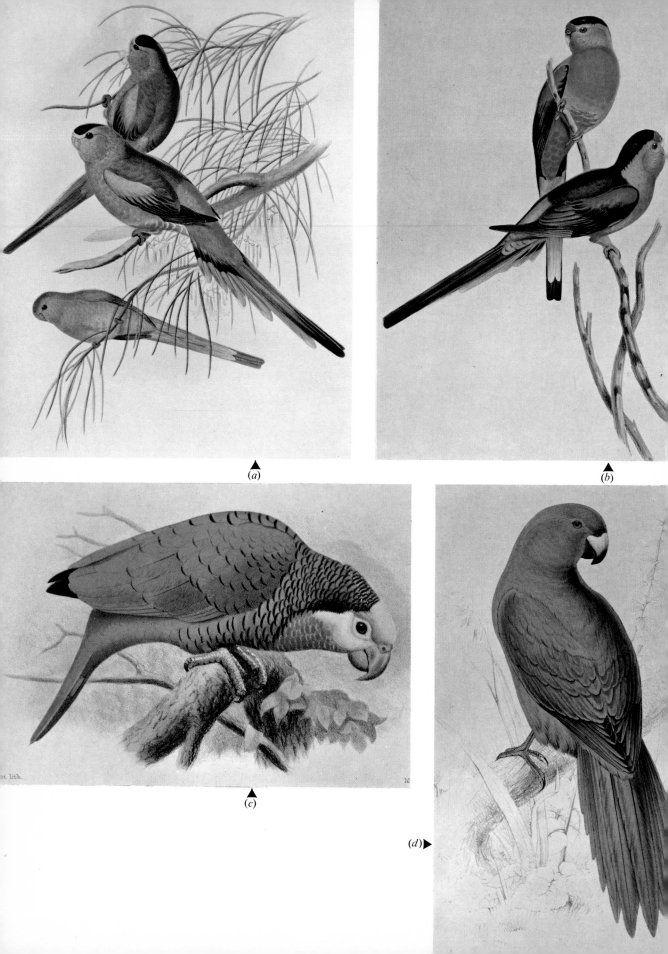

(a)

(b)

(c)

(d) ▶

he writes, "hence they could neither cook their food nor warm themselves during the cold weather. The bird took pity on them and, flying to the home of the gods, stole a blazing brand and carried it back to earth. On its return flight its formerly white forehead was scorched by the flames; hence its name *alae*, signifying a burnt forehead."

Notwithstanding a reverent tolerance by the Polynesians of the alae, which, before the coming of the white men in the late eighteenth century, was doubtless distributed over the whole main archipelago (probably once including Lanai) its fate since the evolution of Western ways has been a poor one, and it has suffered much from introduced predators and perhaps more particularly the drainage of wetlands that still continues apace. Once common on Hawaii, the largest island, and Maui, it is now quite extinct on them. On Niihau, where it was also

Hawaiian gallinule *N. W. Cusa* 1966

common, it was "hardly known" in 1939, and probably became extinct shortly afterwards. On Kauai, where it is believed to be more numerous, the population was estimated as no more than 100 to 150 in 1962, and as "200 birds maximum" in 1966; and on Oahu the estimate was 50 to 100 in 1962. The Molokai population is unknown (though birds have been counted up to a total of nineteen in various parts of the island

---

PLATE 22 (*a*) Golden-shouldered paradise parakeets, male (centre), female (upper), and immature *John Gould and H. C. Richter* 1869; (*b*) Beautiful parakeets, two males *John Gould and H. C. Richter* 1848; (*c*) Bahaman parrot *H. Goodchild* 1904; (*d*) Antipodes kakariki *Edward Lear* 1831

in the 'sixties); but it seems unlikely that the world numbers of the race now exceed 300.

Very little has been done for the Hawaiian gallinule, apart from unsuccessful attempts to reintroduce it by translocation to Maui and Hawaii. On Oahu the only remaining stronghold is in the Kawainui Swamp on the windward (eastern) side – most other wetlands having been already drained for development; and by 1965 this island's population was estimated to have been reduced to between twenty-five and fifty birds. The well-known propensity of the species to become tame and breed on suburban and parkland waters does not appear to extend to this race, which seems disinclined to prospect such suitable habitat.

TAKAHÉ
Notornis mantelli

The badge-bird of the Ornithological Society of New Zealand, the big flightless gallinule that is now one of the most famous "survival species" in the world, is one of the few living birds described from fossil material. Bones excavated at Waingongoro and Wanganui in North Island by the pioneer New Zealand naturalist Walter B. D. Mantell, a son of Dr Gideon Mantell of the Royal College of Surgeons, reached Sir Richard Owen at the British Museum, and were described by him in 1848 as *Notornis mantelli*, Waingongoro being subsequently designated as the type locality.

Soon afterwards bones also reached the British Museum from Timaru in South Island, which were referred to the same species. By 100 years later, the New Zealand paleontologists and archaeologists had become so active that the bones of *Notornis* are now known from at least six localities in North Island and twenty-two in South Island, with a few possible exceptions dating from after the end of the Pleistocene Ice Ages, and (of these) at Waingongoro and perhaps Pataua in North Island and eleven places in South Island dating, mainly by their associations with Polynesian relics, from after the first human colonization of New Zealand in about A.D. 950. At Pyramid Valley in east-central South Island, as carbon-dating suggests, the *Notornis* bones are probably post-1600; and those discovered recently in Takahé Valley in south-west South Island are, by C_{14}, not earlier than 1785. Even if the living *Notornis* had not been discovered, the Survival Service Commission would have had it on its list as a bird extinct since 1600.

Notornis was, in fact, found alive in 1849, at Duck Cove on Resolution Island in the Dusky Sound area of south-western South Island by some sealers. Although they are reported to have kept their single captive alive for several days and then eaten it, it was skinned by a competent but unknown taxidermist and, through W. B. D. Mantell, soon reached the British Museum. Mantell got hold of a second specimen, which, though caught by a Maori in 1851 at Deas Cove, opposite Secretary Island[1] in Thompson Sound, also in Southland, was also skilfully skinned and is now in New Zealand's Dominion Museum. The third specimen was found in Southland again, 9 miles south-east of the south end of Lake Te Anau, by a rabbiter in December 1879, skinned by J. Connor, forwarded to London, bought there in 1882 by Oscar Loebel for the then large sum of £110, and presented to the Dresden Museum, where it was named *Notornis hochstetteri* by A. B. Meyer in 1883. This name is available for the South Island population if its racial status can be upheld, which is rather doubtful: though South Island bones (especially those of the leg) appear to be mostly smaller than the corresponding few we know of from North Island, there is much size variation. The type specimen of *Notornis mantelli hochstetteri* disappeared from the Dresden Museum in the Second World War.

All the subsequent live sightings or hearings of takahés (except one) have been in Southland. James Park, another pioneer New Zealand naturalist who is now believed but was doubted by some contemporaries, "saw or heard" the big flightless gallinules in 1881 at Cascade Burn and on the south branch of the Matukituki River, and in 1888 at five places in the Dusky Sound area, thus bringing the "records" up to ten. The eleventh in South Island was made in the takahés' present headquarters on the 7th August 1898, when Donald Ross collected a bird on the shore of Middle Sound, Lake Te Anau, about 25 miles from the south end of this great lake in the heart of Fiordland; skinned by the Otago Museum's taxidermist Jennings, it is in Dunedin to this day.

For years the Ross specimen was believed to be the last of the takahés, and for fifty years *Notornis* was considered extinct by all the textbook writers, despite rumours to the contrary, spurned by admittedly reasonable editors and authorities. Some of these rumours were quite probably false – for instance, circumstantial reports of two birds, one larger than the other, from the "Milford Track" in northern Southland in or before 1940, and other similar "sightings". But a very good account of a takahé was given (in 1953, after its "rediscovery") by W. A. Cumming from his memories as a young leading seaman on H.M.S. *Challenger* in late January 1910; one bird was doubtless seen on the shore of Gear Arm in Southland's George Sound by Cumming and some companions in a cutter 50 feet away, and from his excellent account could not have possibly been confused with its nearest relative, the New Zealand pukeko or purple gallinule (*Porphyrio porphyrio melanotus*).

The most important of the resuscitated records of the missing half-century 1898–1948 comes from North Island, and was published in 1959, by W. J. Phillipps, as experienced and careful a naturalist as any in New Zealand. In the autumn of 1894 a takahé was collected by the surveyor Norman Carkeek, and its skin was brought to Roderick A. McDonald of Horowhenua, at whose homestead it was kept for many years. As we have already seen, all the other evidence of the North Island takahé is based on fossil or subfossil bones, and it is a tragedy that the only skin of a specimen seen alive by a European should now be destroyed or lost. Maoris who saw the bird identified it as a *mohoau* (bush wanderer), already an exciting rarity to their elders (and not confused with the *pukeko*). There seems every reason to believe that the North Island takahé is extinct, but only since the end of the last century.

The South Island takahé was rediscovered in

---

[1] Secretary Island was originally recorded as the locality, but Dr R. A. Falla has told us that it was probably Deas Cove, as Hector later ascertained from the Maori concerned.

Takahé *D. M. Henry* 1958

valley, Falla believed that a total of 100 birds (including non-breeders and chicks) were resident in the area.

Since those exciting days of 1948–9, the takahé reserve has been carefully investigated by trained teams of ornithologists and ecologists, and under careful control the birds have been banded, filmed for science and television, and watched and measured by behaviour and longevity students. The present range of *Notornis* is now known to be the wild country (the wildest in the wildest part surviving in New Zealand) of the Murchison Mountains between the Middle and South Fiords (or Sounds) of Lake Te Anau, and of the Kepler Mountains between South Fiord and Lake Manapouri, mostly between 3,300 and 3,800 feet above the forest line and in the zone of scrub and tussock-grasses. The area of the Takahé Valley and Point Burn still houses the main colony, which has been stable since it was discovered: the full population is now known to be certainly more than the first educated guess of 100 in 1949; but it is certainly well under 500 – probably of the order of 200 to 300 birds scattered in small groups over about 200 square miles. Preliminary calculations from the careful banding programme indicate an annual mortality of about 20 per cent of birds that have reached the age of one year. The normal clutch of eggs is two, and double brooding and renesting have been proved in some cases.

There is no doubt that under the protection of the New Zealand Government, national (and international) public opinion, and the very inaccessibility of the site (most takahé-watchers have to get to their birds by float-plane or amphibian), the takahé will continue to be the living, and not a fossil, symbol of New Zealand ornithology. It is a fine example of a relict bird that has been discovered, properly investigated, and dealt with in time. Its chief enemies are introduced predators, especially stoats, and the rival grazing pressures of introduced herbivores, particularly deer. Both predators and rival herbivores are under a broad campaign of control by the Wildlife Service of the Department of Internal Affairs. A small population has been kept captive since 1950 by the Wildlife Division for avicultural trials – so far not

1948 by a man who had collected all the records he could of old sightings, and set out for Southland with a group of young companions, having rediscovery as their single purpose. In April they heard an unfamiliar bird sound and found a footprint on the mud of western Lake Te Anau. Undiscouraged by the fact that the footprint was similar to that of a bittern or a pukeko, they returned on the 20th November with cameras and netting and found, filmed, and caught two fine takahés straight away, releasing them after examination and measurement. They also saw a third bird. Dr G. B. Orbell, the first man to see a live *Notornis* for half a century, had no difficulty in persuading the New Zealand Government to declare – before the year was out – a close prohibited zone of no less than 434,000 acres (the size of an average English county) to protect the range of less than 600 acres in which the 1948 birds were found.

To cut the story short, early in 1949 Orbell led another expedition to "Takahé Valley" above Te Anau with J. H. Sorensen and Dr R. A. Falla of the Dominion Museum. They made a four-day ecological survey of the valley's flora and the takahés' feeding habits, found nests with eggs and chicks, saw twelve or fourteen adults, and estimated at least twenty breeding pairs in the valley; with a small population in an adjacent successful, as the gallinule has not yet been proved to breed in captivity. A new pair was introduced to the captive colony at the Mount Bruce Reserve on North Island in 1966 to try for positive breeding.

Some ecologists think that the shrinkage of the takahé's range into its last Southland refuge (200 square miles of which is now a declared sanctuary) has followed a climatic change, and may be more natural than man-promoted. It seems doubtful whether the withdrawal is in fact entirely "natural", though it may be partly so. All the not inconsiderable fossil evidence shows a range of the big flightless gallinule well over both islands right up to prehuman times, and a steady shrinkage of it during nearly 1,000 years of purely Polynesian occupation, to the extent that, with the possible exception of a small part of North Island, with a very small, doomed population, probably only Southland was the takahé's headquarters on the arrival of Captain Cook. Polynesian hunters continued to exert pressure after the European landings; a moa-hunter shelter (dated not earlier than 1785) in Takahé Valley excavated in 1948 yielded not only *Notornis* bones, but those of *Megalapteryx didinus*, the latest of the moas known to have lived, and other relict birds besides. As we see elsewhere, the takahé is only one of many "Pleistocene" birds that have suffered total or partial extermination in New Zealand and elsewhere; an extermination in which, in New Zealand as elsewhere, Stone Age hunters have played a very important part. Although the civilized successors of the Stone Age men have often made things even worse, at least they can correct their own mistakes. The Polynesians truly seem to have been the major depopulators of *Notornis*, and the Europeans, for once, appear almost wholly as stoppers of the rot.

Family Rhynochetidae: kagu

KAGU
Rhynochetos jubatus

About 750 miles from Australia, and halfway between it and Fiji, lies the combined archipelago of New Caledonia and the Loyalty Islands, a rather isolated tropical group with between seventy and eighty native breeding land birds. Some of these are peculiar to the islands, especially to the only large island, New Caledonia itself, a 220-mile ridge, 25 to 30 miles wide (6,221 square miles), rising jaggedly from the sea to mountains of over 5,000 feet in places. New Caledonia's history (as that of all islands) has close relevance to the status of some of its birds. First discovered by Captain Cook in 1774, it was then populated by Melanesians; apart from a few traders and, since about 1840, Marist missionaries, white men did not settle in New Caledonia in any number until France annexed it in 1853, when the Melanesian population was about 70,000. By 1936 the human population had declined to a little over 53,000, of which about one-third were whites: but at present it numbers about 40,000 Melanesians, about 33,000 Europeans, and a few thousand others.

The remarkable kagu of New Caledonia is placed in a suborder all its own of the crane-rail order, or Gruiformes; the true affinities of this mysterious and virtually flightless forest bird are still rather uncertain. It was discovered shortly after the French annexation and was formally described in 1860, when it was probably widespread over the forest of the whole island. In the nineteenth century its range already showed a withdrawal into the mountains of the interior and the forest of the steeper valleys, where the birds live in pairs, each of which occupies a large territory and travels a great deal in search of snails and other invertebrates. A report of 1960 shows no evidence of further change in status, despite what were most probably exaggerated rumours of extinction in the central and north-western forests; but the kagu is certainly in grave danger of extinction after a long history of early snaring by Melanesians, and of hunting and trapping by Melanesians and Europeans (up to at least forty or fifty years ago for the plume trade), the destruction of habitat by lumbering, mining, and burning, and the introduction of

Kagu *N. W. Cusa* 1966

predators and rival foragers, particularly the dog (after the French annexation) and the pig.

Today the Colonial Government, backed by the active and sophisticated new Ornithological Society of New Caledonia, fully protects the kagu by law, and permits capture and export only for exceptional scientific purposes. A scheme is under consideration to create a park in the Rivière Bleue area that will, in effect, be a kagu reserve. All efforts are being watched anxiously by the zoological world; the demise of the kagu would be an affront to human dignity and skill, as nearly all extinctions of species now are – but, and more particularly, the loss of a unique subfamily from the living avifauna would be a scientific disaster.

Kagus entered aviculture more than 100 years ago; their peculiar and beautiful nuptial display, indeed, was for the first time described from a pair in the London Zoo by G. Bennett of its staff in 1863. They were not successfully bred in captivity, however, until 1920, in New South Wales, after earlier near-successes in Australia. In mid-1964 at least eleven birds were captive in four mainstream zoos of Europe, but none of them bred in captivity. While the most interesting and unusual behaviour of this curious mollusc-eating forest bird well merits a captive group or two for study, the prospect of a useful zoo bank for natural "replanting" seems at present remote.

Family Otididae: bustards

GREAT INDIAN BUSTARD
Choriotis nigriceps

The largest flying birds are undoubtedly swans; an exceptional mute swan cob may reach 50 pounds 10 ounces, and the noble trumpeter swan of North America male 38 pounds. Swans can alight on water, which gives birds of their extremely high weight an advantage. If we use weight (and not wingspread) as the criterion, the largest birds that normally alight on land are bustards. The king of them all is doubtless the great bustard, males of which in Central Asia have reached a measured weight of 46 pounds 3 ounces. A claim of 40 pounds has been made for the subject of this essay (males average 18 to 22 pounds), and the vast kori, or giant, bustard of Africa has been confirmed at a weight of 30 pounds, and claimed at 40. There is intercontinental competition for the largest land bird, as we can see: but it is certainly a bustard.

As may be readily imagined, there is nothing but pessimism for the ultimate future of these magnificent birds. In Africa they will probably survive for a considerable time, although in dwindling numbers, because so much of that continent is very sparsely populated when compared with many other parts of the globe. Almost everywhere else, however, they are quickly dying out, not only because closer settlement and increasing land-development steadily reduce the type and amount of suitable habitat available for the birds, but also because their large size makes them all too tempting a target for the trapper and for persons armed with any type of firearm.

Doubtless marching with their size and range requirements, each breeding pair of the bigger bustards seems to demand an immense territory in which to live; and in many places this is no longer available. All the large bustards are birds of the grasslands – some of the open upland plains, others of the drier savannah country of Africa; and, although they are to some extent adaptable to the more open type of cultivation, generally speaking they are too shy and wary to put up with the constant disturbance caused by agricultural development.

The great Indian bustard does not differ from its close relations elsewhere in its preference for the (once vast) grassy plains and open wastelands. Everywhere now, however, it is rare, decreasing, and near to extinction in the subcontinent that is its home. Its distribution has been very hard for past scholars of Indian ornithology to summarize, and the précis that follows derives largely from accounts published by W. T. Blanford in 1888, E. C. Stuart Baker in 1912, S. Dillon Ripley in 1952 and 1961, and R. S. Dharmakumarsinhji of Bhavnagar (who has studied its ecology and life history for years) in 1958. The nineteenth-century range of the species, the earliest and broadest we know of, extended north to West Punjab east of the Indus and to east Punjab. East beyond the Jumna its former existence on parts of the Gangetic plains of Uttar Pradesh, Bihar, and West Bengal, where it is now unknown, may have been casual, in fact non-breeding, as it is in most of Orissa and the Eastern Ghats. It ranged south through eastern Sind, Rajasthan, Madhya Pradesh, north-western Orissa, Gujarat, and Maharashtra to Andhra Pradesh, Mysore, and northern Madras as far as Tiruchchirappalli. After about 1924 it appears to have become extinct as a breeder in well over half its old range – in the southern and eastern parts of it: in most of Madhya Pradesh, most of Maharashtra, Andhra Pradesh, most of Mysore, and Madras. Since about 1938 it has become reduced to a tiny remnant in West Pakistan and East Punjab, and survives in a very scattered population in Rajasthan, western Madhya Pradesh, Gujarat, Maharashtra, and probably Mysore. It has few

demesnes that can be regarded as headquarters: one of them, lately well-studied by Dharmakumarsinhji, survives in the old state of Saurashtra in Gujarat, and is recommended as a nature reserve, though not yet declared to be one. Here, as Dharmakumarsinhji points out, a good population persisted as long as the princely rule with its severe game laws and shikari wardening system persisted; that is to say until the later 1940s. Though here, and indeed throughout the whole range of this bustard in India, the species has been officially protected by all states since the new Indian Board for Wild Life advised it in 1952, enforcement of law has been very difficult indeed. The wardening of bustard range has not yet begun. If started in time, it could be an instrument as efficient as the shikari system of the more enlightened and game-minded former princes, maharajahs, and other rulers. To point this out is in no disparagement of the Government of India, which had as a duty to construct in a few years a new game system to take the place of the feudal one. In England the feudal game system was equally effective – as far as conservation was concerned; England's advantage over India is that its feudal game system disappeared much earlier, and the evolution of a substitute for it was able to proceed gradually, with the rise of a democratic society over many years of trial and error, without undue disturbance of most of the indigenous game animals.

One of the reasons why the great Indian bustard is certainly very rare, but not at present very easy to map, is that educated public opinion in India and West Pakistan is not fully aware of its endangered state. So much coveted a giant bird is easily recognized, and would doubtless be more often reported did observers realize that the Wild Life Boards wanted to know about it, and kept a file.

Habitat destruction, which marched with the improvement of agriculture on the subcontinent's plains, has been a strong factor in the decline of the great Indian bustard: but illegal hunting may be stronger in many important areas. The propensity of the species to wander, which it shares with other large bustards, provides another reason why it is being exterminated by illegal hunting with increasing rapidity. However, the older adults settled in stable territories

Great Indian bustard *Waterhouse Hawkins* 1831

Unfortunately, too, the large bustards are conspicuous wherever they may be. They favour open country where the grass is short enough to enable them to keep a close look-out for intruders, and in the breeding season, incredibly unobtrusive though the hen birds may be, the males strut about their territories, with measured tread and neck or gular pouches so blown up that at a distance the observer has the impression of a truly huge white bird.

If approached by a person on foot, they move off with long strides and at an equal pace, but they fly readily enough if the intruder gets nearer, and make off with an immensely powerful flight. Regrettably, the birds are not so circumspect if approached by a hunter on horseback or in a vehicle; hence the steady decline in population, all brought about by human predation.

In feeding habits the bustards are virtually omnivorous, taking largely grains and insects, but also picking up small snakes, or even birds and mammals that do not move away from them. The nest is a mere hollow in the ground perhaps slightly lined with grass; one drab or olive egg is normally laid, although two eggs are not greatly exceptional. Some small species lay five or even six eggs.

Lately R. S. Dharmakumarsinhji has kept a population of great Indian bustards, and successfully reared the species in captivity for the first time. Bustards do fairly well in mainstream zoos; the great bustard, *Otis tarda*, of Eurasia has been consistently bred lately in the Budapest Zoo, Hungary (which takes a special interest in the native birds of Hungary) and since 1962 also in West Berlin. The Houbara bustard, *Chlamydotis undulata*, has also been recently bred in the small but highly efficient and scientific zoo at Tel Aviv University in Israel. Whether these successes will lead, one day, to an aviculture bank of *Choriotis nigriceps*, history will show.

are sedentary (it is the young that wander), and it is certainly feasible to protect established breeding populations in such areas of their habitation as might lie within a national park or equivalent state reserve. Unfortunately, however, young bustards may travel great distances from their favoured breeding-grounds to other areas, usually at lower altitudes, where they prefer to spend some of the winter months. In Africa and Australia it is certainly true that, whereas the big bustards may be well cared for in their nesting localities, they are being subjected to immense and ever more destructively efficient hunting pressures on their off-season feeding-grounds.

Order CHARADRIIFORMES
Family Charadriidae: plovers

NEW ZEALAND SHORE PLOVER
Charadrius (Thinornis) novaeseelandiae

The New Zealand shore plover or tuturuatu was originally discovered on Captain Cook's second voyage to New Zealand, by his naturalists, father and son J. R. and G. Forster, in Dusky Sound on the south-west coast of South Island some time between the 26th March and the 1st May 1773. It was found also in Queen Charlotte Sound at South Island's north end in 1773 or 1774 by the same expedition, and formally named *Charadrius novae-seelandiae* by J. F. Gmelin in 1789. As soon as New Zealand was first really colonized by Europeans, it was also found in Wellington Harbour on North Island, in 1840.

In November of the following year J. D. Hooker and Robert M'Cormick collected a bird on the remote Auckland Islands, some 250 miles south of the main archipelago, which was named *Thinornis rossi* by G. R. Gray in 1845 after James Clark Ross, leader of the famous *Erebus* and *Terror* Antarctic expedition that included the two famous naturalists. *C.(T.) rossi* is now identified as a vagrant New Zealand shore plover in subadult plumage, and the 1841 record is the only one for the species on the Aucklands.

Subsequent records show that the New Zealand shore plover was at least widespread, though perhaps nowhere common, on the main archipelago of New Zealand in early European colonial years. In South Island it was found on the Taieri coast in 1844, in Otago in 1872, and by 1880 on the Cargill River and at Okarito. Not only at Wellington was it found in North Island before 1880, but also at Whangapoua, Lake Rotorua, the Piako River, Manukau Harbour, and Tauranga. Since about 1880, however, there has been no known record of it from either big island: it seems to have become extinct in the main archipelago within forty years of the first New Zealand settlements.

Only in the Chatham Islands does this interesting plover now survive. In its main island days some believed that it was migratory, and that the breeding headquarters was on South Island, the North Island records being of winterers, though this cannot now be proved. On the Chathams, where it was first discovered on the main island (Chatham Island proper, or Wharekauri) in 1871, it appears to have been resident not merely on Wharekauri, but on the southerly outlying Pitt Island (Rangiauria) group, including Rangiauria itself, Mangare, South East Island (Rangatira), and at least a visitor to the northerly outlying islets, the Sisters. But by 1937, when Charles Fleming and E. G. Turbott visited the Chathams, it was already apparently confined to Rangatira. Here they camped from the 16th to the 31st December, studied the plover's behaviour, counted fifty-two pairs and estimated a population of about 140 individuals on the island.

The world population of *Charadrius novae-seelandiae* was thus, in the last days of 1937, confined to an area of 540 acres, or under 1 square mile. Fortunately the introduced cats and rats, a legacy from the colonial and whaling days of the Chathams, have never reached Rangatira, though they have been doubtless the first factors in the extinction of the plover in the rest of the Chathams. Still rat-free, Rangatira still had a shore plover population "holding its own" in 1961, when B. D. Bell visited it. Bell believed that the plover possibly might still also breed in small numbers in some even remoter islets of the Chathams. Mangare, the Fourty-Fours (eastern outliers), and the Sisters deserve new visits; ornithologists (as far as we know) have not sailed round the last two outlying islands for very many years.

The shore plover is protected by New Zealand law, and naturally protected by the remoteness and rat-free nature of Rangatira, where its only enemies are natural predators – the red-billed gull (which was seen to eat chicks by Fleming and Turbott) and possibly the southern great skua. There is a good case for controlling Rangatira (and other islands in the Chathams) under full nature reserve status.

Family Scolopacidae: snipe, sandpipers, etc.

ESKIMO CURLEW
Numenius borealis

The little whimbrel, *Numenius minutus*, is so close to the Eskimo curlew that not all the best systematists of the day have declared their stand on its true position. Some say the two belong to the same species and some say not; and some good authorities simply sit on the fence and say they may belong to the same species.

This difference of opinion does not alter the fact that the Siberian bird, the little whimbrel, is a not very rare bird. Though rather little is known of its breeding distribution in eastern Siberia (and possibly north-western Mongolia), a fairly substantial population appears to migrate across the equator to winter in the Australasian faunal zone of the East Indies, and on the (mainly north-east) Australian coasts; it straggles occasionally to New Zealand.

The American counterpart of the little whimbrel (senior by virtue of its earlier Linnean name) is famous as one of the rarest birds of the world. The Eskimo curlew's eggs have not been seen for a century; and for the last quarter of a century the only sightings of this once locally abundant species have been of about fourteen individuals, in ten separate years (though in every one from 1959 to 1966), on spring migration on the Texas coast. It was last seen in its winter quarters in South America in 1939, in Argentina; on its autumn passage in 1932, in Newfoundland Labrador, and on Long Island, New York; and on proved breeding-grounds in 1865! Its continued survival is a miracle and a mystery, celebrated lately in a tender novel by Fred Bodsworth (*Last of the Curlews*, 1956).

The Eskimo curlew is so far known from only one fossil; its bones have been found in Kansas in a deposit of Middle Pleistocene age, probably over 200,000 years old. It was first discovered for science by the pioneers of the great Hudson's Bay Company system of traders in Canada's northlands, who found it in the spring at Fort Albany in James Bay and Fort Severn in Hudson Bay (both now in Ontario) and sent specimens to J. R. Forster (the discoverer of the previous bird in this book) in London, who named it *Scolopax borealis* in 1772, evidently thinking that this smallest of the curlews was closer to the snipes (it is, in fact, a very characteristic curlew). The species was recorded again by the Hudson's Bay Company prospector Samuel Hearne, who made formidable journeys from Churchill (now in Manitoba) on Hudson Bay through Keewatin into central Mackenzie, and found two kinds of curlew common about Hudson Bay (probably most in the Churchill area), one of which was doubtless the Eskimo curlew. In 1822, after nearly three years of incredible privations in the first Franklin expedition, the talented naturalist Dr (later Sir) John Richardson discovered the first Eskimo curlew's nest at Point Lake on the Coppermine River in central Mackenzie on the 13th June. Richardson also recorded what he believed to be Eskimo curlews on spring passage north from Saskatchewan River between Carlton and Cumberland, when he was in this part of Saskatchewan, in May, on the first Franklin expedition in 1820 and on the second in 1825.

The Eskimo curlew, so far known only from the Canadian north, became fast recognized as a migratory passenger through the United States by Audubon's closest friend and colleague, John Bachman (America's first great expert on migration), in South Carolina in the 1830s. Audubon himself first saw it between the 29th July and the 12th August 1833, when he encountered dense flocks on fall passage at Bradore Bay (Bras d'Or Harbour) at the eastern end of Quebec's Labrador shore – the first record for the province, almost needless to say; his famous plate of it (p. 240) was published in the following year.

With the opening up of the Middle West, and the rise of the shotgun throughout North America, mass shooting began to overwhelm this naturally tame and confiding bird, in the later years of the nineteenth century, just when the very interesting pattern of its flyways was being established. We can now be certain that the shape of the Eskimo curlew's year in its heyday

Eskimo curlews, male (upper) and female *John James Audubon* 1834

was this: a short breeding season in the Canadian northern summer beyond the tree-line, provedly in Mackenzie and (as most authorities have guessed) probably also in Alaska, possibly in Franklin (the Canadian Arctic archipelago) and Quebec's Ungava Bay area, and conceivably in Keewatin and the Ontario part of Hudson Bay and James Bay; followed by a migration down the eastern flyway of North America near or along the coast, across the Caribbean and through South America via Brazil to winter quarters in Argentina and southern Chile, as far south normally as Chubút in northern Patagonia and Chiloe Island (there is one possible record, perhaps of a stray, from the Falkland Islands over a century ago). The return passage, by an unknown route up South America, began to diverge from the fall route in central America (there are single spring records from Guatemala and Mexico), skirted the Texas shore of the Gulf of Mexico, and pursued its way north to the breeding-grounds up the central Mississippi flyway.

The migration routes in North America, which are well known from nineteenth-century and early twentieth-century records,

exposed the Eskimo curlew to hunters in the central states in spring and the eastern seaboard of Canada and the U.S.A. in fall. On the spring passage the flocks were large until about 1875, and modest until 1890, after which birds came through, when they did at all, singly or in tiny groups; the Nebraska passage was fairly strong until 1879; the Alaska passage until 1878; the Missouri passage until 1894. The last years in which spring migrants were seen on breeding-grounds were in 1863, 1864, and 1865, when Roderick McFarlane collected some thirty clutches of eggs east of Fort Anderson, at Rendezvous Lake and at Franklin Bay, all in north-western Mackenzie, since when, as far as we can discover, there has not been a further record for Mackenzie.

Clearly there must have been a nesting nucleus for longer than that in the vast barren grounds of Alaska and the Canadian North – and, for that matter, there must still be one, somewhere. Much further east, the only record for Franklin is of small flocks seen by Ludwig Kumlien passing northward in June 1878 at the head of Cumberland Sound. Where were they going? Northgoing Eskimo curlews persisted in

Alaska until 1882, and the bird was last recorded from the Anadyr' peninsula of easternmost Siberia, opposite, as late as about 1890 (there is only one other record from this area of Russia, in August 1881, and no evidence that the species may have bred in the U.S.S.R.).

The petering out of the spring passage through the central United States makes pathetic reading. The last Eskimo curlews were seen or shot in Arkansas and Michigan in 1883, in South Dakota and Oklahoma in 1884, in Minnesota in 1885, in Louisiana in 1889, in Indiana in 1890, in Iowa in 1893, in Kansas and Missouri in 1902, in Nebraska in 1926; abnormally far east spring migrants were last seen in Massachusetts in 1916, and in 1906 an exhausted spring bird settled on a ship in the Atlantic halfway between Newfoundland and Ireland. No spring migrant has been seen anywhere but in Texas since 1926; the Texas records since then, all from Gainesville except two from Rockport, are 1945 (two birds), 1950 (one), 1952 (one), 1959 (one), 1960 (one), 1961 (two), 1962 (two), 1963 (one), 1964 (two) and – the last year whose records are available – 1965 (one). The reappearance of this bird in Texas has been indeed a surprise and an ornithologists' excitement; and speculation about the breeding-grounds of this tiny but regular remnant has already influenced the design of some expeditions to Canada's barren northlands in the last few years, though so far without success.

The evidence of the reverse migration shows the same sorry succession. Fall passage sightings that were also the last records for provinces and states are: Illinois 1872, Ontario 1873, Ohio 1878, Pennsylvania and Newfoundland 1889, Prince Edward Island 1901, Nova Scotia 1902, Quebec 1906, Wisconsin 1912, Maryland and Bermuda 1913, Massachusetts 1916, Maine 1929, Newfoundland Labrador and Long Island (New York) 1932, South Carolina 1956, New Jersey 1959, and Bahamas 1963 (one shot). Possibly the later records suggest that the last breeding-ground of the last of the curlews may be in Ungava or Franklin.

In the nineteenth century the fall passage was strong (that is, composed of fair-sized flocks) in Newfoundland Labrador until 1892, in Quebec to 1891, in Massachusetts to 1883, in Maine to 1879, and in Bermuda to 1874. There was a big enough fall population for storms of the prevailing westerlies to catch a few off course and drive them across the Atlantic to live long enough to be seen or shot in England in 1852 (two) and 1887, Scotland in 1855, 1878, and 1880, and Ireland in 1870. Most of these sightings are linked with exceptional storms.

There is no such fall population now, and study of the South American quarters of the species gives us nothing but confirmation of the slenderness of the thread by which the survival of the little curlew hangs. Though the birds have been recorded in the past in, or on their way to, winter quarters, in Brazil, Uruguay, Paraguay, Argentina, and Chile, the only sightings in the present century appear to be in Argentina. The last seen in the south was near General Lavalle, in the province of Buenos Aires, on the 17th January 1939.

Law came too late to protect the birds from shooters. The case of the Eskimo curlew is one of the few where global rarity can be exclusively ascribed to modern explosive hunting. All conservationists agree that the surviving breeding-grounds of *Numenius borealis* must somehow be found. So must the wintering grounds. Most also agree that the design of a programme to restore the species would be difficult. Meanwhile, efforts are being made to restrict disturbance at migration time on the Texas coast in March and April.

HUDSONIAN GODWIT
Limosa haemastica

This lovely rare wader, the American counterpart of the Eurasian black-tailed godwit, bears a great resemblance to the Eskimo curlew, not in its form, but in its life history, migration, and distribution. In its survival status it differs from the Eskimo curlew by virtue of having been generally agreed to have become out of danger by 1958, after a long period in which it was thought to be, like the Eskimo curlew, rapidly declining. Its story is told here largely because, out of the six endangered American bird species specifically mentioned in Franklin Delano Roosevelt's National Resources Treaty (ratified in 1941 by eighteen Latin-American countries

Hudsonian godwits, summer (left) *John James Audubon*, and winter (right) *John Audubon* 1835

and the United States and Canada), it is one of the two that, since the ratification of the treaty, have recovered and are for the present out of danger. The trumpeter swan (p. 186) is the other.

The historical picture of the Hudsonian godwit shows an astonishing parallel to that of the Eskimo curlew. Its nest, for instance, was first found by the original discoverer of the Eskimo curlew's nest – near Fort Anderson in Mackenzie, by Roderick MacFarlane on the 9th June 1862. Its full breeding range is almost (though not quite) as mysterious as that of the Eskimo curlew; so far, proved nests are known only from MacFarlane's locality, from the Mackenzie River delta to the west of it and – quite lately in the present century (1948 and since) – from the Churchill area of Hudson's Bay in Manitoba, not far from where it was first discovered by Isham of the Hudson's Bay Company well over two hundred years ago. It is suspected, but not yet formally proved, to breed in Keewatin in the high interior of Southampton Island, and possibly on the peninsula south of Repulse Bay opposite that large island, and on Akimiski Island in James Bay – and in Franklin in the Cumberland Sound area of Baffin Island.

The migrations of the Hudsonian godwit from its obviously not fully known breeding-grounds in the Canadian northlands also clearly resemble those of the Eskimo curlew in its classic times. In fall the main migration appears to flow from James Bay to the eastern seaboard of North America, by Canada's Maritime Provinces, the lower Great Lakes, New England, and the West Indies. The birds winter in Patagonian Argentina, southern Chile, the Falkland Islands, and Tierra del Fuego. In North America the spring migration flows by the Mississippi flyway north, and from May to July strays reach Alaska (though there is no indication that any breed west of Canada). Winter strays have reached New Zealand rather often, apparently "caught up" with flocks of the Pacific race of the bar-tailed godwit – the commonest winter waders of all the Arctic-American ones in that country.

Perhaps the Hudsonian godwit survived the shooting pressures on the central and eastern flyways of North America in the nineteenth and early twentieth centuries because it was never so tame or confiding as the more vulnerable Eskimo curlew, and was certainly always far more numerous (despite our ignorance of its full breeding range). Nevertheless it was considered to be "almost extinct" in the 1920s by such deep analysts as the late A. C. Bent. Only in the 1950s – and, we believe, through a change in public opinion, and an improved ability of huntsmen (that is, shooters) to identify protected birds in North America – were there real signs of a recovery of the population. By 1956 transit flocks were improving in size in several of the national wildlife refuges of the U.S.A., to the extent that 370 birds were seen together on spring passage at Squaw Creek in Missouri. The trend continues towards increase; and for the first time most North American bird watchers can log this handsome bird on their life tally for the price of a car trip at the right time: though *Limosa haemastica* is still a rare one.

Family Laridae: gulls and terns

AUDOUIN'S GULL
Larus audouini

Most of the gull family – "seagulls", as they are often called (but not very accurately, because many species either range far inland or may live on lakes and other waters) – are birds of wide distribution. For the most part, too, they are great opportunists as far as their almost omnivorous tastes in food are concerned; and they may be found scavenging around ships, harbours, and in some cases even towns.

However, this species, with its prominent red bill, is curiously rare and local as well as unusually shy and wary. It seems always to have been confined to the Mediterranean, where earlier records indicate that it had a fairly wide distribution. Even at the beginning of the present century, although as a breeding species usually found on more remote islands and islets, it was recorded as being sparingly seen on the shores of Tunisia, Spain, France, Majorca, Sardinia, Malta, Corsica, Elba, and even in one colony off the Syrian coast. It was always a species that loved rather deep water and nested colonially, although quite apart from other gulls. Now, however, it must be considered a seriously endangered species, for its total population is lately estimated to number under 1,000 birds. It is known to breed, now, on the coasts of Morocco and Tunisia, on the Chaffarine archipelago east of Melilla, where about 500 pairs were found in 1966 (here protection has now been lifted by the Spanish military authorities!), on islets near Corsica and Cyprus, and in a few small colonies in the Aegean Sea.

Any wandering the birds may now do cannot take them very far, apparently, for there have been no recent records outside the limited breeding areas, and the birds are known almost exclusively to frequent rocky islands; they are seldom seen near level or sandy coasts. One breeding colony at present being closely studied contains nearly eighty individuals; other known ones have only about a dozen. The present position is therefore such that, unless some arrangements can be made for Audouin's gull to be given full protection measures, the species is unlikely to be with us much longer.

It is difficult to be precise about reasons for the precarious status of these birds. Perhaps the species has always been comparatively uncommon, although there is no doubt whatever that the last half-century has seen a steady decline in its population. It is generally considered that wide predation of eggs by fishermen, and more recently by collectors, must have had a very serious effect, and that egg-thieving by other species, such as the herring gull, must also have been a contributory factor. The clutch size is reported as being two or three eggs, and the nesting habits do not seem to differ from those of other species, the usual untidy nest being constructed of rough grasses and similar material.

There are two other gulls whose range limits them to the Mediterranean area – the Mediterranean gull and the slender-billed gull; but neither is readily confused with the Audouin's species, and we may perhaps outline the differences. Audouin's gull, as already mentioned, is essentially a species that prefers rather deep water; but the other two are both coastal birds. The slender-billed gull inhabits coastal marshes and lagoons, while the Mediterranean gull breeds on islets in similar lagoons or in lakes.

Audouin's gull – which looks a little like a common gull, but with a red, not yellow, bill – is intermediate in size between that and the herring gull. The other two, however, are considerably smaller; both have red bills, but the Mediterranean gull has a black instead of a white head, and the slender-billed gull has a noticeably long bill and carries its head tilted downwards. The ends of the wings of the three species also show marked dissimilarities when in flight: whereas those of Audouin's gull are conspicuously black, those of both others are white – entirely so in the case of the black-headed bird, and no more than just tipped with black in the slender-billed species.

It must be reiterated that the population of the shy, island-haunting Audouin's gull has reached numbers that are almost catastrophically low. Its position is not improved by the dangerously scattered nature of the surviving colonies and by the differing nationalities of those who control them.

Order COLUMBIFORMES
Family Columbidae: pigeons

MADAGASCAR TURTLE DOVE (SEYCHELLES RACE)
Streptopelia picturata rostrata

The headquarters of this pretty Indian Ocean dove is on the island of Madagascar, the home of its "typical" – or first-described – race, *S. p. picturata*. Five islands or island groups near Madagascar also have good races of the species: so does the more distant island of Diego Garcia in the Chagos Archipelago, and also the archipelago of Seychelles. The native form, *S. p. rostrata*, of the latter is now in grave danger of extinction.

The Seychelles turtle dove formerly existed throughout the granitic group, as well as on some of the coralline group of islands of the Seychelles colony, in the western Indian Ocean, where it was characterized by its rich red head and redder back compared with the grey upper parts found in the Madagascar birds. The past tense is necessary because the native race, in its pure form, is perhaps now confined to the two neighbouring islands, Cousin and Cousine, and even there (or at least on the former) not all of the doves retain their ancient hereditary characteristics.

At some period typical Madagascar birds were successfully introduced into the Indian Ocean islands of Réunion and Mauritius, and from the latter into the Seychelles; tragically, it now seems inevitable that the attractive local ones are doomed. Although doves continue to be common almost everywhere, there has been a rapid decline in the number of individuals showing the local racial characteristics; and to halt the present trend towards impurity of stock would prove an impossible task. It has been said that careful weeding out of those birds on Cousin and Cousine showing affinities with the typical race is now vital if the endemic one is to survive; but even so the impurities are there, and the position clearly cannot be retrieved.

In future the Seychelles turtle doves must be regarded as mere hybrids of little ornithological importance, but they will doubtless survive and multiply, because in so many parts of the world it seems that there is a hardy member of the group, which is able to maintain or increase its numbers however much man's activities may threaten them.

All over the Seychelles the birds are widely spread at lower levels, living in the "plateau" country, as it is called, of small bushes and trees or among the coconut palms. They feed on seeds of all kinds and, being also fond of copra, are commonly seen strutting, bowing, and cooing around the drying-grounds in typically turtle-dove manner. Their nests are the usual loosely interlaced platforms of twigs and roots, and the normal two white eggs are laid.

Most turtle doves do well in captivity, and *Streptopelia picturata* has bred in aviculture since 1907. The translocation of some of the present tiny stock of *S. p. rostrata* from Cousine (where hybridization with *S. p. picturata* may not yet have swamped the indigenous stock), might prove a valuable experiment.

GRENADA DOVE
Leptotila wellsi

The Grenada dove is a normal-sized turtle dove, 11 or 12 inches long, and not at all striking, because it is dull brown above and wine-coloured below, with none of the black or white markings found on the much commoner and quite similar zenaida dove of the West Indies. It is in fact a very drab bird. It is also very rare, so much so as to be nearly extinct.

The one possibility is that the Grenada dove may be barely surviving in an extremely limited area on its island in the Lesser Antilles, West Indies. There has been no estimate of remaining numbers, and for long it was considered virtually extinct, particularly after 1929, when a report merely stated that one had been heard in arid scrub near Point Saline. Specimens were seen, however, in 1961 and 1963, the observations being in a rather dry zone of 30 to 40 inches of rainfall, far removed from the forest area where there is a yearly fall of 200 inches.

The species is endemic to Grenada, and it is from that island it was originally described in 1884. It is known that the birds were formerly more numerous on the same island; they are said also to have existed on nearby Glover's Island and Green Island, although they could not be

Grenada dove *Albert E. Gilbert* 1966

found on the latter in 1929. Destruction of habitat must have had some adverse effect; but apparently it is difficult to find adequate reason for the present extreme rarity of the species. Also put forward as a contributing factor is the likelihood of some food competition by the very numerous violet-eared dove, of which there seems to have been a noticeable increase in population.

Like so many island species that are now in real danger of extermination, it is fast disappearing before any real knowledge of its habits has been gained. Even its call is unknown; and, although there is one dubious record of a nest built by a bird in captivity, there are no available details of its breeding in the wild state.

Order PSITTACIFORMES
Family Psittacidae: parrots

KAKAPO *or* OWL PARROT
Strigops habroptilus

"Rarity is the attribute of a vast number of species of all classes in all countries. If we ask ourselves why this or that species is rare, we can answer that something is unfavourable in its conditions of life: but what that something is we can hardly ever tell."

It was with this quotation from Darwin's *Origin of Species*, published in 1859, that G. R. Williams of the New Zealand Wildlife Service opened his admirable (1956) analysis of the history of New Zealand's rare kakapo. He somewhat belied it by finding several good historical

reasons why this extraordinary near-flightless parrot is rare. Rare it is, indeed, as we shall see.

As the fossil and subfossil evidence shows, the kakapo was once distributed over probably all the moist, mossy, main climax forests of *Nothofagus* beech throughout the two main islands of New Zealand and also Stewart Island. Bones reputed to have been collected on the remote Chatham Island archipelago are certainly kakapo bones, but may have been mislabelled as regards their origin, though there were strong traditions among the Chatham colonists that kakapos were common on the island in early European times.

This queer, big parrot, eater of berries, leaves,

Kakapo *John Gould and H. C. Richter* 1869

and shoots, and occasionally lizards in the beech forests, boomer in the New Zealand night in the wooded hills to about 4,000 feet, breeder and rooster in rock crevices or long burrowed tunnels, seems already to have been a decreasing bird when the Europeans first discovered it in the 1840s. It was first scientifically named by G. R. Gray in 1845 on material sent to London from Dusky Sound in south-west South Island.

Of twenty-five sites at which kakapo bones, fossil or subfossil, have been certainly found, two in North Island and six in South Island lie far beyond any place where the kakapo has been recorded since 1840, and can also be assigned with some confidence to the period after the Polynesian colonization of New Zealand in about A.D. 950. It seems right to conclude that the early withdrawal of this vulnerable parrot, at least from its old range in southern North Island and eastern South Island, was a consequence of the hunting pressure of New Zealand's first humans, who were, technically, Stone Age men. Williams's view that the kakapo "was a diminishing species before Man was able to exert any marked effect on the birds or their environment" may thus need modification. The simplest theory to account for the kakapo's crash is that it started in Polynesian times, and was rapidly accelerated after the European culture took hold of New Zealand in the mid-nineteenth century, largely as a consequence of

introduced predators (particularly stoats) and of forest clearance (by 1922 the forests of New Zealand had already been cut down to 11,500,000 acres from the original 40,000,000) and possibly the effect of introduced vegetarian competitors, especially the red deer. After 1950 there are records of the kakapo from only eight places on South Island, and one on Stewart Island, where the last was seen alive near Seal Point in 1959 and feathers were found at nearby Port Pegasus in 1951. On North Island the last certain sighting was in the Huiaran Range in 1927, and Williams believed that the kakapo was extinct by about 1930. However, typical nocturnal boomings or drummings were heard early in 1961 by surveyors in the beech forests, at between 4,000 and 5,000 feet, in the Omarukokere valley of an eastern tributary of North Island's Ngaruroro River, not very far from where one had been heard in the Kaimanawa Range in 1915, and in a region where Williams, five years earlier, had said it might survive; so the possibility of the continued life of the species in North Island cannot be discounted.

The post-1950 South Island records are all in Southland's Fiordland except one at the Red Pike River in Otago's lakeland in 1951. The other seven are grouped in the Cleddau area above the head of Milford Sound; in the Wild Native River area at the head of Bligh Sound; at Mount Pisgah, western Lake Te Anau; and in the Coronation Peak area. Quite a respectable population was found as late as 1958 in the Cleddau watershed. The Wildlife Branch of New Zealand's Department of Internal Affairs, which regularly patrols the known parts of Fiordland (the last refuge of several of New Zealand's survival species), believed the 1960 population to be well under 200 birds, and the 1961 population to be under 100, with about thirty in one area of northern Fiordland.

Several attempts have been made in the past to introduce kakapos on island reserves with beech cover, for instance in Southland's Dusky Sound area, where R. Henry, caretaker of the

PLATE 23 (*a*) Red-faced malkoha; (*b*) Tristram's woodpecker; (*c*) Ivory-billed woodpecker, North American race; (*d*) Narcondam hornbill; (*e*) Prince Ruspoli's turaco *N. W. Cusa* 1966

N.W.CUSA.

(a)   (c)

(b)   (d)

Night parrots *John Gould and H. C. Richter* 1869

pioneer Resolution Island Reserve from 1894 to 1908, introduced at least 370 living birds. None survived the predation of stoats (with which the island swarms) for very long. In North Island introduced stock did not survive on Little Barrier Island beyond 1903, or on Kapiti Island beyond 1912, except for one long-lived individual, apparently blind, seen and photographed by the late A. S. Wilkinson in 1934. In 1961 five birds were caught by the Wildlife Branch for avicultural breeding experiments, but the last survivor of these died in 1964. The kakapo reached the London Zoo collection in the nineteenth century, but has never bred in captivity.

The kakapo's last haunts in New Zealand are in the wildest hill-beech areas, and to this day are relatively inaccessible and seldom visited. It is clear that any figures of its surviving population are speculative – though based on a careful analysis of some remarkably thorough explorations of chosen areas. More kakapo surveys are, needless to say, essential before we can be sure

PLATE 24 (*a*) Rufous scrub birds, two males *John Gould and H. C. Richter* 1869; (*b*) Noisy scrub birds, adult male (lower) and immature *John Gould and H. C. Richter* 1848; (*c*) Kokakos, South Island race (upper) and North Island race *J. G. Keulemans* 1888; (*d*) Saddlebacks, South Island race, adult (upper) and immature *J. G. Keulemans* 1888

that this highly specialized and indeed unique parrot, which is classed in a subfamily all its own, can survive to remain a joy to bird watchers and a scientific subject of ornithologists. Its demise would, indeed, be not only a moral disaster, but a scientific one.

NIGHT PARROT
Geopsittacus occidentalis

This nocturnal ground-living parrot of the spinifex zone of Australia's dry interior must be one of the rarest birds in the world, if it still exists. It was first discovered by the surveyor Robert Austin in an isolated spinifex patch in the granite "breakaway" country 8 miles south-west of Mount Farmer in the Murchison district of west-central Western Australia. By 1884 it had been collected in South Australia in the Gawler ranges and nearby Lake Gairdner in the south of the state, and near Lake Eyre further north, where it was recorded at Macumba and as even numerous south-east of Oodnadatta. But since that year it has never been seen in South Australia.

In Western Australia its discovery locality was searched again in 1959: none was found. Indeed, the only evidence of its survival comes from

Martin Burgoin, who in years between 1912 and 1935 found it in the spinifex country north-east of Mount Farmer at Nicholl Springs, Bolger's Soak, Pinyerina Pool, and Windich Spring. It has never been seen since then, unless a record reported from Western Australia in 1960 be confirmed. From 1937 it has had total protection in Australia. The protection may have come too late.

Very little is known of the habits of this eater of spinifex seeds and nester in hollows tunnelled in tufts of tussock or porcupine grass (its nest was once found in South Australia). A record of unsuccessful breeding in European aviculture in 1877 needs confirmation. Possibly nothing more of importance may ever be known of this remarkable bird, which was recorded almost entirely from arid, unpopulated areas, and may by now have become extinct through natural causes. For the time being the night parrot stays in the Red Data Book, with a red sheet representing the gravest danger of extinction.

GROUND PARROT
Pezoporus wallicus

Closely related to the night parrot, Australia's ground parrot once had a mainly coastal distribution on the plains between hills and sea all round southern Australia and Tasmania from southern Queensland to north of Perth in Western Australia. Although those authorities who have divided the species into three races may perhaps have done so rather unjustifiably, it is useful to keep the names for the populations here, for their survival status differs considerably.

The Tasmanian population, *P. w. leachi*, is in no danger of extinction, though this button-grass and moorland species, of rather quail-like habits, has doubtless withdrawn with the development of arable land. It is still common on the island's west coast, and, though generally rather rare elsewhere, has been reported from several places near the suburbs of Hobart within the last decade. The form on the islands in the Bass Strait – now extinct on Flinders Island, where it was common a century ago – may belong either to the Tasmanian or eastern population.

The eastern or typical population, *P. w. wallicus*, was probably common on all the coastal plains from Brisbane to beyond Adelaide 100 years ago. It is now in some danger, probably extinct in Queensland, restricted to a few places in New South Wales, rare in South Australia, and perhaps now restricted in Victoria only to Frazar and Marlo islands, unless the Bass Strait island survivors also belong to this group.

It is the western population that is in the gravest danger. *P. w. flaviventris* was, indeed, thought to have become extinct in 1913, though in the early days of the opening up of Western Australia it was present all along the coastal plain from north of Perth to Albany. By 1912–13

Ground parrots, two males *John Gould and H. C. Richter* 1869

it was known only from Irwin's Inlet and from the wet flats around Denmark, particularly at Wilson's Inlet, where nests were found. After that, no birds were seen in the state until the early 1940s, when Charles Allen found it at Cheyne Beach, and 1952, when J. W. Baggs rediscovered a population (he saw four) in December near Irwin's Inlet, at Bow River. Since then this very rare ground parrot has been seen by several parties in 1962 and 1963 in the Cheyne Beach area. It is protected by law and can only be collected or exported under licence.

The range withdrawal of this interesting, rather small parrot is probably due to several causes – first, perhaps, the cultivation and burning of its coastal grassland, and, perhaps equal second, hunting (by man) and persecution by introduced predators. It has been said to have bred in captivity, but no successful rearing has been confirmed.

KAKARIKIS
Genus *Cyanoramphus*

The kakarikis, to give them their Polynesian-Maori name, are the parakeets that have penetrated farthest into the southernmost Pacific archipelagos, and, at Macquarie Island, once even to the threshold of the Antarctic. The genus has a distribution centred on New Zealand, with six known species, of which two are already extinct and the other four, or at least some races of every one of them, are in danger of extinction. *Cyanoramphus* is a genus at the very edge of the world range of parrots and, as an edge-group, is more vulnerable than most. Island forms lead a more hazardous and, in the geological sense, normally a shorter life than the species and races of mainlands. The story of this genus is worth telling, because it illuminates most facets of the survival problem, including extinction. Species by species, it runs:

New Zealand kakariki, *or* red-crowned parakeet, *Cyanoramphus novaezelandiae*

Most widespread of all the kakariki species, this had eight good races in historical times. In New Caledonia (the only Melanesian part of the range of the genus) lives *C. n. saisseti*, which has been known as Saisset's parakeet; though thought rare in 1929, it was evidently not so in 1946. A race on isolated Lord Howe Island, *C. n. subflavescens*, is extinct, having been last certainly seen in 1869. Native to equally isolated Norfolk Island, *C. n. cookii* survives on this small island, only 5 by 2½ miles, but is rare and in need of investigation.

The "typical" race, *C. n. novaezelandiae*, was beyond doubt distributed over virtually the whole of the main islands of New Zealand and their more closely offlying islands through the times of the Polynesian colonization (as fossil evidence confirms) and into European times. In these, at first abundant, this pretty little parrot of catholic vegetarian tastes seems to have withdrawn, or been driven to survival in the remoter upland wooded tracts and on most of the nearer offlying islands (including Stewart Island and its satellites); in the latter it still flourishes well. The population of those more distant ones, the Auckland Islands, is indistinguishable from the mainland form and survives well on Adams and Enderby islands. The Macquarie Island race, *C. n. erythrotis*, the only known member of the family to have reached what could reasonably be described as polar regions, became extinct not later than 1913. The large, hardy race on the distant outlier Antipodes Island, *C. n. hochstetteri*, survives well in this uninhabited place. Another large race, *C. n. chathamensis*, is confined to the distant Chatham Islands, where it was rare enough to be thought extinct by some observers in 1840, but survives fairly well to this day in some localities, especially on South East Island (Rangatira). Likewise the subtropical race on the distant, northerly, small Kermadec archipelago, *C. n. cyanurus*, was once reported as extinct, but was later found to survive and is apparently not in danger.

Antipodes kakariki, *Cyanoramphus unicolor*

The remote New Zealand outlier, uninhabited Antipodes Island, is only 5 miles long and 3 miles wide (its group occupies 24 square miles), yet there are two good species of kakarikis in the tussock and prickly fern and scrub of this windy place. Doubtless the origin of the two species is by double-invasion from the same old ancestry, *C. unicolor* having arrived first, perhaps in the

Pleistocene Ice Ages, and the native race of the New Zealand kakariki, *C. n. hochstetteri*, often known as Reischek's kakariki, in recent times. The two share the little island quite happily, and neither appears to be in present danger of extinction. As seems to be the rule among very closely related or "sibling" species in the same area, the two apparently have a rather different food ecology; the Antipodes kakariki (larger than Reischek's) appears to scavenge far more than the other on the fat of the skins and carcases of the casualties in the big penguin colonies.

Yellow-crowned kakariki, *Cyanoramphus auriceps*

This is obviously an ancient sibling of the red-crowned kakariki of the New Zealand mainland, and has a different food-preference from it, being less dependent on ground plants. On the main islands, once widespread, it has shown recovery from a withdrawal in European times and has expanded fairly recently (from the analysis of Dr R. A. Falla and his colleagues) to the extent that it is now "moderately common in larger forest tracts in both North and South Island (central mountain chain of North, mountains from Nelson to Fiordland in the South Island)". It is found, too, like the red-crowned or New Zealand species, on various near outliers, including the Solanders, and the "typical" race, *C. a. auriceps*, extends, like that of *C. novaezelandiae*, to the Auckland Islands. But the Chatham population is of a different subspecies, *C. a. forbesi* (often called Forbes's kakariki), and, originally found on Pitt, Mangare, and Little Mangare islands in the southern part of this distant archipelago, has been – at least since January 1938 – confined to Little Mangare Island, on whose 2 or 3 acres of thick vegetation about a hundred birds then survived; in 1962 the number was believed to be about the same.

Orange-fronted (*or* alpine) kakariki, *Cyanoramphus malherbi*

The rarest of a trio of New Zealand siblings, this most montane of the kakarikis was "by no means uncommon in the wooded hills surrounding Nelson", according to the writings of the great New Zealand ornithologist Buller in the 1880s. There is no evidence that this small species (rather hard to tell from the others at a distance in the field) has been found elsewhere than in South Island hill scrub and wood-edge from Nelson to Fiordland. Records since Buller's day certainly indicate a withdrawal, for in 1962 G. R. Williams could cite only four separate later reports, mostly unconfirmed. However, it was reliably recorded in the Nelson Lakes National Park in 1964–5. It is undoubtedly rare, and may always have been so; but, as Williams says, "it is not possible to estimate the degree of its rarity".

Tahiti kakariki, *Cyanoramphus zealandicus*

Probably first collected by the naturalists of Captain Cook's voyages, this may have been confined to Tahiti, where it is now extinct, the youngest specimen having been taken in 1844.

Raiatea kakariki, *Cyanoramphus ulietanus*

This very distinct species is known from two specimens collected by G. R. Forster on the remote Pacific island of Raiatea (then known as Ulietea) in May or June 1774 on Captain Cook's second expedition. It was not recorded on W. Anderson's visit in November to December 1777, and it has never been seen since.

The kakarikis, then, have shown a pattern of extinction and withdrawal typical of native island birds. An unknown but certainly important factor in this extinction has been nature. An even more important factor has been colonizing man. But as with many (not all) island birds, some comfort for the future comes from the late exploits of aviculture. The New Zealand and yellow-crowned kakarikis are now easily bred in captivity, and have been reared in Europe since 1872 or before; the orange-fronted kakariki, though never imported since (as far as we can discover), bred in France in 1883.

SOME AUSTRALIAN GRASS PARAKEETS
Genera *Neophema* and *Psephotus*

The night parrot, the ground parrot, and the kakarikis all belong to a tribe of thirty-two

Turquoise grass parakeets, male and female *Peter Slater* 1966

species (of which, as we have seen, two or possibly three are already extinct) often known as the Platycercine parakeets or grass parakeets – for most of them are small (and some very colourful) species adapted to life in open country. They are exclusively Australasian in their distribution, as are the larger, short-tailed cockatoos with which they are linked, on the family tree, by the familiar cockatiel or cockatoo-parakeet, *Nymphicus hollandicus*. Australasia, and possibly Australia itself, is now believed to be the original theatre of evolution of the parrot order and family.

While the most famous of all the grass parakeets, the budgerigar, *Melopsittacus undulatus*, is one of the few birds of the world of which wild flocks of over 100,000 can still be encountered (and is the ancestor of one of the few new domestic birds of the industrial age), a number of the Platycercines are rare. Among them are several – indeed most – members of the genera *Neophema* and *Psephotus*, respectively containing seven and five peculiarly Australian and Tasmanian species.

The elegant grass parakeet, *N. elegans*, of southern Australia is in no danger of extinction and has, indeed, been expanding west in West Australia in the last thirty years. The blue-winged grass parakeet, *N. chrysostoma*, mainly of Victoria and Tasmania, seems to be in little danger; years in which it has been reported rare appear to have been times of abnormal migration across the Bass Straits and in Tasmania, though its population in continental Australia has shrunk in this century. The orange-bellied parakeet, *N. chrysogaster*, is however very rare: of its two races, the "typical" Tasmanian form, *N. c. chrysogaster*, is known from scarcely any specimens, and lately has been seldom sighted; it is very hard indeed to tell in the field from the blue-wing, and has perhaps not been satisfactorily identified by an expert since 1956; and the continental form, *N. c. mab* (not a very well-marked race), has not been seen near Sydney in the present century, has but once been recorded from Victoria, and has not been seen in a fair-sized flock in South Australia since the late 1920s.

The rock parakeet, *N. petrophila*, of the coasts and islands of South and Western Australia is, in many areas, the most numerous grass parakeet, though now becoming scarce in some; it is in no global danger. The ancient range of the turquoise grass parakeet, *N. pulchella*, is not clear, though it was reported a century ago as far north as 20° S. in Queensland, and a third of a century ago in southern Queensland, New South Wales, Victoria, and South Australia. In 1945 it was breeding near Sydney, and had been reported breeding also in two other places up to 200 miles inland in New South Wales. It was later believed to have only a scattered distribution from Sydney to eastern Victoria. However, in the early 1960s it was reported at least three times from areas in Queensland where it had not previously been seen, and it appears to be staging a recovery.

For the distribution of *Neophema splendida*, the splendid (or scarlet-chested) grass parakeet, we largely rely on the latest edition (1962) of D. L. Serventy and H. M. Whittell's excellent *Birds of Western Australia*. Apart from statements that the species was once known from western New South Wales and Victoria, all records with localities and approximate dates come from Western and South Australia; indeed only about fourteen places have been named in all the available literature, of which four are in South Australia, including the only breeding record at Pudnooka on the Murray River over fifty years ago. These places

Splendid grass parakeets, two males (left) and female
John Gould and H. C. Richter 1848

are widely scattered, and over half of them had their sightings between 1939 and 1960, which suggests that there may have been more competent ornithologists in Australia in that period than before (which we already know), but at least that this elusive parakeet may not be decreasing. The seventh *Neophema*, Bourke's grass parakeet, *N. bourki*, is definitely increasing. More adapted to the desert than its congeners, it has been found in a scattered range in the mulga of central and western New South Wales; in Alice Springs in Northern Territory; and the Musgrave Ranges to the south of Alice on the South Australian border. Pending more exploration of the central desert, Western Australia rates as its headquarters; for about fifteen years a spread from the central desert has continued which reached the westernmost coast in 1963.

Of the five *Psephotus* parakeets, the blue-bonnet, *P. haematogaster*, of the eastern and central interior and the Nullarbor area of south-east Western Australia seems in no danger of extinction. Neither is the common "red-backed parrot" of south-eastern Australia, *P. haematonotus*, or the "mulga parrot", *P. varius*, of the central deserts. But of all the rare Platycercines the beautiful parakeet, *P. pulcherrimus*, and the paradise parakeet, *P. chrysopterygius*, may now be the rarest. The beautiful parakeet is an eastern species that seems to have occupied an area never more than 500 miles across in south-east Queensland and just over the border of central New South Wales, nesting in termite castles, perhaps once as far north as the Tropic of Capricorn near Rockhampton. It now seems to be restricted to a few places in the sparsely timbered grassland of the upper tributaries of the Darling River on both sides of the border between Queensland and New South Wales, having been thought extinct in the early twentieth century and having been "rediscovered" in the early 1920s. Though it is impossible for the present strength of Australian ornithology, competent though it is, to work through all the possible terrain of any of these rare parrots, the population of the beautiful parakeet in the wild was estimated at not more than 150 birds in the early 1960s.

The tropical paradise parakeet, *P. chrysopterygius*, another nester in termite castles, has two good races. The hooded form of Arnhem Land *P. c. dissimilis*, has been found only in the Northern Territory, and that very seldom, from Pine Creek (possibly Darwin) and the Mary River south-east to the McArthur River on the Gulf of Carpentaria. It seems to have been always rare. The Queensland or golden-shouldered race, *P. c. chrysopterygius*, was first discovered over a century ago between Croydon and Normanton not far from the Gulf of Carpentaria at the root of the Cape York Peninsula. Later a population was discovered at the Watson River, also in the Gulf of Carpentaria drainage. It has always been very local and rare in this area of north Queensland, and has been lately believed to have a total population of fewer than 250 wild birds. Despite the strongest legal protection, a bird-dealer was arrested when catching some for the avicultural trade in 1963 and heavily fined in the following year.

The century-old activities, now illegal, of Australian suppliers of the international cage-bird trade have been thought to be one of the most important contributions to the present rarity of so many of these beautiful grass parakeets. Enlightened aviculture, on the other hand, has no part in the encouragement of this unlawful trade and has also made important contributions to the other side of the account. The *Neophema* and *Psephotus* parakeets generally do very well in sound captivity: of the rare ones, the blue-winged was bred in Europe since 1879; the orange-bellied lately in Australia; the turquoise in Europe over a century ago (a good captive stock is now building up in Europe and Australia); the splendid in Australia since 1932, in Europe since 1934, and in the U.S.A. since 1947; the beautiful in Europe since 1878 (perhaps 1876), though there is little, if any, captive stock of it now; and the paradise in Europe since 1912, in the U.S.A. since 1939 or 1940, and in Australia (some in artificial termite castles) since 1930. Already, then, there is the foundation of a zoo bank of some of the most beautiful birds in the world.

SEYCHELLES LESSER VASA PARROT
Coracopsis nigra barklyi

The genus *Coracopsis* embraces two species of parrots found widely in Madagascar and in the neighbouring Comoro Islands. Of these, the lesser vasa parrot has four races: the "typical" form, *C. n. nigra*, described by Linnaeus in 1758, is found in the east of Madagascar, *C. n. libs* in the west, and *C. n. sibilans* is native to two of the Comoros, Grand Comoro and Anjouan. None of these forms seems in any danger: but the outpost population in the Seychelles, *C. n. barklyi*, named by E. Newton a century ago, has full status in the Red Data Book.

Also known as the black parrot and locally as the *cateau noir*, this interesting little parrot, whose genus doubtless proves that it colonized the Seychelles from Madagascar, is apparently now confined to one small hilly area on the western side of Praslin Island of the Seychelles group, in the western Indian Ocean. It was, indeed, first described from Praslin, and has never been recorded elsewhere in the archipelago. Its present range coincides with the surviving patches of palm forest on the island, and, although there must be some association between the birds and certain palms, its nature is still not fully known. The details, if discovered, would certainly be interesting, because there are other places in the world where parrots have this close association with certain palm trees even

though their food supplies are not confined to them. The distribution of the Seychelles parrot is not governed by food; the berries on which they feed are found in many other parts of Praslin.

The population of the birds seems to be chiefly located in the Vallée de Mai, where most of the world's coco-de-mer plants are found. The valley is carefully preserved, and, so long as this state continues, the birds should survive.

The subspecies is undoubtedly rare, because it is so localized, although commonly seen in certain localities. The precise numbers of the birds have not been estimated, but the population must still be quite good. An observer in 1959 saw twelve birds in one afternoon, and in 1962 thirteen were seen feeding together.

These parrots are a dark sooty brown, slightly lighter on the under parts; a very good representation of the form appears on one of the Seychelles postage stamps. Like so many other parrots, they usually reveal their presence at first by their piercingly shrill whistle, which it is said, they often give also, and with rather an eerie effect, in the night.

Nothing seems to be known about the breeding habits of this black parrot, although one young bird is reported to have been taken from a hole in a casuarina tree.

AMAZON PARROTS OF THE WEST INDIES
Genus *Amazona*

Amazona is the genus of the Amazon parrots, the most familiar and famous of all the talking cage parrots of the days of sail and the West Indiamen – the "pieces-of-eight" parrots of Long John Silver. Of the twenty-eight species that were alive in historical times (which from the bird point of view we take as since 1600), exactly half were found in the West Indies – and twelve were full natives of the West Indies and of nowhere else in the Americas. Not all of them are in danger of extinction: but the fate of the genus in the West Indies gives us an interesting parallel with that of the kakarikis in the New Zealand region and the pretty grass parakeets in

Australia. Though the West Indies were colonized quite early by Amerindians, who began to extinguish their most specialized native animals long before Columbus dropped anchor in 1492, it is since the Columbian colonizations that (as far as we can tell) the colourful indigenous Amazon parrots of the archipelagos have come into danger, and mainly, we can be sure, through the destruction of the native climax forest and its clearance for agriculture; partly also through the introduction of firearms.

From the Bahamas, through the Greater and Lesser Antilles, the distribution of Amazon parrots (for details of which much use has been made of the tireless researches of James Bond) through the arc of the West Indian archipelagos runs as follows:

Bahamas, Cuba, and the Cayman Islands

The Cuban parrot, *A. leucocephala*, is the sole parrot in these islands, and has been a member of their fauna for at least 60,000 and possibly as long as 150,000 years, for its bones have been identified in a deposit probably of Upper Pleistocene age on New Providence Island in the Bahamas, which may have been laid down early in that part of the Ice Ages. The Cuban parrots of the present day have four good races. The typical *A. l. leucocephala*, named by Linnaeus in 1758, has now doubtless withdrawn, with the felling of woodlands, from a wide original range, but is still common in wilder districts of Cuba and the Isle of Pines. The two races in the Caymans – *A. l. caymanensis* on Grand Cayman and *A. l. hesterna* on Little Cayman and Cayman Brac – are also restricted but not uncommon in their surviving range, though the latter is now very rare on Little Cayman. But the status of the present Bahaman race, *A. l. bahamensis*, causes great concern. No Bahaman parrot has been seen in historical times on New Providence, or on Crooked Island, where bones have been found in a cave with associated Amerindian culture of about 3,000 to 1,500 years ago. The subspecies has been reported from Andros, Long Island, and Fortune Island, but certainly disappeared from these years ago. On Abaco it was common in the 1930s, still in fair numbers around the south of the island in the 'forties, and perhaps hanging on in the 'fifties; but it has been

lately sighted only once. On Acklin, where it was common in the 'thirties and held to be fairly common in the 'forties, it is now believed to be extinct. Only on Great Inagua does it still survive in any strength. The last remnant of the race is found in the northern part of this rather large and still relatively wild island; but the population has not been closely estimated, though it is doubtless under 1,000 birds; and, though it is protected by law, the law is hard to enforce.

Jamaica

The island of Jamaica has two native Amazon parrots, of which *A. collaria*, the yellow-billed parrot, is clearly a counterpart of, and very closely related to, the Cuban parrot. The handsome black-billed parrot, *A. agilis*, distinguished in the field by a red wing-flash, is less common and widespread than the yellow-billed parrot, and does not range so high in the mountains, being absent from the eastern (Blue Mountain) end of the island where the yellow-bill is common in some places. Neither species appears to be in danger of extinction.

Hispaniola

The Hispaniolan parrot, *Amazona ventralis*, is a handsome Amazon peculiar to the Dominican Republic and Haiti, including Haiti's Gonave Island. It is common in Hispaniola, and, though on Gonave now restricted only to the heights, is in no danger of extinction.

Puerto Rico

The Puerto Rican parrot, *A. vittata*, was once represented by a district race, *A. v. gracilipes*, on neighbouring Culebra and Vieques islands. Though common in 1899, this form was extinct by 1912, even before it was formally named in 1915, and is known to science by only three specimens. If forest clearance on the main island had not been arrested, the typical race, *A. v. vittata*, on the main island might well have become extinct too. Most of the climax forest in Puerto Rico was already destroyed by the end of the nineteenth century. Once widespread over the island, the species was, early in the present century, already restricted to the forested slopes of El Yunque de Luquillo in the east, to the then

Puerto Rican parrot, typical race *G. Mützel* 1883

wooded valley of the River Arecibo in the north-central region, and to some coastal mangrove swamps. By 1931 it was a relict in the Sierra Luquillo alone, where it survives in what is fortunately, now, the Luquillo National Forest – comprising some 5,600 acres of the 8,500 acres (at most) of climax forest left in the whole of Puerto Rico. Its status here was still "present and safe" in 1943; and in 1958–60 several estimates by José Rodriguez Vidal and other experts estimated the world population of the species, all in the National Forest, at not more than 200. In the habitat available, this may prove to be a viable population – saved beyond doubt by forest dedication and protective legislation. Unfortunately, the Hispaniolan parrot has recently been introduced in Puerto Rico. Competition may result, further depleting the population of the indigenous species, already harassed by egg-eating margays, smallish tree-climbing wild cats introduced from Central America.

Guadeloupe and Martinique

In the French Lesser Antilles, some 300 and 400 miles respectively from Puerto Rico, two Amazon parrots once lived whose scientific names are based only on early eighteenth-century written descriptions (not specimens), notably (but in the case of the Guadeloupe

parrot not solely) those of the fine naturalist J. B. Labat, whose book was published in 1722. The Guadeloupe parrot, *A. violacea*, and the Martinique parrot, *A. martinica*, appear to have been quite valid forms, even if nobody has ever reported them since the time of Labat, and they have doubtless been extinct for two centuries. (It should, however, be added that James Bond, whose opinion is to be respected, has lately questioned their having existed.) Obviously closely related, the parrots of Guadeloupe and Martinique may have been races of the same species, and possibly also of one of the fine species of parrots still surviving on the island between: the imperial parrot of Dominica.

Dominica

This island, like Jamaica, is blessed with two living parrots, typical of the four surviving Lesser Antillean birds that, as James Greenway points out, "represent a very old group [of Amazons] and a relict population, the relationships of which are now obscure". Big and colourful, the Antillean relicts can only be described, with Greenway's word, as astonishing. Dominica's imperial parrot, *A. imperialis*, is doubtless the most striking of all; and on this rather large island has now retreated to the forest of the higher mountainous country, where it has been scarce since the 1920s and is now undoubtedly rare. It shares the forests with the fine red-necked parrot, *A. arausiaca*, which lives mostly on lower mountain slopes and was still reported as fairly common and widespread in the 1940s. Forest destruction, shooting, and trapping continued widely in Dominica, however; and, though both these parrots are nominally protected by law, nobody can feel that their future is assured until a large area of wooded mountain can be set aside as a forest reserve. The imperial parrot is perhaps more vulnerable, although more inaccessible, than the red-neck; but both deserve the special care of the government of the island, with scientific help and control.

St Lucia

The handsome St Lucia parrot, *A. versicolor*, is suffering the same, apparently inexorable, decline as the other big Amazons of the Lesser

St Lucia parrot *H. Goodchild* 1902

Antilles. Indeed, it may be declining faster. In the 1940s it was found widespread, though nowhere in large numbers, in the forests of several mountain massifs. By the 1950s it was restricted to the central part of the islands, where it has been lately found only at moderate heights. It is probably under shooting pressure by pigeon hunters; and by live-bird hunters, for a high price is paid for any Lesser Antillean parrot in good condition. Many are shot in the hope of their being "wing-tipped".

St Vincent parrot *H. Goodchild* 1903

St Vincent

The rather small island of St Vincent, only about 18 by 11 miles, has its own remarkable, big parrot, *A. guildingi*. James Bond and the late Robert Porter Allen both think that it may never have been very numerous. It does not seem to have decreased quite so fast as the Amazon of the larger St Lucia, perhaps because the island, though smaller, is less cultivated, and because it does not seem so dependent on montane forest and nests occasionally near sea-level. It was still doing locally well at all heights in the late 1960s, and Allen thought, then, that several hundred might still exist, most in the north but some also in the southern hills. All the same, for the last four decades at least, there has been illicit gunning on the island (though less than on St Lucia), especially in the open pigeon season; and no conservationist can be happy until some special protective measures are taken.

Trinidad and Tobago

Close to the South American mainland, Tobago and Trinidad have no full Amazon parrot species purely of their own, and none in danger of extinction. The common Amazon parrot of the mainland, or orange-winged parrot, *Amazona amazonica*, has however a special Trinidad-Tobago race, *A. a. tobagensis*, which is abundant on both islands. Besides this, the typical mainland race of the yellow-headed parrot, *A. ochrocephala*, which has a wide continental distribution, has a small outpost population that is resident but rare in a few localities in Trinidad.

Netherlands Antilles

The Netherlands Antilles, at the end of our chain of parrot-islands, have an Amazon species mostly to themselves: mostly, because the typical race of the yellow-shouldered parrot, *A. barbadensis*, is found not only on Aruba but on the coast of Venezuela opposite. Another race, *A. b. rothschildi*, is resident in the islands of Bonaire, Blanquilla, and Margarita. Neither race is in danger at present.

Every one of the living *Amazona* parrots here mentioned has been kept in captivity (this need produce no surprise), and even the two extinct ones most probably have, if we know the habits of Amerindians and the early post-Columbian colonists. However, the genus is not a very good breeder in captivity, and, while a few of the rare ones are present in zoos for avicultural experiments, the only ones of the fourteen here treated that have reared young in aviculture (as far as we can find) are the Cuban parrot – of which the Bahama race reared a young one in England in 1909 (though it soon died) – and the two commonest species (mainland birds essentially), the common Amazon (possibly as early as 1801 in Rome!) and the yellow-headed parrot (first in the U.S.A. in 1936). There is, by present indications, small chance of a zoo bank for at least five magnificent birds that really seem in serious ecological trouble in their shrinking island homelands.

Imperial parrots *H. Goodchild* 1902

Order MUSOPHAGIFORMES
Family Musophagidae: turacos

PRINCE RUSPOLI'S TURACO
Tauraco ruspolii

This representative of an African family of outstandingly beautiful birds is in danger of extinction because of its unusual rarity and extraordinarily localized habitat. As far as is known, it is found only in an area of not more than about 10 square miles of juniper woods with dense evergreen undergrowth. A limited nearby area of the Ethiopian highlands is virtually unexplored, but this turaco does not exist in apparently similar woodlands closer at hand, while another species is commonly found nearby.

Turacos of one species seldom tolerate the presence of individuals of another, and we can scarcely hope that this particular one will be found to have any wider distribution.

Prince Ruspoli's turaco was described by Salvadori in 1896, when a specimen of this hitherto unknown species was found among birds in the Genoa Museum collected by Prince Ruspoli, who was killed by an elephant during an expedition to the Rift Valley of Abyssinia. For a very long time the species was known only

from that single type specimen; indeed, it remained so for forty-six years, until shortly after the Abyssinian campaign in the Second World War, when five specimens were obtained near Yavello, in southern Ethiopia, some 60 miles east of Lake Abaya, where the first one was obtained.

There seems to be little doubt that Prince Ruspoli's turaco is closely related to the white-cheeked turaco, *T. leucotis*; among its characteristic features are conspicuously white tips to the long feathers of its crown. The sexes are alike in colouration, and both are typical examples of African forest turacos, being stoutly built, bantam-size birds with short rounded wings and rather long tails; all the birds are crested, and most of them have a deep blue or iridescent green colouration.

Another group of the same family lives in more open or woodland country; these birds have dull grey and white or brown and white plumage, and are known as the "go-away" birds – an onomatopoeic name derived from their drawn-out, nasal, and rather mewing "ker-way" call. The forest turacos, however, are much more striking, particularly when seen in flight, on account of their handsome red wings. They used to be called "plantain-eaters", but fortunately this entirely unsuitable name was abandoned some years ago. All turacos are fruit-eaters; but in the wild state they do not eat bananas.

One of the most interesting facts about these attractive birds concerns their plumage colouration. In most birds bright colouring is produced by refraction from the feather structures – in other words, it is produced optically; but the green in the turacos is an actual pigment, one called turacoverdin, about which little is yet known. Even more remarkable is the fact that the glorious purplish-red colour of their wings is also a pigment, unique among all animals, and with considerable copper content. It is known as turacin, and it can be dissolved by alkali.

When a bird species becomes rare for any reason, it is not uncommon in Africa for parts of its carcass to be in demand for various imaginary medicinal and other uses. Among some African tribes turaco wing feathers are greatly prized as adornments. Such uses can constitute a grave added hazard to already endangered birds.

All forest turacos are quite noisy birds, many uttering an explosive series of loud, far-carrying notes, but they are wary and not at all easy to see among the foliage. Before taking to their somewhat laboured-looking flight, they will rapidly ascend or move through a tree in a series of prodigious hops or with almost mammal-like quick runs along the larger boughs. Their nests are seldom found, being quite inconspicuous shallow platforms of small twigs, really no more bulky than doves' nests, and often cleverly hidden in a tree or in dense creeper. Two white eggs are laid.

Order CUCULIFORMES
Family Cuculidae: cuckoos

RED-FACED MALKOHA
Phaenicophaeus pyrrhocephalus

This member of the cuckoo family is the only species in its genus, and, although there are no figures for its population, which would in any event be virtually impossible to estimate, they must now be very low. The birds are undoubtedly rare and decreasing. As long ago as 1955 they were reported to be declining very seriously, and the cause is likely to be associated with a severe reduction in their forest habitat. There are indications that the species has never been particularly common; but so much of its former range has been opened up for human occupation and agriculture that even the original status could not have been maintained.

The red-faced malkoha is peculiar to Ceylon, and its range appears now to be restricted to a few patches of heavy jungle in the Central and Uva provinces, up to about 5,000 feet. It is essentially a bird of the tall forest, in which it is said to favour the undergrowth, and it is reported as having been formerly more widespread in the highlands and wet zone of central and south-western Ceylon. There are two unusual and inexplicable records from Travancore on the Indian mainland, one made in 1931, the other in 1935, but there have been no further records from the Indian continent, and an exhaustive search by one of India's most renowned ornithologists, Dr Salim Ali, failed to reveal it. He subsequently pointed out that the country of southern Travancore is entirely unsuited to this cuckoo's needs.

Apparently the species has no safeguard under Ceylon's legislation to protect fauna and flora, and it is difficult to think of any practicable way of saving it from extinction. If restricted habitat is the reason for its decline, the malkoha is almost certainly doomed, because destruction of the original forest is not likely to stop.

This cuckoo (as in the case of many other genera), makes its own nest, lays white eggs, and hatches them like normal birds. Not a great deal has been written of its habits; but it is said to live chiefly on fruit and also to take small insects. A very early report of this species said that its flesh was "well-flavoured"; so perhaps human predation may have contributed to its downfall.

Order STRIGIFORMES
Family Strigidae: typical owls

SEYCHELLES OWL
Otus insularis

By no stretch of imagination can any members of the owl family be described as easy subjects for an accurate census survey. This particular

Seychelles owl *N. W. Cusa 1966*

species, sometimes called the bare-legged scops owl, is no exception, for like most owls it is crepuscular and nocturnal in its movements, thus making extremely difficult any reliable counts or other observations of it.

It is an inhabitant only of the main granitic island of Mahé, of the Seychelles group in the western Indian Ocean, where, among the inhabitants, it is known as the *scieur*. Presumably in former times such a bird must have existed on other islands of the group, but at present, unhappily, it is confined to Mahé. There it is extremely rare and, although reported recently, must be yet another Seychelles bird that is very

near the verge of extinction. With no records since 1906, it was considered already extinct, particularly because searches carried out between 1931 and 1936 failed to reveal it. In 1959, however, it was located in very small numbers at one place in the mountains of Mahé and can be said to breed there.

Our knowledge of the species is virtually nil. There are three examples only – in the British Museum; and from them the birds are seen to be about the same size as the European little owl. In colour they are a pleasant russet brown above and below; the feathers have black shaft streaks, which are more prominent on the under parts. Nothing whatever seems to be known about the habits of the species.

Why the Seychelles owl should have dwindled to such a minute population can only be a matter for surmise. No doubt, as has been suggested, destruction of habitat and disturbance generally must have had a very adverse effect. But the plausible view is that competition by the introduced South African barn owl has been chiefly responsible, and that this will eventually eliminate the endemic bird.

NEW ZEALAND LAUGHING OWL *or* WHEKAU
Sceloglaux albifacies

The laughing owl of New Zealand is indeed peculiar, for it is alone in its genus and may represent a relict of a very early colonization of the archipelago by its family. Relict it is indeed, for like so many New Zealand birds it has withdrawn to an extent that the number of living people who may have seen it or heard its banshee shrieks, barks, hoots, and mews can be counted on the fingers of one hand.

From the evidence of subfossil bones, it appears that this owl was once part of the fauna of New Zealand's distant Chatham Islands. Only two specimens appear to have ever been taken on North Island, of which one is lost, and the other is the type of the great New Zealand naturalist Buller's *Sceloglaux rufifacies* published in 1904, which is accepted as a valid subspecies. Maoris told the early nineteenth-century Europeans that their whekau was formerly plentiful in the Urewera district; but the only European encounters with the North Island form appear to have been on Mount Egmont in about 1856, at Wairarapa in about 1868, at Porirua at an uncertain date, possibly at Little Barrier Island, at Te Karaka in Waikohu in 1889, and in the Kaimanawa range in 1890, where G. J. Garland appears to have been the last man to have found it. The race is on the extinct list of the Survival Service Commission.

New Zealand laughing owl, South Island race
N. W. Cusa 1966

The South Island whekau, *S. a. albifacies*, was first collected by Percy Earl at Waikouaiti on the Otago coast, and the species was formally named in 1844 from one of his specimens. It was fairly abundant in Otago then, and indeed was not rare there, or in Canterbury and Nelson, in the drier districts, for most of the nineteenth century. But by 1900 the population was clearly collapsing (specimens were taken on Stewart Island in the far south in about 1880, since when the owl has never been encountered again there). Dr Falla and his colleagues accept the specimen found in 1914, by Mrs A. E. Woodhouse at

Blue Cliffs in south Canterbury, as the last fully substantiated record of the species.

A "last substantiation" of over fifty years' standing would normally be enough for reasonable faunists to list the South Island whekau as extinct. But the laughing owl is still in the Red Data Book, and not on the extinct list, by the weight of subsequent evidence, even if none of it appears to be confirmed by specimens (who wants to break the law by collecting them?) or by independent witness. Reputable naturalists believed they heard the scarcely mistakable night sounds of the laughing owl on the Gouland Downs in north-west Nelson in 1916, and logged these owls by both ear and eye there in 1919. Other post-1914 sightings were reported from the Hakataramea district in south Canterbury, from Lake Wanaka in Otago, from Lake Te Anau in Southland; the last strong claim comes from Nelson in the north, where one was believed to have been seen in about 1939 just below the top of Mount Maud, in Aniseed Valley.

The general opinion of New Zealand ornithologists is that the whekau may, indeed, just survive. Its old range was on the plains (as the fossil records confirm – all but one are from the Polynesian period of after A.D. 950), but "penetrated deeply into the mountains of the central chain", as Dr Falla and his colleagues have put it. Here, doubtless, is its last refuge; and it has been probably driven there as much by stoats and other predators of European introduction as by any other factor. It is, of course, now fully protected by law, but further conservation measures must surely await its rediscovery. If the whekau still survives, it will most probably be found by one of the increasing number of naturalists' survey parties camping and night watching (and listening) in the highland bush of alpine South Island, on what is now beginning to be a systematic search for several of the indigenous relict birds of New Zealand.

In the nineteenth century, the laughing owl was sometimes kept in captivity by pioneer New Zealand naturalists, and was even successfully bred in aviculture, in a large packing-case nestbox, by one of them, W. W. Smith.

Order CAPRIMULGIFORMES
Family Caprimulgidae: nightjars

PUERTO RICO WHIP-POOR-WILL
Caprimulgus noctitherus

This nightjar has surely what must be the most peculiar history of any rare bird – or indeed of any bird, if we consider purely the order of circumstances in which we have come to know about it. No other bird can have first been discovered as a fossil; then realized to be alive; next, thought to have become extinct; and finally have been rediscovered with the aid of a tape-recorder.

Fifty years ago Alexander Wetmore excavated some deposits in the Catédral and Clara caves near Morovís in Puerto Rico. They were of early prehistoric date; that is, contemporary with one of the earlier cultures of Amerindians in the West Indies – closer in time to the end of the last Ice Age than to the present day. Among many bird bones that he found, some of which

Puerto Rico whip-poor-will *Albert E. Gilbert* 1966

are certainly those of extinct species, were some that he recognized as belonging to a hitherto unknown form of nightjar, which he named *Setochalcis noctitherus* in 1919 – putting it in a genus already proposed for the common whip-poor-will of North and Central America, to which it was obviously closely related. When Wetmore dug the bones up, he thought the form of bird they belonged to was extinct: but almost at once he found that the skin of a female whip-poor-will, collected in 1889 at Bayamón in

Puerto Rico, belonged to a bird of the same form as the bird of his bones. It was clear then that the form might be still alive; and Wetmore himself saw birds that he believed (doubtless rightly) belonged to it during his spell of work at the Insular Experimental Station at Rio Piedras – though none after the 23rd December 1911.

Since then the Puerto Rico whip-poor-will was generally thought to have become extinct; and most authorities have until lately held it as a race of the common whip-poor-will, *Caprimulgus vociferus*. Held first a fossil and extinct species, it had thus been held a living species, then an extinct species, and then, by relegation, an extinct subspecies. It is here accepted as a living, full species.

Puerto Ricans had recognized a special and "different" night voice from that of the common whip-poor-will at least since 1900. In 1961, on an expedition, George B. Reynard of Cornell University tape-recorded this voice in the field one night in March. Later in the year he returned with a group to the area of Bayamón and Río Piedras in north Puerto Rico near San Juan, played the recording back, with amplification, and lured a male whip-poor-will into collection range. By flash photographs, and a field study of the area lasting in all nine months, a small and apparently flourishing population was rediscovered of what, on the evidence of the new specimen and the very great voice difference, is now recognized by some ornithologists as a native whip-poor-will of full specific rank.

The curious history of this species is such that it is impossible yet to say whether its population is a last relic of one once widespread in Puerto Rico. Nightjars are hard to plot and map without extensive and difficult nocturnal surveys. The destruction of Puerto Rican forests, however, must surely have localized the whip-poor-will; and many ground-nesting birds have been seriously reduced in the island – particularly by the introduced mongooses. Further field work is necessary before the real range in the island of *C. noctitherus* is fully worked out, and conservation measures can be prescribed for it.

Order CORACIIFORMES
Family Bucerotidae: hornbills

NARCONDAM HORNBILL
Aceros narcondami

This hornbill has so far been recorded only from Narcondam, which is one of the Andaman Islands lying between the 10th and 14th parallels in the Bay of Bengal. The group has 204 islands; the larger ones consist of a maze of hills covered with thick tropical forest, separated by creeks and straits. It is possible to believe that so strongly flying a bird as a hornbill may yet be found to exist on several of them despite the fact that Narcondam is the most isolated well-wooded island of the archipelago, lying some 80 miles east of North Andaman Island, and closest of them to Burma and the Mergui Archipelago, where the wreathed hornbill, *A. undulatus*, is our bird's nearest relation and possible ancestor; the Narcondam hornbill may even be a subspecies of the wreathed.

This Narcondam species is listed as a very rare bird because it is known from a very small number of specimens, and so few people have seen it. Forty years ago its population was reported at about 200 birds, on its rather small home island. But the ornithologists who have worked in the Andaman Islands must be few indeed, and none, as far as we know, have visited Narcondam for many years. It may well be that the species is not at present greatly endangered – even if it turns out to be confined to Narcondam. A certain amount of timber is nowadays exported from the Andamans, and some plywood is produced there, but so far, probably, destruction of forest habitat has not vitally affected the status of any forest-haunting birds.

Hornbills are essentially birds of the forest, feeding on fruits and berries and moving about over considerable distances to favoured trees wherever – as the birds seem to appreciate with uncanny precision – the various kinds of fruits are ripening. Extensive knowledge of the biology of other species in the hornbill family has shown that they are strange and interesting creatures, particularly in their nesting habits.

When the female bird has repaired to the tree cavity that has been chosen for the nest hole, in most cases she then walls herself in with mud plaster, made from soil mixed with the bird's saliva, handed to her in pellet form by the male. A small hole is left through which the cock feeds the hen during the whole period of incubation. In some species the female then leaves the nest cavity, and the young are fed by both parents; in others, the male continues to feed his hen and family until the young are ready to fly.

Order PICIFORMES
Family Picidae: woodpeckers

TRISTRAM'S (WHITE-BELLIED BLACK) WOODPECKER
Dryocopus javensis richardsi

The handsome white-bellied black woodpecker extends over almost the entire oriental region; that is, South-East Asia and the East Indies as far east as Bali, including Borneo and the Philippines. It also ranges into the more temperate Palearctic subregion in China and Korea. Some authorities have maintained that as many as fifteen races exist, but Dr Vaurie's most recent book on Palearctic birds upholds only six. However, no scholars differ about the validity of the rare Korean subspecies discussed here, which is usually known as Tristram's woodpecker, *D. j. richardsi*. The modern style of incorporating one basic vernacular name in that of each race of a species is sometimes a little awkward, which is how "Tristram's white-bellied black woodpecker" certainly sounds.

It is just possible that this bird may be surviving in one or two localities in the western Kyungki and Chungchong provinces of central

Korea. The most recent reliable breeding records were at Kumnung in 1950 and Kwangnung in 1955, but since then there have only been two (not fully verified) reports at Songri Mount, and a third (also unconfirmed) at Kangwon-Do as recently as 1962; and verified reports in December 1965 and May 1966 on Solak Mount.

The subspecies was formerly more numerous in central and southern Korea, and it existed also on the island of Tsushima, where it has long been killed off. Records of one kind and another were not uncommon even until the time of the Korean War, but more recently they have been exceptional, and for several years now the birds have not been seen or heard in their former stronghold in the Kwangnung National Park. There, too, they have either been eliminated or have moved away, and it is feared that the species may now be extremely rare, or even extinct.

The woodpeckers are protected by law, and the Kwangnung area and Solak Mount (free from human disturbance) have in addition been declared a natural monument and a national nature reserve; Songri Mount is also well protected against hunting, and if the birds are surviving somewhere in these areas there can be some hope of their continuance. However, it is feared that, if they have not gone already, they have reached a point of no return, and that circumstances have proved too much for them. Quite apart from the disturbance caused by two wars, and the construction of strategic and other roads, these woodpeckers have undoubtedly been subjected to a good deal of shooting; but the greatest factor of all in their decline must have been a gradual destruction of their native forest habitat.

There can be little doubt that the position of all those species which may be termed the large woodpeckers is grave all over the world. There is an impressive danger list of these attractive birds, in North America, South America, Europe, and Asia – in fact everywhere except Africa, where human population densities are still not great enough to bring about much disturbance in the vast areas of natural, evergreen forest habitat, although these have really no chance of ultimate survival.

To begin with, the big woodpeckers are so large that each pair requires a very considerable quantity of forest for a territory; and in many countries inadequate areas of original big timber have been left to hold them. The other trouble is that, as a rule, they are highly specialized birds, which feed on particularly large grubs found only in the biggest trees, and have proved quite unable to adapt themselves to secondary growth or introduced trees of any kind. Worse still, it appears that all the large woodpeckers demand, for their nesting holes, trees that are in fact forest giants; and the absence of these seems to discourage breeding. The more that comes to be known of the habits and breeding biology of the larger woodpeckers, the more obvious seems their doom.

It is always unfortunate when any bird disappears, particularly if, like a woodpecker, it is certainly beneficial rather than harmful to human interests. This applies almost as much to a subspecies as it does to a full species, although it is of course to some extent fortunate, as in this instance, when there are races of the same species still not endangered over a wide range.

Not a great deal is recorded of the habits of these fine, 16-inch-long woodpeckers, which are largely black, but have a considerable amount of white on under parts, wings, and rump, and striking scarlet red heads in the case of the males. Female birds are similarly clad, but lack the red on their heads and cheeks. It seems to be the rule for the birds, when not breeding, to be rather solitary in their movements; and they are said to like resting high in a tall tree. When in that position they show a characteristic habit – swaying their heads and bodies slowly from side to side.

OKINAWA WOODPECKER
Sapheopipo noguchii

This remarkable and distinctive woodpecker, in a genus all its own, was not described until 1887, shortly after it had been discovered in the dense forests and bamboo groves that then clothed most of its homeland: the rather large island of Okinawa, in the Ryukyu archipelago south of Japan.

Much has happened to Okinawa in the last

eighty years – much deforestation and, lately, war destruction and disturbance. By 1945 this woodpecker (sometimes known as Noguchi's or Pryer's woodpecker) was apparently confined to the still dense forests near Hedo in the northernmost part of the island. Since then there have been very few reports of it; and no information from which its surviving population can be estimated. Whatever this population is, it is doubtless small, and, equally without doubt, in need of investigation and safeguarding.

The Okinawa woodpecker is a shy bird, red on its back, pink-bellied, brown-breasted, pale-throated, brown-faced; the males have a red cap, the females a brown one. Its tail is brown, and its wings dark brown with three bright white flash-marks. It is of the size – 10 inches long – of average woodpeckers, but quite impossible to mistake for any others of them.

IVORY-BILLED WOODPECKER
Campephilus principalis

The largest and grandest woodpeckers in the world are the three species that most authorities assign to the genus *Campephilus*: the Magellanic woodpecker, *C. magellanicus*, of southernmost Chile and Argentina, whose range extends to the Antarctic beech forests of Tierra del Fuego; and two species of the northern New World, the imperial woodpecker, *C. imperialis*, of Mexico, which is very rare, and the ivory-billed woodpecker of the south-eastern United States and Cuba, one of the rarest birds of the world.

James T. Tanner, the scholarly historian and eager field-investigator of the two rare northern species, has exhaustively analysed the history of the North American ivorybill in his classic Audubon Report of 1942 – the first of a great series of studies of endangered North American species sponsored by the National Audubon Society. The pattern of the former distribution of the ivorybill emerges from his map as the once heavily wooded bottomlands of the whole Mississippi river system north to some distance beyond its confluence with the Ohio River; the once heavily wooded bottoms of the other principal rivers of Mississippi State, Alabama, Georgia, and South Carolina; and the once

heavily wooded swamps of Florida. Its decline to near-extinction has accompanied, with appalling precision, the relentless logging of the giant sweet gums, red oaks, and other huge trees of the Mississippi's great alluvial ribbons, 40 to 80 miles wide, and the big bold cypresses, water oaks, and black gums of the south-eastern states. The ivorybill story is the classic example of the consequences of habitat-destruction.

The North American ivorybill was first described from South Carolina by the great pioneer English explorer Mark Catesby early in the eighteenth century, and, from Catesby's description, given its present scientific name by Linnaeus in 1758. Not even Audubon, who, a century later, nick-named it – a study in scarlet, black, and white – the "Van Dyke" and wrote about it often, could have had reason to guess that after only one more century it would be the most sought-after and worried-about great bird of the United States. Tanner's map of the situation in 1930 showed that the ivorybill hung on then, as proved after exhaustive surveys, in perhaps only one surviving stand of virgin forest in eastern Louisiana, the Singer Tract near Tallulah; in only one in South Carolina, the Santee Swamp; and in perhaps seven in Florida – the Apalachicola River Swamp, the Wakulla-Wacissa Swamp, and Gulf Hammock in the north; and Jim Creek, Highlands Hammock, Big Cypress Swamp, and the Shark-Lostman's River Swamp in the more southerly parts of the peninsula. Since each pair of ivorybills, as Tanner found, needs up to 2,000 acres of mature forest with large old trees, and the sound of the saw was coming nearer and nearer to these last refuges, the prospects of survival were gloomy indeed when Tanner published his report. Many who read it believed the bird was doomed. It may be; but it is not dead yet.

It is likely that the ivorybill was already extinct in the southerly region of Florida when Tanner's report was published; the last records of it are from Highlands Hammock in 1937 and from Big Cypress about the same year. Despite the Audubon Society's all too reasonable suggestion, on Tanner's advice, that the Singer Preserve in Louisiana should be selectively logged, leaving old trees for the woodpeckers, the last great virgin hardwood bottomland swamp on the whole North American continent was logged out in 1943, one tree that was felled containing an ivorybill's nest and eggs. A lone female ivorybill lingered about that year; and a Fish and Wildlife Service biologist reported a bird in 1944. Never since has there been an ivorybill in the classic locality in which the late Arthur A. Allen and Peter Paul Kellog made the only extant movies and sound-recordings of wild ivorybills.

In north Florida no records of ivorybills exist for the Wakulla-Wacissa area after 1937. The Apalachicola Swamp was made a 1,300-acre sanctuary before the last ivorybill was seen there in 1950, or possibly 1952. The sanctuary dedication was too late. One of the present writers made a pre-dawn canoe trip in May 1953 to a big cypress in this swamp with the last roost-hole known to have been occupied here; but when the sun came up no trumpeting ivorybill came out to greet it. However, not far from Gulf Hammock, on the north-west side of the peninsula, where no bird had been since 1934, an unconfirmed but probable sighting of a bird was reported in 1963.

The decade of the 1950s had passed without a confirmed sighting of ivorybills anywhere in North America (setting aside the unconfirmed Apalachicola record of 1952). Ten years without an ivorybill – and most American ornithologists had given up hope. But in 1961 and 1963 unconfirmed though reliable reports came from South Carolina, where no bird had been seen in the Santee Swamp since 1937. Even more remarkable, in Big Thicket, a large pine-swamp with cypress and sweet gum in eastern Texas between the Trinity River (where the ivorybill had been last reported in 1904) and the Neches River (last report 1885), Whitney Eastman and his colleagues found two pairs and an odd female in 1960 and 1961; and positive reports came from the same area in 1963. Parts of Big Thicket explored by James Tanner in 1938 with negative results had been thoroughly logged over; but the ivorybills of the 'sixties had chosen one of the very few extant areas of near-virgin bottomland forest surviving in the whole of Texas. In 1963 there was also a report from an undisclosed locality not very far to the east of the Neches River, over the Louisiana border; if, as is highly

probable, this was an ivorybill, it was the first to have been seen for forty years in western Louisiana; however, an extensive search of Louisiana in February 1965 failed to find ivorybills or (it was judged) any favourable habitat.

In December 1966 John Dennis began a new search of Big Thicket for the U.S. Department of the Interior, and early in that month encountered an ivorybill at a range of 50 to 60 feet in a cypress swamp. Eventually he established that at least five and possibly as many as ten pairs were surviving in Big Thicket, though (at the time of writing) no proof of breeding, or photograph, was obtained. The birds were feeding on insects in pine slashings – areas worked over for lumber – and not (as was usual) in untouched timber. This has led to an approach by the Bureau of Sport Fisheries and Wildlife to local timber-owners to plan the rotation of their forests, and preserve surviving stands of old timber, in the interests of this wonderful bird.

Campephilus principalis principalis, then, survives by the skin of its ivory bill. It is hard to make much further comment. The preservation of the really big areas of climax forest necessary for the safe existence of the North American ivorybill has been an insuperable problem in the past. The Big Thicket and Santee habitats survive at present, as some do in Florida, with just an acreage worthy of the ivorybill. They could and should be kept, in the hope that this smallest of relict woodpecker populations (perhaps half a dozen birds capable of breeding) will provide a reservoir for the colonization of the regenerated climax forest that everyone trusts may be permitted to grow again in conserved and planned areas of the classic wetlands of the south-eastern United States. Many people think that the future of the beautiful bird that Audubon, the patron prophet of North American conservation, loved so much is forlorn. But it would be bad conservation ethics and bad conservation science to think it hopeless.

The Cuban race of the ivorybill, *C. p. bairdi*, first formally named a little over a century ago, has had a fate almost identical with that of the North American race, as the mixed hardwood forests were slashed away, here not only for lumber but also to make way for the sugar industry. Its old range was from one end of the big island to the other; but nearly fifty years ago most of its haunts were written off as "former range" in ornithological accounts of Cuba. Populations seem to have survived until the 1930s in the west near Artenusa in Pinar del Río province and possibly in the Zapata Swamp in Matanzas. But by 1956, when George R. Lamb surveyed the bird for the Pan-American section of the International Council for Bird Preservation, its only known haunts were east of Mayari, and in the Sierra de Cristal and Sierra de Moa pine-woods not very far from Guantánamo in Oriente, at the eastern end of the island. In July of that year a very thorough search by Lamb could find a population of only twelve or thirteen birds here. Apart from sightings in 1963 and 1968, no further information is available: it is as badly needed as is a Cuban nature reserve and forest park dedication for the "carpintero real", together with an effective management, protection law, and enforcement policy.

Imperial woodpeckers, male (upper) and female
R. M. Mengel 1964

IMPERIAL WOODPECKER
Campephilus imperialis

James T. Tanner's study published in 1964 shows that the "original" range of the world's largest woodpecker was – in simple terms – virtually the whole of the pine-oak forests of the western Sierra Madre, the western backbone of the northern half of Mexico, above 6,500 feet in the north and 8,000 feet in the south.

Here, Tanner believes, the population collapse that has taken place during the last fifty years is primarily due to shooting rather than the steady lumbering of the pines, which is highly selective as presently practised and leaves many large trees standing. The lumbering, however, has brought many workers to the upland forests, and wages for them to buy firearms with. His map of this beautiful bird's place-records shows only two localities in south-west Chihuahua, two in western Durango, and one in northern Nayarit that the bird has been recorded from since 1960. A long journey he made with his son David Tanner in 1962 through the virgin pine forests of Durango's uplands showed no more than some disused nesting or roosting holes; new farmers moving into the area told them that the birds had recently disappeared. Later, Alan Phillips found a few on a big trip in the Sierras; but only a very few.

Clearly the Sierra pinelands need a thorough survey before we can be sure that this woodpecker's status is disastrous; but it looks bad.

Order PASSERIFORMES
Family Acanthisittidae: New Zealand wrens

BUSH WREN
Xenicus longipes

Of the family Acanthisittidae, which are rather primitive song birds peculiar to New Zealand, only four species are known. Two of these, the rifleman, *Acanthisitta chloris*, and the rock wren, *Xenicus gilviventris*, are in no danger of extinction. But the bush wren may be, and its congener the Stephen Island wren is extinct.

A forest foliage-creeper, the New Zealand bush wren has three races – on North and South Islands, and on the Stewart Island archipelago. The former range of the North Island subspecies, *X. l. stokesi*, may always have been limited to more southerly latitudes, and indeed the form is still based upon only two specimens taken in about 1850 on the Rimutaka range. Until 1949 – a century later – these were thought by most authorities to be the only evidence of the (previous) existence of the North Island bush wren; but on the 13th June 1949 A. T. Edgar saw one in wet forest just below Lake Waikareiti. There are other sight records of birds that may have been of this species from at least four other areas of North Island; but none has been confirmed, and the race is obviously very rare indeed.

The South Island form, *X. l. longipes* (the typical form of the species, first discovered in 1773 by Forster in Dusky Sound on Cook's second expedition), once (probably) occupied the woodlands of the whole mainland of South Island, whence it has withdrawn since 1880 into the hills and particularly to the wildernesses of Fiordland, where its populations are now scarce and sporadic, and it can certainly be classed as rare, and as becoming rarer. The Stewart Island form is also very rare: *X. l. variabilis* was once apparently widespread over the archipelago, but has not been seen on the main island since 1951, and appears now to be almost (if not quite) confined to the South Cape Islands. Here it survived on Big South Cape until 1964; but was absent from this rather long island in 1965, when it had become very rat-infested. Because of the rats, a population was translocated from Big

North Island bush wren *Robert Gillmor* 1966

South Cape to Kaimohu in 1964, and was surviving in the following year, when four birds were seen; otherwise it may survive only on South Cape Island and Solomon Island, and perhaps another outlier, Kotiwhenu.

This rather reluctant flier and ground and tree-bole feeder may be particularly sensitive to predation by rats and other introduced predators. Another species of bush wren, *X. lyalli*, the Stephen Island wren, had probably progressed to flightlessness and was a very definite species – perhaps already a relict of a once more widespread species – when fate overtook it in 1894, in the shape of the lighthouse-keeper's cat on Stephen Island in Cook Strait. All the specimens that existed (about twenty of them) were collected by this cat in that year; and no bird has ever been seen since, of this species exterminated by an introduced predator.

Family Philepittidae: asities

SMALL-BILLED FALSE SUNBIRD
Neodrepanis hypoxantha

Much has been written about the oddity of the fauna of the Malagasy region, consisting of Madagascar and its offshore islands, and there are still differences of opinion on its origin. It seems certain enough that most of the region's birds came originally from Africa, and that there has been subsequent immigration from the continent's mainland. It is also reasonable to surmise that at some time there was a land connection with Africa, but precisely when this was can only be imagined. Some authorities favour the Oligocene time.

Many Madagascar species are considered to belong to African superspecies, but the fauna shows many features that cannot yet be explained. There are certainly three bird families endemic solely to the Malagasy Republic – the Vangidae or vanga shrikes, the Mesitornithidae (Mesoenatidae) or roatelos or mesites, and the Philepittidae or false sunbirds and asities. Some hold two groups of rollers also as endemic Malagasy families. It is to the Philepittidae that *Neodrepanis hypoxantha* belongs; and its family contains only two genera, *Philepitta* and *Neodrepanis*, each of which has only two species. This small-billed false sunbird must be an extraordinarily rare forest-haunting species, because it is known only from nine specimens, collected in only three places in forests east of Tananarive in central eastern Madagascar; so rare that the great Franco-Anglo-Americaine expedition to the island in 1932 could not find it. It is listed as a rare and threatened species; the possibility exists that it has already been extinguished, particularly now that there has been so much recent destruction and exploitation of original forests. However, it may survive in the Siniaka forest between Fanorana and Lake Alaotra; fairly large areas of this extensive stretch of forest have not yet been cut over. A close investigation is needed to see whether a relict population survives, followed by the confirmation of strict nature reserve status for any forest area in which it may be found.

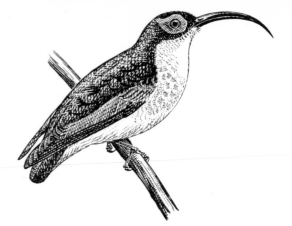

Small-billed false sunbird *Robert Gillmor* 1966

The other species in the same genus, *N. coruscans*, known as the wattled false sunbird, is confined to forests of the eastern slope of the island's highland plateau. Until recent years the genus was often classified with the African true sunbirds of the family Nectariniidae, and this persisted until it was shown that the Malagasy birds had a long, strongly margined first primary wing feather, instead of the rudimentary or minute one found in the sunbirds. So like true sunbirds are the false ones, that it was not until 1933 that both species were seen to be different, and that the small-billed species was seen to differ from the wattled one because of its bright canary yellow, instead of olive grey, under parts.

Few details are known about the habits of the commoner bird, but nothing at all is known of any aspect of the biology of the small-billed species. Judging from the few notes about the former it seems that both species are likely to be quiet and sluggish inhabitants of the thick forest undergrowth, quite unlike the rather demonstrative sunbirds, although similarly fond of visiting flowers in search of small insects, instead of the more normal practice of seeking them on the bark of the branches. False sunbirds are said to be close relatives of the pittas and the New Zealand wrens in the Old World, as well as to the tyrant flycatchers of the New World.

It is generally agreed that all the four primitive perching birds in the Philepittidae family on Madagascar Island derive from the same ancestor, although the asities (*Philepitta*) are markedly different in appearance. The velvet "pitta" or asity shares the damp forests of eastern Madagascar with the false sunbirds; the smaller Schlegel's "pitta" is found in the forests of north-western Madagascar. Neither has the long, thin, down-curved bill, or the slender form, of the false sunbirds; instead, they are plump, stocky birds with short bills and typically pitta-like appearance, although they do not live on the ground like the true pittas or ant-thrushes of the family Pittidae. They are slow-moving birds of the forest undergrowth or lower tree storey, feeding on fruits and berries; they permit very close approach before taking alarm. They too are entirely dependent on the moist, evergreen forests for their livelihood, and, unless better care can be taken of Madagascar's original timber, a whole family of two unique genera will quickly disappear. For the island to suffer such irreplaceable losses would be tragic.

Family Atrichornithidae: scrub birds

SCRUB BIRDS
Genus *Atrichornis*

This peculiarly Australian family of primitive singing birds has only one living genus and two species. Both are very reluctant and ineffective fliers, and now have a relict distribution in two very widely separated areas of the Australian continent.

The rufous scrub bird, *A. rufescens*, from when it was first discovered about a century ago until about half a century ago, was distributed in a strip from the Macpherson Range at the very south-east corner of Queensland, east of the New South Wales water-parting to the Bellingen area a little over 200 miles south, in scrubby forest. Since then its range has withdrawn to the north, and until lately it has been confined to the Lamington National Forest, which lies mainly in New South Wales but ranges into Queensland on the north side of the Macpherson Range; the latter has a good scrub bird population. The chances of survival of the population seem good, protected as it is by forest reserve management and by law: but it is a rare relict that still needs a sheet in the Red Data Book.

The rufous scrub bird's western counterpart, the noisy scrub bird, *A. clamosus*, of Western Australia, was given a sheet in the Red Data Book later than the rufous species – not because it was commoner, but because it was thought to be extinct. Its history is interesting. It was discovered in 1843 by the pioneer Australian naturalist John Gilbert at Drake's Brook, Waroona (just within the Darling Range), at Augusta, and at King George's Sound; at the last locality it was seen and collected by others until the early 1880s. In 1889 A. J. Campbell collected the last museum specimen at Torbay near Albany in early October, and heard the noisy bird calling in November at Boogidup Lake near Wallcliffe. After this the bird came to be generally accepted as extinct, despite unconfirmed records of a possible nest near Torbay inlet, a rather doubtful nest in 1897 25 miles east of Albany, and a hearing in 1920 near Boogidup Creek.

On the 5th November 1961, doubtless to their complete surprise, Charles Allen and P. J. Fuller saw the noisy scrub bird at Two People Bay, east of Albany; and the presence of a singing male was confirmed by H. O. Webster on the 17th December. Soon it was found that a small colony had survived in the densely scrubby slopes of Mount Gardner just south of Two People Bay, where many members of the Royal Australasian Ornithologists' Union (and a good number of ornithologists from other countries) have since seen these birds – back from the dead. At the R.A.O.U. annual congress of 1963, which took place partly in Albany, it was possible to announce that, with the influence and help of Prince Philip, who has taken a keen personal interest in the bird, the town site proposed at Two People Bay was to be shifted to the northern end and away from the scrub birds' territory at the southern end. It is believed that this alternative plan will go through; and meanwhile a national park of 13,500 acres is being set up covering most of the area now known to be inhabited by or suitable for the species, whose population was, in 1966, thought to be at least fifty, and probably eighty.

Doubtless the scarcity and narrow survival of the noisy scrub bird is primarily due to the clearing of scrub in the coastal districts of north-west Western Australia. Introduced cats, rats, and other predators may also have made life difficult for this very weak flyer. But at least the noisy scrub bird now has reserve management, and a quickly tightened licence-law (1962), under which no collection can be made without a permit, and no permit will be given within 4 miles of Mount Gardner. By April 1967, 11,460 acres had been declared a fauna reserve (under a full-time warden) and vested in the Fauna Protection Advisory Committee.

Family Alaudidae: larks

RAZA ISLAND LARK
Alauda razae

During the Tertiary era, volcanic action formed the islands of the Cape Verde archipelago, which lie in the South Atlantic Ocean about 350 miles off Dakar, Senegal. They fall into two groups known as the Windward and the Leeward, and between two of the larger islands, São Vicente and São Nicolão, lies the tiny one of Raza, which is only about 3 square miles in extent.

Raza is the home of a lark, not recorded from anywhere else, that has been classified as related both to the skylark and to the crested larks, but closer to the first. Indeed, it has the same colour-pattern as the common skylark of Europe, and a bill of the same shape, although considerably longer and stronger.

The increased bill size is really the only great difference in this Cape Verde bird, because it is very like the skylark in movements and has a similar short crest, which is raised in the same way. The song, too, is poured out when in mounting flight, although the male bird ascends vertically instead of in spirals; it has been suggested that this may be an adaptation to life on a particularly small island. The large bill may also be an adaptation, enabling the birds to dig for grubs, which they do with skill.

No estimate is available of the population of Raza's endemic lark species, which must be considered both rare and always endangered because of its extraordinarily restricted distribution. It is also not known whether it has always been so localized, or whether it formerly existed on other islands of the group. It was discovered on Raza by the well-known collector Boyd Alexander as long ago as 1898, and even at that time he did not record it from any other locality.

During the Pleistocene, the Cape Verde Islands without doubt had a cool, wet climate, but, although the weather is kept cool by the ocean current, the lower levels of the islands are now very desert-like, with a short tropical rainy season in the autumn. Probably the Raza Island larks will remain safe only so long as their habitat remains largely undisturbed.

Family Sturnidae: starlings

ROTHSCHILD'S STARLING
Leucopsar rothschildi

Often a bird is rare for the simple reason that it has evolved on an island or on some equally restricted zone such as an isolated mountain – within which confined range it may be further localized by some particular habitat requirement. Nevertheless the population of the species may be in a perfectly healthy state and well up to maximum numbers for its limited area, so that there is no question that the birds are in any way threatened. Because of its rarity, moreover, the species may take some time to come to the knowledge of the average bird-dealer. However, those in the cage-birds trade suddenly recognize the existence of a species that might command good prices because it is rare in zoological gardens or private collections. Quickly, then, the birds are obtained and advertised, and come to be in considerable demand. As the demand grows, so more and more of the (almost inevitably) unscrupulous local trappers seek specimens. The usual heavy losses occur, not only in the catching but also during transportation to zoos, aviculturists, and shops; and at once the species is in grave danger of extinction.

All this appears to be precisely what is happening to Rothschild's starling, a bird that has a very restricted distribution on the one island of Bali (about 2,000 square miles), in Indonesia. The species was not described until 1912, and the Bubunan area on the island's northern coast, where the original type specimen was collected, seems to be the zone wherein it is still localized.

Rothschild's starlings *N. W. Cusa* 1966

is likely to prove excessive. In mid-1965 exactly 100 were reported in twenty-six zoos. Unfortunately these starlings do not yet appear on the local list of protected birds, but it is reported that one proclaimed nature reserve affords protection to part of their natural habitat. Rothschild's starling is an unusual and interesting species, the only one in its genus, which is classified as being very close to that of the typical mynahs. Fortunately the avicultural population, doubtless far greater than the purely zoo population, gives us some hope of a zoo bank. The species was first bred in captivity in 1931 in the late Alfred Ezra's private collection in England; and, of the 100 zoo birds in 1965, nineteen had been reared in captivity.

Until very recently the birds were described as quite abundant in this particular locality; but so many have lately been appearing in the hands of bird-dealers that the present population drain

---

Family Callaeidae, wattled crows

SADDLEBACK *or* TIEKE
Creadion carunculatus

New Zealand has three surviving families of birds all its own – the kiwis, the New Zealand wrens (p. 268), and the Callaeidae or "wattled crows", which consist of three genera in the historical fauna, each with one species. In spite of rumours to the contrary, one of these, the extraordinary huia, *Heteralocha acutirostris*, of North Island, became extinct in about 1907. The other two, as we shall see, are relict survivors.

The two living Callaeids are often called by their Maori names *tieke* and *kokako*. Most New Zealanders simply call them crows. But saddleback is a good name for the tieke: although the bird's plumage is mostly glossy black, its mantle is dark chestnut. Its face wattle is reddish-orange.

The North Island race of saddleback, *C. c. rufusater*, first discovered by Europeans at the Bay of Islands in 1722, was widespread in the days of early colonization, but had disappeared on the mainland north of the lower Waikato by 1870 and from all inhabited parts by 1907. There are reports of mainland birds surviving until 1935, but these are unconfirmed. The later strongholds were on coastal islands, but the last birds seem to have been killed off by cats on Little Barrier Island before 1900, and in the

present century its only headquarters has been Hen Island, or Taranga (1,775 acres), at the mouth of Hauraki Gulf. Here it has always been abundant, and has increased from between 300 and 500 birds in 1939 to at least 1,600 and probably over 2,000 in 1963 in a habitat practically untouched by man. Since 1925 various experiments have been made in the translocation of saddlebacks from Taranga to other islands, including Kapiti (a failure), a recolonization of Little Barrier (which also failed), and a trial on Big Chicken, or Marotiri, in 1950 (a third failure). But in 1965 twenty-two birds were seen with seven young ones on Middle Chicken, or Whakahau (168 acres), where twenty-three had been introduced the same spring (1964). And for the first time this race also bred in captivity in 1965, in Mount Bruce Native Bird Reserve.

The story of the South Island saddleback, *C. c. carunculatus*, reads in much the same way. It was discovered by Forster in Queen Charlotte's Sound on Cook's second expedition, in 1773 or 1774, and was widespread from there through the main island to Stewart Island in early European times. By 1890 it was still thriving at least in Fiordland on South Island; but after then the remaining mainland population quickly disappeared, as soon also did the population on

Stewart Island. By the early 1930s it was confined, like the northern birds, to small islands – in particular, and perhaps solely, to Solomon and Big South Cape islands off the south-west coast of Stewart Island. Both these islands became infested with rats in the 1960s. On Solomon, where about 200 birds were estimated in the nesting season of 1931, only about twenty birds were present in 1965. On Big South Cape the population, strong in 1961, was also down in 1965. Fortunately, birds were translocated from Big South Cape to Stage Island and another Stewart outlier, Kaimohu, in 1964, and were already breeding on both islands in 1965; and in July 1965 thirty more saddlebacks were caught on Big South Cape and freed on the Inner Chetwode Islands in Cook Strait near where Forster discovered the race. But the future of the southern saddleback seems disturbingly unsafe since the rats invaded its last natural stronghold, despite the protection of law and the energetic translocation experiments of the New Zealand Wildlife Service.

KOKAKO
Callaeas cinerea

Of the handsome kokako there are two subspecies, one, *C. c. wilsoni*, in North Island, the other, *C. c. cinerea*, in South Island; and, although both are now rare, the second is the nearer to extinction.

The kokakos show the same pattern of retreat as the saddlebacks, though their disaster has not been so great. The North Island race, discovered at the River Thames in 1835, was soon found to be widespread in the early days of Europeanization, and has withdrawn in range during it to the remoter parts of the island's interior. Here, though scattered, fair populations were surviving, some quite well, in over fifteen areas, some of which, for instance in North Auckland, were places where the race was reported extinct as long ago as 1900. This still wide distribution is comforting, despite its clearly relict pattern.

The South Island form is not surviving by any means so well. Discovered first by Forster on Cook's second expedition of 1773 in Dusky Sound, and found early to have a more or less island-wide distribution, in places common, it was already scattered and rare by 1889, and by the 1940s was collapsing fast: it disappeared from Stewart Island at that time, and has been reported only a few times in the last two decades; in 1946 at the head of Lake Monowai in Southland, in 1954 or 1955 at Mokihinui in Nelson (unconfirmed), in 1958 in the Wilkin Valley at the head of Lake Wanaka in north-west Otago, in 1961 on the Nelson slope of the Maungatapu Saddle, in 1962 near Havelock in Marlborough (unconfirmed), and also in the 1960s near Picton. If the unconfirmed records are subsequently backed by new sightings in the same areas, the pattern will still be one of a race in wide but last-ditch relict scatter, more probably as the result of predation by introduced stoats and other predators than from the destruction of habitat.

It will be a tragedy if these attractive birds cannot regain their former status, because they are often confiding towards human beings, and utter pleasing, flute-like notes. Their song in the breeding season has been described as among the best heard in New Zealand. They are a uniform dark bluish-grey, with a black band from nostrils to eye; and they have conspicuous face wattles, orange with a blue base on the South Island bird, but all blue on the North Island one.

Family Corvidae: crows

HAWAIIAN CROW
Corvus tropicus

Hawaii's native crows were doubtless sailing and harshly cawing overhead when Captain Cook was killed by the Hawaiians in Kaawaloa Cove in 1779. Their ancient beat was on the western, drier side of Hawaii, the biggest island of the Hawaiian archipelago – and there is no evidence that they have ever (since the Europeans first came to the islands the year before) been found anywhere else but on Hawaii's Kona coast; that is, along the 75 miles or more from Puuwaawa to Kau, on the forested slopes from 1,000 to 8,000 feet on the sides of Hulalai (8,269 feet) and the western and south-western lava flows of great Mauna Loa.

Hawaiian crow *N. W. Cusa* 1966

From all accounts, the native crows were numerous until farmers moved up the slopes in the early 1890s, cleared forest, and waged direct war on birds they considered vermin. George C. Munro, Hawaii's bird historian whose field studies covered the Kona coast from 1891 to 1937, found little change during that period in the crows' gross range, but a great reduction in their numbers. Common in flocks in 1891 all over, they could muster only a few scattered individuals in the Kau and Puuwaawa forests at the time of the 1936-7 bird survey. In the present decade a further collapse causes real concern to all, and to the Hawaii Audubon Society in particular; William V. Ward, who made the first tape-recording of the crow in August 1961, believed that there were then very few (twenty-five to fifty) birds. A recent population estimate, confirmed by W. M. Ord and David Woodside, is of about (and probably at least) 250 birds, however. In 1965 Dillon Ripley reported that the birds were scarce on the north Kona coast, where formerly it was possible to see fourteen to twenty-four in a day on the Dillingham Ranch alone.

Unfortunately the crow's range is outside the national park in south-eastern Hawaii, though it is fairly well protected in the Puuwaawa-Kau lava-flow areas of private ranchland. But protection, now legal, is still hard to enforce in places, and the dedication of some tracts of the remaining dry hill forests of the west, as reserves for this and other fauna and flora, seems essential.

Family Troglodytidae: wrens

WREN
Troglodytes troglodytes
(some island races)

The wren family is of American origin, and the familiar European jenny wren (which the North Americans call the winter wren) is the only member of it whose range extends into the Old World. It doubtless colonized the Old World via the Bering Straits or the Aleutian Islands (where a chain of races now lives), spreading west to reach, eventually, the remotest outlying islands of western Europe – Britain, Ireland, the Outer Hebrides, St Kilda, Shetland, Faeroe, and even Iceland. This may have happened in the Pleistocene period, and everywhere the birds have settled more or less as residents. Isolated populations, particularly those on islands, have tended to form good races; and indeed thirty-five races of the species are at present accepted.

Some of the island wren populations accepted as valid races are small enough for the Red Data Book, even though their present size may be well adjusted to the carrying capacity of their isolated homes. On St Kilda, the remotest archipelago of the British Isles, whose three larger islands and two great towering stacks provide most of its 2,107 acres, the native wren, first described as a full species (*Troglodytes hirtensis*) by Henry Seebohm in 1884, has ever since excited the interest of ornithologists and conservationists. Early in the present century W. H. Hudson announced its extinction – which, like Mark Twain's death, was somewhat exaggerated. Despite the urgent work of egg-collectors in those days, most of the St Kilda wrens live and nest in such inaccessible places on the towering cliff-sides and puffin slopes of St Kilda (some are $\frac{1}{4}$ mile high) that even the most ruthless zoologist could never find them.

St Kilda wren *N. W. Cusa* 1966

In fact the most thorough count of a big sample of the St Kilda wren population, which was made by Kenneth Williamson in 1957, gives us an estimate of not fewer than 460 breeding birds in the whole archipelago. There have been many previous sample counts, in which one of the present writers took part in 1939, and the pattern of fluctuation that emerges seems quite normal for a population on an island where the climate in no two seasons is quite the same. The St Kilda wren, as Williamson correctly concludes, "is in an extremely healthy and flourishing state". St Kilda is extremely inaccessible, and is a rigidly wardened national nature reserve; and these facts are certainly no hindrance to its continued survival.

Though the Fair Isle, the southernmost island of Shetland, is almost exactly the same size as the combined St Kilda archipelago, so different is the carrying capacity of the land that the population of the native race was counted, also by Williamson in 1957, as ninety-eight breeding birds, or less than a quarter of St Kilda's. Williamson himself discovered the racial status of the Fair Isle wren, which he named *Troglodytes troglodytes fridariensis* in 1957, during his long period of office as director of the finest bird observatory in Europe. It is limited in habitat (like many island wrens in the boreal zone) by being almost exclusively a bird of the steep cliffs and rocky inlets. Quite simply, St Kilda has at least five times as much of this habitat as the Fair Isle.

The Fair Isle wren's population, according to

Williamson, fluctuates between the narrow limits of ninety to a hundred breeding birds. Even if it is a world population of a subspecies, it seems to be in no predictable danger on this island, which is virtually a wardened sanctuary of the National Trust for Scotland as well as the home of a bird observatory.

However, some island forms of the wren may need watching. The isolated Pribilof Islands in the Bering Sea, for example, have a race, *T. t. alascensis*, on their two main islands, St Paul and St George, and the population seems variable and very low on the former, less low on the latter, and certainly needs further investigation on both by the custodian of the islands, the United States Fish and Wildlife Service. Lately the form on Copper Island, the lesser of the two Komandorski Islands off Kamchatka, has been referred to this race. All small island races need a scientific population survey from time to time – which is perhaps the only moral of this essay, apart from its demonstration that a small world population, tuned to an unchanging habitat, can be stable, viable, and safe.

HOUSE WREN
Troglodytes aedon
(some island races)

The house wren, one of the most familiar wrens of the Americas, has a vast distribution all the mainland way from southern Canada to Tierra del Fuego, and has almost as many recognized subspecies as the jenny wren – to be precise, thirty-one. Of these, eleven are confined to islands or island groups; and some of them really do appear to be in danger of extinction. In fact, two already are extinct.

The Clarión house wren, *T. a. tanneri*, is confined to the small Isla Clarión, in the rather isolated Revillagigedo archipelago, nearly 600 miles off the west coast of Mexico. The bigger Isla Cozumel, off Quintana Roo on the east coast of Mexico, has *T. a. beani*. *T. a. carychrous* lives on the middle-sized Isla Coiba, off Veraguas, south-west Panama. Down in the south Atlantic the outlying, big Falklands archipelago has *T. a. cobbi*. There is no evidence that any of these races is in danger, though the Clarión wren should be watched. It is in the Lesser Antilles, the theatre of the only excursion of the species into the West Indies, that a group of races has a past and present survival story.

Apart from the Zapata wren, *Ferminia cerverai*, which was discovered thirty years ago in Cuba's Zapata Swamp, to which it appears to be confined and where it is common (though in the Red Data Book as a precaution), there is no member of the wren family at all in the whole West Indies, except for the house wrens of the Lesser Antilles, Tobago, and Trinidad, and migrants of this species from North America reported from Cuba and the Bahamas. The wren family, though successful, has hardly "discovered" the West Indies, in the evolutionary sense. Judging by the Antillean distribution, the main wren colonization, as far as it has gone, has been from the south – that is, from the direction of Trinidad, which at present shares a widespread race, *T. a. albicans*, with the eastern South American mainland all the way down to southern Brazil. North of Trinidad there is, or was, a chain of races that is worth examining from south to north, with the help of the researches of James Bond in particular.

Tobago

T. a. tobagensis is abundant and in no danger of extinction.

Grenada

More of a "house wren" here than in the rest of the Lesser Antilles, *T. a. grenadensis* is not uncommon, and is widely distributed both in the inhabited lowlands and the mountain forest.

St Vincent

A quarter of a century ago *T. a. musicus* was widely distributed, at least in the lowlands, of both the leeward and windward coasts, and was common in the ravines around the base of the Soufrière. Now it is localized and scarce, with full status in the Red Data Book.

St Lucia

Now exceedingly rare, the St Lucia house wren, *T. a. mesoleucus*, has, for nearly two decades, been apparently confined to the neighbourhood of Le Marquis and Petite Anse, below

St Vincent house wren *Albert E. Gilbert* 1966

Morne la Sorcière on the windward coast. The race, which may even be extinct, needless to say has full status in the Red Data Book.

Martinique

Already probably rare in 1879, the last specimen of *T. a. martinicensis* was taken in 1886, since when it has been neither seen nor heard, and is regarded as extinct.

Dominica

T. a. rufescens is still common and widespread in this island, and in no danger of extinction.

Guadeloupe

When first discovered in 1878 this race, *T. a. guadeloupensis*, was already very local and usually found only in secondary woodland growth in the hills. The last specimen was collected in 1914 near Sainte Rose. Despite searches by experienced ornithologists in 1924, 1930, 1937, and more lately, it has never been seen or heard since 1914, and is presumed extinct.

The exception of Dominica suggests a rule that there is a gradient in the house wren's vulnerability from the presumed newer to the older-colonized islands. In Dominica, as in Grenada, the house wren seems to have adapted itself to suburban life during the forest clearance and can now survive in their densely populated lowlands – just as it survives well in the commuter belt of so many North American cities. In the rest of the islands it has probably become reduced by the forest clearance, but has maybe also suffered acutely from the predations of introduced mongooses and rats, and perhaps, in St Lucia, the large native boa *Constrictor orophias*. Its success in Dominica is also interesting because this island is mongoose-free. As far as we know, no legal or material protection is given to the relict populations in St Vincent and St Lucia.

Family Mimidae: mockers and thrashers

MARTINIQUE BROWN TREMBLER
Cinclocerthia ruficauda gutturalis

This species, the sole member of its genus, is peculiar to the Lesser Antillean chain from Saba to St Vincent, whence six races have been acceptably described. Those on Guadeloupe (including Grande Terre), Dominica, St Lucia, and St Vincent are now at least not uncommon, and in most cases common in the mountain forests and in no apparent danger of extinction. However, the most northerly race, *C. r. pavida*, is perhaps becoming relict. It is now confined to the higher points of Saba Island, where it is not uncommon; on St Eustatius it is rare, though lately recorded from the "Quill"; on Nevis it is still numerous on Nevis Peak; it is rare on St Christopher, where it was perhaps confined to Mount Misery; and it is moderately common in forested areas of Montserrat, the only other island of its old, known range – for its existence on Barbuda is very doubtful.

The Martinique brown trembler seems to be in a much worse state than this, and has full status in the Red Data Book. *C. r. gutturalis* was formerly confined to and common on its island, but as early as 1879 was known to be pursued by gunners and becoming local. By the 1930s energetic ornithologists could hunt in vain for it; and by 1951 the best that James Bond could write of it was that it was "still fairly common . . . in the southern half of Martinique (e.g. near Trois-Ilets), and one was collected in 1949 at the base of the Pitons du Carbet". It was able to survive the continued rain-forest clearance for sugar-cane and the hunting of rat or mongoose on this island to early 1964, when a very few localized pairs were reported by H. G. Dowling: later in the same season he could not find any. Despite international representations, no attempt has yet been made to give it legal or administrative protection.

WHITE-BREASTED THRASHER
Ramphocinclus brachyurus

The white-breasted thrasher, sometimes known as the white-breasted trembler because it may also "tremble", though not really like the brown trembler, forms – like that other bird – a Lesser Antillean species in a genus all its own. The two genera are, indeed, markedly different from any other mockers or thrashers, and are obvious relics of an old evolutionary line; no two authorities agree about their nearest living relatives, though they are quite close to each other.

When science discovered the white-breasted thrasher in the nineteenth century, the species was living on Martinique and St Lucia only. The populations are racially distinct. On Martinique, *R. b. brachyurus* was not uncommon about the time of its naming in 1818, and widespread. But a specimen taken in the Presque-île de la Caravelle in 1886 was the last heard of it for many years, and it was, indeed, thought to be extinct. However, James Bond was told by an old woodman in about 1930 that the *gorge-blanche* survived on the slopes of Mont Pelée in the days of his youth – presumably before the violent eruption of 1902; and a very small population was rediscovered on the Caravelle isthmus in 1950, when a specimen was taken on the 15th June; and Dr Bond saw a pair there in 1966.

R. b. sanctaeluciae of St Lucia was fairly numerous about the time of its first description in 1886, but was rare, local, and confined to the north-east by 1927, when a group was found in the scrub woods between Castries and Le Marquis. By 1932 it may have been confined to the area east of Morne la Sorcière, in a lowland region around De Barra and Grande Anse. It was reported again in 1961, but now must have a tiny population, though it has lately been found on the Morne above Castries. Protective measures seem essential for this dying species of high scientific interest. Largely terrestrial, the white-breasted thrasher may be even more seriously threatened by introduced predators than by the wood- and scrub-clearance in some parts of Martinique and St Lucia.

Family Pycnonotidae: bulbuls

DAPPLED BULBUL
Phyllastrephus orostruthus

In the evergreen mountain rain forests of the higher altitudes in tropical and subtropical Africa, many of the birds live in the forest canopy. The bird observer or collector working under such conditions has few opportunities to see or get to know his subjects. Indeed, his knowledge of many will for a long time be limited to dim shapes glimpsed in silhouette as they bustle through the highest foliage.

Often they are silent, but sometimes they carry on an indefinite low chattering, and always there are parties of several species feeding together; it is often difficult, if not impossible, to single out individuals.

In 1932 there was a first ornithological exploration of Namuli Mountain in northern Mozambique, a large "island" massif, rising to over 8,000 feet above the monotone of *Brachystegia* woodland. On this mountain the grassy slopes of the lower levels peter out at about 4,500 feet, and above them are steep-sided ridges and gullies clothed with dense, moist forests of big timber. The bird parties moving about in the canopy of this gallery forest always include many bulbuls, and identification is made more difficult by the fact that representatives of at least four species are usually mixed up together. The four concerned are the yellow-streaked bulbul, *Phyllastrephus flavostriatus*; the olive greenbul, *P. fischeri*; the mountain greenbul, *Arizelocichla nigriceps*; and the stripe-cheeked greenbul, *A. milanjensis*. If these parties move down to the lower forest storey in their foragings, they are joined by yet a fifth species, the little green bulbul, *Eurillas virens*.

From one of these mixed parties of bulbuls and other species a bird was collected in August 1932, which was quite unlike any bulbul previously obtained, and this became the type specimen of a new species named *Phyllastrephus orostruthus*. Because of the very unusual olive-green spotting on its pale yellow breast, the bird was given the vernacular name of dappled mountain bulbul, although its author at the time expressed disapproval of such compound names, which, though clumsy, are in common use. As he said, it is unfortunate that no one nowadays has the courage to coin short, acceptable terms such as robin, martin, and swallow. He wished to call the new bird the "dappul", as being an entirely suitable name for a bulbul with such exceptional characteristics, but the editor of the journal in which the bird was described preferred a more conservative approach.

One other example of the same species was seen on Namuli Mountain, but nothing like it was noted again until three years later, when another single individual was obtained, over 700 miles further north, in the Amani Forest of the Usambara Mountains in Tanzania. This is the type of a rather brighter coloured subspecies; and, remarkably, it was collected in a patch of forest where, for various reasons, dozens of other bulbuls had been obtained over a period of years. The fact that no individual of this species had been seen in all that time gives some indication of its rarity. As the collector said (and he had been living in the neighbourhood for more than five years), if the bird had not been extremely rare he should by the law of averages have seen it earlier. Since those first collectings of the two subspecies, in 1932 and 1935, the southern bird has not been seen again by anyone, and the northern one only by a collector who obtained another four examples thirty years later in the area of the type locality, in the Usambara Mountains. Both races have an unusually clear and liquid, robin-like song; beyond this nothing is known of the biology of this bulbul. Perhaps the species, although rare, is not yet truly endangered.

OLIVACEOUS BULBUL
Hypsipetes borbonicus

In many people's minds, the two Indian Ocean islands of La Réunion (also called the Ile de Bourbon) and Mauritius are associated with what may be described as the beginnings of the extinction of bird species. The former, which has been a French possession since 1643, lost its dodo-like bird, the solitaire, in 1746; and Mauritius – which was held by the Dutch from 1638 to 1710, and by the French from 1715 to 1810, when it became British – lost the last of its famous dodos in 1681. It can certainly be said that the Mauritian dodo is the epitome of all extinct animals. "As dead as the dodo" is now a figure of speech; the dodo, however, was no imaginary bird, but a magnificent flightless one belonging to a group or family, classified as very closely related to the pigeons and doves (and, by one late authority, perhaps to the rails). It may be mentioned in passing that the island dependency of Mauritius, Rodriguez (40 square miles), also had its own solitaire species, which became extinct in 1791.

At present both Réunion and Mauritius have rather better records for their endangered birds than an immense number of other islands about the world. Both at present have some rare birds, but few seem to be in immediate danger of extinction, and, if any are, they have become so perhaps more through natural calamities than through the actions of the inhabitants.

On both islands, one of the rarest birds is the olivaceous bulbul, of which each has its distinctive subspecies, differing slightly in colouration. The "typical" race, *H. b. borbonicus*, lives on Réunion: the present writers have no estimate of its population, but do know that it must be very small. Records disclose that there has been some destruction of the birds by poachers and trappers using guns and birdlime, but the greatest damage to the population was undoubtedly brought about by the cyclone of 1948; after this but one was seen in a long search in 1951. There seems to have been a recent recovery, however, for the birds were noticeably increasing in the more inaccessible forest in 1964, and were described as actually common in the forests in 1966.

The Mauritius subspecies, *H. b. olivaceus*, is also rare and local; indeed, it is probably now the rarer of the two. Even as long ago as 1912, its population was considered dangerously small, and, although cyclones may have been a factor in its decline, it must regrettably be admitted that the destruction of original forest by human beings must have contributed a great deal.

The island of Mauritius was once covered with thick forest, but at present little more than 20 per cent of it remains woodland, and the area in which this bulbul – or merle, as it is locally called – can now exist is limited. On Réunion the position is a little better, because much of the island is still densely forested and very inaccessible. The birds have recently been given legal protection, and some recovery will be assisted by the fact that part of their habitat has been established as a strict nature reserve. They keep to the damp and forested areas, and do not seem to descend below 3,300 feet on the leeward side of the island, although they wander a good deal lower on the windward side; very little, apparently, has yet been recorded of their biology or breeding. Although these birds are classified as bulbuls, some of the few notes that we have of their rather furtive habits suggest that, when observed in the field, they give the impression of being very thrush-like. They are about the size of a true thrush, and are similarly brown above and paler below, with orange bill and legs. The few whistled notes that have been described are also melodious and thrush-like, and are not likely to be associated with the somewhat more raucous but gay notes generally heard from the bulbuls.

PLATE 25 (*a*) White-breasted thrasher; (*b*) Martinique brown trembler; (*c*) Rufous-headed robin; (*d*) Mauritius olivaceous bulbul; (*e*) Dappled bulbul *Robert Gillmor* 1966

(a)

(b)

(c)

(d)

(e)

(a)

(b)

(c)

(d)

GILBERT

Family Muscicapidae
Subfamily Turdinae: thrushes

RUFOUS-HEADED ROBIN
Erithacus ruficeps

Some sixty years ago – in 1905, to be precise – Japanese bird collectors working in the ever-green original mountain rain forest, among the mist-shrouded peaks of the Tsinling Mountains, in Shensi Province, west central China, obtained three specimens. Their skins were sent to Lord Rothschild at the Tring Museum in Hertfordshire, England, where in 1907 the birds were described by Hartert in the *Bulletin of the British Ornithologists' Club* and first given the name quoted above. Those three specimens remain the only examples of the species ever to have reached any museum, and no one saw the rufous-headed robin again, or even heard of it, for another fifty-eight years.

On the 15th March 1963 Dr Elliot McClure, an ornithologist living in Malaya, set his mist-nets in the shrub growth around a radio relay station on the summit of Mount Brinchang, at about 6,600 feet above sea-level. This peak is in Malaya's Cameron Highlands, and Dr McClure's surprise can be imagined when an inspection of his nets on that evening revealed that he had captured quite a beautiful little bird, undoubtedly belonging to the thrush family, but not like any of its representatives that he had ever seen or read about before.

Dusk had fallen, and Dr McClure – although he did not wish to destroy this unique bird – happily appreciated the importance of identification and record. He therefore kept the bird in a cage overnight, and, although he released it into the forest again in the morning, this was not done before it had been colour-photographed when held in the hand. Fortunately the photograph was an entire success, and it has been reproduced, with an account of the discovery, in the *Malayan Nature Journal*.

PLATE 26 (*a*) Hawaiian thrush, Kauai race; (*b*) Omao; (*c*) Teita olive thrush; (*d*) Grand Cayman thrush *Albert E. Gilbert* 1966

Because the Cameron Highlands are so many hundreds of miles from Tai-pai-sham, the type locality of *Erithacus ruficeps* in China, the identity of the photographed bird was not even suspected; and its description was sent to prominent ornithologists in America and Britain for their opinion.

The bird was just over 5 inches long, with a wing of 3 inches, and was a pleasing slaty grey on its back and breast with a broad black stripe below its eye and encircling its white throat, but with a striking orange-red head-top and neck. The description circulated enabled one of the ornithologists to guess correctly the identity of this beautiful and remarkable little bird; and the photograph stands (alongside the three skins, which are now in the American Museum of Natural History, New York, which purchased Lord Rothschild's Tring collections) as the fourth record of it.

The Japanese collectors of 1905 left no record of the habits of the rufous-headed robin, or of the circumstances under which they secured their birds. The world, in fact, knows nothing whatever about the biology of the species – not even whether it is found abundantly in the Tsinling Mountains, whether it is obtrusive in its habits, or whether it sings at all sweetly like its near relations the redstarts and others.

A pleasant surprise awaits the first ornithologist who is lucky enough to explore this particular locality in China, and factual information about the rufous-headed robin will certainly not be the only prize that he will bring back.

The utter lack of knowledge of this species makes clear the desperate need for investigation of many little-known areas of the world, and for precise status surveys of an immense number of apparently rare birds. It may be a misrepresentation to describe this robin as rare, and it may be an exaggeration to suggest that it is endangered. It is merely one among a vast assemblage of birds that are presumed to be rare merely because they are known from so few specimens or records. Hardly anyone can appreciate how many such birds exist; if the list were to include those that (like this robin) are known from three or four specimens, the total would be immense. Even those species known from a single example would fill several pages.

SEYCHELLES MAGPIE ROBIN
Copsychus sechellarum

The population of this gay, confiding little thrush-sized songster has become so small that only the very greatest fears can now be expressed for its survival. It will be a tragedy if it is allowed to become extinct; and the story of its gradual disappearance is an indictment of the lack of attention given to the conservation of bird life in the Seychelles islands, and the absence of control over a great deal of indiscriminate destruction by human beings.

A hundred years ago the *pie chanteuse* – as this steel-blue bird with conspicuous white wing coverts is locally called – was reported as being common on the islands of Marianne, La Digue, and Félicité, although becoming rather scarce on the large island of Mahé. It was for long recorded also on Aride, Frégate, Praslin, and Silhouette; and about the 1930s it was introduced into the island of Alphonse, which lies some 250 miles to the south-west of the Seychelles group. Gradually its range has shrunk. By 1940 the bird had disappeared from Aride and Marianne, and had become so rare elsewhere that for a time Alphonse was considered its main stronghold – although by 1962 it was so depleted even there that only one bird could be found. Since then the species has gone completely from all of the islands in which it formerly existed, and it now appears to survive only on the small island of Frégate, whence the latest available information puts the total population as being down to a mere twelve birds. As recently as 1960, repeated checks on Frégate estimated the survivors as numbering ten pairs or twenty individuals; the decline thus continues to be extremely disturbing.

Man alone is to blame for the disappearance of this bird, mostly because of his introduction of cats and rats to the Seychelles islands, but in part also because children and others have been allowed to kill the birds with catapults or by any other means. In 1960 the remaining twenty birds were said to be healthy and doing well, but fear was expressed that cats, which were noticeably increasing on the island, would prove to be a serious threat.

More recently, over fifty cats on Frégate have been destroyed on the initiative of the island's owner, who is very much concerned about the survival of the birds. It was hoped that this action would increase the robin's chances of survival, but its numbers still go down, and only the most rigorous and immediate protective measures can now save it.

It has been suggested that environmental changes are responsible for the widespread decrease in the *pie*'s populations, brought about by increased cultivation and planting of coconut palms. But this supposition became difficult to maintain when the birds thrived so well after their introduction into Alphonse Island, and there is little doubt that predation by human beings and undesirable exotic mammals is in fact solely to blame.

Seychelles magpie robin *Rena M. Fennessy* 1966

A recent suggestion is that two introduced bird species may also be having an adverse effect on the magpie robin's chances of survival – the Indian mynah, because of its direct competition for available food supplies; and the cattle egret, which is suspected of physical predation. The population of the latter was said in 1965 to have grown to about 100 birds from an original introduction of four individuals, brought to the island to compete with insect plagues. The author concerned stated that the egrets have dealt effectively with some of the insects, but do not seem to mind supplementing their diet with warm-blooded animals. He described how he had watched a cattle egret take a fairy tern chick from its nest in a tree.

It is tragic that the confiding nature of this little magpie robin, which ought to be appreciated by all those fortunate enough to have it with them, should have contributed towards its downfall. With typically robin-like movements (that is, with their tails usually carried at a jaunty upward angle), the *pies* spend much of their time feeding on the ground, and they are not averse to continuing their search for food very close to buildings. Generally, however, they prefer bushy undergrowth, where they like to scuffle about beneath the trees, particularly among the fallen leaves.

They have an agreeable habit of slowly lowering the expanded tail before jerking it up high over the back again. Attractive courtship behaviour has also been described: the birds, poised with fluffed-out plumage, wings and tails drooping to the ground and beaks pointing skywards, slowly undulate their heads from side to side.

The food of the magpie robins consists largely of insects of all kinds, but it is stated that they also have a liking for small lizards.

This bird is yet another example of an interesting island species that is sliding into extinction for entirely avoidable reasons, and before the world has had time to learn much of its biology. The nest of the Seychelles magpie robin must often have been seen and watched, yet there do not seem to be more than the briefest accounts of it. One nest was taken from the base of a coconut palm leaf frond and described as an untidy bundle of dry coconut fibres, in the centre of which a neat cup of finer grass and other material measured about 4 inches in diameter and $2\frac{1}{2}$ inches deep. Another author stated that the nests were generally an untidy collection of roots and leaves, which might even include paper and feathers, but he, too, stressed the neatness of the inner cup.

As for the eggs, it is said that only two of them form a clutch, and it seems that there is still no reliable account showing their precise colour or measurement. In one case a single nest only was found with eggs, and these were said to be plain white; in another instance the eggs were said to be blue.

There are altogether seven other species of the genus *Copsychus*, one of them existing in Madagascar, and all the other six in Asia, from India to the Philippines.

CEBÚ BLACK SHAMA
Copsychus niger cebuensis

There are two subspecies of the black shama, both of them found in the Philippine Islands: the "typical" race, *C. n. niger*, which exists (in no danger so far) on the islands of Balabac, Calamianes, and Palawan; and this, *C. n. cebuensis*, which is restricted to Cebú and is extremely localized there. Without doubt it was much more widespread on the same island even until quite recently, but now it is very rare indeed, and, although there is no estimate of the population numbers, they must be very low, because an expedition that sought the birds in 1956 saw only one example, and this, unfortunately, was collected.

The Cebú black shama is a bird that favours the dense thickets of original or undisturbed forest, and, although it has been seen in some very dense second growth, it is generally not a species that will stand, or in any way cares for, interference with its forest habitat. There is another shama, a different species of the same genus living on Cebú Island, that is far more numerous, apparently because it has succeeded in adapting itself to all kinds of exotic or man-made cover, such as second growth of any form, hedges around cultivated fields, bamboo thickets, and gardens. For this reason it is a very common bird; and, unless the Cebú black shama is quite soon to become extinct (and indeed it may already have disappeared), it too must quickly learn to live in an exotic or degraded habitat.

Birds of the Philippine Islands in general, and of Cebú in particular, will indeed have to adapt themselves to human proximity if they are to survive at all. Any species there that remains too demanding in its requirements can have little hope for the future, because in few other places can the forests have so widely disappeared.

Although Cebú is one of the ten large islands of the Philippine archipelago, with a total area of about 1,700 square miles, it has long been one of the most densely populated. To begin with, a great deal of original forest was left alone, because the population grew little more than rice, and that on the coastal plain. But, with the arrival of grain and root crops, cultivation spread inland, and, because Cebú does not rise to any great height, the spread was almost general, and the forests were gradually cut down to satisfy man's hunger and greed. Naturally the position was helped by the shameful practice known as shifting cultivation – of planting a few annual crops until the fertility of the soil is exhausted, and then moving on to repeat the wasteful process elsewhere. Finally, the human populations themselves began to expand: and now there are few if any relict patches in which the forest birds can eke out a precarious existence. Collectors even as long ago as 1906 reported great difficulty in finding any such cover.

Before the Second World War, there were signs that the local Department of Forestry would save some birds' lives by means of their reforestation programme on Cebú Island, where large acreages were being restored. But by 1945 the humans had cleared all the ground again and had extended the depredations elsewhere. Although the foresters are now working once more, it is almost certain that their efforts have come too late to save all the birds and more species will perish than most people realize.

Any summary of the prospects facing the Cebú black shama must point to the permanent disappearance of the subspecies; and, although it is fortunate that the other race is still found on three islands of the archipelago, the better preservation of its forest habitat must be considered, lest it should follow the same course.

The *Copsychus* thrushes belong to a genus that contains eight species, and two of them have the unusually large number of seventeen races each. Their ranges are similar, one extending from the Andaman Islands across India to China and Malaysia and as far east as the Philippines, and the other from Ceylon as far east as Java.

STARCHY
Nesocichla eremita

Much has been written about the probable origin of the land birds of the Tristan da Cunha group of islands, which lie on what is known as the mid-Atlantic ridge and, roughly speaking, midway between the southern tips of Africa and South America. Evidence points to colonization from South America (though a few of the indigenes have probable African affinities); but the matter is uncertain. During some thousands of years, while the distinctive differences between the island forms developed, there may have been no tendency for wandering among the resident land birds. There is no record that any subspecies has been wind-driven from one island to another, although the distances involved are quite small.

Even today, on Tristan da Cunha, examples are constantly found of the American purple gallinule, *Porphyrula martinica*, which have finished up as far away as 37°15′ S. and 12°30′ W. in their attempted migrations about North America or the West Indies. Of course these birds arrive at Tristan sadly emaciated; there are six records that they have reached even as far as the Cape Province of South Africa.

Certainly the origin of most Tristan da Cunha land birds is not to be found in Africa, and this typical thrush, known as the starchy, or hermit thrush, has no very close relations there. It behaves like most other thrushes, but shows no liking for trees or woodlands, although it has been said to have features in common with a forest-dwelling West Indies species. The claim has been made that it is more closely associated with the bird of the *Turdus* genus that exists in the Falkland Islands and Tierra del Fuego.

Not only is the ancestral origin of the Tristan starchy a matter for conjecture, the meaning of the name starchy is also unknown. But, as one account of the birds of the Tristan group points out, the name "gives some impression of the perkiness and sociability of the species".

It seems that the first specimen of a Tristan starchy was collected as long ago as 1816; but, although several bird skins were brought back to England from that early expedition, only two survive and this was not one of them. The expedition concerned was the military one that first took possession of the island. One of its members was a Captain Carmichael, and it was he who collected the birds and wrote a few notes on Tristan's avifauna. His skins were first lodged in a private museum, but this collection was disposed of by public auction in 1819: although a catalogue of the sale has been subsequently published, all the lots have disappeared with

Tristan starchy *Albert E. Gilbert* 1966

one exception. This was Lot 115 of the sale's twentieth day, and consisted of two birds that found their way into the Berlin Museum, where one of them, the Tristan "bunting", was later (in 1873) described by Cabanis. It is also known that Lot 143 of the sale was an "unknown thrush from Tristan da Cunha", but the specimen perished somewhere, and the starchy had to be rediscovered before it was described by Gould in 1855.

There are three subspecies of this thrush, each of them restricted to an island of the group: *N. e. eremita* on the main island of Tristan, *N. e. gordoni* on Inaccessible, and *N. e. procax* on Nightingale. The birds of all of them seem to be quite numerous within the limits of their restricted habitat. No precise or recent estimates of actual numbers are available, but in 1952 the population of the "typical" race on the main island was estimated at between 200 and 400 birds. It is not believed that the birds' status has greatly altered anywhere, at any time.

Birds restricted to islands such as these must always be regarded as to some extent endangered, particularly from introduced predators, and it is known that the birds on the main island are kept much in check by feral cats and rats.

Although typical thrushes in almost every way, these Tristan birds have, not unexpectedly, developed some peculiarities during their long establishment in the group. Perhaps the most marked of these is an adaptation of the tongue

that enables the birds to feed by egg-sucking and to take advantage of nourishment offered by broken and abandoned sea birds' eggs, particularly those of the great shearwaters.

The starchies are inconspicuous birds both in colouration and habits. Not only can they be described as rather plain brown birds, but they are distinctly shy, and largely silent. They have a call, of course, and this is recorded as being a soft chirping, combined with some sibilant, wheezy notes to make up a so-called song. So unobtrusive generally are these thrushes that in the 1920s they were thought to be extinct.

The countryside on Tristan da Cunha, below 2,000 feet, is quite thickly wooded with a juniper-like growth, the woodlands being interspersed with considerable areas of grass cover, particularly the tussocky *Spartina*. Above 2,000 feet are areas of ferns, cranberry, and mosses, and these gradually give way higher up to lichens and bare shale. The thrushes are birds of the tussock-grass localities, where they live for the most part on a plentiful insect supply. Their nests, too, are placed in thick clumps of the *Spartina* a few inches above the ground-level, and are rough cups of grass-stems, tussock-fronds, and a few leaves or bits of moss. Their eggs are described as being pale blue, blotched and speckled with browns and mauves. It is said that, although the birds range up to as high as 4,000 feet, they have not been seen to visit the seashore and can be noticed only occasionally on the cliffs.

THRUSHES OF HAWAII
Genus *Phaeornis*

The Hawaiian thrushes of the genus *Phaeornis* are represented by two species only, the small *P. palmeri*, the omao or puaiohi, found only on Kauai Island, and the larger *P. obscurus*, the "Hawaiian thrush". Of the latter there is the one "typical" race in the main island of Hawaii, *P. o. obscurus*, and another, *P. o. myadestinus*, which (like the small bird) is restricted to Kauai.

The larger bird was earlier represented by three other island subspecies, *P. o. lanaiensis* of Lanai, *P. o. rutha* of Molokai, and *P. o. oahensis* of Oahu, but these were last seen or heard in

1931, 1936, and 1825 respectively, and are considered extinct.

The birds on Lanai seem to have started their decline shortly after Lanai City was built in the mid-1920s and the island's human population increased with extraordinary rapidity. Soon the thrushes had completely disappeared; and it is suggested that introduced poultry diseases may have affected them, as well as the extensive habitat destruction and constant interference. Of the race *P. o. rutha* we have been told very little, and it may have become extinct before 1936; but that year is quoted as the final one, because it was then that a careful search on Molokai, even in the virgin forest areas, failed to reveal any sight or sound of a thrush, though G. C. Munro thought he heard one sing. Rats were seen in the trees, however, and this probably explains why the birds had disappeared. Of the bird of Oahu Island, Munro, in his book on the birds of Hawaii, tells an interesting story. The subspecies is listed as having become extinct in 1825, because that was the year in which the endemic thrush of Oahu was collected by Bloxam, who was naturalist on the ship H.M.S. *Blonde*, which brought the bodies of King Liholiho and Queen Kamamalu from England to Honolulu in 1823. Bloxam mentioned in his 1825 diary that he had collected a brown thrush, the "only songster on the island", but his specimens were later lost, the race became extinct, and there is now no known example of it in any museum.

Of sombre brown plumage and about 7 inches long, the Hawaiian thrushes have characteristic thrushy songs, and their loud, fluty, whistled notes cannot fail to attract attention. As might be expected, immature birds have brown plumage spotted with buff.

Different vernacular names are given to these thrushes on the various islands. It has been suggested that most of them are corruptions of the name *amani*, and that this in turn is shortened from *manu-a-Maui*, meaning a bird of the demigod Maui. It is understandable that such fine songsters should have been dedicated to this Polynesian deity.

Mostly birds of the forest, the thrushes of Hawaii have become both localized and very rare, and their populations seem to be steadily decreasing. It is feared that they must now be in considerable danger of extinction. The prime cause of this position is doubtless the reduction of their forest habitat.

Very little is known about the precise status of the typical race of the larger Hawaiian thrush, and, though it was common in 1891 (at least around the 2,000-foot levels, but scarcer at higher altitudes), only one individual was seen in a 1936–7 survey, on the eastern slope of Mauna Kea. In 1940, however, it was found not to be rare in the neighbourhood of the Hawaii National Park, being recorded as "numerous" in the forest north of the Makaopuhi crater, and less common on Kilauea Volcano and on the slopes of Mauna Loa between 8,000 and 8,500 feet.

The *P. o. myadestinus* race of Kauai is similarly little known and, as with its near relation, very few examples have been seen in the field. It was described in 1887 from specimens collected a few years earlier, and at least we know that the birds were still common in 1899. Concern was first felt when searches carried out in 1928, 1931, and 1932 failed to reveal any trace of the birds, but in 1936 several were found in an area remote from any settlement, at an altitude of about 3,700 feet on the mountain of Kaholua-manu. In 1941 and 1960 the birds were seen to be still thriving in the same area of undisturbed mountain forest habitat, and it was noted that they too had the habit, recorded for the typical race, of flying out into the air on buzzing wings and singing a few loud notes as they returned to a perch.

As for the small omao, also of Kauai, this seems to be the rarest of the three surviving forms. Apparently it has always been endemic to the one island, and, although no doubt formerly found throughout the forested parts, it is now restricted to two quite small areas. The specimen from which the species was originally described in 1893 was for long unique, and it was recovered from a rat that had taken it; the collector returned twice to Kauai in the 1890s but did not succeed in getting another example. The birds are skulking, and in their flight low under the trees are extremely difficult to follow. Though reported by Walter Donaghho in 1940, they were believed extinct in 1950, but were rediscovered in 1960 by Frank Richardson and John Bowles after a massive search of this least deforested of all the Hawaiian Islands. They saw at least fifteen individuals. During four visits between 1962 and 1964 ten birds were recorded; and two were seen on one day in February 1964. It has been suggested that the present population is about thirty birds.

It is most unfortunate that there has still been no exhaustive or detailed study of this vanishing genus, for not only is our knowledge of the status of the birds still rather scanty, but the breeding biology of both species is virtually unknown, and no eggs have ever been recorded. Rumour has it that two broods are reared in a season.

The omao seems always to have been described as rare, but no complete explanation has been put forward for the remarkable decrease in the range and numbers of the "Hawaiian thrush". In the 1890s they were recorded as common on several islands, yet forty years later in some localities their extinction was complete, even in areas where they had formerly been very numerous, and elsewhere reductions were obvious. The decreases have taken place at different times on different islands, and it can only be presumed that in some way the birds are strangely specialized in their habits or feeding, and unable to adapt themselves to changed circumstances, in the way that has been so evident among some Old World thrushes.

Early authors have provided us with a certain number of field notes, but these are incomplete. The feeding habits of the two species do not seem to differ greatly from those of other birds of the family, for they are both frugivorous and insectivorous, favouring the berries of various forest trees and shrubs and also feeding widely on spiders and insects of all kinds – even winged ones, which are said to be caught in fluttering rushes along the ground or dashes into the air. These thrushes have also been reported to like caterpillars: there are records of local incursions by strange birds into new areas in seasons of caterpillar pest. It is often thought that insect-eating birds may reduce the basic population of noxious insects. Whether this is so or not, the thrushes of Hawaii may more certainly contribute to plant colonization and recolonization by scattering seeds about the forest floor because they prefer to swallow berries whole.

The larger species often sings on the wing – a habit unusual in a thrush. The performance usually takes the form of a lavish outburst of notes as the bird flies down into the lower cover from a perch in a tall tree. The smaller species has the same habit at times, although its song is very different and consists of little more than a simple trilling.

We have mentioned that the thrushes on Hawaii are mostly birds of the forest. The reason for this qualification is that on the Hawaiian mountains of Mauna Loa most individuals are to be found in the wet *ohia* forest; but some live on the lava flows between altitudes of about 7,000 and 9,000 feet above sea-level. No reason has been put forward for this very strange choice of such contrasting habitats, and, whereas the forest denizens are said to build their nests at a good height in trees, those on the lava flows are described as building on ledges inside deep, horizontal cracks. Birds of the smaller Kauai species are somewhat different in general habits as well as in their call notes, for they seem restricted to forest: although they go up into larger trees to sing, for much of the time they prefer to stay in the undergrowth, where they perch on the lowest twigs and branches.

TEITA OLIVE THRUSH
Turdus helleri

All over the world, destruction of habitat is continuing rapidly as human populations expand. Wherever human beings take over virgin countryside, one of the first things they seem to do is destroy the original forests, particularly those with big timber. Both in South America and Africa, to name just two of the continents concerned, there has within very recent times been the most appalling eradication of evergreen rain forests. Throughout Africa, mountain forests have suffered in this way, and it is only in the remotest areas that anything remains but the scantiest relict patches; and these are being cut into almost daily.

As far as the larger and more conspicuous mammals are concerned, there have been some extensive measures to ensure their survival by the proclamation of national parks, or equivalent sanctuaries. But the birds do not receive the same consideration; and the gradual thinning out of forest species is becoming increasingly serious to their status. Several bird races at least are now so localized that their status has passed beyond rarity far enough to give cause for anxiety, even though they may not yet have reached the point of mortal danger.

Many African mountain forests have been cut off from each other so long that it is not unusual for the more isolated ones to house distinctive subspecies of wide-ranging birds; the olive thrush, *Turdus olivaceus*, which as a species has a vast range, has many such. In general habits and movements no different from the better-known thrushes of the same genus in Europe, it was first described, from the Cape of Good Hope, by Linnaeus in 1766. Since then ornithological exploration has continued to discover more forms, now held to be races of it; sixteen in all were listed by S. Dillon Ripley in 1964, several of them peculiar to a single mountain range.

The Teita olive thrush has been seen once on Kilimanjaro, at about 6,500 feet; but this bird may have been a straggler, for the form is otherwise known only from four patches of forest on the Teita Hills in southern Kenya, above 5,000 feet, which together do not amount to more than 1,000 acres of suitable habitat. In 1953 two or three birds were seen on Mbololo, in 1964 none could be found on Ngangai, and in 1965 about eight were seen in the Ngangao Forest. It is treated as a distinct species because of its much darker head, and, if not merely a race of the olive thrush, it is certainly a very close relation indeed. The relict forest patches unfortunately lie outside of the Tsavo National Park, which is in the same district. They have been constantly subjected to ruthless cutting for firewood, though in 1965 the District Commissioner said that further reduction of the forest was unlikely. There seems to be most hope for the thrush's future if it also breeds on Kilimanjaro after all. If it does, it must overlap there with a known race of the olive thrush, and its identity as a separate species would be beyond doubt.

GRAND CAYMAN THRUSH
Turdus ravidus

Most countries have a true thrush of the genus *Turdus*, similar in size, movements, and general habits to the "robin" of America or the blackbird of Europe. Practically all of these birds have many other characteristics in common, such as ten wing primary feathers, twelve tail feathers, and a spotted first plumage in young birds; and for the most part they are fine songsters. As it happens, this particular West Indies bird is not so proficient vocally as many of its relations, for, although its song is pleasing and prolonged, it is rather weak and is perhaps better described as not much more than a warbling.

The Grand Cayman thrush is now certainly about as near extinction as possible; it may even be that it has already gone for ever. Described by Cory in 1886, it is endemic and has always been entirely restricted to the island of Grand Cayman, about 180 miles west of Jamaica in the Caribbean. As long ago as 1911, a professional bird-collector said that he could find the species only in two very remote patches of woodland; his specimens were the last to be obtained, and the latest record seems to be of one seen in 1938. This last sighting was in the extreme east of the island, and, if the bird survives at all, it will be only within that area. Writing in 1966, James Bond logs the species as "possibly extinct".

The disappearance of this fine thrush will be a great tragedy. Although destruction of its woodland habitat must have been partly responsible for a decrease in its numbers, there is no apparent reason why it should not be adaptable to changed conditions as so many *Turdus* thrushes have proved to be. There is no good explanation for its extreme rarity. It was, or is, a very handsome thrush, of a pleasing slate-grey with white on its lower tail coverts and abdomen, and strikingly coral-red bill, feet, and bare ring around the eye. The Grand Cayman thrush is yet another species that has practically gone before adequate details of its biology have been made available, and when even its nesting is entirely unrecorded and apparently unknown.

Subfamily Sylviinae: Old World warblers

NIHOA MILLERBIRD
Acrocephalus kingi

This small, plain-coloured bird, dull brown above and brownish-white below, is a typical-looking reed warbler of active habits, with the slender bill that characterizes the members of this genus of insect-eating birds. Its sexes are alike, and immature birds resemble their parents; there is neither prominent colouration nor other simple trait by which they can be readily distinguished in the field.

The Nihoa millerbird is to be found only on the small Hawaiian island of Nihoa, and is among the world's rarest and most endangered birds. Almost the only encouraging fact is that its entire range falls within a proclaimed reserve, the Hawaiian Islands Natural Wildlife Refuge. With this measure of protection, it is a reasonable hope that the birds may survive; but there can be few other species whose range is so restricted. The whole known range of the species is within an area recorded as no larger than 156 acres, and its real habitat consists of an even smaller area within this tiny range.

In spite of this extreme restriction, and although the total population of Nihoa millerbirds is now thought to number only somewhere between 100 and 200 individuals, the world's knowledge of their habits and general biology is very slight, and of their population status imprecise. Even their breeding biology is virtually unknown; it is believed that only one nest has been found, that containing a single (partly incubated) egg.

There are far too many islands around the world whose wildlife – fauna and flora – is seriously endangered because of man's folly. Over and over again there are instances of the introduction of rats or other alien predators, to the detriment of all endemic creatures, and in some cases the rapidity with which not only animal but also plant species have disappeared has to be seen to be believed. Before it is too late, every possible precaution must be taken to prevent unannounced landings, by military or other personnel on all islands, wherever they

may be, that have not yet been affected by exotic introductions. The possibility of experimental translocation of birds to Kure and Midway is being presently considered.

Nihoa millerbird *Albert E. Gilbert* 1966

It may well be wondered how this reed warbler came to be called a millerbird. The explanation is that it is a very close relative of the Laysan millerbird (*A. familiaris*) of the same genus, which got its name from its partiality for feeding on large "miller" moths. For some time, indeed, the two were considered to be of the same species.

The species of Laysan (in the same archipelago) has been extinct since 1923, because lack of suitable vegetation prevented any chance of its recovery from an initial setback. The whole of its natural habitat was devastated by introduced rabbits; and the later occupation of Laysan Island by armed forces removed any possible chance of survivors.

There are rather more accounts available to us of the habits of this extinct millerbird than of the Nihoa species. The Laysan bird was widely distributed over its island, existing wherever there was suitable grassy vegetation. In such cover it moved about unobtrusively – although it also came into gardens and approached closely to human habitations in its search for food. George Munro, in his book on Hawaiian birds, tells us how millerbirds came into laboratories while work was going on, and hunted their favourite moth food among the rafters. He adds that at night the birds even continued their searches by lamplight, taking insects of all kinds, particularly beetles, and moths which they swallowed whole, wings and all.

The Nihoa millerbird was not found by the 1891 Rothschild expedition to the Hawaiian group, because difficult conditions prevented a landing on that island. It remained undiscovered until the 1923 landing by the Bishop Museum expedition; and from examples then collected the bird was named by Dr Wetmore after Lieut.-Cdr S. W. King, who was in charge of the expedition and the minesweeper *Tanager*, which carried it. To close with Munro's words, it is the difficulty of effecting a landing on the island that helps to isolate Nihoa's endemic millerbird; and we must hope that these conditions may continue to keep the place in its primeval condition.

SEYCHELLES WARBLER
Nesillas sechellensis

The tenuous hold on existence kept by many birds endemic to oceanic islands is beginning to emerge with quite monotonous regularity. But no amount of reiteration seems adequate to bring about the change of outlook in public planners, and the various authorities that alone can save what must now be agreed to be the impressive list of these island birds, which could well become extinct in our time.

This inconspicuous little warbler, with subdued olive-green head and back and dull yellow under parts, is yet another species that has to be numbered among the rarest birds of the world, about which all too few people are feeling concern. The total world population of the species was counted as thirty individual birds in 1959 and estimated as about forty-five in 1965. The birds' distribution is about as limited as could be imagined. The fact is that all of them are to be found only on the one rocky island of

Seychelles warbler *Albert E. Gilbert* 1966

the granitic group of the Seychelles colony, called Cousin, which has a total area of no more than about 60 acres.

The species was first described in 1877 from Marianne Island in the Seychelles archipelago, and possibly may have existed also on Cousine, a different island from Cousin. It has been extinct for years on these islands. Oddly enough, it has never been recorded on the island of Praslin, which is separated from Cousin by no more than about 1½ miles of sea. It may be possible to say that the Seychelles warblers are in no more danger of extinction now than they have been since they became extinct elsewhere, and that their numbers probably constitute a healthy population for the limited amount of habitat available on their tiny last island. The important point is that any accidental introduction of rats or similarly undesirable immigrants, or even any more natural calamity such as an outbreak of fire on so minute an island, could bring about the end of the species very rapidly. For the moment perhaps the birds are safe, but, if tragedy is to be avoided, every precaution is required. Positive steps must certainly be taken to ensure that the island of Cousin remains little disturbed, and that it will never be visited by any boats or ships that might have rats, cats, or similar predators aboard.

The local name for the Seychelles warbler is *petit merle*, and it is reported as having a very sweet and mellow little song, not unlike that of the European blackbird, although much more subdued. As might be expected, the species is entirely insectivorous, taking caterpillars and other insects from the branches of small trees and bushes, or less often from the ground.

The birds are fairly catholic in their choice of habitat, and may be noted in mangrove swamps, among low undergrowth along the shore, or even in coconut-palm groves. They move about quite unobtrusively, singly or in pairs; and their flight is noticeably weak and fluttering. Breeding is said to take place from October until March. It is not quite clear whether the nest is the typical open cup of the warbler family, or whether it has some characteristic differences; it has been described as an oval cup measuring 3 inches in diameter and about 1½ inches deep, made of dry grass and such vegetable fibres as strips of coconut leaf. There is another record, however, which states that it is suspended in a fork of two twigs like that of the paradise flycatcher. No particular trees or bushes seem to be chosen for nests, which have been recorded in mangroves, bamboos, and other trees and bushes, at heights of from 5 to 15 feet from the ground. Doubtless this puts them out of reach of the two species of predatory *Mabuya* lizards on the island. One record suggests that in secluded places the birds tend to nest in close proximity to one another. The two eggs of the normal clutch are said to be white, heavily blotched and spotted with brown.

Information lately reached the Survival Service Commission that the related Rodriguez warbler, *Bebrornis rodericanus*, of the Indian Ocean island of Rodriguez, had a population of perhaps only ten to twenty birds in October 1964 and was in danger of early extinction.

Subfamily Malurinae: Australian warblers

WESTERN BRISTLEBIRD
Dasyornis brachypterus longirostris

This rather big warbler, 6 inches long, has two quite separate populations in Australia, sometimes regarded as two species, if only because the western form has a chestnut-red rump, unlike the "typical" race (sometimes split into two races), which appears to be in no danger of extinction in the eastern parts of Victoria and New South Wales.

The distinctive western bristlebird, *D. b. longirostris*, has a history of distribution not unlike that of the noisy scrub bird (p. 271). It was discovered by John Gilbert on the Swan River, near Perth, in 1839, and named by John Gould in 1840; it has never been recorded near Perth since. Specimens were collected at King George's Sound from 1868 into the 1880s, and there was a colony near Wilson Inlet from 1907 until it was destroyed by a bush fire in 1914. After that it was for long believed to have been a relict form of south-west Western Australia that had, simply, become extinct. But, like several Australian birds, it "returned from the dead" in February 1945, when one was collected at Two People Bay, near Albany, by K. G. Buller. Nothing more was heard of it until April 1961, when it was rediscovered in the Two People Bay area by G. F. Mees and J. R. Ford, at the Waychiniup River; and in 1962 and 1963 it was found by many members of the Royal Australian Ornithologists' Union to extend from this river to Two People Bay and Taylor Inlet, where it will doubtless share the protection now being designed for the even rarer and habitat-particular noisy scrub bird.

Western bristlebirds, two males *John and Elizabeth Gould* 1848

This shy warbler, of reed beds and short scrub in coastal marshes, spends a good deal of its time on the ground, and, like the noisy scrub bird, is usually detected by its voice – a loud succession of varied notes. Now that the Royal Australian Ornithologists' Union is dealing with it, we can expect the strong cadre of Western Australian ornithologists to work out its range and population in detail. Meanwhile what details are available of it remain most emphatically in the Red Data Book.

EYREAN GRASS WREN
Amytornis goyderi

This little bird has been found only in a very localized area, just to the north of Lake Eyre in South Australia, and near the Macumba River, which flows into the lake there. The species is known only from two specimens collected in 1875, both of them now in the British Museum, London; and – as an indication of its rarity – the species was not reported again until 1931, when only one pair could be found in the area of its old habitat. Not having been seen again in the intervening period, despite extensive searches by some very competent ornithologists, the bird was by 1958 thought to have become extinct. Yet on the 3rd September 1961 it was found still to be surviving at Christmas Waterhole near the Macumba, about 25 miles north of Lake Eyre.

The Eyrean grass wren, then, has been encountered only three times in close on a century. We cannot conclude from these encounters, in a vast, wild, and inaccessible area, that it is doomed – though it may, of course, be a relict naturally on the decline. Only time, and even more thorough surveys, can show. Certainly the semi-desert area it lives in is under no human pressures or assaults on habitat of a kind that could affect it. It has been suggested that feral cats may have been responsible at some period for a decrease in its numbers: but by no means all conservationists can agree with this claim. Has the species always been rare and localized within a very small area? Those who followed the experiences of the late Donald Campbell in his prolonged, and finally successful, efforts to break the world speed record for a

motor-driven vehicle, in the British-built car Bluebird on Lake Eyre's flats, will know something of the vagaries and harshness of the climate there. To them it will seem that natural causes are more likely to have been responsible for the plight of the grass wrens, heath wrens, or emu wrens than exotic predators.

Although this particular species is so very rare, the genus with which it is classified has eight other species, widely spread all over Australia, and it is from them that a considerable amount of information can be deduced about habits. Except that the birds tend to be shy and wary, observers with any knowledge of Africa and its avifauna would quickly decide that these grass wrens in the field are remarkably like the African warblers of the *Prinia* group. Typically warbler-like in all their actions, they are agile little birds, brisk in movement and always exploring hither and thither in pairs or in small parties, their unusually long tails carried at a jaunty angle, high above the back.

Their favoured habitat is low scrub, particularly salt-bush. One of their habits that is not very warbler-like is to spend much time on the ground, running and hopping about with remarkable speed. Their food seems to consist of both insects and small seeds. They utter clear call notes and sing a pleasing but subdued little song. Their nests are open cups of coarse dry material, such as leaves or bark, lined with finer grass, plant-down, and animal hair. Their eggs are typically warbler-like – white profusely spotted with reds and browns and clouded with greyish-lilac.

Apart from their lively movements, grass wrens are not particularly conspicuous in their rather dull brown plumage with paler under sides. An unusual feature by which they may be identified is the prominent thin white streaking all over their upper parts. A special characteristic of the Lake Eyre bird is its strikingly thick and rather sparrow-like beak.

This Eyrean species was named after an explorer, G. W. Goyder, who lived from 1826 to 1898 and was Surveyor-General of South Australia. At least five other species in the genus are named after well-known Australian personalities. The generic term is derived from the Greek girl Amytis, the daughter of Astyages.

Subfamily Muscicapinae: Old World flycatchers

CHATHAM ISLAND ROBIN
Petroica traversi

In the most south-easterly group of the remote Chatham archipelago, about 500 miles east of the main islands of New Zealand, H. H. Travers collected some little birds late in 1871 that W. L. Buller named *Miro traversi* in the following year. He found them on the main island of the group (and second largest in the Chatham Islands), Pitt Island, which is about 9 miles by 5 miles, and on Mangare (3 miles north-west of it and about 1 mile long). About twenty years later others were collected on tiny Little Mangare, or Tapuaenuku, a steep islet 50 yards south of Mangare with barely 1 acre of dense bush and vine on its top.

From all accounts, Tapuaenuku had become the sole habitat of this peculiar flycatcher about fifty years ago – by which time much of Pitt had been cleared of bush, and Mangare had lost most of its vegetation from the combined activities of goats, rabbits, fires, and wind. The robin may have finally become extinct on Mangare as a result of the hunting of cats introduced to control the introduced rabbits.

When Charles Fleming visited Little Mangare on the 2nd January 1938, he confirmed that the islet was the last stronghold of the "black robin" of Chatham, as it has been sometimes called. With E. G. Turbott, he floundered through the scrub, riddled with petrel-burrows, on top of the island. They saw robins belonging to about twelve pairs, and estimated from the density of occupation of the cover they could survey (in which the birds were tame and territorial) that from twenty to thirty-five pairs lived in the whole of the island's cover.

Since 1938 there have been few visits indeed to Tapuaenuku, and the only one we can find trace of was during a survey in 1962 of the Wildlife Branch of New Zealand's Department of Internal Affairs, which reported the robins in occupation of their habitat, and found generally that the bird life of the south-eastern group was in a satisfactory state.

Supposing its population to be the same, now,

as on Fleming's visit in 1938, the Chatham Island robin is not quite the rarest bird in the world. But it is certainly the most restricted; no other wild species can provedly be limited to 1 acre! The interesting thing is that its population, at least for the time being, appears to be viable in its tiny – and fortunately rat-free, axe-free, and indeed for years at a time man-free – world of Tapuaenuku.

Modern systematists now place *Miro* in the genus *Petroica*. The nearest relative of the Chatham Island robin is the common New Zealand robin, *P. australis*, of North, South, and Stewart Islands, of which it is the representative in the Chatham archipelago. However, its entirely brownish-black plumage (New Zealand robins have cream, pale yellow, or whitish breasts), smallish size, and distinctive proportions justify its position as a full species.

Chatham Island robin *J. G. Keulemans* 1907

For the time being Tapuaenuku's inaccessibility and steepness makes it a natural sanctuary, and the Chatham Island robin is protected by law. All the same, plans are afoot to promote the regeneration of the lost bush of Mangare, parts of Pitt, and neighbouring South-East Island. If these succeed, the possibility of a translocation has not been forgotten. Species with stocks smaller than the present population of *Petroica traversi* have been able to thrive after such opportunities have been provided.

Subfamily Monarchinae: monarchs

TAHITI FLYCATCHER
Pomarea nigra

The variety of land birds on islands is, as can readily be understood, a function of their remoteness. If we were to sweep east across the scattered archipelagos of the vast Pacific, which have been colonized by birds, as by humans, mostly from the west, we should find a list of native land birds (excluding the non-breeding migrants) of about 127 in the Solomons, seventy-seven in New Caledonia, fifty-four in the Fiji archipelago, thirty-three in the Samoan Islands, seventeen in the Society Islands, eleven in the Marquesas, and only four on distant Henderson Island. Easter Island, the most easterly of all, has no native land birds whatever – though, now, it has three introduced species.

Even to this day the Pacific Islands have not been thoroughly explored for their birds; and the story of this blackish monarch flycatcher is as much a story of our ignorance as of rarity. The location of the tale lies mostly in the Society Islands. Here, in 1773, Captain Cook's second voyage paused at the lately discovered island of Maiao (or Tubuaï Manu, recorded then as Mamao), and J. R. Forster, the ship's naturalist, collected the species for the first time. Later in the eighteenth century it was discovered farther east (and proved to be breeding by the collection of a young one) on the main island of Tahiti, and given its earliest name, by Sparrman in 1786, on specimens from there.

In the early nineteenth century the French exploring ship *Coquille* collected a flycatcher on Maupiti, a mountainous, wooded island, which is the westernmost fair-sized one of the Society group. It was named as a different species by Lesson and Garnot in 1828; but their *Muscicapa pomarea* is now recognized as a race of the Tahiti species, and takes the name *Pomarea nigra pomarea*.

Between the 4th and 7th October 1773, on the second Cook voyage, Forster went ashore on Tongatapu, the principal island of Tonga, 1,500 miles west of Maupiti. He saw birds of which he wrote a detailed description, and this can be compared with his own description of the Tahiti birds he had seen and collected. Unfortunately, he took no specimens and made no drawing of them. However, his description was so precise that the late Gregory Mathews felt able to name the Tongatapu flycatcher *P. n. tabuensis* from it, in 1929, as a third race of the Tahitian flycatcher.

Tahiti flycatcher, typical race *N. W. Cusa* 1966

The subsequent history of this flycatcher's races is interesting. On Cook's third voyage in 1777, the good naturalist W. Anderson was ashore on Tongatapu between the 9th June and 10th July, but did not see the bird of Forster at all. Indeed, nobody has seen it since Forster, and it is presumed extinct. Of the Maupiti bird there is no further news, as far as we can find, though we cannot presume it also to be extinct, as the island has hardly ever been visited by naturalists. Nobody seems to have found the "typical" race again on Maiao; and on Tahiti the residents had reported it extinct until Rollo H. Beck, leader of the great Whitney South Sea Expedition of the American Museum of Natural History, found it again in 1921 in the island's hills. As his colleague R. C. Murphy observed: "It still thrives in the mountain fastness of the queen of isles".

If it had not been for the Whitney expedition,

the whole species might have been (wrongly) on the extinct list of the Survival Service Commission. The Tahiti flycatcher's story owes as much, still, to the pioneer naturalists of two centuries past as to those of the present. To put it mildly, further investigations are needed before its real status can be guessed.

TINIAN MONARCH
Monarcha takatsukasae

When the time comes for more detailed biological surveys of the birds of the many small Pacific islands of Micronesia to be carried out, two things will doubtless be discovered. One is that more bird species than have hitherto been realized are not only rare but also in real danger of extinction; the other, that several more species will be found to have become extinct before anyone could be aware of their plight and avert the catastrophe.

There are literally thousands of islands in the area known as Micronesia, a name derived from the Greek and meaning "small islands". Collecting on most of them has been limited, and some of the very smallest have never been visited. One group constitutes the Marianas, of which there are fifteen well-wooded islands, or rather fourteen single islands and one group of three islets; these form a chain 450 miles long and have a total land surface area of 247 square miles.

Tinian is one of the Mariana Islands, lying approximately in 15° N. Some five or six collecting expeditions have worked on it in the present century. Nevertheless, there is not a great deal of detailed information about the status of Tinian's birds; but it is known that this monarch is a very rare species. It has been found only on this one island, whence it was described by Yamashina in 1931; and the latest available estimate is that the population numbered only between forty and fifty birds in 1945, though the account of another observer in the same year makes it sound a little commoner.

The monarchs are now considered a subfamily of the true flycatchers, and the Tinian species is a good-sized member of the group. It is a handsome bird, with grey head-top and reddish-brown back; below, the reddish colour

Tinian monarch *N. W. Cusa* 1966

is paler; its rump and under-tail coverts are white; and it has prominent white wing bars and outer tail feathers. It is a bird of the scrubby woodlands with typically flycatcher movements, including quick fluttering dashes after winged insects. The nest and eggs (of which two or three form a clutch), as well as the young, have been fully described.

SEYCHELLES PARADISE FLYCATCHER
Terpsiphone corvina

Africa has several flycatchers of this genus of the monarchs – the beautiful paradise flycatchers. There are seven or eight species on the African mainland, and, in addition, this *veuve* (as it is locally named) is endemic to islands of the granitic group of the Seychelles colony in the western Indian Ocean; another, the *coq des bois*, is restricted to the islands of Mauritius and Réunion; and a third exists on Madagascar and in the Comoro group.

This Seychelles *veuve* was formerly more widespread and doubtless known on several of

Seychelles paradise flycatchers, male (upper) and female *Rena M. Fennessy* 1966

the islands. It certainly existed quite recently, on those of Praslin and Félicité, surviving on the latter island certainly until 1936. As long ago as 1906 it was also recorded on Curieuse Island; and it probably once lived on Marianne. Now, however, it survives only on the comparatively small island of La Digue, where it still seemed to be tolerably numerous in 1960, though it had been reported as becoming rarer in 1940. It must be considered endangered because the restricted nature of its habitat could easily lead to tragedy. Calamity of any kind, whether natural or through some exotic introduction, could quickly cause havoc among any such one-island population. Those who are interested in the conservation of wildlife and natural resources cannot fail to put the Seychelles colony on the short list of those countries that have wildlife species of all kinds sliding towards irreplaceable destruction, until someone in authority decides to show the world what conservation can achieve. Most people who visit the islands stress the constant destruction of bird species by the local inhabitants. Although there are laws to protect the endemic avifauna, enforcement is a problem, for the local police have lately seemed quite unconcerned about wildlife of any kind.

All the paradise flycatchers are alike in habits and movements; gay, active little birds, mostly darting hither and thither or fluttering out into the air in pursuit of their insect prey, their acrobatic movements attractively displaying their long tail feathers. These restless actions are always accompanied by conversation in the form of a stuttering succession of short whistles. At times a bird will sit motionless on a twig, now and then launching itself into the air to take a passing insect with a snap of its bill.

The nests built by the flycatchers of this group are famous for their fine structure, built well out along a pendant twig so thin that virtually no predators such as cats, rats, or snakes can get at the nest. It has been stated that, as soon as a pair of birds have chosen a suitable fork, they

PLATE 27 (*a*) Eyrean grass wrens, two males *John Gould and W. Hart* 1876; (*b*) Piopios, South Island race (upper) and North Island race *J. G. Keulemans* 1888; (*c*) Kauai oos, adult (lower) and immature *J. G. Keulemans* 1900; (*d*) Stitchbirds, male (upper) and female *J. G. Keulemans* 1888

(a)

(b)

(c)

(d)

(a)

(b)

(c)

(d)

(e)

(f)

first pile into it a little pad, 1½ inches thick, of plant-down or fluff mixed with fine grass, and then build up the sides to a height of about 3 inches with coarser material. Next the lining is much trampled down: the result is a delightful little cup, which is finally bound together and sewn to the twig with an outer network of threads from spiders' webs.

The eggs are described as being white or pale blue, marked with brownish and reddish spots that tend to be thicker and to form a zone around their larger ends. Some authors have stated that two or three eggs form a normal clutch; but nests found very recently by a visitor to La Digue were stated to contain a single egg only.

It is feared that the small size of the broods that seem to be reared will not make recovery any easier if the status of the birds' population is permitted to sink lower than it is at present. Although the birds range freely through the denser foliaged cover, they tend to nest on the edge of clearings, perhaps where danger can be better observed. This is unfortunate, because the clearings on an island so populated by humans as La Digue are usually along roads or paths; in such places attention is drawn to the nests, and many are knocked down or disturbed.

Subfamily Pachycephalinae: whistlers

PIOPIO *or* NATIVE THRUSH
Turnagra capensis

The piopio (the name is an onomatopoeic Maori word from the bird's call) is a repetitive, loud, clear songster that is most thrush-like in voice and plumage, to the extent that the confirmation of its recent New Zealand records has had to be firm – for even experienced field-men can confuse it on a hasty sighting, or even sometimes hearing, with the widespread introduced song thrush. The piopio is certainly very rare indeed; but just how rare it is can only be discovered by hard field studies on both North and South Island of New Zealand, in each of which a race survives. The North Island race, *T. c. tanagra*, is white-throated and grey-breasted; the "typical" *T. c. capensis* is striped and streaked with brown and white below and the more likely of the two to be confused with the song thrush. In fact the "native thrush" of New Zealand is no thrush; authorities like Ernst Mayr would put it among the whistlers, a subfamily of fair-sized flycatchers.

It is certain that the piopio was widespread on both islands, except perhaps in northern North Island, at the time of European settlement, and that its rapid decline on both began about the 1880s with the introduction of stoats and other predators – especially feral cats – and forest clearance. The species was first collected (like other rare New Zealand birds) by Forster on Cook's second voyage, at Dusky Sound, South Island, in 1773.

In the last quarter-century confirmed records in both islands are few – though some have shown that earlier unconfirmed records from certain areas were valid. Of the North Island form the presence of a population in the area of Lake Waikaremoana and Lake Waikare-iti from 1938 at least to 1955 seems certain, and there is no evidence that it has disappeared; and a group in the Wanganui-Waitotara area in 1950 can be traced back through intervening sightings to 1887, when what may have been the last museum specimens were taken there. Other reports from the 1940s in the neighbouring Patea region (otherwise known to have been inhabited to 1923) and from the Gisborne-Wairoa area in the east need confirmation, but later ones from the Okataina-Tarawera bush and the upper reaches of the Ruakituri River are probably valid.

In the South Island there have been very few, if any, confirmed records since the subspecies

PLATE 28 (*a*) Oahu alauwahios, adult male (upper) and immature, 1899; (*b*) Kauai akialoas, male (upper) and female, 1892; (*c*) Kauai nukupuus, male (lower) and female, 1892; (*d*) Maui parrotbills, male (lower) and female, 1896; (*e*) Palilas, male (upper) and female, 1890; (*f*) Crested honeycreepers, adult (lower) and immature, 1894 *F. W. Frohawk* vanished from Resolution Island in Fiordland when the stoats took over about 1900. However, there has been a trickle of records since then, published but unconfirmed, some at least of which are very likely to be valid – in Fiordland from the Glaisnock Valley at the head of Lake Te Anau in the early 'thirties, from near Lake Hauroko in 1947, and from Caswell Sound in 1949; in western Otago from the lower end of Lake Wilmot in the Pyke Valley in 1963; and from near Mount Zetland in the hills by Tadmor, in Nelson, in 1948.

The piopio survives so tenuously that it has one of the rare red sheets in the Red Data Book. That work treats all species alike, purely measuring, as best its compilers can, their likelihood of survival and extent of present danger. But the piopio surely deserves a special campaign, of the kind the New Zealand naturalists have cooperatively organized so well with Government support – for other Red Data Book species. It is more than a unique species – indeed, all species are unique. It is probably classable at least as of a unique tribe – perhaps a tribe of the whistlers; it may even prove to rate status as a unique subfamily, if it thrives well enough to receive an intensive study of its behaviour. It is, in fact, an important scientific curiosity as well as a considerable distributional mystery. We feel sure the New Zealanders may soon survey and study it, and save its status as a consequence.

Family Meliphagidae: honeyeaters

KAUAI OO
Moho braccatus

Though the one native bird family of the Hawaiian archipelago, which we shall meet presently (p. 305), is doubtless of American origin, as are some other members of its native bird fauna, most of its natural land birds are clearly colonists from the south-west, from the Australasian fauna of the main oceanic islands of the Pacific. One of the bird families that has provided natives for the Hawaiian Islands is that of the honeyeaters. Hawaii's two native genera of this rather large family, of which 162 species have been alive since 1600, suggest that it was long ago colonized at least twice by the same family, one of the genera, *Moho*, evolving into four species in the archipelago.

Already in recent historical times, four of Hawaii's five handsome honeyeaters have become extinct – *Chaetoptila augustipluma*, the peculiar kioea of the island of Hawaii in about 1859; Hawaii's oo, *Moho nobilis*, by about 1934; the Molokai oo, *M. bishopi*, perhaps by 1904, certainly by 1915; and the Oahu oo, *M. apicalis*, by 1837. Left only is one relict in the least man-disturbed big island of the group; the Kauai oo (pronounced oh-oh), *Moho braccatus*, sometimes called the ooaa (oh-oh-ah-ah).

Even on Kauai, under increasing human pressures and habitat destruction, the native oo has withdrawn into the heights where the mountain forest survives. First named by the American ornithologist Cassin in 1855, it was common all over the Kauai forests from sea-level in the north to Mount Waialeale at over 4,000 feet in George Munro's time in 1891, and still not uncommon when he left the island in 1899. But on four return visits to Kauai in 1928–36 Munro never saw it, though he once thought he heard one sing in 1936. Walter Donaghho, another veteran of Hawaiian ornithology, was sure he heard another deep in the forest in 1940, but this record was unconfirmed. Not until Frank Richardson and John Bowles together penetrated the Alakai Swamp forest area around 4,000 feet in July to August 1960 was the Kauai oo found again: "twelve individuals [were] seen or heard". In 1962 two more were seen and several others heard in this heartland of the rugged island, and in 1963 two feeding in Alakai Swamp were watched by W. M. Ord.

The Kauai oo, then, is another island relict, disturbingly rare, protected by law, clearly unable to adapt itself to the new conditions now overtaking even Kauai. This is a situation with which readers, by now, are perhaps familiar.

STITCHBIRD or HIHI
Notiomystis cincta

Of New Zealand's three native honeyeaters two, the bellbird and the tui, are common and successful; but one, the stitchbird, is now relict. It is the only species of its genus, and peculiar to New Zealand's North Island, where it was first apparently discovered at the Bay of Islands by W. Yate in 1835.

The Rev. W. Yate evidently encountered the stitchbird at the very northern limit of its old distribution, for the honeyeater never seems to have been recorded further north up the Auckland peninsula. But over all the rest of the North Island (and over the offlying Barrier Islands and Kapiti) it once roamed, sucking nectar from the pohutukawas and other New Zealand flowers; and with the European settlement it quickly withdrew in range. Found commonly all over the mainland by 1840, it was rare north of the line between Taranaki and the Bay of Plenty (except on the Barrier Islands) by 1872, though still fairly common further south. By 1878 there were apparently none left north of the lower Waikato. By about 1885 it was extinct on the mainland, and probably also on Great Barrier Island.

The hihi, as the Maoris call it, has survived only on unspoiled wooded Little Barrier Island for eighty years.[1] The island, of 7,000 acres, rises to the high peak of Mount Hauturu (2,378 feet) at the entrance to Hauraki Gulf. Upon it, the population of the stitchbird (already virtually the world population) was apparently in its greatest danger when the formidable Austrian collector Andreas Reischek was ashore there in the 1880s. Possibly as a consequence of his own and fellow-collectors' activities (the stitchbird was in great demand by museums in those days), he spent three weeks on Little Barrier without seeing one, saw only one in five weeks in 1882, and was twelve days ashore in 1884 before he saw (or collected) one. Fortunately Little Barrier was proclaimed a sanctuary in 1896 – an early piece of conservation legislation that may have overcome an early survival crisis. From then access to the reserve was by permit only; and the stitchbird turned the corner. In 1919 the pioneer bird photographer H. Guthrie-Smith got the first "stills", and found the first nests of the unique bird. Since the Second World War few years have passed without some report on it.

Owing to the roughness of Little Barrier's bushy mountain terrain, the population of the stitchbird (like all honeyeaters a roamer, working the heights at some seasons, and the sea-level when the pohutukawa or *Phormium* flax is in flower) has never been ascertained; though a breeding-season campaign by a trained and athletic group might well get a close measurement of it. There is no doubt that during the 'forties the population was increasing, and that it has been maintained since; indeed, it is well-established and viable, in the opinion of Dr R. A. Falla and other authorities. Nevertheless, it seems doubtful, from the accounts of the numbers encountered by parties in defined parts of the island, whether the world population of the hihi can be much over 100.

Family Zosteropidae: whiteyes

TRUK GREAT WHITEYE
Rukia ruki

The Caroline Islands, which form part of the mass of islands dotting the Pacific Ocean known as Micronesia, consist of forty-one clusters of islets or single islands, of which three are volcanic rock, one is sedimentary rock, and the rest are coral atolls.

Truk Island is really one good-sized island in a cluster of about 100 others, collectively known as the Truk Group. It has extensive and varied vegetation cover, with some slopes, lowlands, and stream verges clothed in dense forest, and higher hill-sides covered with grass and scrub. The bird life is quite abundant, and includes one

[1] There have been unconfirmed reports of its survival recently in the Ruahine Ranges, according to G. R. Williams's survival analysis of New Zealand birds of 1962; and a record from Ngugnuru, near Whangarei in 1936, Williams suggests, "could refer to birds blown from Little Barrier some fifty miles to the south-east".

representative of the genus *Rukia* into which Micronesia's four "out-size" whiteyes have been placed. There are other and more normal-sized members of the whiteye family throughout the Pacific, but the "greater" ones, as they are known, lack any pale ring of feathers round the eyes and are nearly half as big again as the birds of that vast assemblage of "normal" whiteyes that ranges throughout the tropics and subtropics of the Old World.

Just why this Truk species should be, or seem to be, so uncommon is not understood. Virtually nothing is known of the birds or their habits; but they must be very rare indeed. A most competent collector spent more than a year on the island about 1870 without finding the species, and it was not until 1895 that it was discovered. It is thought that its population has always been small, and that it may exist only in one or two secluded areas. Ornithologists ashore for fourteen months about 1900 and two and a half years in 1957–60 did not record it.

The Truk great whiteye differs from all its relations by lacking any green colouration in its plumage; it is sepia all over – slightly darker on the primary wing feathers, and paler on the under side of the wings. Its bill is black and legs reddish-orange. Nothing appears to have been recorded about its nesting habits, nest, or eggs.

PONAPE GREAT WHITEYE
Rukia sanfordi

The four species of these unusually large *Rukia* whiteyes of the Pacific are all strangely localized and regrettably little known. All exist only in Micronesia. One is found on the two Palau Group islands of Babelthuap and Peleliu; one on Yap of the Caroline Islands; one on Truk Island of the same group; and this one only on Ponapé, which is also one of the Caroline Islands.

Like its three near relations in the same genus this Ponapé bird must be extremely rare, if the experiences of recent collectors are true indications of its status. Mention could be made here of the point that some professional museum collectors might have more regard for endangered species than is often apparent, or that they

Ponapé great whiteyes *N. W. Cusa* 1966

might be better controlled by those who employ them. With island species, the greatest care must be taken in establishing a rare bird's precise status, before deciding to collect it.

The Ponapé great whiteye was discovered no earlier than 1931, simultaneously by collectors for Japanese ornithologists and for the American Museum of Natural History; and was described almost simultaneously by Takatsukasa and Yamashina on the one hand, and by Ernst Mayr on the other, in the same year. Since Mayr's printed paper was mailed (that is, published) on the 4th November and that of Takatsukasa and Yamashina on the 23rd November, Mayr's *sanfordi* has priority over the others' *longirostra* by less than three weeks, as an adjective to be applied (now) to *Rukia* to make its proper Linnean name. The task of nomenclature has a few such adventures! Mayr's collector Coultas found the birds were feeding at the flowers of one kind of gum-tree seen at 2,000 feet above sea-level; on that occasion seven birds were taken. When the island was visited again in 1947, only four birds were seen, at 700 and at 900 feet, and one of these was collected. Beyond the fact that the call has been described as loud and deep-throated, nothing whatever seems to be known of the habits or breeding biology of the species.

The four Micronesian large whiteyes were formerly placed in four separate genera, and, although there is of course a possibility that they derive from several ancestors, it seems more likely that they have evolved from one.

Family Drepanididae

HAWAIIAN HONEYCREEPERS

The Hawaiian Islands, the greatest and most isolated archipelago of the North Pacific, stretch westwards, with some northing, in a 1,000-mile belt from the great island of Hawaii to Midway and Kure. Geologically they are young islands, of volcanic origin; it is unlikely that land capable of supporting forests can have existed for much more than 5,000,000 years, or since the middle part of the Pliocene period. Some of its island life communities are considerably younger: it has been estimated that the land surface of Lanai (141 square miles), the smallest of the major islands, is less than 200,000 years old, which means that its fauna and flora must have evolved into its present form as late as the Upper Pleistocene.

Nevertheless Hawaii has many unique taxa (the plural of taxon, meaning a systematic group of any level, such as genus, tribe, subfamily, or family) of plants and insects – and one native family of birds that is now almost wholly in danger of extinction. Of the twenty-two full species of the Hawaiian honeycreepers, eight are already extinct and eight others are currently considered to be in danger of extinction and are accordingly in the Red Data Book. Of the six remaining, as species in no global danger, three have each at least one valid race in danger. A short account will therefore here be given of the whole family.

The Hawaiian honeycreepers are doubtless of American origin (several other Hawaiian bird indigenes are of Australasian origin via Polynesian islands), and Dean Amadon's most careful field and museum study suggests that their ancestral colonists were indeed of nectar-feeding honeycreeper type. What family they belonged to when they were blown over the ocean, perhaps in Upper Pliocene times, it is not possible now to be certain of: but the most likely one seems to be the Emberizidae, a big family that (according to some authorities) embraces as subfamilies, amongst others, the buntings and American "sparrows", the tanagers, and the American honeycreepers. The last, known as the Coerebinae, are by some thought to be a "rag-bag" subfamily; that is, one composed of elements that may look alike although of different origin – in this case believed to be partly from tanagers, partly from the American wood warblers or Parulidae. It would also be possible that the Hawaiian honeycreepers' ancestors might have been true finches of the family Fringillidae. One thing is certain: the Hawaiian honeycreepers are now a valid and well-differentiated family, which can, indeed, be divided into two subfamilies – the more primitive Drepanidines, which retain the honeycreeping habit, and are indeed nectar-feeders, most with long or rather long bills; and the Psittirostrines, which have evolved into sharp-billed insect-eating forms, sickle-billed insect-eating forms, and finch- or even parrot-billed seed-eating forms, though some still take nectar. One of the insect-eaters, the rare akiapolauu, has a strong straight lower mandible used for pecking wood; its curved upper mandible is used for prizing; and it occupies a "woodpecker" niche in what is left of its range in the forests of Hawaii.

Before any of the twenty-two species of Hawaiian honeycreepers became extinct, all but two of them were confined to the six main islands of the archipelago – from east to west, these are Hawaii (much the largest, 4,030 square miles), Maui, Lanai (the smallest), Molokai, Oahu, and Kauai. Twelve were confined to one island. Of the rest, four were distributed over some or all of the main islands without racial distinction, while five ranged over some or all of the main islands with a different (and sometimes well-marked) race in each. The Laysan "finch" is now the only representative of the family west of the main islands, where formerly there was also a distinct race of the apapane on Laysan. It can thus be seen that a considerable evolutionary radiation has taken place, perhaps in a few million years, which is, geologically, a short time. The Drepanididae are very probably the youngest of all the families of birds.

Geologically, the eastern main islands are the most recently formed and show least marine erosion; Kauai on the west is the oldest. Hawaii reaches a height of 13,825 feet at Mauna Kea, and has two other active volcanoes, Mauna Loa and Kilauea.

Measurable genealogical tradition points to

the first human settlement of the Hawaiian Islands, probably from Tahiti, over 2,500 miles to the south, in about the sixth century A.D. The earliest radiocarbon dates from Polynesian kitchen charcoal establishes that camps were on Kauai by about 1230, Oahu by about 1004, and Hawaii by about 950 – which last is the same date as the first Polynesian colonization of New Zealand, also from Tahiti. New Zealand is about the same distance from Tahiti (to its north-west) as Hawaii.

The Polynesians in New Zealand (p. 16) destroyed a large proportion of its fauna long before the European settlement. But they did not find so highly specialized and defenceless a fauna when they colonized the Hawaiian Islands (it was a much newer fauna), and appear to have settled down as neolithic farmers and fishermen without unduly slashing the widespread forests or killing off the wild animals. It is true they hunted the néné geese, and took hundreds of the more colourful of the honeycreepers to make their great royal feather robes. But nobody can prove that they endangered any species. The crash, if it can be so described, of the Hawaiian honeycreepers came some years after Captain Cook discovered the archipelago in 1778. It really dates from the second half of the nineteenth century, and is due to the widespread clearance of the native forests for agriculture and strongly also to the predation of introduced mongooses and other animals, to the competition of introduced birds, and provedly also to the inroads of disease carried by introduced birds and mosquitoes. Only seven species were discovered in the eighteenth century and three more in the first half of the nineteenth century. All the other twelve were discovered and named by 1893, at a time when many of them were already becoming rare; one was named when already possibly extinct.

In a systematic order, here are the Hawaiian honeycreepers and their fate. The Linnean racial names, omitted here, are listed in Dr Dean Amadon's monograph (1950) in the *Bulletin of the American Museum of Natural History*.

Subfamily Psittirostrinae: insect- and seed-eaters

Amakihi, *Loxops virens*

Four and a half inches long, dull green above, yellowish below, with a dark, sharp decurved bill, this insect-gleaner is still, fortunately, one of the commonest native birds of the archipelago, especially on Kauai. It has a race on each main island. Only on Lanai has a race become scarce, since the mid-1920s, when Lanai town was built and all but a small part of the forest cleared for pineapple plantations.

Anianiau, *Loxops parva*

Yellowish, and a little smaller than the amakihi, with a straight sharp bill, this insect-eater is still reasonably common on its native island of Kauai, especially in the proposed reserve of the Alakai Swamp forest in the high interior, at around 4,000 feet.

Greater amakihi *or* **green solitaire,** *Loxops sagittirostris* (extinct)

Discovered by the collector H. C. Palmer in 1892 on the lower Hilo slopes of Mauna Kea, Hawaii, this bird seems to have been already rare when found, at a time when its forest was being felled for sugar-cane. It was heard and seen by R. C. L. Perkins in 1895 in the Wailuku River area, and last collected by H. W. Henshaw in a rather small patch of dense forest in the same region in 1900. Since then it has been sought hard and often, but has never been seen or heard again. It must have become extinct in or shortly after 1900.

Alauwahio *or* **creeper,** *Loxops maculata* (one extinct race)

A dull-coloured bird $4\frac{1}{2}$ inches long, with yellowish under parts on most races, and a straight, sharp bill, this tree-trunk-creeping eater of insects was represented by a race on each of the six main islands. The Hawaiian race is much reduced in numbers since the nineteenth century. The Maui race, not uncommon in 1928, was less common in 1936 and much reduced, though surviving, in 1951. Quite common in

1913, the Lanai race did not survive the forest clearance and was last seen in 1937. The Molokai race was evidently much reduced by forest clearance; George C. Munro and W. Alanson Bryan found it "still quite common" when collecting in 1907, but it became so rare that it had been thought extinct for over a decade when N. Pekelo Jr saw two birds in 1961; three were seen in 1962, and one in 1963. On Oahu the native race was fairly common in the 1890s, sought in vain in 1935, but reported in 1950 as still to be found (and rare). Only the Kauai race seems to have a respectable population: several hundred were seen in the Alakai Swamp by Frank Richardson and John Bowles in 1960, and it seems to have been common around the 4,000-foot contour here ever since it was discovered eighty years ago.

Akepa, *Loxops coccinea* (one extinct race)

This bird of 4½ inches has a short, pale bill, rather like that of a siskin, though it is a caterpillar- and spider-catcher. Males of the Hawaii race are bright orange-red, females green above and yellow below. This race was plentiful in the last century, especially above Mana on the slopes of Mauna Kea at around 5,500 feet, and was still fairly common high in the Kau district in 1938. Since then it has been irregularly sighted, though there was a small but apparently stable population on the northern slope of Hulalai volcano in 1950, and birds have been seen elsewhere (several in the Hawaii National Park) at heights from 2,000 to over 13,000 feet – where the corpse of one was found frozen in a pool on Mauna Loa in 1943.

The males of the Maui race vary from dull yellow to brownish-orange. This form was collected by R. C. L. Perkins last in 1894, not long after it had been first discovered, and was since then long sought vainly and thought extinct until Amy B. H. Greenwell met a party of three in koa forest in 1950 at about 2,500 feet on the south slope of Haleakala volcano. So the species may still (just) survive on Maui. As far as anybody knows, it has never been represented on Lanai or Molokai. Oahu's race was discovered as early as 1825, was collected for the last time at Waialua by H. C. Palmer in 1893, and seen for the last time in the same area in about 1900 by Perkins, since when it has doubtless been extinct. On Kauai the race has males and females both greenish above and yellow below, and was common at around 4,000 feet in the high forest when George Munro collected it "from flocks" in 1891; it survives, but in reduced numbers, mainly in the Alakai Swamp area at this height, where Richardson and Bowles found it uncommon in 1960, but occasionally in parties of twenty or more.

Akialoa, *Hemignathus obscurus* (presumed extinct)

The akialoa was a greenish-yellow bird, dark-mantled, and about 6½ inches long, of which 1½ inches (more with males) was a thin, strongly decurved crevice-probing bill, with which it hunted insects. It was found on three islands.

The Hawaii race, well distributed over the forests in 1891–5, especially on the Kona side (western, or leeward) of the island, must have collapsed quickly afterwards, for, apart from an unconfirmed report from the windward side in 1940, it has never been recorded since 1895, despite long searches of the suitable surviving forest. It must be extinct. The Lanai race was last surely seen by Perkins in 1894, not long after it was discovered; though it is possible that Munro saw and collected one in or after 1911, this needs confirmation. This race, too, is surely extinct. The Oahu race was first discovered as early as 1834, and last surely seen as early as 1837; later reports, though by reliable observers, in 1892 (Perkins), 1937 (Harold Craddock), and 1940 (J. de A. Northwood) are not fully confirmed. The birds seen were probably young iiwis (p. 311). There are too many examples of "extinct" species coming back from the dead for such reports to be simply discounted: but meanwhile the Oahu akialoa, and the species as a whole, should be regarded as extinct until further evidence shows otherwise.

Kauai akialoa, *Hemignathus procerus*

The last living akialoa is distinct enough from the late forms of Hawaii, Lanai, and Oahu to rate status as a full species. It is a brightly greenish-yellow bird, slightly bigger than the common akialoa, with a sickle bill well over 2 inches long in both sexes – nearly 2½ inches long in males. Quite numerous on Kauai in 1891, soon after it was discovered and indeed to the end of the nineteenth century, it was already rare by 1920 and never seen by the indefatigable Munro in his visits between then and 1940.

However, Walter Donaghho reported it on the upper plateau in 1941, as Valdemar Knudsen did in 1957; and in 1960, in the Alakai Swamp area at around 4,000 feet, one bird was seen by David Woodside and another by Richardson and Bowles. Another bird was seen in April 1965 by Lawrence Huber. This most specialized of the insect-probing honeycreepers is thus hanging on by the skin of its longest of sickle-shaped bills, and has full status in the Red Data Book.

Nukupuu, *Hemignathus lucidus* (two extinct races)

About the same bodily size as the akialoa, the nukupuu has (at 1¼ inches) a shorter sickle-shaped, insect-probing bill. It is known only from three of the main islands. The yellowish Maui race was discovered in the early 1890s and last collected by Perkins in 1896 on the northeast side of Haleakala at between 4,000 and 4,500 feet, since when it has never been seen, despite intensive searches.

Also doubtless extinct is the green and yellow Oahu race, first collected in about 1837 in the Nuuanu Valley and still common up to about 1860, when the lower belt of koa forest was cleared. It has never been seen since.

The Kauai race, yellow with white under parts, was discovered by Scott B. Wilson at Kaholuamanu in about 1887, seen again by Munro in 1891, and at the head waters of the Hanapepe River at 4,000 feet or more in 1898, when he logged it as already rare and localized; he reported it last in 1899. Since then it was thought to be extinct, until in 1960 it was rediscovered by Richardson and Bowles, who saw two in the highland Alakai Swamp. Two were seen in 1961, three in 1964, and one in 1965 (Warren King). Like the Kauai akialoa, it has full status in the Red Data Book.

Akiapolauu, *Hemignathus wilsoni*

Representative of the nukupuu on Hawaii, the olive-mantled akiapolauu, with its yellowish under parts, differs from it specifically – largely by the shape of its lower mandible. That of the nukupuu, though half the length of the upper mandible, curves with it. That of the akiapolauu is straight and touches the upper mandible only at its tip. With this instrument the bird chips at bark for the insects underneath, holding its probing upper mandible out of the way.

The akiapolauu, though not scientifically named until 1893, was known to be common in the forests of Hawaii, down to low altitudes, in 1825 and continued so until the clearance of the lower woodlands in the 1860s. By 1891 it had withdrawn uphill (with the forests), but was still common on the western, Kona side of the island above 3,500 feet. As further, higher felling, and the destruction of much undergrowth by cattle and pigs proceeded, this "woodpecker-honeycreeper" became rarer, and was certainly uncommon by 1937, though still found in or near the borders of the unfelled Hawaii National Park from 1938 onwards. Indeed, in 1948–50, it was "found to be rather common really" by P. H. Baldwin and L. P. Richards at between 3,900 and 7,750 feet on the north-east slopes of Mauna Kea and the eastern slopes of Mauna Loa. It is nevertheless regarded as being in danger of extinction, with the big refuge of the Hawaii National Park as its life insurance, in or near which further sightings are recorded for 1961, 1964, and 1965.

Maui parrotbill, *Pseudonestor xanthophrys*

This olive, short-tailed bird, 5½ inches long,

Akiapolauus, male (upper) and female *J. G. Keulemans* 1893

with its yellow eye-stripe and remarkable hooked parrot-bill, is a hunter of beetle-grubs under the bark, and in the twigs (which it crushes), of the koa tree in the surviving forests of the island of Maui. It represents the nearest thing to a parakeet reached in the adaptive radiation of the Hawaiian honeycreeper family, and was first discovered by H. C. Palmer in the early 1890s. By 1894 it was found by H. W. Henshaw to be already rare and localized on the north-west slope of Haleakala Mountain at around 4,500 feet, where the koa trees (since largely gone in this area) were already suffering from insect pests and were dying or dead.

Since then the survival of the parrot honey-eater (which does not eat honey) is known only from an unconfirmed sighting in or shortly before 1928 near the Haleakala crater, and from a certain sighting of two birds by L. P. Richards on the 4th December 1950 about $\frac{1}{2}$ mile north-west of Puu Alaea, at 6,400 feet on the north slope of Haleakala.

Ou, *Psittirostra psittacea*

This rather big bird (6 to 6$\frac{1}{2}$ inches) has an olive mantle and lighter under parts; the males have yellow heads. Its pale, thick, finch-like bill has a parrot-hook, though not so marked as that of the Maui parrotbill. In the early 1890s it was common on all the six major islands (including Maui), feeding largely on fruits and wandering considerably with the fruiting seasons, probably from island to island – no valid island race has been described.

Judging from reports to 1950, a small but viable population may survive on Hawaii in the Upper Olaa Forest Reserve and the Hawaii National Park (near the Napau crater). On Maui it is either very rare or extinct; on Lanai, though believed to be increasing in 1923, it became extinct in about 1932; on Molokai, though it may have survived until the first decade of the present century, it was sought in vain in the 1940s and is also extinct. Its extinction on Oahu since the beginning of the century – it was almost gone by 1894 – is linked by some authorities with the competition of introduced rats for one of its favoured foods, *Freycinetia*. Even on least-disturbed Kauai it is now very rare, and has lately been reported only by

Walter Donaghho in 1940; by Richardson, Bowles, and Woodside, who saw three in the Alakai Swamp at around 4,000 feet in 1960; by W. M. Ord in 1963 (two) and 1964 (three); and by Warren King in 1965 (two).

Laysan "finch", *Psittirostra cantans*

This finch-like honeycreeper, 6 to 7 inches long and resembling a thick-billed canary, is the only survivor of its family now in the western part of the Hawaiian archipelago. It was first discovered by a picnic-party on the uninhabited island of Nihoa in the 1880s, though named first from specimens taken on Laysan at the end of that decade. The Nihoa race, which is different from that of Laysan, had a viable population estimated at 500 to 1,000 birds in a report published in 1941, at 800 to 1,200 birds in December 1961 and at 3,000 to 4,500 in September 1964, and is obviously in no danger of extinction. The Laysan race, though captured in some numbers for aviculture at about the time of its discovery, was still very common in 1891 and in that year and later was introduced on to remote Midway, where it has since been destroyed. By 1923 the Laysan population had become small as a consequence of the destruction of vegetation by the introduced rabbits; but, with the clearance of the rabbits, it recovered, to the extent that in 1938 it was estimated at at least 1,000, and in 1958 at the surprising population of 10,000. It is in no present danger.

Palila, *Psittirostra bailleui*

A thick-billed, finch-like honeycreeper, 6$\frac{1}{2}$ inches long, of the island of Hawaii, the grey-backed, white-bellied palila, with yellow head and breast, was doubtless common in all the mamane-naio woods of Hawaii when first discovered ninety years ago, though in the early 1890s Perkins found it already withdrawing from some of its former range on the western Kona side of the island. It is a fruit-eater that tends to wander in flocks outside the breeding season.

In the present century it has decreased further; by 1946 its colony on Mauna Loa was said to have disappeared – though the habitat there appears to remain suitable for it. Probably its only viable colonies now are near the tree-line in the high woods on Mauna Kea, where it was apparently thriving in 1946. In 1960 Roger Tory Peterson and Eugene Eisenmann saw thirty to forty there; but in 1961 it was reduced to only a few scattered groups of five to fifteen birds. However, W. V. Ward, who saw a Mauna Kea colony in 1961 (and tape-recorded the bird's voice) believes it is once more increasing; and in 1964 five were recorded again on Mauna Loa.

Great koa "finch" or hopue, *Psittirostra palmeri* (extinct)

This is another of the finch-like honeycreepers, which was adapted to feed primarily on the green beans of the koa acacia, though it also ate caterpillars in the breeding season. A big, 9-inch, golden and orange bird, it was discovered by H. C. Palmer in 1891 at Puulehua in Kona, the western side of Hawaii. R. C. L. Perkins, who collected a series in 1894 in the koa forests in Kona and Kau on the west and south slopes of Mauna Loa, believed the whole population might assemble at a fruiting koa grove. Though Munro, who collected with Palmer and Perkins and well remembered the hopue's powerful and peculiar fluty whistle had just such a thing described to him in 1937 by a guide in Kona who had heard it a year or two before, there is no confirmed evidence of the survival of the species since Perkins encountered it in 1896.

Lesser koa "finch", *Psittirostra flaviceps* (extinct)

Some koa finches collected by H. C. Palmer and George C. Munro with hopues feeding on koa seeds in Kona, western Hawaii, were recognized as of a different, smaller species by Walter Rothschild and named by him in 1892. This species, which is doubtless a valid one, was last seen before Rothschild described it, for Palmer and Munro collected their series in September and October 1891, and nobody has seen the lesser koa finch before or since.

Kona "finch" or grosbeak finch, *Psittirostra kona* (extinct)

Hawaii Island had no fewer than five members of this finch-like genus; no other island has had more than one. The Kona finch (so called from the Kona district of western Hawaii where alone it was found) was a small (6-inch) olive, whitish-bellied bird with the heaviest bill of all the family, apparently adapted specially to crushing the hard, dry seeds of the naio tree. It was discovered by Scott B. Wilson in 1887, collected in some numbers by Palmer and Munro in 1891, and collected by Perkins in 1892 and 1894. Apart from a record of a pair at Honaunau in 1891, all the birds were seen or collected about 10 miles north of that place in an area about 4 miles square on the south-west slopes of Mauna Loa, where they were working through open naio woodland at around 4,500 feet. Despite extensive searches of this rough area of recent lava flows, and other zones, no Kona finch has ever been seen alive since Perkins's trip of 1894.

Subfamily Drepanidinae: nectar-feeders

Apapane, *Himatione sanguinea* (one extinct race)

This, the commonest surviving Hawaiian honeycreeper, is a deep crimson bird, $4\frac{1}{4}$ inches long, with black wings and tail and white lower belly and undertail. Its bill is slender, sharp, and slightly downcurved, and it feeds on flower nectar (that of the ohia particularly) and insects, flying strongly with buzzing wings and sometimes wandering from island to island. It is found in the surviving forests on all the main islands without racial distinction, and is the only member of its family (as far as we know) to have been recorded (vagrant) from Niihau, west of Kauai. On Hawaii it is abundant, and was material for many of Paul H. Baldwin's vigorous ecology studies in the Hawaii National Park between 1937 and 1949. In fair numbers on Maui, it is now scarce on Lanai and rare on Molokai. It is still common on Oahu, and on Kauai, where it is, indeed, abundant in the high Alakai Swamp area. It is less abundant than it was lower down on this island, where at Kaholuamanu it was so numerous in 1891 that the air was filled with its continuous buzz.

Apapane colonists once reached Laysan years ago on the prevailing wind and established a race that, when described in 1892, was very much paler. By no means rare in 1902, this race was destroyed through the gradual reduction of its habitat by rabbits imported in 1903. Alexander Wetmore, ashore in 1923, may have witnessed its final demise; upon his arrival he could find only three birds on this small island. A sandstorm then blew for three days, after which there was not a bird to be seen, by him or anybody since.

Crested honeycreeper, *Palmeria dolei*

This 7-inch bird is blackish with a remarkable pattern of thin longitudinal pink stripes on its head and body, pink wing bars, an orange-red eye-ring, eye-line, and nape, and a bushy white crest on its forehead. Its beak is thin and sharp. Like the apapane, it feeds on ohia and other flower nectar, and insects.

Formerly it inhabited Molokai, where nobody has seen it since W. Alanson Bryan saw a small group on the wing in 1907. It still inhabits Maui, where it was discovered in the late 1880s by Scott B. Wilson, and was at least locally abundant on this island until 1895. In the present century it has become very rare; George C. Munro searched much forest for it in vain in 1936. In 1942, however, Paul H. Baldwin discovered one at 6,300 feet on the Haleakala extinct volcano; and he found others on its slopes in 1943, as L. P. Richards did in 1950, when up to four were seen and five or six others heard $\frac{1}{2}$ mile north-west of Puu Alaea at about 6,500 feet. The bird was heard by W. M. Ord in 1963, and seen again in January 1965; but only better news of this strange and beautiful bird could take it out of the Red Data Book.

Ula-ai-hawane, *Ciridops anna* (extinct)

This small red bird, $4\frac{1}{4}$ inches long, with dark wings and tail, greyish-white neck and head, and black crown had a short bill and was probably adapted to feed on the fruit of the hawane palm. It was confined to Hawaii, where it was discovered in about 1859, and was once perhaps widely distributed on both the windward and leeward sides in Hilo and the Kohala Mountains, and in Kona, where it was rare. By 1892, however, its population was very small, and the specimen that H. C. Palmer took near the headwaters of the Awini River on Mount Kohala on the 20th February of that year is probably the last seen alive by man. Munro believed he saw one at Kahua in 1937, but was not certain.

Iiwi, *Vestiaria coccinea*

This bird, nearly 6 inches long, is larger and less abundant than the apapane, with which it can be confused. It is vermilion, its wings black with a white flash, its tail black and its bill pink, long, sharp, and strongly downcurved. It eats the nectar of ohia, mamane, and other flowers, and insects – particularly caterpillars.

Like the other honeyeating honeycreepers, this active bird flies strongly for considerable distances as different areas come into flower. It was formerly recorded from all six main islands without racial distinction. It is still common enough in many parts of Hawaii – for instance, the Hawaii National Park. On Maui it is now very scarce. On Lanai, where it was recorded as fairly common in 1923, it diminished year by year until it disappeared entirely by 1929. It is doubtless also now extinct on Molokai, where none was seen in the thorough bird survey of 1935–7, or has been seen since. It is scarce on Oahu. However, a good population survives in Kauai, where it was abundant in the last century; in 1960 Richardson and Bowles found it abundant, or reasonably so at least, in the Alakai Swamp area at around 4,000 feet in the interior of the island.

Mamo, *Drepanis pacifica* (extinct)

The glossy, black, 9-inch mamo, with its rich yellow rump, undertail, and thighs, and yellow shoulder and wing-flashes, was certainly the finest of the Hawaiian honeycreepers, a nectar-feeder whose skin was in much demand for the feather-cloaks of the Hawaiian kings. Nevertheless the forest clearance by the white colonists seems to have been the cause of its decline, and its final downfall may have been hastened by shotgun feather-collectors, of whom one, in 1880, bagged as many as a dozen in a day. Native originally to all Hawaii's forests of the leeward and windward sides and Kohala in the north, it was decreased but still not extremely rare in the early 1880s, when the feather-collectors began to attack it. But it died out in the 'nineties. The last specimen seems to have been taken alive by R. H. Palmer deep in the Olaa forest, and the last bird was seen by H. W. Henshaw in the Kaumau forests at 1,000 feet above Hilo in 1898.

Black mamo, *Drepanis funerea* (extinct)

Endemic to Molokai, where clearly the representative of the mamo, this 8-inch black bird with a longer and more downcurved beak than the mamo's, used to take nectar from lobelias and other flowers. It was discovered by R. C. L. Perkins in the Pelekunu Valley in 1893, and recorded by him as rare in that year when much forest habitat had already been destroyed on the island. Private collectors worked the Pelekunu hard after Perkins's discovery, and in 1907, when Munro and Bryan visited the valley, they found none, though they managed to collect three males further east at Moanui.

Apart from an unconfirmed rumour of a sighting in the Wailau Valley a few years before 1936, the Moanui collection was the last record of living black mamos. Hard searches were made, in vain, for it in the surviving Molokai forests in the 'thirties and 'forties.

Hawaii is now the fiftieth state of the United States of America, with a strong forestry and national park service, and a fine cadre of private conservationists grouped round its flourishing Audubon Society and other organizations, notably the Bernice P. Bishop Museum in Honolulu. Western man, with his forest-slashing, introduced predators, and competitive alien birds and their diseases, and his days of rarity collecting, has given the youngest bird family a trouncing of which an aftermath of perilous rarity remains. A few of the lovely Drepanidids are still common; but the state of most survivors is a challenge to all of us – and of course to the modern, forward-looking proud Hawaiians in particular. The survival story of the Hawaiian honeycreepers is not half told. What will the rest of it read like when the present century is out? Time alone will show. The succour of the survivors arouses enthusiasm: but enthusiasm is not enough. What is needed is more research, more nature reserves – in fact, more spending of money. Only thus can our technological civilization's erosion of the native animal community of the great Hawaiian archipelago be arrested.

Family Parulidae: American wood warblers

BACHMAN'S WARBLER
Vermivora bachmani

In July 1833 John Bachman collected two specimens, and saw several others, of a "new" warbler a few miles from Charleston in South Carolina, and in the same year the species was figured from his material and formally named after him, by his greatest friend, John James Audubon.

Dean Amadon, when he discussed Bachman's warbler a hundred and twenty years after its discovery, was doubtless right in thinking that it was already a relict species when it was first found. It may well be a bird that, when first recognized by modern science, was already, quite naturally, on the way to extinction. It is not, however, extinct yet. After Bachman found it, it was not found again for over half a century; it

was next collected by Charles S. Galbraith, a dealer in decorations for women's hats and a pillar of the preposterous plume trade, who obtained, at Lake Pontchartrain in Louisiana, on spring passage, one in 1886, six in 1887, and thirty-one in 1888.

Gradually, since then, a picture of an extra-ordinarily rare migrant summer visitor to the south-eastern United States, and (certainly at the end of the last century) winterer in the deep south and Cuba and the Isle of Pines, has been pieced together. There are few now living who have seen Bachman's warbler, but it still appears, quite unpredictably and in tiny numbers, in the summer, mainly between Missouri and South Carolina. Its first nest was found by Otto Widmann in 1897 on the St Francis River in south-east Missouri on the Arkansas border. It has nested, in appearance quite desultorily, also in Arkansas, Alabama, and Kentucky, and possibly once even near Indianapolis in central Indiana, and has been seen and heard in the breeding season in the present century also in Virginia, North Carolina, Louisiana, and Mississippi. In South Carolina it was not seen again until sixty-eight years after Bachman collected it: Arthur Trezevant Wayne took it again near Mount Pleasant in May 1901, and proved breeding in I'On Swamp, Fairlawn, in Christ Church, Charleston County (probably Bachman's locality) in various years between 1905 and 1919. It then vanished from I'On, only to be discovered in the area again in the breeding season by C. Chandler Ross in 1938 and by Henry Kennon in 1946. A male sang (and was recorded on tape) near Washington in 1955. Birds have been observed in the area of Fairlawn and Charleston at spring passage and breeding time intermittently into the 1960s (one male sang for three or four consecutive seasons at Folly Beech without attracting a mate), though the later records have been of non-breeding birds; and there are recent records also from near Lorton, Virginia and on Bulls Island, South Carolina. The only bird so far reported in 1966 was a spring male at Birmingham in Alabama.

The population must now be smaller than it was even in previous years. There has been no detectable spring or fall passage of any strength for more than half a century; indeed, just a few individuals have been singly spotted. It is nearly eighty years since rather a large migrant party was identified, through the death of twenty-one on a night in March 1889 by striking the lighthouse beacon at Sombrero Key in Florida. None has been seen in Florida on passage since 1909.

The natural habitat of Bachman's warbler is in swampy river bottoms. Large areas of these still survive (though very few with pristine timber) both inside and outside the national wildlife refuge chain. The bird is protected by federal and state law. Research may confirm that Bachman's warbler has been discovered towards the end of its natural evolutionary life, perhaps (for once) unhastened by man. Only a study of the ecological requirements of the species can determine its probable future. It is doubtless the rarest present North American native songbird, as Roger Peterson puts it.

GOLDEN-CHEEKED WARBLER
Dendroica chrysoparia

This bird was first discovered in its winter quarters in Guatemala and described in August 1860 by the English ornithologists Sclater and Salvin. It was not until many years later that the breeding-grounds of this handsome black-and-white, yellow-faced Parulid were found to be confined, as they still are, to a relatively small area of Texas – the "cedar-breaks" (the cedar is in fact the juniper *Juniperus ashei*) of mature trees, 25 to 40 feet high, in very restricted areas of the Edwards Plateau in Texas.

Lately Roger Peterson has defined the breeding range as from near San Angelo, Rocksprings and the northern part of Uvalde County, eastwards locally to near Dallas, Waco, Austin, and San Antonio. Roger Pulich's recent survey, which he reported in 1962, shows that each pair of golden-cheeked warblers needs 2 or 3 acres of suitable habitat, and that a 400-acre block of cedar-break country normally holds only some twelve to fifteen pairs. He believed the total population was probably not over 14,000 birds.

The golden-cheeked warbler, then, is in a far better state than Bachman's warbler, or the rather similarly tree-restricted Kirtland's warbler (below) of Michigan. Its estimated population would signal no global danger were it not for current tendencies in Texan agricultural practice, which involve heavy brush removal and the eradication of the cedar stands to increase the grassland area. Despite the bird's strict protection by federal law, the preservation of substantial areas of old growth cedar-breaks seems essential for the future of the species, as it is also, and as strongly, on botanical grounds.

Despite this bird's first recognition in its winter quarters, not very much is known about its migration. Some reach Nicaragua at Matagalpa; but others appear to winter in southern Mexico, Guatemala, and Honduras.

KIRTLAND'S WARBLER
Dendroica kirtlandi

The first Kirtland's warbler ever taken as a specimen was collected by Samuel Cabot Jr in

October 1841 on shipboard between Abaco in the Bahamas, and Cuba. Cabot was on his way to collect the then quite unknown birds of Yucatan, and the specimen went unnoticed in his collection until 1865, long after the species had been truly discovered by Charles Pease.

Pease's bird was collected by him on the 13th May 1851 near Cleveland, Ohio, given to his father-in-law Dr Jared P. Kirtland, a most talented naturalist, and by Kirtland given to the great ornithologist Spencer Fullerton Baird, who published the Linnean name – after his old friend – in the following year. We now know that the Ohio bird was near its goal on spring migration, and that the 1841 bird must have been near its goal on fall migration.

Kirtland's warbler, whose story has been sedulously unfolded by the late Josselyn Van Tyne and Harold F. Mayfield, deserves to be the State Bird of Michigan. It nests now only in the jack pine stands of the Lower Peninsula of Michigan, and has never been proved to winter anywhere but in the Bahamas, where there are recent records from Cat, Eleuthera, New Providence and Grand Bahama islands – five in 1964. As far as anybody knows, this was its specially limited range when it was first found 100 years ago: if it is a relict (as it certainly appears to be – for the jack pine range touches the Yukon and extends in a great belt through Canada, the western Great Lake states, and Maine as far as Nova Scotia), then it had probably become a relict naturally, before European culture began to make its deep ecological disturbances of North American wildlife.

By the end of the nineteenth century the Bahamas had already been established by Charles B. Cory and other collectors as the winter home of this typical American songbird; but its nest and nesting-ground were not discovered until 1903 by Norman A. Wood in Oscoda County, Michigan. "Every nest since the first has been found within 60 miles of this spot," writes Mayfield in his admirable book *The Kirtland's Warbler*, published in 1960.

To cut short a long story of patient exploration and record-sifting, Van Tyne and Mayfield had established by 1951 – the year of an exhaustive cooperative census of all the singing males that could be found (432) – that the species was restricted in its breeding range to a gross area of the Lower Peninsula of Michigan less than 85 miles from north to south and 100 miles from east to west. Within this area at least one occupied territory was found in ninety-one different square-mile blocks. Only a small part of the chosen habitat was in fact occupied by the birds: the parts nearest the centres of greatest abundance of jack pine, particularly those densely covered with small jack pines (*Pinus banksiana*) between about 6 and 18 feet high. These are young trees growing after a felling or – more significantly – regenerating after a forest fire. Indeed, the warblers are apparently compulsive fire-aftermath colonists, arriving in a juvenile jack pine stand with some punctuality between six and thirteen years after the fire that gave rise to the regeneration. The more ordered replantings have had a slower colonization because they have taken longer to produce the thickets liked by the warblers.

Mayfield and his band of field colleagues repeated the 1951 census of singing males ten years later; the 1961 figure was 502. It is clear that lately Kirtland's warbler has had a stable population of about 1,000 birds at the beginning of each breeding season. It could, therefore, appear to be in rather little danger, favoured as it is by public opinion in both Michigan and its sole winter home in the Bahamas. But the peculiar circumstances of its preference for fire-aftermath jack pine stands has led to some further expensive (and very acceptable) insurance. Already the United States Forest Service has set aside 4,010 acres in the jack pine country of the Huron National Forest in cooperation with the Pontiac Audubon Club, the Michigan and Detroit Audubon Societies, and the Michigan Natural Areas Council. Within the area, prescribed and controlled burning will provide the birds with a succession of suitable young stands of jack pine for breeding. Furthermore, the Michigan Conservation Department has also established three management areas especially for this warbler, each of 4 square miles, on State Forest land.

Protected by strict state and federal law, and by this fine and imaginative management programme, the Kirtland's warbler has a case history that sets an example.

SEMPER'S WARBLER
Leucopeza semperi

This 6-inch bird, big for a wood warbler, belongs to a peculiar genus of its own, of quite uncertain relationship. Confined to the West Indian island of St Lucia in the Lesser Antilles, it was first described by P. L. Sclater in 1876, and doubtless represents a relict form of some old evolutionary trend in the exclusively American family of the Parulids. The Parulids are the ecological parallels of (though quite unrelated to) the Sylviine warblers of the Old World, and occupy the same niche in nature – on the whole more colourfully, though Semper's warbler, the *pied-blanc* of the St Lucians, is dull grey above and whitish below, with pale feet.

Very little is known about this extraordinary rare relict bird, which has full status in the Red Data Book. Formerly not uncommon over all its home island's mountain forests, it has been decreasing since the first decade of the present century, and has been provedly encountered only three times in the last four decades: in 1934, when Stanley John collected it on the summit of the Piton Flore; in March 1947, when John saw it in the forest between Piton Lacombe and Piton Canaries; and in 1961, when John saw one on the east coast at Louvet. A bird heard singing in 1962 in the remains of St Lucia's high forest was believed to be a Semper's warbler; but this report is unconfirmed.

James Bond suspects that Semper's warbler may become extinct before the twentieth century is out. It is a bird of low forest growth and

Semper's warbler *Albert E. Gilbert* 1966

probably nests on or very near the ground. Dr Bond has never seen or heard it during the many weeks he has spent in this habitat on St Lucia in the height of the breeding season.

An ecological survey of the fauna and flora of all the relict forests of the Antillean (and some other West Indian) islands seems abundantly necessary – as readers of other slender case-histories similar to that of Semper's warbler must doubtless now agree. Without such a survey, the possibility of saving this and other rare forms can never be worked out, far less a plan for its survival rescue by sanctuary management. Perhaps some of the West Indian bird rarities will themselves be declared national monuments, and a programme made for them similar to the one lately begun for some of the rare birds of Japan, such as could doubtless also be designed for some of the Hawaiian rarities.

Family Ploceidae: weavers

SEYCHELLES FODY
Foudia sechellarum

The fauna of the Seychelles islands gives the conservationist cause for very great anxiety. Much of it is unique; it is of great scientific significance, when studied with the flora, for the understanding of the origins and adaptations of living communities within their habitat; it helps the zoologist to solve problems of ancient land connection with, and dispersal from, the continental mainland, as well as of the evolution of isolated island forms. These invaluable faunal resources have steadily diminished through the colonization of the islands by man; and in several parts of the Seychelles the position is so bad that some rare land birds are now very near the point of extinction.

The fody – or *toq toq*, to give it the rather pleasing local name – is the only weaver bird endemic to the Seychelles. Its ancestral population probably spread to the islands from Madagascar or the Comoros, and is thought to have had its origins among the African widowbirds or more probably the queleas. Whether the *toq toqs* were originally red birds, like their close relatives in nearby island groups, is not known; but, if they were, there has been an evolutionary change in their colouration, for they are now dull brown with only a little yellow on their faces.

Seychelles fody *Fenwick Lansdowne* 1966

The species had in 1959 a total population of between 400 and 500 birds only, and is now restricted to the small islands of Frégate, Cousin, and Cousine, and thus to a total area of about 1,000 acres. Formerly it existed also on the islands of Praslin, La Digue, and Marianne. The conditions on Marianne, where the bird was first collected by E. Newton in 1866, show clearly why the birds have disappeared from it. Marianne was once well known as a refuge for several rare birds; but now it is devoid of all interest, with neglected coconut plantations and introduced domestic predators, and the original vegetation has been utterly destroyed. During the last century another *Foudia*, the flaming red cardinal, *F. madagascariensis*, from Madagascar, was introduced into the Seychelles. Because of the extinction of the *toq toq* from the three islands last mentioned, it has been thought that competition from the introduced "cardinals" might have been the cause. But close investigation of their ecology and behaviour has shown that they occupy separate ecological niches and are reproductively isolated noncompetitors.

Family Fringillidae: finches

TRISTAN GROSBEAK
Nesospiza wilkinsi

The remote South Atlantic Tristan da Cunha archipelago consists of three rather small volcanic islands: Tristan itself, which is the largest and northernmost; Inaccessible, the westernmost; and Nightingale, the smallest and southernmost. The name given to the group derives from the fact that the islands were discovered in 1506 by the Portuguese admiral Tristão da Cunha. The islands (excluding Gough) contain only four resident species of land birds; one rail, one thrush, and two finches. The particular finch here under review has just two subspecies: the "typical" race, which is restricted to Nightingale Island, and the other, *N. w. dunnei*, which is peculiar to Inaccessible. Inaccessible Island is ornithologically famous as the home of a unique flightless rail, *Atlantisia rogersi*,

locally known as the "island cock". So far, this island has escaped invasion by the introduced rats that have become such a pest on the main island; and everyone must hope that it will always be spared this threat.

It is rather strange that the Tristan grosbeak should have remained so long undescribed. Though there had been several much earlier naturalists' visits to the islands, it was not until 1923 that P. R. Lowe named it after G. Hubert Wilkins (later Sir Hubert Wilkins), who collected a single specimen on Nightingale Island on the 2nd May 1922 during the voyage of the *Quest*, which carried the Shackleton-Rowett expedition to the southern Atlantic. Dr Lowe mentioned that another specimen he examined, from Inaccessible Island, which had been collected on the 16th October 1873 by the *Challenger* expedition and had been in the British Museum collection since then, was of the same species, but he did not give it a racial name. In fact, it was not until 1952 that Y. Hagen named this race *N. w. dunnei* in an account published in Oslo, of the birds of Tristan da Cunha, recorded during the Norwegian Scientific Expedition there in 1937 and 1938. He gave the name after J. C. Dunne, who in 1946 wrote a full account of the vulcanology of the Tristan islands. Hagen rightly recognized the yellower colouration in the Inaccessible Island birds, and the marked difference in their smaller size of bill. Reports have also stated that the call of *N. w. dunnei* differs and is harsher in tone.

As may be imagined, notes on the biology of the birds living in these remote islands are not very extensive or detailed, but from information available it seems that the Tristan grosbeak is very specialized in its feeding habits. The birds apparently depend for their main source of livelihood on the seeds of the juniper-like *Phylica nitida*, which tree species densely woods some areas of both Nightingale and Inaccessible islands, up to a level of about 2,000 feet above sea-level. The large, strong bills of the grosbeaks enable them to deal most effectively with these hard seeds, which are picked either from the trees or off the ground and efficiently husked before eating. Woodland is not so extensive on Inaccessible Island as it is on Nightingale; and the birds there not only move about more and are harder to estimate in numbers but (it is said) also tend to be more insectivorous. On Nightingale Island the *Phylica* woods are denser, and the birds of the typical race *N. w. wilkinsi* feed more exclusively on the seeds and wander little, rarely even out into the tussock grass areas. It has accordingly been found easier to determine the likely numbers of the Nightingale birds. In 1957 it was estimated that their population numbered not more than about ninety birds – thirty pairs and another thirty young of the year. The population on Inaccessible was then probably a little higher, but could be estimated only between the rather broad limits of 70 to 120 birds.

These numbers are small. Though it is perhaps true that the population density of each race is satisfactory when compared with their available habitat, both subspecies must be looked upon as to some extent endangered. They should be given

Tristan grosbeak, Nightingale race *Robert Gillmor* 1966

all possible protection. Their woodland habitat is often subject to extensive storm damage; and there must be constant guard against any possibility of rat-introduction to these two at present uninhabited islands. Neither island is of any great size. The area of Nightingale is not much more than about 1 square mile, and at its highest point it is only 1,200 feet above sea-level. Inaccessible, although about seven times larger and rising to a height of 6,760 feet, has sides to its quadrilateral that are still only about 2 miles long.

The Tristan grosbeak breeds in the southern midsummer, in December and January, and those few of the partly domed nests that have been seen were placed near the ground in clumps of the *Spartina* grass. Two eggs appear to form a clutch – pale blue mottled with mauve and brown. From the few observations made on the young, it appears that they are fed on a few insects, but mainly on seeds; and not the seeds of the *Phylica* that the adult birds prefer, but those of the island crowberry shrub *Empetrum*.

TRISTAN FINCH *or* TRISTAN BUNTING
Nesospiza acunhae

According to Ernst Mayr and Dean Amadon, the two species of *Nesospiza* from the Tristan group seem to belong to the Fringillidae, or true finch family, and are perhaps close to the serins, which would point to an African origin of these colonists. It is interesting that the Gough sparrow, or Gough bunting, *Rowettia goughensis*, of Tristan's outlier Gough Island, about 250 miles to the south-east, is so close to the South American buntings of the genus *Melanodera* that some authorities put it in that genus, and it doubtless reached the very isolated island from the South American continent. It is in no danger of extinction.

It is possible, however, that the *Nesospiza* birds may, after all, be buntings. Their nesting habits hint at this. Until more systematic and behaviour work is done on them, either of the above vernacular names can thus be used. They could have reached Tristan long ago: of its main islands, all of volcanic origin, parts of Nightingale (by radiometric dating) are about 18,000,000 (or perhaps a little more) years old and of Miocene age. Inaccessible is from 5,000,000 to 7,000,000 years old and of Pliocene age. Big Tristan itself (40 square miles) is the youngest – a Pleistocene island (still volcanically active) that has been in existence less than 1,000,000 years.

The main Tristan islands have a total bird list of sixty forms, but this includes its only two extinct ones, nine "possibles", ten rare vagrants, and seven frequent visitors; the thirty-two breeding species and subspecies comprise one penguin, fifteen petrels, three albatrosses, one skua, one tern, one noddy, three thrushes, five "buntings", and two rails. Of land birds there are only six species – a rail on Inaccessible; a moorhen, or gallinule, on Gough; a thrush, which has one subspecies each on Tristan, Inaccessible, and Nightingale; one bunting restricted to Gough; and two buntings or finches already noted, with a race on Nightingale and a race on Inaccessible – one of them formerly also had a race on Tristan.

The species under review here has been called the "small-billed Tristan sparrow", and several other vernacular names have been used. Despite the uncertainty of its true relationship, we here propose to say "Tristan finch", if only to celebrate the contrast of its normal finch-sized bill with the grosbeak bill of its "sibling species", the Tristan grosbeak.

The Tristan finch is so called because it was originally described on material from the main

island in 1873. It was then already extinct there, having possibly been exterminated by introduced cats and rats. At present the "typical" race is restricted to Inaccessible Island, and, although the birds there are now considered identical with the form extinct on the main island, they might have been considered distinct if more specimens from Tristan had been available for comparison.

Tristan finch, Nightingale race *Robert Gillmor* 1966

In 1957 the population of the "typical" race was estimated to be not fewer than several hundred birds on the 6 square miles of Inaccessible Island. No estimate was available, however, of the *N. a. questi* race (like the Tristan grosbeak, also collected first by Hubert Wilkins on the 21st May 1922) on the 1 square mile of Nightingale Island, and there have been no recent accounts of ornithological exploration in the Tristan group. We may mention that the islands were virtually uninhabited between late 1962 and 1964, at the end of which year Tristan da Cunha was reoccupied by the islanders, after their absence in Britain following the volcanic eruption in 1962 near their settlement of Edinburgh.

Both races of this finch are at present common enough within their limited habitat, but because of their restricted distribution – and because the two eggs that form the normal clutch laid yearly are in a nest built on or close to the ground in a clump of grass – they would quickly be threatened if, by any unlucky chance, rats or cats were inadvertently introduced on to the islands. We must indeed hope that every possible care will be taken to ensure that this does not happen. It is similarly important that the error made on

Tristan should not be repeated – that is, of permitting goats to become feral and damage the natural vegetation. "Wild" goats have now, however, apparently been eliminated from Tristan. Moreover, the pigs (now also eradicated) that became wild and were doing so much damage on Inaccessible Island must not be reintroduced.

The climate of the Tristan islands, contrary to some popular misconceptions, is quite equable, with sea-level temperatures of between a maximum 75° F. and a minimum 34° F. The annual rainfall averages about 50 inches, and, as the soil is fertile, there is good grass cover at lower altitudes, while up to about 2,000 feet the slopes are well wooded with a juniper-like *Phylica*. Strong gales are the trouble, and it is interesting to note that, although the ancestral stock of the land birds undoubtedly originated over 2,000 miles away both in Africa (probably) and in South America (as we may infer from the Gough sparrow and from the frequency with which the American purple gallinule strays to Tristan), those species that are established have become very sedentary, and there is no apparent contact between the distinctive island subspecies.

Family Emberizidae: buntings

IPSWICH SPARROW
Passerculus princeps

The New World is doubtless the evolutionary home of the bunting family, and has the greatest number of them. One particularly large group consists of many species, most of which have inconspicuous streaky brown plumage; these, doubtless because they are superficially like the common European birds of the genus *Passer*, are known in English-speaking North America as "sparrows". It has long been known that they are quite unrelated to the true sparrows, and instead are closely allied with the Old World buntings, but the vernacular word "sparrow" is now so firmly established for them that it will no doubt remain. Indeed, an ornithologist from Africa might be excused for suggesting that these sparrowy brown American buntings remind him strongly, by their general plumage characteristics, of the large group of grass warblers known as the cisticolas.

The Ipswich sparrow, named by C. J. Maynard in the *American Naturalist* in 1872, is so called because the type specimen from which the species was described was collected at Ipswich, Massachusetts. The birds are now found breeding only on Sable Island off Nova Scotia, where the population is already dangerously localized because of the small size of the island. Even this small habitat is unfortunately being steadily reduced in area, because the island is being steadily eroded by the sea. Upon the present circumscribed area of Sable Island, the population of Ipswich sparrows might really be called quite dense, because in 1962 the place was divided into seventeen counting areas and these produced a total of fifty-eight birds. The species must thus obviously be considered very rare. It requires no imagination to appreciate how truly scarce and thinly scattered the birds must be throughout their wintering areas.

These winter homes are described in the *Check List* of the American Ornithologists' Union as lying along the United States Atlantic coast from Massachusetts south to Cumberland Island in South Georgia; some casual instances have been recorded in two coastal areas, Old Orchard in southern Maine and Wolfville in central Nova Scotia, as well as in two just inland, Cambridge in Massachusetts and New Haven and West Haven in Connecticut.

The erosion of Sable Island, by reducing the breeding habitat, is obviously a prime danger to the future of the Ipswich sparrows. But there can be little doubt that another contributing factor in their decline is the rapid development of holiday resorts along the eastern or Atlantic seaboard of the United States, all of which must be interfering very greatly with the birds' wintering places.

Ipswich sparrows need undisturbed sand-dunes if they are to survive, and, as the Fish and Wildlife Service has written, there is a very urgent need to persuade private owners of coastal property to leave their sand-dunes in the natural state. It is true that there are three appointed reserves that may help a great deal by preventing the spread and development of housing estates: the National Seashores at Cape Cod and Cape Hatteras, and the Chincoteague National Wildlife Refuge. But their areas are inadequate for full protection, and the help of private landowners must be invoked elsewhere.

Many of the New World buntings are fine songsters, and this one is in voice very similar to a closely related species, the savannah sparrow. Indeed, some taxonomists consider that the Ipswich sparrow is no more than a well-marked subspecies of the savannah one. There is certainly no doubt that the former is well marked, because it is a much larger and paler, sandy-coloured bird, and the two could never be confused in good field conditions. Although there has been no very detailed investigation, a good deal is known about the habits of the Ipswich sparrow, and, like many others, it lays four or five eggs; it could increase quickly if its preferred habitat were left undisturbed.

DUSKY SEASIDE SPARROW
Ammospiza nigrescens

Like the Ipswich sparrow, this also is a bird of the Atlantic Ocean coast. Now a rare and local species, in some danger of extinction, the dusky seaside sparrow for a time occupied a unique position among the birds of the world, as its population had increased through the influence of the most modern scientific development; the space rocket. Its principal home is in the marshes around and behind Cape Kennedy, formerly and on many maps still known as Cape Canaveral, where stringent military security measures ensured for some years a minimum of disturbance by wandering human beings, and prevented commercial development of that part of the eastern United States coast. There is every reason to believe that in this security area some temporary improvement of the dusky seaside sparrow's population did result. The occasional firing of rockets was doubtless something to which the birds soon became accustomed. But

this situation was too good to last; and another form of scientific progress has nullified the benefits that the birds at first derived from the removal of human disturbance.

To improve the living conditions of the workers at the rocket centre, there have been recent extensive draining projects and widespread mosquito control measures. These have greatly altered the birds' domain. What were purely coastal salt marshes (which constituted the sparrows' specialized habitat) became fresh, brackish, or even dry areas in which there was a rapid change both in the vegetation and the fauna. Plant species foreign to the terrain as well as new predators, were able to gain access to it; and much of the area is now entirely unsuited to the seaside sparrows.

The total population of the birds is now estimated at fewer than 500 individuals. The type locality was at the Indian River; and the distribution a decade ago was given as being the eastern Orange and northern Brevard counties of central eastern Florida, near Indian River City, at Titusville, on Merritt Island, and on the adjacent mainland along the St Johns River. The species seems always to have had a localized range in this salt marsh area; but it certainly used to be much more widespread and numerous there, particularly on Merritt Island, where it was believed there were fewer than 200 in 1964, and along the St Johns River, with only ten birds seen in 1962 and more recently none at all.

Biological studies of the species have established its habitat needs as well as the remedial measures necessary to restore its *status quo*. But whether restoration will be possible is doubtful, because it would need re-flooding of the area by salt water to eliminate all the alien species, plant and mammal.

The dusky seaside sparrow is the only seaside member of the group that is found breeding in this particular area of Florida, and it is, as its name implies, the darkest. It is about 6 inches long and has under parts strikingly striped with black and white; it is in every way much darker than either of the other two seaside sparrows – the one next mentioned, which is resident in southern Florida, and the more northern *A. maritima*, which breeds from Massachusetts to North Carolina. So dark is it, in fact, that one local name given to it is "black shore finch". Although all three sparrows are treated as distinct species in the American *Check List*, some ornithologists consider that at least the Cape Kennedy bird is likely to be a subspecies of *Ammospiza maritima*, which was described from New Jersey.

This dusky species has a buzzing call, rather like that of its northern relation. Its nest, placed just above high-water mark, is made of grasses with a finer lining; and three or four eggs are thought to form a normal clutch.

CAPE SABLE SEASIDE SPARROW
Ammospiza mirabilis

Man's recent development and alteration of Florida's coastline and marshlands have already eliminated much of the natural habitat on which many specialized wild animals depend for their living and being. Yet another North American sparrow-bunting, the Cape Sable seaside sparrow, has consequently become rare and to some extent endangered. This particular species is not so strictly coastal in its choice of habitat as the other two seaside sparrows, to which it is closely related. It is an entirely marsh-haunting bird and found within so very limited an area that suitable places for its feeding and breeding are constantly being narrowed or eliminated.

Ammospiza mirabilis was originally described from Cape Sable, which is a peninsula of the Everglades National Park, jutting out into the Gulf of Mexico from the extreme south-western tip of Florida. Until quite recently, it still existed in the type locality; but apparently it is no longer found there. The present distribution of this entirely resident, or non-migratory, bird is described as being solely within south-western Florida, but only from the Ochopee marshes near Everglade south-east towards the head-waters of the Huston River, and from the mouth of Gum Slough to the Shark River basin.

The Cape Sable sparrow may prove to be the last new species of bird to be discovered in the eastern United States of America. It was described as recently as January 1919 by A. H. Howell, and is a very distinctive little species,

much greener in general colouration than all the other sparrows likely to be found among the sand dunes or coastal prairies and marshes. It is also much more contrastingly white below than any other south Florida sparrow.

The birds are protected by law, and their future is perhaps to some extent assured by the fact that many of their numbers live within the Everglades National Park. But land-drainage projects, farther to the north, are already having an adverse effect on the ecology of this great wildlife sanctuary. The habitat of the small population of this species, which fluctuates but generally shows a declining trend, is now highly and unnaturally unstable. The size of the population is uncertain, though it has lately been estimated at certainly fewer than 1,000 and probably fewer than 500 birds. Outside the national park, there is a constant and menacing process of real estate development, which has already much infringed former strongholds of the sparrow. Within it, threats, some natural but others newly strong, include fires, droughts, hurricanes, and encroachment by mangroves. Mangroves have lately invaded areas of estuary grasses and reeds in many parts of the world, because the silt brought down in rivers as a result of bad farming practices in the hinterland has provided ideal conditions. Mangrove seeds have been able to germinate in silt where hitherto pure sands have prevented any such spread. It has also been suggested that parasitism by some cowbirds, which limits the breeding success of the buntings, may thus limit their recovery rate when conditions improve.

The best hope for the survival of this rare sparrow is the acquisition of further reserve land for it outside the national park. If already drained lands can have their original water table restored, one immediate consequence will be a reduction in the present serious fire hazard. This is a reversal of present trends not yet fully accepted, far less adopted, in the state of Florida, and is much hoped for by conservationists.

In habits, these Cape Sable birds do not differ greatly from some other closely related members of the large and greatly diverse group of typical New World buntings within which one prominent taxonomist has classified a total of 157 species.

REPTILES

About 5,000 living species of reptiles survive on our planet at present. There are thus still rather more kinds of reptiles than of mammals, but fewer than of birds. Though much more primitive than either mammals or birds, and indeed, back in the Secondary or Mesozoic Era, ancestral to both (and themselves of Carboniferous period origin – that is, of the Primary or Paleozoic Era), the reptiles cannot be described as a relict class. Their great heyday of the Secondary, when they produced the largest land animals the world has known, is over. Some of their surviving groups are indeed relict. There are no longer any reptiles that truly fly. But in the tropics particularly the reptiles still thrive, and successfully occupy places in nature to which they are beautifully adapted. Modern lizards, indeed, are as young as birds, first appearing in the Jurassic period; and snakes are even younger, being first known from Cretaceous deposits. In their ideal habitat they have a pattern of abundance and rarity not provedly much different from that of the mammals and birds – though no species of reptile seems to reach the order of numerical abundance of the most successful mammal and bird species.

Despite the variety of the world's reptiles, the I.U.C.N. has not yet been able to complete a file of their rare and endangered forms so large and detailed as that of the endangered higher vertebrates. Active herpetologists are very much rarer than mammalogists, who in turn are rarer than ornithologists. However, the work is now in hand and it should be possible in the future to do more justice and give better protection to these interesting animals.

Reptiles are just as vulnerable to the human pressures that have made the other rare vertebrates rare: perhaps a little less than the others to hunting (except in some cases like crocodiles, a few snakes, and sea turtles), and to the introduction of competitors. The S.S.C. offers here some sample cases that have been studied as deeply as those of higher rare vertebrates, in the hope that their story may encourage a wider interest in the survival problems of the class.

Order RHYNCHOCEPHALIA
Family Sphenodontidae: tuatara

TUATARA
Sphenodon punctatus

This remarkable New Zealand animal is indeed a relict – the last survivor of a very ancient order of reptiles. It is the only living animal that preserves virtually unchanged the basic anatomical features of the reptiles of late Primary (Permian) times well over 200,000,000 years ago – notably the arrangement of its skull bones and structure, especially its complete palate and well-developed pineal (or central, third) eye.

The tuatara can therefore, and with some reason, be regarded as a living fossil, and the scientific and educational importance of its conservation assumes special dimensions. Indeed, if the tuatara were allowed to die out, we should lose the only living model of land vertebrate life whose order flourished almost as early as that of the Coelacanth fish, *Latimeria*.

The tuatara is confined to the main archipelago of New Zealand, where it has been deeply studied by W. H. Dawbin and other herpetologists. At the Polynesian invasion of about A.D. 950, as fossil and subfossil records show, it was widely distributed over both North and South Islands. By European times it had either been exterminated by the Maoris, or (as some think) extinguished by climatic and ecological changes, to the extent that it had disappeared from both mainlands, and is now found on only twenty coastal islands, of which three are in

Cook Strait and belong geographically to South Island, and the rest lie off the north-east coast of North Island. Two mainland groups surviving on North Island have been kept going by translocation.

Dawbin's recent surveys suggest that the surviving population on half the inhabited islands (all so far studied in detail) may be of the order of 10,000 or a little over. The biggest population is on Stephens Island in Cook Strait. It is, for the time being, safe – particularly as the New Zealand Government has for years, as Dawbin reports, "maintained a very strict protection on tuataras, so that permits are required even to visit the islands on which the animals occur and the penalties for unauthorised handling are very severe".

The tuatara lives in burrows, and is sensitive to predation by cats, rats, and other introduced predators. It lives and breeds slowly; fertilization may occur ten months before its eggs are laid, and the eggs may take fifteen months to hatch. The lizard-like reptiles grow very slowly, may not reach maturity for over twenty years, and – if undisturbed – may probably live for a century.

Order TESTUDINES
Family Testudinidae: tortoises (including freshwater "turtles")

MUHLENBERG'S, or BOG, TURTLE
Clemmys muhlenbergi

This small water tortoise is described by Roger Conant as a "gem of a turtle, indeed almost a collector's item". Possibly collecting for captive culture may have contributed to the present rarity of this animal of the eastern United States, which formerly ranged from near sea-level in the state of Connecticut to western North Carolina, living up to 4,000 feet in the slow streams and bogs of the southern mountains. But it is certain that land-drainage and "reclamation" has been the main cause of the present very fragmented and relict distribution of this turtle.

Although pockets of relative abundance still exist, according to a very recent report from P. C. H. Pritchard, these are almost all in areas presently scheduled for building development.

GALÁPAGOS GIANT TORTOISE
Testudo elephantopus[1]

The Galápagos Islands, 500 miles west in the equatorial Pacific from the mainland of Ecuador, are of volcanic origin and have never been connected with any mainland. They arose from the sea in a series of volcanic disturbances in the later Tertiary Era, and acquired their present topography mainly in Pleistocene times – that is, in the last 1,000,000 years. It is thought unlikely that the principal members of the present plant and animal community of the islands arrived much before the end of the Pliocene period that immediately preceded the Pleistocene.

Young though they are, the flora and fauna of Galápagos contain many peculiar kinds that have evolved in isolation into genera and species unique to the archipelago and into many races and even a few species unique to particular islands within it. There is even one tribe of birds peculiar to the archipelago, the Geospizini or Darwin's "finches", that is doubtless descended from a bunting ancestor that colonized it by flight and favourable wind and is still part of the American buntings' subfamily, the Emberizinae.

The rapid evolution of the Galápagos fauna was so obvious and inspiring to Charles Darwin on his visit to the archipelago in H.M.S. *Beagle* in 1835 that – more than any of his many other discoveries on that momentous voyage – they started the train of thought that culminated in his *Origin of Species* of 1859.

Among the material that lit the fuse of Darwin's theory of organic evolution by natural selection were not only the "finches" now named after him, but the giant tortoises he found, so different on each main island. We now know

[1] Some modern workers use the genus *Geochelone*.

from fossil evidence that the (smaller) ancestors of the Galápagos giant tortoises were present on the South American mainland in the period of the Miocene (the one before the Pliocene). We are certain, too, from parallel evidence elsewhere in the world, that the land tortoise ancestor of *Testudo elephantopus* and its swarm of island forms in the Galápagos could have colonized the archipelago across 500 miles of sea, and each separate substantial island within it, as some land tortoises can float and survive for long periods in sea water. All the Galápagos land animals appear to be of American origin except one, the land mollusc, *Tornatellides chathamensis*, which is doubtless of Polynesian (and therefore faunally Australasian) origin and may have floated to its present home from islands about 3,000 miles to the west!

The Galápagos archipelago was discovered in 1535 by the Spanish conquistadores of Panama, and in the seventeenth century was already a haunt of buccaneers of several nations, who were followed in the early nineteenth century by whalers. However, it was not properly settled by humans until a few years before Darwin's visit. The earliest Spaniards found the islands a *galápagar*, a place where tortoises abound, and after the tortoises they have been named Galápagos ever since. Buccaneers, sealers, and whalers knew the world's largest tortoises well, and found them an easy source of excellent meat; big ones can weigh 500 pounds. C. H. Townsend, who analysed the logbooks of about 105 whalers, found that (not to mention what their crews ate on the spot) they carried off over 15,000 giant tortoises between 1811 and 1844, or an average of 122 tortoises per vessel. And during this period there were far more operating whalers than 100 – over 700 in the American whaling fleet alone.

Scientists, when they came to collect and name the Galápagos tortoises, were already examining the aftermath of an appalling slaughter; and the destruction and removal of island tortoises by ships' companies continued through the nineteenth century. The hunting ceased on the different islands only when the tortoises became so rare that the hunters could not profitably find them.

Modern systematists now regard the array of Galápagos giant tortoises, extinct and surviving, as island races of one species – though, in the days of the scientific naming of the different forms, which virtually ended in 1907 (collection for museums and zoos went on later), at least sixteen Linnean names were given to various specimens, all originally as full species. Five forms have been so described from what is much the largest island, Albemarle (Isabela), which seem to be acceptable at least as valid races, each centred around one of its five large volcanoes. These volcanoes, originally separate islands, but now joined by what (most probably in Pleistocene times) was a lowering of sea-level (or elevation of sea-bottom, or both) of 300 feet or more, are still "islands" in a vast and (even to tortoises) largely impenetrable, rough, lowland, lava plain. Apart from these, each of ten other islands – that is, all the other larger ones except Bindloe (Marchena), and the small island of Tower (Genovesa) – has, or had, its own form of giant tortoise. Two names have been given to tortoises of the second largest island, Indefatigable (Santa Cruz), and two to tortoises of Charles (Floreana), but these are doubtless synonymous – that is, descriptive of an already named form: there is considerable individual variation within the whole species, or subspecies. The extinct tortoise of Barrington (Santa Fé), though collected by hunters over a century ago, was never collected scientifically and has not been named, though a few remains of shells and bones might prove enough for a systematist to erect a valid name for it. In the short island-by-island account that follows, the racial names (still in need of some revision) are not given, nor are the present official Spanish island names; in all deference to the Ecuadorian Government and the geographers, it is the convention in zoological accounts to use the old English island names.

Abingdon. Plentiful in 1822, and until hunted down in the 1840s, the Abingdon giant tortoise was very rare indeed by the end of the nineteenth century, and survived as a tiny population by 1962, several previous scientific expeditions in the 'thirties and 'fifties having failed to find it altogether. A careful exploration in 1964 found only dead tortoises – twenty-eight of them in holes and fissures – most of which appeared to be over five years dead. Goats had been introduced to this island between 1957 and 1963 and had cleared much vegetation.

James. Fourteen tons of James tortoises were collected by one ship in 1812; and this form continued to exist in declining but reasonable abundance until the 1840s. By the 'seventies there were so few in penetrable country that they were no longer worth hunting. Early in the present century (in 1906) a few were collected for museums. The form still survives, and may not have been seen by some recent expeditions to this uncolonized island, owing to the appalling difficulty of travel on the sharp lava flows of the eastern side of the island. Here a population of unknown size certainly survives: and the fact that only two were seen in 1961, two in 1962, and two in 1963 does not mean that the virtually impenetrable terrain may not hold considerably more. A few more tortoises were found in 1966.

Jervis. The Jervis tortoise is based, scientifically, on only one specimen of unknown origin (the type) and another taken by the California Academy of Sciences expedition on Jervis in 1905. No Jervis tortoise has been found since by any of the rather few explorers of this island, including a party from the Charles Darwin Research Station that searched almost the whole island thoroughly in May 1963. The type specimen is only doubtfully from Jervis, and the 1905 specimen resembles a south Albemarle form and may have been introduced on Jervis by hunters. Nevertheless, good tortoise trails on Jervis testify to a once-flourishing population.

Duncan. Rather abundant from 1848 to 1863, judging by some hunters' records, the Duncan tortoise seems to have continued to be reasonably so until the California Academy expedition collected eighty-six in 1905–6. Since then only small numbers had been encountered by field surveyors on this rather small island up to 1962, when three were seen. A thorough exploration by Miguel Castro in 1963–4 established a total population of the order of 140. Much endangered by rats, this population was thought non-breeding and was apparently down to ninety-two in 1967. Eggs have therefore been lately taken on Duncan by the Charles Darwin Foundation to rear young for translocation when they are big enough to withstand rats.

Indefatigable. Abundant in 1812 and until the 1840s, the Indefatigable form was thought no longer worth hunting by the 1870s. However, although the island was settled in the 1930s, there is still good and fortunately inaccessible tortoise country in the west-central part of the island (scheduled now as a nature reserve) where more than 1,000 individuals have now been marked and the population is estimated as possibly up to twice as many.

Barrington. A population known to hunters in 1839, when they took twenty-two or more, was last seen in 1853, when hunters took at least one. The island form is doubtless extinct; a tortoise seen alive in 1957 was one of at least two introduced from Indefatigable Island the year before.

Chatham. Judging by hunters' records, a large population of the tortoise of this island suffered heavy human predation from 1813 to 1863, after which it collapsed. The form was rare in 1875. The California Academy expedition could collect only two live animals in 1905–6. Still surviving about 1942, and just so in 1955 and 1957, the Chatham form was thought to be extinct by 1960. Many small ones were sold to the soldiers of the American base in the early 'forties; this may have contributed significantly to its disappearance. This is, fortunately, not yet complete; in 1964 the island naturalist Jacob Lund found two tortoises, hatched in about 1959, kept as pets on a remote smallholding, and heard of others such still living on the island.

Hood. The Hood tortoise was decliningly abundant from 1831 to the late 1840s, when it was virtually hunted out; though hunting continued until 1853, it was no longer worth the effort in 1875. The expeditions of the present century encountered very few individuals: three in 1906, two in 1929. A Hood tortoise seems to have been killed in 1942; a small individual was seen in 1957; and two were found in 1963, of which one at least was alive in 1964. Five were found in a more thorough search in 1966. The vegetation of this island has been progressively impoverished by goats throughout the present century.

Charles. Very abundant in 1812, when 400 to 500 (or more) were taken, the Charles tortoise population was inexorably reduced by hunters until it was small in the 1840s and, by hunters, reported extinct in 1875. Possibly it was already extinct by about 1850: three taken in 1882 may have been of stock translocated from another island, and are the last seen on Charles, where the giant tortoise is certainly now extinct.

Narborough. The Narborough form is based on only one specimen taken by Rollo H. Beck, leader of the California Academy expedition in 1906. Nobody has ever seen a giant tortoise on this island since. Yet the race must survive. Narborough, the driest of the larger islands, has its most extensive humid and vegetated quarter on its southern slopes. This, like the rest of the island, is surrounded by a vast wilderness of almost impassable, barren lava flows, which have discouraged the tortoise-hunters of the past and so far checked most field explorations of present conservationists. Until the most inaccessible oasis in the whole archipelago is explored, the fate and status of the Narborough tortoise must remain a mystery. However, fresh droppings were found on the southern slopes by J. Hendrickson and others early in 1964.

Albemarle. The five forms of Albemarle tortoise are based on the five principal volcanoes of this, by far the largest, island of Galápagos: the north volcano, or Volcán Wolf; the north-central volcano, or Volcán Darwin, above Tagus Cove; the central volcano, Volcán Alcedo or Cowley Mountain; the south-central volcano, or Sierra Negra, above Villamil; and the south-west volcano, or Cerro Azul, above Iguana Cove. The last two forms are not very distinct, and the Villamil population may have to be "sunk" within the Iguana Cove race. This is now recognized as the "typical" form named by Harlan in 1827 as *Testudo elephantopus*.

The figures available from steady hunting from 1833 to the end of the nineteenth century

indicate the survival of a fairly substantial population up to the 1860s, though by 1875 it was clear that some at least of the races were reduced in numbers. In the present century there is enough evidence to give us a rough idea of the status of each. The Volcán Wolf race was fairly numerous in 1905–6, still numerous in 1957, not uncommon in 1960–4, and 2,000 or more in 1967. The Volcán Darwin race, tolerably numerous in 1875, was fairly so in 1905 and still breeding (by the evidence of dead young and the trails of adults) in 1953 and 1957. However, fresh droppings were seen in 1963, a good number of adults were discovered in 1965, and the population was flourishing in 1966, and sixty-five in 1967 by the count of the Charles Darwin Research Station. The Volcán Alcedo race, already rare in 1905–6, was of uncertain status until 1963, when Miguel Castro found the droppings of a respectable population, which was seen feeding on the grassy crater floor from a helicopter early in the following year. In 1966 Eric Shipton, in two days of survey, counted seventy-nine. The Darwin Station estimated a population of 174 in 1967. The Villamil race, still abundant in 1875, had become rarer and was still hunted in 1902 and 1905, though it was recorded as abundant in 1906 (doubtless after search in a different part of this largest "volcano-island" area of Albemarle); in 1957 it was certainly reduced in numbers, at least near the penal colony at Villamil, though it survived in 1960–2 and 1964, when it was said to be still exploited by settlers. The Iguana Cove race, numerous in 1905–6, and common enough in 1928 to enable 180 to be caught by the New York Zoological Society, also persisted in 1960–2. Taking all five races together, the Albemarle tortoises were still fairly plentiful in 1957 and persisting in 1965.

To sum up the whole species (or subspecies), entirely viable populations of giant tortoises at present survive in the western, nature-reserve sector of Indefatigable, and on at least three of the five volcanoes of Albemarle. The Narborough population is a mystery. Small and endangered populations survive on Hood, Chatham, James, Duncan, and probably Abingdon. Ignoring those of Jervis, the tortoises of the other two islands – Barrington and Charles – are doubtless extinct.

In mid-1965 no fewer than 177 Galápagos giant tortoises of various forms (forty-three of them unidentified to races) were reported to the International Zoo Year Book as captive in at least fifty-eight of the world's zoos. The International Zoo Year Book made censuses of rare animals in zoos in the seasons 1962–3, mid-1964, and mid-1965. Of the Chatham tortoise a pair was at the Bronx Zoo in New York in all three censuses, a female in the Prague Zoo in 1964 and 1965, and an individual in the Rapid City Zoo, South Dakota, in 1964. Of the Hood race two males were in the San Diego Zoo, California, in 1962–3 and 1964, though apparently not in 1965. Moreover, tortoises referred, not simply to the full species, but to the "typical" south Albemarle race, *T. e. elephantopus* (or its synonym *T. e. vicina*), were recorded from thirty-four zoos in 1964 to the number of 114, of which twenty-one were logged as having been bred in captivity; while in 1965 at least forty-three zoos claimed 106 of this race.

The Galápagos giant tortoises are certainly very long-lived, and occasionally have reached a proved age of over 100 years. While the successful hatching and rearing of eggs in captivity has been recorded in detail fewer than thirty times (the latest from the San Diego Zoo in 1958, and yearly since 1961), it seems possible that a much larger number have, in fact, been captive-bred, and that over 10 per cent of the 1964 zoo stocks may have been so. The 180 south Albemarle tortoises caught in 1928 by the New York Zoological Society and dispersed over various zoos and other establishments in the southern U.S.A., Bermuda, Panama, and Australia did not have breeding success until 1939, in Bermuda, and probably contributed the stock (or some of it) that bred later in Miami in Florida, the Honolulu Zoo, and San Diego.

The origins of present zoo stock, the racial status of the specimens, and the full details of zoo breeding records may be in need of a fresh look – including systematic study of the many living specimens and some shells and bones, and a fresh dig in the zoo archives. Besides the Chatham and Hood forms, the rare Abingdon form was represented by a female in the Oklahoma Zoo in 1962–3 and 1964, and by an individual in the Rapid City Zoo in 1964, but apparently was in no zoo in 1965. Of the rare Duncan form the Bronx Zoo had two females in 1962–3 and 1964, one female in 1965; the National Zoological Park in Washington, D.C., may have had two individuals in 1962–3 and 1964, one in 1965; the Rapid City Zoo logged one in 1964. In 1965, twenty-two Indefatigable tortoises were in ten zoos, and a female of the north Albemarle race had been living for some time in the Bronx.

These identifications, quoted from the International Zoo Year Book, may in some cases need revision; but it is certain that five races of Galápagos giant tortoises, deserving full status in the Red Data Book, linger on wholly or partly in zoos, and that the establishment of a real zoo bank needs more serious research and organization than is at present being done. If undertaken, it could march well with the big drive now being mounted by the Charles Darwin Foundation for the Galápagos Islands, whose field station at Academy Bay on Indefatigable has been operating fully since 1962, and whose conservation officer, Sr Miguel Castro, has been working on the tortoises since before then. The object of the drive is a full assessment during the 1960s of the wild status of all surviving races, notwithstanding the vast difficulties of field travel on the rougher lava fields. All the uninhabited islands, and western Indefatigable, have already been declared nature reserves, and all Galápagos tortoises are now everywhere protected by law.

MEXICAN GOPHER TORTOISE
Gopherus flavomarginatus

The genus *Gopherus* is the only member of the true tortoise subfamily (the Testudininae) native to North America, with four species, all of which can burrow powerfully. The Texas tortoise, *G. berlandieri,* the desert tortoise, *G. agassizi,* of the west, and the gopher tortoise, *G. polyphemus,* are smallish animals in no present danger (the first two, threatened by the pet trade, are now protected by law); but the relatively giant Mexican gopher tortoise is becoming very rare, and may already be extinct in the desert states of the far south-west United States. In Mexico it may now be limited only to relict groups in the states of Chihuahua and Durango, where it is threatened by the local people who hunt it for food. In its open habitat it is very easy to find and catch, and its decline gives rise to deep concern.

Family Cheloniidae: sea turtles

GREEN TURTLE
Chelonia mydas

Probably the most valuable reptile in the world, the green turtle could be of greater importance as a food-animal on the coasts of the tropical seas if its grave over-exploitation during the present century could be corrected. Numerically it still has a rather large population; but its breeding-grounds are so seriously reduced and in danger that the Survival Service Commission has a sheet for it in the Red Data Book.

The green turtle was formerly common in most of the world's oceans where the temperature is never less than about 68° F., and has often wandered into cooler waters. In the Caribbean area it has now virtually or entirely vanished from its breeding beaches in Florida's Dry Tortugas, the Bahamas, and the Cayman Isles, and survives largely by virtue of the Tortuguero protected hatchery in Costa Rica, whence some 20,000 hatchlings have been annually flown to different parts of the Caribbean in the last decade (by Dr A. Carr of the Caribbean Conservation Corporation) for release and restocking. These experiments continue. In the South Atlantic, Ascension Island is still an important nesting ground. A colony on the coast of Turkey between Fenike and Samandag in the Mediterranean is being over-exploited.

Headquarters in the Indian Ocean were formerly the Seychelles and the Mascarene Islands (Mauritius, Réunion, and Rodriguez), where the turtles are now very scarce. Aldabra, north of Madagascar, was once the only site of mass nesting by the green turtle in the western Indian Ocean. In 1967 only five laying turtles could be found. The islanders of Bajun, off East Africa, have developed an important business since 1950 of live turtles caught with sucker fish. A newly discovered colony on the South Arabian coast is being over-exploited.

In the Pacific it is still common in the Hawaiian Islands, and in the west millions of eggs are still laid on Malayan beaches, and perhaps 1,000,000 eggs are collected annually in the Philippines. The eggs of the Bornean population, whose main breeding beaches are on three uninhabited islands of western Sarawak, are now partly farmed in special hatcheries to keep up the output of from 1,000,000 to 2,000,000 eggs taken from the "nests" of rather less than half the estimated 10,000 females that come ashore annually to lay in the sand.

The egg-harvest is doubtless the main drain on the breeding population of green turtles, except in some areas of Malaysia and Costa Rica where it is controlled. But the market in adults caught at sea (mostly for turtle soup) is still of the order of 15,000 to 20,000 live animals yearly in North America and Europe alone. This of course involves direct predation on females of breeding age. New exploitations are increasing the demand for pelagic-taken turtles: turtle oil is valuable to the cosmetics and luxury soap industry, and a new highly advertised exploitation of the skin (of the forequarters alone) for shoe leather is developing fast. It is certain that, if present practices continue, the green turtle's once legitimate role as part of the harvest of the tropical seas will be over, unless control can extend to an international agreement to cease pelagic turtling and enforce the ban.

ATLANTIC HAWKSBILL
Eretmochelys imbricata

Dr Archie Carr, expert on the world's turtles, has lately reported a "change in the survival outlook for the hawksbill" – once the main source of the tortoiseshell of commerce. When he first visited Tortuguero, a breeding beach of the species in Costa Rica, in 1954, plastic imitations had killed the market for tortoise-shell. However, the situation has since materially changed, as a 1966 paper by Dr Carr (with his colleagues Hirth and Ogren) shows. To quote their summary:

"A mature hawksbill had no commercial value [in 1954], except as food for the small segment of the local population that eats the species. At the present time there is a resurging demand for genuine tortoiseshell, and this, along with a steady outlet for hawksbill calipee to the 'green turtle' soup trade, and with the recent appearance of a strong market for turtle skins for making into leather, allows a fisherman to realize as much as $14 for a few pounds of easily prepared and transported products from a single hawksbill. In a region in which this sum is more than the pay for a usual week's work, the motivation to kill hawksbills, legally or other-wise, is understandably strong. Add to these developments the general spread of seaside human populations and the perennial killing of hawksbill yearlings wherever they can be found, to be polished and mounted for the curio trade, and the survival outlook for *Eretmochelys* seems gloomy.

"The localized character of the reef habitat and the attraction of reefs to fishermen and skin-divers bring people into extensive contact with the hawksbill, perhaps more than with any other species; and its diffuse nesting range makes it hard to protect at breeding time. The future of all the sea turtles is obviously precarious. The hawksbill may at present be the most seriously threatened of the lot."

The hawksbill nests periodically or sporadi-cally on most undisturbed Caribbean shores, and from Bermuda through the West Indies and along the Atlantic coast of South America to Brazil. A female laid a clutch of eggs on the beach at Juno in southern Florida in 1959 – the only U.S. record. On beaches used by green turtles the hawksbills nest earlier, and there is evidence that, like the green turtles, they may lay every other year or at three-year intervals.

Atlantic ridley *Barry Driscoll* 1966 (*see* overleaf)

ATLANTIC RIDLEY
Lepidochelys kempi

The breeding-place of this rare sea turtle was discovered only in the early 1950s, on a section of almost uninhabited beach between Tampico and Soto la Marina in Tamaulipas, on Mexico's Gulf coast. It has also been established that occasional individuals may nest as far north as Padre Island in Texas and south to Alvarado in Veracruz, Mexico. The animal has never been found in the Caribbean proper, though the Gulf population, doubtless the world population, ranges across the Atlantic to the European coast.

Dr A. Carr believes that a nesting or *arribada* may take place about three times a year, each on different beaches at the Mexican headquarters, and estimated at least 40,000 females present at one of them. However, an exploitation, already begun, not only of eggs but of flesh for soup, may seriously threaten this species in its one main headquarters, and therefore globally. The eggs have been harvested excessively, and a practice has arisen of catching the egg-bearing females on their way to the nesting beaches, and breaking them open in order to get the eggs. The situation is being carefully watched, as there has been no proper *arribada* since 1963 and no big one since 1953. The early 1967 *arribada* involved only about 2,200 turtles, and nearly all the beach eggs were illegally poached.

Fortunately, Mexico is now actively protecting the ridley in Tamaulipas, and it is probable that fewer eggs were taken in the two *arribadas* of later 1967.

Family Dermochelyidae: leathery turtle

LEATHERY TURTLE, LEATHERBACK, *or* TRUNKBACK
Dermochelys coriacea

This peculiar turtle formerly enjoyed a wide distribution in tropical seas and has wandered into cooler waters as far north as Norway and as far south as Chile. It was common in the last century on many coasts, especially off western India and around Ceylon.

It has declined in recent years. Indeed, the only known egg-beaches lately reported – apart from a possible beach in New Guinea – are at Tortuguero Beach and Matina in Caribbean Costa Rica; in Surinam and French Guiana; on the coast of northern Zululand in Natal, South Africa; and along the $7\frac{1}{2}$ miles of Trengganu Beach in Malaya, where between 850 and 1,700 females are believed to lay annually. This last has been managed as a hatchery since the 1960s; and the establishment of a similar hatchery for reintroduced leathery turtles is being tried in Ceylon.

The future of this species, now beginning to show a relict distribution, may ultimately depend on beach-control, practised now as a means to the restoration of rational and reasonable egg harvesting. However, good populations have recently and encouragingly been found on beaches in some of the other countries mentioned above.

Family Pelomedusidae: river turtles

SOUTH AMERICAN RIVER TURTLE
Podocnemis expansa

Since the early European explorations of South America over 300 years ago, this freshwater turtle has been famous as a primary food animal of the Amerindians of the Amazon and Orinoco. Laying in sandbars and sand islands of these great rivers, the turtles were exploited for eggs (in the old days collected and piled in 20-foot heaps), oil, and meat. A hundred years ago, though, over-cropping began to tell, and the turtles' range began to withdraw.

Formerly abundant from the mouth of the Amazon to that of its tributary the Rio Negro, the river turtle has now withdrawn to the higher waters and to nesting sands less favourable and more subject to flooding, while on the Orinoco the major nesting beaches are now confined to the Isla Pararuma, Playa del Medio, Playa Blanca, and Cabullarito, between Cuidad Bolivar and the Atures rapids, though there are at least five lesser ones.

The days when the river turtles were so abundant that they even impeded the passage of boats are over. The animals are legally protected in both Brazil and Venezuela; but enforcement is poor except in parts of Venezuela, where lately stock has been successfully translocated to

South American river turtle *Barry Driscoll* 1966

Lake Valencia in the highlands west of Caracas. Here artificial egg-beaches have been constructed with some success; and the controlled use of a natural food resource is once more possible.

Family Chelidae: terrapins

SHORT-NECKED TORTOISE
Pseudemydura umbrina

First described as lately as 1907, this water tortoise, unique to its genus, is found only in an extremely limited region of three small swamps in the "crabhole" country of Bullsbrook, about 20 miles north-east of Perth, Western Australia. All recent examples have been found in a few isolated spots in a swamp area of radius less than 2 miles, though it is possible that the species ranged earlier over swamps now drained and developed for agriculture in a narrow strip for

40 miles north and south of Perth.

Extremely rare, the short-necked tortoise is now legally protected, and a headquarters of about 540 acres has been purchased and dedicated as a nature reserve for it. (In 1967 the Perth–Carnarvon coaxial cable was rerouted around this sanctuary to avoid disturbance.) In this area zoologists of Western Australia University estimated 200 to 300 animals in 1967.

A small group in captivity and under study in the South Perth Zoo has laid eggs but not yet successfully reared young.

Order CROCODYLIA
Family Crocodylidae

CUBAN CROCODILE
Crocodylus rhombifer

Peculiar to Cuba, where it formerly ranged over Matanzas Province in the island's central west, and was found on the Isle of Pines, the Cuban crocodile may now be confined only to the last relic of full swamp-land in the Zapata Swamp – an area not much more than $\frac{1}{2}$ square mile. Z. Vogel, who reported on the locality early in

1965, estimated about 500 individuals in it, most of which were certainly subadults. It is possible that a few may survive in Matanzas and on the Isle of Pines; but the tiny headquarters of the species is doubtless its only important refuge; and here it has to compete with the much commoner Cuban population of the American crocodile, *C. americanus*, a larger animal.

The relict swamp area of Zapata is now designated a "crocodile refuge"; and young are

Cuban crocodile *Barry Driscoll* 1966

sequestrated there by the keepers until they grow to a certain size. A stock is also kept in the Havana Zoo, part of which has been exchanged with other zoos. Ten zoos, not including Havana, which had about twenty, reported fourteen individuals in captivity in mid-1965.

Persecution for hides, which doubtless brought the species to its present extremely restricted rarity, is now unlawful, and the Cuban Government charges the finders of all animals outside the crocodile preserve to bring them to it.

Order SQUAMATA
Family Iguanidae: iguanas

GALÁPAGOS LAND IGUANAS
Genus *Conolophus*

The peculiar land iguanas of the Galápagos belong to a genus all their own. The Galápagos land iguana, *C. subcristatus*, was formerly found on Narborough, Albemarle, James, and Indefatigable and its satellites Seymour, South Seymour, and South Plaza. The very distinct Barrington land iguana, *C. pallidus*, is confined to the island of its name.

These most interesting animals have suffered much the same fate as the giant tortoises on some islands, being reduced by human predation for skins, by the predation of introduced cats (at least on Seymour), and by the reduction of vegetation by farmers, and (particularly) feral goats. On Narborough, the largest uncolonized and least penetrable island, a good but quite unmeasured (indeed at present unmeasurable) population persists. On Albemarle, still partly unpenetrated, reports of rarity in the first half of the century seem due to shallow exploration, and the surveys of the 1960s suggest that this largest island of the archipelago may (with the possible exception of Narborough) have the largest surviving population. On James, however, where Charles Darwin found the animal very common in 1835, it may have been extinct by 1905, when only bones were found by the California Academy expedition; and, despite an unconfirmed report of survivors in the present decade, the main survey of 1960–2 was negative. Indefatigable, which may have had rather a large colony until the first decade of the century, had only a few in the 1950s and 1960s. On Seymour, where common earlier in the present century, the iguanas were few in the 'sixties. On South Seymour, where a good population lived in 1922, the iguana may have been cleared out during the recent military occupation; only one mummified specimen was found in 1954. On the small island (about 100 by 150 yards) of South Plaza, however, where the goats have been cleared, a good population was found in 1957, and, although over forty were killed for skins in 1960–1, the population since then has been

PLATE 29 (*a*) Bachman's warbler; (*b*) Golden-cheeked warbler; (*c*) Kirtland's warbler; (*d*) Cape Sable seaside sparrow; (*e*) Dusky seaside sparrow; (*f*) Ipswich sparrow *Fenwick Lansdowne* 1966

(a)

(b)

(c)

(d)

(f)

(e)

J.F. LANSDOWNE
·1905·

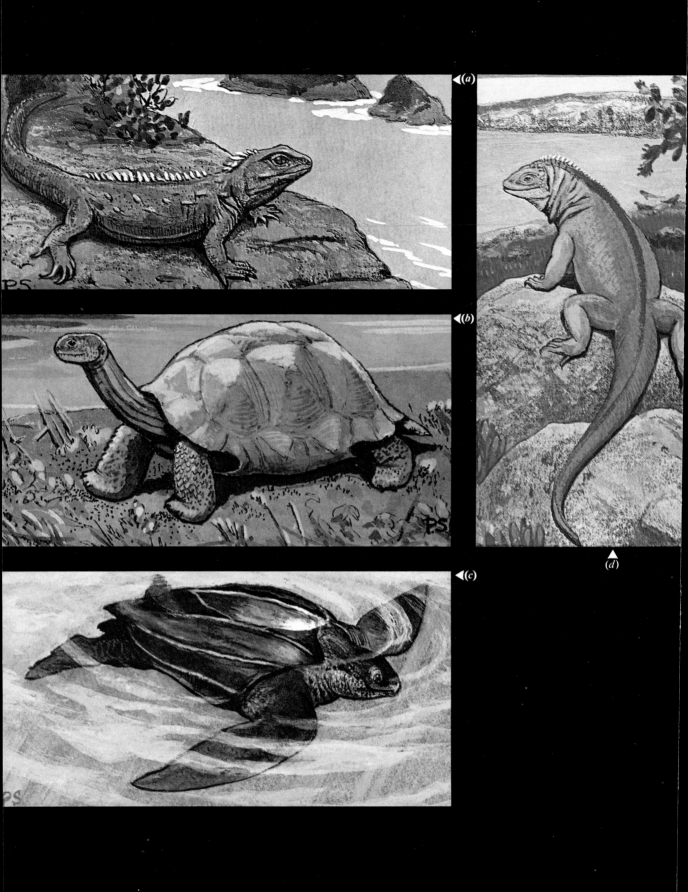

(a)

(b)

(c)

(d)

reported as still thriving and was estimated by one observer as between 50 and 100.

The Barrington land iguana, though reported as rare by the 1930s, was quite abundant in 1957 in numerous colonies scattered over the eastern side of the island (the west was unexplored on this visit). There seems to have been a decline since then, for in the early 1960s the population was estimated at about 300, and contained very few young and a preponderance of large, old adults.

The future of both these precious species is generally agreed to depend on the present goat-clearance programme on the islands. Goats, in clearing cover, expose the vulnerable young to the predation of Galápagos hawks (another endangered species, p. 203), especially on Barrington.

Family Varanidae: "super-lizards"

KOMODO DRAGON
Varanus komodoensis

The world's largest lizard, discovered only in the present century, and not named until 1912, was formerly found in the Indonesian islands of Komodo, Rintja, and (part of) Flores, and islands of its old range, and within the population were individuals of over 13 feet. By 1963 there may have been a few still in Rintja and Flores, but the population, estimated at no more than 300, was largely based on Komodo, and it was quite unusual to see one as much as 10 feet long.

Komodo dragon *Cécile Curtis* 1966

perhaps (though this is not confirmed) on Poeloe Padar.

By the 1930s, despite protection by the then Dutch Colonial Government (which has been carried on by the present government), this hunting and carrion-feeding giant lizard was already reduced to a few hundred individuals. It was still, however, found on the three main

While the Indonesians, out of respect for tradition as much as for the law, do not kill the giant lizards, they are over-effective rival predators of its main prey of deer and wild pig. There is thus an urgent need to declare a good-sized reserve on Komodo, where the game can be reserved for the dragons.

Though the Komodo dragon was bred during the Second World War in the Djakarta Zoo, no details of this are available. In mid-1965 there were seven dragons in zoos outside Indonesia, all collected under licence, though only the Sydney Zoo may have had a pair.

PLATE 30 (*a*) Tuatara; (*b*) Galápagos giant tortoise, Indefatigable race; (*c*) Leathery turtle; (*d*) Galápagos land iguana *Peter Scott, Brooke Bond* 1964

AMPHIBIANS

As we descend the evolutionary scale from the higher vertebrates to the lower, the amount of detailed information available to scholars on the geographical distribution of rare species becomes progressively sparse.

A world survey of endangered amphibians (of which class there are at present about 2,400 known living species) is beyond the current information resources of the Survival Service Commission. Fortunately, however, the interesting frogs, toads, newts, and salamanders of the North American continent have long been the joy and study of a cadre of well-informed herpetologists: and a valuable sample of the world situation, largely from this region, is given below by a distinguished American zoologist.

RARE AND ENDANGERED AMPHIBIANS
by Coleman J. Goin[1]
of the University of Florida, Gainesville

A careful estimate indicates that, so far as we know, nearly 500 species of animals have become extinct on this earth since the time of Christ. To the best of my knowledge, this list does not include any amphibians, but several of them are on the verge of extinction at the present time (one species may be already extinct), and man's activities make it probable that the number of threatened species will increase rapidly in the near future.

The amphibians as a class differ from the other groups of vertebrates in that they are seldom the immediate objects of man's destructive proclivities. Few if any of them are considered vermin, and as a consequence they seldom become primary goals of vermin-control campaigns. Also, few of them are of enough economic importance to have suffered from direct human exploitation. They are more apt to be threatened indirectly through man's unwise tampering with the environment, and to pass from the scene unnoticed and unmourned.

A cursory search of the literature shows that, of the several species and subspecies of amphibians that seem to be in danger of extinction at the present time, the majority are found in the continental United States. I do not believe that this is because my fellow Americans are more bent on eliminating species than the members of other nations are, but rather because the rapid increase in land development in the United States in the last several decades has done much to restrict the habitats available for amphibians. By their very nature, amphibians are dependent upon moisture in their environment to protect their soft, scaleless skins. Another very real, though undocumented, danger to amphibians is the destruction of their food supply through insect-control campaigns. And all that the ichthyologists have to say about the evils of stream pollution applies to many amphibians as well. I believe, though, that the most serious threat to some of our amphibian populations is simply the elimination of suitable habitats by the excessive use of bulldozers, draglines, and concrete mixers.

Let us examine some of these forms that are thought to be either extinct or on the verge of extinction.

Black toad, *Bufo exsul*
This small species is restricted to Deep Springs Valley, an isolated desert basin within the Inyo Mountains that is adjacent to the Death Valley system in Inyo County, California. The size of the actual breeding population has been

[1] Much of the information on the amphibians discussed here was obtained from the list of rare and endangered wildlife species compiled by a Committee of the Bureau of Sport Fisheries and Wildlife, United States Department of the Interior. I should like to express particular appreciation to Dr James A. Peters, of the United States National Museum, Washington, D.C., and Miss Alice G. C. Grandison, of the British Museum (Natural History), London, for special advice and information.   C.J G.

estimated at anything from under 1,000 up to 10,000 individuals. Actually, we do not really know how many there are. It is known, however, that the population is endangered as a consequence of drainage and irrigation practices in the valley; in certain instances, at least, the flow of water was modified after the egg-laying period, so that the young were killed by drying up before they metamorphosed.

Pine-barrens tree frog, *Hyla andersoni*

The actual limit of distribution of this frog is in doubt. But the main – virtually the entire – population is restricted to the pine-barrens region of New Jersey. There are one or two small colonies in North Carolina, and it may also occur in Georgia. The areas of New Jersey suitable for this frog have been drastically reduced by the rapid development of housing and industries and by the control of water-levels for recreation and industrial purposes. Now the remaining portion of suitable habitat, about 1½ square miles, has become the object of political machinations. The Port of New York Authority wants to absorb this swampland, which is essentially all that is left of the habitat of this frog, for the establishment of a multi-million-dollar airport for jet airliners. Conservationists are trying to protect the swamp: they claim that it was given to the Federal Government as a bird sanctuary, and that its use for any other type of development is an infringement of their constitutional rights. The further course of this case is in the hands of legislators and courts. The pine-barrens tree frog stands either to maintain its *status quo* so far as its habitat is concerned or to become extinct in favour of the jet age. I for one shall support the frog.

Mountain chicken, *Leptodactylus fallax*

This big frog is now restricted to the islands of Dominica and Montserrat in the Lesser Antilles. It is a dietary favourite of the people who live in the mountains of these islands, and is almost certainly endangered by the expanding, meat-hungry population. A few years ago the Government of Dominica considered undertaking an active conservation programme for this species, but I have been unable to find whether it was ever initiated.

Texas blind salamander, *Typhlomolge rathbuni*

This counterpart of the blind white salamander of Europe seems to be the only American salamander that may be in danger of extinction. It is known from deep wells and underground streams in caves of Hays County, Texas. Although some people consider it to be on the verge of extinction, I am not sure this is so; for I doubt whether man is at present in a position to over-collect underground waters in regions where there are extensive limestone caves and caverns. It is true enough that very few individuals are now to be seen in the wells and caves from which it was originally known – and, if indeed these are the only localities in which it exists, it is close to total extinction. However, it may well be that there are numerous untapped caverns that house rather large populations of this salamander. If I seem too optimistic here to my conservation-minded friends, I should like to point out that the Georgia blind salamander, *Haideotriton wallacei*, known originally from only one cave, has now been found in other localities and can be more readily collected today than it could be twenty years ago.

Olm, *Proteus anguinus*

The blind white salamander of the underground waters of Yugoslavia was at one time excessively collected. It is now very strictly protected by the Yugoslav Government, and severe penalties, in some cases terms of imprisonment, are imposed on poachers.

In addition to this species, I know of at least three local races of more widespread species that appear to be on the verge of extinction.

Vegas Valley leopard frog, *Rana pipiens fisheri*

This race of the widespread leopard frog was formerly found in the neighbourhood of Las Vegas, Vegas Valley, Clark County, Nevada, where it was restricted to springs and seepage area. Man's activities in this region, the capping of springs and other measures that involve water-control, have pretty well eliminated the habitat of this race. Added to this difficulty is the fact that the large bullfrog, *Rana catesbeiana*, was introduced into the area and perhaps became predatory upon the young of the Vegas Valley leopard frog. The present status of this frog is in doubt. The last known specimens were collected in 1942, and it may be that the sub-species is already extinct.

Golden frog, *Atelopus varius zeteki*

This is one amphibian of my acquaintance that seems to be endangered by collecting while its habitat is being preserved. It occurs in El Valle de Antón, Panama. This valley, roughly oval, is about 2 miles in diameter and is entirely surrounded by mountains except for one place, where the Río Antón breaks through the mountain to drain the valley to the west. The valley is now a popular tourist resort with large hotels; one of the attractions for the tourist is to see these bright golden frogs sitting on the rocks and plants around the edge of the streams. People have collected them, and friends of mine who visit the valley at regular intervals tell me that it is now getting extremely difficult even to see a golden frog alive in the valley, much more to collect one. The frog is so well known to tourists that lapel pins modelled after it are sold in the shops in Panama.

Santa Cruz long-toed salamander, *Ambystoma macrodactylum croceum*

This rare salamander is at present known from only two localities in mid-coastal California. One of these is Valencia Lagoon, Río Del Mar, near Aptos, and the other about 4 miles west of Watsonville, Santa Cruz County, California. It seems to be on the verge of total extinction, primarily because of land and subdivision developments, and perhaps also in part because of excessive zeal in collecting these rare animals by both professional and amateur biologists.

Compared with the numbers of threatened birds and mammals, this is a meagre list. It might be wondered why anyone should feel perturbed about the probability or even possibility that these few amphibians might reach extinction.

I believe that one of the best summaries of the reasons why populations of animals should be saved from extinction is that given by Lee M. Talbot in *Wildlife* (Vol. 3, No. 1) the official journal of the Kenya Wildlife Society, Nairobi, Africa. Mr Talbot lists five reasons why it is logical for man to save any species of animal

from extinction. They are: economic, scientific, cultural, moral, and democratic.

Two of the species listed above are of economic value: the mountain chicken and the golden frog. I do not know how many people have travelled to El Valle de Antón, and spent the night in a hotel just for an opportunity to see the golden frog, but I do know that some have done so, for I have talked to them. Scientific knowledge of all wildlife is still very far from complete; and the small and inconspicuous amphibians are perhaps less well known than any of the other vertebrate groups. Obviously we can gain more scientific knowledge from species that are still with us than from those that have become extinct. The cultural reason for conservation has been discussed often by much more learned and more elegant zoologists than myself. I simply want to list myself as one of those who feel that all forms of wildlife are important parts of nature and that there is a satisfaction in just knowing that they are there. Dr Talbot points out that a great many people (and I am one of them) feel it is simply not morally right to destroy completely any form of life, and that this thread of feeling runs through most of the world's great religions. And here I should like to quote two sentences from his article: "Many of the exterminations in the past were accomplished before anyone realized what was happening. But now we can usually see what is happening and recognize when we are exterminating a species, which in most modern cases brings the moral argument forcefully into focus". The final reason is democratic. There has been much in the world's news in recent decades about the rights of minorities under the democratic process where the majority rules. If minorities do have rights, it seems only fair that the con-servationists who want to preserve species from extinction should have their rights as well as other minority groups in these days of democracies.

I should like to close by pointing out once again that (as it seems to me) the most imminent danger to many of our species and subspecies of amphibians is not from vermin-control, preda-tion, poaching, or even over-collecting for scientific purposes, but rather from the loss of the habitats on which these delicate, soft-skinned animals are dependent.

FISHES

RARE AND ENDANGERED FRESHWATER FISHES[1]

by Robert Rush Miller
of the University of Michigan

INTRODUCTION

Serious efforts to protect and increase vanishing species of animals have been limited almost exclusively to the birds and mammals. Easily observed and readily identified in numerous popular guides, these often colourful animals have a large following of terrestrial mankind. In sharp contrast, most freshwater fishes are seen with difficulty in their natural habitat, and many are hard to identify, except by the specialist. A scarcity of popular guide-books, the existence of these animals beneath the water, and the comparative dearth of information on their biology have forestalled the recognition and treatment of the problem of conserving vanishing freshwater fishes. Most of the species that have been recognized as endangered are small and rather inconspicuous and find their chief value in scientific study and research. Only a few are large enough, or of sufficient sport value or economic importance, to have become widely known, except for the aquarium fishes.

Whereas virtually all the distinct species of birds and mammals of the world have already been found, new species of fishes are continually being discovered, even in such long-studied areas as Europe and the eastern United States. Consequently the framework of information available to conservationists of the warm-blooded vertebrates is quite different from that under which the fish conservationist must operate. In large parts of the world (South America, for example), our ignorance of the fauna imposes formidable obstacles to designing a conservation programme. Thorough surveys by competent workers (of which there are few) must be carried out before a useful list of endangered world fishes can be prepared and effective measures proposed for their preservation.

In 1961, committees concerned with the conservation of cold-blooded vertebrates were established by the American Society of Ichthyologists and Herpetologists, and these began to identify and investigate the current status of rare and endangered species in the United States. In 1964, an eleven-man committee was formed within the Survival Service Commission of the I.U.C.N. to look at this problem for freshwater fishes on a world-wide basis. Also in 1964, the President of the American Fisheries Society appointed a Committee on Endangered Species, and a Committee on Rare and Endangered Wildlife Species was established in that year within the United States Bureau of Sport Fisheries and Wildlife by the Secretary of the Interior. All of these groups are working together with others vitally interested in devising means for saving threatened wildlife.

REASONS FOR DECLINE

A variety of factors have, directly or indirectly, seriously affected the welfare, and thus influenced the decline, of freshwater fishes over large areas of the world. Modification of natural environments by man continues with increasing speed as his populations expand and his technology advances. Intensive industrialization, rapid urbanization, the spread of exotics, and water pollution have been particularly hard on native biotas. Water demands imposed by the rapidly growing numbers of people make urgent the need for effective action if samples of our native aquatic biotas are to be preserved. Aquatic habitats, especially freshwater ones, are particularly vulnerable to ecological changes brought on by man's activities, for these often make impossible the continued existence of organisms that are inescapably bound to water. Direct habitat changes have resulted from

[1] The author of this article, and Dr Ethelwynn Trewavas, the author of the one that immediately follows, have both supplied valuable bibliographies, which have been placed with the Library of the Zoological Society of London, where they are available for consultation by students.

deforestation and over-grazing, bringing floods, erosion, and heavy siltation. Lowering of the water table has eliminated populations as streams, marshes, and springs have disappeared. Diversion of water for irrigation has reduced fish populations; so has the dredging and channelization of rivers and the ditching of streams. Construction of dams and hydroelectric projects has cut species off from large segments of their original distribution. Pollution from a variety of domestic and industrial wastes has made barren habitats formerly productive. In the past decade or so, the wide use of powerful new insecticides on agricultural crops has resulted in the destruction of fish populations. During the same period, fish-management practices that employ increasingly potent piscicides (with rotenone as the active ingredient) have brought about mass eradications of native fishes in various parts of the world, including South America, India, and the United States; the aim of such projects is to improve sport fishing, but thorough evaluation of the method remains to be made. Some success in curbing the intentional destruction of native species has been achieved recently in the United States.

The deliberate or accidental introduction of foreign fishes in various parts of the world has often had dire consequences for native species, especially in areas with depauperate faunas. For example, aquarium fishes released into desert waters populated by local endemics are causing serious problems in the survival of the native forms; and in Lake Victoria, Africa, the native species are being threatened by the introduction of cichlids of the genus *Tilapia* and of the predatory Nile perch, *Lates niloticus*. In 1965 G. S. Myers emphasized that one of the most widely stocked species, the mosquito-fish, *Gambusia affinis*, has seriously affected native fishes in many places. The penetration of the sea lamprey, *Petromyzon marinus*, into the Great Lakes of eastern North America is a dramatic example of how an exotic predator drastically changed species composition.

DOCUMENTATION

Although the need to obtain accurate information on vanishing fishes was stressed in 1949 by G. S. Myers, only in the United States has a recent organized effort resulted in a published compilation on endangered species. Over the greater part of the world there is no up-to-date information. Documentation for change, depletion, and extinction of fishes in the American Southwest was summarized (by the present writer) only in 1961.

At least fourteen species of North American freshwater fishes are now suspected or believed to be extinct, since they have either not been taken in recent years or the only locality where they are known to have existed no longer provides a suitable habitat. These fishes constitute the following:

Blackfin cisco, *Coregonus nigripinnis*

Once abundant in deep waters of the Great Lakes (Michigan and Huron), it has not been reported since 1955. Recent decline and disappearance have resulted from predation by the introduced sea lamprey and from continued heavy commercial fishing for larger fish during the 1940s and 1950s.

Deepwater cisco, *Coregonus johannae*

Formerly abundant in the deeper waters of Lakes Michigan and Huron, it has not been taken since 1951, for reasons given above.

Thicktail chub, *Gila crassicauda*

Formerly abundant in rivers, ponds, marshes, and lakes of the Central Valley (with their adjacent drainages) of California, the species was last taken in 1957. Drastic changes of its habitat by man, and very probably competition with, and predation by, exotic species, have resulted in its disappearance.

Pahranagat spinedace, *Lepidomeda altivelis*

This localized endemic was first collected in 1891 in the isolated Pahranagat Valley, Nevada, in the course of Pleistocene White River. It became extinct between 1938 and 1959, evidently through modification of its habitat and competition with introduced species such as carp and mosquito-fish (*Gambusia affinis*).

Stumptooth minnow, *Stypodon signifer*

Described in 1880 from a spring on the Chihuahuan desert near Parras, Coahuila,

Mexico, this relict was last collected in 1903. Thorough search in 1953 indicated extinction, evidently due to habitat disturbance coupled with industrial and domestic pollution.

Harelip sucker, *Lagochila lacera*

Formerly distributed in clear streams tributary to the central part of the Mississippi valley, in eastern United States, this specialized fish has not been taken since 1900. It is believed that siltation has been the principal cause of its extinction.

June sucker, *Chasmistes liorus*

Formerly abundant in Utah Lake, Utah, to which it was confined except for a spawning migration up the tributary Provo River, this lake-adapted species has not been observed since the mid-1930s. The severe drought of that time, coupled with domestic use of the Provo River, evidently dealt the species a fatal blow through the prevention of its annual spawning migration.

Mexican blindcat, *Prietella phreatophila*

Described by J. Carranza in 1954 from a small well in northern Coahuila, Mexico, this novelty may no longer occur in the type locality, the only known place of its existence. Whether it will be found elsewhere in the region remains to be seen.

Ash Meadows killifish, *Empetrichthys merriami*

This species, known only from Ash Meadows, Nye County, Nevada, just east of Death Valley, was last collected in 1948. Strenuous efforts by James R. Deacon and others to obtain specimens in recent years have failed, and the fish is now probably extinct. The reasons for its disappearance are not known, but exotic species (bullfrogs and crayfish, as well as fishes) may have contributed.

Leon Springs pupfish, *Cyprinodon bovinus*

This species, confined to Leon Springs near Fort Stockton, Texas, was described in 1851 and has not been taken since. Efforts to obtain it in 1938 and 1950 failed. Extinction is believed to have resulted from habitat disturbance and the planting of exotic fishes.

Parras pupfish, *Cyprinodon latifasciatus*

This distinctive species, like *Stypodon signifer* (*see above*), is restricted to a desert basin in Coahuila, Mexico, where it was last collected in 1903. Long usage of the spring habitat for washing clothes, industrial pollution, and modification of the natural environment contributed to the extinction of this fish.

Sharphead darter, *Etheostoma acuticeps*

This was described on the basis of six specimens taken in 1947 and 1949 above a dam on the South Holston River, Tennessee. The area has since been inundated by the impounded reservoir. Repeated attempts to secure additional specimens have failed.

Trispot darter, *Etheostoma trisella*

This recently described species is known only from two specimens obtained in 1947 and 1954 from the Coosa River drainage of north-eastern Alabama. Repeated attempts by ichthyologists to secure additional specimens proved fruitless. Since 1960, the type locality has been inundated by a reservoir, which destroyed the only known area of suitable habitat.

Utah Lake sculpin, *Cottus echinatus*

Like its associate, the June sucker (*see above*), this lacustrine species has not been collected from Utah Lake, Utah, the only place where it is known to have existed, for about forty years. Perhaps the species did not survive the low lake levels caused by the drought of the mid-1930s, or, if it did, subsequent habitat changes and the establishment of foreign fishes may have exterminated remnant populations.

About two dozen North American freshwater fishes fall into the category of endangered species – that is, those whose continued survival without assistance is questionable. Some of the better documented of these are discussed below.

Gila trout, *Salmo gilae*

This species and its close relative, the Apache trout of Arizona, are native only to the Gila River basin of New Mexico and Arizona. Both were formerly abundant, but habitat destruction, leading to erosion and lowered stream levels, and competition with exotic trout, have seriously depleted these game fishes until pure stocks are now almost gone. Efforts are being made to restore suitable habitat and to establish refuges for the preservation of these trouts.

Moapa dace, *Moapa coriacea*

This relict represents a monotypic genus restricted to warm springs in southern Nevada. It has declined markedly in recent years through habitat alteration for commercial development of the springs and the establishment of exotic species, particularly the mosquito-fish, *Gambusia affinis*, and the Mexican molly, *Poecilia mexicana*. Recent estimates (1965) indicate that the population numbers between 500 and 1,000.

Desert dace, *Eremichthys acros*

Like the above species, this is a monotypic, warm-spring genus confined to a very restricted area in north-western Nevada. Disturbance of habitat for irrigation has reduced populations, but the species is not yet seriously threatened. A portion of the undisturbed habitat should, however, be set aside if this genus is to persist.

Modoc sucker, *Catostomus microps*

Known only from one short stream in north-eastern California (Rush Creek near Adin, Modoc County), this fish was not collected between 1934 and 1967. Two ichthyologists, working independently, discovered residual stocks in the spring of that year. Protection of its habitat from man-made changes is required if the species is to survive.

Cui-ui, *Chasmistes cujus*

The lake suckers of the genus *Chasmistes* were more speciose and widely distributed in Pliocene and Pleistocene times, and survive today only in two restricted areas of western United States (one species, *C. liorus* of Utah Lake, is probably already extinct: *see above*). The cui-ui is now confined to Pyramid Lake, Nevada, a restriction of its former range. It is of economic value to the Indians of the region and of great scientific importance as a relict. Its welfare is under study by the Nevada Fish and Game Department, which has imposed catch limits on non-Indians and is attempting to restore spawning access and

habitat and to increase efforts for artificial propagation.

Klamath sucker, *Chasmistes brevirostris*

This sucker, related to the cui-ui, is also declining and may need assistance soon to assure survival.

Pahrump killifish, *Empetrichthys latos*

This is the only surviving species of a distinctive genus confined to the desert region just east of Death Valley. Originally it lived in three springs in Pahrump Valley, Nevada, but within the past decade one of these failed and another was filled in by the ranch-owner. Until 1963, when goldfish were introduced into the third spring and vegetation was removed, the last remaining population was doing well. Estimated numbers reached a subsequent low level of twenty to thirty individuals, but have risen slowly, and a 1967 census yielded at least 1,300. The species can be reared and maintained in captivity (this is currently being done), but the native habitat should be designated a preserve, and the species should also be established in a natural refuge, to assure survival.

Checkered killifish, *Cualac tessellatus*

This monotypic, relict genus is known only from the outlet of a warm spring in San Luis Potosi, Mexico, where it is not abundant. The spring area is the water source for nearby towns and is subject to modification for domestic use; introduction of foreign species is contemplated and could prove disastrous – not only to this fish but to three other highly distinctive, localized species representing two other families. *Cualac* has been estimated to constitute only 1 per cent of the total fish population known from the area. Since the spring contains a noteworthy fish fauna, a very interesting turtle, and probably other aquatic organisms of scientific value, its preservation would maintain a significant variety of forms rather than simply a single species.

Devils Hole pupfish, *Cyprinodon diabolis*

This species, perhaps the most restricted vertebrate known, is confined to a single spring hole in Ash Meadows, Nye County, Nevada, about 30 miles east of Death Valley and within a detached part of Death Valley National Monument. The population size fluctuates between about 200 and 500 individuals. Although protected by a high fence and locked gate, the species is so localized that an attempt should be made to establish a population elsewhere in nature. All attempts to culture this pupfish have failed.

Comanche Springs pupfish, *Cyprinodon elegans*

This species formerly abounded in large springs at Fort Stockton, Pecos County, Texas, and in Phantom Lake and adjacent springs near Toyahvale. Now it inhabits only irrigation ditches near Toyahvale, since the springs at Fort Stockton have gone dry. Lowering of the water table and introduction of aggressive exotic fishes have greatly reduced its numbers in the past two decades. A suitable area within its present range should be set aside for it as a sanctuary.

Owens Valley pupfish, *Cyprinodon radiosus*

This species is known only from Owens Valley, California, at the eastern base of the Sierra Nevada. It was thought to have been extinct since 1942, but a breeding population was located in 1964 in the Fish Slough region north of Bishop, Mono County. The near extinction of the fish resulted from habitat destruction through drainage of swamps and marshes as well as from predation and competition from introduced species. Plans are under way to re-establish the species in its natural (rehabilitated) habitat as well as to seek a natural refuge for its preservation.

Clear Creek gambusia, *Gambusia heterochir*

This species is restricted to the headwaters of a single creek in Texas with a population under 1,000, but probably once enjoyed a wider distribution. It is threatened by competition and hybridization with the mosquitofish, *Gambusia affinis*, and, unfortunately, by the proposed construction of a dam that would alter its very restricted habitat.

Pecos gambusia, *Gambusia nobilis*

Originally limited to springs and westward-flowing tributaries of the middle third of the Pecos River basin of New Mexico and Texas, this species has now disappeared from New Mexico and no longer occurs in several springs (such as Leon Spring and Comanche Springs) that it once inhabited in Texas. Lowered water tables and competition from exotic species have contributed to its decrease. The species still occurs about Toyahvale, Texas, and should be protected there.

Big Bend gambusia, *Gambusia gagei*

This very restricted species, originally known only from two springs in and near Big Bend National Park, along the Rio Grande in Texas, was in 1957 reduced to two males and one female. From this meagre stock the population grew to an estimated 1,000 individuals, but it has been threatened with extinction twice since then, despite the fact that the species is now receiving protection in Big Bend National Park, its only known place of occurrence. Continued surveillance of these populations is vital, to preserve the habitat and protect the species against competition with the aggressive exotic mosquito-fish, *Gambusia affinis*.

Gila topminnow, *Poeciliopsis occidentalis*

Formerly common in the lower Gila River basin of Arizona and northern Sonora, Mexico, this species is now restricted to only two localities. Its widespread depletion is attributed to habitat destruction and the introduction of exotics, especially the mosquitofish, which completely replaced the native species in one creek withing a two-year period. The topminnow is still thriving at Monkey Spring, on a private ranch, which should become established as a wildlife monument.

Maryland darter, *Etheostoma sellare*

This species, one of the rarest of its tribe, is restricted to one or two streams tributary to Chesapeake Bay, Maryland. It was based on two specimens taken in 1912, and, despite repeated efforts by various collectors, it was not taken again until 1962, when a single young was secured. In 1965, however, a breeding population was finally located by Frank Schwartz. Until more is known about its biological requirements and distribution, the only proposed measure is to avoid disturbing the habitat.

PROTECTIVE MEASURES

A few fishes now receive formal, though not always effective, protection: the Australian lungfish; the blind cavefish of Mammoth Cave, Kentucky; and the Devils Hole pupfish of Death Valley National Monument are the only ones that come to mind. The passage in 1964 in the United States of the Land and Water Conservation Fund Act does appear to provide a means for protecting some critically endangered species. It is obviously impossible to build a shrine around every threatened species. Careful selection of habitats or habitat types that include a variety of rare or endangered organisms, both invertebrate and vertebrate, including plants where possible, will be more effective in preserving biota than choosing isolated species.

For those species that may be propagated in captivity, "refugia centres" may be established for their maintenance until suitable natural areas can be set aside as refuges for their perpetuation.

The International Biological Programme is concerned with the identification and preservation of habitats or areas of special biological interest, particularly those known to contain a variety of relict species or threatened biota. Once identified, such areas should be brought to the attention of the I.B.P.

The selection of truly representative areas that contain a maximum number of habitats and threatened species is a first necessity. Adequate means of providing protection to such habitats must also be assured, either by measures that will prevent direct disturbance of the habitat by man or through effective security patrol to enforce the legal protection granted.

FRESHWATER FISHES OF AFRICA

by Ethelwynn Trewavas
from the British Museum (Natural History)

INTRODUCTION

Dr Miller's introduction to his article on fishes is valid in every detail for Africa and Asia too, but in these continents urbanization has not gone so far as in North America and Europe. It is therefore theoretically possible to learn from European and American experience to avoid the mistakes made there.

In swiftly developing countries, the balancing of the claims of development and conservation needs constant vigilance on the part of the conservationist. If industrial pollution or the use of pesticides makes a body of water unfit for fish life, the destruction of a natural resource ensures that the debit side of the operation is demonstrable to everyone. But other operations that alter the composition of the fish fauna have ill effects that are more subtle, harder to predict, and of less general appeal.

The natural distribution of plants and animals, including fishes, is a very instructive clue to the geological history of the areas concerned and to their past climatic history. The reading of the course of evolution relies on the assumption that the present inhabitants of a river system, a swamp, or a lake arrived there by natural means and not by the intervention of man.

For these reasons the mere prevention of extinction of a fish species does not satisfy the scientific conservationist. It should be conserved in and with its natural habitat, or, if the claims of the developer outweigh this and conflict with it, then every effort should be made to study and record the whole of the endangered habitat and its biota, both for fundamental scientific reasons and as a base-line from which to understand the subsequent changes.

In Africa as elsewhere each river-system has its characteristic fauna, and still more strikingly each lake. Endemism and the inter-relationship of the endemic forms of different bodies of water are of the greatest interest.

ENDEMISM IN MONTANE REGIONS

In the tropics trout and black bass, so dear to the angler from temperate regions, are not indigenous and can thrive only in the uplands. In Africa such regions form "islands" in the midst of vast tracts of land where the temperature is never low enough for cold-water fishes to breed. The fish fauna of the mountains is often sparse, and for this reason the angler, going into the hills for a cool weekend, feels justified in supporting the introduction of trout and black bass. This has been done in Kenya and South Africa.

In Kenya Van Someren (in 1952) did not report any native fishes in the trout-streams whose bottom-fauna he described, but these streams have been explored only locally and not by the best methods for catching fishes adapted to hiding under rocks or clinging to them. The presence of such genera as *Chiloglanis*, *Leptoglanis*, *Amphilius*, and *Garra* is to be expected, and their relationship to the invading trout is unknown.

Oreodaemon quathlambae D. W. Ovenden 1966

An example of apparent extermination in South Africa is *Oreodaemon quathlambae*. This was a cyprinid fish reaching a total length of about 4 inches. Because it differed from other African Cyprinidae in the small and numerous scales (sixty-five to sixty-eight in the lateral line) and in the pharyngeal dentition, it has been given a separate generic name.

It inhabited a stretch of the River Umkomazana in the Drakensberg range, Natal, at an altitude of about 5,300 feet. The source of this river is at about 9,000 feet, whence it descends by cascades and waterfalls and a torrential reach to the flatter valley in which the fish was collected. The course of the river in this valley is strewn with rounded boulders, stones, and sand, and the river easily changes its course in time of flood. About 1 mile below there is a waterfall high enough to prevent upstream migration of fishes. In a letter to Dr Greenwood, Mr R. S. Cross describes this environment, in which *O. quathlambae* must have existed undisturbed by any predator-fish for thousands of years.

Now the severity of flood-spates has been increased by the removal of vegetation by grazing cattle, and this, combined with the

introduction of trout, which both compete with it as fry and prey on it as adults, has meant the end of *O. quathlambae*.

So far it has not been found in any other of the Drakensberg streams, but a drawing of it is given as a guide to anyone who may have the opportunity to search in the less accessible waters of the range. Quathlamba is the Sesuto name for that part of the Drakensberg along the Natal-Lesotho border.

In 1943 Barnard noted that the whole of the freshwater fauna of the Cape Province was endangered by the introduction there of trout and black bass, and he took the best preliminary action open to him in writing a review of what was known of the natural fish-fauna at that time, redefining the species and giving precise information on their type localities. He regarded this as the starting-point for the field survey of the region that he said was desirable.

In West Africa a contrast is provided by Mount Nimba, a mountain 5,800 feet high at the meeting-place of the borders of Mali, Liberia, and Ivory Coast, which has been made a nature reserve and surveyed. The fishes have been described by Dr J. Daget (1952 and 1963), and the one species unknown elsewhere was considered doubtfully endemic because the genus is imperfectly known.

The fish-fauna high on such tropical mountains is mainly a depauperate fauna. On the lower slopes of Mount Ruwenzori, however, are several lakelets that have been stocked with *Tilapia* from the neighbouring Great Lakes, without being fully surveyed first. We may never know if these originally contained any fishes.

ENDEMISM IN THE AFRICAN GREAT LAKES

There is nowhere in the world in which endemic species-flocks have developed on such a scale as in the African Great Lakes, and the family overwhelmingly contributing these is that of the Cichlid fishes. In Lake Malawi (Nyasa) basin about 194 species of this family have been recorded, all but three of which are endemic. In Lake Tanganyika 134 have been described, only two of which exist also outside the lake basin. At present these provide such rich and under-exploited fisheries in themselves that there is no excuse for interfering with them by making dangerous introductions. (One or two suggestions to do so have happily not been carried out.) The contribution that their study is likely to make to our knowledge of the course and nature of evolution hardly needs stressing.

Lake Victoria also contains its own immense species-flock, and in this case there is danger of altering the ecological picture, first by over-fishing and then by trying to remedy the deficiency created by the introduction of species from other lakes.

Fortunately there is a research station on the shore of Lake Victoria, the East African Fresh-water Fisheries Research Organization, which for two decades has been a repository of increasing knowledge of the lake fish-fauna. Its small staff and visiting scientists have built up a consider-able body of knowledge of a complex situation that is changing all the time. Financial con-siderations must limit the rate at which this work is done. Already the stocks of the two most important economic species, the endemic cich-lids *Tilapia esculenta* and *T. variabilis*, have been so much reduced (at least relative to the demand) that species from other lakes have been intro-duced, though how effectively remains to be seen. There is some evidence that one of the introduced species is hastening the decline of one of the endemics by competition at the fry stage. The present position is reviewed by Welcomme in *Nature* of the 1st October 1966.

It would be hard to say that any species of Lake Victoria is threatened with extinction, and conservation of a species cannot be given priority over maintenance of a fishery in such an area of expanding population. Conservation measures can be justified to the three riparian governments only if they also combat a threat to the fisheries. But, from the beginning of its establishment, the E.A.F.F.R.O. has included description of the fish-fauna of the lake in its programme. Dr P. H. Greenwood, a member of its staff from 1951 to 1957, has published and is still working on a series of reports on the species-flock of *Haplochromis* and derived genera, and new species are still being found and studied by present and recent members of the staff, Dr M. Gee and Mr R. Welcomme. An interesting popular account of this species-flock was given by Greenwood in 1964.

In 1965 Greenwood reported on a new collection from Lake Nabugabo, a small lake that has been separated from Lake Victoria for only 4,000 years by a sandspit about 2 miles wide. Among the six species of *Haplochromis* in it, only one can be identified with a Lake Victoria species; the other five differ from their nearest Lake Victoria relatives in the same kind of way that these differ among themselves, and they are regarded as endemic species, surely some of the youngest known.

Earlier studies on the cichlids of Lake Edward show that there is a distinct but related species-flock there, as well as in Lake Kivu. Thorough studies on these, and on the smaller flock of Lake Albert, still remain to be done.

The numbers of non-endemic and endemic species of Lakes Victoria and Kioga, Edward and George, and Albert are given by Greenwood in his essay of 1964.

ENDEMISM IN THE SMALLER LAKES OF EAST AFRICA

The small lakes of the eastern Rift Valley, Magadi, Natron, and Manyara are so charged with salts that the fish-fauna is limited and perhaps exists only in favourable localities such as the springs that feed them. The valleys are so hot that the danger of human interference is minimal.

In Lake Magadi lives the small *Tilapia*, *T. grahami*, which has been studied recently by Dr Malcolm Coe.

In Lake Natron, a closely related species, *T. alcalica*, abounds in certain localities, but there is also a non-endemic species in this lake or in the river that feeds it, the Southern Uaso Nyiro. This is an isolated population of *T. spilurus*, and so far is known only from a few museum specimens. It is of scientific interest as a link between the main area of distribution of this species in the eastern drainage of Kenya and the site of fossilized members of a Lower Pleistocene population on the shores of the Kavirondo Gulf. I would therefore recommend to naturalists for conservation and study the aquatic fauna of Lake Natron and the Southern Uaso Nyiro.

Lake Manyara has its own well-characterized species of *Tilapia*, *T. amphimelas*. This may be present also in Lake Eyasi, a little to the west.

Lake Kitangiri provides an example of the confused situation that may result from introduction without preliminary survey. Recent surveys have recorded the presence of three species of *Tilapia*. One, *T. melanopleura*, was certainly introduced by the accidental overflow of a stocked dam in one of the inflowing rivers. The second, *T. esculenta*, probably got there in the same way, having been stocked in the dam from Lake Victoria. The third, *T. amphimelas*, may be native to Lake Kitangiri, but we cannot now be certain. *T. esculenta* and *T. amphimelas* appear to be hybridizing freely.

This may provide a good fishery, but from the point of view of zoogeography Lake Kitangiri must now be written off as a fishpond.

ENDEMISM IN CRATER-LAKES OF THE NORTH-WESTERN CAMEROONS
Lake Barombi-ma-Mbu or Kumba

Lake Barombi-ma-Mbu has a surface area of less than 2 square miles and a maximum depth of 364 feet (average 226 feet). It is surrounded by steep cliffs, interrupted to the south-east by a gorge into which the overflow of the lake escapes over a shallow sill and along a rocky bed to join the River Mungo, which itself continues by a series of rapids towards the sea. The lake is said to be too deep to be stirred by the wind, so that bottom organisms are probably restricted to a peripheral zone and fish-life to the periphery and the surface.

No biological survey of the waters has been made, but the latest report (Trewavas, 1962) on the fishes listed eight species, only one of which is known to exist elsewhere. To this should be added a ninth species that has since been collected in this lake and was formerly attributed, probably because of a mistake in labelling, to another lake, Barombi-ba-Kotto. It should probably (as here) be added to the endemic list of Barombi-ma-Mbu.

The non-endemic fish is *Barbus batesii*, a member of a section of the genus *Barbus* given to ascending streams for spawning, even if this entails jumping rapids.

Six of the endemic species are Cichlidae, known for their explosive radiating evolution in the Great Lakes of Africa. Four of them are members of the genus *Tilapia*, and the two

others are so peculiar as to be made each the type of a separate genus, related to *Tilapia*.

A species of *Epiplatys* (a small cyprinodont) has been collected alive from this lake and is being studied in aquarium by Col. Scheel of Denmark. It seems to be at least a distinct subspecies, related to *E. sexfasciatus*.

Clarias maclareni is a catfish that seems to be endemic too, but its relationship to other species can only be determined when the taxonomy of the whole genus is better known. It is possible that *Clarias* could make its way into the lake along the outlet stream.

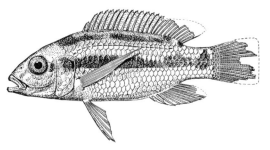

Tilapia eisentrauti D. W. Ovenden 1966

Tilapia eisentrauti, *T. lohbergeri*, *T. linnellii*, and *T. steinbachi* are four well-characterized endemic species, and to judge from their structure and dentition are likely to have different ecological requirements. I would expect *T. eisentrauti* to be an aufwuchs-feeder; *T. lohbergeri* may feed on both aufwuchs and phytoplankton; *T. linnellii* has much in common with species known to be detritus-feeders, but the large mouth and simplified dentition of adults suggest a change to a more carnivorous habit; *T. steinbachi* is probably dependent on phytoplankton. The breeding habits of all are unknown.

Barombia maclareni. The monotypic genus is characterized by few and prominent teeth, which act as forceps for picking up food-organisms. The stomach contents of the type-specimen included the remains of a trichopterous larva.

Although a similar dentition is developed in *Labidochromis* of Lake Nyasa and *Paralabidochromis* of Lake Victoria, the general structure of *Barombia* shows that it is unrelated to these.

The single type-specimen was labelled as from

Lake Barombi-ba-Kotto, but the species has since been found in Barombi-ma-Mbu by M. Thys van der Audenaerde, from whose colour-photograph the information for the picture on Plate 31 was obtained. The original label was probably a mistake, since Mr Maclaren, the collector of the type, visited both lakes.

Stomatepia mariae. The genus is related to *Tilapia*, from which it differs in the narrow head, large mouth, and simple outer teeth, and to *Pelmatochromis*, from which it differs in having tricuspid inner teeth and no papillose hanging pad in the pharynx.

This monotypic genus is confined to Lake Barombi-ma-Mbu. The species is recorded to a length of about 5 inches. The habits are unknown, but the structure suggests that it may have been derived from a *Tilapia* with a diet of plankton or aufwuchs by adaptation to a more carnivorous mode of life, feeding in mid-water on insect-larvae or young fish.

This little group of species is vulnerable because of the small size of the habitat. At present I know of no particular threat to it. On the southern slopes is the little town of Kumba (formerly Johann-Albrechtshöhe), near which there is a medical research station.

Since the lake is at an altitude of approximately 980 feet above sea-level, it is a welcome cool resort from the hot and humid coastal towns. The botany and zoology of the surrounding forests are of great interest and have been the subject of a good many studies.

Danger of disturbing the ecological picture of the lake might come from the following actions:

1. The introduction of a predaceous fish for angling.

2. The indiscriminate use of pesticides – bilharzia is present along the northern shore.

3. An attempt to improve the fishery, at present only at subsistence level, by introducing another species without adequate study.

4. Pollution, unlikely unless some new industry should be established here.

The authorities should be aware of the great interest of the present fish fauna, and should be ready to control any threat to it.

On the positive side, a handbook on the natural history of the area might be written to suggest rival occupations to angling and shooting and a basis for conservation measures when these become necessary. A book has been written by Prof. Eisentraut (1963) on the vertebrates of the Cameroon Mountain, but he did no detailed work in the Kumba area. In contrast to the fishes, the other vertebrates have no endemic species in the area, although four endemic races of mammals are described. The Eisentraut expeditions provided some new knowledge of the bionomics of the birds and mammals, but more is required, and the fishes themselves are worth special study.

Lake Barombi-ba-Kotto

Lake Kotto is smaller than Lake Kumba (surface area $1\frac{1}{4}$ square miles, maximum depth 20 feet, average 12 feet 6 inches), and has a seasonal connection with the River Meme. Like Kumba (or Barombi-ma-Mbu), it is considered to have been formed by a volcanic gaseous explosion, after which a volcano erupted in the middle of the basin, nearly filling it with its ejecta. The cone remains as a wooded island in the middle of the lake.

If we remove the supposed endemic genus *Barombia* from its list, the degree of endemism is much less than in the higher and more isolated lake. Among the six species recorded from Lake Kotto, one species and one subspecies appears to be endemic.

Pelmatochromis loennbergi is related to *P. guentheri* and *P. kingsleyae*. The former inhabits West African rivers from Sierra Leone to the Benito, including the River Meme; the latter takes its place farther south in the Gabon and Ogowe. The true status of *P. loennbergi* can be known only when the life-history, colours, and habits of all three have been studied.

Tilapia mariae dubia. The typical subspecies, *T. m. mariae*, is found in the River Meme, and further study is necessary to confirm the closer relationship of the lake form with that of the Ogowe.

The low degree of endemism in this lake would be of little interest if it did not appear to relate it to the Ogowe rather than to the Meme, which is now its only outlet. Another species, named after the lake *Tilapia kottae*, has been recorded also farther south and belongs to a series of forms in which specific limits are hard to define.

Since fish-culture and fish-stocking are now being practised in the Cameroons, Lake Barombi-ba-Kotto and its fauna should be studied, before they are interfered with, to extract what information they can yield about the past history of these river-systems.

ENDEMIC SPECIES OF THE RIVER FWA, CONGO

The River Fwa is a tributary of the River Lubi in the Kasai system, about 84 miles from Luluabourg and 96 miles from Lusambo. It runs between limestone hills and is fed by the clear upsurging waters of springs. It has been described by Dr J. Schwetz (1947), who went there in the course of his medical duties to investigate the occurrence of schistosomiasis among visitors and natives. The region is one of outstanding beauty, and Dr Schwetz caught and preserved some of the fishes that could be seen

Cyclopharynx fwae and (inset) its pharyngeal plate
D. W. Ovenden 1966

swimming in the clear blue water. They were described in 1948 by Dr M. Poll, who identified thirteen species. Seven of them, including one cichlid, were the common species of the area; the other six, all cichlids, were new to science and have been found nowhere else. Dr Poll assigned two of the endemics to the genus *Haplochromis*, and proposed new genera, one for each of the other four, naming them *Haplochromis rheophilus*, *Haplochromis callochromis*, *Schwetzochromis neodon*, *Neopharynx schwetzi*, *Callopharynx microdon*, and *Cyclopharynx fwae*.

The first two were placed in *Haplochromis* because of a resemblance between *H. rheophilus*

and *H. moeruensis*, but their real relationship has still to be determined when more material is available. The new genera were given this rank because of their specialized dentition in both jaws and pharynx.

The dentition of cichlid fishes becomes so readily adapted to special diets that it is not in it that clues to relationships are likely to be found. The Fwa endemics are probably a true species-flock and deserve study both for their ecological and their phylogenetic relationships. Any attempt to clear the habitat of the bilharzia and its vectors should be coupled with the preservation of both the beauty of the area and its fish-fauna. It is possible that the six species are really endemic to the Fwa, for, although the river is not cut off from the Lubi, it contrasts with the turbid waters of that river in its limpidity and also in spreading into lake-like basins because of the copious supply of water from its springs. A lake, even quite a small one, seems always to stimulate its cichlid inhabitants to explore all the ecological niches offered and in doing so to speciate.

Nevertheless the same or related species should be looked for in the vast Congo basin. There are certain superficial features of squamation and colour-pattern that suggest that they may be near one of the source-groups of some of the genera of lakes Tanganyika and Nyasa.

THE INTEGRITY OF THE FISH-FAUNAS OF RIVERS

In Africa the fishes most commonly used to stock ponds or dams are species of *Tilapia*. Every river in tropical Africa has its species or group of species of *Tilapia*, and it is rarely necessary to bring fry from a pond in one river system to stock a water in another. At least fishery officers are asked to look first in the home river-system, and to test the local *Tilapia* for growth, utilization of natural food, and palatability. In Lake Kariba, although a species from the Kafue and Upper Zambezi was stocked, it was the local, middle Zambezi *Tilapia* that succeeded.

There is sometimes a call to stock a predatory fish to control the undue increase in *Tilapia* numbers. In this case also it is wise to avoid introducing a predator into a river-system where it did not previously exist. Its effect on the fauna unused to it cannot be predicted.

If, on consideration, it still seems advisable to violate these principles, it is the duty of the fishery officer to record the introduction and as much of the *status quo ante* as he can find the time and personnel to establish. If he cannot find the personnel locally, he should seek the co-operation of some international body or large research organization to supply it.

PLATE 31 (*a*) Pine-barrens tree frog; (*b*) Black toad; (*c*) Golden frog; (*d*) Olm; (*e*) *Barombia maclareni*; (*f*) Gila trout; (*g*) Moapa dace; (*h*) Desert dace *D. W. Ovenden* 1966

(a)

(b)

(c)

(d)

(e)

(f)

(g)

(h)

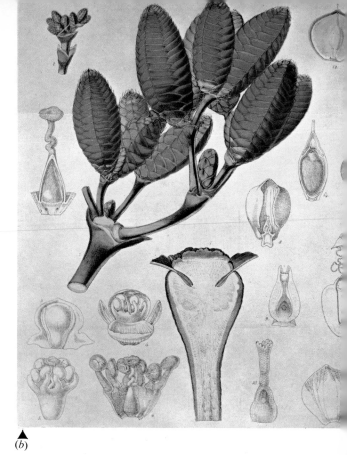

(a)

(b)

(c)

(d)

PLANTS

THE CONSERVATION OF RARE AND VANISHING SPECIES OF PLANTS

by F. Nigel Hepper
Principal Scientific Officer,
The Herbarium, Royal Botanic Gardens, Kew

THE GENERAL SITUATION

The preservation of plant species can be satisfactorily achieved only by conserving the habitats in which they live. The plant communities thus maintained have themselves an intrinsic value from an ecological point of view. If the area is of sufficient size and of a climax type of vegetation, it will be self-perpetuating.

Animals are dependent upon plants, either directly or indirectly, for food and shelter; so, by the conservation of the habitat, animals will benefit at the same time and rare and local ones will be preserved. Selection and choice of an area for conservation can often be to the mutual advantage of the flora and fauna – as well as being financially attractive. Sometimes the plants are dependent on the animals, particularly in respect of their seed-dispersal mechanisms. It is well known that birds eat berries and excrete the seeds, but curiously, the subterranean fruits of an African cucumber, *Cucumis humofructus*, are sought out and eaten by aardvarks, which deposit the seeds in their dung; their digestive juices may break down the seed-coat and facilitate germination. The relationship between a plant and its insect pollinator is apparent in the remarkable adaptation of each to the other.

The preservation of certain plant species must therefore be considered in relation to their biology or autecology. Placing too much emphasis upon the saving of an individual species must not detract from the conservation of the vegetation of an area where the flora is of outstanding interest. The Survival Service Commission has this point very much in mind, and it is indeed obtaining information for the Red Data Book on rare plant species with this end in view. That a particular area contains the only known surviving plants of even a small and obscure species may, however, constitute a powerful lever in saving the whole habitat. Any measures proposed for the conservation of a habitat will inevitably concern non-biologists, and the importance of "vanishing species" in public relations should not be overlooked.

The achievement of these aims is another matter, and it may well give grounds for despair. Two factors accentuate the urgency of the problem: the enormous increase in the world's human population, which can only be satisfactorily controlled by public education, and, closely related to this, the extreme rapidity with which physical changes can now take place by scientific and mechanical means. For example, vegetation is of course rapidly affected by the use of chemical weed-killers. Aerial spraying of such chemicals can reach enormous areas, and reservoirs of wild vegetation in otherwise inaccessible places may be eliminated. Zohary rightly said in 1959 that "modern mechanized methods of agriculture, industry and building have not only inflicted heavy damage on such relics of nature as have withstood man's interference during millennia, but have entirely upset the equilibrium which until recently existed between man and his vegetal environment."

The overriding need for increased food production for the world's growing population has

PLATE 32 (*a*) Purple-stained Laelia orchid, *Laelia purpurata* – used extensively for hybridization, it is now in danger of extinction in eastern Brazil *L. Constans* 1852; (*b*) Welwitschia, *W. bainesii* – a well-known feature of the desert of Angola and South-West Africa, it was once thought to be very rare *W. Fitch* 1863; (*c*) Californian big tree, *Sequoiadendron giganteum* – now carefully safeguarded in special reserves *W. Fitch* 1854; (*d*) Flamboyant, *Delonix regia* – well known in tropical gardens throughout the world, but limited in the wild to one forest reserve in Madagascar *Bojer* 1829 frequently been held to rule out the conservation of nature. Already, however, this attitude is undergoing a change. For instance, on the Scottish island of Rum the Nature Conservancy has lately found that more meat can be obtained from red deer than used to be marketed from the sheep and cattle formerly kept on the island. In East Africa it is now being recognized that the production of protein from wild animals is an efficient way of utilizing resources. Nobody would wish to starve a human population for the sake of a rare plant. But who knows which of today's weeds and wild species will become the progenitors of tomorrow's new crop plants or yield valuable medicines? Huge sums are already being spent in many countries on screening plants for alkaloids, cancer-curing drugs, and other chemicals. Even so, only a small fraction of the world's total flora has yet been analysed.

The key to the discussion of these matters is, I think, to be found in the wastage and inefficient use of land. Short-term results may be achieved, for instance, by the cultivation of hill-slopes or watersheds; but the long-term effects may be disastrous to the water supply for wide areas of agricultural land downstream. Removal of the natural vegetation in such cases means a faster run-off of rain water, increased flow of the river for short periods with possible flooding of low land, and lack of water in the rivers at other times of the year. Conservation of the natural vegetation in such sites, with judicious selection of the areas and subsequent good land-management, can be of mutual advantage to all interests, and especially to those concerned with food-production.

Rapid destruction of the natural vegetation, and its replacement by either monoculture or ill-conceived methods of agriculture, has taken place with disastrous results. The process of change continues at an alarming rate in many parts of the world with varying effects, and from the biological point of view the effects may be final and irreversible. For this reason, it is vitally important to conserve original or primary vegetation before it has lost its diversity of species. In the tropics a remarkable number of totally distinct species may exist within a relatively small area. Destruction of the natural vegetation such as a forest is invariably accom-

panied by burning of the unwanted material. The trees may be felled and set on fire and the ground beneath cultivated for a period. For instance, in São Paulo, Brazil, when the crops become uneconomic after a few years, tilling ceases and the resulting grass cover may be used for cattle. Even without the cattle, very little woody growth will appear, and this will be composed of a much smaller number of species than formerly existed in the region. Nothing like the original forest will return, either because the seeds have been burnt, or because, when they germinated during the period of cultivation, the seedlings were eradicated.

There is evidence, however, that this succession is not the same in Amazonia, or in the climatic forest zone of tropical Africa, where a thick secondary forest develops unless the grass is burnt every year. The secondary forest would in time give way to high forest physiognomically resembling the original primary forest, but it would be floristically poorer, with the rarer species lost in the process. It must also be admitted that not enough is known about the ability of plants to re-establish themselves when once they have apparently disappeared. Whereas mammals breed conspicuously, and their numbers and whereabouts can be readily assessed, many plants reproduce vegetatively, or their propagules remain dormant for many years. In any case, it seems that vegetation and competition between species is in a delicate state of equilibrium; and the rarer the species is, the more easily it may be exterminated by even a minor change.

To secure a conservation plot from encroachment by burning, by illegitimate farming or wood-cutting, or even by too many authorized visitors, the area must be large enough to be viable – and large enough also for the local climatic conditions to stay unaltered. In a tropical rain forest, for instance, the high humidity and still air must be maintained, which can be guaranteed only by having a large reserve or a smaller one surrounded by similar forest. Population pressure must be avoided. Properly controlled national parks and nature reserves act as the last refuge for many important species. Unfortunately, without proper control or supervision, they can act as magnets for visitors whose depredations destroy the very objects one seeks to preserve. Thus for particularly important areas access, especially by road, should be strictly limited and enforceable laws enacted. In the tropics, where the situation is often the most critical, these recommendations are usually difficult to carry out. Again it must be emphasized that the size of the area is important, and that now is the time to act while there is some primary tropical vegetation, with its diversity of species, still intact.

Many countries have declared strict reserves, and more are required, but it should not be thought that formation of actual reserves is the only method of preserving rare species. Often it will prove impracticable to form a reserve to save a particular species that is locally widespread but whose continued existence is threatened in some way. A different approach may be necessary to prevent its numbers from being reduced to the danger level. Measures may include the control of burning of grassland to diminish the intensity of fires. In many countries rank grass is cleared by burning during the dry season, and it has been found that deliberate firing soon after the cessation of the rains, while the grass still retains a considerable percentage of moisture, has a beneficial effect on the vegetation. But when the fires take place during the driest part of the year, either by accident or by design, the excessive heat generated is sufficient to modify the flora by killing all but the more resistent species.

Other measures may include the regulation of water flow, to avoid lowering the water-level in marshes and the severe effect this would have on the specialized plant communities. Open water with its aquatic species can give way to marsh, and marsh can be eliminated altogether when the water table is lowered by some change that may be far removed from the site itself. Another similar consideration concerns the podostemons (family Podostemonaceae), which are beautifully adapted for survival in rocky tropical streams with a fluctuating flow. These minute flowering plants encrust certain rocks in streams where the water is fast-flowing and well aerated. At the height of the rainy season they are completely submerged, but, as the rains decrease and the water-level falls, they become increasingly exposed. A succession of development may be noted, with the plant-bearing buds just below water-level; while just above the water-level the open flowers are exposed. Further out of the water on the now exposed and more or less dry rock the plant body becomes shrivelled, with its capsules already bearing ripe seeds. It will be seen from this sequence of events that a circumstance such as the construction of a dam upstream, allowing an even flow of water, would be disastrous for the podostemons, many of which are extremely rare.

INFORMATION-GATHERING

It seems fairly evident that precise information on the existence and distribution of plant species is considerably more difficult to obtain than for at least the larger animals, whose numbers and species are much fewer. The present state of knowledge of the distribution of plants in vast areas of the world is still rudimentary. Often the only records to be found in floras and monographs are compiled from herbarium material, which may not give an accurate account of either the range or the frequency of a species. While herbarium records constitute a valuable means of assessing the general distribution of any species, they need to be backed up by local observations. A local observer can also report on new developments affecting rare species. On the other hand, local information intended for the Red Data Book must be assessed centrally by the Survival Service Commission if it is to present a true international picture of the status of a species; for, although a new development may threaten the entire population of a species in one place, the same species may be abundant elsewhere. Local observations can sometimes be dealt with through existing regional organizations, and it is, of course, important that the Survival Service Commission should work in close cooperation with them.

Certain well-known vanishing species come to mind at once, but there are countless others recorded from a single locality whose present real status is unknown. By working through a standard flora for a country or region, it is possible to extract the names of rare endemic species. Unfortunately, large parts of the world are still without such floras; and many of the existing ones are not up to date as far as distribution, taxonomy, or nomenclature are concerned. Enough has been said above concerning the need for information about the distribution of the species; and now a word should be added about the relevance of taxonomy and nomenclature. Correct identification of the species is a necessary first step, and the right name should then be applied. Recognition of the plant in the rank of species, subspecies, or even variety may differ according to the opinion of the author concerned, and this should be considered when using published work. Failure to take this into account could cause the same organism to be entered under two or more different names and in different ranks.

For any threatened species, it is useful to know its approximate original range of distribution in the recent past, as well as having an accurate indication of its present restricted area. Ecological information must also be obtained as to the nature of its habitat and whether it has changed. Historically the habitat may have been altered by human action such as protracted land-clearance, drainage, flooding, fire, afforestation, or building operations; or it may have been affected by over-grazing or trampling by animals. Climatic changes may influence the habitat in a surprisingly short time; and the climate should therefore be taken into consideration. Present-day assessment of the causes of the decrease or the threatened extermination of the species should be considered in detail on much the same lines as the long-term changes mentioned above. New economic uses for the species may threaten its continued existence. An epidemic disease or other affliction not previously of great importance can adversely affect a species already in a precarious position. Sometimes alien species compete too successfully with the native vegetation and constitute a serious threat to the original species. For instance, Australian species of *Acacia* (Leguminosae) and *Hakea* (Proteaceae) have shaded out the native flora in parts of South Africa, and the South African species *Arctotheca calendula* (Compositae) and *Homeria breyniania* (Iridaceae) have replaced much of the native flora in parts of Australia.

For effective measures to be taken to preserve a particular species, further detailed biological information may be necessary. The relationship of the species to other plants in the community must be investigated, as well as its methods of reproduction. The production of viable seed may depend on certain factors such as the presence of the right species of insect pollinators. In some plants, vegetative propagation is more important than sexual reproduction, and in such cases there may be special requirements for its successful accomplishment. For various and sometimes obscure reasons a plant, like *Polygala cowellii* (Polygalaceae), may no longer establish itself in nature. This Puerto Rican species is now limited to old trees, and attempts to reproduce it have failed. Suggestions for measures to be taken to preserve a vanishing species can be best recommended by an informed local person or one with specialist knowledge. Basic information about the possibility and desirability of preserving the species must also be sought. In the case of each species under consideration convincing

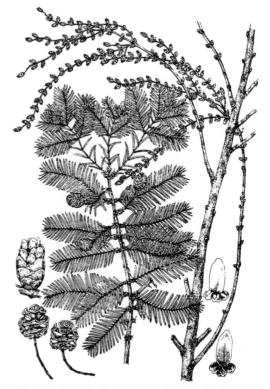

Dawn redwood, *Metasequoia glyptostroboides*. Discovered in China in 1941; few trees remain in the wild. *From "Arnoldia" 1948. Drawing supplied to "Arnoldia" by Dr H. H. Hu*

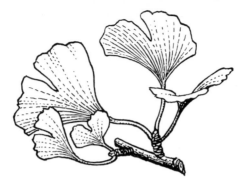

Maidenhair tree, *Ginkgo biloba,* and (above) detail of twig and leaves. A "living fossil" long planted around Buddhist temples, it is believed still to grow naturally in central China. *S. R. Badmin* 1966

arguments, whether scientific, aesthetic, or economic, must be put forward so that rapid protective measures will be taken.

PARTICULAR CONSIDERATIONS

The cultivation of plants in danger of extinction can only be regarded as a last resort in cases of extreme urgency. Many species are difficult to maintain in the artificial conditions available in botanic gardens, and they are likely to be subject to the variations in treatment that may result from changes in supervisory staff and financial stringencies in the countries concerned. It is as well, however, that some species, such as the "living fossils" *Metasequoia glyptostroboides* and *Ginkgo biloba* (Taxodiaceae), which are known to survive as relicts only in central China, are already safely in cultivation. Even so, it is to be hoped that the wild plants will remain in existence. Often a species is introduced into cultivation from perhaps only one gathering; and all other plants are propagated from this. Such artificial selection is producing a cultivated plant considerably different from those in the wild state. In 1965 Stearn pointed out the danger inherent in cultivating plants with a limited gene complement, and their susceptibility to attack

by disease on an epidemic scale. Wild species of economic crops constitute an important gene reservoir, as has been found from research on the potato (*Solanum tuberosum*) and on other major world crops. Already some ornamental species are known only in cultivation. For example, *Franklinia alatamaha* (Theaceae) has not been seen in its native locality in Georgia, U.S.A., for more than a century, and it is certainly extinct in the wild; *Camellia granthamiana* (Theaceae) is known from only one plant in Hong Kong; *Cyclamen libanoticum* (Primulaceae) has only one known wild population in Lebanon; the flamboyant, *Delonix regia* (Leguminosae) is known from one valley in Madagascar; the Chilean crocus, *Tecophilaea cyanocrocus* (Tecophilaeaceae) has a very limited distribution in Chile; and the parrot's bill, *Clianthus puniceus* (Leguminosae) is already extinct in various former localities in North Island, New Zealand.

Some rare species are of great scientific interest from the morphological, evolutionary, or phytogeographic point of view. These plants are seldom spectacular and may not attract popular interest, but scientifically they can be far more important than others of horticultural merit. Every possible effort should be made to preserve them in their own habitats. If, however, some of them could be brought into cultivation while they are still available, there would be a good cause for utilizing certain botanic gardens for this purpose. For instance, several Flacourtiaceous species with their flowers borne on the leaves – *Mocquerysia multiflora, Phylloclinium paradoxum*, *Phyllobotryum soyauxianum*, and *P. spathulatum* in tropical Africa – are all held to be unique relict species of great evolutionary interest. Many examples of phytogeographical interest are available: on rocks in Guinea is found *Pitcairnia feliciana*, the only representative of the family *Bromeliaceae* growing naturally outside Central and South America, and in Seychelles about six individuals remain of *Vateria seychellarum*, the only member of *Dipterocarpoideae* outside Indo-Malaysia.

Island floras present a particular problem for the conservation of their species, usually due to immense population pressure in a confined area. Even unpopulated islands, such as Aldabra, are constantly being threatened with modern developments that would largely eliminate the wildlife. Much has been written about the specialization that has taken place in both plants and animals, especially on certain islands or archipelagos such as the Galápagos Islands, with 42 per cent of the species endemic, and Hawaiian Islands with about 90 per cent endemic as well as many endemic genera. The situation is now so desperate in Hawaii that as many as possible of the rare endemics are being cultivated to save them from extinction. Elsewhere there are even endemic families. Thus Medusagynaceae is a monogeneric family with the single species *Medusagyne oppositifolia*, formerly known from Mahé Island in the Seychelles. It existed on one mountain top in a rain forest rich in other endemics, but it was apparently extinct by 1962. The famous Kerguelen cabbage, *Pringlea antiscorbutica* (Cruciferae), is said to be in great danger because of the depredations of animals and the spread of a species of *Acaena*. In Fiji only a few trees remain of *Pullea perryana* (Cunoniaceae), which is the only member of the genus recorded from a locality east of New Guinea.

Mountains, like islands, often have a high degree of endemism. Unlike islands, they are not usually subject to great pressures, although continued encroachment on their lower slopes may ultimately obliterate a considerable part of the vegetation. At higher altitudes, the many specially adapted species are particularly vulnerable to any unusual factors, such as concentrated grazing or fire, and action is needed to protect

them. Rocky hills and cliffs are vulnerable from quarrying, which of course utterly destroys the plants. In Malaya the limestone hills are being destroyed in this way, and the species, such as *Chirita sericea* (Gesneriaceae) and the palms *Maxburretia rupicola* and *Liberbaileya lankawiensis*, each of which occurs on one hill, may be threatened. The site of a spectacular tree, *Gigasiphon macrosiphon* (Leguminosae), in Kenya is threatened by mining, and the area of the forest in Tanzania where it also exists is very small indeed.

Mention could be made of many other vulnerable habitats where specially adapted species grow. Even deserts are no longer safe, and the species are particularly sensitive to change. In the floristically rich semi-desert of Somalia many endemics are being destroyed by over-grazing and subsequent erosion, while in northern Mexico and south-western United States the smaller cacti are subject to intensive collection by commercial interests which threaten their existence. It might be appropriate to mention here that, although large old plants of the remarkable *Welwitschia bainesii*, also called *W. mirabilis* (Gnetales), are favourite museum material, the species is in no danger of extinction. It is much commoner than was formerly realized since it extends from Angola to South-West Africa, where it is actually protected.

The species of certain groups of plants are in danger in many parts of the world. Cycads, for instance, are interesting relicts, and many species occupying limited areas are in precarious balance with their environment. Certain species of *Encephalartos* in East Africa and of *Bowenia* in Australia come into this category. The species of *Macrozamia* in Queensland are in imminent danger of extinction by fire, clearing, and grazing interests, and their eradication is being urged as they are poisonous to stock. Many Gymnosperms are likewise in grave danger of extinction in various parts of the world. Some of the more famous ones, such as the Californian big tree *Sequoiadendron giganteum* (Taxodiaceae) and the cedar of Lebanon *Cedrus libani* (Pinaceae), are now safeguarded in reserves. Others are less secure, such as the Japanese *Picea koyamai* (Pinaceae), which was reported fifty years ago to grow in one small grove of about a hundred

Cedar of Lebanon, *Cedrus libani,* and (above) detail of cone and flowers. Used for Solomon's Temple and Egyptian palaces; survives only as scattered relicts and in cultivation. *S. R. Badmin* 1966

trees, and even then to be in danger of extinction; and *Abies nebrodensis* is said to be known from only one tree in Sicily.

Of all flowering plants, perhaps orchids (family Orchidaceae) have a special popular fascination. It is difficult to assess with any degree of accuracy the number of natural orchid species comprising this single distinct family, but a reasonable estimate would be in the order of 17,000 natural orchid species, apart from the vast number of artificial hybrids and selected forms that often differ markedly from their parents and from the natural species. It is due to the widespread horticultural interest in orchids that many species are in danger of extinction and, as a contrast, why orchids have been chosen by the Survival Service Commission as a special project for conservation.

Curiously enough, in spite of their numerical abundance, orchids do not create a vegetation type, nor do they often form a significant part of a habitat. The tropical epiphytic species growing upon trees possess aerial roots of a characteristic type that is almost unique to this family. They have the ability to absorb moisture from the atmosphere and prevent water loss by their cellular outer covering, the velamen. Maintenance of the epiphytic species depends,

therefore, on the availability of trees on which they can live, and enough atmospheric moisture for their roots. Furthermore the trees must be old ones, with horizontal branches big enough in diameter to support the orchid plants. It follows that a policy of forest working by which old trees are selectively and progressively felled as they reach a certain size and age will soon eliminate the epiphytic orchids. Even those that have become established in the canopy of the forest would hardly have time to reach maturity, much less produce enough seeds to maintain the continuity of the species. The forest may still, to all intents and purposes, remain a forest under such a procedure; but the effect upon the orchid population would be nearly as disastrous as clear felling.

In eastern Brazil, several species of *Laelia* occur as epiphytes in forest along the narrow coastal belt. *L. purpurata* is one of these whose fate is at present in the balance through reduction of its habitat, and particularly through the depredations of orchid hunters. This species is one of the parents of the numerous *Laelia* hybrids that are immensely popular with orchid-growers, and is itself variable in colour and form. Local spare-time orchid-hunters, finding this a profitable pursuit, have for some time collected large numbers of plants of *L. purpurata* and other species, hoping that one or two at least would turn out to be of particular merit. Such individuals are sold for a handsome profit, while the less desirable plants are discarded, to the deprivation of the natural population.

The collection of wild orchids has reached such proportions in North India that their export has become big business with regular consignments reaching European and American airports for distribution by dealers. The latter freely advertise in horticultural magazines, and the short-term profits must be considerable. In the long run, however, the natural supply will diminish, and that of the rarer species is likely to cease altogether as they are exterminated. In Brazil, the orchid-hunters are already becoming dismayed at the depletion of the choicer species; and the same situation may occur elsewhere where orchids are over-collected on a commercial scale.

WHAT IS BEING DONE TO CONSERVE PLANTS?

The needs have been summarized above, and it is quite clear that they are pressing needs. What, then, is being done about them? The inter-relationship of animals and plants has been known for a long time, but it is only in recent years that the important implications of this inter-relationship have been fully appreciated in the management of nature reserves. This awareness should have important repercussions on botanical aspects, since it is still true to say that zoological conservation dominates the movement. Nevertheless, the need to protect plants for their own sake is becoming increasingly accepted by those in authority and by the scientific world in general. For instance, the main theme of an international conference in 1966 was the "Conservation of vegetation and of its constituent species in Africa south of the Sahara"; delegates from some twenty-five countries were present. The aim was to stress to the governments of each African country the need for the conservation of plant life by providing authoritative scientific accounts in a readily obtainable report of the present position and future requirements. The I.U.C.N. itself has taken the principal lead in this field by initiating a scheme for the protection of plant species in cooperation with the Conservation of Terrestrial Communities Section of the International Biological Programme involving the employment of a full-time senior botanist on the work.

In many countries throughout the world governments, societies, and individuals are now actively encouraging botanical conservation. As the work gains momentum, it is hoped that the world will be the richer for its continuing diversity of plants, as well as of animals.

ACKNOWLEDGMENTS

The President of the I.U.C.N. joins with the writers and editors in offering grateful thanks to Peter Scott, who originated the idea of this volume and who has meanwhile worked untiringly to make the Red Data Book the effective instrument of the Union's Survival Service action programme for safeguarding gravely endangered species. A special acknowledgment is due also to E. J. H. Berwick (Secretary-General of the I.U.C.N.) and Sir Hugh F. I. Elliott (former Secretary-General of the I.U.C.N.), who have been constant sources of strength and constructive suggestion in the preparation of this volume.

The Red Data Book represents a summary of the collated results of work by a great many biologists and conservationists now engaged upon research on survival. It is quite impossible to acknowledge here all our informants by name; they are acknowledged on the relevant sheets in the scientific publication. But a special group has taken a helpful interest in the present volume, and has been kind enough to check over, and when necessary rewrite, some of the species essays. The writers' and editors' thanks are thus offered to the Chairmen of the S.S.C.'s special committees: A. G. Bannikov (wild horse), John J. Calaby (marsupials), Archie Carr (marine turtles), T. H. Harrisson (orang utan), P. F. Hunt (orchids), Karl W. Kenyon (seals), Ernst M. Lang (zoo liaison), R. R. Miller (freshwater fish), Jean-Jacques Petter (Madagascar), W. T. Schaurte (rhinoceroses), Qassim bin Hamad al Thani (oryx), G. K. Whitehead (deer), and J. Zabinski (European bison); and to the following equally patient and learned experts: J. W. Aldrich, Dean Amadon, Robert F. Andrle, Oliver L. Austin, Phyllis Barclay-Smith (Secretary of the I.C.B.P.), Erwin L. Boeker, James Bond, Roland Clement, Jean Delacour, G. P. Dementiev, R. S. Dharmakumarsinhji, R. A. Falla, E. P. Gee, Albert Earl Gilbert, Alice G. C. Grandison, Bernhard Grzimek, W. W. H. Gunn, Barbara Harrisson, Raymond Lévêque, George Lowery, Harold F. Mayfield, Brooke Meanley, Lady Medway, William M. Ord, James A. Peters, L. A. Portenko, Peter C. H. Pritchard, S. Dillon Ripley (President of the I.C.B.P.), David W. Snow, James T. Tanner, L. H. Walkinshaw, Philip Wayre, Alexander Wetmore, David B. Wingate, and Yoshimaro Yamashina.

The writers appreciate, and have used, the firm foundation of information about endangered higher vertebrates provided by the classic publications of the American Committee for International Wild Life Protection: Glover M. Allen's *Extinct and Vanishing Mammals of the Western Hemisphere with the Marine Species of All the Oceans* (1942); Francis Harper's *Extinct and Vanishing Mammals of the Old World* (1945); and James C. Greenway Jr's *Extinct and Vanishing Birds of the World* (1958). The research files on which Roger Tory Peterson and James Fisher based their lists of extinct and endangered birds in *The World of Birds* (1964) were made available to the Red Data Book and have also been used.

The writers and editors are grateful to the following living artists for the use of their work, and (when specially commissioned) for their patience with the briefing of it: S. R. Badmin, Cécile Curtis, N. W. Cusa, Barry Driscoll, Rena M. Fennessy, Albert Earl Gilbert, Robert Gillmor, D. M. Henry, Shigekazu Kobayashi, Fenwick Lansdowne, Robert M. Mengel, D. W. Ovenden, Peter Scott, Peter Slater, Charles F. Tunnicliffe, and Maurice Wilson. Works by some of these artists have been used through the courtesy of Messrs Brooke Bond, for years supporters of the conservation cause, or through that of the American Committee for International Wild Life Protection and other conservation bodies who have published books and journals in which they first appeared. Gratitude must be expressed, too, to the shades of some great illustrators of past classic works—John James Audubon, Bojer, L. Constans, W. Fitch, F. W. Frohawk, H. Goodchild, Elizabeth Gould, John Gould, W. Hart, Waterhouse Hawkins, J. G. Keulemans, Edward Lear, G. Mützel, P. Oudart, H. C. Richter, J. Smit, Archibald Thorburn, and Joseph Wolf.

Further, the editors would like to thank the officials of the Zoological Society of London, and of the British Museum (Natural History), for kindly granting permission to reproduce here some of the classic plates preserved in their libraries. R. A. Fish, Librarian of the first, has been especially helpful in promoting research. Thanks are also due to R. Desmond, Librarian, the Royal Botanic Gardens, Kew.

The editing of the final manuscript, and the preparation of the illustrations, was done by Yorke Crompton, house editor of George Rainbird Ltd, and his assistant Julia Trehane, with the collaboration of James Fisher. The text incorporates most of the information available to the S.S.C. by the end of 1966, and some highly important information about specially interesting species published up to the spring of 1968.

Full bibliographical references to the facts cited in this volume can be found in the S.S.C.'s Red Data Book.

ICONOGRAPHY

The sources below are arranged in chronological order. The plate and page numbers at the ends of the references indicate the places of the illustrations in this volume.

Botanical Magazine, 1829: Plate 32(*d*).

JOHN EDWARD GRAY, *Illustrations of Indian Zoology*, 1830–2, Vol. 1: p. 237.

EDWARD LEAR, *Illustrations of the Family of Psittacidae, or Parrots*, 1839–2: Plate 22(*d*).

JOHN GOULD, *The Birds of Europe*, 1837–8: Plate 21 (*b*).

JOHN JAMES AUDUBON, *Birds of America*, 1827–38: Plates 18 and 20, pp. 187, 214, 227, 240, 242.

OEILLET DES MURS, *Iconographie Ornithologique*, 1845–9: p. 207.

JOHN GOULD, *The Birds of Australia*, Vol. 3, 1848: Plate 24(*b*), p. 293. Vol. 5, 1848: Plate 22(*b*), pp. 250, 254. Supplement, 1869: Plate 22(*a*), Plate 24(*a*), pp. 246, 249.

LINDLEY and PAXTON, *Flower Garden* III, 1852–3: Plate 32(*a*).

Botanical Magazine, 1854: Plate 32(*c*). 1863: Plate 32(*b*).

DANIEL GIRAUD ELLIOT, *Monograph of the Phasianidae*, Vol. 1, 1872: Plate 19(*a, b, c, d*).

ANTON REICHENOW, *Vogelbilder aus fernen Zonen: Abbildungen und Beschreibungen der Papageien*, 1873–83: p. 257.

WALTER LAWRY BULLER, *A History of the Birds of New Zealand*, 1st edition, 1873: Plate 21(*a*). 2nd edition, 1888: Plate 24(*c, d*), Plate 27(*b, d*).

JOHN GOULD, *The Birds of New Guinea*, 1875–88, Vol. 3: Plate 27(*a*).

SCOTT BARCHARD WILSON and ARTHUR HUMBLE EVANS, *Aves Hawaiienses: The Birds of the Sandwich Islands*, 1890–9: Plate 17(*a*), Plate 28(*a, b, c, d, e, f*).

WALTER ROTHSCHILD, *The Avifauna of Laysan*, Vols. 1 and 2, 1893: Plate 17(*c*), p. 308. Vol. 3, 1900: Plate 17(*b*), Plate 27(*c*).

Avicultural Magazine, 1902, Vol. 8: pp. 258, 259. 1904, Vol. 2: Plate 22(*c*), p. 258.

WALTER ROTHSCHILD, *Extinct Birds*, 1907: p. 295.

ARCHIBALD THORBURN, *British Mammals*, 1920–1, Vol. 2: Plate 4(*a, b*), Plate 5(*a, b*), p. 61.

Arnoldia of the Arnold Arboretum, Harvard University, U.S.A., Vol. 8, 1948: p. 356.

JAMES COWAN GREENWAY Jr, *Extinct and Vanishing Birds of the World*, 1958: pp. 191, 233.

YOSHIMARO YAMASHINA, *Birds in Japan: A Field Guide*, 1961: Plate 16 (*b, c*).

The Auk, American Ornithologists' Union and University of Kansas, U.S.A., Vol. 8, No. 1, 1964: p. 268.

WILDFOWL TRUST, *Annual Report*, 1964: p. 198.

INDEX

The figures in bold type refer to illustrations.

363

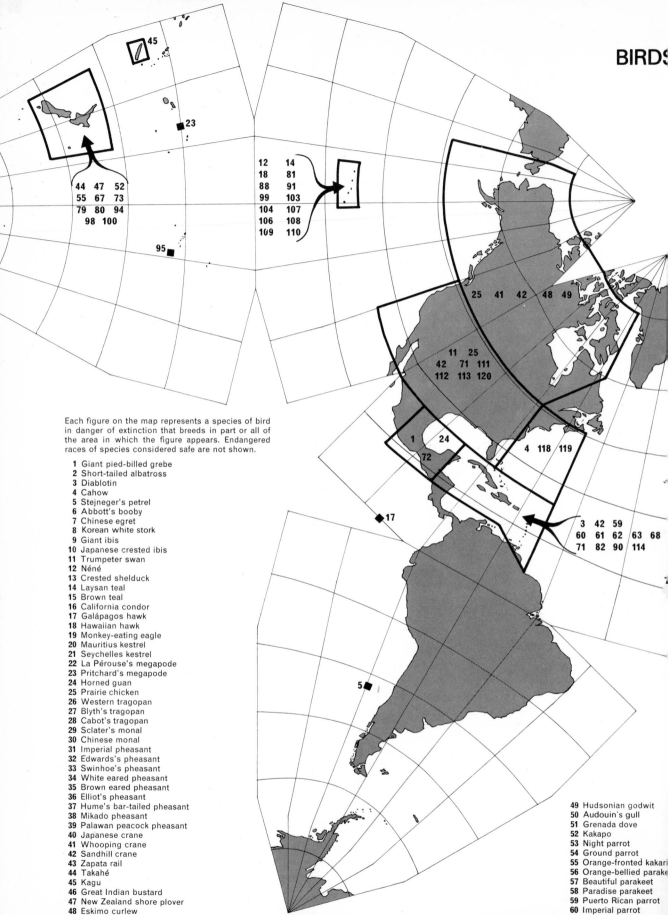

BIRDS

45

23

44 47 52
55 67 73
79 80 94
98 100

12	14
18	81
88	91
99	103
104	107
106	108
109	110

95

25 41 42 48 49

11 25
42 71 111
112 113 120

1 24

72

4 118 119

17

5

3 42 59
60 61 62 63 68
71 82 90 114

Each figure on the map represents a species of bird in danger of extinction that breeds in part or all of the area in which the figure appears. Endangered races of species considered safe are not shown.

1 Giant pied-billed grebe
2 Short-tailed albatross
3 Diablotin
4 Cahow
5 Stejneger's petrel
6 Abbott's booby
7 Chinese egret
8 Korean white stork
9 Giant ibis
10 Japanese crested ibis
11 Trumpeter swan
12 Néné
13 Crested shelduck
14 Laysan teal
15 Brown teal
16 California condor
17 Galápagos hawk
18 Hawaiian hawk
19 Monkey-eating eagle
20 Mauritius kestrel
21 Seychelles kestrel
22 La Pérouse's megapode
23 Pritchard's megapode
24 Horned guan
25 Prairie chicken
26 Western tragopan
27 Blyth's tragopan
28 Cabot's tragopan
29 Sclater's monal
30 Chinese monal
31 Imperial pheasant
32 Edwards's pheasant
33 Swinhoe's pheasant
34 White eared pheasant
35 Brown eared pheasant
36 Elliot's pheasant
37 Hume's bar-tailed pheasant
38 Mikado pheasant
39 Palawan peacock pheasant
40 Japanese crane
41 Whooping crane
42 Sandhill crane
43 Zapata rail
44 Takahé
45 Kagu
46 Great Indian bustard
47 New Zealand shore plover
48 Eskimo curlew

49 Hudsonian godwit
50 Audouin's gull
51 Grenada dove
52 Kakapo
53 Night parrot
54 Ground parrot
55 Orange-fronted kakari
56 Orange-bellied parake
57 Beautiful parakeet
58 Paradise parakeet
59 Puerto Rican parrot
60 Imperial parrot